COMPUTER ARCHITECTURE AND DESIGN

ELECTRONIC SYSTEMS ENGINEERING SERIES

Consulting Editor **E L Dagless**
University of Bristol

Special Consultant **D W Barron**
University of Southampton

OTHER TITLES IN THE SERIES

Advanced Microprocessor Architectures *L Ciminiera and A Valenzano*
Optical Pattern Recognition Using Holographic Techniques *N Collings*
Modern Logic Design *D Green*
Data Communications, Computer Networks and OSI (2nd Edn) *F Halsall*
Microwave Components and Systems *K F Sander*
Tolerance Design of Electronic Circuits *R Spence and R S Soin*

COMPUTER ARCHITECTURE AND DESIGN

A. J. van de Goor
Delft University of Technology

The first half of this book was translated and revised by: **M. P. de Kluyver** and **M. Korsloot**

Produced in association with: **Vereniging voor Studie en Studentenbelangen – Delft**

Addison-Wesley Publishing Company
Wokingham, England • Reading, Massachusetts • Menlo Park, California
New York • Don Mills, Ontario • Amsterdam • Bonn
Sydney • Singapore • Tokyo • Madrid • San Juan

The programs presented in this book have been included for their instructional value. They have been tested with care but are not guaranteed for any particular purpose. The publisher does not offer any warranties or representations, nor does it accept any liabilities with respect to the programs.

Many of the designations used by manufacturers and sellers to distinguish their products are claimed as trademarks. Addison-Wesley has made every attempt to supply trademark information about manufacturers and their products mentioned in this book. A list of the trademark designations and their owners appears on page viii.

Cover designed by Crayon Design of Henley-on-Thames
and printed by The Riverside Printing Co. (Reading) Ltd.
Illustrations by Chartwell Illustrators.
Typeset by Columns of Reading.
Printed in Great Britain by The Bath Press, Avon.

First printed 1989. Reprinted 1990.

British Library Cataloguing in Publication Data
Goor, A. J. van de
Computer architecture and design.
1. Microprocessor systems. Design
I. Title
004.2′56

ISBN 0–201–18241–6

Library of Congress Cataloguing in Publication Data
Goor, A. J. van de.
Computer architecture and design.

Bibliography: p.
Includes index.
1. Computer architecture. 2. Microprocessors.
I. Title
QA76.9.A73G66 1989 004.2′2 88–16615
ISBN 0–201–18241–6

To Anny
and our children Han, Jacky and Rinske

Foreword

Computer Architecture and Design is a fine introduction to today's computers. The book is based on the microprocessor, a component built on a single, very-large-scale integrated circuit with several hundred thousand transistors, but this is in no way limiting and in fact is likely to turn out very forward looking. In the next few years all but a few supercomputers and the ageing, traditional mainframes and minicomputers which serve as 'code museums' for the last three decades of programs and data will be built on the microprocessor.

According to the Preface, Professor van de Goor's book is aimed at introductory courses in computer architecture and design. I feel it goes well beyond this level given its approach, insight, breadth and extensive references. It should be useful to anyone engaged in the design of systems using microprocessors. While the book uses the Motorola 68000 microprocessor as the core, with extensions using the VAX architecture, an overall taxonomy for the various architectural dimensions is always provided to give the reader a full view of architecture.

The 68000 is a justifiable model to use since it is the core of three revolutionary machines: the workstation (Apollo and SUN), the finest personal computer (Apple Mac) and a fully fault-tolerant computer (Stratus). In addition, the structure of nearly all microprocessor-based systems today is around Motorola's VME bus, which is described along with the more elegant, but less used, Nubus. Justifiably absent is the I/O processor as embodied in the Intel and IBM 360 . . . 3090 Series channels – these structures, although complex, are not especially interesting or useful to anyone except their designers.

In five years, I suspect that virtually all important new computers will utilize a simple pipelined architecture – the RISC or reduced instruction set computer. Several new companies (for example, MIPS Computer) and nearly all semicomputer companies (for example, Motorola 88000) are introducing microprocessors using this approach. Chaper 15 provides the basis for understanding this shift.

I heartily recommend this book. All the important basic principles are introduced and described in a well-developed context by an experienced teacher and fine engineer who understands how to build computer systems.

C. Gordon Bell
Vice President R & D,
Ardent Computer

PREFACE

The advances achieved in computer systems have been very remarkable. Since the introduction of the first electronic computers in the 1940s, they have now reached a point of general acceptance to the extent that high school curricula include courses to familiarize students with the use of computers for applications such as text processing and database management. Courses in problem solving are also being offered, using programming languages such as BASIC or Pascal. It is safe to predict that many introductory college level computer science subjects will be included in the curricula of high schools.

This trend, however, causes an upward pressure on the material to be covered at the college level. The low price and wide acceptance of microprocessors creates a need for their architecture and organization to be covered in greater depth. The aim of this book is to allow computer science, computer engineering and electrical engineering students, and practising professionals, to master the terminology and concepts used to describe computers, and to provide them with a frame of reference for evaluation and comparison.

Aims and audience

The progress in technology has enabled microprocessor systems to have a level of functionality and performance only achievable by large computers of a previous generation. Packaging density has reached the point where a single microprocessor chip includes, in addition to the CPU, caches, memory management facilities, multiprocessor support and support for extended functionality (for example, floating-point operations) via a co-processor interface. In order to achieve a high execution speed, acceleration mechanisms such as pipelining and prefetching are used.

It is the aim of this book to provide a foundation for understanding, evaluating and comparing alternative design principles used by state-of-the-art microprocessors and minicomputers. Studying the manufacturer's manual on a new microprocessor then becomes a process of recognition and classification.

Rather than basing the text on a theoretical computer, the architectures of current microprocessors and minicomputers with a widespread acceptance have been used. Examples are taken primarily from the Motorola MC68000 family, abstracted to the relevant level of detail. The DEC VAX-11 architecture has been used as a second source, while examples from other architectures are used only to illustrate important concepts or alternatives. Although the Intel 80X86 architecture is being used widely in many personal computers, it is less suited to illustrate important architectural concepts because of its irregularities and inconsistent structure. Programming examples are mainly given using the language Pascal.

The material is presented at a level and depth suitable for

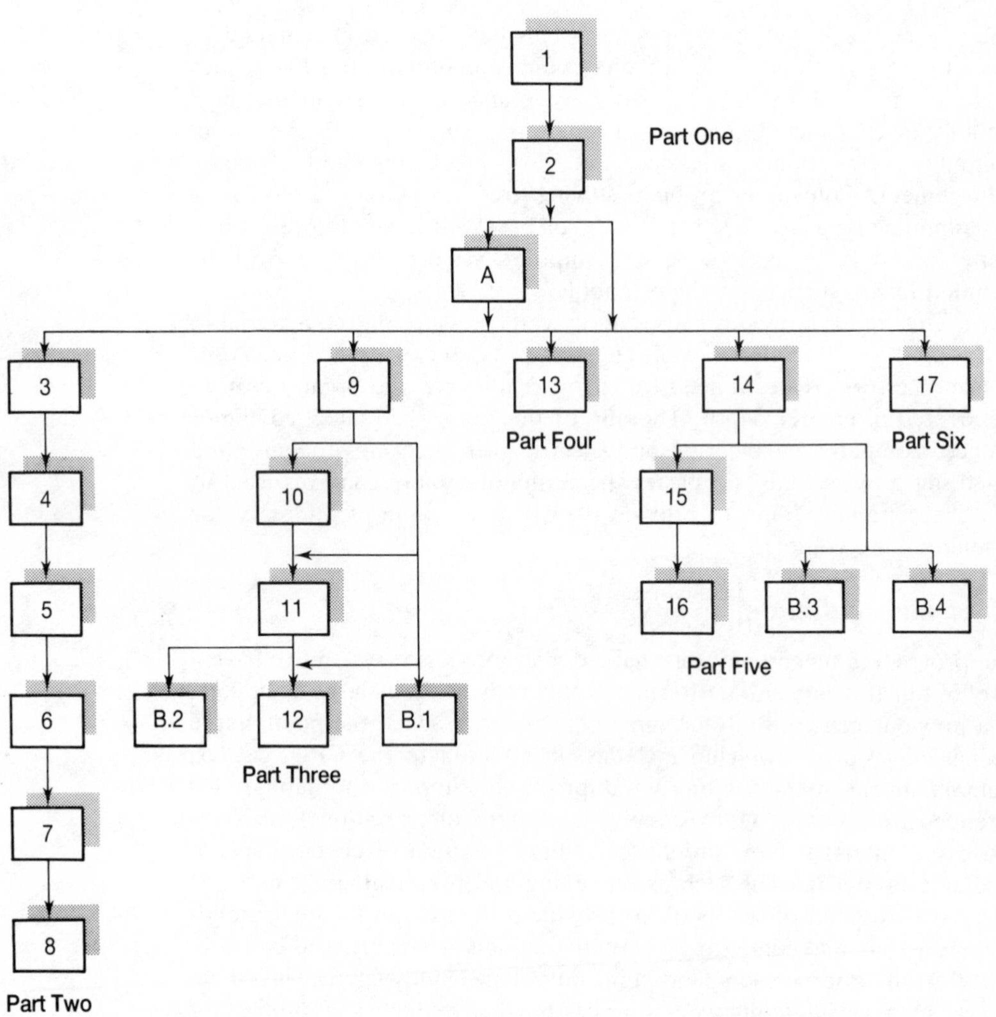

intermediate and advanced undergraduate courses in computer science, computer engineering and electrical engineering curricula. Currently, the book is being used as a text for two courses: Computer Architecture (covering Part One, Part Two and the first chapter of Part Three) and Computer Organization (covering the remainder of the book). The material in Part Three (operating system interface), Part Four (buses), Part Five (acceleration) and Part Six (trends) has been presented in such a way that each part can be taken in isolation as an optional subject for a course. The first chapters of Parts Three and Five serve as an introduction/overview for the remaining chapters of those parts. These remaining chapters are also organized so that they can be taken in isolation. The flowchart opposite shows some possible paths through the book.

The material in this book is complementary to that covered in courses on compilers and operating systems. When a bottom-up approach is taken, these courses can be given after the courses covering the compiler and operating system interface. When a top-down approach is preferred, compilers and operating systems should be covered first.

The reader should have some knowledge of programming languages and preferably some understanding of computer hardware at the introductory level.

Practising professionals can use the book to keep up to date with the latest developments in computer architecture and organization, and to become aware of how these developments interrelate.

Organization

The book is organized into several parts. Part One provides an introductory overview. Part Two discusses the compiler interface. Part Three covers the operating system interface. Part Four discusses buses and can be seen as the hardware interface. Part Five covers acceleration mechanisms, while Part Six covers modern trends, with the accent on non-conventional architectures.

A special language, such as IPL or ISP, could have been used for describing the operation of instructions. Instead, a notation similar to that used in processor manuals has been chosen, because it is closer to the real world and easier to learn. Rather than including a special chapter on the history of computers, the historical evolution of the different concepts is presented together with those concepts. Each chapter starts with an overview of the topics to be discussed and ends with a summary and a set of exercises. The solutions are available at the back of the book to aid self-study. A Glossary of terms has been added for the reader's convenience. An overview of the MC68020 has been included in Appendix A to give the reader a frame of reference for a complete architecture. This appendix is not intended to be comprehensive. Special topics are covered in Appendix B.

Part One Introductory

- **Chapter 1**, **Introduction**, defines computer architecture and introduces a set of quality measures, followed by a classification of computer architectures.
- **Chapter 2**, **Machine Levels**, addresses the levels of abstraction in computer systems (machine levels), together with an analysis of the proper choice of the level to be supported by the architecture. It also addresses software portability.

Part Two The Compiler Interface

- **Chapter 3**, **Data Representation**, illustrates the way in which data, as defined in high-level languages, is represented at the computer architectural level. It also covers data structures, such as stacks and queues, which support the run-time system.
- **Chapter 4**, **Machine Languages**, introduces the basics of instruction set design without going into detail into the different classes of instructions. Instruction formats, the number of operands, and the specification alternatives for opcode, data type, data location and data value are presented.
- **Chapter 5**, **Addressing**, introduces the notion of addressing and addressing modes, together with mechanisms for compact specification of operands (which includes addresses). Addressing modes are used for accessing data elements in arrays, records and stacks. In addition to the MC68000, the VAX-11, NS32000 and Nebula architectures are used to illustrate implementations of addressing mechanisms.
- **Chapter 6**, **Operations on Data**, covers operations on data. It describes the classes of operations, such as move, logical and arithmetic, together with the properties of each class. The effect of multiple-precision arithmetic on data representation is shown, and the handling of range and domain errors is treated.
- **Chapter 7**, **Program Flow Control**, covers the sequence of instructions, condition codes, conditional operations, such as branches, and architectural support for iteration mechanisms.
- **Chapter 8**, **High-Level Program Structures**, deals with groups of instructions – that is, procedures and modules. Binding mechanisms, run-time models and subroutines, and function and module mechanisms are presented conceptually and illustrated with examples from the MC68020 architecture.

Part Three The Operating System Interface

- **Chapter 9**, **Operating Systems**, presents the architectural support for operating systems: process protection, synchronization and switching. It also covers interrupt handling and virtual machine monitors.
- **Chapter 10, Memory Management,** introduces virtual memory and discusses the mapping of virtual addresses on to physical addresses. Relocation, paging and segmentation are presented as mapping mechanisms. Memory protection alternatives are also presented. The introduced concepts are illustrated with some current implementations.
- **Chapter 11, Input/Output,** covers input and output device properties and different types of I/O operations – that is, programmed, overlapped or autonomous I/O. Issues such as I/O in virtual or physical space and properties of I/O processes are addressed.
- **Chapter 12**, **Exception Handling**, covers error and exception handling, together with program debugging support (which typically uses a similar mechanism).

Part Four The Hardware Interface

- **Chapter 13**, **Bus Systems**, introduces the basics of bus systems – concepts such as arbitration, addressing, data transport, interrupts and error handling are presented. Examples are taken from the Multibus II, the Nubus and the IEEE-488 bus, while the VME bus is covered in more detail to show how the different concepts fit together.

Part Five Acceleration

- **Chapter 14**, **Acceleration Mechanisms**, starts with an overview of how program execution can be accelerated and is followed by a discussion of the acceleration mechanisms that can be found at the implementation level of a computer system. It includes caches, pipelining, interleaving and co-processors. The chapter ends with a discussion of the acceleration mechanisms used in the MC68000 family. Some of the concepts introduced in this chapter are detailed in Chapters 15 and 16.
- **Chapter 15**, **Reduced Instruction Set Computers**, presents the basics behind reduced instruction set computers (RISC). It shows how compiler technology can be used to simplify the hardware and to achieve faster instructions. Register windows and delayed branches are presented, together with the RISC II architecture used to show the synergism of the RISC concepts.
- **Chapter 16**, **Multiprocessor Systems**, is devoted to multiprocessor systems, with special attention being paid to interconnection

networks and tightly coupled multiprocessor systems with shared memory. Data consistency issues are also discussed.

Part Six Trends

- **Chapter 17**, **Architectural Trends**, covers trends. It starts with an analysis of the Von Neumann model, indicating its shortcomings. A new taxonomy is presented, based on the work of Treleaven, which allows for the classification of newer computational models. A short description of each of the eight models is given.

Acknowledgements

The first nine chapters of this book are essentially an updated version of the book *Computerarchitectuur* by A. J. van de Goor and H. A. Spanjersberg, written in the Dutch language. I would like to thank H. A. Spanjersberg for his contribution to this Dutch version, especially for his skilful editing, which often involved rewriting parts of the text.

The basic research for the remainder of the book has been done by many students, of whom I would like to mention J. Karbaat and C. van Reeuwijk, who undertook the first attempt to compile the large amount of available information, and M. J. Druzdzel who collected the information on non-conventional architectures.

I owe special acknowledgements to M. Korsloot and M. P. de Kluyver, who translated the original Dutch version and were instrumental in getting the remainder of the book into its current form. Jointly we went through many iterations of restructuring and of incorporating newer and better examples. They also made the writing of this book fun.

I would also like to express my appreciation to Addison-Wesley for the pleasant way we have been able to complete this book.

The author and publishers would like to thank: the Association for Computing Machinery Inc. for permission to reproduce Figures 14.15, 14.16 and 14.22 from A. J. Smith (1982) Cache memories, *Computing Surveys*, **14**(3), 473–530 and Figures 16.20 and 16.21 from J. Archibald and J. L. Baer (1986) Cache coherence protocols: evaluation using a multiprocessor simulation model, *Trans. on Computer Systems*, **4**(4), 273–98; and the Institute of Electrical and Electronics Engineers Inc. for permission to reproduce Tables 15.2 and 15.3 from D. MacGregor and J. Rubinstein (1985) A performance analysis of MC68020-based systems, *IEEE Micro*, **5**(6), 50–70 and Figure 10.14 from W. W. Chu and H. Opderbeck (1974) Performance of replacement algorithms with different page sizes, *Computer*, **7**(11), 14–21.

Finally, I would like to thank my wife Anny, and our children, for their patience and understanding.

A. J. van de Goor

April 1989

For reasons of simplicity, the pronoun 'he' is used to relate to both male and female throughout the book.

Contents

PART ONE

INTRODUCTORY

The introductory part of this book defines the notion of computer architecture and distinguishes the three design levels (architecture, implementation and realization) involved in the process of evolving from idea to finished product. It describes the characteristics a good architecture should have and outlines a classification of traditional architectures.

The different levels of abstraction in a computer system, which are also called virtual machines, are presented. Computer architecture is defined to be the highest level of abstraction that is implemented in hardware. Conversion mechanisms to go from higher to lower levels of abstraction are described in relationship with the problems of software portability to a new architecture.

1 INTRODUCTION

Good judgement comes from experience. Experience comes from bad judgement.

– Jim Horning

It is common practice to introduce a certain discipline by starting with the explanation of its terminology. This chapter, therefore, introduces the basic terminology and definitions used in computer architecture. First, the three design levels (architecture, implementation and realization) are introduced and explained, followed by the characteristics of a good architecture. A classification of the different traditional architectures is given in the final section of this chapter.

1.1 Design levels

In nearly all fields of engineering design, the process of evolving from idea to finished result is divided into smaller steps. For instance, in building a house, the architect lays out the design while various contractors take care of the different building aspects, such as bricklaying and carpentry. This is equally true in computer science. The division is explained in the following sections. First, the design levels are identified. Then, the reasons for this division are given, followed by a discussion of how these design levels influence each other.

1.1.1 Design level identification

In the design and specification of systems in general, and of digital computer systems in particular, three different design levels can be distinguished: **architecture**, **implementation** and **realization**. This tripartite division is explained in the following subsections, with the help of an analogy from daily life, a clock.

Architecture

'The architecture of a computer system can be defined as its functional appearance to its immediate users.'

Amdahl, 1964

The 'architecture' can be regarded as the appearance of a system. The term *architecture* was probably first applied to computers by Buchholz (1962) in the description of the Stretch computer. Yet it is obvious that, viewed in the light of this definition, every mechanism in fact has an architecture, so that the concept of 'system architecture' is much older.

When children are taught to tell the time, they are taught the architecture of an analog clock (although children nowadays perhaps learn to tell time from digital wristwatches). They learn that there are two hands – the long hand, which indicates minutes, and the short hand, which indicates hours – and that the position of both hands together indicates the time. When they can distinguish this architecture from the realization of the clock, they can use a wristwatch as easily as a church clock to see what time it is.

The architecture of a computer is normally defined in a descriptive document, IBM calls it 'Principles of Operation'. Figure 1.1 shows the architectural description of the Motorola MC68020 ADD instruction as included in the MC68020 user's manual (Motorola, 1985). Such an architectural description starts by identifying the performed operation and the assembler syntax. It then gives the applicable data types,

Operation: Source + Destination → Destination

Assembler syntax: ADD <ea>, Dn
ADD Dn, <ea>

Attributes: Size = (Byte, Word, Long)

Description: Add the source operand to the destination operand using binary addition and store the result in the destination location. The size of the operation may be specified to be byte, word or long. The mode of the instruction indicates which operand is the source and which is the destination as well as the operand size.

Condition codes:

X	N	Z	V	C
*	*	*	*	*

N: Set if the result is negative, cleared otherwise.
Z: Set if the result is zero, cleared otherwise.
V: Set if an overflow is generated, cleared otherwise.
C: Set if a carry is generated, cleared otherwise.
X: Set the same as the carry bit.

Instruction format:

15 14 13 12 11 10 9 8 7 6 5 4 3 2 1

1	1	0	1	Register Dn	Opmode	Effective address Mode	Effective address Register

Instruction fields:

Register field: Specifies any of the eight data registers.
Opmode field:

Byte	Word	Long	Operation
000	001	010	<ea> + <Dn> → <Dn>
100	101	110	<Dn> + <ea> → <ea>

FIGURE 1.1
Architectural description of the MC68020 ADD instruction.

followed by a short description of the actions performed by the instruction and the effect that these actions have on the condition codes. The last part of the architectural description shows the instruction format (binary representation) and the use of the different fields within that format.

Implementation

The 'implementation' (or organization) of a system means '*the logic structure that gives shape to the architecture*'. One could say that the architecture describes *what* happens and the implementation describes *how* it happens. Returning to the example of the clock, the implementation describes how the energy is supplied to make the hands turn

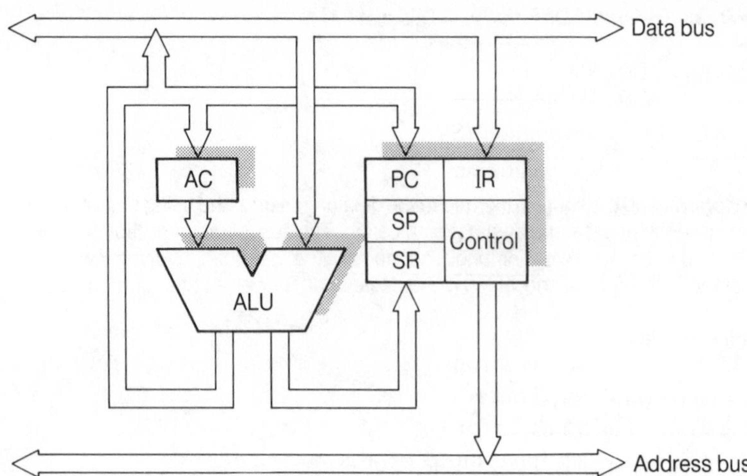

FIGURE 1.2

Basic implementation of a CPU.

(gravitation, elasticity, electricity) and how the time-keeping precision is achieved (balance, pendulum, crystal, tuning fork, AC power frequency).

Figure 1.2 shows a simplified representation of the implementation of a central processing unit (CPU), which has an arithmetic and logic unit (ALU), a single accumulator (AC), a program counter (PC), a stack pointer (SP) and a status register (SR). The instruction register (IR) contains the instruction that is being executed, while control and timing is performed by the control section. Sometimes this control section is implemented in the form of a program (called a **microprogram**).

In computer design, several implementation choices must be made: the choice between a serial or parallel (byte/word oriented) data flow, hard-wired or microprogrammed instructions, decisions of how to encode information, considerations about the cost/performance ratio for a given implementation, and so on. A given architecture should not be a constraint to the implementation. As just discussed, the implementation designer is free to choose in a large number of areas – for example, the choice between electrical or mechanical propulsion when implementing a clock. A good architecture will not limit this freedom, so a certain architecture can lead to a multitude of implementations.

Realization

The realization is '*a concrete version of the implementation*'. It determines which components will be used, how these components will be interconnected and how they will be positioned with respect to each other. Other realization aspects are component reliability, maintenance, cooling, shielding, packaging, and so on.

Table 1.1 Technologies used in the IBM/360 family and its successors.

Model	Technology	
360	Small-scale integration (SSI)	1 . . . 10 gates/chip
370	Medium-scale integration (MSI)	10 . . . 100 gates/chip
303x	Large-scale integration (LSI)	100 . . . 10 000 gates/chip
43xl	Very-large-scale integration (VLSI)	> 10 000 gates/chip

The realization is strongly connected to the continuous development of components. This is exemplified by the different generations of the IBM/360 machines – for an architectural description see Amdahl (1964) – all of which have more or less the same architecture, but later models use newer technologies, or at least higher packaging densities (see Table 1.1).

1.1.2 Reasons for a level structure

At first glance, the division into three design levels may appear to be somewhat artificial and the reader may wonder whether this division is a purely theoretical matter, without any practical relevance. When the complete design of a computer system is considered, it can be concluded that it is almost impossible for a designer to design such a complex system alone. So the system design process must be split up into separate activities, a process which is called **division of labour**. There are two possibilities for the division of labour: horizontal and vertical division. For a computer consisting of the following subsystems, CPU, memory and input/output (I/O), the **horizontal division** means that each subsystem is designed independently – that is, with its own architecture, implementation and realization. **Vertical division** means that the architectural phase is relevant to the whole system, rather than to each subsystem independently, after which the implementation and realization phases come into action.

The horizontal division has disadvantages with respect to the vertical division. A disadvantage is that decisions must be made about the division of units that have not yet been defined, because the architectural phase is postponed until all work has been divided. Conway (1968) has stated that this always leads to a design reflecting the human organizational structure of the design team, instead of a construction serving the intended design as well as possible.

A second disadvantage is that the horizontal division burdens the designer of the subsystem with all of the aspects (that is, all three design levels) of that subsystem: the functions, the language aspects needed to make a subsystem function, the choice of components, the positioning of components, and so on. This means that a designer must master a large variety of disciplines and technologies.

However, the third disadvantage, which is the most serious one, is the inconsistency in the overall architecture, terminology and description of the system. It is apparent that, in the horizontal division of labour, the design of every subsystem indeed satisfies the interfaces, which have been agreed upon, but that every designer will have met these interfaces in his own way. As a result, the methodology is hard for the end user to understand, because there is no **unity of concept** at each design level. This unity-of-concept principle is important for design quality. The underlying line of thought is as follows. A computer system is meant to serve a certain class of users, so these users, or at least some of them, should be able to understand the architecture of that design; that is why it should be possible for one single person to understand, master and design the complete architecture, which is only possible when the design is consistent. This goal can only be reached by having one single person, or at most a small number of closely co-operating people, draft the design. Brooks (1975) describes the problems involved in the design of the first operating system for the IBM/360. Before the architecture had been completed by a small team, too many people were already involved in implementing the operating system, causing *ad hoc* architectural extensions.

Thus, as the foregoing illustrates, horizontal division is not very useful in practical computer design situations. Therefore, vertical division of labour is not only preferred, but should be mandatory.

1.1.3 Reduction in mutual influence between levels

In the previous subsections, the three design levels have been discussed and the interfaces between these levels pointed out. One design level may influence the others. This influence is self-evident in the hierarchical order architecture → implementation → realization, but it also holds the other way round. To reduce this mutual influence, it is important to define the interfaces between these levels as clearly as possible, giving a maximum freedom of choice within each level.

At the architectural level, an example of the importance of clearly defined interfaces between design levels is the IBM/370 architecture, which has served as a well-defined standard allowing many different implementations and realizations. At the implementation level, a similar example is the definition of the VME bus, the system bus for many computer families, among them the Motorola MC68000 computer family. Thanks to such a standard, a manufacturer can compose a variety of systems (consisting of a CPU, I/O and memory) with varying cost/performance ratios. In these computer systems, the CPUs can be replaced by more powerful models without making hardware and/or software changes in peripherals. For the user's benefit, other manufacturers can now supply hardware for computers of this type.

These examples illustrate the reduction in mutual influence, in the case in which connections between units are realized according to an accepted standard. Still, it is crucial that the designer, who is occupied with one level, familiarizes himself with the other levels; that is, the designer should, so to speak, 'peep over the wall' around his own design level. An example of this peeping over the architecture–implementation–realization walls is the move from the MC6800 8-bit architecture to the MC68020 32-bit architecture. The lower costs of memory elements justified the use of larger primary memories, which resulted in the need for a larger addressing space, while the development of more powerful digital components motivated the addition of more complicated functions to the architecture.

1.2 Characteristics of a good architecture

The quality of an architecture is determined by the accessibility of the various functions. Obviously, the desired functions must all be available, but that is not all. Even if certain functions are available, using them can be complicated and annoying, because of operating instructions that are hard to handle and remember. An architecture that is straightforward in use is often called 'clean'. The question of whether an architecture is good or bad cannot be answered in a standard way; it is a matter of balance, judgement and taste. However, a set of desirable characteristics can be given with which to judge an architecture (Blaauw, 1985). These characteristics are explained in the following subsections.

1.2.1 Consistency

An important characteristic of a clean architecture is **consistency**. This means that, with a partial knowledge of the system, the remainder can be predicted. If, for instance, the instruction for taking the logarithm has to be added to the instruction set, this operation will, in a clean architecture, already have been defined largely on account of other, earlier defined operations. The data and instruction format should be the same as for other arithmetic operations. Rounding, precision and significance should be handled like other results. Taking the logarithm of zero should produce a similar exception as, for instance, that of division by zero.

An example of an inconsistent design is the different size of the immediate operands of the MC68020 ADDQ (ADD Quick) and MOVEQ (MOVE Quick) instructions. For the ADDQ instruction, the immediate operand is a 3-bit, unsigned integer (ranging from 1 to 8, where the binary code 0 specifies the value 8), but for the MOVEQ instruction, the immediate operand is an 8-bit two's complement integer (with a range between −128 and +127).

Starting off at the point of consistency, three other characteristics or design principles can be derived from it. These are orthogonality (not mixing separate functions), propriety (not introducing irrelevant functions) and generality (not restricting functions). As will be seen, still more principles follow from these.

1.2.2 Orthogonality

In a good architecture, conceptually independent functions are kept separate in their specifications. This principle is called **orthogonality** or sometimes 'separation of concerns'. This term stems from mathematics, where it was originally used to describe the property of a set of co-ordinates that are related such that a change in position along any one of them causes no change in the positions along any other co-ordinate.

Referring once more to an example from the world of the watchmaker, the standard functioning of a clock can be enhanced by providing a luminous dial and hands and by adding an alarm facility. These are independent functions and the principle of orthogonality would be violated if the alarm could only operate with a lighted dial (or worse, if the dial could only be lighted if the alarm was ringing). The MC68020 architecture has a MOVE operation whereby the source as well as the destination operand can specify an effective address, which consists of a mode and a register field. Most other MC68020 instructions, such as ADD (see Figure 1.1), can only specify an effective address for one operand while the other operand can only specify a data register. From this, it can be stated that, in the MC68020 architecture, the specification of the operation is not orthogonal to the specification of the operands.

1.2.3 Propriety

In a good architecture, the specified functions logically belong to the essential requirements of a system. This principle is called **propriety**. Thus, for an analog clock, hands and a dial are proper. The opposite of propriety is **extraneousness**; that is, the introduction of something alien to the purpose to be served. An example of a system that violates the propriety characteristic is the gear box in a car. Shifting gears is not proper to driving; it is only required because of the limited effective torque range of the engine. An automatic gear shift agrees better with demands for propriety in the architecture of a car.

An example of propriety in computers is the representation of integers and especially the unique representation of zero in the two's complement notation. In this notation, the representation of zero corresponds to the definition and use of zero in mathematics, where the number zero is unsigned. Both the one's complement and the sign magnitude notation have distinct positive and negative zeros. Therefore, both integer representation mechanisms require architectural rules like 'plus zero equals minus zero' to prevent behaviour contrary to mathematical conventions. This kind of impropriety is of no help to the user in solving his problems.

Another example of impropriety is the MC68000 CLR instruction which executes a read cycle before performing the desired write. Reading an operand is not proper with respect to the instruction 'Clear' and can even cause disastrous results – for example, when trying to clear a write-only command register in an I/O device. (This bug has been corrected in the MC68010 and following processors.)

Parsimony

One of the principles that follows from propriety is that a good architecture is also economical, in the sense that functions not proper to the system should not be present. Even if a certain function can be included in the design without further expense, the designer should still ask himself whether the function is proper to the concept of the computer. It is, for example, easy to include an instruction in the MC68020 architecture to take the one's complement of a 32-bit floating-point number, as this can be done without extra hardware. However, this instruction is of no use, so its inclusion would violate the principle of parsimony.

Transparency

The principle of transparency is also derived from the principle of propriety and means that the choices made at the implementation or realization level have no influence on the architecture; in other words, these choices are **transparent** to the architecture. Hence, the specification of a certain level should not be influenced in any part by the implementation of lower levels. This principle is often defined as 'information hiding' (Parnas, 1975). For example, when dialing long distance, the user must not be bothered with the choosing of channels and exchanges through which the call is routed. All the user wants to do is to dial the number of the person he wants to talk to.

In computer science, an example where this principle is violated is the implementation of a pipeline in RISC-like processors, which use the technique of a delayed branch to achieve a higher performance. This implementation feature, whereby the instruction following a branch is always executed regardless of whether the branch is taken, is not shielded from the architecture and the architecture must know whether or not the underlying implementation uses a delayed branch.

1.2.4 Generality

The ability to use a function for several purposes is denoted in the concept of generality: the designer should be aware of the fact that users will be inventive beyond his imagination and that needs may change beyond his ability to predict them. Therefore, the designer should not limit a function by his own notions regarding its use, unless these notions have become widely accepted by experience.

As an example, consider the I/O structure of a computer. Computers were originally designed for computation only, and I/O was exclusively intended for the exchange of data with the peripherals available at that time (for example, punched card readers, tapes and line printers). Soon, people tried to use this same data exchange mechanism for not only peripherals, but also for process control, which is conceptually different. This could not be achieved without making major changes in the existing I/O structure, because no process control facilities were available. This shows that the original I/O structure was not general enough to realize the needs of the inventive users. Present computer systems usually have a more general I/O structure, which makes a variety of applications and connections possible.

Another example is the use of immediate operands with values 2π, π, $\pi/2$ and $\pi/4$ in a computer where trigonometric functions are used frequently. The use of any constant as an immediate operand, instead of only these four, would have satisfied the generality characteristic. Generality can be achieved by completeness and open-endedness.

Completeness

When all functions of a given class are provided in an architecture, the architecture is called **complete**. For example, if a computer incorporates multiplication, it might also be expected to provide the inverse operation, division. If the machine has instructions for fixed-point addition, multiplication and division as well as floating-point addition, it might also be expected to have instructions for floating-point multiplication and division as well.

Theoretically, completeness can be accomplished by providing all functions determined by the product of a set of orthogonal properties, where the set of data types may be one property and the set of operations another property. An example of completeness is the logical operations of the DEC System-10 (DEC, 1969), as shown in Table 1.2. In this architecture, all 16 possible logical operations are present, which illustrates completeness. As far as the frequency of use is concerned, it appears that the instructions AND, OR and NOT are the most commonly used instructions. Leaving out the other 13 logic operations would have saved opcode space and would be justifiable because these 13 functions

Table 1.2 Logical operations of the DEC System-10.

Operand A	0 1 0 1	
Operand B	**0 0 1 1**	**Operation**
0 SETZ	0 0 0 0	0
1 AND	0 0 0 1	A AND B
2 ANDCA	0 0 1 0	~A AND B
3 SETM	0 0 1 1	B
4 ANDCM	0 1 0 0	A AND ~B
5 SETA	0 1 0 1	A
6 XOR	0 1 1 0	A XOR B
7 IOR	0 1 1 1	A OR B
8 ANDCB	1 0 0 0	~A AND ~B
9 EQV	1 0 0 1	~(A XOR B)
10 SETCA	1 0 1 0	~A
11 ORCA	1 0 1 1	~A OR B
12 SETCM	1 1 0 0	~B
13 ORCM	1 1 0 1	A OR ~B
14 ORCB	1 1 1 0	~A OR ~B
15 SETO	1 1 1 1	1

can be realized by the other three. This example clearly illustrates that completeness can lead to proliferation by introducing a superabundance of instructions (possibly violating the principle of parsimony).

The waste of space in coding and therefore the excessive memory use can be reduced by using a decomposition of the orthogonal properties. An example outside the field of computers is a set of screwdrivers consisting of a set of bits and a few different handles into which they fit. In this way, a lot of material can be saved while still providing a full set of screwdrivers.

Open-endedness

Finally, to provide generality, a clean architecture is **open-ended**: as provision for future developments, it is wise to reserve extra space, such as opcode space and address space. If, for example, a processor with 128 instructions has a 7-bit opcode field, no extra instructions can be included in later models of the same architecture. One of the most commonly mentioned constraints of the DEC PDP-11 architecture is its 64 kbytes address space, which limits the maximum size of program and data modules. When the first machine of this family was introduced, common memory sizes were 16 or 32 kbytes. The design, at that time, was open-ended to future expansion of memory size. The VAX-11 (of the same firm) now has an address space of 4 Gbytes. Open-endedness is a sign of modesty on the part of the designer, indicating that he does not know every development now and in the future.

1.3 Classification of computer architectures

Classifying objects, which are changing dynamically in time, is a difficult task. It requires predicting the direction in which these objects will develop. Classification requires a careful investigation of even the least important details in order to test them and to find all aspects that are possible criteria. Out of these aspects, only a few are chosen, because the fewer criteria there are, the clearer the classification. Humans know only three dimensions, a sheet of paper can express only two. Using more than two criteria is risky, while using more than three introduces the danger of being misunderstood.

There is one other aspect related to classification schemes. Once classification schemes are accepted, they have a considerable influence on future thinking. In the case of systems that are still in development, the danger is that the ways of thinking will be limited to the classified cases.

A widely accepted classification has been proposed by Flynn (1966). This classification is very popular and can be found in almost every book on computer architecture. Flynn's classification is based on the identification of two different, independent concepts: the **instruction stream** and the **data stream**. The instruction stream is defined as '*the sequence of instructions as performed by the machine*' and the data stream as '*the sequence of data called for by the instruction stream (including input and partial or temporary results)*' (Flynn, 1966). The classification is based on the multiplicity of both streams (that is, single or multiple) and leads to the following four classes, as shown in Figure 1.3:

(1) **SISD:** The class of *s*ingle *i*nstruction stream/*s*ingle *d*ata stream computers comprises the conventional von Neumann architectures where only a single instruction is processed at a time, operating on a single data stream of operands and results.

(2) **SIMD:** In SIMD computers, a single instruction operates on several data elements simultaneously. According to Flynn, pipelined computers should be included in this category. A classic example of an SIMD architecture is the ILLIAC-IV (Barnes, 1968), where 64 processing elements concurrently execute a single instruction under control of a central control unit. Although a significant speed-up

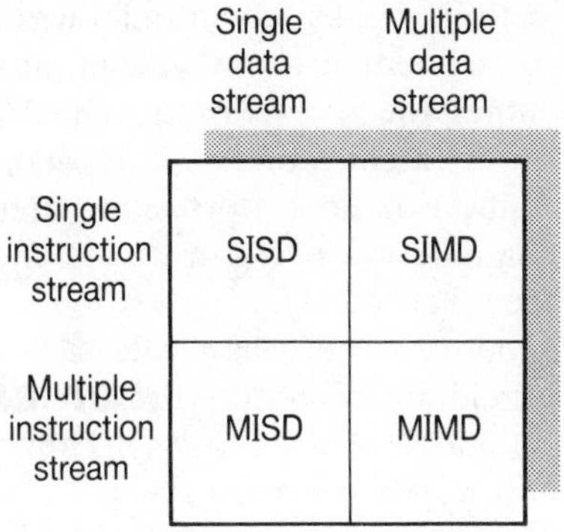

	Single data stream	Multiple data stream
Single instruction stream	SISD	SIMD
Multiple instruction stream	MISD	MIMD

FIGURE 1.3
Flynn's classification of computers.

can be found for problems and algorithms that fit an array of 8×8 processing elements, such a layout is not well suited to other problems that cannot be shaped into a (square) matrix form.

(3) **MISD:** Although Flynn proposes an example of an MISD architecture, a real embodiment of such a system still has to take place. The category MISD can be considered an anomaly of this classification.

(4) **MIMD:** This class is very broad because it comprises all multiprocessor systems, with either private or shared memories, loosely or tightly coupled, and so on. A more extensive discussion of MIMD architectures can be found in Chapter 16.

The problem with this classification is that its resolution is too small, since the class of SIMD computers comprises nearly *all* parallel computers excluding multiprocessor systems. Also, the ambiguity in the meaning of 'data stream' has led to the confusion for pipelined computers (although Flynn placed them in the SIMD class). Table 1.3 lists computer systems for each of the three existing categories.

Table 1.3 Flynn's classification.

SISD	SIMD	MIMD
MC68020	ILLIAC-IV	IBM 370/168MP
VAX-11/780	ICL DAP	UNIVAC 1100/80
NS32000	Staran	C.m*
IBM 360/91	MPP	Cray Y-MP
Cray-1		
Cyber-205		

Flynn's classification speaks about instructions, which are performed by the machine sequentially and which operate on passive data. This classification assumes the sole existence of traditional computers, leaving no room for novel architectures where data is active, or where functional units, like unification processors (logic computers) or reduction engines (reduction computers), perform the computation instead of instruction streams (see Chapter 17).

There are a number of newer classifications that consider the latest developments in the field of computer architecture – see Kennaway (1983), Vegdahl (1984) and Treleaven (1984). However, it must be said that they have not been widely accepted (yet).

SUMMARY

- The notion of 'architecture' can be defined as the functional appearance of an object to its user. This definition is not restricted to computer systems, as every object has an architecture.

- Other characteristics of an object are its implementation (the structure that gives shape to the architecture) and its realization (the concrete, tangible version of the implementation).

- When looking at the architecture of computer systems, an architecture is considered well designed or clean when it meets design characteristics such as consistency, orthogonality, propriety, parsimony, transparency, generality, completeness and open-endedness.

- Consistency means that with a partial knowledge of a system the rest can be predicted.

- Orthogonality means that conceptually independent functions are kept separate in their specifications.

- Transparency means that no implementation aspects are included in a definition at the architectural level.

- Generality allows functions to be used in a broad range of applications.

- Open-endedness requires that a system should have room for growth.

- Flynn's classification is based on the differentiation of single versus multiple instruction and data streams. This results in the following classification of traditional computers: SISD, SIMD, MISD and MIMD. Novel architectures, such as data flow, do not fit into this classification scheme.

EXERCISES

1.1 Determine whether the following items belong to the architecture, the implementation or the realization level:

(a) Instructions in some architectures have a source Src and a destination Dst operand. The distinction between the following instruction forms is at which level: ADD Src, Dst versus ADD Dst, Src.

(b) The choice of adding a floating-point processor via special hardware or via microprogramming.

(c) The choice of using an ALU chip of manufacturer M1 or M2.

(d) The conditions under which the carry bit is set as a result of an add operation.

(e) The data path/control level of a computer.

(f) The alternative of executing the ADD.W (add two 16-bit integers) instruction in one cycle with a 16-bit ALU or in two cycles with an 8-bit ALU.

1.2 The addition of a new function, for example log (*x*), can be done in the hardware or in the firmware (microprogramming) of the machine. Indicate whether the following statements are true or false:

(a) The addition of a new function in firmware is transparent to the architecture. (This means that the architecture of the machine does not have to be changed or extended.)

(b) The architecture can be designed such that it is transparent whether the addition of a new function is done at the hardware or firmware level.

1.3 Check whether the following statements are true:

(a) Vertical division of labour results in a consistent architecture.

(b) Horizontal division of labour is the best approach to system design.

(c) The design of a good architecture requires a large team where decisions are made democratically.

1.4 A good architecture has to satisfy the following characteristics: consistency, orthogonality, propriety, parsimony, transparency, generality, completeness and open-endedness. Determine for each of the following architectures with which characteristic it is in conflict:

(a) A given architecture allows the operation ADD, SUB and MUL to be applicable to all data registers D0 through D7. The DIV operation is only applicable to D6 and D7.

(b) The architecture of the MC68000 does not support operations on complex numbers such as $a + b * i$. It has been proposed to extend the architecture with one new instruction which can add two complex numbers.

(c) A given architecture did not support operations with constants. To compensate for this, the architecture was extended to allow for operations with the constants 10 (for decimal arithmetic) and π (for trigonometric functions).

(d) The economic use of memory is a worthwhile goal. An architecture with an 8-bit opcode field has been designed with 255 defined instructions.

(e) The signalling of insufficient bits for the result of an ADD operation is done via the overflow bit, while for a SUB operation it is done via the carry bit.

(f) An architecture has the following instructions: ADD, MOV, MUL, DIV, COM (complement). The SUB instruction is missing because the availability of the COM plus ADD instruction was considered adequate.

(g) An architecture supports the following operations on integers: ADD, SUB, MUL, DIV, MOV and COM. For floating point, it supports the operations: ADD, SUB, MOV and COM, because of the expense of the MUL and DIV operations.

(h) A particular computer supports all 16 Boolean operations.

1.5 Which criteria did Flynn use to classify the architectures of traditional machines? To which class does the MC68020 architecture belong and to which class does the ILLIAC-IV belong?

References

Amdahl, G. M. *et al.* (1964). Architecture of the IBM/360. *IBM Journal of Research and Development*, **8**(2), 87–101.

Barnes, G. H. *et al.* (1968). The ILLIAC IV computer. *IEEE Trans. on Computers*, **C-17**(8), 746–57.

Blaauw, G. A. and Brooks, F. P. (1985). *Computer Architecture*. Technical University of Twente: Netherlands.

Brooks, F. P. (1975). *The Mythical Man-Month*. Addison-Wesley: Reading, MA.

Buchholz, W. (1962). *Planning a Computer System*. McGraw-Hill: New York.

Conway, M. E. (1968). How do Committees invent? *Datamation*, **14**(4), 28–31.

DEC (1969). *PDP-10 Reference Handbook*. Digital Equipment Corporation: Maynard, MA.

Flynn, M. (1966). Very high speed computing systems. *Proc. of the IEEE*, **54**(12), 1901–9.

Kennaway, J. R. and Sleep, M. R. (1983). Novel architectures for declarative languages. *Software & Microsystems*, **2**(3), 59–70.

Motorola, (1985). *MC68020, 32-bit Microprocessor User's Manual*. Prentice Hall Incorporated: Englewood Cliffs, NJ.

Parnas, D. L. *et al.* (1975). *On the Design and Development of Program Families*. Technische Hochschule Darmstadt, Fachbereich Informatik, Forschungsbericht BS I 75/2.

Treleaven, P. C. and Lima, G. I. (1984). Future computers: Logic, data flow, . . ., control flow? *Computer*, **17**(3), 47–57.

Vegdahl, S. R. (1984). A survey of proposed architectures for the execution of functional languages. *IEEE Trans. on Computers*, **C33**(12), 1050–71.

2 Machine Levels

Hope is a good breakfast, but a bad supper.
– Francis Bacon

2.1 Machine level identification
2.2 Conversion mechanisms between machine levels
2.3 Implementation of new levels
2.4 Tradeoff between hardware and software
2.5 Software portability related to machine levels

Chapter 1 showed how the architecture of a computer system can be regarded as a functional description of that computer system, as seen by the user. The question now arises: Who is the user? Is it the person using an application program – for example, an aircraft designer using a CAD/CAM package? The programmer of that application program? Or the systems programmer? In fact, the question itself gives us a clue to the answer, as in each case we can speak of a user, the major difference being the level at which the user uses the system. The aim of this chapter is, therefore, to discuss the various machine levels existing in a computer system, the mechanisms used to convert from one level to another and the level to be chosen for hardware implementation. Finally, the architectural requirements for the portability of software from one system to another are analyzed.

2.1 Machine level identification

In deciding which instructions are to form the 'machine language' of a computer system, the designer needs to seek a balance between the performance, on the one hand, and the complexity of the machine and the overall cost of the hardware and software, on the other hand. Historically, high-performance requirements have created a need for powerful instructions, which required many high-speed electronic circuits, thereby raising the cost. In contrast, the requirements for a general-purpose system have necessitated instructions of a less specialized nature. As a consequence, this tradeoff for general-purpose computers has usually resulted in simple machine languages, which are hard for humans to understand. On the contrary, high-level languages, such as ALGOL and Pascal, are designed to protect the user against tiring details, and they allow for higher productivity in terms of program development as well as maintenance. One of the reasons for this is that high-level language programs are more readable (although some people can write unreadable programs in any language) and provide constructs with which the problem can be solved more easily.

Figure 2.1 illustrates how the simple operation of assigning the sum of two numbers to a variable is programmed in a high-level language (Pascal), an assembly language and a machine language (MC68020). From this example, it is clear that it is preferable to write programs in a high-level language. If this is not possible for one reason or another, the use of an assembly language is preferable to a machine language.

Figure 2.1 depicts three language levels existing in a computer system. Figure 2.2 shows yet another machine level (not shown in Figure 2.1), located between assembly and machine language, referred to as the **operating system** level. (Note that the levels in Figure 2.2 are organized according to the user's point of view. The assembly level is higher than that of the operating system because the operating system functions are available to the user.) This level handles such matters as input/output (I/O), memory management, process scheduling, and so on. It is called a **hybrid** level because it consists of two different classes of instructions executed in different ways. One class consists of machine language instructions, while the other class allows for process creation, synchronization and I/O. The different mechanisms used to execute these two classes of instructions will be discussed in more detail in Section 2.2.4.

In machines made until the early 1960s, the machine instructions were realized directly in hardware. However, the introduction of microprogramming by Wilkes in 1951 meant that each instruction of the machine language could be translated into a sequence of microinstruc-

High-level language level (Pascal):

```
A := B + C;
```

Assembly language level (MC68020):

```
MOVE.W  B, D1
ADD.W   C, D1
MOVE.W  D1, A
```

Machine language level (MC68020) (in bits):

```
1000:  MOVE.W  (0x2002).W,D1     0011 0010 0011 1000
                                 0010 0000 0000 0010
1004:  ADD.W   (0x2004).W,D1     1101 0010 0111 1000
                                 0010 0000 0000 0100
1008:  MOVE.W  D1,(0x2000).W     0011 0001 1100 0001
                                 0010 0000 0000 0000
2000:  A
2002:  B
2004:  C
```

FIGURE 2.1
Different language levels.

tions specifying the control signals for the electronic components in every detail (Wilkes, 1951). The complete set of microinstructions can be considered as a language in itself, resulting in a new (virtual) machine level.

Therefore, most current computers can be regarded as containing five machine levels, denoted as L1–L5, respectively (Figure 2.2). An extension is formed by the electronic circuits, indicated as L0. There are six interfaces between these levels, signified as I0–I5. Levels L0 and L1 together form the hardware of a system. The term 'hardware' is ambiguous, because sometimes only level L0 is considered to be the 'hardware' and L1 the 'firmware'. Levels L2–L5 are called the software. Level L5 consists of dedicated application programs, particularly adapted to the needs of an end user – for example, a payroll program. In terms of Figure 2.2, computer architecture can be defined as '*the description of the interface between the hardware and the software*' – that is, the interface I1. The levels below I1 form the real machine while all the levels above I1 comprise the virtual machine – that is, the user is under the impression that a machine exists, but in reality it is a simulated version of the machine.

Each manufacturer publishes manuals for its computers, called *Machine Language Reference Guide*, *Principles of Operation* or *Hardware Reference Manual*. These manuals cover interface I1. Programs at this level are executed by the microprogram or by the hardware directly (when the technique of microprogrammed interpretation is not used). Hardly any manufacturer publishes manuals on the hardware instructions used by the level L1 machine (the I0 interface), thereby leaving a certain degree of freedom to choose any implementation.

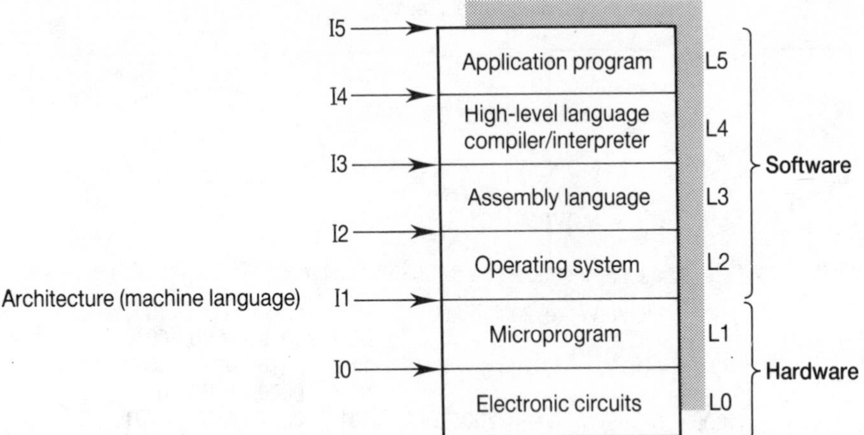

FIGURE 2.2

Machine levels in a computer system.

2.2 Conversion mechanisms between machine levels

Section 2.1 showed how the programmer prefers to program in a level above machine language and certainly above the microprogram level. The question that arises now is how a machine with such a low-level language can execute a program written in a higher-level language. In other words: How is a program converted from one level to another? In answering this question, we will only consider the conversion from a higher to a lower level, as the reverse is almost never possible. At a lower level, it is no longer possible (or at least very difficult) to recognize what operation was originally intended by the programmer. This reduces the quality of reporting errors, with messages related to statements in the original high-level program. This supports the plea for defining an architecture at a level that closely resembles the high-level language. However, instructions with an increased complexity tend to decrease system performance and increase implementation complexity. The quest for architectures with an ever-increasing level has led to the surge of reduced instruction set computers (RISC), as described in Chapter 15. Figure 2.1 shows that, from looking at the instructions at the lowest language level, it is not possible to tell to which higher-level statement they belong. This is often referred to as a **loss of semantics**. This large difference in semantics between the machine language and the high-level language used is called the **semantic gap**. To go from one level to another, compilation, interpretation or a combination of both can be used. The combination involves the introduction of an intermediate language.

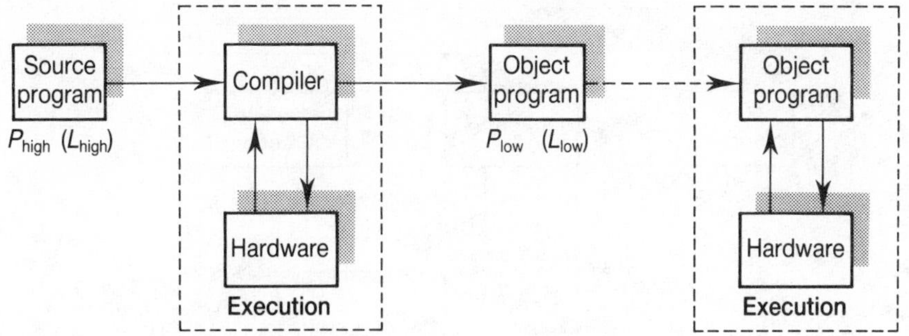

FIGURE 2.3

Compilation from L_{high} to L_{low}.

2.2.1 Compilation

During the compilation of a **source** program P_{high} (which is written in the high-level language L_{high}) into an **object** program in a lower-level language L_{low} (which can be handled by the machine), each statement of the program P_{high} is replaced by a series of instructions from L_{low} such that together they have the same effect as the original statement from P_{high}. This conversion process eventually results in the creation of a program P_{low} in language L_{low}. The conversion process is accomplished by a program called a **compiler** (usually written in L_{low}), which accepts the original program P_{high} as input data and generates the object program P_{low} as output data. After compilation, this object program is loaded into the machine for execution (Figure 2.3). During execution, the source program P_{high} is no longer needed and can be removed from memory, although it should be saved because virtually no program is correct the first time. The development of compilers is a complex task, which is too detailed to be discussed here, but an excellent reference on this subject is Aho (1985).

2.2.2 Interpretation

When a program P_{high}, written in language L_{high}, is interpreted at level L_{low}, a special program, called an **interpreter**, is required. The interpreter takes one instruction from the program P_{high}, analyzes it and causes a series of instructions at level L_{low} to be executed with the same effect. This process continues until the complete program has been executed (Figure 2.4).

The advantage of this conversion mechanism is that an interpreter is often relatively small, making it easier to port a language to (re-implement it on) a new machine rather than a compiler. Another reason for using interpretation can be that the source language makes demands on the dynamic behaviour of data types and structures, making compilation impossible, for example, because the data type of variables changes during execution from integer to floating point. APL is an example of a language that permits this kind of change during execution.

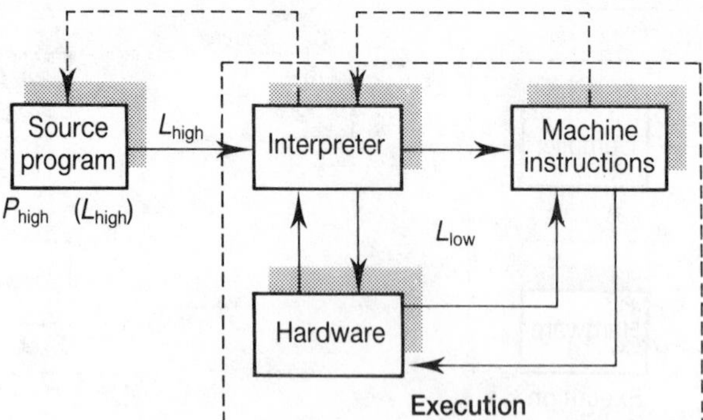

FIGURE 2.4
Interpretation of L_{high} at L_{low} level.

This implies that *early binding* (the fixation of data types and structures at compile time) is not possible during the compilation of APL and must be postponed until execution time.

The disadvantage of interpretation is that the execution of the source program is generally slower than that of an object program produced by a compiler, because each higher-level language statement has to be analyzed, after which an equivalent sequence of lower-level language instructions has to be executed. The difference in speed is typically a factor of ten. As interpretation consists of many complicated activities, it is therefore time consuming, which is made worse by the fact that instructions that have to be carried out frequently (for example, in loops) have to be interpreted over and over again, every time they are executed.

Traditional instruction sets do support early binding because of the resulting execution time efficiency and because many languages, such as FORTRAN and ALGOL, were designed with early binding (and this efficiency) in mind.

2.2.3 Combined compilation and interpretation

The combined compilation and interpretation mechanism uses an intermediate level language L_{int}, with a level between L_{low} and L_{high}. A program P_{high}, written in the source language L_{high}, is compiled into a program P_{int} in language L_{int}. Program P_{int} is then interpreted at level L_{low} by an interpreter (Figure 2.5).

The combined compilation and interpretation mechanism improves program portability (see Section 2.5), while also having the advantages of both methods. For example, the intermediate level language L_{int} can be chosen such that the translation process is easy, the object program P_{int} is small and the compiler can be small as well. On the other hand, the intermediate level language L_{int} is easier to interpret than the higher-level language L_{high}. However, the execution speed of completely compiled

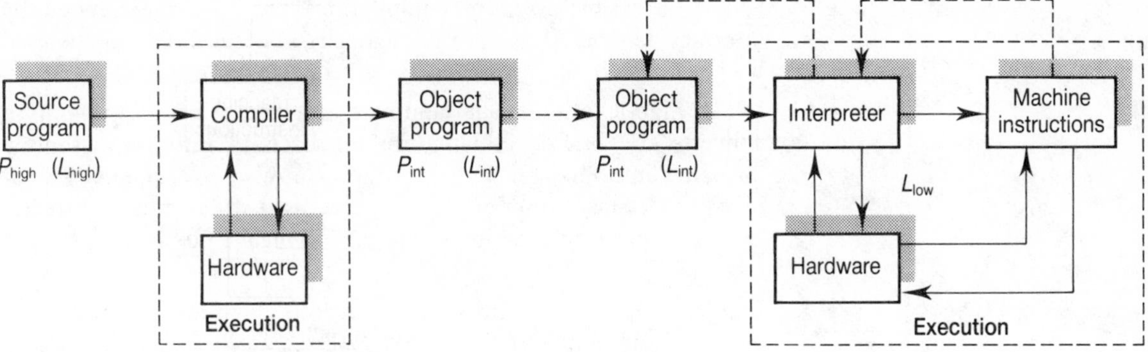

FIGURE 2.5

Combined compilation and interpretation.

languages cannot be usually reached, due to the relatively slow interpretation process.

Choosing the intermediate level language L_{int} at a fairly high level can result in the preservation of much of the semantics of the source program. This clearly improves the possibilities for accurate error reporting, since the original meaning of a statement is still known. Consequently, an error can be connected to the corresponding statement in the source program that in fact caused the error. A good example of this method is P-code as an intermediate level language between Pascal and machine code.

2.2.4 Commonly used conversion mechanisms

The conversion mechanisms used between the levels of Figure 2.2 are as follows:

- L0: The instructions the microprogram is written in (defined by interface I0, where L_{high} = I0) are interpreted by the electronic circuits of L0.
- L1: The microprogram at L1 interprets the machine language of I1 with instructions of I0, so L_{high} = I1 and L_{low} = I0.
- L2: L2 is a hybrid level. Some instructions of I2 are identical to those of I1 – for example, the ADD instruction. These identical instructions are passed from I2 to I1 to be interpreted by L1. The other I2 instructions are typical operating system functions, such as *Time_of_Day* or *Print_a_Message*, which are interpreted by L2.
- L3: At L3, it is possible to speak of a virtual L3 machine, with a language L3 as a possible interface to the user. However, most users refrain from using assembly language and prefer to make use of languages that are still higher than L3. The assembler translates

(this is a simple form of compilation) the language defined by interface I3 (called assembly language) into the language defined by I2 (which is the operating system interface).

- L4: A high-level language compiler, interpreter or a combination converts the high-level language interface I4 into the assembly language interface I3. This interface can also be called a *virtual machine* because it appears to the user as if the computer directly executes programs written in the language defined by that interface.
- L5: The application program interprets high-level application-oriented commands, such as *Print_Salary_of_Mr_Johnson*, in terms of the language defined by I4.

2.3 Implementation of new levels

The language L_{int} introduced in the combined compilation and interpretation mechanism can be considered a new virtual machine. In the same way, using compilation and interpretation, it is possible to introduce a new virtual machine with certain desired qualifications at each level. It goes without saying that this new virtual machine can be converted to a lower level using one of the three mechanisms described in Section 2.2.

The previous sections showed that creating a new, higher, level does not always imply that a lower level has been completely substituted, since, in Figure 2.2, I1 is a subset of I2; or, in other words, I2 is created by extending I1 with new instructions (such as for file handling).

Another, often-used, method for extending a language is via special facilities, procedures and functions, built into the language. This method is used where the existing language defined by Ix is almost adequate for the desired application and where language Ix offers adequate extension possibilities. The procedure mechanism is a very commonly used implementation mechanism for these extensions. Typical examples are the addition of trigonometrical and statistical functions, or the addition of a graphical toolbox. All these extensions result in the virtual machine Iy of Figure 2.6.

The advantage of this method lies in the fact that the extensions can be made in language Ix, and, as the user is probably familiar with this language, he can create or adapt these extensions himself. The disadvantage is that the efficiency of the extensions greatly depends on the efficiency of the compiler or interpreter used and that the extensions are constrained to fit the framework of the language Lx. For example, it would be very hard to write procedures in Pascal to extend this language to enable real-time processing.

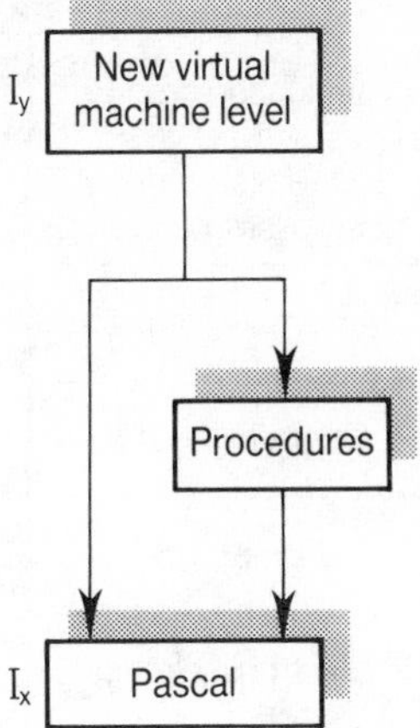

FIGURE 2.6
Language extension with procedures.

2.4 Tradeoff between hardware and software

Before examining the tradeoff between hardware and software, it is important to understand the distinction between them.

- Together with the memory and the peripherals, the electronic circuits that can carry out the microinstructions directly form the **hardware**.
- The microprograms that realize the machine, as specified by the manufacturer, are referred to as **firmware**. However, it is not uncommon to include the firmware when talking about hardware.
- The complex of algorithms and programs designed and brought together to solve certain user problems, to manage accounts and to control and determine the course of events inside the machine is referred to as **software**. More specifically, the latter is called **system software** and the former **application software**.

With due regard to certain borderline cases, it is possible to characterize every operation as either hardware or software. This implies that the designer of a computer system must make an implementation choice about the level at which a certain function is to be introduced: if he chooses L0 or L1, then the function is implemented in hardware; if he chooses a higher level, then the function is performed by software. This decision is a matter of judgement. On the one hand, the designer wants to adhere as closely as possible to the highest language level that has to be supported by the machine and he wants to deliver a product with a high performance. On the other hand, the machine must not become too complex, as regards maintenance and use, and the cost of the electronic

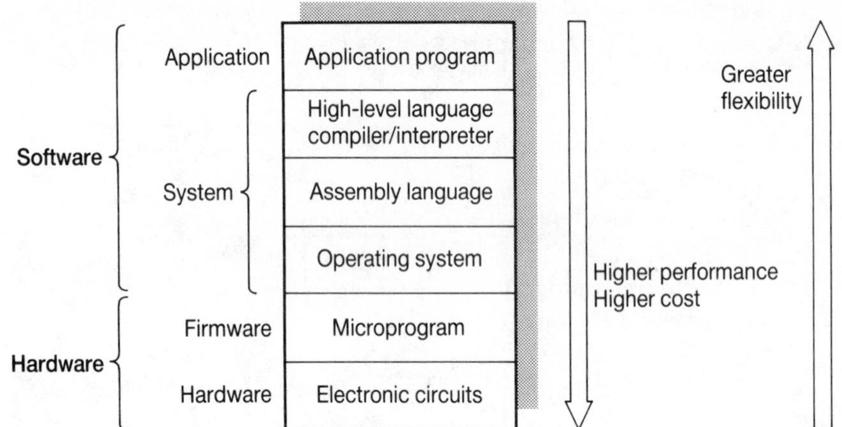

FIGURE 2.7

Effects of implementing functions at different levels.

components should not be too high. Finding a good balance between these two is not always easy. Of course, this is not the only point at which the designer must consider the tradeoffs. As shown in Chapter 1, a tradeoff is also necessary when the characteristics of an architecture are determined.

Figure 2.7 supplements Figure 2.2 in that it illustrates the different levels of a computer system together with the notions of hardware, firmware and software. This figure again demonstrates that shifting the implementation of functions towards the hardware implies an increase in both speed and cost, and that substituting hardware functions by software offers greater flexibility and user friendliness at the cost of speed. In currently available machines, this tradeoff has usually led to low-level machine languages (I1 in Figure 2.2), which are realized in hardware in the older machines. The introduction of microprogramming techniques caused a shift from hardware to software (firmware) because larger instruction sets and more complex instructions became economically feasible. In more recent machines, this trend has reversed itself, tending towards realizing software functions in special hardware, such as floating-point processors and memory management chips, because of the availability of low-cost hardware. Consequently, the central microprocessor has to implement a less extensive instruction set and the overall system can achieve a higher performance. This high performance is dependent on the development of advanced compilers, which can fully exploit the possibilities of each processor.

Sometimes, the designer may wish to leave the decision as to how certain functions are to be implemented (either in hardware or software) to the user. The user then has the option of realizing certain functions, such as double-precision integer operations, floating-point operations, decimal arithmetic or vector operations, in different ways, depending on the requirements. These implementations can be made at different levels. Some possibilities are:

- L4: Write programs in a high-level language to simulate the required functions.
- L3: Write programs in assembly language to simulate these functions.
- L1: Write microprograms to simulate the required functions with the existing hardware (provided that the microprograms can be changed).
- L0: Add special hardware that performs the required functions.

For the last two solutions to be possible, the designer has to make provisions in both the architecture (by adding extra instructions) and the implementation – for example, by adding 'writable control store' for a microprogram. The responsibility for ensuring that any of these four solutions is 'transparent' to the user lies with the designer, who must endeavour to see that the software does not need changing if another implementation is chosen at a later date.

The foregoing discussion has shown that most existing machines use a fairly low level of machine language and that the use of high-level languages is strongly recommended for programmers. Some computers were designed to execute such a high-level language directly, such as the SYMBOL computer of Iowa State University (Smith, 1971) and the JOVIAL Direct Execution Architecture (Chu, 1980). There are, however, some drawbacks attached to this approach. Since there is a wide range of high-level languages, due to the many different application areas, each language would need its own separate processor, because a computer with a very high-level language as its machine language will have great difficulties in executing another high-level language. Another disadvantage is that the efficiency is generally low, because some actions have to be performed over and over again during the interpretation of a program (remember that the machine is interpreted and not translated), whereas many actions have to be performed only once during a compilation process (for example, syntax analysis).

Nowadays, in order to exploit chip technology, computer architects are turning away from the concept of designing architectures with an ever-increasing level, and tending instead towards more simple architectures, such as RISC. In conclusion, therefore, it can be stated that future machines will definitely have to adhere to high-level languages in terms of the machine language primitives, but that a translation step will be necessary. This difference between the architecture and the language

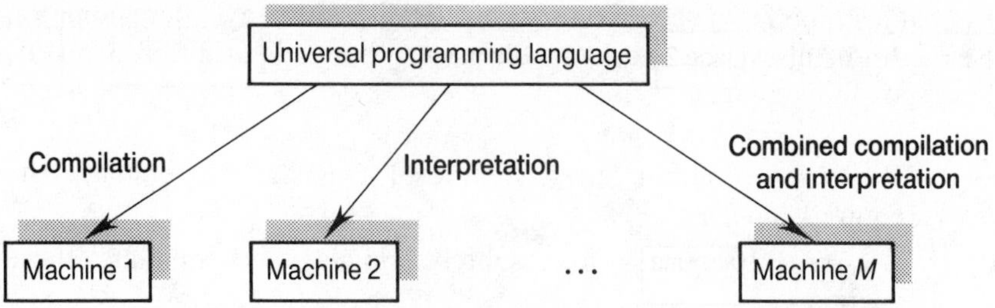

FIGURE 2.8
Universal programming language.

level is necessary in order to offer the freedom of implementing more than one language on the same architecture in an efficient way.

2.5 Software portability related to machine levels

The large variety of existing and future computer systems (and in particular machine languages) has led to the question of **software portability**; that is, the possibility of executing programs written for a computer of brand and type X/A on a computer of brand and type Y/B with little or no effort. Portability is a very important consideration in the introduction of newer (better) architectures and it also allows for protection against too strong a dependency on one manufacturer. This becomes more important as the amount of software, which represents a substantial investment in time and money, increases.

Referring to the different machine levels discussed in Section 2.1, it is natural to question at which level this portability must be realized. In the following subsections, some proposals are given, using different machine levels.

2.5.1 Universal programming language

The most obvious solution to the portability problem at level L4 is to use a **universal programming language** (Figure 2.8). It should be possible to implement such a language on all brands and types of machines (via compilation, interpretation or a combination). It is then easy to move programs from one system to another. A further advantage of this solution is that it requires only M different compilers and/or interpreters (assuming M different machines), which is the absolute minimum, compared to the number of compilers needed for other solutions, as will be seen later.

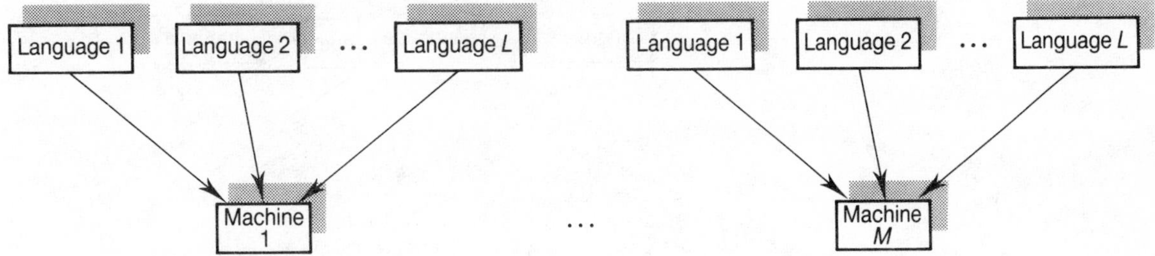

FIGURE 2.9
Brute-force approach.

Attempts to gain acceptance for such a universal language have so far failed (perhaps for some of the same reasons as the synthetic language Esperanto); programmers in a particular application area make specific demands on the language being used and do not want to pay (in the sense that they may be difficult to learn or less efficient to use) for facilities that are not needed or wanted.

2.5.2 Brute-force approach

The **brute-force approach**, which also enables portability at level L4, proposes a direct implementation of every language on every machine (Figure 2.9). No matter what language and machine is chosen by the user, the virtual machine that executes this language is available. If there are L languages and M different machines, $L * M$ implementations of compilers and/or interpreters are required. Considering the vast number of languages and machines already available and the fact that new languages and machines are constantly appearing, this would be a never-ending task. Notwithstanding, this approach is, in fact, the one that best approximates the existing situation.

2.5.3 The UNCOL Language

Because of the large number of compilers and/or interpreters needed with the brute-force approach, attempts have been made to try to find a solution that does not raise the number of implementations by the product of the number of languages and the number of suitable machines ($L * M$), but by the sum ($L + M$). Such a solution would require only one compiler for every new language or for every new machine.

The solution to this approach was to define a new virtual machine to be used as the basis for the implementation of the different languages (Figure 2.10). The machine language of this virtual machine was called UNCOL (Universal Computer-Oriented Language) (Strong, 1958) and was intended to be implemented on all machines. The UNCOL solution has been adopted by certain manufacturers in the sense that their assembly language is the UNCOL of a family of computers, such as the

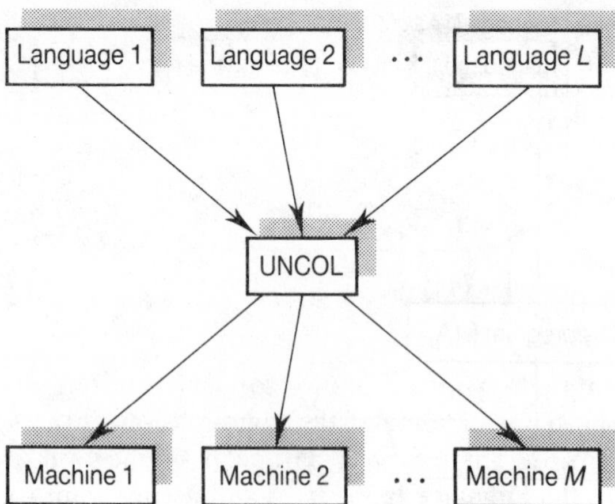

FIGURE 2.10
UNCOL solution.

IBM/360 family or the MC68000 family. Other manufacturers, such as SUN, consider the language C (Johnson, 1978) as their UNCOL language.

2.5.4 Simulation

Porting software written in a high-level language from one architecture to another is generally feasible, assuming the language is also available on the target machine. In contrast, the task of porting machine language programs is much more difficult. Such programs can be executed on a machine with a different architecture by simulating the old machine on the new architecture. This can be done in three ways:

(1) **Interpretation**: This is a rather cumbersome process, since each instruction of the old architecture must be decoded and interpreted at the assembly language level (L3, or even a higher level) of the new machine.

(2) **Emulation**: This can be seen as interpretation at the microprogramming level (L1). The microprogram of the new machine is adapted to execute the machine language of the old machine. The advantage of this approach is the substantial gain in execution speed compared to interpretation.

(3) **Combined interpretation and emulation**: With this method, the most frequently occurring parts of an instruction are emulated – for example, the part for 'instruction fetch' and 'decode' – whereas less frequent parts are executed interpretively. This is equivalent to the approach shown in Figure 2.6, but with Pascal (Ix) replaced with I0 (the microprogramming language). The machine language I1 is

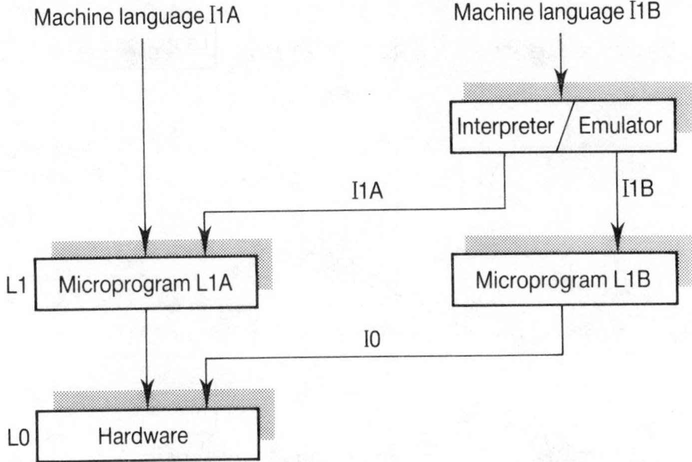

FIGURE 2.11
Combined simulation and emulation.

extended with the 'fetch' and 'decode' instructions executed by the microprogram (equivalent to the procedures in Figure 2.6). An example of this approach is shown in Figure 2.11, where machine language I1B is supported on a machine primarily designed to support I1A.

Generally, the most difficult part of this method is the simulation of the old I/O instructions on the new hardware. Because there can be a significant difference in the way the processor and devices communicate, directly mapping one system on to another is nearly always impossible. Furthermore, a new system generally has other peripherals, different from the old system, such that routines like a 'printer driver' cannot be ported without changes.

The emulation and combined methods were used successfully by, for example, IBM during the introduction of the IBM/360 family. IBM simplified the conversion of existing software written on older machines, such as the IBM 1401, by providing the IBM/360 with emulation software.

A straightforward method of emulation is the one where the new machine has different **modes** through which the machine language of an older architecture is directly available. The mode is used to choose between the different microprograms, which can be supported by special hardware for the sake of efficiency (Figure 2.12). Examples of this are the IBM/370, which emulates the IBM/360 machines, and the VAX-11/780, which can mimic the PDP-11 series. In the latter case, the difference in instruction sets is very large.

Machines that simplify the emulation of other architectures need a flexible microprogramming structure that does not rely on automatically

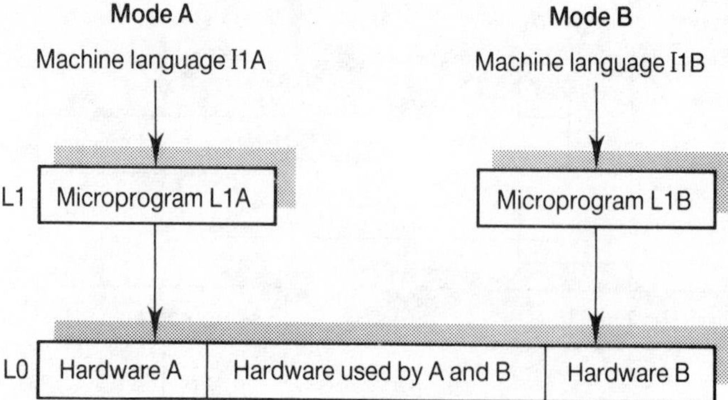

FIGURE 2.12
Emulation by means of machine modes.

activated hardware circuits for an optimal execution of its 'own' architecture. Because this is the case with high-speed versions of the IBM 360/370 and PDP-11 models, these machines are less suited to emulate other machines. Machines that use the mode concept, and are made to support only a few (and frequently only one) other architectures, need less flexibility and can therefore make more extensive use of hardware support that is machine language dependent.

2.5.5 Virtual machine monitors

An application program nearly always uses the facilities of the underlying operating system. However, newer generations of hardware often also offer new generations of operating systems, which may be attributed to new concepts in the design of the operating system, such as the process model of Chapter 9 or to new hardware concepts, such as virtual memory. This causes a portability problem because application programs are usually bound to the original operating system, due to the special facilities provided by that operating system. This problem may be solved by introducing a special operating system, called the **virtual machine monitor**, whose only function is to offer a number of independent, virtual, L1 machines. The virtual machine monitor presents each user with an interface I1V which appears identical to the I1 interface the user used to see (Parmalee, 1972). The newly introduced level is then called L1V (Figure 2.13). L1V is called a **virtual machine**, and it can support different operating systems simultaneously (including L1V itself), of course at the cost of extra overhead. This concept has been used, for example, by IBM where VM/370 (Virtual Machine/370) is the virtual machine monitor. Other aspects of virtual machine monitors, including their implications for the architecture of a computer, can be found in Appendix B.

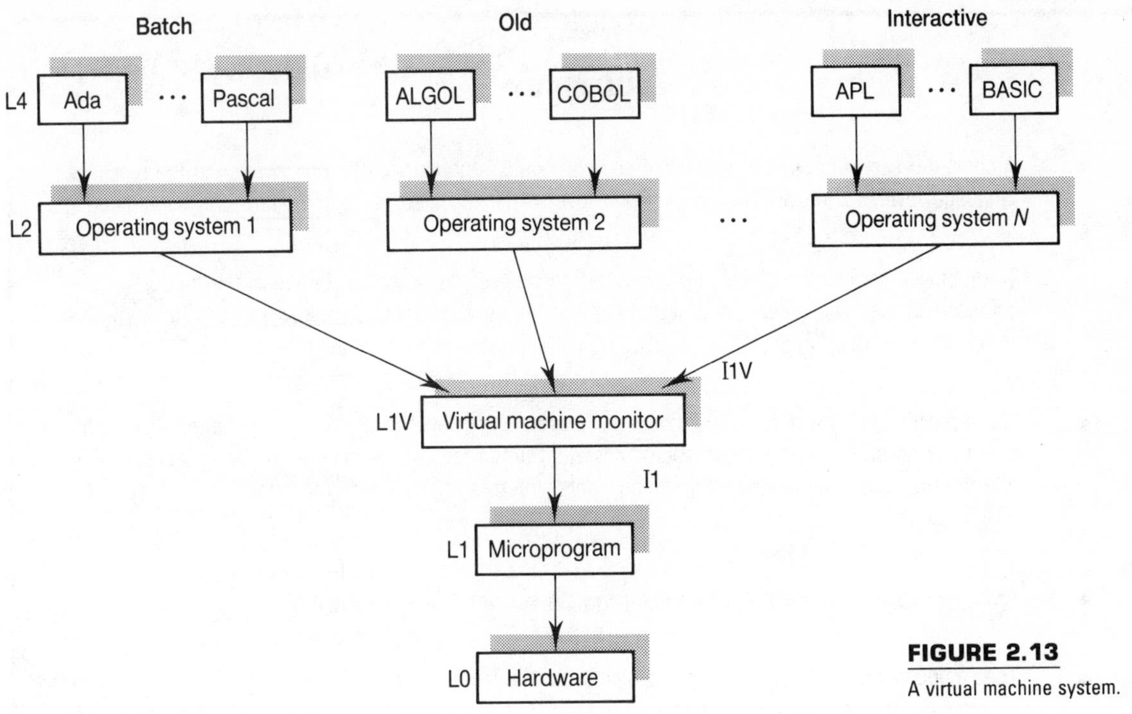

FIGURE 2.13
A virtual machine system.

SUMMARY

- A computer can be shown to consist of several levels, ranging from the hardware, via the machine language level, to the application program level. At each level, an architecture can be defined.

- Traditionally, computer architecture has been defined as the interface between the hardware and software levels. The selection of the functions to be supported by hardware is a task of the computer architect.

- Three mechanisms exist for converting from one machine level to another: compilation (execution only after an entire program has been translated), interpretation (execution and translation evenly intermixed) and combined compilation and interpretation (first compilation, followed by interpretation).

- New levels can be added to an existing system via procedural extension.

- The computer architect usually has a choice as to the level at which he can add a new function to a computer system. Generally, it can be stated that the lower the chosen level, the higher the performance and cost.

- For software portability (the migration of a program from one system to another), it is essential that there is at least one level at which both systems are equivalent. Depending on this level, several techniques for software portability can be distinguished. At the architectural level, other architectures can be simulated via interpretation, emulation or a combination of these. Portability at the operating system level can be accomplished via a virtual machine monitor.

EXERCISES

2.1 Which language level (high-level language, assembler or machine language) is usually preferred for solving a problem and why?

2.2 Why is interpretation usually much slower than compilation?

2.3 Which conversion mechanism is generally preferred when going from a high-level language to machine language?

2.4 Which conversion mechanism is used to go from I1 to I0 (see Figure 2.2)?

2.5 At which levels can a new function be added to a computer system? Which level do you prefer when a high execution speed is required? Which level do you prefer when, as a user, you wish to be able to specify the new function, and which mechanism should be used for this specification?

2.6 Which way of simulating an older architecture on a new machine do you prefer given the following requirements:

(a) The older architecture is similar to that of the new architecture (such as the PDP-11 and the VAX-11) and programs for the old architecture should run at top speed on the new architecture.

(b) The new architecture is microprogrammed in a flexible way while programs for several older architectures have to be run on the new architecture.

(c) Computers that have to be very fast do not use microprogramming. Programs of an older architecture have to be run on such a high-speed computer.

2.7 The Intel 80386 processor can simulate the 8086 architecture via a special mode bit. Is this a form of emulation or interpretation?

2.8 How can higher-level language programs, which contain operating system dependencies, be ported?

2.9 Why can languages such as APL not be compiled?

2.10 What is a virtual machine?

2.11 What is a virtual machine monitor?

References

Aho, A. V. *et al.* (1985). *Compilers: Principles, Techniques and Tools*. Addison-Wesley: Reading, MA.

Chu, Y. (1980). A Jovial Direct Execution Computer. In *Proc. of the International Workshop on High Level Language Computer Architecture*, University of Maryland, College Park, MD, pp. 17–32.

Johnson, S. C. *et al.* (1978). Portability of C programs and the Unix System. *The Bell System Technical Journal*, **57**(6), 2021–48.

Parmalee, R. P. *et al.* (1972). Virtual storage and virtual machine concepts. *IBM Systems Journal*, **11**(2), 99–130.

Smith, W. R. *et al.* (1971). A large experimental system exploring major hardware replacement of software. In *Proc. AFIPS SJCC*, pp. 601–16.

Strong, J. *et al.* (1958). The problem of communicating with changing machines: A proposed solution. *Comm. of the ACM*, **1**(8), 12–18.

Wilkes, M. V. (1951). *The Best Way to Design an Automatic Calculating Machine*. Report of Manchester University Inaugural Conference, Manchester.

PART TWO

THE COMPILER INTERFACE

The compiler interface is that part of the architecture of interest to the compiler designer. Other parts, such as I/O and memory management, are of interest to the operating systems designer. The architectural constructs that comprise the compiler interface are used by the code generated by compilers, as well as by application programs written in assembly language.

This part covers the way data is presented in computers together with the operations on that data. The basic concepts behind and the tradeoffs to be made in machine languages, which includes the instruction set, are presented together with a chapter on the methods of addressing data and instructions. The mechanisms available for making decisions in programs and changing the flow of control (through branch and loop instructions) is discussed next. The way architectures support high-level structures, such as subroutines, procedures, functions and modules, together with activation records, concludes this part.

3 Data Representation

Sometimes the best helping hand you can get is a good, firm push.
– JoAnn Thomas

Although the devotion of a chapter to the representation of data in a book about computer architecture may not seem appropriate at first, on second thoughts, data representation is a crucial element in the design of a computer architecture. It is important, not only because rules about the types of data and the ranges of their values must be devised, but also because the choice of data formats is dependent on the concepts upon which the architecture is based. Indeed, the choice of data types can greatly influence the efficiency with which operations can be performed.

3.1 Classification of data

Data present in computers can be divided into three categories:

(1) **User-defined data**: Data explicitly specified by the user in a program. The structure and characteristics of such data are usually determined by the capabilities of the programming language used.

(2) **System data**: Data implicitly generated by the computer system when a program is being executed. This category of data (with its own structure and characteristics) is often referred to as the **run-time environment**, part of which will be discussed in Chapter 8. The main exponent of this category is the stack, which will be discussed in Section 3.5.

(3) **Instructions**: The program being executed can be considered as a composition of data, again with its own structure and separate characteristics. This category will be discussed in Chapter 4.

Before going on to discuss the user-defined data types, let us first look at the type of data encountered in daily life. Although this data can be represented in all kinds of shapes and forms, it can roughly be divided into two groups: numbers and symbols.

Numbers can be written in many different ways, some of which are listed here.

- **Cardinals** (also called **natural numbers**). For example:

  1; 2; 3; . . .; 11 345; . . .

- **Integers**: The set of cardinals, both positive and negative (including zero). For example:

  . . .; −282; . . .; −1; 0; +1; . . .; +9210; . . .

- **Rational numbers**: The set of integers and fractions. For example:

  $-1\frac{1}{4}$; $^{22}/_{7}$

- **Real numbers** (also called **floating-point numbers**): This set includes those numbers that cannot be expressed as fractions. Examples are:

  $\sqrt{3}$; $\log_2 (13)$; $\sin (\pi/4)$

- **Complex numbers**: These are frequently used in mathematics. They consist of a real part and an imaginary part. For example:

  $4 + 3i$; $2 - 3i\sqrt{3}$

Symbols are used for the symbolic representation of data, such as letters, pictograms and drawings, and have an even greater variety

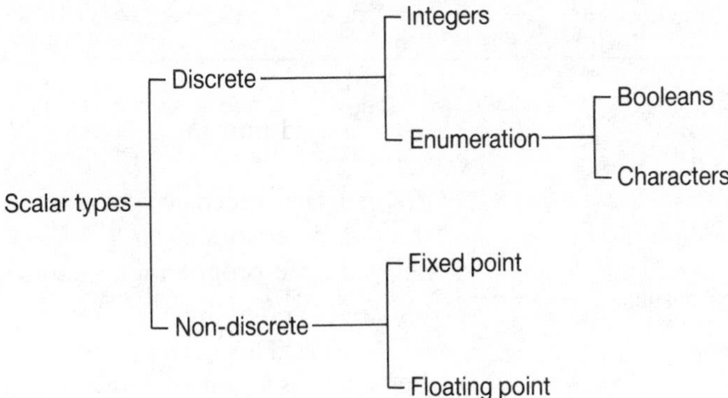

FIGURE 3.1
Classification of scalar data types.

of manifestations than numbers. Letters (upper and lower case), also called characters, and words, formed by combining letters, are the most important symbols for a computer architect. Examples are:

a; A; b; B; . . .; Hello; World; α; Γ; . . .

Not all of these types of numbers and symbols are relevant to problems to be solved in languages such as FORTRAN, ALGOL or Pascal. These languages also tend to have their own representations of data, thereby differentiating between scalar data types, structured data types and access data types.

3.2 Scalar data types

From an architectural point of view, the scalar data types can be classified according to the scheme shown in Figure 3.1. These data types, used in many programming languages, are images or approximations of the concepts of the surrounding world – for example, the concept of the fraction ⅓. In real life, these concepts must be manipulated. However, as this cannot be achieved directly in computers, several intermediate steps must be utilized, as shown in Figure 3.2. To handle data types in a computer, data must be represented in logical entities, usually bits. Because a 'bit' is an abstract notion, it must be converted into a physical quantity, such as an electric potential or a magnetic field, so that it can be manipulated. This is achieved by the interaction of physical processes. Following, the physical quantities must be converted back to the logical entities (bits), the bits to data types and finally these data types to concepts in real life, achieving the desired manipulation at the conceptual level. The representation of data types in bits and the interpretation of these bits as data types are typically architectural subjects. The different ways in which the most common data types are represented in bits are discussed in the following subsections.

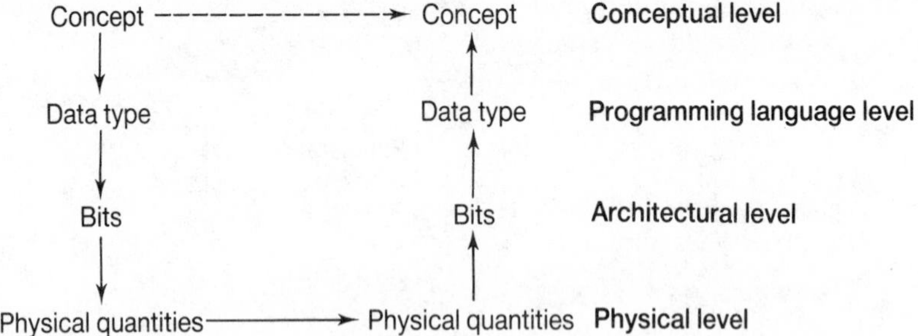

FIGURE 3.2

Representation and conversion of data types.

Every data type has two properties: the set of values that the data can assume (the domain) and the operations that are allowed on the data. The **domain** is characterized by two aspects: the **range**, which is the *number* of values that data can assume, and the **precision**, which is the *distance* between successive data values.

The number of data types that a computer architecture supports is some indication of its power. Rich architectures often support many data types, which means that hardware is available for the mapping of data types to bits, implying a higher efficiency. On the other hand, this increases the complexity and the cost. Simple architectures support a limited number of data types. For example, the first minicomputer, the PDP-8, had only one data type, a 12-bit two's complement integer (DEC, 1970). At the time of its emergence, characters were specified in 6 bits (because 64 different characters were considered sufficient) and so most architectures had word lengths that were a multiple of 6 bits: 12, 18, 24, 36 or 48 bits. Every other data type had to be composed from this basic data type by software. This allows for simple hardware but at the expense of a longer execution time for the 'other' data types.

3.2.1 Integers

Integers are used for exact computations, as control variables for iterations, as indices for arrays, and so on. In computer systems, their range is finite, because their length – that is, the number of bits used for their representation – is limited by the design of the computer. The reader is assumed to know how positive and negative integers can be represented using two's complement, one's complement and sign-magnitude representation – see, for example, Wakerly (1981), Shiva (1985) or Knuth (1969).

Some languages or systems also provide natural numbers, or cardinals, which are a subset of the integers, containing the non-negative values – for example, Cardinal in Modula-2 and Unsigned in C. For n-bit cardinals, the range is $0 \leq x < 2^n$. Unsigned numbers are often used for variables such as counters and for address arithmetic (addresses usually do not assume negative values).

For an architecture, it is important to formulate criteria for the representation of integers:

- Ease of implementation of arithmetic operations (**generality**): The use of Roman numerals for addition, for instance, is an example of the contrary.
- Uniqueness of the representation of the value zero (**propriety**): This simplifies the hardware, because testing for zero, which is done frequently, is simplified.
- Symmetry of representation range (**completeness**): The complement of a number should always be representable, which is not true for asymmetric representations, such as two's complement.

Strict testing of these criteria reveals that the ideal bit representation of integers does not exist, because every representation with a unique bit pattern for zero is asymmetric. Therefore, it is important to consider the consequences when one or more criteria are not met. Usually, the uniqueness of zero is more preferable than the symmetry of the range, as testing for zero occurs frequently and must be kept as simple as possible. The widespread use of the two's complement representation can be attributed to this preference (see Chapter 6). In this representation, the range is $-2^{n-1} \leqslant x < 2^{n-1}$.

Implementing integers introduces two conflicting requirements: range (as large as possible) and size (as few bits as possible). This has led to two solutions: a (number of) fixed-length formats or a variable-length format. The decision to support a number of fixed formats is based upon the reasoning that most integers cover a limited range and therefore need fewer bits. Nevertheless, the user should not be restricted to this. To cite an example, the MC68020 has four integer formats with 8-, 16-, 32- and 64-bit representations (named B: byte, W: word, L: long word and Q: quad word). A variable-length format is not often used, but may be useful in some instances. The problem with a variable-length representation is efficiency: it is necessary to specify the length and the start of the bit field, but bit addressing is less efficient than byte addressing. Consequently, it is necessary to very carefully weigh whether the reduction in the number of bits needed to represent an integer and the greater flexibility are not lost as a result of the increase in bits for address specification and the extra alignment time needed when, say, integers are allowed to start at arbitrary bit positions in a byte.

Operations on integers yield an exact result and follow the laws of arithmetic. An indication should be given when the result is outside the representable range (overflow). High-level language operators appropriate for integers are:

**	exponentiation
*, **mod**, /, **div**	multiplication, modulo and division
+ and −	sign operators (unary operators)
+ and −	addition and subtraction (binary operators)
=, ≠, <, >, <=, >=	relational operators

Not only are the integers of high-level languages mapped into the data types supported by the architecture, but subranges and enumerated types also make use of such a representation. For example, in Pascal, the following enumerated type can be defined:

type *Day* = (*Mon*, *Tue*, *Wed*, *Thu*, *Fri*, *Sat*, *Sun*);

Variables of the type *Day* can only assume the values *Mon* through *Sun*, which the compiler may represent by the integer values 0 to 6.

3.2.2 Booleans

Booleans are the most simple manifestation of an enumerated data type, having only two values. This data type, which is predefined in many languages, can be defined as:

type *Boolean* = (*False*, *True*);

Packing several Booleans into one machine word raises the problem of selection: How must the required element be extracted from the bit vector? This usually requires several extra instructions, so the gain in space is offset by the loss of speed and simplicity.

3.2.3 Characters

In many languages, characters are also a predefined enumerated data type, just like Booleans. A set of characters is needed for the exchange of information between a computer and its users. Consequently, a character set is composed according to specific rules. First, it must contain the letters of the alphabet (preferably both upper- and lower-case letters), the digits and a separation character (usually a space). Punctuation marks, such as the comma, period, semicolon, colon, exclamation point, question mark, brackets and quotes, are indispensable as well, and often there is a need for a currency- and other commercial symbols (&, @). Arithmetical applications require the presence of operators, such as +, −, *, =, and so on.

Another class of symbols needed in a character set is the set of characters that are used to control the communication process and the representation of the characters. These characters are often referred to as **control characters**. Examples of control characters are 'carriage return' and 'form feed'. Table 3.1 shows the so-called ASCII code (American Standard Code for Information Interchange), formally known as the ISO code. It uses the high-order codes 000 and 001 for the control characters. Another code was adopted by IBM, which began with the BCD code (which in turn originated from the Hollerith code for punched cards) and developed it into the EBCDIC code (Extended Binary Coded Decimal Interchange Code).

3.2.4 Fixed-point numbers

Fixed-point numbers are often used in administrative applications, because this data type closely corresponds to the conceptual data representation of the end user. The conversion from its internal representation to an external format – for example, hardcopy – and vice versa can be done easily, which outweighs the disadvantage of more complex and slower internal operations (+, −, * and /). Normally, only a few (and mostly simple) operations are required for decimal numbers.

For the implementation of decimal numbers (composed of decimal digits), the following aspects are important:

- The binary coding of the decimal digits: All digits (0–9) are normally coded in binary, using 4 bits (Table 3.2). This representation is called **BCD** (binary coded decimal) or **packed decimal** notation.
- The position and coding of the sign: When a sign-magnitude notation is used, several options are available. The sign can be placed in the most significant byte, simplifying output, for example, to a printer. Alternatively, it can be placed in the least significant byte, simplifying arithmetic operations, because these always start with the least significant bytes and it is important to know the signs of both operands at the start of an operation: if one of the numbers that is being added is negative, a subtraction (that is, a different operation) must be executed instead of an addition. Positive and negative signs can be coded by using the six combinations of 4 bits not used by the digits (Table 3.2), or they can be coded as, for example, the ASCII characters '+' and '−'. Both methods are in frequent use and are explained in more detail in Example 3.2.

Table 3.1 ASCII code.

	High							
Low	**000**	**001**	**010**	**011**	**100**	**101**	**110**	**111**
0000	NUL	DLE	SP	0	@	P	`	p
0001	SDH	DC1	!	1	A	Q	a	q
0010	STX	DC2	"	2	B	R	b	r
0011	ETX	DC3	#	3	C	S	c	s
0100	EOT	DC4	$	4	D	T	d	t
0101	ENQ	NAK	%	5	E	U	e	u
0110	ACK	SYN	&	6	F	V	f	v
0111	BEL	ETB	'	7	G	W	g	w
1000	BS	CAN	(	8	H	X	h	x
1001	HT	EM	)	9	I	Y	i	y
1010	LF	SUB	*	:	J	Z	j	z
1011	VT	ESC	+	;	K	[	k	{
1100	FF	FS	,	<	L	\	l	|
1101	CR	GS	−	=	M	]	m	}
1110	SO	RS	.	>	N	^	n	~
1111	SI	US	/	?	O	—	o	DEL

Example: The ASCII code for the character ‘>’ is 0b0111110.

Abbreviations for control codes

ACK	acknowledge
BEL	bell
BS	backspace
CAN	cancel
CR	carriage return
DC1	device control 1
DC2	device control 2
DC3	device control 3
DC4	device control 4 (stop)
DEL	delete
DLE	data link escape
EM	end of medium
ENQ	enquiry
EOT	end of transmission
ESC	escape
ETB	end of transmission block
ETX	end of text
FF	form feed
FS	file separator
GS	group separator
HT	horizontal tabulation
LF	line feed
NAK	negative acknowledge
NUL	null
RS	record separator
SI	shift in
SO	shift out
SOH	start of heading
STX	start of text
SUB	substitute
SYN	synchronous idle
US	unit separator
VT	vertical tabulation

Table 3.2 Binary coding of sign and digits.

Digit/Sign	Binary Code	Hex
0	0000	0
1	0001	1
2	0010	2
3	0011	3
4	0100	4
5	0101	5
6	0110	6
7	0111	7
8	1000	8
9	1001	9
+	1010, 1100, 1110, 1111	A, C, E, F
−	1011, 1101	B, D

- The number of decimal digits: The number of digits can be fixed (and is thus implicit, because no length specification is needed) or variable. For variable-length numbers, the length must be specified explicitly (for example, in the operand), and normally a maximum length is enforced by the architecture.
- The number of digits in each byte: In most modern architectures, two basically different formats exist: packed decimal format and unpacked decimal format. The packed decimal format (Figure 3.3(a)) divides each byte into two 4-bit fields, each containing a binary coded decimal (a digit). For internal operations, this format is used most frequently, because of its efficiency. In the unpacked decimal format, each byte is also divided into two 4-bit fields, the zone (Z) and the digit (D) field (Figure 3.3(b)), and specifies one digit. The zone field is chosen such that the Z–D combination forms a printable character. Therefore, the values '3' for ASCII and 'F' (15 in decimal notation) for EBCDIC are often used for the zone field.

Examples 3.1 and 3.2 illustrate how two architectures, the MC68020 and the VAX-11, have implemented decimal numbers in quite different ways.

□□EXAMPLE 3.1

The MC68020 has both the packed and the unpacked decimal format (Motorola, 1985). It uses ten's complement arithmetic, so, for example,

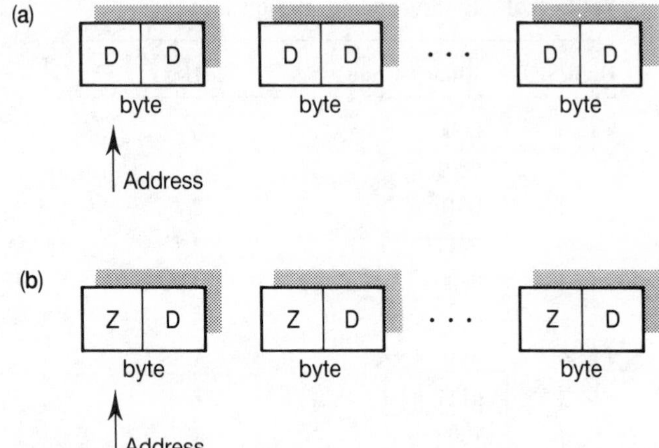

FIGURE 3.3

Decimal formats: (a) packed; (b) unpacked.

-47 is represented as 53. The digits are coded according to Table 3.2 and no explicit sign is used. The length of a BCD number is always one byte (that is, two or one digit(s)), and software must provide longer decimal numbers, by repeated operations on byte operands. In the unpacked format, the zone field can have a user-defined value, making this data type character set independent.

□□EXAMPLE 3.2

The VAX-11 supports three different formats, two of which are unpacked (DEC, 1979). The packed decimal format uses a sign-magnitude representation, where the sign is coded according to Table 3.2 and placed in the low-order half of the least significant byte (that is, the least significant digit). Each byte contains two digits and the length, L, specifies the number of digits, excluding the sign. Therefore, for the number -39, $L = 2$. The length must be in the range 0–31.

In the 'trailing numeric' format, all bytes contain ASCII decimal digit characters (0–9), and a zone field which contains the value 3. The sign is placed in the zone field of the least significant byte and coded as '3' for a positive sign and '7' for a negative sign. Once again, the length specifies the number of digits, which now equals the number of bytes.

The 'leading separate numeric' format is somewhat different. The sign of the number is stored in a separate byte, in front of the other bytes, and it is coded as an ASCII character, with '+' and 'blank' representing a positive, and '−' a negative sign. The length, L, specifies the number of digits, so a string takes up $L + 1$ bytes in memory (one extra for the separate sign byte).

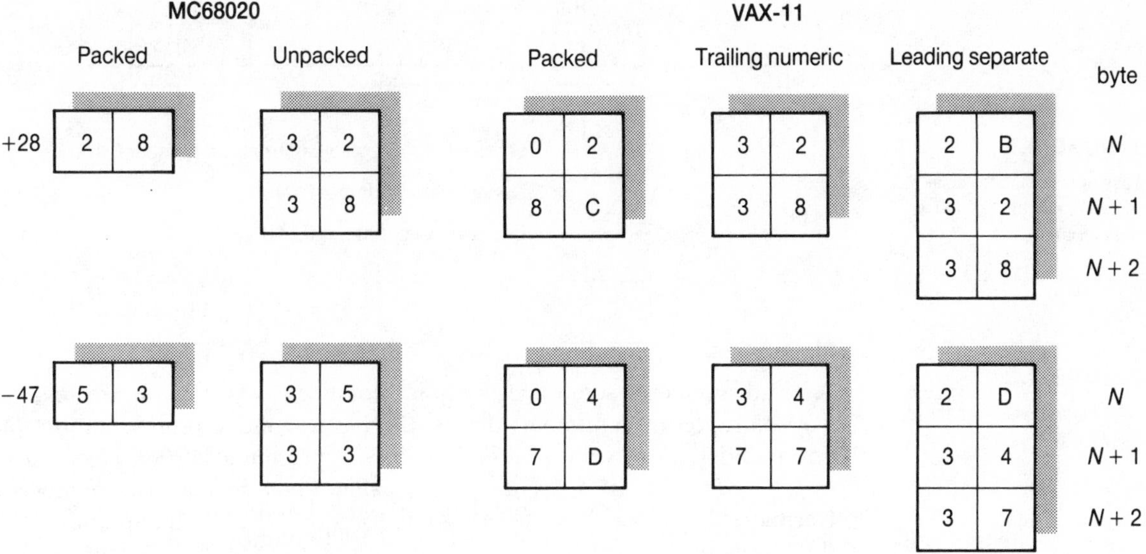

FIGURE 3.4
Different decimal number representations.

Figure 3.4 shows how the numbers +28 and −47 are represented in memory using the formats of the MC68020 and the VAX-11. Note that 2B and 2D are the hexadecimal ASCII values for the characters '+' and '−' (see Table 3.1).

3.2.5 Floating-point numbers

Most high-level languages offer the possibility of declaring variables as **real**; that is, these variables may be given values that are placed between two consecutive integers. In computers, these numbers are represented in floating-point notation. This notation is based on the elements S, the sign, F, the fraction, E, the exponent, and R, the radix, in such a way that the value, V, can be represented as:

$$V = (-1)^S * F * R^E \qquad \textbf{(3.1)}$$

If the radix has the same value for all reals in an architecture, as is normally the case, it need not be specified explicitly.

Computer systems often handle several formats for reals because, on the one hand, memory economy requires a compact format, while, on the other hand, a single compact format is too limited for the required precision and range.

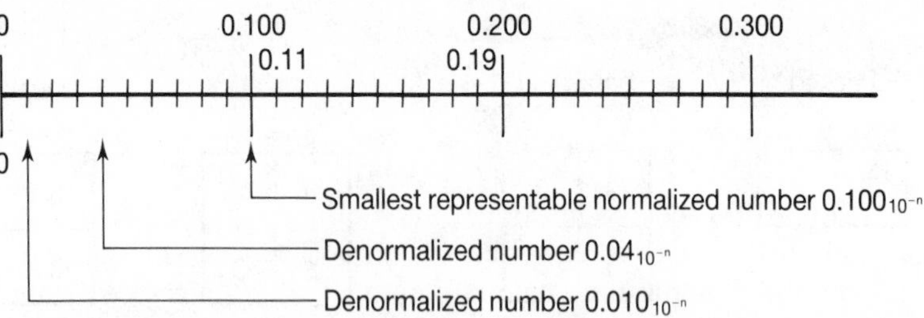

FIGURE 3.5

Loss of precision for small numbers due to normalization.

Normalized notation

A disadvantage of some floating-point notations is that there are several ways to represent a number; that is, there is no unique representation for one number. For example, 37.145 can be represented as 0.037145×10^3 or as 3714.5×10^{-2}. These are called **non-normalized numbers**. **Normalized numbers**, on the other hand, require the decimal point of the floating-point number to have a fixed position such that, for example, the decimal point is to the left of the most significant digit. (Note, however, that when using a binary representation, it is not really appropriate to speak about a decimal point.) In that case, the fraction satisfies Equation (3.2):

$$1 > F \geqslant 1/R \tag{3.2}$$

In the representation of floating-point values the symbol E is usually used as a separator between the value of the fraction and the value of the exponent. The number 37.145 is then represented in normalized form as 0.37145E+2. In the decimal system (R = 10), the fraction must be between 0.1 and 1 to satisfy Equation (3.2).

Note that the normalized notation does not allow the representation of certain numbers close to zero. Figure 3.5 shows the normalized numbers 0.3E−n, 0.2E−n, 0.19E−n, 0.11E−n and 0.1E−n, where the latter represents the smallest normalized number. Numbers smaller than the smallest normalized number are called **denormalized numbers**, and they do not have to satisfy Equation (3.2). Denormalized numbers, such as 0.04E−n, 0.01E−n and 0.001E−n, may then be representable.

Range

The range depends on the number of bits available for the exponent as well as the radix. As shown in Figure 3.5, there is a smallest representable value, in addition, of course, to a largest representable value. Because this set of representations is not closed for the operations

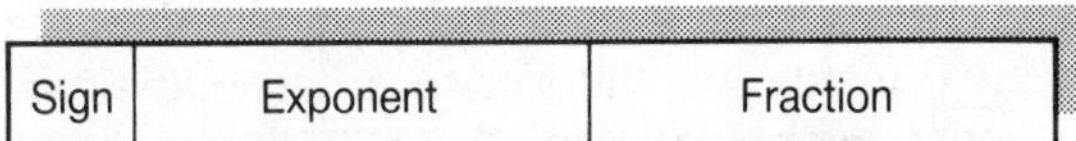

FIGURE 3.6

General structure of floating-point format.

that are allowed on it, computations can produce results that cannot be represented. Just as with integers, this is called **overflow** and, specifically for small numbers, **underflow**. An architecture should have provisions for detecting, handling and signalling overflow and underflow. For example, the occurrence of underflow could be signalled and the underflow could be translated into a value of zero. For overflow, the largest possible value might be used, together with a signal, or 'infinity' may be representable.

Precision

There is yet another set of numbers that cannot be represented, because they are situated between representable numbers; for example, if the fraction contains three digits, then 0.3114×10^{-2} cannot be represented and must be approximated by 0.311×10^{-2}. The precision depends on the number of bits available for the fraction.

Radix

Because of the operations that can be expected, it is desirable for the radix to be equal to a power of the base of the number system used for the fraction. In most computer architectures this is 2, which implies a radix of 2 or a radix equal to a power of two. The IBM/370 has a radix of 16 for reasons of efficiency – to reduce the number of shift operations (Sweeney, 1965). This makes it possible to shift over 4 bits simultaneously for (de)normalizing, while normalizing is required only when the most significant 4 (or more) bits of the fraction are zero.

Structure of a floating-point format

Figure 3.6 shows the format of a floating-point number as adopted by most architectures. This format resembles that of integers.

The single-bit sign field is the first field in the format and inspection of this bit allows positive values to be distinguished from negative values, as is the case for integers.

The exponent field is the next most significant field: the exponent has a greater influence on the value than the fraction. As for the representation of integers, where the significance of bits decreases from left to right, the exponent field should precede the fraction field. The encoding of the exponent value can be done using either an unbiased or a biased notation (Wakerly, 1981). In an **unbiased notation**, the value of the exponent is encoded in the way integers are encoded – for example, by using the two's complement notation. An 8-bit exponent field may then specify values for the exponent in the range −128 . . . 0 . . . +127. Small numbers, which have a negative exponent value, have 1s as the most significant bits of the exponent field whereas large numbers, which have a positive exponent value, have 0s as the most significant bits of the exponent field. This is in contrast to the representation of integers where a large number has 1s in the more significant bit positions. The **biased notation**, also called **excess notation**, eliminates this distinction by adding a bias to the exponent value to be encoded. Exponent values in the range −128 . . . 0 . . . +127 would be represented as 0 . . . +128 . . . +255. Small exponent values would then have 0s in the most significant bit positions.

The fraction field is the least significant field of the floating-point format. Usually, a sign-magnitude notation is used because of the desired separation of the sign (as the first field) and the magnitude (as the last fraction field).

Representation of the number zero

The representation of the number zero in floating-point notation can be a problem. It might be said that any representations with an all-zero fraction should be interpreted as zero, so that the exponent can adopt any value. Again, to resemble the representation of integer values, it is desirable for the exponent field to be also equal to zero.

Hidden bit

When the radix is 2 and numbers are always normalized, the most significant digit (that is, bit) of the fraction will always be a 1 (except for the case where the value is zero). This means that this first 1 does not carry any information and therefore does not have to be stored, which allows the fraction to have one extra bit. Only when the floating-point number is used (in computations) does the 1 need to be present; when stored, the 1 can be stripped off again. Such a bit is called the **hidden bit**. As the hidden-bit technique is used in many architectures, special hardware (floating-point processors) must include this hidden bit in their internal data representations.

Floating-point standards

Floating-point formats have been a challenge to the computer architect for a long time. The enormous differences between the architectures testify to this. Recently, however, a standard used by most newer architectures has been developed: the IEEE Standard (IEEE, 1985). Other formats, such as those used in the PDP-11 (DEC, 1975) or IBM/370 (IBM, 1970), are not discussed here, because they are all slight variations on the IEEE Standard. For details of other formats, the reader is referred to the manual of the corresponding manufacturer.

The IEEE Standard is valid for both software and hardware implementation of floating-point operations. Furthermore, the standard deals with such matters as rounding, overflow and underflow, and other exceptional results that might arise. In the IEEE Standard, four basic formats exist:

- Single format: E = 8 bits, F = 23 bits.
- Double format: E = 11 bits, F = 52 bits.
- Single-extended format: E $\geqslant$ 11 bits, F $\geqslant$ 31 bits.
- Double-extended format: E $\geqslant$ 15 bits, F $\geqslant$ 63 bits.

The exact size of the E and F fields for the extended formats depends on the implementation. The value, V, of a normalized number (including a hidden bit) in the single format is determined as follows. (Note that the decimal point is placed *after* the first bit – that is, the hidden bit.)

$$V = (-1)^s * (1.F) * 2^{E-127} \tag{3.3}$$

where the radix is 2, S is the sign bit, E is an 8-bit exponent in 'excess-127' notation, and F is a 23-bit fraction in sign-magnitude notation, resulting in 24 significant bits (remember the hidden bit). The exponent values 0 and 255 are reserved for indicating special values, such as zero, represented by a sign (+0 and −0), E = 0 and F = 0. To realize arithmetic operations, the hardware or software extracts the fields (S, E and F), the hidden bit is made explicit and the exponent is converted to its real value (two's complement instead of excess code).

The IEEE Standard further provides a representation for special numbers, such as NaN (Not a Number), $+\infty$, $-\infty$ and denormalized numbers. Table 3.3 shows the interpretation of the single format,

Table 3.3 Interpretation of single format in the IEEE Standard.

	E Field Value		
F Field Value	**0**	**1 . . . 254**	**255**
0	$-1^s * 0$	$-1^s * (1.F) * 2^{E-127}$	$-1^s * \infty$
$\neq 0$	$-1^s * (0.F) * 2^{-126}$		NaN

depending on the values of the E and F fields. NaN is, say, the result of 0/0 or $\sqrt{(-5)}$ and can be used for floating-point exception signalling and handling. Values with E = 0 and F ≠ 0 represent denormalized numbers to allow for a greater precision for small numbers.

3.3 Structured data types

Structured data types are composed of a set of data elements that are mutually related. These data elements can be scalar quantities or structured data types themselves. Furthermore, their structure is fixed at compile time and cannot be changed during execution. From this description, it is clear that structured data types can be very complex, which is the reason why most architectures only partially support structured data types. In this section, we look at sets, arrays, character strings and records.

3.3.1 Sets

A **set**, such as used in Pascal, is a collection of values. These values consist of all subsets of the enumerated elements (including the empty set), where the elements only have a scalar data type or belong to a subrange. For example, the set {'A' . . . 'Z', '0' . . . '9'} includes {'A'}, {'C', 'D', '3', '7'}. For the set data type, specific operations have been defined:

*	set membership
+	set union
−	set difference
in	set membership

Bit vectors are often used for the implementation of sets. The compiler is responsible for the translation of every member of the set to a bit in the vector. Logical operations are used for operations on bit vectors. Many architectures, including the MC68020, support bit-field operations, which can be used to extract bit vectors from a word or assign a specific value to a bit vector. Example 3.3 shows a possible implementation of sets, using bit vectors.

□□EXAMPLE 3.3

First, the following type and variable are declared:

type *Day* = (*Mon*, *Tue*, *Wed*, *Thu*, *Fri*, *Sat*, *Sun*);
var *D* : **set of** *Day*;

7	6	5	4	3	2	1	0
—	*Sun*	*Sat*	*Fri*	*Thu*	*Wed*	*Tue*	*Mon*

FIGURE 3.7

Implementation of sets using bit vectors.

The variable D can now be implemented by a bit vector of 7 bits, as shown in Figure 3.7.

The subset *Working_days* is now defined as the subset {*Mon* . . *Fri*}. The test '*Sat* in *Working_days*' can now be implemented by the logical AND of two bit vectors, representing the subsets *Sat* and *Working_days*. *Sat* is represented by a bit vector with a 1 in bit position 5 and *Working_days* has 1s in positions 0–4. The result of the AND operation is zero, so *Sat* is (fortunately) not a working day.

3.3.2 Vectors and arrays

Normally, a **vector** is a one-dimensional and an **array** a multi-dimensional collection of data elements of the same type, where every element can be selected separately by using one or more discrete index values. Usually, however, the notion array also includes one-dimensional vectors.

An array is placed in memory such that the elements take up a contiguous area of memory, which can be done in two ways: column-major ordering or row-major ordering. With **column-major ordering**, the columns of the array are placed in memory one after another. Figure 3.8(b) shows how the array $A[1\ ..\ M,\ 1\ ..\ N]$ is placed in successive addresses. In general, for column-major ordering, the elements are first sorted on the last index, then on the next-to-last index, and so on. This method is used by FORTRAN.

FIGURE 3.8

Orderings of an array in memory.

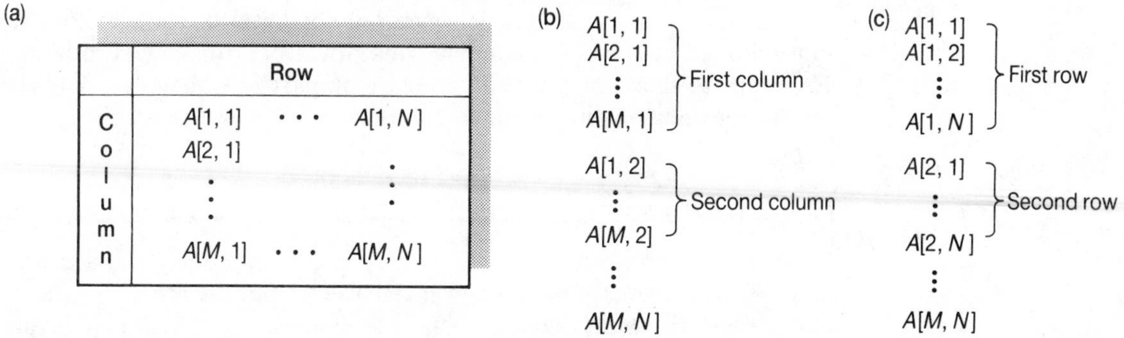

(a)

(b)

(c)

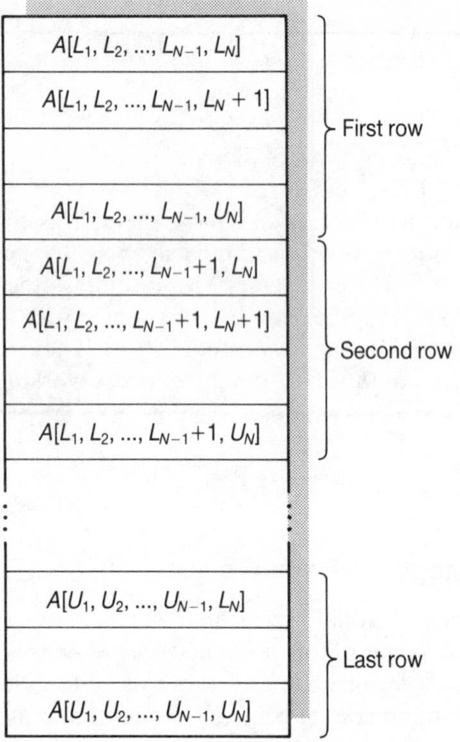

FIGURE 3.9

Memory allocation for an N-dimensional array.

For **row-major ordering**, the rows of the array are placed in memory successively, as shown in Figure 3.8(c) for the array $A[1\,..\,M, 1\,..\,N]$. In general, for row-major ordering, the elements are first sorted on the first index, then on the second index, and so on. Nearly all programming languages (except FORTRAN) use row-major ordering to store arrays. A possible reason for this is that in mathematics involving operations on arrays, the last specified index changes most frequently so elements, stored in adjacent memory locations, are accessed successively.

Figure 3.9 shows the usual allocation of an N-dimensional array $A[L_1\,..\,U_1, \ldots, L_N\,..\,U_N]$, in which L is the lower bound and U is the upper bound of the corresponding subscript, using row-major ordering. Example 3.4 shows how a multi-dimensional array can be allocated such that it does not require one contiguous area of memory.

□□EXAMPLE 3.4

A completely different method of memory allocation for arrays is used by Burroughs (1969). They make use of pointers that eventually point to vectors with a length of the last dimension of the array. Figure

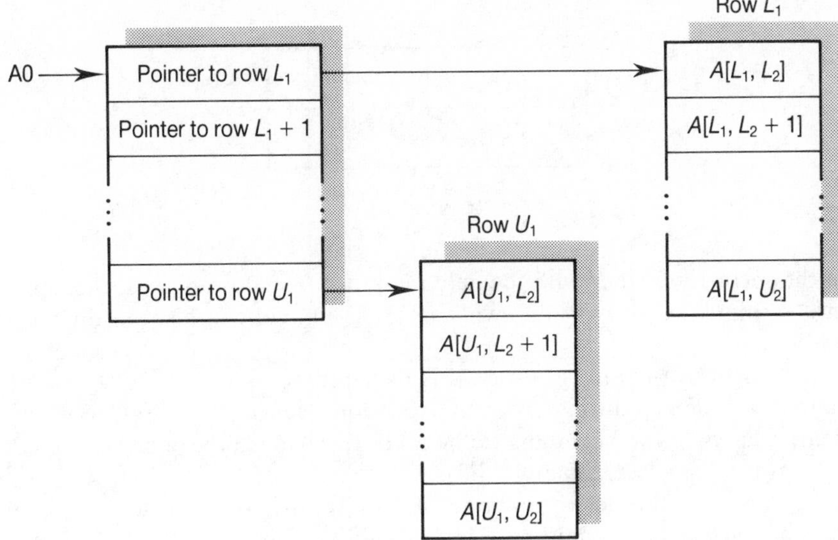

FIGURE 3.10
Memory allocation for arrays, as used by Burroughs.

3.10 shows the method for the two-dimensional array $A[L_1 \,..\, U_1, L_2 \,..\, U_2]$. The advantage of this method is that complicated array subscript calculations are replaced by indirections through the pointers, which are generally faster, but this speed is at the expense of the storage required for the pointer vectors. Obviously, this method can be expanded to arrays with three or more dimensions.

3.3.3 Character strings

A **character string** is a series of characters. Because program source text can be seen as character strings, string operations are important for compilers and assemblers as well as for word processors. Often, character strings are considered as an array of characters, making each character directly accessible. Many architectures, such as the VAX-11 and the IBM/370, support operations on character strings.

3.3.4 Records

A **record** is a collection of data elements, each of which can have a different data type, which is in contrast to an array. These data elements, called **fields**, can be addressed separately by associating a label, the so-called **field identifier**, to the fields. A data element is selected by the name

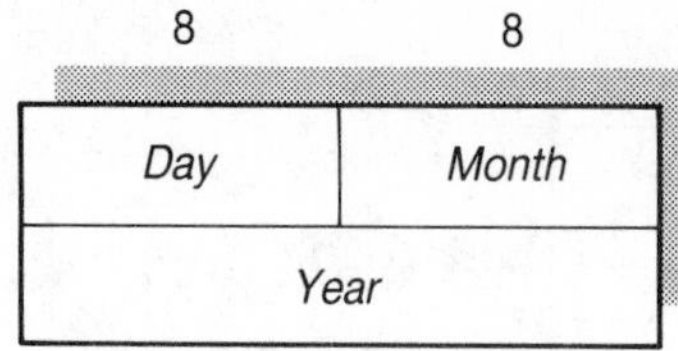

FIGURE 3.11

Memory allocation of record *Birthday*.

of the record, together with the field identifier. A field can be further split into subfields, each with its own name. A subfield can also be divided, and so on.

As the structure of a record is declared at compile time, a record cannot be changed during program execution. Hence, the offset for every field, relative to the beginning of the record, is fixed and can be computed at compile time (see Example 3.5).

To meet the desire for more flexibility, it is possible to include a variant part in the definition. This variant part dynamically defines the structure of a record; that is, the variant part contains several possible (different) definitions, one of which is selected during execution. A **tag field** is included so that one of these definitions can be selected. (See, for example, Wirth (1986) for a more extensive discussion of variant records.)

□□EXAMPLE 3.5

In the following program, variables of the type *Date* have three fields: *Day*, *Month* and *Year*. A field of a record can be specified by the record name, followed by a period and the field name.

```
type Date = record
                Day   : 1 . . 31;
                Month : 1 . . 12;
                Year  : integer;
            end;
var Birthday : Date;

begin
  Birthday.Year  := 1964;
  Birthday.Month := 12;
  Birthday.Day   := 8;
end.
```

Figure 3.11 shows the way this record could be allocated, with each field starting at a fixed position relative to the beginning of the record.

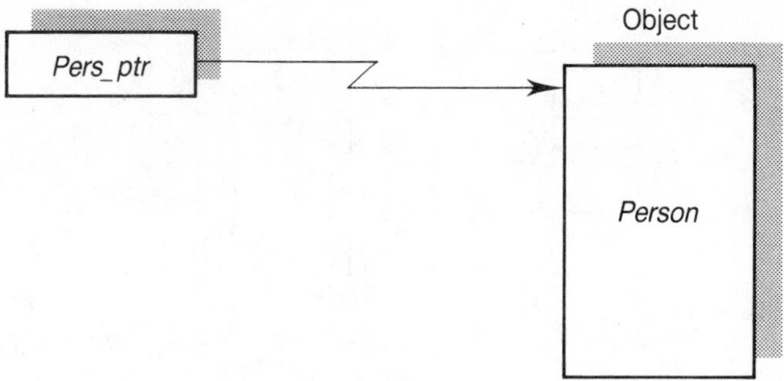

FIGURE 3.12
Pointer type.

3.4 Access data types

The **access data type** opens up the possibility of creating data objects and structures dynamically – that is, during program execution. Identifiers of this type are declared at the start of a program module. In Pascal, they are considered to be pointers; the data type of the pointer is considered to be the data type of the object to which the pointer is pointing. Only the memory required for the pointer is allocated when the block containing the pointer is activated. For example, if the data type *Person* is already declared, then the definition:

type *Pers_Ptr_type* : ↑ *Person*;

means that *Pers_Ptr_type* is an access type pointing to an object of the type *Person*. If *Person* is, say, a record type, then the declaration:

var *Pers_Ptr* : *Pers_Ptr_type*;

would mean a pointer (called *Pers_Ptr*) that points to a record with the same structure as defined in *Person* (Figure 3.12). However, this declaration only creates the pointer object (*Pers_Ptr*), and not the data object pointed to (a record of type *Person*).

The creation of *dynamic* objects is done at statement execution time. Pascal uses the standard procedure **new** for this. Freeing the allocated storage is done in Pascal via the procedure **free** or **dispose** (the name depends on the Pascal version used).

The machine representation of a pointer is normally an address. In most architectures, the arithmetic on addresses is performed via integer operations. In such cases, the integer data type has the same length as an address. Furthermore, to access objects via pointers, it is important that an architecture supports indirect addressing.

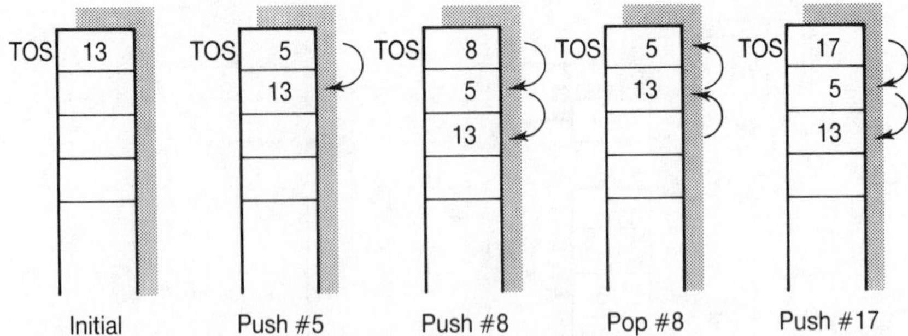

FIGURE 3.13

Basic stack push and pop operations.

Data structures, composed of access data types, such as linked lists and trees, will not be discussed in this book but can be found in several other textbooks, such as Wirth (1986), Knuth (1973) and Wakerly (1981).

3.5 System-structured data types

System-structured data types are used by, for example, the operating system to control the flow of programs inside the computer. A stack is often used to store the state of a process on a context switch, or for activation records during the execution of a program. Queues are often used to form a buffer, for example, for the processes waiting to be scheduled for a processor or for I/O.

3.5.1 Stacks

A **push-down stack** can be considered as a structured data type where values can only be entered or retrieved at one end. The cell containing the last entered value is usually referred to as the top of the stack, or TOS for short. Because the item that was entered last is retrieved first, a stack is also called a **last-in, first-out (LIFO) buffer**. A stack can be compared to a pile of cafeteria trays, in which the tray that was placed on top of the others must be removed before the other trays can be picked up. As entering a value on the stack pushes all the other elements further down, the write operation on a stack is usually called a **push** operation. Similarly, the read operation is called a **pop** or **pull** operation. Figure 3.13 shows a stack for the basic push and pop operations.

As the technique depicted in Figure 3.13 requires all the elements of a stack to be moved when a push or pop operation is performed, a stack is usually implemented with a **stack pointer**, which always points to the top of the stack (TOS). A stack is then a contiguous block of memory

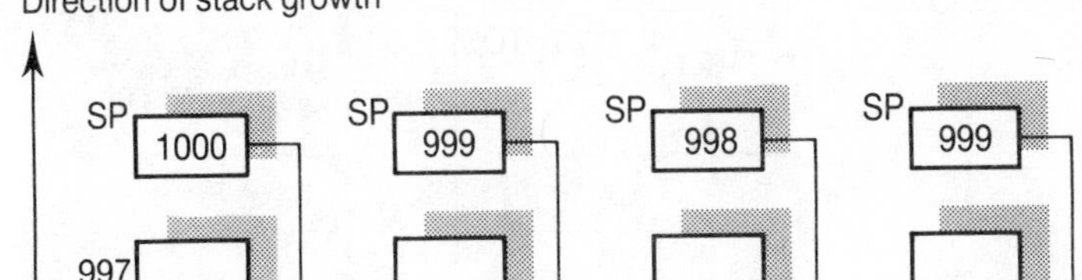
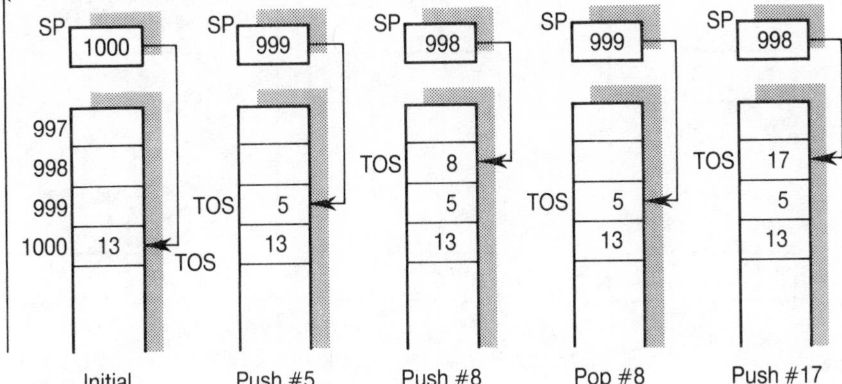

FIGURE 3.14

Use of a stack with a stack pointer.

locations, and when a stack operation is performed, the stack pointer is incremented or decremented, while all the elements remain in the same memory locations.

Care must be taken to ensure that the stack does not exceed the allocated memory area (overflow), because this would result in the loss of some elements or the destruction of adjacent data structures or programs. Another dangerous situation is underflow, which occurs when an attempt is made to pop an item off an empty stack. Left undetected, this can produce unpredictable (and possibly disastrous) results.

For historical reasons, many stacks grow downwards in memory, so that the elements that were pushed first occupy memory locations with higher addresses. Pushing a new element on to the stack involves decrementing the stack pointer first, to point to a new (free) memory location, before the new element is stored in memory (the stack pointer usually points to the top element on the stack). Figure 3.14 shows a stack (with stack pointer SP) during several push and pop instructions.

Because of the LIFO type of organization, a stack is highly suited to support block-structured languages such as Pascal and ALGOL (see Chapter 8). Another important application is its use by compilers for expression evaluation and storage of intermediate results.

3.5.2 Queues

Another data type that is important for systems is the **queue**. A queue is an **FIFO (first-in, first-out) buffer**; that is, the items that are put in first are also retrieved first. Queues are used, for example, by the operating system to store the description of an executable process, which is retrieved when the process is scheduled for execution.

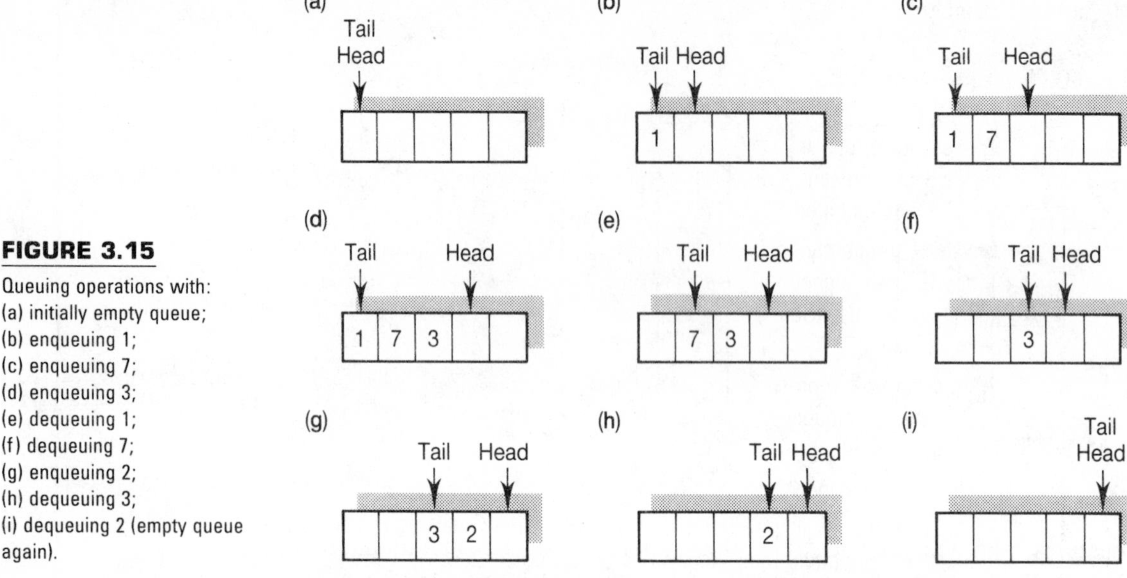

FIGURE 3.15

Queuing operations with:
(a) initially empty queue;
(b) enqueuing 1;
(c) enqueuing 7;
(d) enqueuing 3;
(e) dequeuing 1;
(f) dequeuing 7;
(g) enqueuing 2;
(h) dequeuing 3;
(i) dequeuing 2 (empty queue again).

In contrast to the stack, a queue needs two pointers, a **head** and a **tail**, which point to the location where entries are inserted and retrieved, respectively. In fact, the head pointer points to the first free location after the entry which was inserted last. In the case where the head and tail pointers both point to the same location, the queue is empty. The use of these pointers, and the operations **enqueue** and **dequeue**, are illustrated in Figure 3.15.

The simplest implementation of a queue uses an array of *MAXSIZE* entries, together with two pointers. The problem is that if *MAXSIZE* entries have actually been enqueued (regardless of the number of dequeuing operations), the queue is exhausted (the head pointer cannot be incremented above *MAXSIZE*), which is clearly not desirable. The solution to this problem is to make the array circular; that is, entry 0 immediately follows entry *MAXSIZE* – 1. Now it is only necessary to check that the queue does not overflow or underflow (the head pointer catching up with the tail pointer). More advanced implementations allow queues to be of arbitrary size.

The queue-structured data type is important because many architectures provide support for operating systems via instructions that perform the enqueue and dequeue operations.

SUMMARY

- Data is ubiquitous in daily life with a myriad of representation forms. However, it is not possible to represent all these forms in a computer and so normally a restricted set of data types is implemented.
- The most frequently occurring data types are the scalar data types. This group consists of integers (both signed and unsigned), Booleans (with values *true* and *false*), characters (mostly coded as ASCII characters), decimals and reals (also called fixed-point and floating-point numbers).
- Criteria for the representation of integers are: ease with which the operations can be implemented, uniqueness of the value zero and symmetry of range. Most architectures allow for a few fixed-length formats.
- Booleans require only one data bit and are usually stored in the smallest length integer.
- Decimal numbers can be stored in a packed format (two digits per byte) or an unpacked format (one 'printable' digit per byte). It is preferable to have the sign of a decimal number stored with the least significant digit, to distinguish between add and subtract operations.
- Floating-point numbers should have a format such that they closely resemble integers (for consistency and also useful when reading a 'core dump'). The exponent is, therefore, stored using a biased notation.
- The maximum precision for floating-point numbers is obtained when the number is normalized. A denormalized notation allows greater precision for small numbers. Normalized numbers using a radix of 2 always have their most significant bit equal to 1. When this bit is not stored, which is done to gain precision, it is called a hidden bit.
- Structured data types are composed of a number of elements with the same data type (such as sets, arrays and strings) or with different data types (such as records).
- Sets can be represented by bit vectors.
- Vectors and arrays are usually stored in memory such that they occupy a contiguous area. Most languages store multi-dimensional arrays using row-major ordering; that is, the rows are placed in consecutive memory locations.
- Records may consist of elements with different data types and/or structures. The structure of a record is determined at compile time and elements have a fixed position relative to the beginning of the record.
- Access data types are used to implement dynamic data structures; that is, data whose structure can vary during execution. Examples are linked lists and trees. Pointers are used to access elements of access data types. These pointers can be implemented via indirect addressing.
- In addition to user-defined data types, there are system data types, which are used by, for example, the operating system. The most important exponents of this group are the stack (comparable to an LIFO buffer) and the queue (comparable to an FIFO buffer).

EXERCISES

3.1 Which data types can be classified as discrete?

3.2 Which criteria are important for choosing a representation for integers?

3.3 What are the ASCII codes for A, 9 and ! in binary?

3.4 Show in hex notation:

(a) The packed decimal format for 23.

(b) The unpacked decimal format for 23 using the ASCII zone field.

(c) The ASCII characters 23.

3.5 A given microprocessor has words of one byte (8 bits). What is the smallest and largest number that can be represented using the following representations:

(a) Unsigned.

(b) Signed magnitude.

(c) One's complement.

(d) Two's complement.

(e) Unsigned BCD.

(f) Signed BCD, using a digit for the sign.

3.6 Indicate which of the following statements are true or false:

(a) The representation of floating-point numbers often uses an excess notation for the exponent. This allows integers to be represented as a subset of floating-point numbers.

(b) A floating-point representation with a radix not equal to 2 does not allow for the hidden-bit technique.

(c) The implementation of the set data type, as used in Pascal, can be represented most efficiently in terms of memory use as an array.

3.7 What is a denormalized number and why is it important?

3.8 In the IEEE floating-point standard the value of a single-precision number $X = (-1)^s * (1.F) * 2^{E-127}$. What is the decimal value of the numbers shown in the following table:

	S	E	F
(a)	1	10000011	11 0000 0000 0000 0000 0000 0
(b)	0	01111110	10 1000 0000 0000 0000 0000 0
(c)	0	10000000	00 0000 0000 0000 0000 0000 0

3.9 The IBM/370 floating-point short format consists of a sign bit, a 7-bit exponent field using excess 64 notation, a radix of 16 and a 24-bit fraction field consisting of six hex digits. A number is considered normalized when the first hex digit following the decimal point is not equal to zero. The value of a number is $X = (-1)^s * (0.F) * 16^{E-64}$. What is the binary representation for:

(a) 1.

(b) 65535 (this is $16^4 - 1$).

3.10 In some computer architectures it has been proposed to use the test instruction for 32-bit integers (this instruction determines whether the operand is equal to, less than or greater than zero) for floating-point numbers. Which of the following requirements have to be made regarding the representation of floating-point numbers?

(a) The relative positions of the mantissa, sign and exponent field.

(b) The representation of the value zero.

(c) The representation of the exponent.

3.11 How could the Pascal variable *Strange* be represented:

```
type S = (Mon, 5, March, 10, 1990)
var  Strange : set of S.
```

3.12 Compute for the integer array *A*[5 .. 25, 10 .. 20], where integers are considered to consist of two bytes and the array starts at location 1000, the following:

(a) The total amount of memory required for *A*.

(b) The location of *A*[10, 15] assuming row-major ordering.

(c) The location of *A*[10, 15] assuming column-major ordering.

3.13 Given the Pascal record of Example 3.5, what is the relative position of element *Day* and element *Year*, assuming a byte-addressable memory?

References

Burroughs (1969). *Burroughs B6700 Information Processing System Reference Manual*. Burroughs Corporation: Detroit, MI.

DEC (1970). *PDP-8/e, PDP-8/m & PDP-8/f Small Computer Handbook*. Digital Equipment Corporation: Maynard, MA.

DEC (1975). *PDP-11 Processor Handbook*. Digital Equipment Corporation: Maynard, MA.

DEC (1979). *VAX-11/780 Architecture Handbook*. Digital Equipment Corporation: Maynard, MA.

IBM (1970). *IBM System/370, Principles of Operation*. Form No. GA22-7000. IBM Corporation: Armonk, NY.

IEEE (1985). *IEEE Standard for Binary Floating Point Arithmetic*. ANSI/IEEE Std 754–1985, New York.

Knuth, D. E. (1969). *The Art of Computer Programming*, Vol. 2, *Seminumerical Algorithms*. Addison-Wesley: Reading, MA.

Knuth, D. E. (1973). *The Art of Computer Programming*, Vol. 1, *Fundamental Algorithms*, 2nd edn. Addison-Wesley: Reading, MA.

Motorola (1985). *MC68020, 32-bit Microprocessor User's Manual*. Prentice Hall Incorporated: Englewood Cliffs, NJ.

Shiva, S. G. (1985). *Computer Design and Architecture*. Little, Brown & Company: Boston, MA.

Sweeney, D. W. (1965). An analysis of floating point addition. *IBM Systems Journal*, **4**(1), 31–42.

Wakerly, J. F. (1981). *Microcomputer Architecture and Programming*. John Wiley & Sons: New York, NY.

Wirth, N. (1986). *Algorithms and Data Structures*. Prentice Hall Incorporated: Englewood Cliffs, NJ.

4 MACHINE LANGUAGES

Marriage is an unusual gamble. Both partners win or nobody wins.
– Anonymous

Chapter 2 discussed the different machine levels and their interface in general. This chapter now focuses specifically on interface I1. This interface, which describes the architecture of a computer, constitutes the machine language. First, the frequency distributions of high-level language statements and machine language instructions are discussed, followed by the formats of instructions. These frequency distributions are important for computer architecture because they show the importance of language constructs in terms of how often they are used. An architecture should be designed such that frequently used language constructs can be executed efficiently; that is, have a short execution time and a small number of bits for the representation of instruction(s) executing that construct. The subsequent sections cover the direct and indirect specification of instruction components, and show the dependencies between instruction components.

4.1 Instruction frequency

Currently, most programs are written in high-level languages, because of the higher programming productivity, compile-time error detection and improved maintainability. However, for historical reasons, or in an attempt to achieve higher performance, assembly language is still being used. To gain a better understanding of the requirements of an instruction set, an analysis of high-level languages is desirable.

For instruction analysis, it is important to distinguish between **static** and **dynamic frequency analysis**. With static frequency analysis, the instructions are counted as they appear in programs. The result of this analysis is important for the optimization of memory use. Dynamic frequency analysis, on the other hand, produces instruction counts representing the number of times each instruction is executed by the processor. This analysis is important for reducing the execution time of programs: the processor is designed in such a way that the most frequently executed instructions have the shortest possible execution time.

4.1.1 High-level language statistics

Table 4.1 lists the static frequency distribution of FORTRAN (Knuth, 1971) and Pascal (Shimasaki, 1980) statements. (Note that, for FORTRAN, the construction `IF ( ) STATEMENT` counts as an `IF` as well as a statement, so the total is more than 100%.) In both languages, the assignment statement occurs the most frequently, followed by the **call** statement in Pascal – this is because Pascal promotes the more modern structured, modular approach to programming. In FORTRAN, which is a somewhat older language, the `CALL` statement comes in fourth, after the `IF` and `GOTO` statements.

Table 4.2 further analyzes the frequency distribution of the assignment statement (Tanenbaum, 1978). This implies that most assignment statements are simple: dynamically 66.3% are only data moves, 20.4% require two right-hand side operands and only 13.3% require more than two operands (these operands can vary from constants, variables to function calls). When designing computers, it is important to keep the most frequently occurring cases in mind, so that they can be handled efficiently. With reference to Table 4.2, this means that data moves must be implemented the most efficiently.

Table 4.1 Frequency distribution (%) of FORTRAN and Pascal statements.

Language Construct	Distribution
FORTRAN	
Assignment	41.0
`IF`	14.5
`GOTO`	13.0
`CALL`	8.0
`CONTINUE`	5.0
`WRITE`	4.0
`FORMAT`	4.0
`DO`	4.0
`DATA`	2.0
`RETURN`	2.0
`DIMENSION`	2.0
Others	8.5
Total	108.0
Pascal	
Assignment	37.2
call	31.6
if	19.2
with	3.4
procedure	2.6
var	1.4
repeat	1.3
while	1.1
for	0.7
case	0.7
goto	0.2
Others	0.6
Total	100.0

Table 4.2 Frequency distribution (%) of FORTRAN assignment statement.

Type	Static	Dynamic
One right-hand side term (`A := B`)	80.0	66.3
Two right-hand side terms (`A := A op B`, `A := B op C`)	15.2	20.4
Others	4.8	13.3

Table 4.3 Frequency distribution (%) of operand types.

Type	Static	Dynamic
Constant	40.0	32.8
Simple variable	35.6	41.9
Array element	9.3	9.2
Field of a structure	7.1	11.1
Function call	4.8	1.6
Bit field	3.2	3.3

An analysis of the types of operands used in the Pascal-like language SAL is shown in Table 4.3 (Tanenbaum, 1978). This analysis illustrates that simplicity is a characteristic of the average SAL statement (and of many other languages). Apparently, constants are important, as they account for 40.0% of the operands. Hennessy (1982) composed a frequency distribution for constants found in a collection of Pascal programs (Table 4.4). Most constants in the range 16–255 represent character constants. Table 4.4 reveals that the constant 0 is used very often, which can be explained by the fact that 0 is often used in initialize, test and compare statements – for example, **if** $A > 0$ **then** . . . . The constant 1 also appears often because it is used frequently in elementary count functions, such as $A := A + 1$. As analyses of other languages have produced similar results, this frequency distribution can be considered representative. This implies that the ability to specify small constants as direct operands in an instruction (using immediate addressing) is important. As an example, the MC68020 has the instruction MOVEQ, with an 8-bit immediate value, where the value of the constant is contained within the instruction itself, without having to resort to an extension word. This covers 95.5% of the cases where a MOVE constant is used, as shown in Table 4.4. (Note that other instructions, such as ADDI and ADDQ, also use constants.)

Table 4.4 Frequency distribution of constants.

Constant	Percentage	Cumulative Percentage
0	24.8	24.8
1	19.0	43.8
2	4.1	47.9
3–15	20.8	68.7
16–255	26.8	95.5
>255	4.5	100.0

In conclusion, it can be seen that the use of the various statement types, the complexity of assignment statements, and the complexity of operands and the values of the constants used is far from uniformly distributed over the complete range. In fact, most distributions approximate a negative exponential distribution.

4.1.2 Machine language statistics

Table 4.5 shows the dynamic frequency and dynamic execution time distribution of MC68000 instructions, generated by general-purpose high-level language (HLL) applications, executing under a UNIX-like operating system in a typical engineering environment (MacGregor, 1985). The dynamic frequency shows how often an instruction is executed, whereas the dynamic execution times reflect the percentage of the total execution time the processor spends executing an instruction. The MOVE instruction (in all its varieties) is the most frequently occurring instruction. This could have been expected from, say, the high frequency of the assignment statement in Table 4.1, along with the often-used statement type $A := B$ (see Table 4.2) and from parameter passing as part of the **call** statement. The instructions Bcc (Branch Conditionally) and DBcc (Decrement and Branch Conditionally) together occupy second place. This can be explained by the fact that these two instructions are used for **if**, **repeat**, **while**, **for**, **case** and other statements. While they do not occur too often separately, together they make up about 25% of all Pascal statements (see Table 4.1). The arithmetic/logical group comprises all such instructions as ADD, MUL, SUB, OR, AND, etc. The compare and test instructions are also often used for **if**, **repeat** and other such statements, as discussed for the Bcc and DBcc instructions. The shift and rotate instructions are necessary, for example, for array subscripting, while the clear instruction is useful for initializing data structures. The link and unlink instructions are used to maintain a linked list of local data and parameter areas on the stack for nested subroutine calls.

As before, the statistics of Table 4.5 also closely match a negative exponential distribution. This is a fortunate circumstance for the computer designer, because only a few instructions have a significant influence on the performance of a computer.

Table 4.6 shows the frequency distribution of the addressing modes of the MC68000 (MacGregor, 1985), as discussed in Section 5.2. This table shows the dynamic frequencies of the modes of the effective address (EA) for the source and destination operands. Some instructions have only one EA operand (such as monadic instructions like CLEAR, for example) while other instructions, such as branches, have no EA operands at all.

The most frequently used addressing mode for source operands is base addressing, which is called base displacement by Motorola. This is because variables of the scalar data type and scalars in record data types

Table 4.5 Frequency distribution (%) of MC68000 instructions.

Instruction	Dynamic Frequency	Dynamic Execution Time
MOVE	32.85	36.86
Bcc, DBcc	23.40	18.23
Arithmetic/logical	12.18	13.64
Compare	7.86	7.61
Shift/rotate	3.25	3.19
Test	3.09	2.92
Link/unlink	2.76	3.15
Clear	2.69	3.93
Others	11.92	10.47
Total	100.00	100.00

can be addressed in this way. The program counter (PC)-relative addressing mode, which is called program relative by Motorola, cannot be used to specify a destination EA, as self-modifying code is not allowed. The high frequency of constants in higher-level languages can be found in the immediate mode of Table 4.6. Obviously, this mode cannot be used as destination operand.

The most commonly used destination addressing mode is the register-direct mode. The reason for this is that on-chip registers can be accessed much faster than memory, and require shorter instructions. Consequently, programs use registers as often as possible. The second most frequent destination mode is the register-indirect mode. This may be explained by the high frequency of **call** statements, whereby parameters are passed on a stack using the −(An) addressing mode.

Table 4.6 Frequency distribution (%) of MC68000 addressing modes.

Addressing Mode	Source EA Frequency	Destination EA Frequency
None	35.10	17.28
Register direct: Dn, An	12.50	49.48
Register indirect: (An), (An)+, −(An)	8.24	14.50
Base displacement: (d8, An), (d8, An, Xn)	22.83	10.94
Absolute: xxx.W, xxx.L	0.54	0.00
Program relative: (d8, PC), (d8, PC, Xn)	0.42	—
Immediate: #xxx, Quick	7.77	—
Implied stack	3.08	4.93
Total	90.48	97.13

Clark (1982) has analyzed the frequency distribution of VAX-11/780 instructions, generated by FORTRAN and COBOL programs. When the FORTRAN and COBOL statistics are compared, a large difference in the instruction distribution is evident. The conclusion to be drawn is that, in general, the distribution is strongly dependent on the high-level language used. This is a consequence of the characteristics of a language. In FORTRAN, floating-point numbers are often used, while in COBOL operations on characters and packed decimal strings are used frequently.

4.2 Machine instruction formats

Compared to the statements in high-level languages, instructions that have to be executed by hardware or a microprogram usually have a rather simple format. This can be explained as follows:

- Simplicity implies a higher execution speed, since the data paths can be less complicated. Less hardware also reduces the chance of design errors, improves the reliability and shortens the design time.
- An analysis of high-level languages reveals that simple statements are used most frequently.
- Machine instructions with a very high level cannot be used easily by different high-level languages because these languages differ too much from each other. For instance, the final value of the control variable in a **for** loop is different in Pascal and BASIC. A high-level machine instruction FOR would therefore only optimally suit one language.
- Complex instructions make compilation more difficult, as more special cases need to be considered. Many compilers, therefore, do not bother to include lengthy code-generation algorithms for rarely used special instructions (see also the RISC discussion in Chapter 16).

Before proceeding further, it is important to introduce some terminology. To explain this terminology, reference will be made to the MC68020 ADD instruction (Figure 4.1).

4.2.1 Terminology

An **instruction** consists of several parts, which together specify the operation type and the locations (or values) of the operands. The phrase 'instruction' refers to all of its components. For example, in Figure 4.1, the entire instruction takes up 32 bits, as it includes the displacement *A*. If the

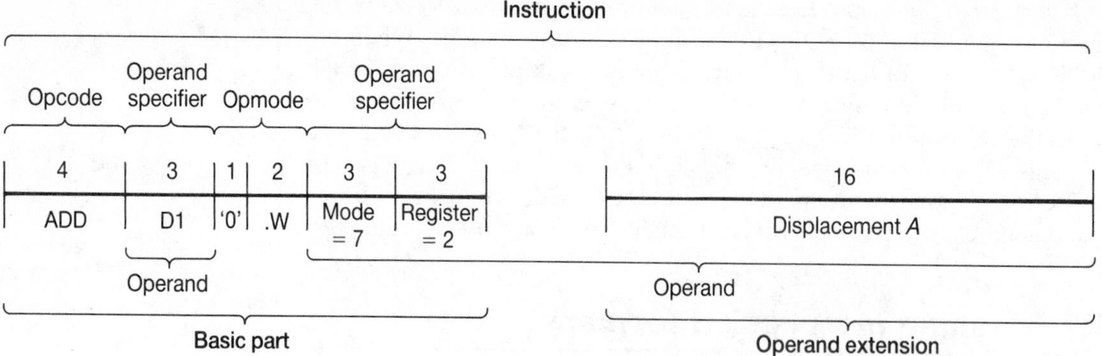

FIGURE 4.1

Instruction terminology: specification of the instruction ADD.W A(PC), D1.

instructions have variable lengths, there is usually a first part (with a fixed length) which specifies the operation and the number of operands. This part will be referred to as the **basic instruction part** or the **first word** of the instruction. In Figure 4.1, the basic part consists of the first 16 bits; the displacement *A* is not part of the basic part.

The operation is usually specified in a field in the basic part, called the **opcode** field. In computers such as the MC68020, the operation is further detailed in the **opmode** field, which specifies, for example, the operand size (W = word in this case) and the direction of the operation (in this case '0', which is memory to register).

An operand specification consists of several parts. The first part, normally having a fixed length, may specify the addressing mode used, a register number or a small constant. This part is called the **operand specifier**. In the instruction of Figure 4.1, the last 6 bits of the first word are an example of an operand specifier. The operand specifier sometimes needs extra data, such as displacements, which are stored after the basic part. This data is referred to as **operand extension words**. Motorola uses the term 'extension words' in the 68000 family, but DEC uses 'extension bytes' in the VAX-11 family. We will use the term 'operand extension', as it is more general. Together, the operand specifier and the operand extension(s), form the **operand**. This operand can be an address, a register specification or immediate data. If this operand specifies a register or a memory location, it can be called an **operand address**. Lastly, the value of immediate data, or the value that is found in the specified memory location or register, is called the **operand value**.

4.2.2 Instruction set classification

The general form of an instruction can be traced back to the time when the attention of computer designers was mainly focused on arithmetic operations. The denotation $c = F(a, b)$ can be seen as the simple mathematical form of a function F that, when applied to two variables a

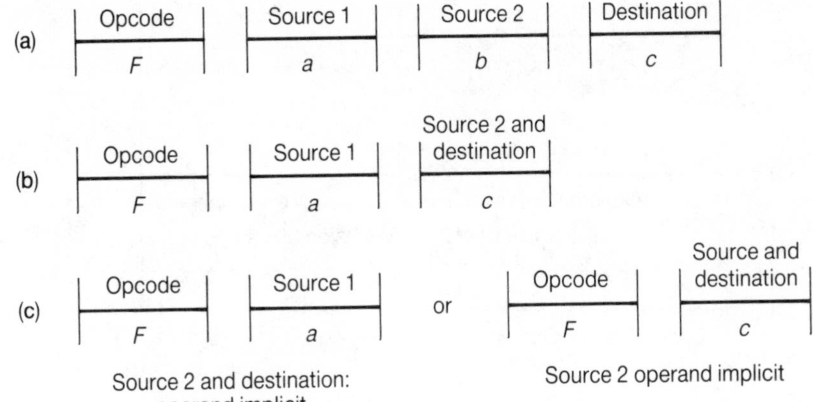

FIGURE 4.2
Instruction formats:
(a) three-address instruction;
(b) two-address instruction;
(c) one-address instruction.

and b (operands), yields the value c. In computer instructions, the *locations* of a, b and c, rather than their values, are usually specified via separate fields. These fields are normally called **addresses**, although this is not entirely accurate because these fields can contain, for example, a memory address, a register number or immediate data. However, in the following, these operand specifiers will be referred to as addresses, in line with standard practice. Therefore, substituting the locations of a, b and c for their values results in the three-address instruction of Figure 4.2(a).

At the time when memory was expensive, designers attempted to reduce the number of bits required by an instruction. One way to do this is by specifying registers (requiring fewer bits), instead of a complete address. An alternative way is to place the destination operand in the same location as one of the source operands, necessitating only two addresses, as in $c = F(a, c)$ (Figure 4.2(b)). Generally speaking, this is not too inconvenient because the result of an operation often replaces one of its operands – for example, when incrementing a loop count ($A := A + 1$). Another advantage lies in the use of subsequent operations on the same operand, such as when adding a term to a partial sum. The disadvantage, however, is that one of the source operands is overwritten, which is a destructive operation.

Often, one of these two operands is located in a register, rather than memory, so only a single memory address and a short register number must be specified. These instructions are usually referred to as **one-and-a-half address instructions**. The memory operand can be a source operand, R = F(R, M), called a memory-to-register operation, or a source and destination operand, M = F(R, M), called a register-to-memory operation.

So far, it has been assumed that the number of addresses specified by an instruction is equal to the number of operands used during the

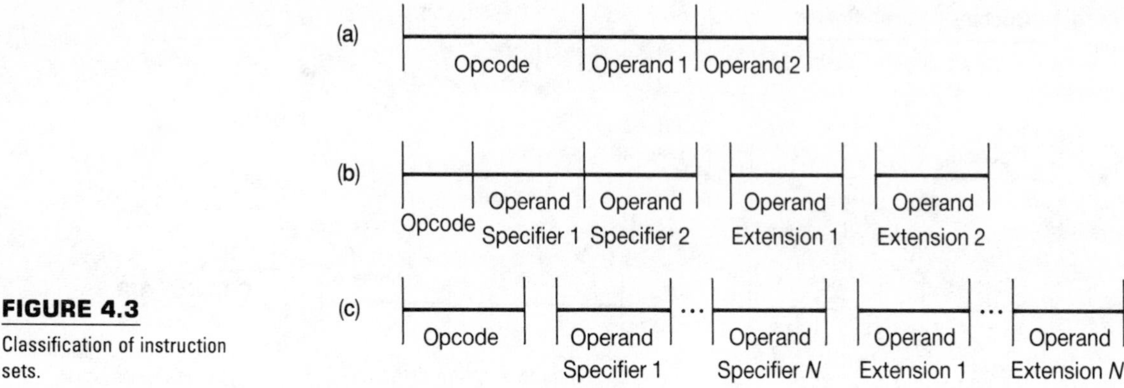

FIGURE 4.3
Classification of instruction sets.

execution of the instruction. A further reduction in the number of addresses can be achieved by assuming that one operand is always the same (usually a register). This is called an **implicit operand**. The other operand is still specified *explicitly*. In older architectures, such as the Manchester MK1 and the UNIVAC I, and also in many older microprocessors, such as the Mostek 6502, the one-address instruction is used (Figure 4.2(c)), where the implicit operand is assumed to be in a so-called accumulator register (AC) or on a stack – that is, AC = $F(a, \text{AC})$ or $c = F(\text{AC}, c)$. The result is stored in this implicit operand. There are also instructions that use the operand specified by the address as the destination operand, in order to store results in memory (c = AC).

The ultimate reduction can be achieved by eliminating all addresses. This instruction format can be found in stack architectures, such as the Burroughs B6700 series (Burroughs, 1969). In such architectures, an operation like MUL pops the two topmost elements off the stack, multiplies them and pushes the result back on to the stack. These architectures, with zero-address instructions, also need one-address instructions to allow memory to be accessed for loading and storing purposes – that is, the move operands between memory and the stack.

Using the preceding terminology, it is possible to classify architectures according to their instruction format (which is heavily influenced by the operand specification part). An overview of three classes is given in Figure 4.3. The first order classification depends on whether the number of operands is fixed (as in Figures 4.3(a) and (b), where it is fixed at two) or variable (Figure 4.3(c)). Instruction sets with a fixed number of operands can be further classified into fixed-length (Figure 4.3(a)) and variable-length instructions (Figure 4.3(b)). This second classification cannot be made for instruction sets with a variable number of operands, as they always have a variable length.

Fixed number of operands

This is the most frequently occurring instruction format, because most computers are designed this way for reasons of simplicity.

Fixed instruction length Instruction sets with a *fixed* number of operands and a *fixed* length (Figure 4.3(a)) are popular for reasons of simplicity and therefore execution speed. In older architectures, fixed-length instructions were used to save (expensive) hardware, because of the easier decoding process. An example of such an architecture is the PDP-10 (DEC, 1969), which is described in Example 4.1. Instructions with a fixed length are also used frequently in architectures where execution speed is a primary design goal, such as in RISC machines, because these instructions are faster to decode and they make it easier to implement acceleration mechanisms such as an 'operand prefetch unit'.

□□EXAMPLE 4.1

Figure 4.4 shows the instruction format of the PDP-10. All instructions have a length of 36 bits, in which 7 bits are used for the opcode specification. The instructions specify two operands, where the first operand is always one of the 16 internal registers (accumulators). The second operand is determined as follows, using the I-field to specify indirection and the X-field to specify a possible index register:

$$
\begin{aligned}
Tmp &:= \textbf{if } I = 0 \textbf{ and } X = 0 \textbf{ then } Displ\\
&:= \textbf{if } I = 0 \textbf{ and } X > 0 \textbf{ then } (X) + Displ\\
&:= \textbf{if } I = 1 \textbf{ and } X = 0 \textbf{ then } M[Displ]\\
&:= \textbf{if } I = 1 \textbf{ and } X > 0 \textbf{ then } M[(X) + Displ]
\end{aligned}
$$

$$
\begin{aligned}
Operand2 &:= \textbf{if } Mode = 0 \textbf{ then } Tmp\\
&:= \textbf{if } Mode > 0 \textbf{ then } M[Tmp]
\end{aligned}
$$

where $M[A]$ means the contents of the memory location with address A. The *Mode* field determines how the intermediate value, *Tmp*, must be interpreted and where the result of the operation is stored:

- *Mode* = 0: *Tmp* is immediate data. The result is written in *Operand*1 (an accumulator).
- *Mode* = 1: *Tmp* is the address of the operand value. The result is written in *Operand*1 (an accumulator).
- *Mode* = 2: *Tmp* is the address of the operand value. The result is written in *Operand*2.
- *Mode* = 3: *Tmp* is the address of the operand value. The result is written in *Operand*1 and *Operand*2.

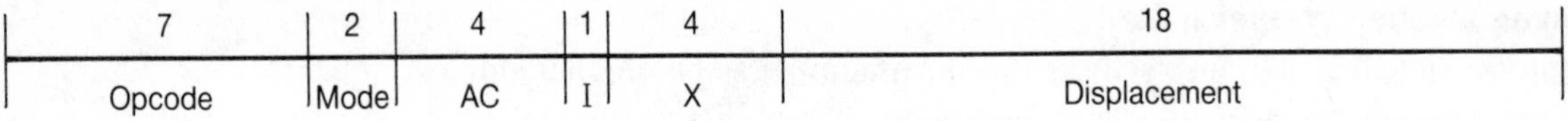

7	2	4	1	4	18
Opcode	Mode	AC	I	X	Displacement

FIGURE 4.4

DEC PDP-10 basic instruction format.

Register-to-register operations are possible because the registers form an overlay with memory; that is, the registers are also accessed when using memory addresses 0–15. This requires a 23-bit operand specifier to specify an accumulator operand. Given the PDP-10's 16 accumulators, this could have been done with 4 bits, saving 19 bits.

Multiple levels of indirection are possible (just as multiple levels of indexing are): if the indirection bit I in the instruction equals one, the 23 low-order bits of the addressed word are interpreted as if they were the least significant 23 bits of an instruction, resulting in another operand address calculation.

Variable instruction length The need for instructions with a *variable* length and a *fixed* number of operands (Figure 4.3(b)) arose when it became economically feasible to build computers with a number (typically 8 or 16) of registers (also referred to as general-purpose registers), instead of a single accumulator. For such architectures, the one-address instruction format of the single accumulator machine is inadequate to specify two operands, while the classical two-operand instruction format occupies too much memory (see Example 4.1), when the memory-referencing operand has to specify a register. So, a special operand format, which requires fewer bits for the specification of a register and more bits for the specification of a memory-based operand, had to be introduced: the one-and-a-half address instruction. Two-address instructions were, however, not entirely discarded, resulting in instructions with a variable length.

It is because of this memory efficiency that many modern architectures have an instruction set with a fixed number of operands and a variable length. Examples are the IBM/370, DEC PDP-11, Intel 80x86, Motorola MC68000 and National Semiconductor NS32000 families.

Variable number of operands

Architectures in which a variable number of operands for a given operation is allowed (Figure 4.3(c)) are rare. An example is the VAX-11 (DEC, 1979), which allows, for most operations, two or three operands in the following way (shown for the VAX-11):

```
ADD2  A, B       ;B := (B) + (A)
ADD3  A, B, C    ;C := (B) + (A)
```

Because of the limitation that only one operator (such as +, −, * or /) may be specified per instruction, the maximum number of operands is three (two source and one destination operand). This covers about 95% of all assignment statements (see Table 4.2). An instruction set with a variable number of operands has a variable length because of memory efficiency. Example 4.2 describes the VAX-11 POLY instruction. The MC68020 CAS (Compare and Swap) and CAS2 instructions with three and six operands, which are an exception to the two-operand instruction format, are explained in Chapter 9.

□□EXAMPLE 4.2

An example of a VAX instruction with three operands is the polynomial instruction:

```
POLY  argument, degree, table_address
```

The definition of this instruction is given by the following example: $P(X) = C_0 + C_1 * X + C_2 * X^2$, where $C_0 = 1.0$, $C_1 = 0.5$ and $C_2 = 0.25$. The instruction for computing this polynomial P(X) is:

```
          POLY X, 2, Ptable
            -
            -
Ptable : .Float  .25    ; C2
         .Float  .5     ; C1
         .Float  1.0    ; C0
```

Complex instructions with an arbitrary number of operands can be implemented in this way.

4.3 Instruction component specification

The three elements included in the execution of an instruction are: the operation, the locations of the operands and the values of the operands. More formally, it can be stated that an instruction spans three different spaces. These are:

(1) The **opcode space**, the set of all possible operations.

(2) The **operand space**, the set of all names (addresses) of the operands.

(3) The **data space**, the set of all possible operand values.

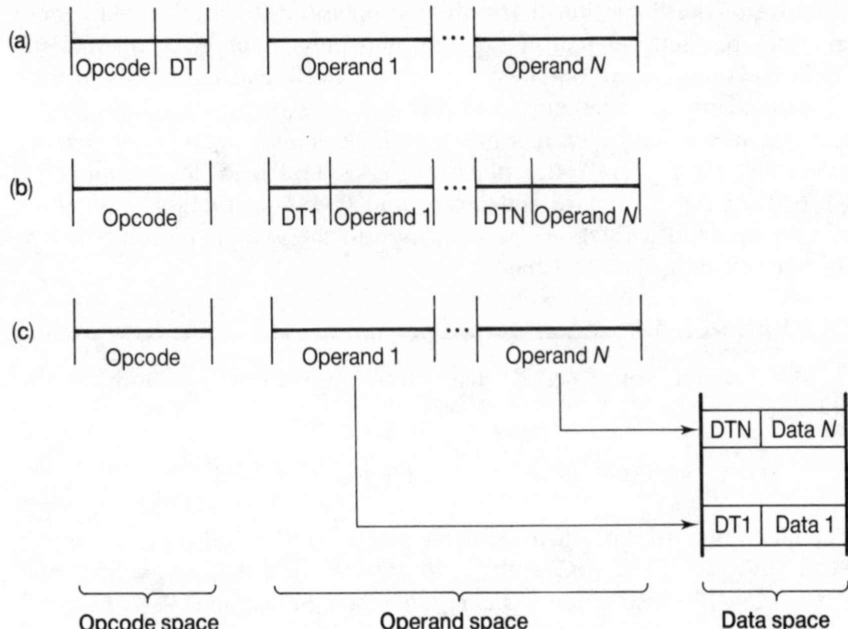

FIGURE 4.5
Data type specification in the three possible spaces.

Although not completely exact, the fields in the instruction and the words in memory are usually referred to as the opcode, operand and data space (these fields are not the actual space but containers for coding the members of a space). Properties of instructions and operands can therefore be specified in each of the afore-mentioned spaces. These properties are: the opcode, the data type, the data space, the data location and the data value. The specification of these properties in relationship to the three spaces is discussed in the following subsections.

4.3.1 Opcode specification

The opcode specifies the operation that must be performed. In theory, the opcode can be specified in one of the three existing spaces. In practice, it is only specified in the opcode space. Most often, the opcode specifies a simple operation, such as ADD, MOV or MUL, but it can also specify more complex operations, such as the VAX-11 POLY instruction (Example 4.2), which consists of a series of add and multiply operations.

4.3.2 Data type and data structure specification

The data type, such as integer word (W) or floating point (F), can be specified in each of the three possible spaces (Figure 4.5).

Data type specification in the opcode space

The most common method of data type specification is where the opcode specifies the data type of the operation (Figure 4.5(a)) in addition to the operation. This normally requires that all operands have the data type required by the operation. Instructions can be as follows:

```
ADD.W   R1, R2        ;Add integer word
ADD.F   R3, R4        ;Add floating
```

Operations on operands with different data types cannot be usually carried out directly. A way to solve this problem is to introduce special conversion instructions. In some architectures, this conversion is done by subroutines. The VAX-11 is an example of an architecture that supports conversion instructions. It has instructions to convert between all data types (byte, word, long word, floating, double floating). For example, the statement *Float*1 := *Float*2 + *Word*1 can be translated into:

```
CVTWF   Word1, R1     ;Convert word to floating
ADD.F   Float2, R1    ;Add floating
MOV.F   R1, Float1    ;Store result
```

This method for data type specification implies that the data types must be known at compile time and that statements with operations on data with different types should not occur too often. Most languages, such as ALGOL, FORTRAN and Pascal, require that the data type of all identifiers be specified explicitly – for example, in Pascal, **var** *X*, *Pi*, *Epsilon*: **real**; – or that they be derived from the name – for example, in FORTRAN, identifiers starting with one of the letters `I–N` are considered to be integers, while the rest are considered to be reals, unless explicitly declared otherwise. This requirement on data type specification allows data type checking to be done by the compiler, while the amount of memory required to allocate these variables, the data type of the operation and the necessity for possible conversions can also be determined statically during the compilation process. This early binding of data type to identifiers improves the efficiency of the eventual program execution. Because many high-level languages support early binding, most traditional architectures specify the data type in the opcode space. This implies that there must be a separate instruction for every data type. The IBM/370, to cite an example, has 15 different ADD instructions which means that an equally large number of opcodes is required.

Data type specification in the operand space

This method demands that every operand specifier be accompanied by a data type specification (Figure 4.5(b)). This method has not been used in

3	48
Tag	Machine word

Tag	Type
0 0 0	Single-precision operand
0 0 1	(Stuffed) Indirect reference word (IRW, SIRW)
0 1 0	Double-precision operand
0 1 1	Mark stack control word (MSCW)
1 0 0	Step index word (SIW)
1 0 1	Data or segment descriptor (DD, SD)
1 1 0	Used by software (uninitialized)
1 1 1	Program or return word (PCW, RCW)

FIGURE 4.6

Burroughs B6700 tag types.

any commercial machine, to the best of the author's knowledge. A variation on this scheme is used in the Nebula architecture (Nebula, 1982; Szewerenko, 1981).

Data type specification in the data space

Data type specification in the data space (Figure 4.5(c)) can be done by using **tags**. This means that *every* memory word is extended with a field, the tag field, which specifies the data type of the word. Architectures that use this method are called **tagged architectures** (Feustel, 1973), examples of which are the Burroughs machines B5000, B5500, B6700, . . ., as described in Example 4.3. In this architecture, every memory word (which is 48 bits) is extended with a 3-bit tag. With a data type, such as double-precision floating point, which requires more than one memory word, each memory word must still have a tag.

□□EXAMPLE 4.3

In the B6700 and B7700, every 48-bit word is extended with 3 tag bits, resulting in a total word length of 51 bits. The interpretation of these tag bits is given in Figure 4.6 (see Burroughs (1969) for a more detailed explanation). Single- and double-precision operands can be distinguished (with tag values of 0 and 2, respectively), while integers are defined as a natural subset of the single-precision, floating-point numbers, thus requiring no tag of their own. Simple Boolean or character variables are stored as a 48-bit entity, because byte addressing would require one tag for each byte, resulting in too much overhead.

The advantage of tags is that the data type – a property of the data – is stored together with the data. It enables both **generic operation specification** – that is, specification of the operation independently of the data type(s) – and implicit data type conversion. This could be of value to such languages as APL and SNOBOL, where the data type of a variable can vary dynamically – that is, with each program statement. Both languages, however, also require that the data structure of an identifier can be varied dynamically, implying that an identifier, being a character, can change after a statement to a vector of integers and change again to a matrix of reals. This has far-reaching consequences for memory management, which cannot be handled at the instruction level.

A second advantage of tags is that operands can be checked (because all words in a machine have a tag field). For example, when an instruction, due to a hardware addressing error, fetches an operand that is tagged as an instruction, this would be detected.

A disadvantage of tags is that every memory word must have its own tag, which requires extra memory. This overhead becomes larger when the basic unit of storage is relatively small – for example, one byte. In such a case, a tag of 3 or 4 bits could mean an overhead of 50%. Therefore, machines with a tagged architecture usually have a large basic unit of storage – the Burroughs, for example, has a 48-bit word. A single character, normally requiring 8 bits, must then be stored in a 48-bit container. However, as characters are usually part of a string, six characters can be packed into one word.

A second disadvantage of tags may be a lower execution speed, because the size of the operand is not known until the data is fetched (the data length must be derived from the tag that is fetched with the data). Furthermore, the data type of the operation is not known until the data has been fetched. Sending an operation and its operands to a dedicated execution unit (such as an integer arithmetic unit and a floating-point arithmetic unit) is therefore slowed down. Storing the result of an operation requires an extra read cycle to determine the data type of the destination.

A third disadvantage is that architectures using tags have an extra overhead in instruction space and time because they need special instructions to initialize these tags.

These disadvantages probably explain why tags are not often found in commercial machines. However, many architectures optimized for the programming languages LISP and PROLOG do have tags to support the dynamic data type concept of these languages at the architectural level.

Data structure specification

The structure of data can take on many forms, from a simple scalar variable to an array or record. Most high-level languages, however, do not support operations on structured data types. Instead, a program is written which decomposes the structured data type to the level of scalars on which the operations can be performed. This is illustrated in the following program segment which shows how the matrices A and B are multiplied such that $R = A * B$:

```
const N = 100;
var   I, J, K   : integer;
      R, A, B   : array [0 . . N, 0 . . N] of integer;

begin
  for I := 0 to N do
      for J := 0 to N do
          begin
              R[I, J] := 0;
              for K := 0 to N do
                  R[I, J] := A[I, K] * B[K, J] + R[I, J];
          end;
end;
```

An architecture that only supports arithmetic operations on scalars would be sufficient to execute this program. This means that the specification of the data structure is not supported by the architecture, but that a sequence of instructions is executed to simulate the data structure.

Due to the large variety of ways in which data can be structured, most architectures do not support structured data. Instead, the mapping of these structures on to those supported by the architecture is left to the compiler or interpreter, with a few exceptions. Architectural support for vector and string operations are not uncommon, as well as architectural support for accessing array elements, using descriptors.

Vector and string operations are supported by several architectures as the former can be useful for the inner loop of a matrix operation, which is of interest to scientific applications, while operations on character strings (such as move and compare) are important for text processors, interpreters and compilers. The specification of an operation as a vector or string operation is usually done in the opcode space (via a special instruction) while the length of the data structure is specified via an extra operand, or as the first data element with the data.

Descriptors can be used to support the access of array elements, although conceptually they can be used to specify any data structure. To support the access of a scalar in a data structure, a descriptor contains all the information describing the data structure. For example, the descriptor of Figure 4.7 may be used to describe the vector $A[L\ .\ .\ U]$ of floating-point numbers. The fields of the descriptor contain all the information required to access an element of vector $A[L\ .\ .\ U]$. The first three fields specify the data length of the array elements and the lower and upper bound of the array. The data length in the descriptor is often used for address computations, but not for generic operations. The last field contains a pointer to the data of array A.

An advantage of descriptors, which is also the main reason for their existence, is that they can automatically perform all operations for

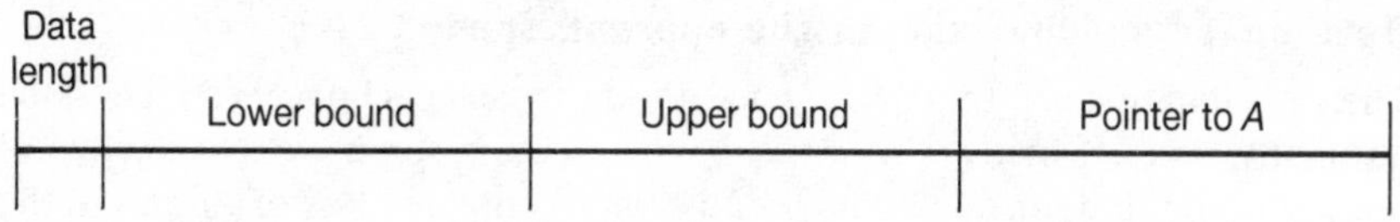

Data length	Lower bound	Upper bound	Pointer to A

FIGURE 4.7
Descriptor for array $A[L..U]$.

accessing an element from a structure. When, for example, $A[I]$ has to be accessed, I can be automatically checked to determine if it is a valid subscript ($L \leqslant I \leqslant U$), after which the correct memory address for $A[I]$ can be computed, because the length of the elements of the array, I and the begin address of A are known.

A disadvantage of descriptors is the special hardware required to handle them (they can be considered as special instructions for accessing data elements in a structure). Optimizing compilers can often generate code whereby many of the functions performed upon data access using a descriptor can be eliminated. For example, when it can be deduced that the subscript will always be within its range, as in the following:

```
const N = 100;
var   I : integer;
      A : array [0 . . N] of integer;
begin
  for I := 0 to N do
      A[I] := A[I] * 25;
```

no run-time checks are needed. Descriptors do not allow for such a refinement and may even introduce a performance penalty.

4.3.3 Data space and data location specification

Although the previous subsections referred to a single data space, it is necessary for the instruction to specify the data space it is referring to. Some frequently occurring data spaces are: main memory and general-purpose registers. Others are the I/O space, the stack space and special registers (status register, for example).

The data space can only be specified in two places, the opcode space or the operand space. It cannot be specified in the data space itself, as the data space is the subject of the specification, and cannot be referenced before it is known.

Data space specification in the opcode space

Occasionally, the opcode space is used to specify the data space. The MC68020 instruction PEA (Push Effective Address) implicitly refers to the stack data space. In architectures with a special I/O space, the instructions IN and OUT implicitly refer to this I/O space.

Data space specification in the operand space

The specification of the data space in the operand space can be done implicitly and explicitly. An *implicit* specification might use the order of the operands to determine which data space is meant. For example, in the PDP-10 instruction format of Figure 4.4, the first operand (AC) always refers to one of the 16 general-purpose registers, while the second operand always specifies a location in the main memory. The *explicit* specification of the data space in the operand space is the most commonly used method. Some example instructions of the MC68020 with explicit data space specifications are:

```
EOR.W    D3, 0xF874.W     ;D3 specifies the register space and 0xF874
                          ;specifies the word location 0xF874 in the
                          ;main memory space
DIVS.W   #8, (SP)+        ;#8 specifies the constant 8 in the instruction
                          ;stream and (SP)+ specifies the stack space
                          ;while the stack pointer is incremented
```

Data location specification

After the data space has been specified, it is necessary to define the data location. This indicates where the data can be found within the selected data space, and so is often specified relative to the start of a data space. A data location could, for example, specify which register is used in the register data space.

4.3.4 Data value specification

The data value can also be specified in the three available spaces, although the data space is most frequently used for the specification of data values. The operand space is used to specify the location of the data, which is normally a memory location or a register. Special places for data value specification are the opcode and the operand space.

Data value specification in the opcode space

The specification of small constants in the opcode space is often done to save memory. For instance, the MC68020 instruction MOVE.L #0, Mem needs two 16-bit words to specify the immediate (long word) data. In the instruction CLR.L Mem, this value is specified by the opcode, reducing the instruction by two words. Other examples of such instructions are INC and DEC, which increment or decrement a variable by 1. Table 4.4 shows that the constants 0 and 1 may together account for 43.8% of all constants, which justifies including these constants in the opcode space.

Data value specification in the operand space

This method is used in nearly all architectures to specify immediate data (constants). Table 4.3 shows that 40.0% of all operands in assignment statements are constants. Furthermore, it has been shown that most constants are small: 68.7% are smaller than 16, according to Table 4.4. Specifying constants in the operand space increases the execution speed because no reference to a constant in memory has to be made, thereby saving an extra memory read operation. In addition, it saves memory, since the bits specifying the address of the constant are not needed.

4.3.5 Indirect instruction component specification

In the previous subsections, instruction components (data type, data structure, and so on) were specified directly in the opcode, operand or data space. However, this is not always necessary. Each of the instruction components can be specified indirectly, via an index into a table or via a pointer, for example. Although in theory all components can be specified indirectly in each space, discussion of all the possible combinations would become tedious. Therefore, in the following, we discuss only the most important one, the indirect specification of operands.

Indirect operand specification means that the location, normally containing the value of the operand, now contains a reference to the operand. Indirect operand specification is important in those cases where the address has to be computed at run time. This may be the case when an element from a structured data type has to be accessed or when an access data type is being used. Because arithmetic operations, such as those performed on addresses, are most efficient when register operands are used, indirect operand specification usually implies some form of register-indirect addressing mode.

4.4 Dependency between instruction components

An instruction comprises the following components (whether or not specified explicitly): operation, data type, data space, data location and data value. However, these components are not completely independent. For example, there is a relation between the data type and the operation: not every operation is sensible for every data type (consider multiplying characters). Another relation can be found between the data type and the length of the data: some data types imply a fixed length. Many such dependencies exist of which only the case of compound operands will be discussed here.

Normally, a single data object is specified by one operand. To

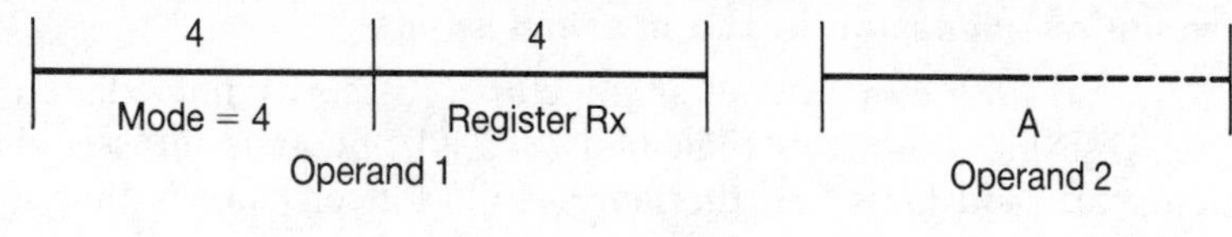

FIGURE 4.8

VAX-11 index addressing mode.

allow for more complicated address calculations, it may be necessary to use several operands (mostly two, each of which may consist of several components), which together determine the location of the data object. This is called a **compound operand**. In this case, there is a dependency between the operands in the operand space as some operands are determined by those preceding them (see Example 4.4).

□□EXAMPLE 4.4

In the VAX-11, it is possible to address an array element $A[I]$ directly, by using the index addressing mode. The value I (an index relative to the begin address of A) is specified by the first operand and can be found in a register (Rx). This first operand also specifies the index mode, whereas the begin address A is specified by the second operand as a *normal* VAX-11 operand, whereby all addressing modes may be used. This means that the address A can be specified identically to any other VAX-11 instruction operand.

Figure 4.8 shows the VAX-11 operand specifier for operand 1, which specifies the index addressing mode (mode = 4). The index register is scaled; that is, multiplied by the data length (in bytes). This length (specified by the data type in the opcode space) can be 1, 2, 4 or 8 bytes. Operand 2 is a normal operand with the usual format and specifies the begin address of A. The location of the array element is now determined as follows:

$$Loc := value\_operand\_2 + (Rx) * data\_length$$

SUMMARY

- When measuring the frequency distribution of machine language instructions, it is striking that only a small subset of all instructions is used most frequently. Furthermore, these statements illustrate the simplicity of most operations and operands. For example, 40% of all high-level language statements are assignments, while two-thirds of the time, the right-hand side of the assignment contains a single element (such as a variable or a constant).

- For instructions, it is important to distinguish between the basic instruction part (usually the first word of an instruction, always with a fixed length) and optional instruction extensions (with a variable length).

- The basic instruction part usually specifies the operation (in the opcode field) and the addressing modes for the operands (in the operand specifiers).

- The extension words are used for displacements, immediate data, and so on.

- Instructions can be classified according to the number of operands, as three-address, two-address, one-address and zero-address instructions. A variation of the two-address instruction is the one-and-a-half address instruction, where one address consists of a short register address.

- When an instruction is executed, its operation, the location, the data type and the values of the operands must be determined. These properties can be specified in the opcode space, the operand space (including the instruction extensions) and the data space (usually main memory or the register set).

- A tag is a set of bits attached to every word to specify the data type of the corresponding word. Architectures that use tags are called tagged architectures. They allow generic operations.

- A descriptor describes the structure of structured data. Descriptors are used to access elements from a data structure and allow many operations involved in the access operation (such as subscript checking) to be done implicitly.

EXERCISES

4.1 Indicate whether the following statements are true or false:

(a) Static instruction frequency analysis is important for optimizing the execution time of a processor.

(b) Dynamic instruction frequency analysis is important for optimizing the program size.

(c) The analysis of higher-level language programs has shown that most statements in those programs are rather complex.

(d) There exists a rather direct relationship between frequently used higher-level language statements and machine instructions.

4.2 (a) Which is the most frequently occurring higher-level language statement?

(b) Which form of that statement is most frequent?

(c) Which two operand types of assignment statements are most frequent?

(d) The distribution of values of constants is not uniform. Constants in the range 0–15 represent about 10%, 20% or 65% of all constants. Which is correct?

4.3 Of the following list of pairs of classes of MC68020 instructions, which of each class is executed more frequently and why?

(a) Move vs. Bcc and DBcc.

(b) Bcc and DBcc vs. arithmetic/logical.

(c) Arithmetic/logical vs. shift/rotate.

4.4 (a) Why is the register-direct addressing mode used frequently?

(b) Why is the register-direct addressing mode used more frequently for destination than for source operand specification?

(c) How can you explain the relative high frequency of the immediate mode?

4.5 Instruction sets can be classified according to their length and number of operands, as follows:

- Fixed length, fixed number of operands.
- Variable length, fixed number of operands.
- Fixed length, variable number of operands.
- Variable length, variable number of operands.

(a) To which class does the basic instruction set of the MC68020 belong?

(b) Which class is preferred for high-performance implementation?

(c) Which class offers most flexibility?

(d) What is the disadvantage of class 1?

4.6 The specification of the data type can be done in the operand space. This:

(a) requires more bits to represent the operands.

(b) requires a larger instruction set (more instructions).

(c) is optimal for languages that require data types to be declared.

(d) requires the use of tags.

4.7 Indicate whether the following statements are true or false. The use of tags has the following advantages:

(a) Saves memory.

(b) Allows for data types to be dynamic.

(c) Allows for generic operations.

(d) Allows for faster instruction execution.

(e) Eliminates the need for conversion instructions.

(f) Allows integers to be represented such that they are a subset of floating-point numbers.

4.8 Constants are used frequently, and they can be encoded in the opcode, operand or data space. In which space would you encode the following constants and why?

(a) Zero.

(b) Small constants – for example, in the range 1–7.

(c) Large constants.

4.9 Descriptors can be used to describe data structures.

(a) Which data structures do they usually describe?

(b) What is the main purpose of a descriptor?

(c) Does a descriptor perform bounds checking?

(d) What information has to be available in a descriptor for it to perform the scaling operation?

(e) Do descriptors allow for generic operations?

References

Burroughs (1969). *Burroughs B6700 Information Processing Systems Reference Manual*. Burroughs Corporation: Detroit, MI.

Clark, D. W. and Levy, H. M. (1982). Measurement and analysis of instruction use in the VAX-11/780. In *Proc. 9th Annual Symposium on Computer Architecture*, April 1982, pp. 9–17.

DEC (1969). *PDP-10 Reference Handbook*. Digital Equipment Corporation: Maynard, MA.

DEC (1979). *VAX-11/780 Architecture Handbook*. Digital Equipment Corporation: Maynard, MA.

Feustel, E. A. (1973). On the advantages of tagged architectures. *IEEE Transactions on Computers*, **C–22**(7), 644–56.

Hennessy, J. *et al.* (1982). Hardware/software tradeoffs for increased performance. In *Proc. of the Symposium on Architectural Support for Programming Languages and Operating Systems*, March 1982, pp. 2–11.

Knuth, D. E. (1971). An empirical study of FORTRAN programs. *Software Practice and Experience*, **1**(2), 105–33.

MacGregor, D. and Rubinstein, J. (1985). A performance analysis of MC68020-based systems. *IEEE Micro*, **5**(6), 50–70.

Motorola (1985). *MC68020, 32-bit Microprocessor User's Manual*. Prentice Hall Incorporated: Englewood Cliffs, NJ.

Nebula (1982). *Nebula Instruction Set Architecture*. MIL-STD 1862A, US Department of Defense.

Shimasaki, M. *et al.* (1980). An analysis of Pascal programs in compiler writing. *Software Practice and Experience*, **10**(2), 149–57.

Szwerenko, L. *et al.* (1981). Nebula: A new architecture and its relationship to computer hardware. *IEEE Computer*, **14**(2), 35–41.

Tanenbaum, A. S. (1978). Implications of structured programming for machine architecture. *Comm. of the ACM*, **21**(3), 237–46.

5 ADDRESSING

Happiness is belonging, not belongings.
– Elisabeth Harvey

This chapter discusses the concept of addressing, in addition to some general properties of addressing. Basic addressing mechanisms for scalar data types and addressing mechanisms for addressing data elements in structured data types are covered. The chapter concludes with a section on compact operand specification.

5.1 General properties of addressing

Instructions and data are stored in the memory of a computer. The physical structure of such a memory can be conceived of as follows: the memory consists of units (called *words* or *bytes*), each of which consists of a fixed number of memory elements (called *bits*), where each unit can contain both instructions and data. Each unit has a unique name (called an *address*), formed by a combination of bits, such that the number of address bits is equal to $\log_2 (N)$, with N being the maximum number of units. The classical computer architectures (based on the von Neumann model) are very closely related to this physical memory structure.

As no physical distinction can be made between the units containing instructions and those containing data elements, it is possible for a program to change instructions (including addresses). This method, by which programs change themselves dynamically, was used in the early days to write compact programs with great ingenuity. Currently, insights into programming techniques have changed such that this method of programming has been rejected, because it results in unreadable programs that are therefore hard to maintain.

In the following subsections, some general properties of addressing, such as address resolution, alignment, the order of bits, bytes, words and address spaces, are discussed.

5.1.1 Address resolution and data alignment

The **address resolution** specifies the smallest possible amount of information (in terms of bits) that can be addressed directly by an architecture. The absolute minimum is a single bit. Some architectures, such as the iAPX432 (Intel, 1981), are capable of directly addressing a single bit. However, an address resolution of a single bit is not often used because it requires a large number of address bits and extra time to align the data such that it is in the correct position for an ALU or the memory subsystem.

Most modern architectures code instructions in groups of bits that have lengths of 8 bits (VAX-11), 16 bits (MC68020, IBM/370) or a multiple thereof. This reduces the length of an address by 3 or 4 bits compared to bit addressing and reduces the alignment time.

Many classic architectures have the same address resolution for both data and instructions (consistency and simplicity). Table 5.1 shows the address resolution for data and instructions for some well-known architectures. The B1700 and the iAPX432 allow instructions to start on any bit boundary and to have a length that is not a multiple of 8 or 16 bits. The advantage of this is a more compact encoding of instructions, at the expense of a larger instruction address – for example, 3 bits more

Table 5.1 Address resolution in existing machines.

Resolution	MC68020	VAX-11	NS32000	IBM/370	B1700	B6700	iAPX432
Instructions	16	8	8	16	1	48	1
Data	8	8	8	8	1	48	8

than machines that use byte addressing. An address resolution of 16 bits for instructions is a result of the fact that the machines concerned (MC68020) have many instructions that can be contained in 16 bits. This means that, in a 16-bit, word-organized memory, many instructions can be fetched in a single memory cycle.

To compensate for the lack of single-bit resolution, some architectures possess special facilities (instructions or operands) to make bit addressing possible (Example 5.1).

□□EXAMPLE 5.1

The MC68020 has instructions to test, clear, change or set a single bit within the destination operand. The bit number can be specified as an immediate operand or can be present in a data register. The following instructions are examples of this:

```
BTST.B   #3, Dst    ;Test the third bit in the byte located at Dst
BCLR.L   #0, D1     ;Clear bit 0 in data register 1
BSET.L   D, D2      ;Set bit 31 in data register D2 (assuming D1
                    ;contains the value 31)
```

If the destination operand is a data register, the bit numbering is modulo 32, to allow bit manipulation on all bits of the data register. If the destination is a memory location, the bit operation is performed on one byte, using the bit number modulo 8. Bit number zero refers to the least significant bit.

Alignment is the requirement that data and/or instructions should be placed in memory such that (although the address resolution may be 8 bits) 16–bit words have to have addresses that are multiples of 2 (an even or word-aligned address) and 32-bit long words have to have addresses that are a multiple of 4 (a long word-aligned address) (Figure 5.1). This is an implementation requirement to allow for a higher execution speed.

If a 32-bit long word can have address 0001, which means that bytes 0001, 0002, 0003 and 0004 form the long word (Figure 5.1), a 32-bit machine must execute two memory read cycles, to fetch this data. If the data is aligned, it can be guaranteed that a 32-bit operand can be fetched in a single memory cycle. In general, aligned data (even when it is not

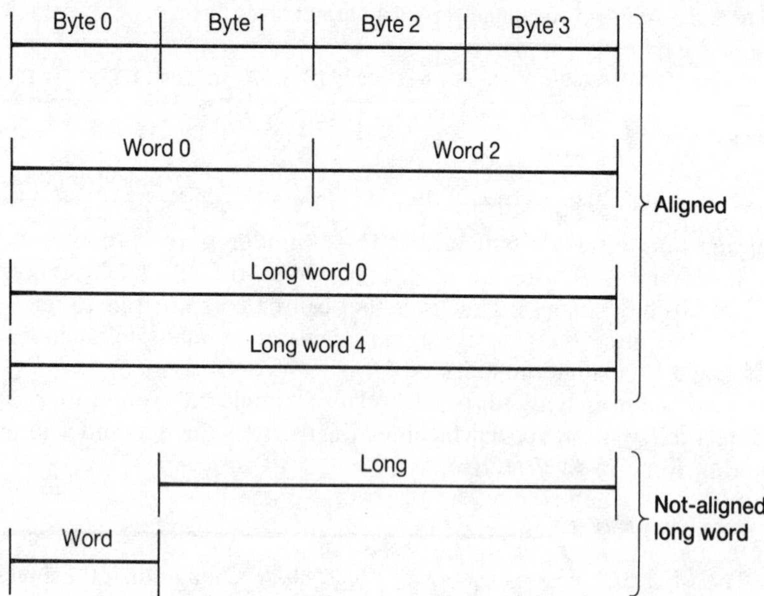

FIGURE 5.1
Alignment.

required) is preferred – that is, words on word boundaries, long words on long word boundaries – because of the increased performance. Many architectures, including the MC68020, which only require byte alignment for data, require word alignment for stack data because of stack operation efficiency.

5.1.2 Bit, byte and word order

Figure 5.2 shows the numbering of bits in a byte, word and long word for the MC68020. This is done systematically from right to left, starting with the least significant bit (LSB) position. The numbering of bytes in a 16-bit

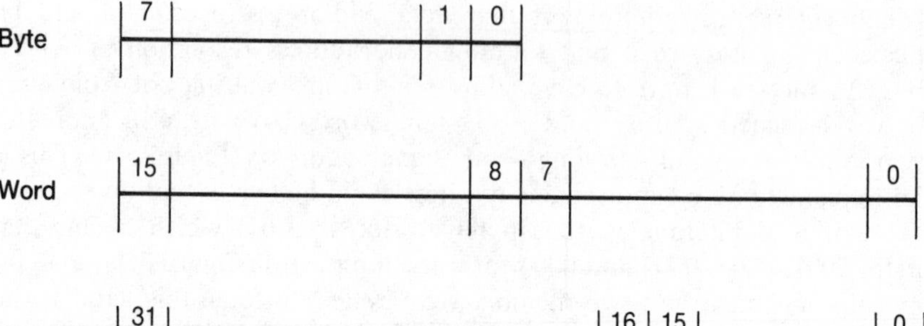

FIGURE 5.2
Bit numbering in the MC68020.

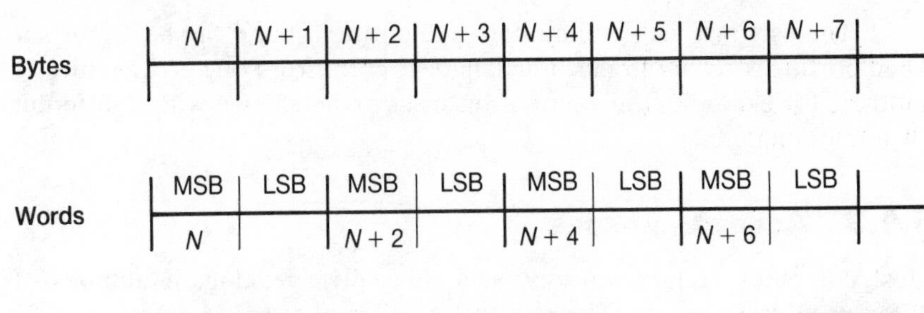

FIGURE 5.3
Byte order in the MC68020.

word and a 32-bit long word for the MC68020 is shown in Figure 5.3. This is done from left to right, which is inconsistent with the numbering of bits in a byte. For example, a 16-bit word consists of 2 bytes, the left byte having the lowest number. The address of a word or long word is the address of the lowest numbered, most significant byte (MSB), as pictured in Figure 5.3.

Not all architectures have the same structure (in terms of bit, byte and word order) as the MC68020 (Figure 5.4(a)). A more consistent bit and byte numbering scheme can be found in the IBM/370 (Figure 5.4(b)), where both bits and bytes are numbered from left to right. Another approach can be seen in the VAX-11 and the NS32000 (Figure 5.4(c)), where bits and bytes are numbered from right to left. For a further discussion on bit and byte orders, the reader is referred to the paper by Cohen (1981).

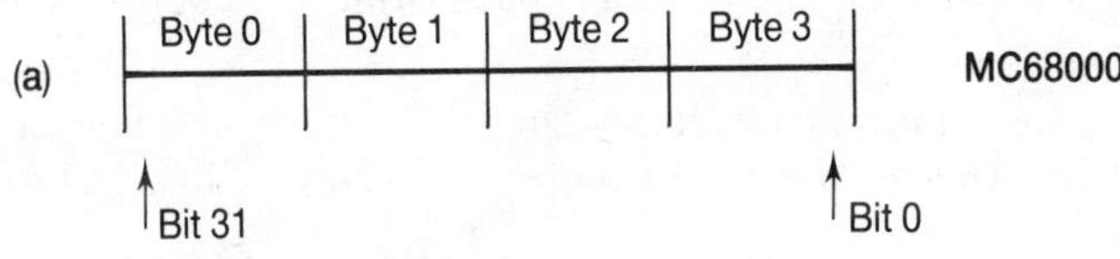

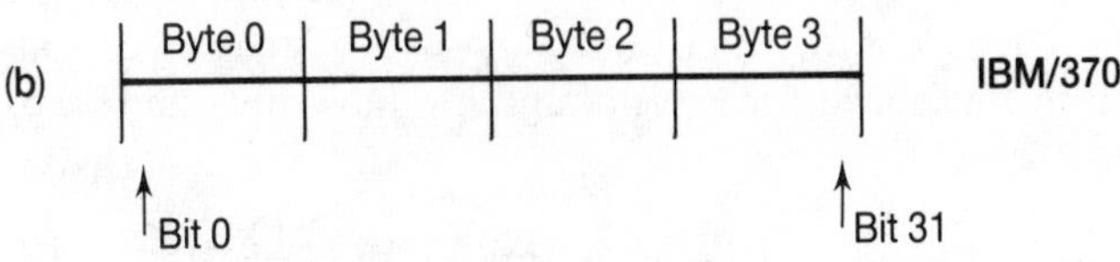

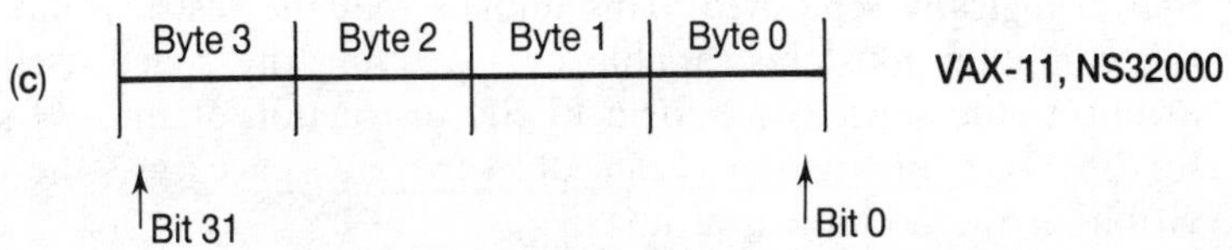

FIGURE 5.4
Diversity of bit and byte numbering schemes.

The way in which bit and byte numbering is done can be important when porting software in machine language form from one architecture to another; for example, the value of bit masks may change with a different bit numbering.

5.1.3 Address spaces

Most computer architectures possess, logically speaking, a number of different address spaces. The reason for this is that some spaces imply a certain use. The most important spaces are:

- **Working store or register space**: This is the space containing the general-purpose registers; for example, the MC68020 has eight data and eight address registers in this space. The advantage of using these registers is their compact operand specification (3 or 4 bits), which favours the instruction length. This saves memory and allows a faster instruction-fetch cycle. Furthermore, register access times are much shorter than memory access times.
- **Main memory space**: This space contains the programs and data. Main memory space (also called memory space) is sometimes logically further divided into a constant space (for constant data-like tables), a space for global data, a space for local data, a space for procedure parameters, and so on.
- **I/O space**: This space is used for the addressing of peripherals. It might be desirable to introduce this space in an architecture when I/O instructions require a different timing than memory and when I/O does not take up any memory space (which can be valuable for small address spaces).
- **Stack space**: Many architectures support a stack mechanism in a direct way. This means that data elements can be addressed on the stack.
- **Control space**: This space contains, for example, the program status word (PSW) or status register (SR), memory management registers, cache control registers, and so on. Vectors can also be specified in this space for use in handling interrupts and traps (see Chapter 9).

All these spaces can exist separately, both logically and physically:

- **Spaces logically separated**: This implies that the instruction set of the computer must be capable of specifying the space used; for example, the stack space for a PUSH instruction or the I/O space for an OUT instruction. Logically separate spaces are therefore visible at the architectural level.

- **Spaces physically separated**: Physically separate spaces are implemented separately by means of special hardware, as might be done for performance reasons; for example, the register space is often implemented this way, because it must be able to be accessed quickly. This is transparent at the architectural level; it is only visible at the implementation level.

The **overlay** technique enables spaces to overlap. To cite an example, the stack could be implemented as part of the memory space, which causes the logical stack and memory spaces to share the same physical space.

The specification of the desired logical space can be done via one of the methods described in Chapter 4: in the opcode space (via special instructions) or in the operand space (by specification of register, stack or memory). By using overlays, which is sometimes called **memory mapping** because overlays are usually done on to main memory space, it is possible, for example, to overlay the I/O space on to main memory space. Example 4.1 showed how, in the PDP-10, accumulators overlay the lower memory locations, so register–register instructions are implemented by specifying the second register operand as a memory address (the first operand is always a register).

Figure 5.5 shows the logical address spaces of the MC68020, which are placed in three, physically separated, spaces: the register, the control and the memory space. Nowadays, the registers are placed in a separate space in nearly all architectures. A logical overlay (of the registers) with memory is not desirable, because the memory addresses are longer (require more bits and therefore also a longer decoding time) and because extra hardware is needed for the overlay mechanism.

All other logical spaces of the MC68020 form a *logical* overlay with the memory space. Except for the control and register spaces, all spaces are also *physically* implemented as part of the memory space. The boundary of the I/O space in memory is not fixed by the MC68020 architecture but is implementation dependent.

.The advantage of a logical overlay is that no special instructions (opcodes or operands) are needed for communication between the spaces, as the power of the complete instruction set is available. This makes the architecture simpler and better organized. Although this overlay is at the expense of the space left for main memory, Figure 5.5 shows that these overlays take up a rather limited amount of space, making the advantage (no need for special instructions) more than outweigh this disadvantage. For architectures with a large address space (32-bit addresses), this disadvantage is small; therefore, such overlays are currently used in many architectures.

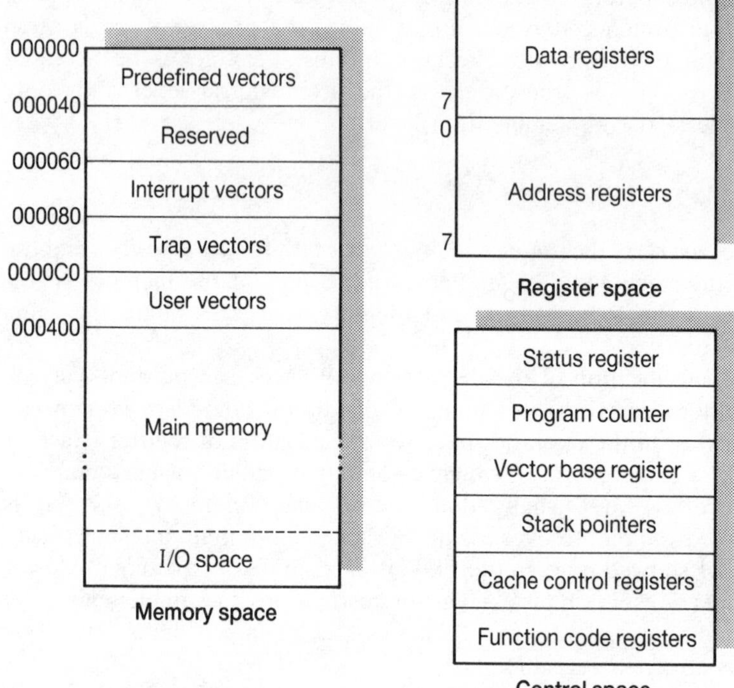

FIGURE 5.5

Address spaces of the MC68020.

5.2 Addressing modes

The representation of scalar and structured data types has been discussed in Chapter 3. This section discusses how objects of a scalar data type can be addressed when they are declared in isolation or when they are part of a structured data type. The methods for addressing data can be classified according to the number of address components needed to specify the operand value or the location of the operand (Figure 5.6). The multi-component addressing class comprises all modes that can be formed by combining elements of the zero-, one- or two-component addressing classes. It is not useful (nor possible) to discuss all but a few members of this class. The other classes are discussed in the following subsections. Example 5.5 shows how to specify the operand value 12345 for all addressing modes. Table 5.2 shows the addressing modes of the MC68020, and will be used as a source of examples.

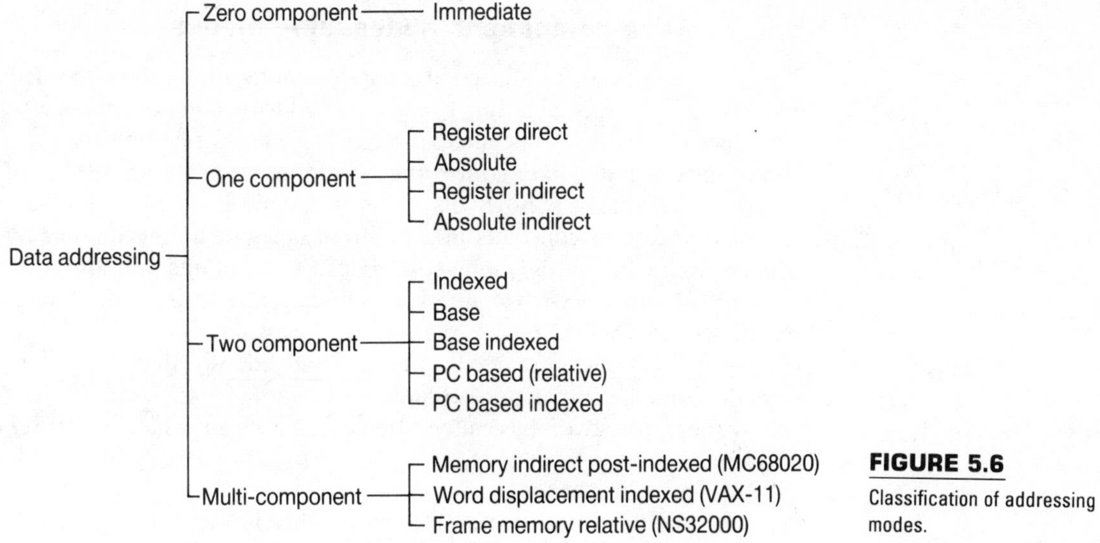

FIGURE 5.6
Classification of addressing modes.

Table 5.2 MC68020 addressing modes.

Mode	Register	MC68020 Name	Syntax	Effective Address Computation
0	reg#	Data register direct	Dn	ea = Dn
1	reg#	Address register direct	An	ea = An
2	reg#	Address register indirect	(An)	ea = (An)
3	reg#	Address register indirect post-increment	(An)+	ea = (An), An = (An) + N
4	reg#	Address register indirect pre-decrement	−(An)	An = An − N, ea = (An)
5	reg#	Address register indirect displacement	(d_{16}, An)	ea = d_{16} + (An)
6	reg#	Address register indirect indexed	(d_8, An, Xn)	ea = d_8 + (An) + (Xn)
6	reg#	Memory indirect post-indexed	([bd, An], Xn, od)	ea = (M[(An) + bd]) + (Xn) + od
6	reg#	Memory indirect pre-indexed	([bd, An, Xn], od)	ea = (M[(An) + bd + (Xn)]) + od
7	0	Absolute short	xxx.W	ea = (next word)
7	1	Absolute long	xxx.L	ea = (next 2 words)
7	2	Program counter relative	(d_{16}, PC)	ea = d_{16} + (PC)
7	3	Program counter indexed	(d_8, PC, Xn)	ea = d_8 + (PC) + (Xn)
7	3	PC memory indirect post-indexed	([bd, PC], Xn, od)	ea = (M[(PC) + bd]) + (Xn) + od
7	3	PC memory indirect pre-indexed	([bd, PC, Xn], od)	ea = (M[(PC) + bd + (Xn)]) + od
7	4	Immediate	#xxx	data = (next word(s))

Note that the term Xn stands for the complete index operand Xn.SIZE * SCALE, where Xn selects any data or address register, SIZE specifies the index size (word or long word) and SCALE allows the index register to be multiplied by 1 (no scaling), 2, 4 or 8.

5.2.1 Zero-component addressing modes

The zero-component addressing mode, normally called **immediate addressing**, is a special form, because no address components are used. The operand value is specified directly in the instruction stream. The importance of immediate addressing is obvious from the frequency of its occurrence. Table 4.3 shows that constants typically account for 40% of all operands. Most constants in a program are specified using immediate addressing, which is advantageous because constants are often small numbers (0 and 1 occur frequently). Consequently, it is more efficient to specify the constant, rather than the address of a memory location. Furthermore, constants need not be changed, so that they can be embedded in the instruction stream.

There are two, basically different, places in which to store the immediate data:

(1) Inside the basic instruction part: This is often called 'short' or 'quick' immediate addressing. The constants can only be small (because they have to fit inside the first instruction word or byte), but they use memory most efficiently.

(2) Inside instruction extensions: This method uses constants with a length equal to the basic instruction length or a multiple thereof. The length of the immediate data is normally specified inside the basic part and the data immediately follows this basic part (hence the name 'immediate' addressing).

Example 5.2 outlines the methods for specifying constants in the MC68020.

□□EXAMPLE 5.2

The MC68020 can specify immediate data in the opcode or in the operand space.

Opcode space There are some opcodes that imply that one operand is immediate data, whereas the other operand is specified in the normal way. A further division can be made according to the place in which the immediate data is stored:

- In the basic instruction part: Instructions such as the ADDQ and MOVEQ have reserved space within the basic instruction part for the specification of small constants; for example, ADDQ: $1 \leq C \leq 8$; MOVEQ: $-128 \leq C \leq 127$. The format of these quick instructions is shown in Appendix A (Figures A.4(i) and (j)).

- In extension words: Other instructions with an implied immediate addressing mode store the immediate data in one (for byte and word data) or two (for long word) extension words. Instructions of this kind are, for example, ANDI (AND Immediate), CMPI and STOP.

Operand space Instructions that have one or more general addressing modes can use the source operand to specify immediate addressing (see Table 5.2, mode 7.4). The immediate data is again stored in one or two extension word(s). Examples are ASL.B #2, D0, BTST.L #3, D1 and MULS.W #12, D5.

5.2.2 One-component addressing modes

These simple addressing modes specify the effective operand address by using a single component in the operand specifier. This component can be a register number or an absolute operand address. Both components can be used directly or indirectly.

Register-direct addressing

One of the most frequently used operand addressing modes is the register-direct mode. In this mode, a register number that uniquely identifies the register containing the operand value is specified. This mode is used frequently due to its efficiency and speed. Because few registers are available (typically 8 or 16), a compact operand specification, using 3 or 4 bits, can be achieved. Furthermore, because the register file is normally located on-chip, its access time is very short, compared to memory or even to caches (see Chapter 14). All modern architectures having more than one register support this mode. In architectures with only one register, this register is often specified implicitly.

The MC68020 architecture divides its register set into two groups:

(1) **Data registers**, specified via mode 0 of Table 5.2, which are primarily used to act as source or destination for arithmetic/logical operations.

(2) **Address registers**, specified via mode 1 of Table 5.2, which are primarily used to specify operand addresses.

Absolute addressing

The absolute addressing mode specifies addresses as they are offered to the memory system (called 'absolute' or 'effective addresses'). Absolute addressing is needed in many architectures for the specification of vector,

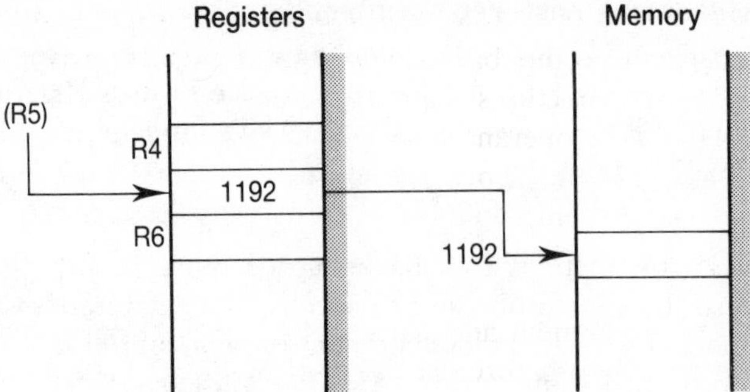

FIGURE 5.7

Register-indirect addressing.

I/O and status register addresses (assuming that they form a logical overlay with main memory). With absolute addressing, as opposed to relative or indirect addressing, no relocation operation (the addition of a displacement to an address) or indirection is required, at the expense of fetching an extension word that specifies the absolute address.

□□EXAMPLE 5.3

The MC68020 supports two absolute addressing modes. The address can be either short (16 bits, see mode 7.0 of Table 5.2) or long (32 bits, see mode 7.1 of Table 5.2). The short address is contained in one extension word and sign extended to form a 32-bit address (this allows for the addressing of the top and bottom 32 kbytes of physical memory), while the long address is stored in two extension words, which are concatenated to form the complete address. Examples are:

```
MOVE.L   0x80B932C6.L, D0     ;32-bit (.L) absolute address
ADD.W    0xFE30.W, D7         ;16-bit (.W) absolute address
ASL.B    0xD9CD.W             ;16-bit (.W) absolute address
```

Indirect addressing

Indirection means that the specified location, instead of containing the operand value, contains the address of the operand value (the effective address). Register-indirect addressing is used very often. It is useful (and necessary) when addresses of data structures are not known until run time, because addresses can be computed with instructions and stored in a register, after which the operand can be accessed via this register. Figure 5.7 shows the way in which register-indirect addressing is performed. The mode (R5) is used, whereby R5 contains the memory address 1192. The notation for this form of addressing is: memory address = M[(R5)].

Indirect addressing with register modification

Several variations on the basic register-indirect addressing mode are possible. Many architectures support addressing modes in which the register containing the operand address is modified before or after usage. Four modes are possible, depending on the direction of the modification (increment or decrement) and the time of modification (pre- or post-modification). As an example, the pre-decrement addressing mode is explained here.

In the pre-decrement addressing mode, the register containing the address is decremented before use, so it points to the next (or previous) data element. The amount decremented is dependent on the data size of the objects. The pre-decrement addressing mode is often used in combination with the post-increment addressing mode. With these two modes, it is possible to implement stacks via a stack pointer (that is, a register pointing to the top element of the stack). If an element is popped off the stack, the stack pointer must be incremented to point to the next element (assuming the stack grows downwards in memory, starting at the higher addresses), using the post-increment addressing mode. An element can be pushed on to the stack via the pre-decrement addressing mode (first decrementing the stack pointer to address the next free location and then using it as an operand address pointer).

□□EXAMPLE 5.4

The MC68020 supports different forms of indirect addressing modes: the basic address register indirect (mode 2 of Table 5.2), possibly combined with pre-decrement or post-increment (modes 4 and 3 of Table 5.2, respectively). Examples of some instructions using indirect addressing are:

```
AND.L     #4, (A4)        ;Register indirect
DIVS.W    (A3)+, D0       ;Post-increment, A3 incremented by 2
                          ;(word!) after use
```

Examples of stack operations using pre-decrement, register indirect and the post-increment addressing mode are:

```
MOVE.W  X, -(A1)          ;Push X on stack pointed to by A1
MOVE.W  Y, -(A1)          ;Push Y on stack pointed to by A1
ADD.W   (A1)+, (A1)       ;Add X to Y and leave result on stack
MOVE.W  (A1)+, Z          ;Pop result off stack pointed to by A1 and
                          ;store it into Z
```

		Displacement	
		Fixed	Variable
Base	Fixed	————	Indexed
	Variable	Base	Base indexed

FIGURE 5.8

Two-component addressing modes.

5.2.3 Two-component addressing modes

Two basic components can be combined to form the two-component addressing modes. One component is usually called the **base** while the other component is called the **displacement**. Usually, the displacement (or offset) is the distance between a base address and the operand address. The base address and the displacement can be fixed (known at compile time) or variable (computed at run time). Because the combination of a fixed base address with a fixed displacement is not sensible (it is a circumstantial form of absolute addressing which has already been discussed), three possible addressing modes remain, as shown in Figure 5.8.

Indexed addressing

With the indexed addressing mode, the (fixed) base address is specified in the instruction stream (comparable to an absolute address). To form the operand address, a variable offset, contained in a register called **index**, is added to the base address. This mode is used when the base address of a data structure, such as a vector, is known at compile time but the exact element position can only be determined at run time. To accommodate operand sizes of several lengths, the index is often multiplied by a **scale factor**. If a vector $A[0\ ..\ 100]$ has data elements occupying 4 bytes, the scale factor is 4, assuming an address resolution of a byte. Given that the base address for vector $A[0\ ..\ 100]$, which is the starting address, is 1000, then element $A[3]$ can be found at address $1000 + 3 * 4 = 1012$.

A level of indirection may also be used. This indexed indirect mode has two varieties: **pre-indexed indirect** and **post-indexed indirect**. When M[X] means 'the contents of memory location X', the formulas for the calculation of the operand address are:

Pre-indexed: address = M[base + index]
Post-indexed: address = (M[base]) + index

In the pre-indexed mode, the offset is added to the base address, producing an intermediate address. The contents of this intermediate address is then used as the operand address. In the post-indexed mode, the base address is used as an intermediate address. Afterwards, the offset is added to the contents of the intermediate address to obtain the operand address. Examples of both modes are given in Example 5.5.

Base addressing

Base addressing is the opposite of indexed addressing, in that the instruction contains a fixed displacement and the (variable) base address is contained in a register. The main difference is that the base address in indexed addressing must always be a full-length address, while the displacement in base addressing may be either short or long. If the offset and the base addresses have the same length, base and indexed addressing cannot be distinguished.

Base addressing is used when the base address of a data block is not known until run time, while the relative position of an item is already known at compile time. Some possible base addresses are:

- The begin address of an activation record: This is the begin address of a block of memory that is allocated upon activation (call) of a program block, a procedure or a function. Fixed displacements can be used to access local variables and parameters.
- The begin address of a parameter block or a record: This is a pointer to the beginning of a set of parameters or a record. Again, fixed displacements can be used to address the required parameter or record element.
- A specified pointer: This is important for the construction and addressing of dynamic structures, such as linked lists and trees.

Base-indexed addressing

In the base-indexed addressing mode, both the base address and the offset are variable, and they are computed at run time. This allows for accessing arbitrary elements in a data structure with a begin address that is not known at compile time.

Program counter-relative addressing

A special class of two-component addressing modes is the class that uses the program counter (PC) as the register containing the base address. In architectures where the PC is one of the general registers, normal register addressing modes can be used for accessing data in the program space. For example, the VAX-11 (DEC, 1979) can use the mode (R15)+ to access immediate operands, because R15 is the program counter. However, if the PC is a special register, an extra addressing mode must be provided to be able to address data relative to the current value of the

Mode	
Immediate	#12345
Register direct	R0
Absolute	1132
Register indirect	(R2)
Absolute indirect	(6003)
Indexed	1138(R4)
Pre-indexed indirect	(R5, 6000)
Post-indexed indirect	(6000), R3
Base	32(R6)
Base indexed	(R6, R7)
PC based	130(PC)
PC based indexed	(PC,R1)

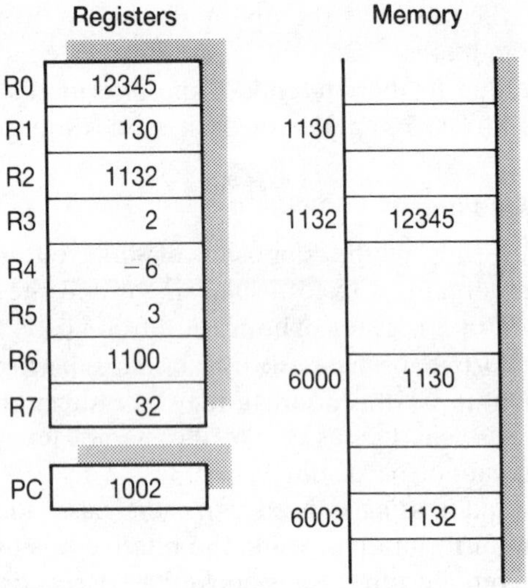

Registers	
R0	12345
R1	130
R2	1132
R3	2
R4	−6
R5	3
R6	1100
R7	32
PC	1002

Memory	
1130	
1132	12345
6000	1130
6003	1132

FIGURE 5.9

Examples of addressing modes.

PC. Because this value (the base address) is variable, there are two possible addressing modes: PC based and PC based indexed (Figure 5.8). The **PC-based addressing mode**, often called **relative addressing**, can normally use variably sized displacements. Because most data and program items are close to the place where they are referenced, short (one byte) displacements are often sufficient. **PC-based indexed** or **relative-indexed addressing** works just like normal base-indexed addressing, except that the PC is used as a base register.

The most common use of PC-relative addressing is in branch instructions, which are essential for implementing most high-level language control structures. Using relative instead of absolute addressing automatically provides relocatable program modules that can be placed anywhere in memory (they are position independent). Addressing data, relative to the program code, is also important if read-only data is a mandatory part of the program. This data can be loaded at the same time as the code and can consist of translation tables (EBCDIC to ASCII) or tables with initial values for iterative computations.

□□EXAMPLE 5.5

Figure 5.9 shows the specification of the operand value 12345 (located in register R0 and in memory location 1132) for all of the zero-, one- and two-component addressing modes discussed. For example, in the pre-indexed indirect mode, adding 6000 to the contents of R5 (= 3) produces the location (6003), where the operand address (1132) is stored.

5.2.4 Multi-component addressing modes

As stated before, all previously discussed addressing modes can be combined to form all kinds of esoteric (and some useful) addressing modes. Although it is not possible to discuss all of them, Example 5.6 outlines some of the combinations for the MC68020.

□□EXAMPLE 5.6

The MC68020 has many addressing modes with an extended form of base-displacement addressing. The addressing can be relative to the address in one of the address registers or to the program counter. A displacement can be specified in different ways:

- Base displacement (bd): An 8-, 16- or 32-bit displacement that is added to the value in the address register or program counter. A bd is always added before any memory indirection takes place.
- Outer displacement (od): A null, word or long word displacement that is added to the calculated address operand, yielding the effective address. The notion 'outer' refers to the fact that it is the last displacement added after any memory indirection.
- Index register (Xn): An index register that is included in the address specification contains a variable offset. It can be used for both pre-indexing and post-indexing. The format of the index operand is Xn.SIZE * SCALE. Xn selects any data or address register as the index register, SIZE specifies the index size as either W (for word, indicating that the 16 least significant bits of the register should be used) or L (for long word size), and SCALE allows the index register value to be multiplied by a value of one (no scaling), two, four or eight.

These elements of relative addressing can be combined, together with the levels of indirection, to form very sophisticated (and complicated) addressing modes. These modes range from 'address register indirect with displacement' to 'program counter memory-indirect pre-indexed, with base and outer displacement'. As an example, the formula for calculating the operand address for the memory-indirect, post-indexed addressing mode is:

$$\text{address} = M[\text{bd} + (\text{An})] + (\text{Xn}) * \text{SCALE} + \text{od}$$

The effective address is calculated in two stages. The first stage is the calculation of an intermediate memory address by adding a base register (An) and a displacement (bd). This address is used to access a (long word) value at the calculated address. This value is indexed with the

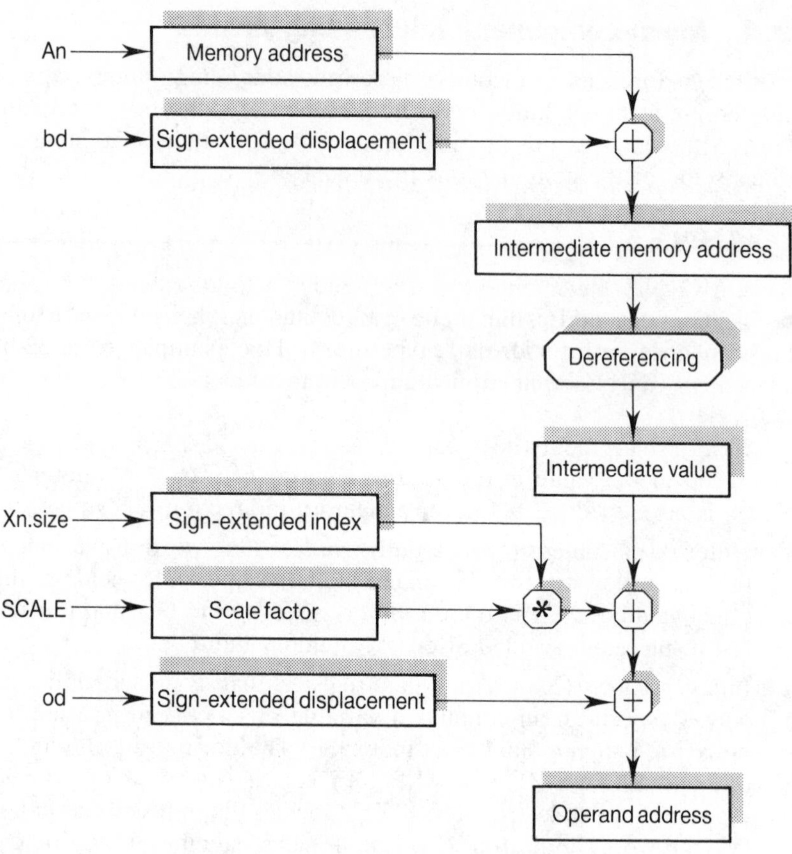

FIGURE 5.10
Memory-indirect, post-indexed addressing mode.

scaled index register (Xn.SIZE * SCALE) and, finally, the outer displacement (od) is added to yield the effective address, as illustrated in Figure 5.10.

5.3 Addressing of structured data

Many data types, discussed in Chapter 3, can be easily accessed by using any of the zero- or one-component addressing modes introduced in this chapter. Structured data types, such as arrays, records and stacks, need a more sophisticated addressing mechanism. The addressing of elements inside these data structures is discussed in the following subsections.

5.3.1 Arrays

For the addressing of array elements, the following aspects are important:

- **Index checking**: The index must stay within the pre-declared bounds of the array. Note that this check need not always be done at execution time, because a compiler is often capable of determining whether the index will be within bounds – for example, when the index is a constant.
- **Scaling**: Scaling is the multiplying of an index by the size of a submatrix or of the data type used. For example, if a 32-bit floating-point number is used in a byte-addressable machine, the scale factor is 4.
- **Element selection**: Selection of the required vector element is supported directly in many architectures by, for example, the indexed addressing mode. For element selection in arrays, special instructions are often provided for index computation.

The address of the element $A[I, J]$ in the array $A[1\,..\,M, 1\,..\,N]$ can be computed in the following way (assuming every element takes up only one memory location, otherwise scaling must be applied, and row-major ordering is used (see Figure 3.8)):

$$\begin{aligned}\text{address } A[I, J] &= \text{address } A[1, 1] + (I - 1) * N + (J - 1) \\ &= \text{address } A[1, 1] + I * N + J - N - 1 \\ &= \text{constant } A_0 + I * N + J \qquad \textbf{(5.1)}\end{aligned}$$

$$\text{where } A_0 = \text{address } A[1, 1] - N - 1$$

The address computation for an element in a two-dimensional array thus requires one multiplication and two additions (assuming that A_0 can be computed beforehand at compile time). The disadvantage of the multiplication (it is time consuming) can be eliminated in many cases, as compilers can replace it by a repeated addition or subtraction within an outer loop. This is called **strength reduction**; that is, replacing a complex operation by a simpler one in an outer loop. This is illustrated in the following program fragment. The Pascal **for** loop for initializing the eighth column of array A can be translated into the MC68020 assembly statements (using Equation (5.1)), where register A0 contains the constant A_0 and D0 is used to hold the variable I.

```
var A : array[1 . . M, 1 . . N] of integer;
for I := M downto 1 do
    A[I, 8] := 0;
```

```
       MOVE.L   #A0, A0          ;A0 contains begin address of A
       MOVE.L   #M, D0           ;D0 contains initial value for I
Loop:  MOVE.W   D0, D1
       MULS.W   #N, D1           ;D1 := I * N
       CLR.L    8(A0, D1.W)      ;J = 8,
                                 ;so address = A0 + I * N + 8
       SUBQ.W   #1, D0           ;I := I - 1
       BNE      loop             ;Until I = 0
```

When the multiplication is replaced by a repeated subtraction, the result is as follows, where A0 again contains the constant A_0 of Equation (5.1) and D0 is now used as index register:

```
       MOVE.L   #M * N, D0       ;D0 := I * N
Loop:  CLR.L    8(A0, D0.W)      ;Address = A0 + I * N + 8
       SUB.W    #N, D0           ;I := I - 1
       BNE      loop             ;Until I = 0
```

Next, the general form of the address of element $A[S_1, S_2, \ldots, S_N]$, which is an element of the array $A[L_1 \,..\, U_1, \ldots, L_N \,..\, U_N]$, is discussed, assuming that A is row-major ordered (see Figure 3.8). To make it easier, the variables d_i ($i = 1 \,..\, N - 1$) are introduced, where $d_i = U_{i+1} - L_{i+1} + 1$; that is, d_i is the number of index values for dimension $i + 1$. d_N can be considered as the size of the array elements (= E addressable units) and the begin address of the array is A. The addresses of array elements can now be computed as follows:

- For array $A[L \,..\, U]$, the address of element $A[S]$ is:

$$\text{address} = A + (S - L) * E$$

- For array $A[L_1 \,..\, U_1, L_2 \,..\, U_2]$, the address of element $A[S_1, S_2]$ is:

$$\text{address} = A + ((S_1 - L_1) * d_1 + (S_2 - L_2)) * E$$

- In general, for the array $A[L_1 \,..\, U_1, \ldots, L_N \,..\, U_N]$, the address of element $A[S_1, S_2, \ldots, S_N]$ is:

$$\text{address} = A + (\ldots((S_1 - L_1) * d_1 + (S_2 - L_2)) * d_2 + \ldots + (S_N - L_N)) * d_N \qquad \textbf{(5.2)}$$

In addition to the foregoing computation, a check must be made to ensure that each subscript (or index) S_i lies within its range; that is, if $L_i \leq S_i \leq U_i$ is true. To simplify this calculation, a descriptor, which is also called a **dope vector**, can be used. For each dimension, the values L_i, U_i and d_i are stored. Furthermore, the number of dimensions N, the start address A and the element size E are stored (the element size is stored in the place of d_N). The element size can be seen as a final multiplication factor to achieve the scaling, depending on the size of the elements.

L_1	U_1	d_1
L_2	U_2	d_2
|	|	|
L_N	U_N	$d_N = E$
N	A	

FIGURE 5.11
Dope vector for *N*-dimensional array.

Using the dope vector of Figure 5.11, the address of an element can now be obtained as follows:

```
address := 0;
for I := 1 to N do
begin
  if (S[I] < L[I]) or (S[I] > U[I]) then trap;
  address := (address + S[I] - L[I]) * d[I];
end;
address := address + A;
```

A dope vector can also contain information like the data type of the elements and/or the total array size (although this is redundant, because it can be computed from the other available data). The begin address A may be replaced by address $A_V = A[0, 0, \ldots, 0]$, which represents the virtual begin address of array A. Use of this virtual origin simplifies the address computation because no subtraction operations are needed to deal with lower bounds. Equation (5.2) then becomes:

$$\text{address} = A_V + (\ldots(S_1 * d_1 + S_2) * d_2 + \ldots + S_N) * d_N \qquad \textbf{(5.3)}$$

The memory allocation of an array is strongly influenced by whether the bounds of the array may or may not change during program execution. **Static bounds** implies that *all* values of L_i and U_i must be known at compile time. FORTRAN and Pascal use static bounds to facilitate the allocation of the array (or vector), so that its total size can be determined at compile time. In FORTRAN, the begin address of the array can be assumed to be a constant during program execution, while in Pascal the offset of the begin address of the array to the start of an activation record is constant. **Dynamic bounds** are used by languages like ALGOL and some dialects of Pascal. They do not require that all (or even any) values L_i and U_i be known at compile time. This implies that the total size can only be determined during execution and that the required memory space can only be reserved at that time. The run-time system, charged with the creation of activation records (for procedure and block entry), takes care of these functions. If more than one dynamic structure must be allocated, the begin address will generally only be known during the generation of the activation record.

Descriptor-based addressing

Descriptors can be used to describe the structure of structured data. The dope vector of Figure 5.11 could be used as a descriptor for an N-dimensional array. Architectures that use descriptors do not usually allow such a complexity because of the amount of hardware involved. A single descriptor typically describes only one dimension of an array. An example of such a descriptor, as used by Burroughs (1969), is given in Example 5.7.

□□EXAMPLE 5.7

The memory allocation for the arrays of Figure 3.10 has the advantage that the multiplication for address computation is replaced by a level of indirection (via a pointer):

$$\text{address } A[I, J] = (\text{M}[A_0 + I - 1]) + (J - 1) \qquad \textbf{(5.4)}$$

with M[X] = the contents of memory location X. The disadvantage of this method is that much memory may be required for storing the pointers (consider, for example, $A[1\,..\,1000, 1\,..\,2]$).

The Burroughs B6700 array descriptor (Figure 5.12) uses indirection rather than multiplication to access array elements. The 20-bit address field specifies the begin address. The size field specifies the size of the array elements; they can be 4-, 6-, 7- or 8-bit characters, single (48-bit) or double (96-bit) precision numbers. When indexing a descriptor, the correct scale factor will automatically be used during address calculation.

The length field specifies the upper bound of the subscript (U_i). The lower bound (L_i) is supposed to be zero and is therefore not specified in the descriptor.

The tag field indicates that the word contains an array descriptor (see Figure 4.6).

The flags field is not of interest to a basic understanding of the descriptor mechanism.

3	5	3	20	20
Tag	Flags	Size	Length	Address

FIGURE 5.12

Burroughs array descriptor.

To access an array element, the indices must be corrected such that the new lower bound is equal to zero. They must then be pushed on the stack in the reverse order (that is, the last index first), because the B6700 has a stack architecture. Figure 5.13(a) shows the stack as generated during the execution of the following program fragment. To access the element $A[I, J, K]$, only the descriptor A has to be accessed (Figure 5.13(b)). The corrected indices are automatically popped off the stack and used as index into an array of descriptors for the corresponding dimension. This is repeated for all dimensions and the final index K selects the requested element.

```
var A : array [L1 . . U1, L2 . . U2, L3 . . U3] of integer;
begin
   ⋮
  A[I, J, K] := 28;
   ⋮
end;
```

```
PUSH 28     ;Push constant 28 on stack
PUSH L3     ;Compute K − L3 on stack
PUSH K
SUB
PUSH L2     ;Compute J − L2 on stack
PUSH J
SUB
PUSH L1     ;Compute I − L1 on stack
PUSH I
SUB
POP A       ;The value 28 gets assigned to A[I, J, K]
```

The operation of POP A in the above program is as follows (see also Figure 5.13):

(1) Operand A is fetched, its tag indicates that it is an array descriptor.

(2) Because it is an array descriptor, the index is popped off the stack. If this index is <0 or >Length (as specified in the descriptor), then trap, else continue with step (3).

(3) The address of the array element is computed by adding the index to the address field of the descriptor, after which the array element is fetched.

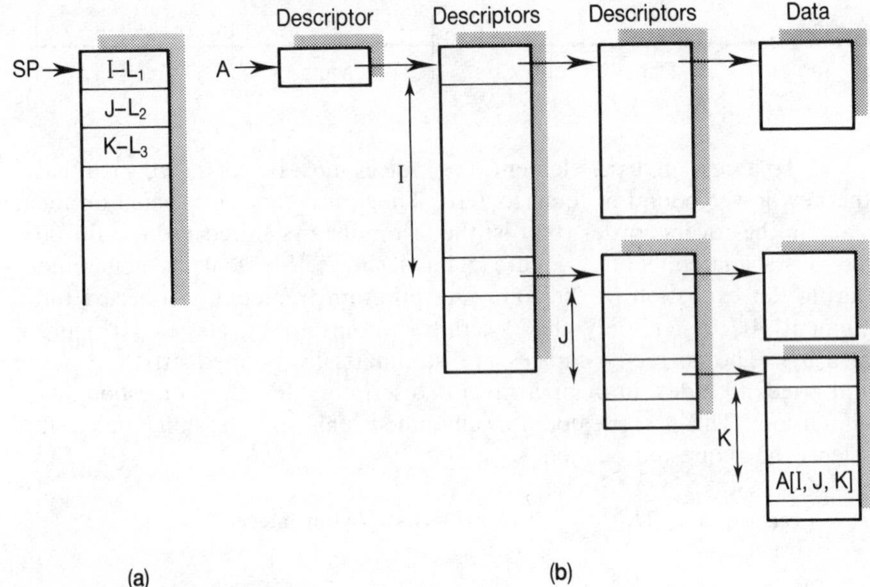

FIGURE 5.13

Burroughs array access.

(4) When the tag of the fetched array element identifies it to be a descriptor, then go to step (2). Steps (2), (3) and (4) will be repeated for each of the subscripts I, J and K.

(5) When the tag of the fetched array element identifies it to be data, this will be the array element $A[I, J, K]$. The constant 28 is popped off the stack and stored at this location, because the operation to be performed was a POP operation.

5.3.2 Records

For the addressing of records and record elements, the most important aspect is that all fields have a *constant* offset relative to the beginning of the record (see Section 3.3.4). Elements can then be easily accessed by using base-displacement addressing. However, if variant records are allowed, fields may have a variable offset relative to the beginning of the record. To make it easier for compilers (and compiler writers), languages that allow variant records often dictate that the fixed part must be declared first, so that the fields in this fixed part still have a fixed offset, relative to the beginning of a record (they can still be accessed with base addressing).

5.3.3 Stacks

Chapter 3 has already indicated that stacks are important in modern high-level languages to store activation records, parameters and intermediate results. Therefore, it makes sense for the architecture to provide some support to implement stacks and to address stack elements. The most frequently occurring support (at least in register-oriented architectures) is the stack pointer register, which points to the top of the stack (the top memory location used).

In stack-oriented architectures, all operations (except load and store) implicitly use stack operands. An instruction such as MUL pops the two top elements off the stack, multiplies them and pushes the result back on to the stack. Only load and store instructions require the specification of an explicit memory address. Apart from the normal arithmetic instructions, stack-oriented machines often have special stack-related instructions such as SWAP (exchange the two top elements), DUP (duplicate the top element) and RSUB (reverse subtract: if the normal SUB operation subtracts the second element from the top element, then RSUB subtracts the top element from the second one). Other, more general, instructions that implicitly use the stack are JSR and RTS, to mention but a few. The JSR instruction first pushes the current value of the program counter on to the stack before performing the jump. The RTS instruction pops the return address off the stack and stores it in the program counter.

In other architectures, it must be specified explicitly that an operation uses operands from the stack. If this is specified in the opcode space, the instructions are normally called PUSH and POP, to add or retrieve an element to or from the stack, respectively. A special version of this instruction pushes, not the operand value, but the effective address of the operand on to the stack – for example, for parameter passing by reference. The MC68020 instruction PEA (Push Effective Address) allows for this.

It is conceivable that one of the operand specifiers is coded such that it represents the top element of the stack (TOS). The implementation of this addressing mode must automatically execute its stack function as a secondary task. The NS32000 architecture contains such an operand specifier (National Semiconductor, 1984). Instructions can then be:

```
MOV  A, TOS      ;Push A on to the stack
MOV  TOS, A      ;Pop A
ADD  TOS, TOS    ;Add two top elements of the stack
ADD  Src, TOS    ;Add Src to the top of the stack
ADD  TOS, Dst    ;Add the top of the stack to Dst
```

If the TOS operand is only used as source operand, the stack pointer is

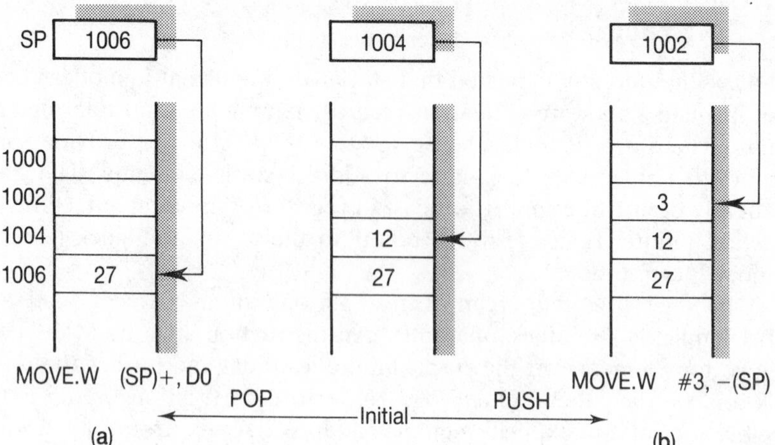

FIGURE 5.14
SP pointing to the top element.

automatically updated afterwards (incremented by the operand length). When the TOS operand only acts as destination operand, the result of the operation is pushed on to the stack by first decrementing the stack pointer (by the operand length) and then storing the result. If the TOS operand is used both as source and destination, the stack pointer remains unaffected and it is used as operand address (the operand is the top element of the stack).

Not many architectures directly support a TOS operand, but many architectures contain the register-indirect addressing mode with an optional post-increment or pre-decrement extension, which is suited to the implementation of stacks in memory. Although all registers are normally allowed to function as a stack pointer (SP), one register is often specially designated to be the system stack pointer (register A7 in the MC68020).

Using the post-increment and pre-decrement addressing modes allows two kinds of stacks to be implemented: one with the SP pointing to the top element of the stack (this stack grows towards lower-numbered memory locations) and one with the SP pointing to the first free location (this stack grows upwards in memory). The first implementation (Figure 5.14) is used most frequently, since it is more sensible to point to something (a value) than to a free location (no value). A philosophical problem is the implementation of an empty stack (where must the stack pointer point to?). The first implementation is more efficient when operands are read and written during the same operation (in this method, the SP can remain unchanged). To push a value on to the stack, the pre-decrement addressing mode is used (Figure 5.14(a)), whereas popping a value uses the post-increment addressing mode (Figure 5.14(b)). With this implementation, the previously mentioned instructions

Table 5.3 VAX-11 frequency distribution (%) of the number of operands per instruction.

Number of Operands	Frequency
0	3.3
1	33.1
2	52.4
3	7.2
4	3.6
5	0.2
6	0.2

using a TOS operand would look as follows:

```
MOV  A, -(SP)       ;Push A on to the stack
MOV  (SP)+, A       ;Pop A
ADD  (SP)+, (SP)    ;Add two top elements of the stack
ADD  Src, (SP)      ;Add Src to the top of the stack
ADD  (SP)+, Dst     ;Add the top of the stack to Dst
```

5.4 Compact operand specification

Operand specifications occur very frequently. Table 5.3 shows the frequency distribution of the number of operands per instruction for the VAX-11 (Wiecek, 1982), which leads to an average number of 1.8 operands per instruction. Because of this number, a compact operand specification is important to achieve savings in the required memory size and bandwidth. There are several techniques available for compact operand specification.

5.4.1 Implicit operands

This method is often used in older architectures, where only one register (called the accumulator) is available. Therefore, the architecture could use the one-address instruction format, with the accumulator always functioning as the second operand. With the increase in the number of general registers, this method can no longer be used. Stack architectures still use this method, whereby only the load and store operations require explicit operands, but all arithmetical and logical operations implicitly use the stack as source and/or destination operand.

Table 5.4 Operand specifier frequency (%) in the VAX-11.

Addressing Mode		BASIC	COBOL	FORTRAN	Pascal
0–3	Literal	9.8	18.1	18.2	15.5
4	Index	4.7	2.1	5.6	7.6
5	Register	34.9	37.9	41.0	45.1
6	Register deferred	9.0	15.3	9.1	2.0
7	Autodecrement	0.5	1.0	0.5	0.7
8	Autoincrement	17.4	4.8	4.1	2.6
9	Autoincrement deferred	0.1	0.2	0.3	0.0
10	Byte displacement	16.3	10.8	13.6	16.6
11	Byte displacement deferred	0.5	1.3	0.6	0.4
12	Word displacement	0.8	0.9	1.5	6.5
13	Word displacement deferred	—	—	0.0	—
14	Long displacement	6.1	7.3	5.5	3.0
15	Long displacement deferred	—	0.3	0.0	—

5.4.2 Register operands

When using registers, those variables (or pointers to variables) that are frequently needed or needed at a given time are kept in registers. Simulations have shown that 32 registers are nearly always sufficient (Radin, 1983). To further reduce the number of required bits for register specification, most register-oriented architectures have 8 or 16 registers. A direct or indirect register operand can then be specified in a compact way, requiring only 3 or 4 bits.

5.4.3 Relative addressing

This method of operand specification is related to the fact that operands are often clustered. This is especially true for activation records, where local variables are allocated a contiguous block of memory. Because of this clustering, it is possible to have short displacements (a byte), which cover most cases. Table 5.4 shows that byte displacements (addressing mode = 10) are used most frequently for the addressing of both data and instructions (Wiecek, 1982). Table 5.5 shows that most displacements in branch instructions are positive (and the distances are small) because these instructions are mainly generated due to **if . . . then** (**. . . else**) statements. Table 5.5 also shows that more than 90% of all branch displacements can be coded in a single byte.

Table 5.5 Conditional branch displacement frequencies (%) in the VAX-11.

Byte Range	BASIC	COBOL	FORTRAN	Pascal
−128 to −17	0.4	0.5	4.5	0.0
−16 to − 1	29.9	0.2	0.8	0.0
Not taken	51.6	43.6	34.4	49.7
1–4	3.1	13.1	13.0	11.0
5–8	1.6	7.8	14.1	2.7
9–16	5.9	11.0	11.1	10.2
17–32	3.5	14.3	8.7	10.5
33–64	1.5	5.5	6.1	4.0
65–127	1.1	1.7	2.3	3.5
Rest	1.4	2.3	5.0	8.4

5.4.4 Pooling

Sometimes, a compiler is able to collect frequently used operands that are scattered in memory into one pool. Base-displacement addressing (with a very small displacement field) can then be used for operand specification.

A special form of pooling can be used for procedures and functions. In this case, the pool consists of a table with pointers to procedures and functions, and a specific procedure can be called using one level of indirection, which reduces the number of operand bits to $\log_2 (N)$, if there are N procedures present. Only the procedure number is needed to access the desired procedure. This method is utilized in many versions of P-code.

SUMMARY

- Because instructions and data are all stored in main memory, it is necessary to address locations in memory when information is required. Depending on the size of the smallest addressable entity, bit resolution, byte resolution or word resolution are the most frequently occurring cases.

- As not only memory contains information, but other spaces as well, it is possible to distinguish between different address spaces, such as main memory space, register space, I/O space, stack space and control space. These spaces can overlap or they can exist separately.

- To specify operands, several addressing modes exist. The most simple one is immediate addressing, where the operand is contained in the instruction stream, so its address is known via the program counter and no memory address need be specified.

- One-component addressing modes only have one element, a register number or an absolute address, both of which can be used directly or indirectly. Furthermore, with register-indirect addressing, it is possible to modify the register contents before or after using it as an address.

- Two-component addressing modes can be divided into base, indexed and base-indexed modes, according to the size and the variability (fixed or variable) of the components. A special version of base addressing uses the program counter and is called PC-relative addressing.

- For the addressing of structured data types, such as arrays and records, several aspects arise. For array elements, bounds checking, scaling and element selection must be performed. This is normally done via, for example, CHK instructions together with an index addressing mode. All the information about an array (bounds, dimension and length of the elements) can also be collected in a dope vector, used for further address calculations.

- Record elements can be addressed with base addressing, as the offset is usually fixed with respect to the base address, while this base address can vary at run time. Stack elements (especially on the top of the stack) are usually addressed via post-increment and pre-decrement addressing modes.

- As operand specifications occur frequently, it is important that they are kept short to use memory efficiently. This can be done via implicit operands (a single accumulator or stack operands) or short register numbers (instead of long memory addresses). Another method is to use variable size displacements, as most displacements are only small and can be often coded in a single byte.

EXERCISES

5.1 What is address resolution? Does it have to be the same for instructions and data? Why is an address resolution of one bit not often used?

5.2 What requirement applies to the numbering of bits in a byte, and the numbering of bytes in memory, bytes in a word and bytes in a long word?

5.3 Indicate which of the following statements are true:

(a) Physical overlay of the I/O space on to memory space is transparent to the architecture.

(b) Physical overlay of the I/O space on to the memory space eliminates the need for special I/O instructions.

(c) Logical overlay of the I/O space on to memory space requires less memory.

(d) Logical overlay of the I/O space on to memory space saves special I/O instructions.

5.4 Why is immediate addressing classified as a zero-component addressing mode? Is immediate addressing used frequently and why?

5.5 Why is register-direct addressing important, what is absolute addressing and where is it used?

5.6 The MC68020 architecture supports stack operations through a combination of addressing modes. Assume that only one stack pointer is needed and that this is denoted by TOS, such that:

- ADD X, TOS means 'add X to top of stack'.
- ADD TOS, X means 'pop top element off the stack and add this to X'.
- ADD TOS, TOS means 'add two top elements of the stack'.

Using this new stack concept, which of the following MC68020 addressing modes are no longer required for stack operations:

D_n; A_n; (A_n); $(A_n)+$; $-(A_n)$; (d_{16}, A_n)

5.7 Which of the following instructions, using the format OPC Src, Dst, can add the two top elements of the stack (SP is used as the stack pointer), and in which direction does the stack grow (towards location zero or towards location infinity) when an element is pushed on to the stack? Is there more than one possibility?

(a) ADD SP, (SP)

(b) ADD (SP), (SP)+

(c) ADD (SP)+, (SP)

(d) ADD −(SP), (SP)

(e) ADD −(SP), (SP)+

(f) ADD (SP)+, (SP)+

(g) ADD (SP)−, (SP)

5.8 Indicate which of the following statements are true or false:

(a) Absolute addressing does not allow for read-only code.

(b) Absolute addressing is required to address I/O locations.

(c) The MC68020 architecture allows for absolute addressing by using the @(A_n)+ addressing mode.

(d) In the VAX-11 architecture, the PC is one of the address registers. This allows for absolute addressing by using the @(PC)+ addressing mode and for the specification of immediate values using the (PC)+ addressing mode.

5.9 What is pre-indexing, what is post-indexing and what is scaling?

5.10 Indicate which of the following statements are true or false. The use of descriptors for describing structured data (such as arrays) has the following consequences:

(a) Automatic index checking can be done at execution time.

(b) Dynamic arrays, whereby the lower and upper bounds are not constants, cannot be supported.

(c) The use of tags is required.

5.11 Why is it important to keep the specification of operand addresses short (require few bits), and which methods are available to accomplish this?

References

Cohen, D. (1981). A plea for peace. *IEEE Computer*, **14**(10), 49–54.

DEC (1979). *VAX-11/780 Architecture Handbook*. Digital Equipment Corporation: Maynard, MA.

Intel (1981). *iAPX432 General Data Processor Architecture Reference Manual*. Intel Corporation: Santa Clara, CA.

National Semiconductor (1984). *NS32000 Programmer's Reference Manual*. National Semiconductor Corporation: Santa Clara, CA.

Radin, G. (1983). The 801 minicomputer. *IBM Journal of Research and Development*, **27**(3), 237–46.

Wiecek, C. A. (1982). A case study of VAX-11 instruction set usage for compiler execution. In *Proc. of the Symposium on Architectural Support for Programming Languages and Operating Systems*, March 1982, pp. 177–84.

6 Operations on Data

The only way to have a friend is to be one.
– Emerson

In this chapter the operations on data, as supported by modern computer architectures, are examined. These operations can be classified into five operation types: data move operations, format transformation operations, code transformation operations, logical operations and arithmetic operations. The most important data types that these operations deal with are characters, bit strings and numbers in various formats (integer, floating point, and so on).

6.1 Classification of operations

In Chapter 3, the relation between the various data types as defined in programming languages and their binary representations was discussed. It appeared that there was a difference between a data element as an abstract concept and the representation of a data element in bits. Similarly, the **abstract operation**, meaning the effect of the operation on abstract data elements, can be distinguished from the effect of the machine operation on the representation in bit patterns. These abstract operations have the advantage that they resemble more closely the human way of thinking about operations. They also allow operations to be separated from data representations, which allows an orthogonal treatment of both subjects.

To obtain abstraction in the definition of a machine operation, this definition must consist of the following parts:

- The abstraction of the required operands from the available bit patterns.
- The description of the abstract operation itself.
- The mapping of the abstract results in the available bit patterns.

Each of these parts can be further divided into a number of steps, resulting in the structure of Figure 6.1, which can be explained as follows:

- First, the data representation, consisting of bit patterns, must be loaded (fetched) from memory. This takes place by associating an operand name (address) with a location in memory (or in one of the registers), followed by reading the bit pattern at that location.
- Next, the fetched bit patterns must be split (deallocated) into separate fields according to the appropriate rules, as, for instance, floating-point numbers are split into an exponent and fraction field.
- To determine the values of the operands represented by the different fields, these fields must be decoded – for example, by adding the hidden bit to the fraction field of a floating-point number.
- After this, an (arithmetic) operation can take place on one or more operand(s).
- Every operation produces one or more results. When the operation is of the arithmetic type, it is possible for the result to fall outside the range of the representation used – the domain (the range of representable values is not 'closed' for arithmetic operations). For example, the product of two 16-bit integers cannot always be represented by a 16-bit integer.

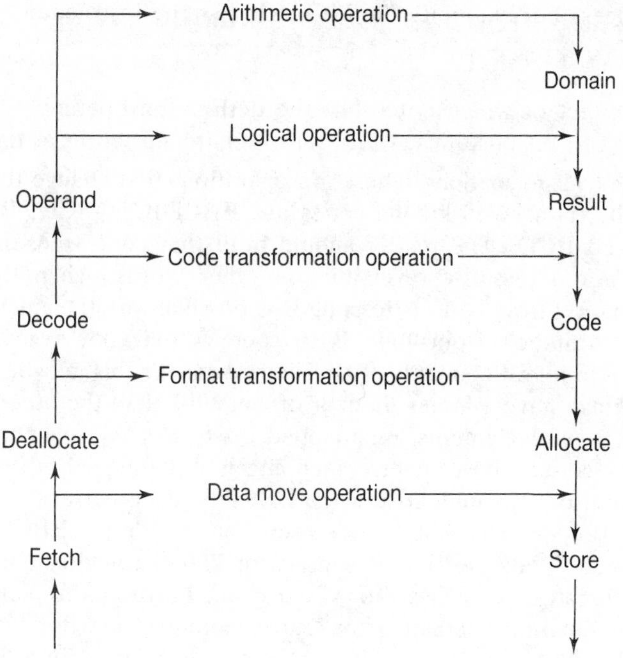

FIGURE 6.1
Operation types.

- The results must be coded to satisfy the specifications of the intended representation.
- The coded fields must be packed into a bit pattern (allocated) in accordance with the representation of the data format.
- When the bit pattern is allocated, it is associated with a location in memory (or a register) again and is linked with the operand name (stored).

Using Figure 6.1, the operation types can be classified as follows:

- **Data move operations**: Data allocation and coding are not influenced by these operations; only the relationship name-data is changed. For example, the MC68020 (Motorola, 1985) has the instruction:

  ```
  MOVE  Src, Dst
  ```

  the effect of which is to make the contents of the memory location determined by the destination equal to the contents of the memory location determined by the source (in short Dst := (Src)).
- **Format transformation operations**: Using these operations, the coding of the data remains unaffected; only the location of the bits

changes. For example, the MC68020 has the instruction:

```
LSL   Cnt, Dst
```

the effect of which is to shift the destination operand to the left over Cnt bit positions, while zero bits are shifted in at the right.

- **Code transformations**: These are operations that change the coding of the data. Well-known codes are EBCDIC, ASCII, BCD and packed BCD. The reader should note that code transformations are not necessarily reversible; in other words, when the transformation from code A to code B is possible for all elements of A, transformation from code B to code A may not necessarily be possible for all elements of B. The reasons for this may be that one code can have a larger number of elements than the other code or that several elements are mapped on to a single element of the other code, whose inverse mapping is not unique. For example, some problems may arise when EBCDIC code is transformed into ASCII code. The ASCII code uses 7 bits, while the EBCDIC code uses all 8 bits, so that it consists of 256 characters, only 128 of which can be converted to ASCII code. Furthermore, some codes have separate characters for 'carriage return' and for 'line feed', while others have the combined function 'carriage return/line feed', with only one character available for this function. The compound character from the latter type of coding can be easily converted to two characters of the former type of coding, but the reverse conversion cannot take place without a fundamental change in the meaning of these characters.
- **Logical operations**: These operations consider the value of the operand(s) as a logical entity or as a set of logical entities and transform these entities. A property of these operations is that when the operation uses representable operands, the result can be represented as well. For example, the MC68020 has the instruction:

```
AND   Src, Dst
```

which performs bit-wise the logical AND operation on the source and the destination, and stores the result at the destination address.

- **Arithmetic operations**: These are data transformation operations that consider the value of the operand(s) as a numerical entity. Furthermore, one of their properties is that the result can lie outside the range of representable values. This can be due to the fact that the result is too large (**overflow**) or too small (**underflow**). or that the required precision is too large (loss of precision). Therefore, after an arithmetic operation, a domain function is necessary to make the result representable again.

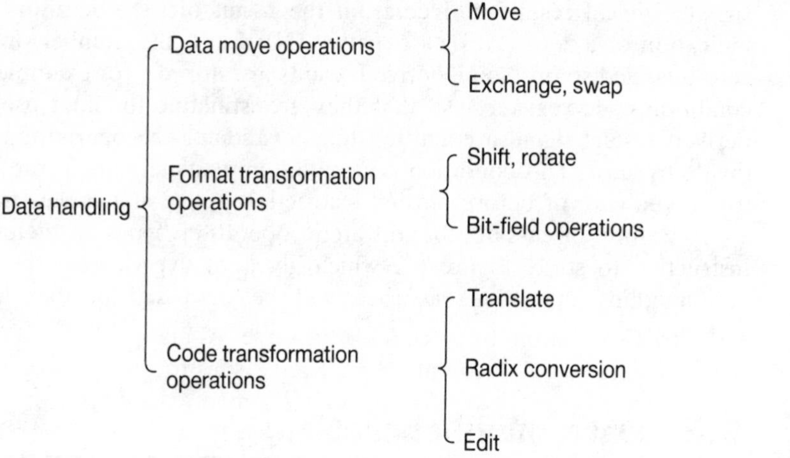

FIGURE 6.2
Overview of data-handling operations.

The data move operations together with the operations for format and code transformations are often called **data-handling operations** (Figure 6.2).

The number of operations in a certain architecture is not restricted. However, generality and parsimony must be taken into account to find a balance between a very large or a very reduced instruction set, thereby also reducing the size of the opcode field. A large instruction set has certain disadvantages:

- Extra expense for hardware implementation, in terms of development time and chip real-estate cost.
- Less compact instruction encoding because of the large number of bits required for the opcode.
- Low frequency of use, because there are many instructions to choose from. Often, more special (or less general) instructions are not generated by the compiler at all because it would become too large and too complex.

Therefore, it is often better to use extra hardware to speed up the frequently used instructions rather than to realize new instructions.

Each operation on data produces a **result** and a **derived result**. A result is the data representation of the outcome of the operation. A derived result is information derived from the operation or from the result of the operation.

Results derived from operations on data are operation dependent. Typical examples are the indication of overflow (V) and carry (C), the detection of a subscript that is out of bounds and the divide-by-zero signal. Typical results derived from the result of the operation are the indication of a zero (Z) or a negative (N) result, the number of leading zero bits, and so on. Some derived results are stored – for example, in the condition code register – so that they are available for later use. Other derived results signal a condition that invalidates the operation, such as divide by zero. This condition is signalled immediately via a trap, so that it is taken care of before normal instruction processing proceeds.

Before discussing the different operation types in detail, it is instructive to study Figure 6.2 which gives an overview of the various data-handling operations as they will be discussed in the following sections.

6.2 Data move operations

Instructions of the data move type require the specification of the following elements:

- The operation, which as a rule, is specified in the opcode of the instruction.
- The data type of the elements. Because data move operations are transparent with regard to the coding of the data, it would suffice to specify only the data length (in bytes). However, for reasons of orthogonality, most instructions require the data type to be specified (byte, half-word, word, double-word, quad word, floating), and to keep the architecture consistent, the specification of the data type is often done in data move operations too. For the MC68020, the data type is specified in the opcode space, while for the B6700 this is done in the data space by using tags.
- The number of data elements, which leads to two classes:
  - (a) A single data element (single move), which can consist of a constant, a simple variable or an element from a data structure (such as an array or a record).
  - (b) Multiple data elements (multiple move), which occurs when a whole data structure (for instance, $A[*]$, all elements from array A) or a substructure (for instance, one column of matrix B, $B[I, *]$, or a subrange of array A, $A[7 \,..\, 15]$) is moved. Direct hardware support for multiple moves is often available for character strings, due to their frequency of occurrence and simple implementation.
- The location of the source operand.
- The location of the destination operand.

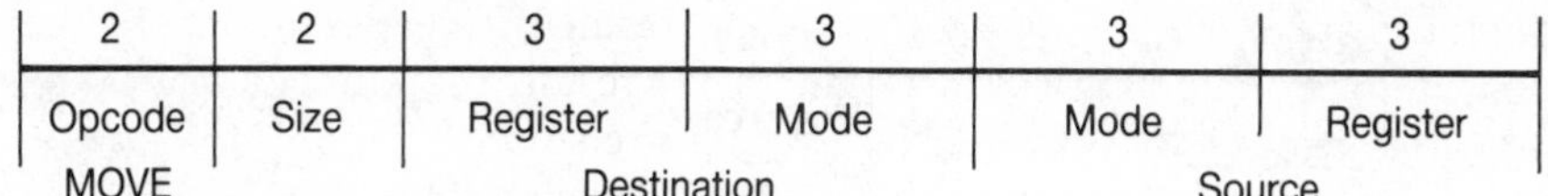

FIGURE 6.3
MC68020 MOVE instruction.

6.2.1 Single data move

With a single data move operation, one single data element is moved. This can be implemented in the following two ways:

(1) Two-step move via registers or stack:

LOAD	Memory to register	PUSH	Memory to top of stack
STORE	Register to memory	POP	Top of stack to memory

This method of data transport is of interest for register- or stack-oriented architectures.

(2) Direct move from memory to memory: In this case, the architecture must be able to specify two memory locations.

Many general-purpose architectures, such as the MC68020, allow both kinds of single data move operations.

□□EXAMPLE 6.1

The MC68020 has the MOVE (MOVE data from source to destination) instruction, which is shown in Figure 6.3. As determined by the addressing mode (see Table 5.2), the source as well as the destination operand can be a register, the top of the stack or a memory address, so all kinds of single move operations are provided. The derived results are stored in the condition codes as follows:

- N: Set if the result is negative. Cleared otherwise.
- Z: Set if the result is zero. Cleared otherwise.
- C: Always cleared.
- V: Always cleared.
- X: Not affected.

Note that MOVE does not produce any derived results as a consequence of the operation (such as carry or overflow). Consequently, in the following, derived results will only be discussed if they are typical or exceptional.

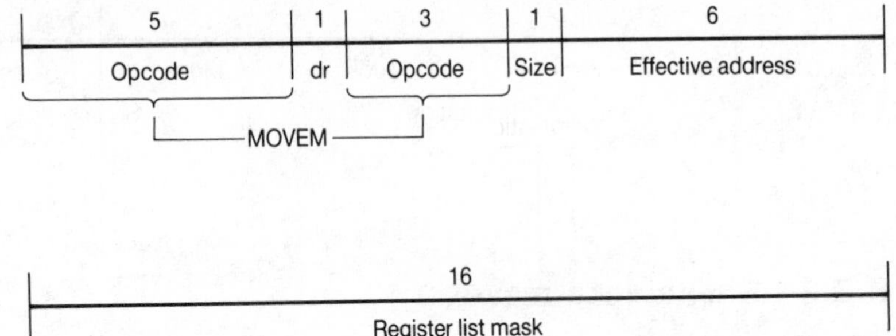

MOVEM register list, <ea>
MOVEM <ea>, register list
if (*dr* = 0) then *Destination* := (*Registers*)
if (*dr* = 0) then *Registers* := (*Source*)

FIGURE 6.4
MC68020 MOVEM instruction.

6.2.2 Multiple data move

With a multiple data move operation, a number of data elements are moved at the instigation of a single instruction. This implies that the instruction, in addition to the location of the source and destination, has to specify the number of data elements, also called the **length**. This can be a single-length specification, where the source and destination operand are of equal length, or separate (possibly different) length specifications. If the source length is greater than the destination length, a choice must be made between cutting the block of data that must be transported at the beginning or at the end (for example, if only *n* data elements can be moved, take the last *n* elements or the first *n*), or not moving any data and raising instead an exception condition.

Assuming a multiple character move with a source length smaller than the destination length, the remainder of the destination block can be filled with 0, blank, a special character defined implicitly or a character that must be specified by the instruction. The use of an implicitly defined character, such as a null character, makes the architecture **character set dependent**. The data elements of a multiple data move operation can be a block of data in memory or the contents of several registers (Example 6.2).

□□EXAMPLE 6.2

The MC68020 has the instruction MOVEM (Figure 6.4), which accomplishes a data move to or from multiple registers simultaneously. The address and data registers involved are specified in an instruction extension word, the register list mask, where, for every register, a bit indicates whether or not the transfer affects the corresponding register. The registers are transferred to or from consecutive memory locations, starting at the location specified by the effective address field in the instruction.

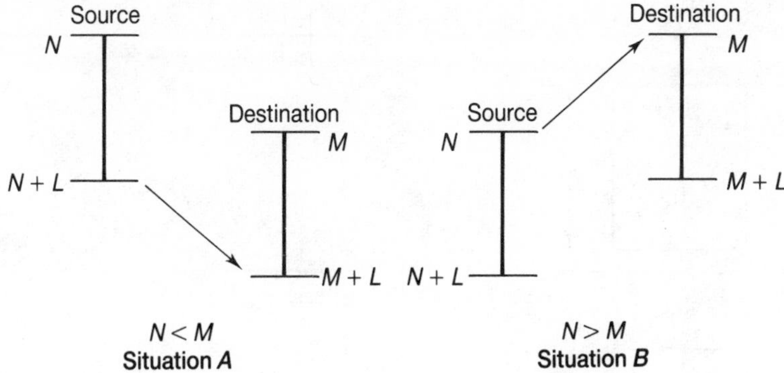

FIGURE 6.5
Source/destination overlap.

When the source and destination are both in memory, a potential overlap of source and destination operands becomes an important implementation aspect. The most simple solution is a **destructive move**; that is, a possible overlap is ignored. This implies that the compiler must guarantee that the overlap will not occur. A more elegant, but also more complex, solution is the **non-destructive move** instruction, where the source data is first written to a buffer or the sequence of element moves is made dependent on the overlap condition. The latter case is shown in Figure 6.5, where the overlap can exist in two situations. Situation A occurs when the source data is at a lower-numbered location in memory than the destination. In such a case, a non-destructive move can be accomplished by starting with the last source element at location $N + L$. In situation B, the source data is at a higher-numbered location in memory than the destination, so the data transport must start with the first source element.

□□EXAMPLE 6.3

The VAX-11 has a three and a five operand move character (MOVC) instruction (DEC, 1979) of which the latter is shown here:

MOVC5 *srclen*, *srcaddr*, *fill*, *dstlen*, *dstaddr*

where *len* is the length, *srclen* is the source length, *dstlen* is the destination length, *srcaddr* is the source byte address, *dstaddr* is the destination byte address and *fill* is the fill byte. The MOVC5 instruction performs a non-destructive multiple data move operation and is character set independent (because the fill byte can be specified). When using the MOVC5 instruction, the following situations can occur, due to the separate specification of both lengths (this is reflected in the condition

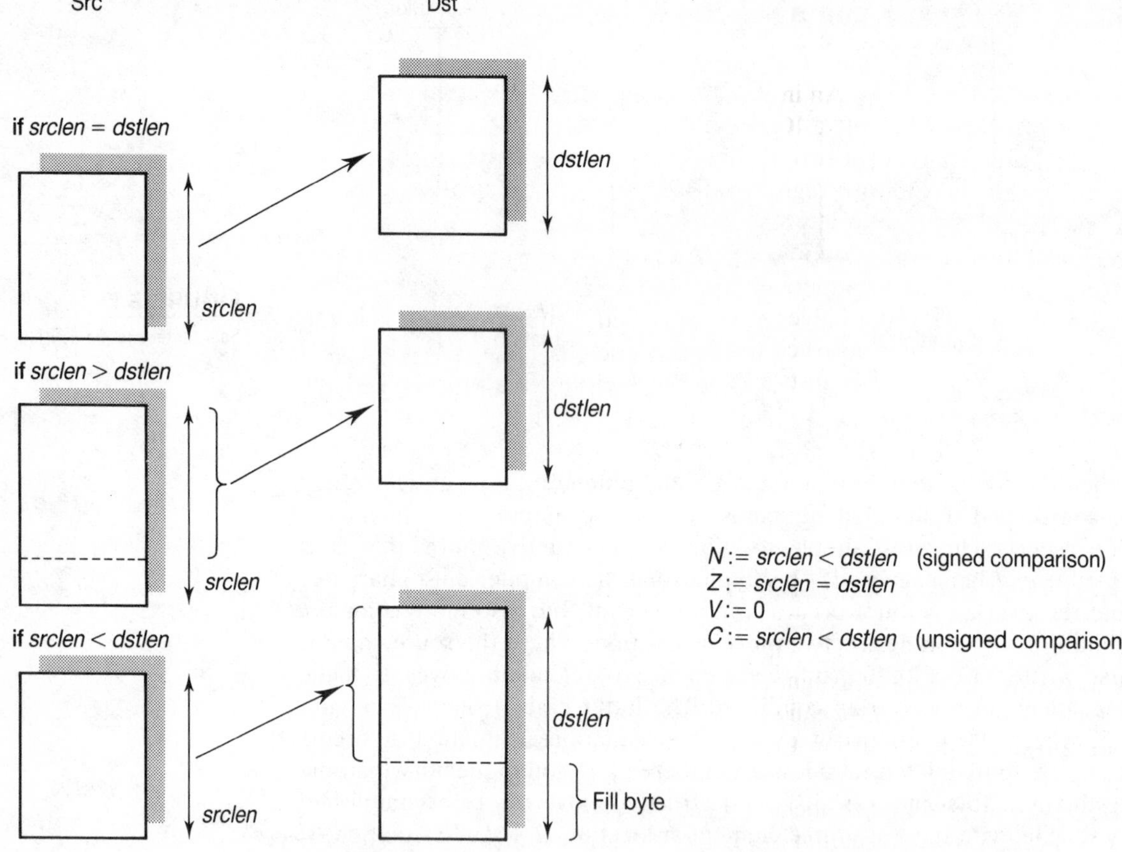

FIGURE 6.6
VAX-11 MOVEC instructions.

codes, as shown in Figure 6.6):

- *srclen* = *dstlen*: A normal move takes place, as both blocks have an equal size.
- *srclen* > *dstlen*: The move operation starts at the beginning of the source and ends when the destination is full.
- *srclen* < *dstlen*: The move operation starts at the beginning of the source and continues until the source is empty. The remainder of the destination is filled with the fill byte, specified by the third operand of the MOVC5 instruction. Often, the character 'blank' is chosen for this fill byte. But, because the fill byte is specified via an operand, it can be any character, meaning that this instruction is character set independent.

6.2.3 Exchange and swap

The exchange instruction is a special kind of move instruction that exchanges two operands. An instruction of this kind is especially useful in sorting algorithms. In the MC68020 architecture, the instruction EXG exchanges the contents of two 32-bit registers. These registers can be two data registers, two address registers or one data and one address register.

The MC68020 also has a special kind of exchange instruction, the swap instruction, where only one operand is specified. This means that certain parts within the operand itself are exchanged. This instruction exchanges the two 16-bit halves of the specified data register and is useful because word-oriented instructions always use the low-order word of a 32-bit register. With this instruction, the high-order word can also be made available.

6.3 Format transformation operations

A format is specified by assigning fixed locations to a coded group of bits (allocation). A distinction can be made between instruction formats and data formats, whereby it must be observed that an assembler regards the instruction formats of the object code as its data formats, since assemblers must compose these instructions from the source code.

Format transformation means the deallocation and subsequent allocation of bit fields. Format transformation operations are normally implemented as shift or as bit-field operations.

6.3.1 Shift operations

Shifting bits, often combined with other instructions, is the simplest form of format transformation. Shift operations are useful in data handling for field selection (for example, in I/O routines or for the decomposition of instructions by an interpreter), with logical operations for bit selection and with arithmetic operations for scaling (normalization), programmed multiplication or division. Figure 6.7 shows five types of shift operations. These shift operations are usually supported by three classes of shift instructions (in which the opcode usually specifies the type of shift operation).

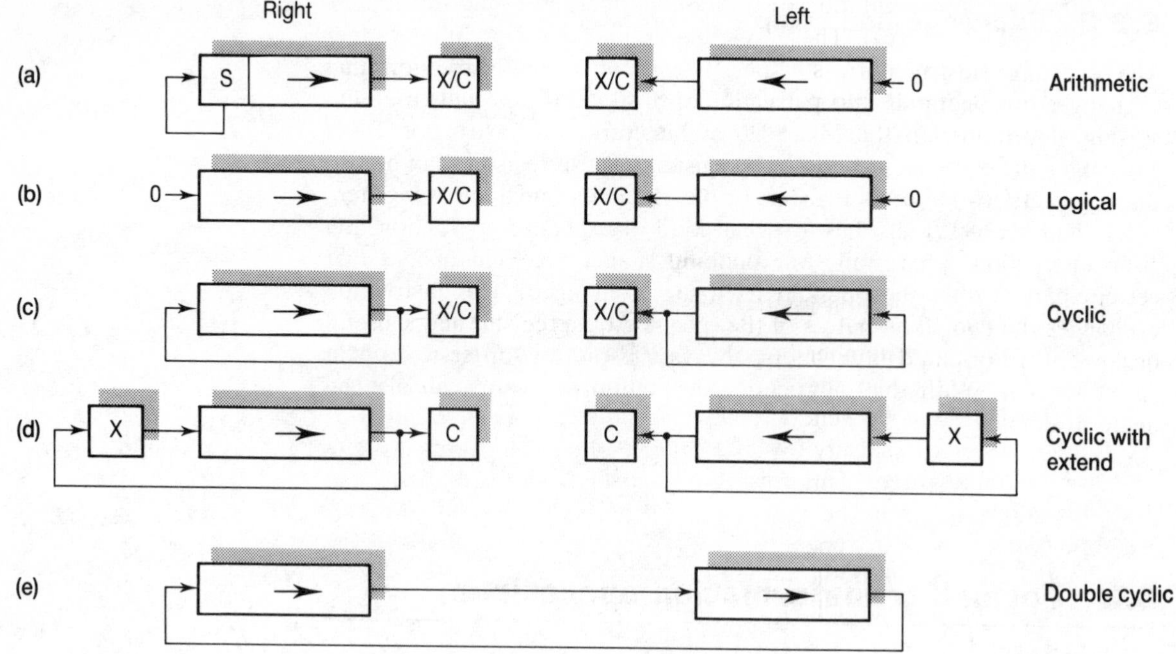

FIGURE 6.7

Shift operation types.

(1) **Arithmetic shift operations** (Figure 6.7(a)): Arithmetic shift operations are implemented as format transformation operations, while functionally they belong to the class of arithmetic operations. An arithmetic shift by N in fact means multiplying or dividing a number by the radix^N (N is the shift count). This can cause overflow or can necessitate truncation or rounding of the result. The sign bit of the operand does not participate in the shift operation in the case of a sign-magnitude representation. With the digit and radix complement representation, the sign bit is replicated with right shifts.

(2) **Logical shift operations** (Figure 6.7(b)): With right as well as left shifts, zeros are shifted in and the bits that are shifted out are shifted into the X and C condition code bits. This type of shift operation is used for bit-field selection and scaling.

(3) **Cyclic shift operations** (Figures 6.7(c), (d) and (e)): In this case, the most significant bit is shifted into the least significant bit position when shifting left and vice versa when shifting right. Some architectures (like the MC68020) use a single-bit extension with cyclic shifting, so the most significant or least significant bit ends up in this extension, and the contents of the extension are shifted to the least or the most significant bit position, respectively. This is a

low-cost implementation of the double-operand cyclic shift operation (Figure 6.7(e)). These double-operand shift operations, which can be simulated by single-operand instructions, are useful for splitting a format into parts.

For the specification of shift operations, the following aspects are important:

- **Type of shift operation**: arithmetic, logical or cyclic. Usually, the type of shift operation is specified in the opcode.
- **Shift count**: The number of positions to be shifted. The shift count can be specified in the opcode, operand or data space. When known during code generation (which implies a fixed value), it is more efficient to specify the shift count as a constant in the opcode or operand space. This may be important for assemblers and interpreters. Often, the shift count is problem dependent and must be determined at run time and specified in the data space. Generally, it is desirable to be able to specify the shift count as a constant or as a variable.
- **Shift direction**: This can be to the left (towards the most significant digit) or to the right. The shift direction can also be specified in the opcode, operand and data space. It is common to specify the direction in the opcode or via the sign bit of the shift count value. The latter is more flexible because the computed shift count can also determine the shift direction. If this method is used, a positive number should indicate a left shift and a negative number a right shift. This allows arithmetic shift operations to be identical to multiplication and division by powers of the radix of the shift operation.
- **A source and destination operand specification**: The source and destination operand are specified in the operand space when specified explicitly. It is possible for one or both to be specified implicitly, but this should be done in line with other instructions (for example, arithmetic operations).
- **Data type of the operand**: Specifying the length of the operand would be sufficient, but for the same reasons as with move operations, the data type is often specified.
- **Single or double operand**.
- **Radix** (2 or 10): In most cases, the radix is 2, except when BCD numbers are shifted. In that case, the radix is 10 and the shifting takes place in units of 4 bits.

□□EXAMPLE 6.4

The MC68020 supports the arithmetic, logic and cyclic shift operations as illustrated in Figures 6.7(a)–(d). The formats are shown in Figure 6.8. With reference to the aspects just discussed, these can be characterized as follows:

- The MC68020 has arithmetic, logic and cyclic shift operations.
- The shift count can be specified in two ways:
  - (a) For register shifts (Figure 6.8(a)): If i/r = 0, the shift count is specified as an immediate value (1–8) in the count field. If i/r = 1, the shift count is contained in the data register (modulo 64, to allow for future double long word or quad word shift operations) which is specified in the register field.
  - (b) For memory shifts (Figure 6.8(b)): The shift count is always 1. The reason for this is that shift operations are performed mainly on registers. Providing the same support for memory shifts as for register shifts would be consistent but would require too much instruction space.
- The shift direction is specified by the 'dr' bit; therefore, it cannot be computed.
- Source and destination are the same; that is, only destructive shift operations are possible. For register shifts, they are specified in the register field, and for memory shifts in the effective address field.
- The data type is not specified, only the length of the operand. For a register shift, byte, word or long word can be specified in the size field. For memory shifts, the size is always word.
- Double-operand shift instructions are implemented by the ROXL/ROXR 'rotate with extend' instructions of Figure 6.7(d).
- The radix is specified implicitly as 2.
- The MC68020 shift instructions set the condition codes in a consistent manner. At the end of the shift operation, both the X bit and the C bit are loaded with the last bit shifted out of the operand. The Z and N bits are set according to the value of the result. The V bit is set if an ASL causes the sign of the operand to be changed, otherwise it is cleared. If a shift count of 0 is specified, the operand and the X bit are not changed, but Z and N are set according to the result, V is cleared and the value of C is made equal to the value of X.

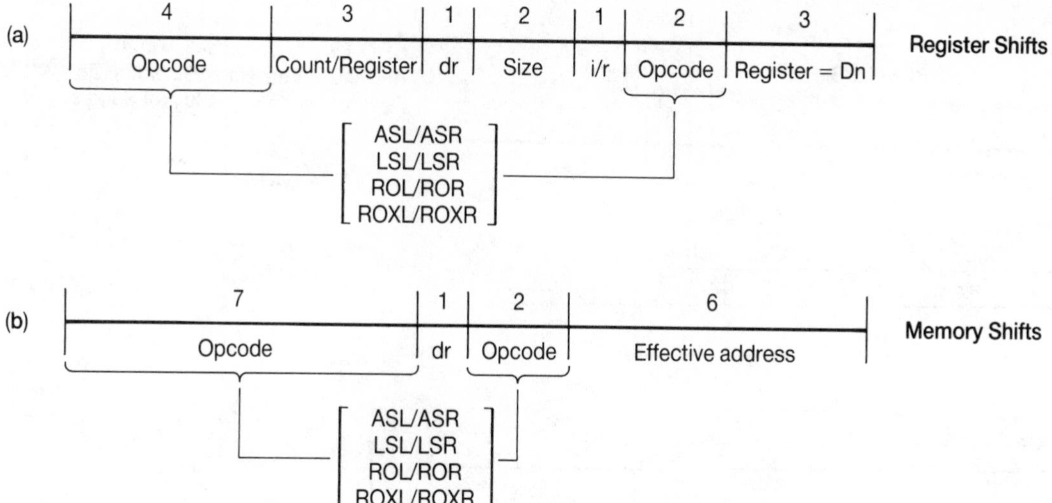

FIGURE 6.8 MC68020 shift instructions.

6.3.2 Bit-field operations

These are operations that specify a bit field as an operand by, for example, specifying the position of the first bit and the length of the bit field. Bit-field operations can be used as alternatives for logical and cyclic shift operations. They are also used for handling packed data (as allowed in the language Pascal).

□□EXAMPLE 6.5

The MC68020 architecture has several bit-field instructions. These can be classified into the following three groups:

(1) Test a bit field and clear, set or complement (change) it if desired (BFTST, BFCLR, BFSET and BFCHG).

(2) Insert a bit field (BFINS) or extract a sign-extended or unsigned bit field (BFEXTS, BFEXTU).

(3) Find the first one in a bit field (BFFFO).

A bit field is specified by three components: a base address (specified by an effective addressing mode), a field offset (specified as an immediate operand or in a register) and the field width (0–31, specified as an immediate operand or in a register).

Figure 6.9 shows the MC68020 extract instructions. The choice between signed (BFEXTS) or unsigned (BFEXTU) extraction allows the bit field to be considered as a signed number, an unsigned number or a bit string. With reference to Figure 3.7, consider a packed array *A*[1 . . 52] of **set of** *Day*. Each array element requires 7 bits. A BFEXTU

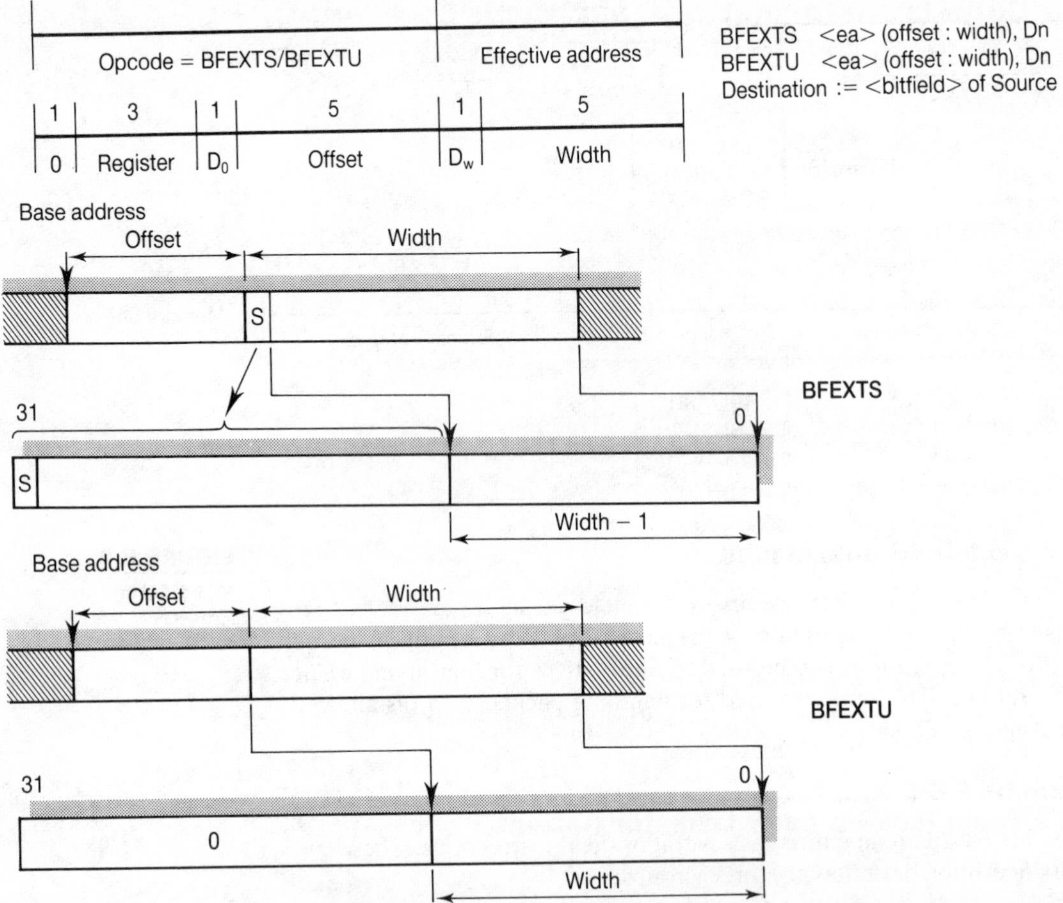

FIGURE 6.9

MC68020 bit-field extract instructions.

instruction could be used to extract, say, the set of working days within a specific week. This bit field should not be sign extended, because the most significant bit does not represent a sign. On the other hand, if an array of integers were to be stored with 7 bits for each integer, the extraction of an integer from this array would require the use of the BFEXTS instruction, because the most significant bit of each integer now represents the sign.

The format of the BFEXTS or BFEXTU instruction of Figure 6.9 is as follows. The effective address field specifies the base address for the bit field and the register field specifies the destination register. The D_o field specifies whether the offset is specified as an immediate value by the offset field or in a register (specified by the 3 low-order bits of the offset field). Similarly, the D_w field specifies whether the field width is specified as an immediate value by the width field or in a register (specified by the 3 low-order bits of the width field).

6.4 Code transformation operations

Code transformations are important because many I/O devices that need to communicate use different codes. A key on the keyboard must produce a unique code inside the computer. Moreover, a unique code in the computer must be sufficient to specify a character that must be displayed on the output device. Similar considerations can be made about other I/O equipment. As a result, it should be possible to represent computer data by different codes, because the keyboard code, for example, does not need to be the same as the display code.

Most data-handling operations are code independent. Move instructions, for instance, are transparent to the bit pattern of the data that must be moved. Other operations, like ADD operations, are code dependent; for example, there is a big difference between whether the data is represented in two's complement notation or in BCD code. With regard to the different demands that high-level languages make upon the data types (character, decimal, integer, real), the demands of I/O equipment (ASCII or EBCDIC) and efficiency requirements for internal representations (the real number 25.373E–10 is not represented internally as 10 characters using 80 bits, but, say, as a 32-bit floating-point number), the computer must be able to deal with different codes and transform data from one code to another. Code transformation operations can be classified as table look-up or algorithmic.

6.4.1 Table look-up code transformations

Table look-up code transformation is generally used for simple character-to-character translation – for example, for I/O equipment. By using tables, different character sets can be easily supported. Many computers have special instructions for this.

□□EXAMPLE 6.6

Figure 6.10 shows the VAX-11 instruction MOVTC (MOVE Translated Character), which has six operands:

MOVTC *srclen*, *srcaddr*, *fill*, *tbladdr*, *dstlen*, *dstaddr*

The fill operand has the same function as in the MOVC5 instruction (see Example 6.3) and makes the instruction character set independent. The characters of the source, specified by source length and address operands, are translated and the result is directed to the destination, also specified by length and address operands. The translation is carried out by means of a table consisting of 256 entries. The table is situated in memory at the

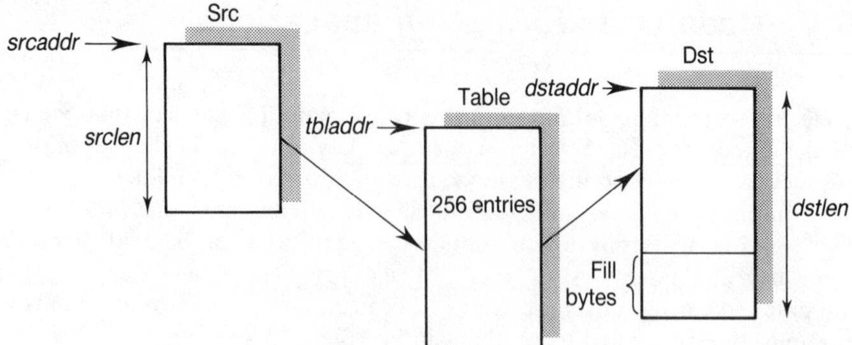

FIGURE 6.10

VAX-11 MOVTC instruction.

location specified by the table address operand. Each character from the source is used as an index into this table and the selected value is stored at the corresponding destination location.

In addition to translate instructions, translate-and-search instructions are often available as well. Translate-and-search operations perform not only the usual translation of characters through a table, but also a number of other functions. The simplest form of such an operation is that where the translation process stops when the result of the character translation is equal to a specified test character. With this instruction, a kind of set-membership operation is performed (does an element belong to a certain set or not?). Text processors and compilers may use this instruction to find a string up to a delimiter (which may be a space or a carriage return).

□□EXAMPLE 6.7

Figure 6.11 shows the VAX-11 MOVTUC (MOVE Translated Until Character) instruction, which has six operands:

MOVTUC *srclen*, *srcaddr*, *esc*, *tbladdr*, *dstlen*, *dstaddr*

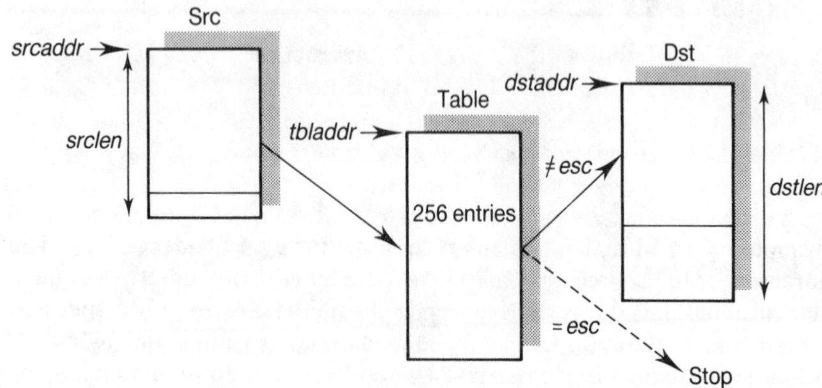

FIGURE 6.11

VAX-11 MOVTUC instruction.

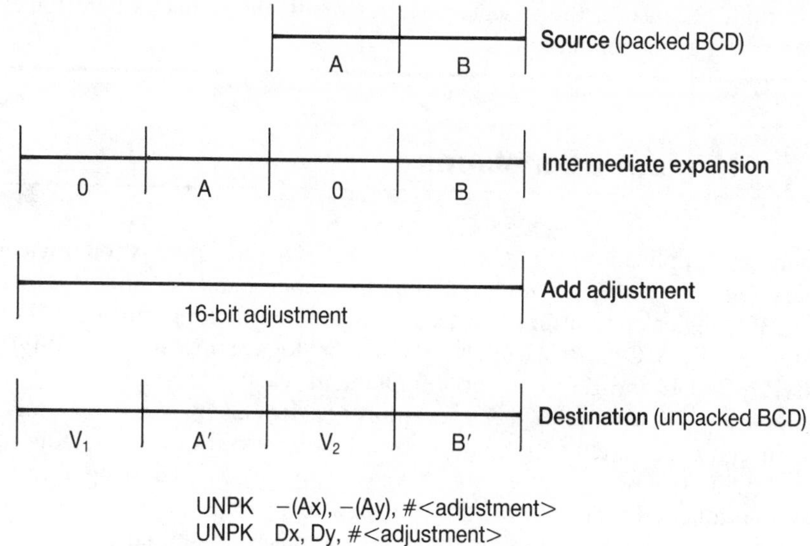

FIGURE 6.12
MC68020 UNPK instruction.

The operand *esc* is the test character. The translation stops as soon as the result of a character translation is equal to this character.

6.4.2 Algorithmic code transformations

Except for the more general instructions that handle characters (mainly used for I/O activities and for compilers to identify delimiters), there are also code transformation instructions that are related to internal representations. Some examples are the translation between decimal and binary representations, between fixed-point and floating-point numbers, and between characters and fixed-point or floating-point numbers.

□□EXAMPLE 6.8

The MC68020 instruction UNPK (Unpack BCD) is an example of an instruction that performs the conversion of a packed internal (BCD) representation to a code that is suitable for I/O. Internally, two BCD digits are contained in one byte (see Figure 3.3(a) and Figure 6.12). For I/O, each digit must be contained in a byte. In the unpack operation, therefore, two BCD digits are separated into two bytes, with the BCD digit residing in the lower nibble (least significant 4 bits). An adjustment is then added to this unpacked value without affecting the condition codes, to give the bytes a form suitable for I/O (ASCII or EBCDIC).

Note that, because of the specifiable adjustment, the unpack operation is character set independent.

6.5 Logical operations

Computer applications in which the result depends mainly on logical operations are rather exceptional. On the other hand, in almost every program, logical operations are used for decision-making purposes. For instance, the MC68020 architecture has the logical instructions BSET, BCHG, BCLR and BTST to set, complement, clear or test a single bit in the operand. Formally, logical operations are defined for single bits only, but in computer architecture, one often has bit strings or bit vectors in mind (without always expressing this explicitly) when logical operations are mentioned. In such cases, the specified logical operation is executed bit-wise on all bits of the operand(s), so this is essentially a vector operation.

Logical vector operations (with fixed-length vectors) are easy to realize because the vector elements are single bits. Furthermore, logical operations can be implemented both cheaply, as a side effect of arithmetic operations, and very fast, because of the absence of carry propagation. For these reasons, the problem for the computer architect is not what instructions can be implemented cheaply and fast, but rather what must be implemented at all.

In some architectures, all 16 logical operations are implemented (see Table 1.2). Most architectures have four logical operations, AND, OR, EOR and NOT, chosen on the basis of their frequency of use. The acronyms EOR and XOR both refer to the same operation, but in this book the MC68020 variant EOR will be used.

Design decisions for logical operations are related to the kind of instructions, the number of operands and the results that can be derived from these operations. For dyadic operations, the minimum number of operands is two; a third operand does not add any function that cannot be obtained by repeated use of two-operand instructions. For reasons of efficiency and the implementation of non-destructive logical operations, some architectures (like the VAX-11) also allow for three-operand logical operations.

□□EXAMPLE 6.9

Table 6.1 shows the logical operations of the MC68020. This set is asymmetrical because, due to the lack of opcode space, the instruction EOR <ea>, Dn is not implemented.

Table 6.1 MC68020 logical operations.

Instruction	Operand Syntax	Operation
AND	Src, Dn	Dst := (Dn) AND (Src)
	Dn, Dst	Dst := (Dst) AND (Dn)
ANDI	#data, Dst	Dst := (Dst) AND data
EOR	Dn, Dst	Dst := (Dst) EOR (Dn)
EORI	#data, Dst	Dst := (Dst) EOR data
NOT	Dst	Dst := NOT (Dst)
OR	Src, Dn	Dn := (Dn) OR (Src)
	Dn, Dst	Dst := (Dst) OR (Dn)
ORI	#data, Dst	Dst := (Dst) OR data

Dn = Data register n; (Src), (Dst) = contents of effective address; #<data> = immediate data.

Derived results of logical operations are produced as a side effect of the operation. In general, logical operations produce a result vector of which certain properties can be derived. These properties can be, for example, signalling an all-zero result and counting the number of bits equal to 0 or 1. These derived results can be generated directly as a side effect of the operation and stored in a special register (for example, the condition code register) or they can be determined by means of special instructions. An example is the MC68020 BFFFO (Find the First One in the Bit Field) instruction, which determines the position of the first 1 in a bit field.

6.6 Fixed-point arithmetic operations

Arithmetic operations (like add, subtract, multiply and divide) can be executed with fixed-point or floating-point numbers, numbers with fixed or variable length and binary or decimal radix. For simplicity, representations of numbers with radix 8 or 16 are classified as binary numbers and arithmetic on data with variable length, when handling only a limited number of lengths, is classified as fixed data-length arithmetic. Fixed data-length arithmetic and variable data-length arithmetic are the topics of the next two subsections, while floating-point arithmetic operations are discussed in Section 6.7.

Chapter 3 dealt with the topic of data types and their representations. Arithmetic operations are executed with representable numbers

Table 6.2 Effect of precision treatment.

Precision Treatment	Representation	Result −1		−0.5		0		+0.5		+1
Truncation	Sign magnitude	−1	→	−0.5	→	0	←	+0.5	←	+1
Truncation	Radix complement	−1	←	−0.5	←	0	←	+0.5	←	+1
Truncation	Digit complement	−1	←	−0.5	←	0	←	+0.5	←	+1
Rounding	All notations	−1	←	−0.5	→	0	←	+0.5	→	+1

and the result must also be representable. This can create the following two domain problems:

(1) The result can be outside the representable range. In such a case, the range function must change the value. When the value of a result is too large in relation to the representation, overflow occurs, and when the value is too small, underflow occurs (this can only occur with floating-point representation). Overflow and underflow can be handled by truncating the high-order bits and signalling this (by setting an overflow bit, for example), or by saving high-order bits together with that signalling.

(2) The result can be non-representable because of the lack of lower-order digits – that is, **precision**, as in the case 1/3 = 0.333 . . . .

Precision treatment implies the selection of a satisfactory representable value for a non-representable number. The best-known methods for this are **truncation** and **rounding**. The result of truncation is representation dependent (Table 6.2). It has a symmetrical effect towards zero for sign-magnitude notation, while the effect of digit-complement (two's complement) and radix-complement notation (one's complement) is towards negative numbers. The result of rounding is equal for all representations and, consequently, is preferred. Rounding, however, is somewhat more difficult to implement because of the mandatory addition of a constant value.

Precision treatment can be performed implicitly (for example, as a side effect of the arithmetic operations) or explicitly using special instructions. With the implicit approach, the superfluous digits are discarded after the operation, while they must remain available with the explicit precision treatment. Some architectures have a so-called mode bit that determines whether implicit truncation or rounding can be done.

6.6.1 Fixed data-length arithmetic

The characteristic difference between arithmetic operations on fixed-point numbers and mathematical arithmetic (arithmetic on the conceptual level, see Figure 3.2) is the limited precision of the numbers. This means that provisions must be made to indicate when the precision is not large enough and, when possible, to extend that precision. Hence, the possibility for extended precision must be considered with every operation.

In this subsection, addition, subtraction, multiplication and division will be discussed in the context of extended precision.

Addition and subtraction

The addition and subtraction operations are considered to be symmetrical, with the exception of subtracting a number from the number zero in the radix-complement notation. This can lead to overflow; that is, $0 - (-2^{N-1})$ causes overflow. As a side effect of these operations, information about the result is usually provided using a zero, negative or positive indication in the condition code register. To enable extended precision with single-precision instructions, the carry/borrow signal is included in the condition code register.

Extended precision for addition and subtraction usually implies operations on data representations that are a multiple of the standard data representation. So, if the standard data type is a 16-bit integer, extended-precision operations are operations on integers with a length of 32, 48, 64, . . ., bits. Programs and subroutines that provide these functions regard the extended-precision numbers as meta-numbers, built from fixed-length numbers that are looked upon as digits of the meta-number (meta-digits) in the extended-precision notation (the meta-notation). The radix of this meta-notation is the modulus of the representation of the meta-digits; that is, if the meta-digits are 16-bit integers, the radix of the meta-number is 2^{16}. The add or subtract operation takes place using meta-digits and a carry/borrow bit, as explained in Example 6.10. Example 6.11 gives instructions that support extended-precision arithmetic.

□□EXAMPLE 6.10

Suppose A, B and R are 48-bit meta-numbers, each composed of three 16-bit meta-digits. A and B are added and the result is assigned to R (Figure 6.13). The addition consists of one 'regular' add operation and two add-with-carry (to allow for extended precision) operations at the meta-digit level. This method allows for integers with arbitrary precision.

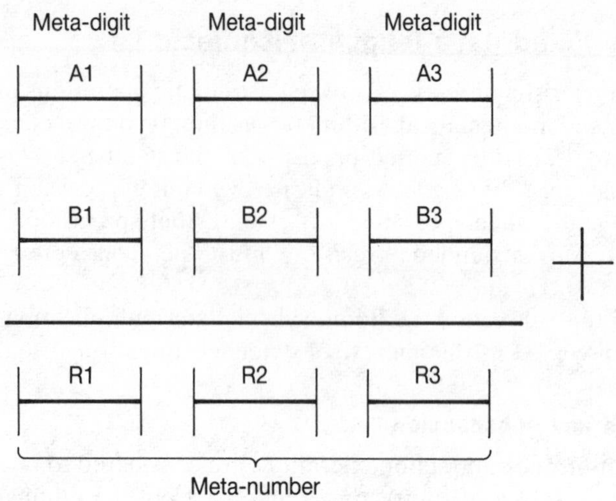

R3 := A3 + B3 ; Derived result : Carry := 0 or 1
R2 := A2 + B2 + C ; Derived result : Carry := 0 or 1
R1 := A1 + B1 + C ; Derived result : Carry := 0 or 1

FIGURE 6.13
Addition of two meta-numbers.

□□EXAMPLE 6.11

The MC68020 architecture has add and subtract with extend instructions which include the X bit as an implicit operand. They allow for addition and subtraction of meta-digits (see Figure 6.13). Furthermore, the NEGX (Negate Binary with Extend) instruction is provided which allows for negating meta-digits. The X bit used in these operations is a special condition code bit which is set and cleared the same way as the C bit, except for the MOVE instructions (see Example 6.1) where it is not affected. This allows MOVE instructions to load and store registers without affecting the X bit, which is important because one form of the ADDX/SUBX instructions can only specify register operands. All three integer formats (byte, word and long) can be specified in the size field. The ADDX, SUBX and NEGX instructions are shown in Figure 6.14.

The ADDX and SUBX instructions have two possible addressing modes:

```
ADDX/SUBX  Dy, Dx
ADDX/SUBX  -(Ay), -(Ax)
```

The second addressing mode is provided for extended-precision operations, where the meta-digits are stored in consecutive memory locations. Because of the MC68020 addressing convention (see Figure 5.3) and the requirement for addition and subtraction for meta-numbers to start with the least significant meta-digit, the use of pre-decrement addressing mode is required.

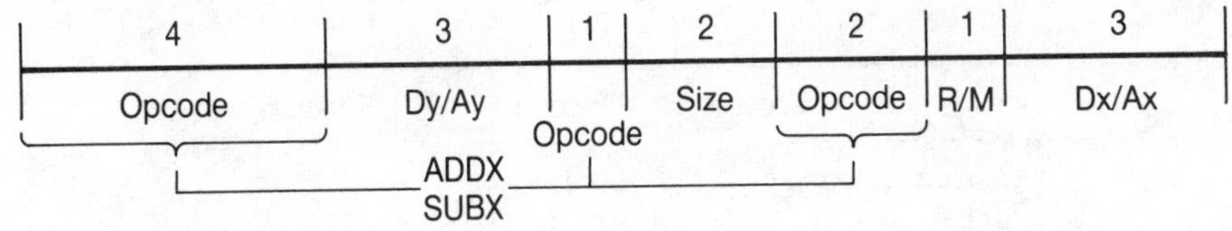

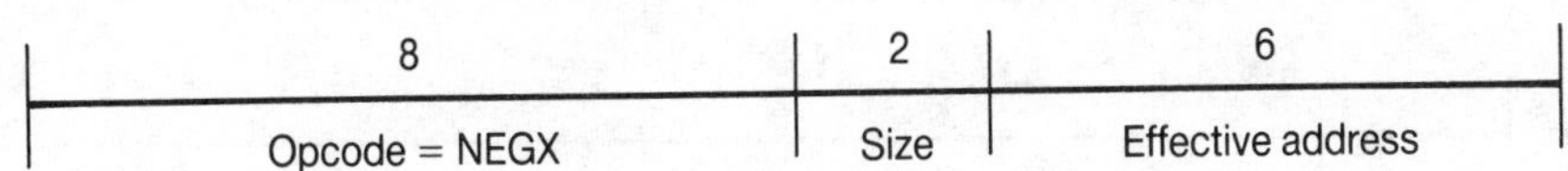

ADDX Dy, Dx
ADDX −(Ay), −(Ax)
Destination := (Destination) + (Source) + (C)

N is set if result < 0, cleared otherwise
Z is cleared if result ≠ 0, unchanged otherwise
V is set if overflow, cleared otherwise
C is set if carry is generated, cleared otherwise
X is set same as C bit

FIGURE 6.14
MC68020 ADDX, SUBX and NEGX instructions.

A three digit meta-number B (with register B pointing to the least significant digit) can be added to meta-number A (see Figure 6.13) as follows:

```
ORI    #0x4, CCR     ;Set Z bit
ANDI   #0xEF, CCR    ;Clear X bit
ADDX   -(B), -(A)
ADDX   -(B), -(A)
ADDX   -(B), -(A)
```

The Z bit for these extended-precision operations is set in the proper way: the Z bit is set only if the current result is zero and the Z bit was already set; this means that the previous and the current result is zero.

Multiplication

The reader is assumed to be familiar with the algorithm for the multiplication of two numbers (Knuth, 1969). The add and subtract operations have a single-length result in addition to a possible overflow indication. The multiplication operation, however, produces a double-length result, which must be preserved for extended-precision operations. Seen from the point of view of high-level languages, however, it is desirable for the data type of the product to be the same as that of both operands; for example, the product of two 16-bit integers I1 and I2 is

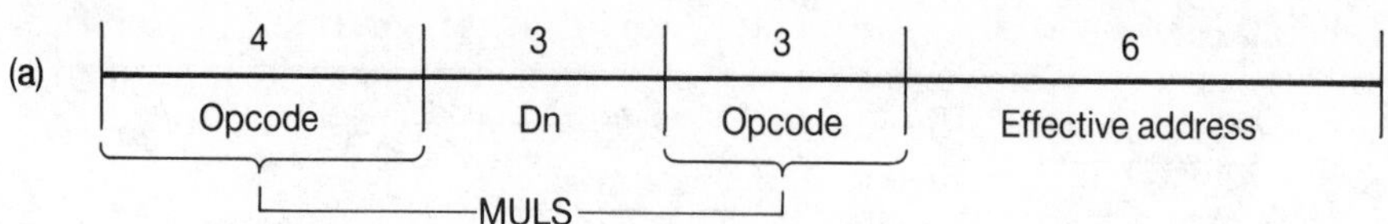

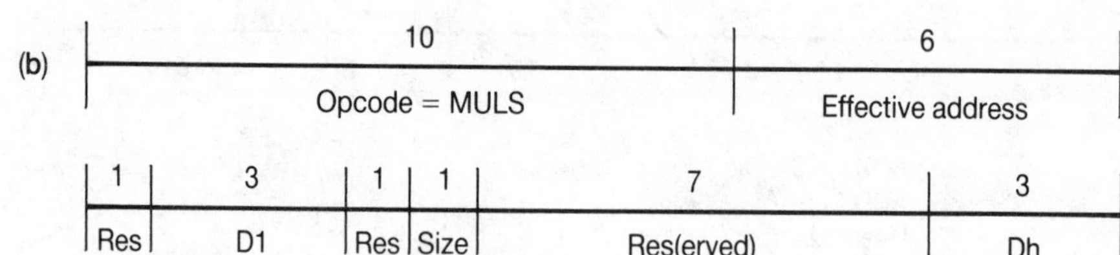

FIGURE 6.15

MC68020 MUL instruction formats.

once again a 16-bit integer, allowing assignment statements like I1 := I1 * I2.

In most computers, it is possible to choose between a single- or a double-length result. Whichever one is desired can be specified in the opcode space, the operand space or the data space (using tags). If the opcode space is chosen, two multiplication instructions are required: one producing a single-length product (the least significant part) and one producing the complete double-length product, or only the most significant part.

□□EXAMPLE 6.12

The MC68020 has two types of multiply instructions, one for signed multiplication (MULS) and the other for unsigned multiplication (MULU). The unsigned multiplication operation is important for extended-precision operations because only the most significant meta-digit has a sign. The MC68020 supports the MULS and MULU operations with three instructions, as shown below. In Figure 6.15, only MULS is shown. Instructions (1) and (3) can be used for extended-precision operations.

```
(1)  MULS.W  <ea>, Dn      16 * 16 → 32   ;Two-operand
                                          ;format, see Figure
                                          ;6.15(a)
(2)  MULS.L  <ea>, D1      32 * 32 → 32   ;Two-operand
                                          ;format, see Figure
                                          ;6.15(a)
(3)  MULS.L  <ea>, Dh:D1   32 * 32 → 64   ;Three-operand
                                          ;format, see Figure
                                          ;6.15(b)
```

The MULS and MULU instructions can have two or three operands. Instruction (1) uses the two-operand format of Figure 6.15(a) and produces a double-length result. Reducing the length of the product is of no use because all data registers are 32 bits anyway. A 16-bit result can be obtained from the least significant word of the result register. Instruction (2) also uses the two-operand format. Instruction (3) uses the three-operand format of Figure 6.15(b). The operation is as follows: the low-order 32 bits of the product of (<ea>) and (D1) are stored in D1 while the high-order 32 bits are stored in Dh.

The option with the specification of the result length in the operand space uses the fact that some operands are implicitly labelled as double-length operands, using two subsequent destination locations, only one of which is specified. Usually, a register pair is used for these locations. This pair can be specified as follows:

(1) Register R and (R OR 1); where R OR 1 means that, from the bit pattern that specifies R (for example, 010 for R2), the least significant bit is set. So, if R = 010, then R OR 1 = 011; that is, R2 and R3 will be used. If R = 011, then only R3 will be used for both results, which means that only the last stored result will be available. If register R has an even number, then the next register is also used, otherwise only the indicated register. This is used in the PDP-11 architecture (DEC, 1975).

(2) Register R and (R EOR 1).

(3) Register R and (R + 1).

Solutions (2) and (3) always yield a double-length result, while solution (3) requires an extra addition to identify the second register.

Division

Just as with multiplication, the result of a division cannot always be represented – for example, 1/3 = 0.333 . . . . To make division exact, the remainder can be produced as well, implying that a division operation produces two results. Because the remainder is always smaller than the divisor, the length of the remainder can be set equal to the length of the divisor.

When division is considered to be the inverse operation of multiplication, the dividend may be a single- or a double-length number. The quotient can be single as well as double length (Figure 6.16). The most frequently used implementations, however, assume a single-length quotient. High-level languages assume a single-length dividend; for instance, I1 := I1/I2, where I1 and I2 are both 16-bit integers.

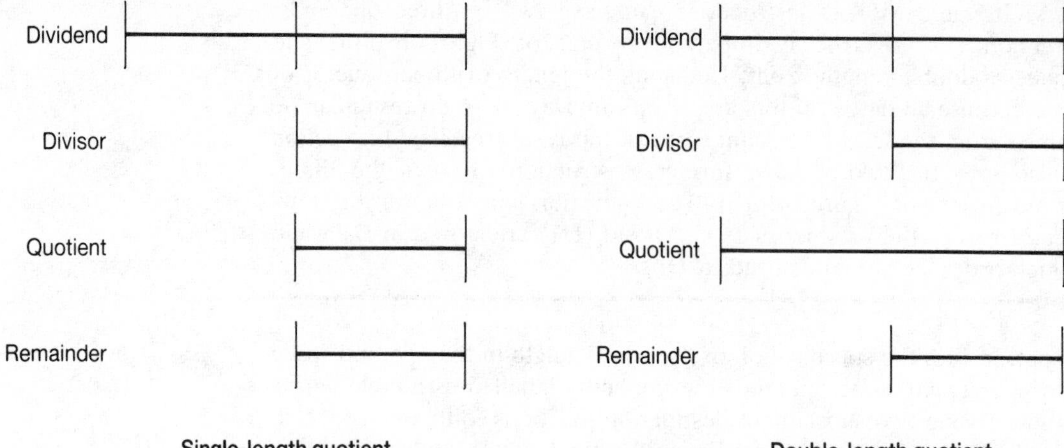

FIGURE 6.16
Quotient length for division operations.

The division operation can be performed in two ways (Table 6.3):

(1) Using Eulerian integer arithmetic: The operators / and REM are used for quotient and remainder. The sign of the remainder is the same as that of the dividend. Let the quotient be $q = m/n$ and the remainder $r = m$ REM n, then the following relations hold:

$$q * n + r = m \quad \text{and} \quad 0 \leq \text{ABS}(r) < \text{ABS}(n) \tag{6.1}$$

(2) Using modulus arithmetic: The operators MOD and DIV are used for quotient and remainder (Wirth, 1986). Let $Q = m$ DIV n and $R = m$ MOD n, where the sign of the remainder equals the sign of the divisor.

Most languages, such as Pascal and C, use Eulerian integer arithmetic, which is also supported by most architectures (MC68020, VAX-11). Some architectures, like the NS32000 (National Semiconductor, 1984), have separate instructions for generating the quotient and the remainder.

Table 6.3 Sign variations for quotient and remainder.

		Eulerian Integer Arithmetic		Modulus Arithmetic	
Dividend	Divisor	/	REM	DIV	MOD
7	3	2	1	2	1
7	−3	−2	1	−3	−2
−7	3	−2	−1	−3	2
−7	−3	2	−1	2	−1

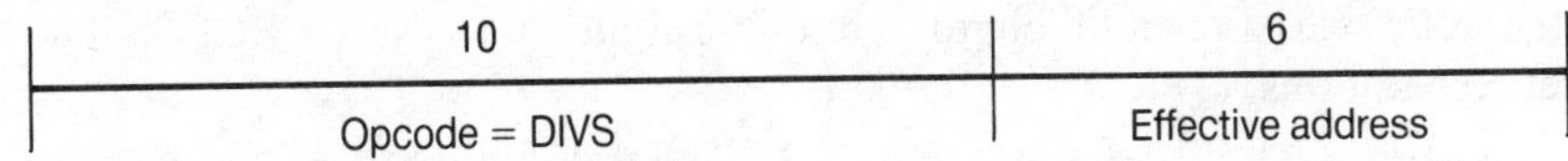

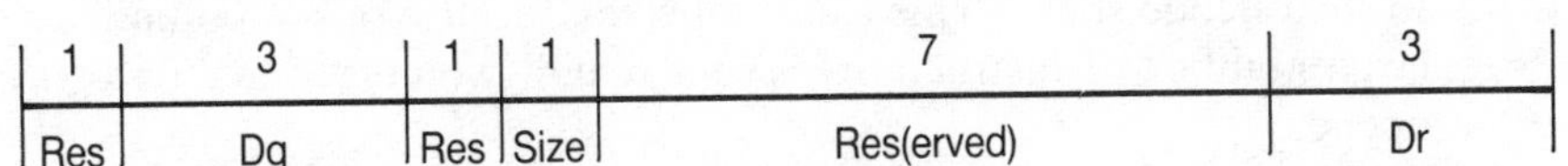

FIGURE 6.17
MC68020 DIV instruction, three-operand format.

□□EXAMPLE 6.13

The MC68020 has signed divide (DIVS and DIVSL) and unsigned divide (DIVU and DIVUL) instructions. The operand specified by the effective address is always the divisor, whereas the destination register(s) contain(s) the dividend. One divide instruction operates on words and three instructions operate on long words as follows:

(1)	DIVS.W	<ea>, Dn	32/16 → 16*r*:16*q*	;Two-operand ;format
(2)	DIVS.L	<ea>, Dq	32/32 → 32*q*	;Two-operand ;format
(3)	DIVS.L	<ea>, Dr:Dq	64/32 → 32*r*:32*q*	;Three-operand ;format
(4)	DIVSL.L	<ea>, Dr:Dq	32/32 → 32*r*:32*q*	;Three-operand ;format

Instruction (1) produces a quotient in the low-order word of Dn and a remainder in the high-order word of Dn. Instruction (3) assumes a quad word dividend in the register pair Dr:Dq and produces a 32-bit remainder in Dr and a 32-bit quotient in Dq.

The two-operand format of the DIVU and DIVS instructions is identical to that of the MULU and MULS instructions of Figure 6.15(a) (consistency!). The three-operand format of the DIV instruction is shown in Figure 6.17.

6.6.2 Variable data-length arithmetic

Operations on integers with a variable length are almost identical to those on integers with a fixed length. The difference is that the length of the operands must be specified.

The most important application for data with a variable length is in the area of administrative data handling, because of the importance of fixed-point numbers with a variable length. Therefore, most machines that offer variable data-length arithmetic limit their use to BCD-coded representations.

The operand length(s) can be specified as follows:

- In the opcode space: This is not efficient because of the potentially large number of instructions (every length would require its own opcode).
- In the operand space:
  (a) By specifying the length as immediate value (IBM/370).
  (b) By specifying the length via a separate operand (VAX-11).
- In the data space:
  (a) By adding a length field to the data (descriptor).
  (b) By adding a special bit pattern (flag) that marks the end of the number. This can be done easily when BCD coding is used, because only 10 of the 16 possible codes represent a decimal number.

6.7 Floating-point arithmetic operations

Floating-point numbers are represented, as shown in Chapter 3, by an exponent and a fraction (including the sign), whereby the value is determined as follows:

$$\text{value} = (-1)^{\text{sign}} * \text{fraction} * \text{radix}^{\text{exponent}}$$

The operations that can be performed on floating-point data are comparable to those of fixed-point arithmetic with the difference that, depending on the operation, certain mathematical laws only hold approximately. For example, the associative law $A + (B + C) = (A + B) + C$ only holds approximately because of the relative error inherent in floating-point operations. This fault can be reduced to be less than:

$$\text{radix}^{\text{exponent}} * 0.5 * \text{radix}^{(1-F)}$$

where F stands for the number of digits in the fraction for normalized numbers (using rounding). In the case of truncation, this fault is twice as large. To reduce the fault, many machines are equipped with double-precision floating-point numbers, having a format with twice as many bits as single precision. These extra bits can be used to extend the fraction

Table 6.4 Sign-magnitude add/subtract operations.

Desired Operation	Sign Op1	Sign Op2	Operation To Be Performed	Effective Operation
ADD.F	+	+	Op1 + Op2	Addition
ADD.F	+	−	Op1 − Op2	Subtraction
ADD.F	−	+	Op2 − Op1	Subtraction
ADD.F	−	−	−(Op1 + Op2)	Addition
SUB.F	+	+	Op1 − Op2	Subtraction
SUB.F	+	−	Op1 + Op2	Addition
SUB.F	−	+	−(Op1 + Op2)	Addition
SUB.F	−	−	Op2 − Op1	Subtraction

field (extended precision) as well as, for some architectures, the exponent field (extended range). The precision of a floating-point number is maximal if the number is normalized. Therefore, most architectures are provided with operations that expect normalized operands and produce a normalized result.

6.7.1 Addition and subtraction

Because floating-point operands consist of two parts, the exponent and the fraction, addition and subtraction take place according to an algorithm that handles both parts. Such an algorithm is described in this subsection. The algorithm requires normalized operands and produces a normalized result.

Add and subtract operations are often translated into *effective* add and subtract operations according to the scheme in Table 6.4. In the following, the algorithms for effective addition and subtraction are discussed.

Algorithm for effective addition

Effective addition means that the operands have the same sign. At the risk of labouring the obvious, it should be noted that addition and subtraction can only take place when the exponents are equal.

The algorithm for effective addition consists of four parts:

(1) A part that checks whether *alignment* is necessary. Alignment is

required when the exponents are not equal:

```
if Exp1 = Exp2 then
  begin                          (* No alignment necessary *)
    ExpRes := Exp1;
    goto c;
  end;
if ABS (Exp1 - Exp2) > Number_of_fraction_digits then
  begin
                                 (* Excessive alignment *)
    if Exp1 > Exp2
    then Res := Op1
    else Res := Op2;
    goto Done;
  end;
```

(2) A part that aligns the fractions:

```
if Exp1 > Exp2 then
  begin
    shiftright Fraction2, (Exp1 - Exp2) digits;
    ExpRes := Exp1;
  end
else
  begin
    shiftright Fraction1, (Exp2 - Exp1) digits;
    ExpRes := Exp2;
  end;
```

(3) A part that adds the fractions:

```
FractionRes := Fraction1 + Fraction2;
```

(4) A part that checks for normalization of the result and normalizes it, when necessary:

```
if fraction_overflow then
  begin                          (* Post-normalize 1 digit *)
    shiftright FractionRes, 1 digit;
    ExpRes := ExpRes + 1;
    if exp_overflow
    then set overflow_indicator;
  end;

Done:
```

Algorithm for effective subtraction

The algorithm for effective subtraction (the addition of operands with a different sign) differs from that for effective addition in parts (3) and (4).

Part (3) differs because the fractions are subtracted. Part (4), the normalization step, is different because, due to the subtract operation in part (3), no fraction overflow can occur. In this case, however, it is possible for a number of leading digits to become zero due to the subtraction operation. So, part (4) must be replaced by the following:

```
if most_significant_fraction_digit = 0 then
  begin                                   (* Normalization *)
    if FractionRes = 0 then
      begin                               (* Special case with 0 result *)
        FractionRes := 0;
        ExpRes := 0;
        goto Done;
      end;
    shiftleft FractionRes, number_of_0_digits;
    ExpRes := ExpRes - number_of_0_digits;
    if exp_underflow
    then set underflow_indicator;
  end;

Done:
```

where a special check has been inserted to check whether the result has become zero.

Guard digit

It is desirable for the result of an operation to approximate the exact result as accurately as possible. Therefore, it is important that the relative error be smaller than the value of the least significant digit of the normalized result. For this purpose, the **guard digit** has been introduced. Guard digits are digits to the right of the significant fraction digits, their purpose being to guard against the loss of digits that can be later shifted left into the fraction during normalization. An example of this is the operation $A - B$ (using radix = 10). An effective subtraction carried out without using a guard digit would cause the least significant digit to be lost, as shown in the following table:

Exponent	Fraction	Alignment	Guard Digit	Operation
2	1.69	$10^2 * 1.69 \rightarrow 10^2 * 1.69$	0	A
1	7.85	$10^1 * 7.85 \rightarrow 10^2 * 0.78$	5	B
1	9.05	$10^1 * 9.05 \leftarrow 10^2 * 0.90$	5	$A - B$

As will be shown in the following, only one guard digit is needed during addition and subtraction to obtain this extra precision.

Addition Two numbers are added; one may be aligned (worst case), and the other may not:

$$\begin{array}{ccccccccl} & a_0 & a_1 & \cdots\cdots & a_{p-1} & 0 & 0 & & \text{number with larger exponent} \\ & 0 & 0 & b_0 \cdots\cdot & b_{p-3} & b_{p-2} & b_{p-1} & & \text{number with smaller exponent} \\ \hline & & & & & & & + & \\ c & r_0 & r_1 & \cdots\cdots & r_{p-1} & r_p & r_{p+1} & & \end{array}$$

In all cases, '$c\ r_0$' (carry bit c and bit r_0) $\geqslant a_0 = 1$, so no left normalization and, therefore, no guard digit is needed. One guard digit can be used for rounding.

Subtraction Three cases can be distinguished:

(1) No alignment necessary (exponents equal):

$$\begin{array}{cccccc} & a_0 & a_1 & \cdots\cdots & a_{p-1} & 0 \\ & b_0 & b_1 & \cdots\cdots & b_{p-1} & 0 \\ \hline & & & & & - \\ b & r_0 & r_1 & \cdots\cdots & r_{p-1} & \end{array}$$

With exponents equal, no normalization and, therefore, no guard digit is required.

(2) Alignment = 1 (exponents differ by 1):

$$\begin{array}{cccccl} a_0 & a_1 & \cdots\cdots & a_{p-1} & 0 & \text{number with larger exponent} \\ 0 & b_0 & b_1 \cdots\cdot & b_{p-2} & b_{p-1} & \text{number with smaller exponent} \\ \hline & & & & & - \\ r_0 & r_1 & \cdots\cdots & r_{p-1} & r_p & \end{array}$$

r_p may be $\neq 0$. Left normalization over one or more digit positions is required if $r_0 = 0$ – that is, if $a_0 = 1$ and a borrow from a_0 occurred – so that one guard digit is sufficient, because, due to alignment = 1, no more guard digits exist.

(3) Alignment $\geqslant$ 2 (exponents differ by 2 or more):

$$\begin{array}{ccccccc} a_0 & a_1 & a_2 \cdots\cdots & a_{p-1} & 0 & 0 & \\ 0 & 0 & b_0 \cdots\cdots & b_{p-3} & b_{p-2} & b_{p-1} & \\ \hline & & & & & & - \\ r_0 & r_1 & \cdots\cdots\cdots & r_{p-1} & r_p & r_{p+1} & \end{array}$$

Left normalization over two or more digit positions is required only if $r_0 = r_1 = 0$. $r_0 = 0$ implies that $a_0 = 1$ and a borrow from a_0 was required by a_1. Yet a_1 borrows from a_0 only if $a_1 = 0$ and a_2 borrows from a_1. If $a_1 = 0$, however, and a_2 borrows from a_1, then $r_1 \neq 0$. Hence, normalization over only one digit is needed, so that one guard digit is sufficient.

The IEEE Standard for base 2 floating-point numbers (IEEE, 1985) provides such a guard digit which, because the radix = 2, consists of a single bit.

6.7.2 Multiplication and division

Both of these operations expect operands of a certain format and produce results of the same format. This means that, in principle, multiplication would produce a double-length fraction. Consequently, a precision operation has to be applied to this fraction to make it fit into the proper format. This precision operation can be truncation or rounding. Supposing the operands are presented in a normalized form, the algorithms are as follows:

	Multiplication		**Division**
(1)	Add exponents	(1)	Subtract exponents
(2)	Multiply fractions	(2)	Divide fractions
(3)	Normalize result	(3)	Normalize result
(4)	Precision treatment (rounding or truncation)	(4)	Precision treatment

6.7.3 Extended precision

Extended precision for floating-point numbers is hard to realize with standard, single-precision, floating-point instructions. This is due to the fact that these standard instructions have been designed such that the operands and the result are normalized. Although floating-point meta-numbers should be normalized, each individual meta-digit should not be. Trying to realize extended precision by using the normal single-precision instructions would lead to a possible overflow or underflow in the exponent fields of every meta-digit. Furthermore, operations on meta-digits require alignment of the operands.

This argument shows that single-precision, floating-point numbers are not the most appropriate meta-digits for extended-precision, floating-point operations. Fixed-length, fixed-point operations are better suited to extended-precision, floating-point arithmetic. To meet the demand for greater precision and sometimes also for a greater range, most architectures provide a double-precision data type together with a dedicated set of operations.

6.7.4 Extremes

The domain function that must make floating-point results representable again must be able to cope with extremes in the range and precision of floating-point numbers.

Extremes in the range

These extremes are related to the maximum and minimum value of the exponent. Exceeding the maximum exponent value results in overflow while exceeding the minimum exponent results in underflow. Overflow and underflow conditions can be attributed to:

- Overflow: A programming error or a range for floating-point numbers that was too small (possibly extended precision required). As this situation may not be left unnoticed, a trap is the most appropriate signalling method.
- Underflow: A result that has become too small. When the result is to act as an operand again, it is usual to continue with the value that is too small (because this value differs only slightly from the correct value) or assign zero to the result. This can be done automatically under the control of a mode bit in the status register of the machine, without carrying out special tests and without interrupting the main program. The alternative is to signal this situation.

The signalling of overflow and underflow conditions should be done such that the correct value can be reconstructed. Solutions, which produce an unpredictable (undefined) result, are not desirable, because this makes correction operations impossible. Signalling can be done in two ways:

(1) By setting a flag (for example, V for overflow and U for underflow) in the condition code register, allowing the programmer to test for this flag.

(2) By generating a trap, which can be masked in some architectures. In the trap-masking mechanism, selective reaction to automatic overflow/underflow detection is feasible, such as assigning a zero value on underflow. It saves the execution time otherwise required for program testing without requiring extra execution time for programmed tests on those conditions, and assigning the value 'infinity' on overflow.

Extremes in precision

These extremes are related to the maximum and minimum number of significant fraction digits. The usual method of handling too large a number of significant digits produced by an operation is via truncation or rounding. Many architectures have a mode bit to select the desired method.

Another issue of concern here is the minimum number of meaningful fraction digits. This number can be greatly reduced by an effective subtraction of two almost identical numbers. The result of the effective subtraction:

$$\begin{aligned} R &= 0.14769588\text{E}{+}5 - 0.14769578\text{E}{+}5 \\ &= 0.00000010\text{E}{+}5 = 0.100000000\text{E}{-}1 \end{aligned}$$

gives the incorrect idea that the normalized result is determined by nine significant digits, while in fact only two digits are significant. There are systems that have some extra bits added to the data format for administering the significance of the result. However, this does not have wide-spread application, because it is preferable to use these bits for extra precision ('How much of one's wealth will one pay to know how much one has?'). The IEEE Floating-Point Standard provides a separate coding for very small numbers (that is, numbers almost equal to zero). This coding is called denormalized numbers. Here, the exponent = 0 and the fraction ≠ 0 (see Section 3.2.5).

SUMMARY

- Instructions produce a result and a derived result. The derived result contains information about the operation and/or the result of the operation. It is usually stored in the condition code register or signalled via a trap.
- Operations can be classified according to the following types: data move, format transformation, code transformation, logical and arithmetic.
- When an overlap exists between the source and destination operands of a multiple data move, special precautions have to be taken to make the move non-destructive.
- It is important for instruction sets to be character set independent.
- Format transformation operations change the bit assignment of their operand. Shift and bit-field instructions are used for this.
- Arithmetic shift operations are a fast and low-cost implementation of multiply and divide operations (by powers of 2). The derived results should, therefore, be the same as for the multiply and divide operations (consistency).
- Bit-field operations should be able to consider the bit field as an unsigned number, a bit vector or a signed number.
- Code transformation operations change the way data is coded; for example, the coding of a character may be changed from ASCII to EBCDIC and the representation of a number may be changed from integer to floating point. These operations are usually implemented using the table look-up method (mainly for conversion between character sets) or the algorithmic method (mainly for conversion between number representations).
- An important consideration for fixed-point arithmetic operations is the possibility for extended precision. To facilitate extended precision on integers: the two's complement representation is preferred; the multiply operation has to be able to produce a double-length result; and the divide operation should be able to accept a double-length dividend.
- The accuracy of floating-point operations can be improved by using a guard digit. A single guard digit is sufficient to improve the precision.
- Extended-precision, floating-point operations cannot be done with single-precision operations; therefore, they require a new data type and a new set of instructions to handle that data type.
- Truncation and rounding are precision operations. They make a non-representable number (due to the lack of sufficient precision bits) representable again.
- Extremes (in the representation of the exponent or fraction) should not produce an unpredictable result, but should be handled such that the correct value can be reproduced or a fixed known value (such as zero) should be substituted.

EXERCISES

6.1 Which two parts form the derived results?

6.2 What is a potential problem with a multiple data move and how can it be handled?

6.3 Which classes of format transformations can be identified? What is special about arithmetic shift operations?

6.4 What is the purpose of code transformation operations? Which two methods of code transformation operations exist, and for what are they used?

6.5 What is the best representation for integers, considering extended-precision operations? What requirements have to be made on multiply and divide instructions on integer operands to allow for extended precision?

6.6 Why does the MC68020 have the extended-precision instruction ADDX −(Ay), −(Ax)? Which condition code bit has to be treated differently from the regular add instruction and how should this be done?

6.7 The assembler syntax of the MC68020 test instruction is TST <ea>. The condition codes are handled in the same way as the MOVE instruction. Write an MC68020 assembler program that tests an *N* meta-digit number, where the address of the meta-number is in address register A1. Each meta-digit is one word.

6.8 Write an MC68020 routine that multiplies two meta-numbers, consisting of *N* meta-digits (of one word). Two versions should be written:

(a) Using only the MULS instruction.

(b) Using the MULU and/or the MULS instructions.

6.9 The IBM/370 floating-point format uses hex normalization; that is, a radix of 16. How many guard digits are required to allow for maximum precision add and subtract operations?

6.10 What is the problem with extended-precision operations on floating-point numbers, using single-precision instructions?

6.11 Which two exceptions can occur when the result of a floating-point operation is out of range? Which precision treatment methods exist and which is more accurate?

References

DEC (1975). *PDP-11 Processor Handbook*. Digital Equipment Corporation: Maynard, MA.

DEC (1979). *VAX-11/780 Architecture Handbook*. Digital Equipment Corporation: Maynard, MA.

IEEE (1985). *IEEE Standard for Binary Floating Point Arithmetic*. ANSI/IEEE Std 754–1985, New York.

Knuth, D. E. (1969). *The Art of Computer Programming*, Vol. 1, *Seminumerical Algorithms*. Addison-Wesley: Reading, MA.

Motorola (1985). *MC68020, 32-bit Microprocessor User's Manual*. Prentice Hall Incorporated: Englewood Cliffs, NJ.

National Semiconductor (1984). *NS32000 Programmer's Reference Manual*. National Semiconductor Corporation: Santa Clara, CA.

Wirth, N. (1986). *Algorithms and Data Structures*. Prentice Hall Incorporated: Englewood Cliffs, NJ.

7 Program Flow Control

It is nice to be important, but it is more important to be nice.
– Anonymous

Natural languages achieve a large part of their expressive power from the word order, even when a limited vocabulary is used. This is also true for computer languages where the vocabulary is called the instruction set. The sequence of executed instructions in a computer program is known as program flow. The computer is required to have the ability to change this flow, depending on certain conditions. The computer must test for these conditions and decide, depending on the result of the test, whether or not to change the program flow. These conditions, as well as the kinds of tests and branches, are important design issues for a computer architect.

Many control constructs like the **for** loop are, conceptually speaking, single operations. Their implementation usually requires a number of instructions: some instructions at the beginning of the loop for setting the initial values and some instructions at the end of the loop for testing the condition to terminate the execution of the loop.

This chapter discusses program flow in relation to high-level programming languages. First, the linear order of instructions is discussed, followed by the non-linear order of instructions. Section 7.3 discusses the architectural support for conditional operations, while Section 7.4 focuses on one aspect of this architectural support: condition use. Finally, iteration mechanisms are described.

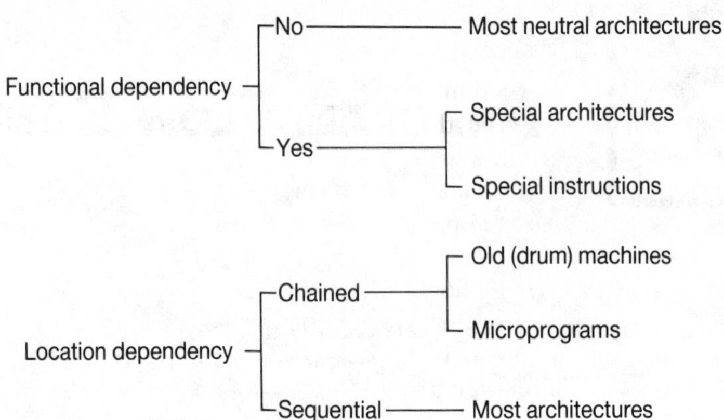

FIGURE 7.1

Functional and location dependency of instructions.

7.1 Linear order of instructions

A program consists of statements, which are normally executed in a linear order. Because every statement is usually translated into one or more successive machine instructions, this implies a direct relationship between the location of a particular instruction and the one that follows it.

Analogous to statements in high-level languages, instructions in computers are generally functionally independent; that is, every instruction can be regarded as a separate syntactic and semantic entity, distinct from both the preceding and the following instruction. Figure 7.1 gives an overview of architectures in relation to the functional and location dependency of instructions.

7.1.1 Functional dependency

In general, every instruction in a computer is an independent syntactic and semantic entity. This property simplifies the implementation, since when N different instructions are present in the architecture, there are $N * (N - 1)$ instruction pairs and $N * (N - 1) * (N - 2)$ instruction triplets, and so on. When repetition is taken into account, these figures become N^2 and N^3, respectively. However, some architectures do have dependent instructions, but in such cases the dependency is limited to a small number of instructions – for example, pairs or triplets. To illustrate these types of instructions, two instructions having a functional dependency on other instructions will be discussed; namely, the **repeat** and the **execute** instruction.

- The function of the repeat instruction is to indicate that one or more subsequent instructions must be repeated a specified number of times. The repeat instruction specifies the number of repetitions together with a special termination condition.

- The execute instruction specifies the execution of another instruction that is located at the address specified by the operand of the execute instruction. This is a kind of subroutine call, in which the subroutine consists of a single instruction. The IBM/370 execute instruction is an example of this (IBM, 1970).

The problem with the functional dependency of instructions is that not every instruction can be accepted as the second instruction in a pair. For instance, repeating a repeat instruction may not be acceptable because the count and the termination condition must be managed for both repeat instructions internally in the hardware, which requires extra hardware and makes the machine status too large. Another reason why a second instruction in a pair is not acceptable is because the instruction pair does not make sense. For example, consider repeating a jump or a halt instruction. Again, hardware would be required to detect and signal this invalid pair. These complexities may be the reason that repeat and execute instructions are not found in many architectures.

The repeat and execute instructions form meta-instructions, together with the instructions that they use as operands. This terminology can be compared with the terminology introduced in Figure 6.13. Here, the meta-digits are the instructions and the meta-numbers are the meta-instructions.

7.1.2 Location dependency

The location of the next instruction depends on the current instruction in two ways (see Figure 7.1):

(1) **Chained**: This means that every instruction specifies the location of the next one. This way was used in some older computers that used a drum (which is the precursor of the disk memory) as an extension of their very small main memory to obtain an optimum overlap between the execution of the current instruction and the drum location of the next instruction. In such a case, the next instruction could be read the moment the current instruction finished executing. Chaining is still often used in microprogramming, particularly in instruction and operand decoding, because the opcodes and addressing modes are used to activate different microroutines. A second, minor, reason for the use of chaining is to fill the 'gaps' that may be caused by unused (spare or reserved) opcodes or addressing modes. These gaps may also be caused by certain combinations that do not or cannot occur. For example, in

a multiway branch, on the result of an arithmetic comparison, only six combinations ($<$, $\leqslant$, $=$, $\neq$, $>$, $\geqslant$) of an eight-way branch are used. When the location of the next instruction is specified within the micro-instruction, the locations of the unused combinations, the gaps, can also be used.

(2) **Sequential**: This means that the next instruction to be executed has the implicit address of the next memory location. This eliminates the necessity to specify the next instruction location. Furthermore, it is important for a fast implementation that the location of the next instruction be predictable (without knowledge of the current instruction), so that the next instruction can be prefetched. Changing this sequence requires branch/jump instructions. Determining the location by means of chaining is generally not applied at the conventional machine level, because it requires an extra operand. The sequential method is therefore preferred, although it requires the architecture to be extended with branch/jump instructions.

An example of sequential location dependency is the delayed branch instruction. This is a (conditional) branch instruction, where the branch is effectuated after the execution of the next sequential instruction. The reason for this is that, in general, the next instruction has already been fetched, and sometimes even decoded, when instruction pipelining is used, so it is profitable to ensure that this instruction is also executed. This results in a performance gain, since the discontinuity in the prefetch unit due to the branch has been reduced. The delayed branch instruction is, in spite of its benefits, not commonly used because of the extra complexity for the compiler or the human programmer – an extra, meaningful, instruction has to be allocated and positioned after the branch. On the other hand, almost all RISC architectures (see Chapter 15) use this technique.

7.2 Non-linear order of instructions

In programming, the order of instructions is not always linear. In many cases, decisions have to be made as to which path of the program is to be executed next. Conditional operations are used to select one of the possible paths.

7.2.1 Decisions

Making decisions in programs is usually done by changing the program flow based on some previously generated result. This creates the necessity for instructions that can change the linear order of instructions conditionally and sometimes also unconditionally. These instructions give the desired flexibility and generality to programming languages and instruction sets. Some examples from the world of high-level programming languages are the Pascal **if** . . . **then** . . . **else**, **case** and **goto** statements. Such programming language constructs require support by the architecture of a computer. This support consists of a number of tests and one or more operations (jumps or branches) based on the results of these tests. In this case, a test is considered as the evaluation of data in order to map it on to a set of mutually exclusive decision criteria, usually condition codes. So, a test is the mapping of the input domain, which consists of all possible input values, to the output domain, which consists of a value for every class of input values.

Decisions are mostly based on the comparison of a number of values. The simplest cases are to compare a value with zero or to compare two values. A more intricate case is to find out if a value is within a range of values.

Comparison of two values

Very often, two values must be compared. In principle, this comparison comprises the ranking of two operand values that are not changed in the course of the comparison. The result is one of the three following conditions: $<$, $=$ or $>$. Often, however, the user wishes to make a compound rather than a simple choice, which results in a choice of two conditions with the following possibilities:

$A < B$ or $A \geqslant B$

$A \leqslant B$ or $A > B$

$A = B$ or $A \neq B$

A possible implementation is via the subtract instruction. However, this has the side effect that the difference is saved in the destination, which causes the undesired destruction of that operand. Therefore, most architectures are equipped with a **compare** instruction, which has no such side effects: the difference is determined only in order to produce the derived results.

Often, it is necessary to rank an operand with zero. The zero operand is, in many architectures, specified implicitly in the opcode by using a **test** instruction.

□□EXAMPLE 7.1

The MC68020 has two instructions for comparing values: CMP and TST (Motorola, 1985). The CMP instruction can compare a general operand with a register, while TST compares a general operand with

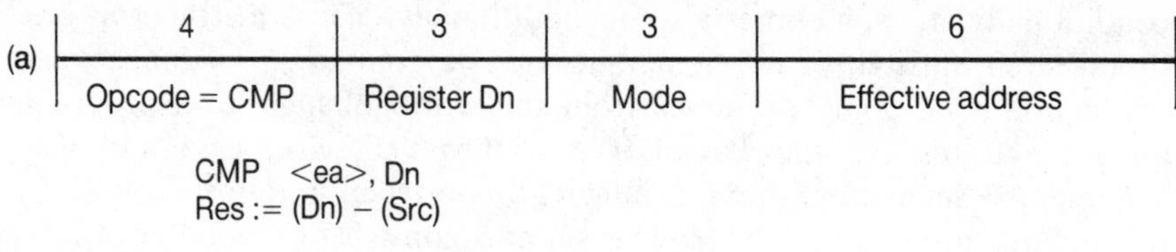

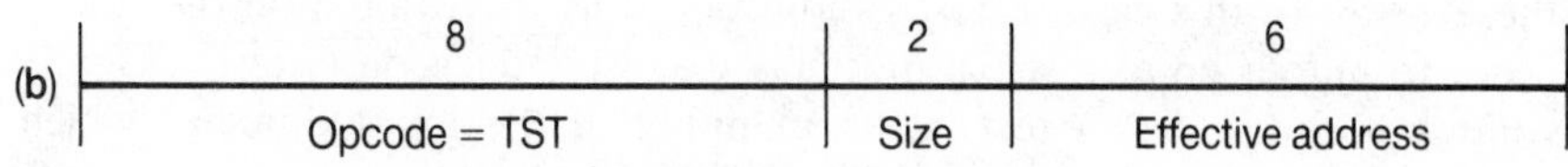

TST <ea>
Res := (Src) − 0
Condition codes: N := (Res < 0)
Z := (Res = 0)
V := 0
C := 0
X := Not affected

FIGURE 7.2

MC68020 CMP and TST instructions.

zero. In many architectures, the instruction CMP A, B computes $A - B$. However, the MC68020 follows the syntax of the SUB instruction, so CMP A, B effectively computes $B - A$, which is consistent. The result of the CMP and TST instructions is reflected in the flags of the condition code registers.

The dynamic frequencies of the MC68020 CMP and TST instructions are 7.86% and 3.09%, respectively (MacGregor, 1985). The total percentage of 10.95% shows their relative importance. Figure 7.2 shows the format of the MC68020 CMP and TST intructions.

Far less commonly supported are the higher-level language functions **max** and **min**. They are a special case of the comparison of two operand values, being combined with an instruction which is executed directly afterwards. For example, the function:

$$A := \mathbf{max}(A, B)$$

can be performed by the MC68020 machine instruction sequence:

```
MOVE.L  A, D0    ;Store A in D0
CMP.L   B, D0    ;Compute A - B
BGE     Ldone    ;If A > B then done
MOVE.L  B, A     ;Else B > A, therefore A := B
Ldone:
```

This sequence could be performed by the following new instruction:

```
MAX.L  B, A
```

The introduction of such new instructions is useful in the following cases:

- When the frequency of use is sufficiently high or when no other method of implementation exists. This is the case for primitive operations performed by instructions such as Wait, Trap and Reset.
- When they save sufficient memory space and execution time compared to a programmed implementation. This includes a gain in instruction execution time due to the elimination of branch instructions, which may have negative consequences for pipelining.
- When it fits in the existing architecture; that is, the existing instruction formats are not (seriously) violated.

Range comparison

This is the ranking of a data item with respect to two elements. It can also be applied to N elements. The latter operation consists of determining the proper position of a data item, assuming that the N elements are sorted on some key. Most architectures have no special instructions for this comparison. The operation is often performed by the repeated ranking of two elements.

With range comparison, an object must be classified according to a certain relation with other objects; for instance:

'A' ≤ Char ≤ 'Z'	alphabetical characters
'0' ≤ Char ≤ '9'	numeric characters
lower bound ≤ index ≤ upper bound	array index

The comparison $A \leqslant X \leqslant B$ can produce (according to the granularity of the result):

- Two possible answers: $A \leqslant X \leqslant B$; $X < A$ or $X > B$.
- Three possible answers: $A \leqslant X \leqslant B$; $X < A$; $X > B$.
- Five possible answers: $A < X < B$; $X = A$; $X = B$; $X < A$; $X > B$.

Range comparison is an important function for the addressing of arrays. In this case, only two possibilities are important, in range or out of range, and the result can therefore be reflected in the condition codes, later to be interpreted by a conditional branch instruction.

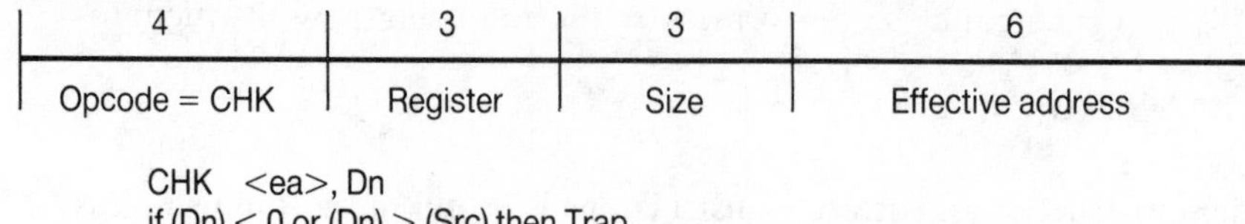

CHK <ea>, Dn
if (Dn) < 0 or (Dn) > (Src) then Trap
Condition codes: N := 1 if (Dn) < 0, := 0 if (Dn) > (Src), else undefined
Z, V, C := Undefined
X := Not affected

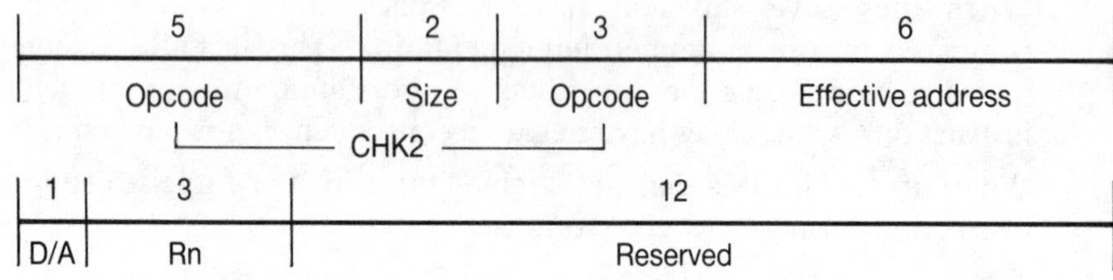

CHK2 <ea>, Rn
if (Rn) < lower bound or (Rn) > upper bound then Trap
Condition codes: N := Undefined
Z := 1 if (Rn) = lower or upper bound, else 0
C := 1 if (Rn) is out of bounds, else 0
X := Not affected

FIGURE 7.3
MC68020 CHK and CHK2 instructions.

□□EXAMPLE 7.2

Figure 7.3 shows the MC68020 CHK and CHK2 instructions, which perform the range comparison. The operand to be compared is specified in the register field: for the CHK instruction this is always a data register, whereas for the CHK2 instruction the D/A field specifies whether this is a data register or an address register. The CHK instruction uses an implicitly specified lower bound of zero, while the upper bound is specified by the effective address. The effective address of the CHK2 instruction specifies the address of the lower–upper bound pair. The instructions set the condition codes, which reflect the result of the comparison, as shown in Figure 7.3, and cause a trap when the operand is out of range.

7.2.2 Conditional operations

Conditional operations may be used to change program flow. They consist of three parts: **testing**, **selection** and **condition use** (Figure 7.4).

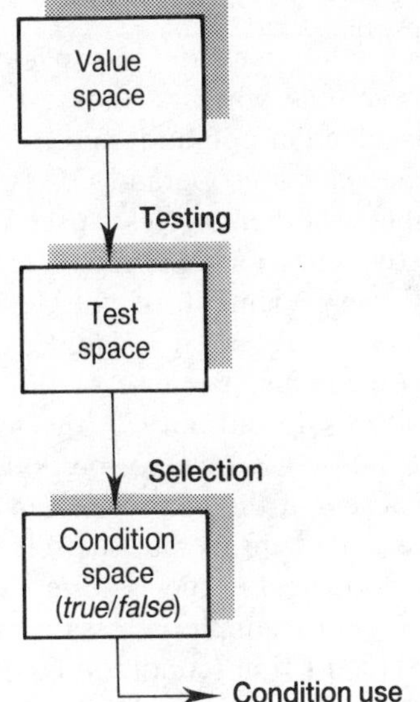

FIGURE 7.4
The execution of conditional operations.

Testing

Testing is the generation of derived results (which form the **test space**) from operations, or results of operations, performed on values taken from the **value space**. For instance, the N, Z, V and C condition codes span a test space of 16 elements. The testing of an integer value results in a representation of this value in one of these 16 elements.

This test function is sometimes performed implicitly; namely, when the condition code bits are set or reset as a derived result of another operation – for example, the ADD instruction. In other cases, this testing must be done explicitly with special test instructions, such as CMP and TST.

The NS32000 has divided the derived results into two groups (National Semiconductor, 1984):

(1) The **implicit** group, which consists of the following derived results of the *operation*: the carry bit (C) and the overflow bit (F).

(2) The **explicit** group, which consists of the following derived results of the *result* of the operation: the Z (the result is equal zero), N (the result, considered as a signed number, is less than zero) and L (an operand, considered as an unsigned number, is smaller than the other operand) bits.

To generate the explicit derived results, separate compare and test instructions are provided, while the implicit condition code bits are set or cleared implicitly for obvious reasons.

Selection

The selection operation maps the test space on to the condition space (see Figure 7.4). It verifies whether the test space contains the elements specified by the selection operand, and the outcome can be *true* or *false*. For example, the selection operand GE (Greater or Equal) of a branch instruction verifies whether the test space contains the element GE.

Usually, the selection operand, due to opcode space restrictions, cannot specify every element of the test space. With the MC68020 architecture, a single subset, such as GE, can be selected from the total test space of 16 elements. Because of the large variety of subsets – for example, the subset GE and not C – the selection of the required subset (in this case GE and not C) cannot be done in one instruction. Only the most frequent subsets of the test space can be selected in one instruction (Table 7.1). The other subsets must be selected by executing two or more instructions, by looking for the required intersection of the subsets of these instructions. For example, a test for 'not equal to zero' can be done in one MC68020 instruction (condition NE), while the test for 'greater or equal to zero' and not 'carry' must be done with a two-instruction sequence (conditions GE and CC).

Condition use

This is the part that uses the Boolean result of the condition space. Usually, the condition use part is performed by a branch operation when the program flow has to be changed. In some high-level languages, the Boolean result of the selection can be assigned as a value to an operand, as in $B := (X \leqslant Y)$, for example. This implies that the condition use part should consist of an operation that assigns the Boolean result of the condition space to some name. For more details see Section 7.4.

7.3 Architectural support for conditional operations

This section shows that the conditional operation can be performed by one, two or three related instructions. It discusses the properties of these instructions, together with the type of architecture where they may be found. Because of the large variety of alternatives for the condition use part, Section 7.4 has been devoted to this subject.

The architectural support for conditional operations is covered in terms of the three parts of Figure 7.4. The specification of these three parts (testing, selection and condition use) can be done in four different ways (Table 7.2), and may require one, two or three instructions. When the conditional operation consists of more than one instruction (cases *A*,

Table 7.1 Conditional tests of the MC68020.

Mnemonic	Name	Formula	Condition
T	true		1
F	false		0
Single condition	code bit		
CC	carry clear		~C
CS	carry set		C
NE	not equal		~Z
EQ	equal		Z
VC	overflow clear		~V
VS	overflow set		V
PL	plus		~N
MI	minus		N
[1]Unsigned			
HI	high		~C.~Z
LS	low or same		C + Z
HS	high or same		~C
LO	low		C
[2]Signed			
GE	greater or equal	N EOR ~V	N.V + ~N.~V
LT	less than	N EOR V	N.~V + ~N.V
GT	greater than	(N EOR ~V) AND ~ Z	N.V.~Z + ~N.~V.~Z
LE	less or equal	(N EOR V) OR Z	Z + N.~V + ~N.V

[1] Unsigned arithmetic: Low: The result of a ranking operation is less than if the carry bit is set (C = 1). High or same: This is the inverse of low (C = 0). Low or same: This is true if low is true (C = 1) or if the result is zero (Z = 1). High: This is the inverse of low or same (~(C + Z) = ~C.~Z).

[2] Signed arithmetic: A signed result (for example, two's complement) is ≥ 0 in the following two situations: (a) if the sign bit is cleared without an overflow detection (N = 0 and V = 0); (b) if, say, the addition of two positive numbers produces a result that causes the sign bit to change, so that the overflow bit is set too (N = 1 and V = 1). The formula for 'greater or equal' becomes N EOR ~V. The other formulas can be derived in the same way as for unsigned arithmetic.

B and *C*), information has to be passed between the instructions. Typically, the condition codes are used for this.

Alternative *A* of Table 7.2 requires three separate instructions for the execution of a conditional operation (instruction 1 for testing, instruction 2 for condition selection and instruction 3 for the condition

Table 7.2 Conditional operation support.

Case	Testing	Selection	Condition Use
A	1	2	3
B	1	2	2
C	1	1	2
D	1	1	1

use). In light of the high frequency of conditional operations, this is very inefficient and therefore not used in commercial machines.

Alternative *B* shows the classical solution for register-oriented architectures. The condition codes are used for information exchange between the two instructions. The first instruction does the test part while the second instruction does the selection and uses the produced condition.

In terms of the MC68020, the test part is performed by instructions such as ADD, MUL, CMP and TST, whereas the selection and condition use part is performed by the conditional branch instructions, Bcc or Scc (see Example 7.4). The reason for this solution is that the test part is often done implicitly (the derived results are generated by ADD, MUL and MOVE instructions, for example) and in register machines test instructions use the instruction format of arithmetic operations (for example, CMP has the same format as ADD and SUB), leaving no room for the specification of the selection and the condition use part.

Alternative *C* is used in stack-oriented architectures and in software-oriented architectures (Pascal P-code). These architectures have no condition codes, but have special instructions that accomplish the test and selection part. This can be done in one instruction, since these instructions do not have to specify any operands. (The operands are specified implicitly as stack based.) Consequently, there is enough space to specify the selection part in the test instruction. The location of the result of the selection part is also determined implicitly – that is, on the top of the stack (TOS). Example 7.3 shows the B6700 implementation of conditional operations.

□□EXAMPLE 7.3

The B6700 GRTR instruction (testing and selection part) is executed as follows (Burroughs, 1969):

if (M[(SP)]) > (M[(SP) − 1]) **then** (M[(SP) − 1]) := True
else (M[(SP) − 1]) := False;
SP := (SP) − 1; decrement stack pointer

The B6700 condition use parts are the instructions:

BRTR / DBTR	Branch if true
BRFL / DBFL	Branch if false
BRUN / DBUN	Branch unconditionally

The BR group of the B6700 specifies the branch address in the instruction (as a relative displacement), while the DB group specifies the branch address implicitly on the top of the stack. The operation of the BRTR and DBFL instructions is as follows:

- BRTR allows for a relative branch destination specified in the Displ field of the instruction:

  if (M[(SP)]) = True **then** PC := (PC) + Displ;
  SP := (SP) − 1;

- DBFL allows for a computed branch destination. This destination is taken, as an absolute address, from the stack:

  if (M[(SP)]) = False **then** PC := (M[(SP) − 1]);
  SP := (SP) − 2;

Alternative *D* requires only one instruction for the complete conditional operation. The use of condition codes is redundant in this alternative, because no information has to be passed. An example of a register-oriented architecture that combines the three parts in one instruction, is the MIPS processor (Hennessy, 1982). This processor has no condition codes and uses explicit compare-and-branch instructions with four operands (a condition, two source operands to be compared and a displacement for the branch target), where the condition is specified as part of the instruction mnemonic.

It is necessary to save the condition codes or the selected condition in the case of an interrupt, because they belong to the status of the interrupted process. Alternative *B* therefore requires space in the status register (SR) to store the condition codes (bits 0–4 of the SR of the MC68020). As alternative *C* stores the result of the selection operation on the stack, no special provisions have to be made in the case of an interrupt. Alternative *D* has no condition codes, so there is nothing to be saved.

7.4 Condition use

The condition produced by the selection part can be used in two different ways: to store the condition or to change the program flow (Figure 7.5).

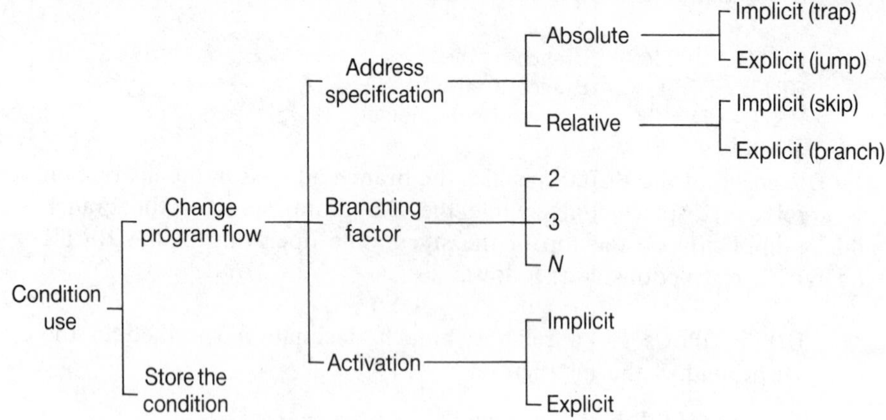

FIGURE 7.5
Conditional use.

7.4.1 Store the condition

Storing the result of the selection part is important in higher-level language statements where this result is assigned to a Boolean variable. Consider, for example, the statement $B = (X \leqslant Y)$. The Scc instruction of Example 7.4 is the proper support for this type of higher-level language statement. The MIPS architecture (Hennessy, 1982) has a four-operand instruction Scc X, Y, B which also includes the testing and selection part.

□□EXAMPLE 7.4

This example shows the elegant solution the MC68020 can provide for the high-level statement $B := (X \leqslant Y)$ using the Scc (Set According to Condition) instruction. This instruction (Figure 7.6) sets all bits of the destination byte operand to 1 if the condition is true and to 0 if the condition is false. This condition can be any of those shown in Table 7.1.

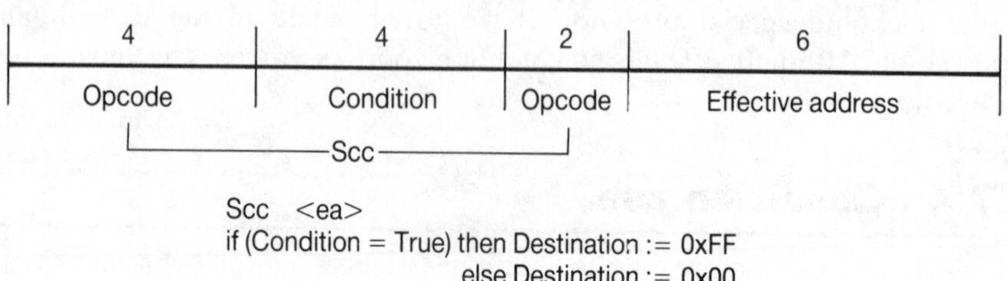

FIGURE 7.6
MC68020 Scc instruction.

7.4.2 Change the order of instructions (program flow)

Using the condition to change the order of the instructions (the program flow) involves the following three aspects (see Figure 7.5):

(1) The **address specification**.

(2) The **branching factor**: the number of conditions that are used (two-, three- and *N*-way jumps, where two-way jumps are implemented most frequently).

(3) The **activation** (implicit or explicit) of the condition use part.

Address specification

The address specification of the condition use part can be done in terms of an absolute or a relative address which can be specified implicitly or explicitly.

Absolute address specification is simple, although it does require the full address, and does not allow for relocatable code. *Absolute, explicit* address specification occurs when the absolute address is specified as an instruction operand of, usually, a jump instruction. This is not a common way of implementing branch instructions because it does not allow for relocatable code. *Absolute, implicit* address specification occurs when the absolute address has been specified before its use (it may be hard-wired). Therefore, at the moment of use, no address specification is required because the pre-specified absolute address is used. Traps and interrupts usually use absolute implicit addresses, enabling automatic jumps to routines at fixed locations, known as **exception handlers**. These jumps are mostly effectuated as a result of exceptional derived results of operations, such as overflow or 'divide-by-zero', or external interrupts, such as 'printer-ready'.

Relative address specification is a form of base addressing (see Section 5.2.3). However, because the program counter is usually used to specify the base address, it is also called program counter-relative addressing. Relative addressing is usually preferable to absolute addressing because it automatically produces relocatable code and the specification of the relative address usually requires fewer bits. *Relative, explicit* address specification is where the instruction specifies the relative address. This is used by most architectures in the form of branch instructions. They have the advantage of being bit efficient and allow for relocatable code (Example 7.5).

□□EXAMPLE 7.5

The MC68020 Bcc (Branch According to Condition) instruction (Figure 7.7) is a two-operand instruction: the first operand specifies the condition to be selected while the second operand specifies the relative

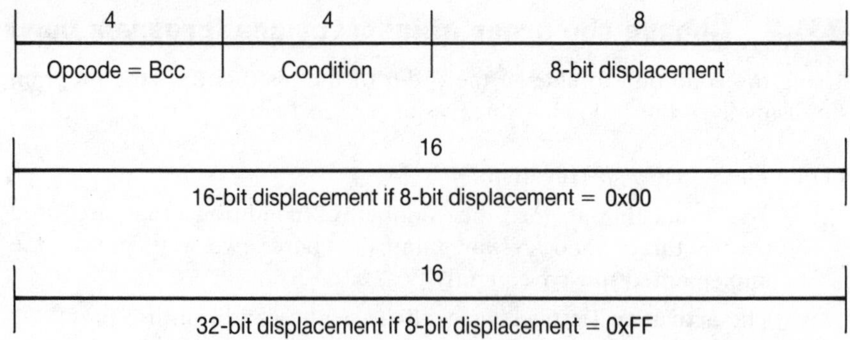

Bcc <label>
if (Condition = True) then PC := (PC) + Displacement

FIGURE 7.7
MC68020 Bcc instruction.

displacement as an immediate part of the instruction. As branch instructions are very common control constructs (Table 4.5 shows that 23.4% of all instructions executed are branch instructions), most architectures, including the MC68020, have a special format for this instruction such that a relative large displacement can be included in the basic instruction part (the first word of the instruction). Table 5.5 shows that, for the VAX-11, this will be similar for other architectures – a byte displacement will be sufficient in 91.6% of the cases for compiled Pascal programs. The MC68020 allows for a compact branch instruction with an 8-bit displacement and also for a branch instruction with a 16- or 32-bit displacement. The 8-bit displacement values 0 and 0xFF determine whether extension word(s) for a 16- or 32-bit displacement will follow.

Relative, implicit address specification means that the relative displacement is specified implicitly. This is usually a fixed displacement of 1. It is used, for example, when the testing, selection and the condition use part must be carried out in one instruction (alternative *D* of Table 7.1), because often there is no operand left for the explicit specification of the address for the condition use part. This was used in some older architectures, where all instructions were of the same length and the relative location was one location further than the next instruction (that is, the PC was incremented by one if the condition was true). The effect of this was that the instruction in the next position (which had to have a length of one word) could be skipped conditionally. Therefore, these instructions were called **skip** instructions.

□□EXAMPLE 7.6

An interesting example of relative, implicit address specification is the IBM/704 CAS (Compare Accumulator with Storage) instruction (Figure 7.8) (IBM, 1955). The IBM/704 architecture uses fixed-length 36-bit

12	1	4	3	16
Opcode = CAS	0	Spare	Index X	Displacement

CAS X, Displacement
if (AC) < (MEM[(X) + Displacement]) then PC := (PC) + 2 ;Skip 2
if (AC) = (MEM[(X) + Displacement]) then PC := (PC) + 1 ;Skip 1
if (AC) > (MEM[(X) + Displacement]) then PC := (PC) + 0 ;Skip 0

FIGURE 7.8

IBM/704 CAS instruction.

instructions which allow the CAS instruction to execute a three-way skip. This example is interesting because it clearly shows how this architecture has influenced the definition of the programming language FORTRAN, and that FORTRAN is more machine oriented than it perhaps should be. The CAS instruction served as a starting point for the definition of the FORTRAN statement `IF (A - B) 10, 20, 30` meaning **if** $A < B$ **then goto** 10 **else if** $A = B$ **then goto** 20 **else goto** 30, where 10, 20 and 30 are labels.

Branching factor

As discussed at the beginning of this subsection, most machines support instructions that offer two alternative ways to continue program execution, either sequentially or by jumping. In other words, the branching factor is two (Blaauw, 1989). Example 7.6 described a three-way branch instruction. Branching factors of N are important for the execution of **case** statements. In this type of statement, a computed value (the **case** selector) determines which path is chosen. Because most machines do not provide special instructions for this, the **case** statement is usually executed using an unconditional jump instruction, with a computable address (which uses base addressing).

□□EXAMPLE 7.7

The VAX-11 has a special CASE instruction (DEC, 1979). The data type (byte, word or long word) of the selector, base and limit operands is determined by the opcode, while the data type of the displacement operands is always word.

CASE *selector*, *base*, *limit*, *displ*[0], . . ., *displ*[*limit*]

Tmp := *selector* − *base*;
PC := (*PC*) + **if** *Tmp* ≤ *limit*
  then (*displ*[*Tmp*])
  else (2 + 2 ∗ *limit*);

A temporary value *Tmp* is computed by subtracting the base operand from the selector operand. The value of *Tmp* is then compared with the limit operand: if it is smaller than or equal to it, a displacement is added to the PC, chosen from a list of displacements on the basis of the *Tmp* value; if *Tmp* is greater than the limit operand, then a jump occurs over the displacement list. For instance, the FORTRAN statement `goto (10,20,30),I` is translated into:

```
CASEL I, #1, #3
.WORD10          ;If I = 1
.WORD20          ;If I = 2
.WORD30          ;If I = 3
                 ;If I < 1 or I > 3 then fall through
```

Activation and conditional instructions

The activation of the condition use part can be done in two ways:

(1) **Explicit activation**: Specific instructions (for example, conditional branch instructions) are used to invoke the condition use part. This is the normal situation.

(2) **Implicit activation**: The invocation of the condition use part occurs as a side effect of other, explicitly specified, instructions. Implicit activation is used when a 'monitoring' function has to be performed to detect exceptional conditions (overflow, underflow or 'divide-by-zero'). Implicit activation can be considered as a conditional operation which is active (enabled) with a scope of many instructions (for example, in the divide-by-zero situation the scope may be the complete program).

The alternative to using a conditional branch instruction to skip a number of instructions is for the instructions themselves to indicate that they should be skipped. This means that the execution of an instruction is conditional. An instruction can be made conditional by specifying that a certain condition must be checked before that instruction is executed. If the condition is not satisfied, the instruction is not executed. These instructions are called **conditional instructions**. An example of an architecture with conditional instructions is the ARM processor (Acorn RISC Machine), where every instruction has a 4-bit condition field (Furber, 1987). If the condition is true, the instruction is executed, otherwise it is skipped.

Another form of conditional instructions is the compare-and-test instructions, where the result (the resulting condition code) depends on the current condition code. These are called **conditional test instructions**, and are important for extended-precision arithmetic. The result of a test instruction for a single-length operand is < 0, $= 0$ or > 0; for extended-precision operands, the condition codes should reflect the value of the complete extended-precision operands.

Table 7.3 Conditional operations of different architectures.

Statement	Alternative *B* (MC68020)		Alternative *C* (B6700)		Alternative *D* (MIPS)	
(10.1)	CMP.L	B, A	PUSH	A	BLE	A, B, end
	BLE	end	PUSH	B	BGE	C, D, end
	CMP.L	D, C	GRTR		S1	
	BGE	end	PUSH	C	end:	
	S1		PUSH	D		
	end:		LESS			
			AND			
			BRFL	end		
			S1			
			end:			
(10.2)	CMP.L	Y, X	PUSH	X	SLE	X, Y, B
	SLE	B	PUSH	Y		
			LEQ			
			POP	B		

Other instructions with conditional side effects are the extended arithmetic instructions, like 'add with carry' and 'subtract with carry'. The resulting side effects must reflect the status of the current meta-digits. This means that the formula for the Z bit is extended with the requirement that the resulting Z can only be true if the current meta-digit and all preceding meta-digits are equal to zero. Thus the Z flag is cleared if the result is non-zero and unchanged otherwise (see Example 6.11 for the ADDX, SUBX and NEGX instructions).

Table 7.3 shows the implementation of the high-level statements:

$$\textbf{if } (A > B) \textbf{ and } (C < D) \textbf{ then } S1; \qquad \textbf{(10.1)}$$

$$B := (X \leqslant Y) \qquad \textbf{(10.2)}$$

for some architectures and alternatives *B*, *C* and *D* of Table 7.2.

7.5 Iteration

The normal mechanism for realizing operations on data elements of a structure (for example, all elements of a vector) is called **iteration** and consists of the repetition of a number of instructions for each of the data elements. The most frequently used iteration mechanisms in higher-level languages are the **for**, **while** and **repeat** statements.

7.5.1 *For* statement

The general form of a **for** statement is as follows:

for <*control variable*> := <*initial value*> **step** <*step value*>
until <*final value*>
do <*statement*>

The Pascal **for** statement is less general because the control variable may change by only +1 or −1, instead of by a step value that may have an arbitrary value, positive as well as negative.

Some important implementation aspects of the **for** statement are:

(1) Checking the initial value: A check of the initial value together with the step value may have to be done in order to determine whether even the first iteration of the loop is allowed. For example, in the statement **for** *I* := 5 **step** +1 **until** 3 the loop may not be executed.

(2) Stop criteria: The loop can be stopped in two ways:

(a) When the control variable gets a value outside the interval determined by the initial and the final value (FORTRAN and ALGOL 60 use this criterion).

(b) When the control value equals the final value (for example, Pascal requires this, because, in such a case, iterations over subranges stop with a control variable that is within the range and can therefore be of the same subrange type).

As far as the above alternatives at the programming language level are concerned, it is not possible to have a single machine instruction that can be used in all cases. This is a good example against the use of high-level instructions! A combination of lower-level instructions is therefore required. The MC68020 supports **for** statements by means of the DBcc (test condition, decrement and branch) instruction (see Example 7.9). The VAX-11 has three instructions to support **for** statements (see Example 7.8).

□□EXAMPLE 7.8

The VAX-11 instruction ACB (Add Compare and Branch) has four operands and functions as follows:

ACB *limit*, *add*, *index*, *displacement*

index := *index* + *add*;
if {(*add* ≥ 0) **and** (*index* ≤ *limit*)}
  or {(*add* < 0) **and** (*index* ≥ *limit*)}
  then *PC* := (*PC*) + *SEXT* (*displacement*); *SEXT* = *Sign-extended*

This instruction supports the general form of the **for** statement. Because the step size is variable (value as well as sign), it can be changed within the loop, as required by, for example, the ALGOL 60 language. The other two instructions AOB (Add One and Branch) and SOB (Subtract One and Branch) are simplified cases using a step value of 1 and −1, respectively, whereby SOB has an implicit final value of 0. These instructions are sufficient to implement, for instance, the Pascal **for** statement.

7.5.2 *While* statement

The **while . . . do** loop is usually not supported by special instructions. The block that must be iterated has a test at the beginning, which causes a jump over that block if the specified condition is false. The last instruction of the block is an unconditional jump to the test at the beginning. Here is a possible translation of a **while . . . do** statement for the MC68020:

```
while A < 5 do      Lbeg : CMP 5,A
  begin                    BGE Lend      ;Branch conditionally
   :                        :   :
   A := A + J;             ADD J, A
   :                        :   :
  end;                     BRA Lbeg      ;Branch always
                    Lend :
```

Another possible translation uses the DBcc instruction (Example 7.9).

7.5.3 *Repeat* statement

The **repeat . . . until** iteration mechanism is, again, usually not supported by special instructions. The block that must be iterated has a test at the end, so this block is executed at least once. This means that this iteration mechanism requires fewer instructions than the **while . . . do** construct, because there is no unconditional jump instruction. Many optimizing compilers can recognize **while . . . do** loops that will be executed at least once and translate these to their **repeat . . . until** equivalent. A possible translation of the **repeat . . . until** language construct for the MC68020 is as follows:

```
Cnt := 100;                   MOVE.L #100, D0    ;D0 := Cnt
do                     loop :
 :
 read(X);                     JSR     READ       ;Read X
 :                            :                  ;Result on
                                                 ;stack
```

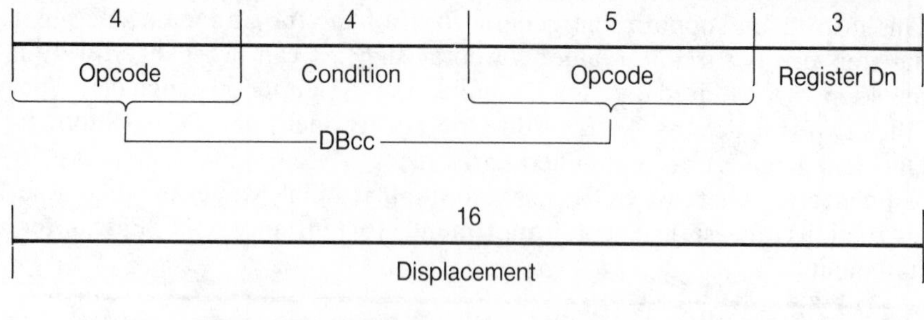


```
DBcc   Dn, <label>
if (Condition = False)
then
   Dn := (Dn) − 1
   if Dn ≠ −1 then PC := (PC) + Displacement
else PC := (PC) + 2                         ; Fall through
```

FIGURE 7.9

MC68020 DBcc instruction.

```
Cnt := Cnt − 1;
  ⋮                          TST     (SP)         ;X = 0?
until (Cnt < 0) or (X = 0);  DBEQ    D0, loop     ;If X = 0 then goto done
                                                  ;Cnt := Cnt − 1;
                                                  ;If Cnt ≠ −1 then goto
                                                  ;loop
                             Ldone:
```

□□EXAMPLE 7.9

The MC68020 has the DBcc (Decrement and Branch According to Condition) instruction (Figure 7.9), which supports the three basic iteration mechanisms. This instruction is placed at the end of the loop for the **repeat . . . until** and the **for** loops, and at the beginning for the **while . . . do** loop. DBcc first tests the condition to determine whether the termination condition for the loop is true. If so, no operation is performed and the loop is terminated. If the termination condition is false, the low-order word of the count value in Dn is decremented by 1 (a counter is defined as 16 bits). If the result is −1, the loop is terminated and execution continues with the next instruction. If the result is not equal to −1, execution continues at the location indicated by the current value of the PC plus the sign-extended 16-bit displacement (positive for **while . . . do** loops and negative otherwise) specified by the DBcc instruction.

SUMMARY

- In conventional von Neumann architectures, instructions are normally executed sequentially, unless instructions are used which deviate from this sequence on purpose; for example, to implement **goto**, **if ... then**, **for**, **call** or **return** statements, or a trap or interrupt occurs.

- For sequential execution, the location of the next instruction can be specified in the current instruction (chaining) or implicitly (the instruction in the following memory location). In the latter case, a program counter is normally used to store the address of the instruction currently being executed.

- For non-sequential execution, a decision has to be made as to which path to choose. This decision is usually based on the comparison of two values and, according to the outcome of this comparison, a branch operation is performed. A conditional operation consists of a test, a selection and a condition use part. The condition use part can store the condition or use it for making a branch decision. When branching, the specified address can be absolute or relative, both of which can be implicit or explicit.

- The sequence 'testing, selection, condition use' can be implemented with one, two or three instructions, according to the chosen architecture. In the most common case, selection and condition use are combined into one instruction, such as 'branch conditionally', while testing is performed implicitly (as a side effect of normal instructions) or by special instructions, such as CMP and TST.

- A special case of conditional execution is the use of conditional instructions which are tagged with a condition field. The condition in this field must be true to execute an instruction, otherwise it is skipped.

- To support iteration mechanisms, such as **for**, **while ... do** and **repeat ... until**, many architectures possess instructions that perform counting, comparison and branching in one instruction.

EXERCISES

7.1 What does functional dependence mean? Why is the repeat instruction not found in many architectures?

7.2 Why is the chained form of location dependency not very popular?

7.3 The comparison of two values may produce any of the following results:

- $A < B$ or $A \geqslant B$
- $A \leqslant B$ or $A > B$
- $A = B$ or $A \neq B$

Which MC68020 branch conditions (see Table 7.1) can be used to test each of these cases, assuming a signed comparison?

7.4 When is the introduction of a new instruction useful?

7.5 The range comparison operation may produce two, three or five results. Show these possible results and indicate which is sufficient for array subscript checking.

7.6 Which three parts constitute a conditional operation? Which part is often done implicitly? What is the purpose of the selection part?

7.7 Why are conditional operations usually not implemented as one instruction? What is the usual implementation form for register-oriented architectures?

7.8 Which two ways of condition use can be distinguished? Which MC68020 instructions are available to support each way?

7.9 When are absolute, implicit branches used to change the order of instructions? Which form of activation of the condition use part is usually used with this way of changing the order of instructions?

7.10 Why is the **for** loop not supported by a single instruction?

References

Blaauw, G. A. and Brooks, F. P. (1989). *Computer Architecture*. Addison-Wesley: Reading, MA. To be published.

Burroughs (1969). Burroughs B6700 Information Processing Systems Reference Manual. Burroughs Corporation: Detroit, MC.

DEC (1979). *VAX-11/780 Architecture Handbook.* Digital Equipment Corporation: Maynard, MA.

Furber, S. B. and Wilson, A. R. (1987). The Acorn RISC machine – an architectural view. *Electronics & Power*, **33**(6), 402–5.

Hennessy, J. (1982). Hardware/software tradeoffs for increased performance. In *Proc. of the Symposium on Architectural Support for Programming Languages and Operating Systems*, March 1982, pp. 2–11.

IBM (1955). *IBM Electronic Data-Processing Machines Type 704 Manual of Operation*. Form No. 24–6661–0, IBM Corporation: New York, NY.

IBM (1970). *IBM System/370, Principles of Operation*. Form No. GA22–7000, IBM Corporation: Armonk, NY.

MacGregor, D. and Rubinstein, J. (1985). A performance analysis of MC68020-based systems. *IEEE Micro*, **5**(6), 50–70.

Motorola (1985). *MC68020, 32-bit Microprocessor User's Manual*. Prentice Hall Incorporated: Englewood Cliffs, NJ.

National Semiconductor (1984). *NS32000 Programmer's Reference Manual.* National Semiconductor Corporation: Santa Clara, CA.

8 High-Level Program Structures

To the optimist all doors have handles and hinges; to the pessimist all doors have locks and latches.

– William Arthur Ward

Many programs written in high-level languages are too large to be comprehended as a single unit. Therefore, they are broken down into a number of small units, or modules, with separate functions. These modules are further broken down into functions or procedures, or, in the case of machine language programs, subroutines. Not only are these smaller units easier to understand, but also the units that activate them, since they may consider the units below them as one command. In other words, a high-level program is implemented as a hierarchy of commands, where each command is implemented as a list of commands for the level below it. This ends at the hardware level, where the commands can be executed by the hardware directly. For machine language programs, algorithms are broken down into smaller units until the instruction level is reached, but for high-level language programs it stops at the statement level. The compiler is therefore left with the problem of translating these statements into sequences of instructions.

This chapter begins with a discussion of functions (note that procedures are considered as functions that do not return a value), followed by the presentation of a run-time model used for the implementation of functions and an overview of the architectural support for functions, including the functional support provided by the MC68020. The concept of modules, as supported by the high-level languages Modula-2 and Ada, is then introduced, followed by the architectural support of modules. A description of the MC68020 module support mechanism concludes the chapter.

8.1 Functions

In modern programming languages, such as Pascal, the use of functions (and procedures) is encouraged, so an increasing percentage of the execution time of a program is spent in the code to activate functions (procedures). An examination of the static frequency of statements declaring and using functions (and procedures) in FORTRAN (1% and 8%, respectively) (Knuth, 1971) and Pascal (2.6% and 31.6%, respectively (Shimasaki, 1980) shows that the function (procedure) is one of the most important constructs in high-level languages.

In general, functions are used for the following purposes:

- **Code length reduction**: If a given sequence of statements occurs at several places in the program, it may be useful to give this sequence of statements a name, so that it only has to be specified once, thereby reducing the amount of code. The function mechanism can be used to activate this sequence of statements.
- **Information hiding**: The specification of a function can (and should) be done such that its caller need not be aware of its inner details. This applies to the algorithms used as well as to the internal data structures.
- **Creation of new levels of abstraction**: The function mechanism may be used to extend the programming level such that it more closely reflects the operations and data structures required by the application. This is essentially the creation of a new virtual machine tailored for a specific application.

8.1.1 Terminology

Figure 8.1(a) shows the block structure of a high-level language program (such as ALGOL or Pascal). A **block** is a sequence of statements and may contain declarations of local data. Inside a block, these local items are visible and accessible via their name; they are not necessarily visible outside the block. In Pascal, blocks are tied to functions or procedures: the body of a function or procedure is a block and this is the only way to create a block.

Blocks can be defined within other blocks. In Figure 8.1(a), program *Main* is the outer or enclosing block of procedures *A* and *B* and function *C*, while *A*, *B* and *C* are inner blocks of program *Main*. Function *C* in turn is an inner block of procedure *B*. The following Pascal program has the block structure of Figure 8.1(a). As this is given to introduce the terminology, it should be studied carefully. The complete program, program *Main*, forms the outermost block of that program.

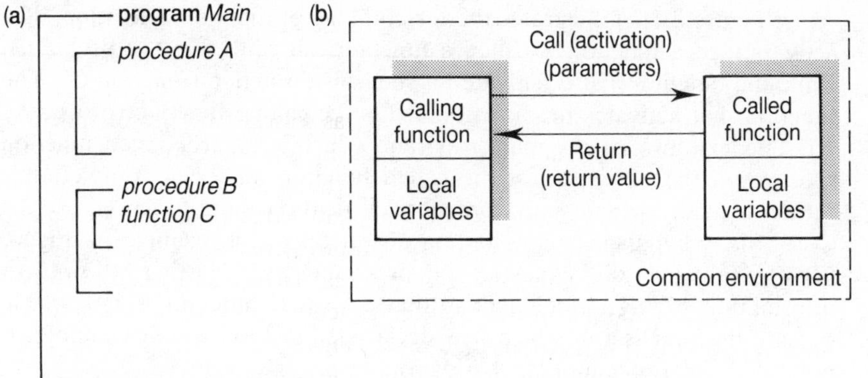

FIGURE 8.1

Block structure and function activation.

```
program Main (input, output);             (* Main program, outermost block*)
  var I, J, K : integer; R : real;        (* Global variable declaration    *)

  procedure A (var X : integer);          (* Function declaration, X is a   *)
    :                                     (* formal by reference parameter  *)
    var J, L, M : integer;                (* Local variable declaration     *)
    begin
    :                              2
    end;

  procedure B (Y : integer);              (* Function declaration, Y is a   *)
    :                                     (* formal by value parameter      *)
    var K, L, P : integer;                (* Local variable declaration     *)
    :
    function C (Z : real) : integer;      (* Nested function declaration    *)
      var J, L, M : integer;              (* Local variable declaration     *)
      begin
        C := . . .                 5      (* Return value assigned to       *)
      end;                                (* function C                     *)

    begin
      :                            4
      J := C(R);                   6      (* Function call                  *)
      :                                   (* R is an actual parameter,      *)
                                          (* the return value is passed to J *)
    end;

begin                                     (* Start of main program          *)
  I := 1;
  K := 2;                                 (* Initialize I and K             *)
  :                                1
  A(K);                            8      (* Function call                  *)
  :                                3
  B(I);                                   (* Function call                  *)
  :                                7
end.
```

Figure 8.1(b) illustrates the terminology of function activation. The activation of a function is called a **function call** (line **6** in the program), while the function that is activated is the **called function** (function *C*). The function that activates the function call is the **calling function** (procedure *B*). This can also be the main program, which is regarded as a function too. When the execution of the called function has been completed, a **return** is made, which gives control back to the calling function.

Many languages allow **nesting** of functions; for example, in Figure 8.1(a), function *C* is nested in procedure *B*. Nesting allows for information hiding, which means that a nested function is not visible outside the function in which it is declared. Function *C*, for example, is not visible by procedure *A* of program *Main*.

As already indicated, the use of functions allows a programmer to partition a program into smaller subprograms, which are conceptually independent of each other. Functions are isolated from the rest of the program, because they can have their own **local data**, which can be of any type, scalar or structured. Local data is declared at the beginning of the function and may not be referenced by functions global to that function. The local data of the outer block (program *Main*) is called the **global data**. The mechanism of local data allows for information hiding.

□□EXAMPLE 8.1

The visibility of names during the execution of the foregoing Pascal program is shown in Table 8.1. That part of the program text where a name is visible is called the **scope** of that name. When names in certain blocks are not visible, the program in that block may not use those names.

When the main program starts executing (line **1**), the global variables *I*, *J*, *K* and *R* are visible, as well as the names of procedures *A* and *B*. Then procedure *A* is called. When line **2** is reached, the global variable *J* is invisible, because procedure *A* has declared a local variable that also has the name *J*; this is called **shadowing**. The global variables *I* and *K* are still visible in *A*, because they have not been shadowed. The local variables of procedure *A*, as well as the formal parameter *X* of procedure *A*, are visible. Reaching line **3**, procedure *A* has returned and the global variables *I*, *J* and *K* are visible again, as in line **1**. The variables local to procedure *A* are not visible any more, which means that global variable *J*, which had been shadowed before, is visible again and the value it had before procedure *A* was called (line **1**) is accessible. A similar situation occurs when procedure *B* is called (line **4**), but in this case the global variable *K* is shadowed by procedure *B* and is therefore invisible during the execution of procedure *B*. Procedure *B* calls function *C*. In line **5**, the local variables of function *C* shadow the local variable *L* from procedure *B* and the global variable *J*.

Table 8.1 Visibility (v) of names during execution of Pascal program *Main*.

Line	program *Main*						procedure *A*				procedure *B*					function *C*			
	I	*J*	*K*	*R*	*A*	*B*	*J*	*L*	*M*	*X*	*K*	*L*	*P*	*C*	*Y*	*J*	*L*	*M*	*Z*
1	v	v	v	v	v	v	—	—	—	—	—	—	—	—	—	—	—	—	—
2	v	—	v	v	v	v	v	v	v	v	—	—	—	—	—	—	—	—	—
3	v	v	v	v	v	v	—	—	—	—	—	—	—	—	—	—	—	—	—
4	v	v	—	v	v	v	—	—	—	—	v	v	v	v	v	—	—	—	—
5	v	—	—	v	v	v	—	—	—	—	v	—	v	v	v	v	v	v	v
6	v	v	—	v	v	v	—	—	—	—	v	v	v	v	v	—	—	—	—
7	v	v	v	v	v	v	—	—	—	—	—	—	—	—	—	—	—	—	—

When a transfer of data to or from the called function is required, this must be indicated in the program text using parameters and return values. **Parameters** are the identifiers used to pass objects of a certain type to and from the called function. A return value is a result passed back to the calling function. In Pascal, this return value is assigned to the function name. Other languages, like C and Modula-2, use an explicit 'return (value)' statement.

Formal and actual parameters can be distinguished. **Formal parameters** are the identifiers that are used in the definition of the function to identify the data and program elements used to communicate with the calling function. The formal parameters are usually specified in a **formal parameter list**, which is placed at the beginning of the function declaration – for example, for procedure *A*, *X* is the formal parameter. The **actual parameters** are the specific data and program elements that must be passed. It is common practice to specify the actual parameters in a list too, which is added to the function call. For example, when procedure *A* is called (after line **1**), *K* is specified as the actual parameter.

Parameters can be passed in several ways, the method used being determined by how an actual parameter expression is evaluated by the calling function. The two most frequently used methods are:

(1) **By reference**: During the execution of the calling program, just before the activation of the called function, the *address* of the actual parameter (for example, the address of the variable *I* or *A*[*J*]) is passed as the parameter. So, a 'by reference' parameter is always passed as an address. As a consequence of this, assignment to such a parameter does have an effect outside the function. In Pascal, a 'by reference' parameter is denoted by a **var** statement in the formal parameter list, as in procedure *A*.

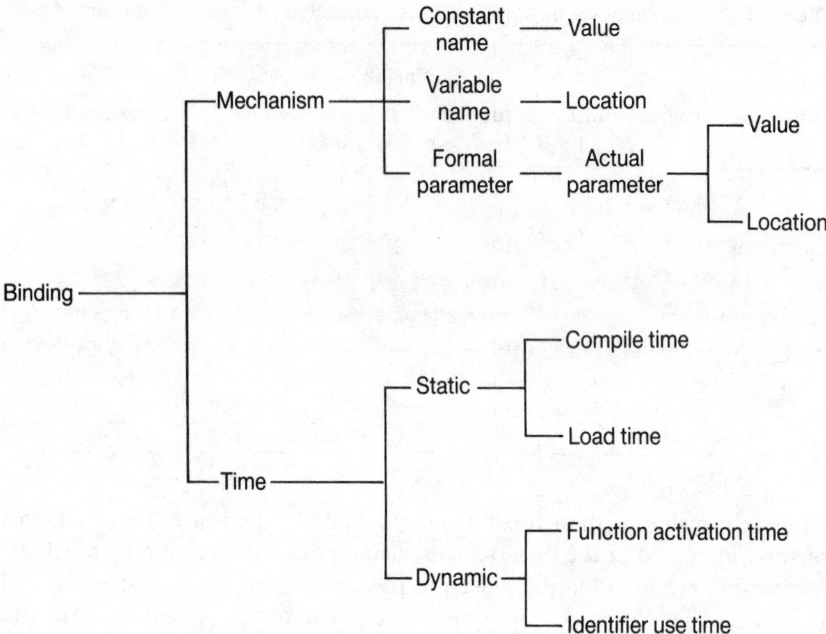

FIGURE 8.2
Aspects of binding.

(2) **By value**: The purpose of the 'by value' type is to pass the *value* of an evaluated expression. The status of a 'by value' parameter inside a called function can be considered identical to that of a local variable. In Pascal, parameters that are not declared to be of type **var** assume the default 'by value' type (as in procedure *B*) and cannot be assigned to.

8.1.2 Binding

The concept of binding consists of the binding mechanism and the binding time (Figure 8.2).

Binding mechanism

The binding mechanism determines *how* a correspondence (binding) between symbolic names (identifiers) and values is made. A binding is, in general, only valid in a limited part of the program, called the scope of a binding.

Identifiers that must be bound can denote formal parameters, constant names or variable names (names used in high-level languages).

- **Binding of formal parameters**: This consists of two parts: binding the formal parameter to an actual parameter and binding the actual parameter to a value. Every programming language has certain rules with respect to the correspondence of formal to actual parameters. The most common rule is the so-called **positional correspondence**; that is, at the moment the called function is activated, the first actual parameter of the list is bound to the first formal parameter. After that, the actual parameters must be bound to a value, which can be either a numerical value or a location. Parameters with name-value binding are called 'by value' and parameters with a name-location binding are called 'by reference'.

- **Binding of constant and variable names**: Identifiers for constant names are bound to a value at compile time, while identifiers for names of variables are bound to a location in which the value is stored. At each position in the program, it is possible to list the constant and variable names that are visible in a block (see Table 8.1). This list of names is called the (run-time) **environment** or **context** of a block. The environment can be different for each activation of a function. If a function activates itself (recursion), each activation will have its own environment. The *local* environment of a function contains the local names of that function; that is, the names that are declared in the current function. In general, a local environment is created (allocated) when a function is called and deallocated when a function returns. Most languages also allow references to the constants and variables of enclosing blocks. These constants and variables are called **non-local** or **free**. The list of possible references outside a block is called the **non-local** environment of a block or function. Variables and constants declared in the outermost block are **global**.

Binding time

The binding time determines *when* a symbolic name is made to correspond with a certain value. This can be done at different times: before program execution (static binding) or during execution (dynamic binding).

- **Static binding**: When an identifier is used, the compiler could search the program text 'outwards' for a block that contains the declaration for that identifier, and use this declaration. This is called **static** or **lexical** binding (lexical, because the textually enclosing blocks are searched). Static binding can be done when the program is compiled or when the program is loaded, just before execution.
- **Dynamic binding**: This type of binding uses the value of the variable whose name is found in the most recent activation of a block containing the declaration of the variable name (constants

are always bound statically). Dynamic binding can be done upon the activation of a function or block, or each time the identifier is used.

Most bindings involve some calculation due, for example, to searches in symbol tables. Program execution will, therefore, be more efficient if binding can be done by the compiler, called **early binding**. For this practical reason, most languages are defined such that the binding of constant and variable names is done at compile time. A good rule of thumb is that compiled languages use static binding, while interpreted languages use dynamic binding (although there are exceptions to this rule). The reason for this is that, in an interpreter, the binding of the identifier to the variable name is done upon each reference to the variable name, while in a compiler this binding is done once at compile time. If an interpreter were to support static binding, it would have to search the lexical scope for each reference to a constant or variable name, which implies analyzing the structure of the program for each reference. This would clearly be inefficient. A compiler cannot support dynamic binding because this requires the availability of the sequence of activations of all blocks, and this is only available at execution time.

8.2 Run-time model

Each function, as used in high-level languages, has its own (run-time) environment. The concept of different environments is difficult to translate into the machine language of conventional computers since they assume only one environment for all program code – that is, any instruction can access any location. The concept of **storage management** is introduced in this section to support these different environments. Furthermore, a stack-based model for the support of static and dynamic binding is described and, as an example, the run-time model of a block-structured language like ALGOL (and Pascal) is discussed.

8.2.1 Storage management

This involves the provision of a storage space by a **storage manager** when a function is activated, to store its environment. When a function has been executed, its environment can be deallocated and the storage space for this environment returned to the storage manager for reuse.

The main problem with storage management is that of **data allocation**. During the execution of a program, the names of that program must be bound to memory locations, which have to be made available (or allocated) for this purpose. This allocation is usually done in a block of consecutive memory locations, so constants and variables with the same scope (declared within the same function) in a source program are located in the same block of memory. Such a block of consecutive memory locations is called an **activation record**, because it is often created (and allocated) when a block or function is activated.

Data allocation can be performed in two ways:

(1) **Static data allocation**: In this case, name-location binding is done during compilation. The compiler allocates storage space during compilation and no storage management is required at execution time. This means that absolute addresses can be used, as the addresses do not change during program execution. With static allocation, a fixed local environment can be provided for all functions of the program. Although some languages such as FORTRAN use this method, it is not in general use because functions cannot be re-entrant or recursive (see Section 8.3). This is due to the fact that multiple activations of a function each require their own local environment, and with this method only the space for one environment is provided.

(2) **Dynamic data allocation**: Blocks are allocated during program execution. This is used, for example, in block-structured languages such as ALGOL and Pascal. Dynamic allocation can be carried out at two different times:

- At function activation time: Activation records (for ALGOL blocks and Pascal functions and procedures) are allocated when a function is activated and deallocated when the function returns. If it can be guaranteed that the block of storage that was requested last will be released first (which is the case with re-entrance and recursion), it is possible to use a **stack** for this type of storage allocation. If a function is activated, a new activation record must be created, and it is put on top of a stack. When the function returns, the activation record is deallocated.
- At identifier use time: This allows storage space for a variable to be provided every time a value is assigned to it. Consequently, more general storage management algorithms are required. As these algorithms are complicated and time consuming, they have a clear performance disadvantage over stack-based storage management. However, the advantage is that the data type and structure of objects is allowed to change from statement to statement. Consequently, only languages requiring this flexibility (such as LISP) use this method. However, other block-structured languages sometimes need to allocate data at object use time. To solve this

problem, most programming languages that use a stack for data allocation provide separate routines for data allocation at object use time by means of a **heap** – for example, for the Pascal access types (see Section 3.3).

8.2.2 Binding support

As described in the previous subsection, activation records are blocks of consecutive memory locations that are allocated when a block or a function is activated. Because this activation has a nested structure for block-structured languages like ALGOL and Pascal, a stack is used for the storage of these activation records.

Activation records

An activation record consists of the following parts (Figure 8.3):

- **Explicit parameters**: This is the area of the activation record in which the parameters that must be passed are allocated. Parameter passing is done by evaluating each actual parameter and pushing the result on to the stack. If the parameter is passed by value, it is sufficient to pass the value of the evaluated actual parameter. If the parameter is passed by reference, the evaluated actual parameter produces an address rather than a value.
- **Implicit parameters**: This is the area used for implicit parameters. It is also known as the administrative area, since it is used by the system to administer information about the run-time model. It consists of the following:
  - (a) **Static link (SL)**: This is a pointer to the activation record of the enclosing function. The SL follows the static nesting order of the functions. This pointer is used for static binding.
  - (b) **Dynamic link (DL)**: This is a pointer to the activation record of the calling function. It is used to find the activation record of the calling function upon a return and may be used for dynamic binding. In many cases, the DL is identical to the SL. However, the values of SL and DL differ for recursive function calls and when functions at the same lexical level call each other.
  - (c) **Return address**: This is the saved program counter (PC), which indicates where execution must continue after the function returns.
  - (d) **Other implicit parameters**: In this area, the contents of general-purpose registers, the program status word, and so

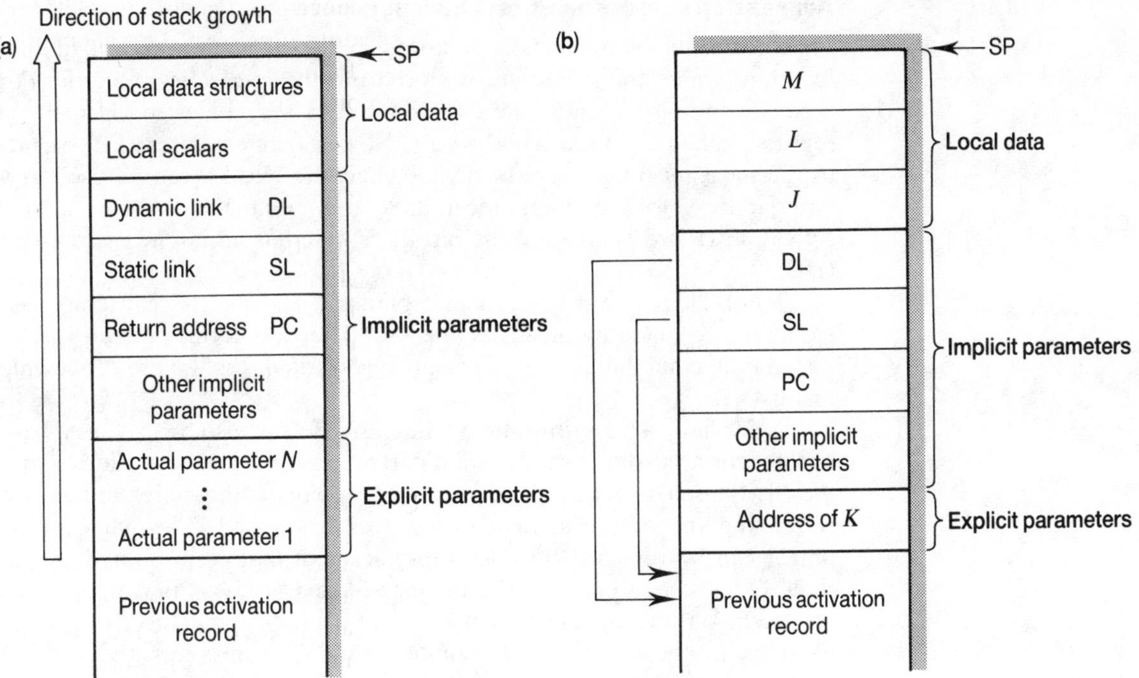

FIGURE 8.3

Structure of activation records.

on, can be saved. Which registers are saved depends on whether they will be changed by the called function.

- **Local data**: This is the area allocated to locally declared scalars and data structures. When a function is called, a new activation record is created on the stack. This can be done as follows. The storage manager has a special pointer – a stack pointer (SP) – which will be used for activation records. When a function is called, a new activation record has to be created. Its length (with the possible exception of local data structures) can be determined at compile time. This length is subtracted from the stack pointer, and the new value of the stack pointer points to the new activation record. When the function returns, the activation record is deallocated by adding its length to the stack pointer. Note that, traditionally, the stack grows towards lower addresses. In Figure 8.3(b), the activation record is shown at line **2** of procedure *A*, which has been called at line **8**. Only one explicit parameter is passed (the address of *K*, because *K* is a by reference parameter). The return address (the value of the saved PC) will be the address of line **3**. The DL and SL point to the activation record of program *Main*. The local variables *J*, *L* and *M* are stored on top of the stack.

Addressing objects in an activation record

The local data of a function is stored in the activation record of that function, while non-local data is stored in other activation records. For accessing non-local data, the SL or the DL may be used. Usually, a register, called the **local name base** (**LNB**) or **frame pointer** (**FP**), points to the most recently created activation record. The FP can be used as a base address for accessing local data and parameters. When a new activation record is created, the old FP is saved as an implicit parameter (DL).

For languages with dynamic binding, accesses to constants and variables are made by means of the DL. The DLs form a linked list, so that the dynamic binding of constants and variables is done by following this list.

For languages with static binding, the FP can also be used as a base register for accessing local data and parameters. To access non-local data, the SL is used to load a base register to point to the activation record containing the non-local data object to be accessed. The name of an object can be replaced by a **level-displacement pair**, represented by the tuple (L, D). L represents the number of lexical levels that have to be retraced from the current lexical level (which corresponds to the number of steps in the chain of SL pointers) and D represents the relative displacement of the object in the activation record. Both of these values can be determined at compile time.

For the binding of parameters, a special pointer similar to the frame pointer is sometimes used. Such a pointer, usually called the **argument pointer** (**AP**), points to the first explicit parameter of the explicit parameter block (see Figure 8.3(a)). This parameter block may be part of the activation record (as has been assumed thus far) but may also be located anywhere in memory. The latter may be of value in FORTRAN which allows the allocation of all data objects at compile time so that parameters do not have to be pushed on to the stack (which is very time consuming). Upon a call, the AP of the current activation record is saved on the stack as an implicit parameter.

8.2.3 The ALGOL run-time model

In order to describe the ALGOL run-time model, we will use the Pascal program presented at the beginning of this chapter because Pascal is an ALGOL-like language. Figure 8.4 shows the stack with the activation records of the program *Main*, procedure *B* and function *C* of that program (line **5**).

The run-time addressing of local scalars, non-local variables, parameters, local data structures and return values is as follows:

(1) **Local scalars**: At first sight, the obvious thing to do would be to use the stack pointer 'SP' as a base register for the addressing of local

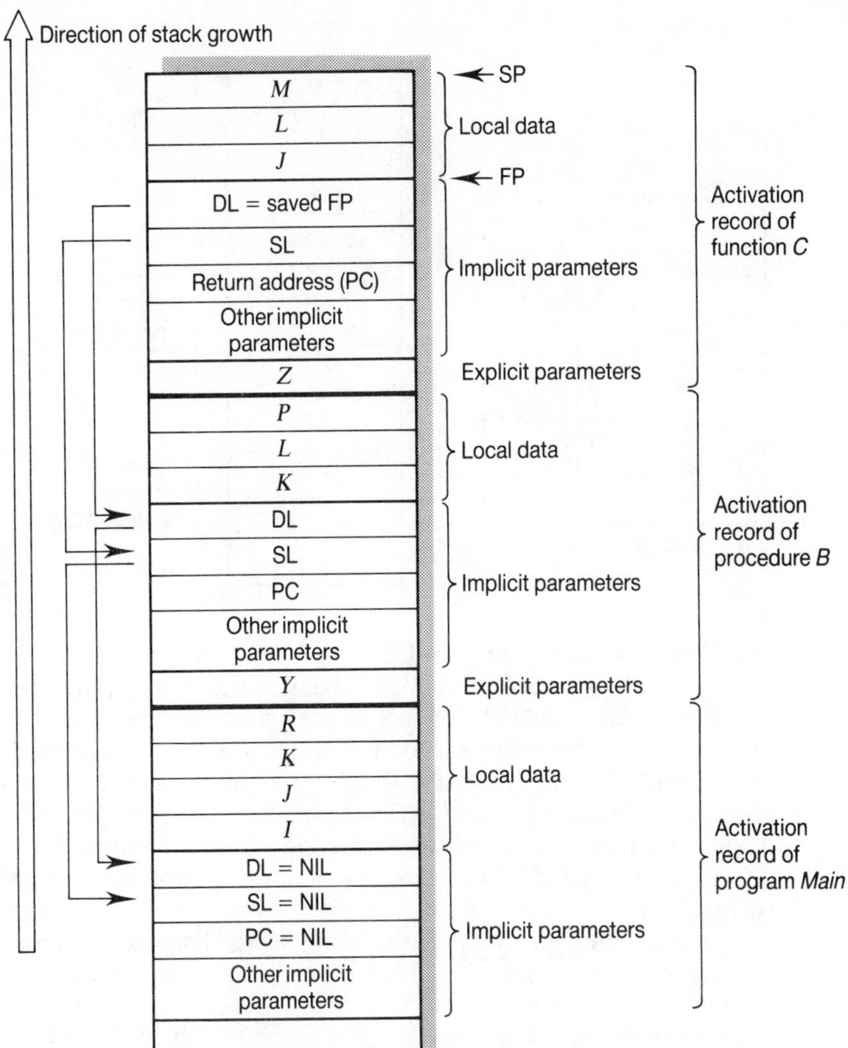

FIGURE 8.4

Stack layout of program *Main* (line **5**).

scalars. The main problem with this is that often the stack is used within the function itself (for example, during expression evaluation). This makes addressing local scalars more difficult, because the displacement relative to the SP is not the same from statement to statement, which makes object programs hard to understand. When local data structures are allowed to be dynamic in size (for example, the ALGOL array $A[1 \,..\, N]$), then the displacement cannot be determined at compile time, which makes base-displacement addressing of local scalars relative to the SP impossible. Therefore, the addressing is done by means of a displacement relative to the FP. For instance, for local variable M of function C in Figure 8.4, this displacement is -3.

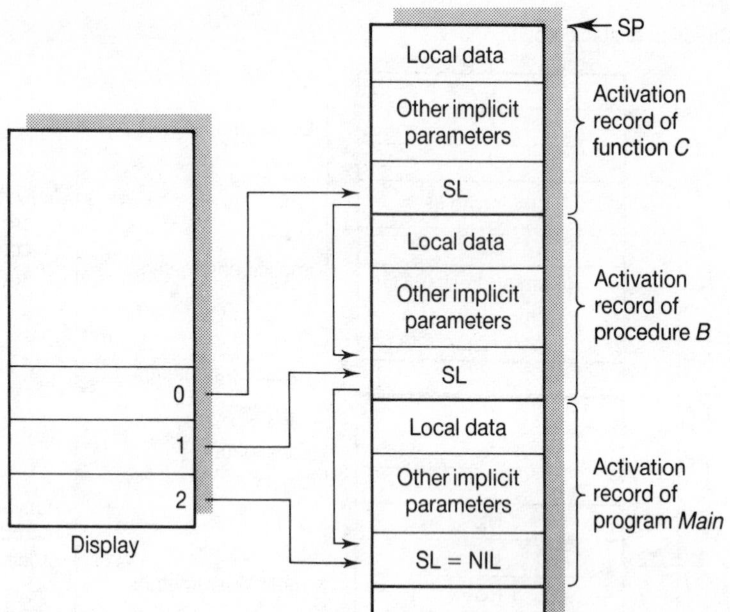

FIGURE 8.5

The display mechanism.

(2) **Non-local variables**: For non-local variables, the addressing is accomplished by means of the SL chain (because ALGOL and Pascal use static binding). To indicate the static nesting level 'L', the value 0 could be used for local data, value 1 for the enclosing block, and so on. Global variable *I* would have a level-displacement value of (2, −1). Two SL pointers must be followed to find the base address of the activation record of *Main*. Then offset −1 must be added to this base address to find the correct address of *I*.

Since the 'pointer chasing' of static links can cause considerable overhead, the **display** was invented. Instead of keeping only the most recent static link in a register, a group of static links is stored. Figure 8.5 illustrates this by using three display registers to access the lexical levels. In this way, a reference to a non-local variable of the current activation record is much faster, since the correct static link is immediately available. In modern languages the display mechanism is less important, since the depth of the static nesting is usually very small (typically 1 to 3). Usually, address registers are used to simulate the display.

(3) **Explicit parameters**: To keep things simple the compiler treats explicit parameters exactly like local variables. The parameters can likewise be referenced by means of a displacement relative to the FP. A special argument pointer (AP) is required if the parameters are not passed via the stack, because then this AP points to the block of parameters somewhere in memory (the AP itself is still saved on the stack).

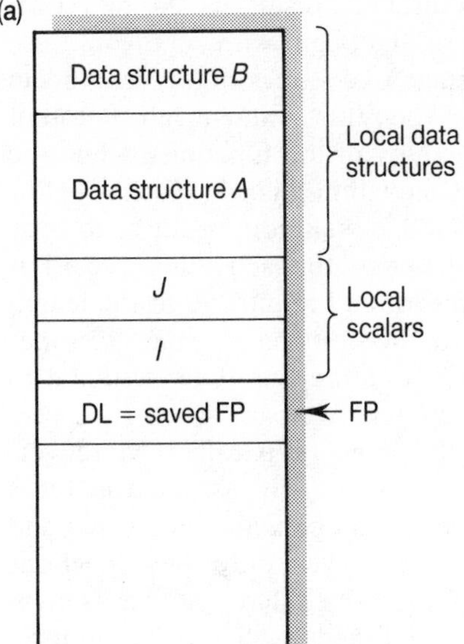

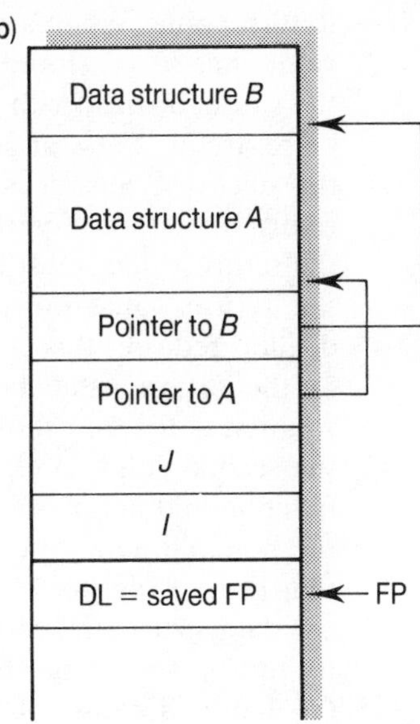

FIGURE 8.6

Addressing of structured data types.

(4) **Local data structures**: With local data structures, storage space for a possibly large number of data elements has to be allocated on the stack. Two different local data structures can be distinguished:

(a) Structured data with a static size: The size of these data structures can be determined at compile time. They can be stored in two ways:

(i) Directly on the stack: In Figure 8.6(a), the integers I and J and integer arrays $A[1\,..\,100]$ and $B[2\,..\,20]$ are shown. The advantage of this method is that the data can be addressed directly using the base-displacement or base-indexed addressing modes using the FP as base register. A disadvantage is that the displacements can be large, occupying extra instruction space and time to fetch.

(ii) Indirectly in the stack, through a pointer (Figure 8.6(b)): In this case, the addressing of an element of a data structure is more complicated. For example, to access $B[X]$, the operand address of $B[X] = (M[(FP) - 4]) - X$.

(b) Structured data with dynamic bounds: This data, for example, integer arrays $A[1\,..\,N]$ and $B[2\,..\,M]$, cannot be addressed directly, because the size of array A is not known at compile time, which means that the begin address of B cannot be determined at compile time. Therefore the indirect method of Figure 8.6(b) has to be used.

(5) **Return value**: When a function returns, its result, called the **return value**, has to be stored somewhere. To begin with, one could use the stack for this, with the advantage that values of any length can be returned. Yet a problem is that the return value is left on top of the stack (because it is the last activity of the function), while the return operation requires that the activation record (which is below the return value) must be deallocated. A solution would be to copy the return value down the stack when the activation record is deallocated, but this creates overhead, and requires that the length of the return value be known to the copying routine. Another solution is to store the return value in a register. This is similar to the second solution except that registers are part of the state of a function and are saved when another function is called. Moreover, the possible data types of the return value are restricted to types that fit in a register – for example, to integers and characters and *not* data structures. Most languages, however, only allow functions to return values of the scalar type, which have a fixed length (probably because of the aforementioned problem). Therefore, many implementations use a register for the return value because this is the fastest method.

8.3 Architectural support of functions

As shown in Section 8.1, one of the most important constructs in modern high-level programming languages is the function mechanism. Computer architectures should, therefore, provide support for this mechanism. Several issues concerning architectural support for functions are covered in the following subsections: parameter passing, call mechanisms, return address location, state saving and restoring, reservation of space for local data and returning storage space. Before looking at these issues, the subject of who has to provide the space to store the activation record will be discussed.

Space to store the activation record can be provided by the calling function, the called function or the system, via the storage manager. The maximum amount of storage space that can be provided by the calling or called function is limited, because that space is part of its own, local space. The system, however, can provide any amount of space up to the limits of the memory subsystem.

The way the space required for the activation record is provided has an effect on the **reusability** of a function. Functions that change themselves can only be used once, and are thus not reusable. As a rule, functions are required to be reusable, because otherwise, for every call, a new copy of the called function (and of its data) would have to be made.

Functions can be reusable in any of the following ways: serially reusable, re-entrant or recursive.

Serially reusable functions can only have one activation at a time. This will be the case when the called function delivers the storage space for the activation record. The next activation can start only when the previous one has finished.

Functions are called **re-entrant** if they are defined such that they can be activated by two or more calling functions simultaneously. This type of function may not change itself and requires a separate space for each activation. This space is provided by either the calling function or by the system.

A **recursive** function is not only re-entrant, but can also call itself, either directly or indirectly through one or more other functions. Just as for re-entrant functions, these functions may not change themselves and every call requires a separate space for its activation record, which has to be provided by the system.

Thus, when the system provides the space for the activation record, re-entrancy and recursion are possible. Therefore, most architectures are designed so that memory allocation is performed by the system.

8.3.1 Parameter passing

The following places can be used for passing parameters:

- **The stack**: In this case, the parameters are pushed on to the stack before the function call is executed. The parameters are addressed as data, local to the called function. This method is very flexible and allows for re-entrancy and recursion.
- **A parameter list**: With this method, a pointer is passed (usually in a register, the AP), which points to the block where the parameters are stored. For languages without recursion, this method has the advantage that only a single parameter, namely the pointer, must be passed.
- **In registers**: The parameters are loaded into registers (or, as is often the case, are already present in registers). These registers can be used by both the calling and the called function. By value parameters as well as by reference parameters can be passed this way (for by reference parameters, the register-indirect addressing mode is needed). The advantage of this method is its speed. A disadvantage is that the number of parameters cannot exceed the number of available registers (as an escape, the stack or a parameter list can be used when, for example, the number of parameters is too large). Usually, however, the number of parameters is rather small, typically from 1–4.

Using the stack for passing parameters is most flexible: it automatically allows for recursion and does not put a limit on the number of parameters. It therefore makes it easy for compilers. The advantage of passing parameters in registers is increased execution speed, but this is at the expense of compiler complexity, because of register allocation issues and the provision of an escape.

8.3.2 Call mechanisms

As function calls occur frequently, many architectures support two types of calls:

(1) **Subroutine call**: These calls are usually used to call routines that do not require their own environment (their own activation record). When they use the environment of the calling function, they cannot be recursive. A typical example of a routine that requires only a simple call is a multiply routine: its storage space is limited and recursion is not required. The MC68020 (Motorola, 1985) supports the subroutine call via the JSR/BSR instructions (Example 8.2). Because of their simplicity, they can be executed very quickly.

(2) **Function call**: These calls are used when the called function requires its own environment, and so are more complex. Most older architectures supported, for reasons of simplicity, only the simple subroutine call; the more complex function call was simulated. Architectures such as the MC68020 do have a function call instruction which is also used to support modules (Section 8.7).

□□EXAMPLE 8.2

The MC68020 has a JSR (Jump to Subroutine) and a BSR (Branch to Subroutine) instruction (Figure 8.7). Both instructions push the return address on to the stack. Program execution then continues at the effective address specified in the instruction. In the BSR instruction, the destination address is not determined by an effective address operand, but by an 8-, 16- or 32-bit displacement, similar to the conditional branch instructions (see Figure 7.7). Very short subroutine call instructions are possible this way. In the JSR instructions, a general operand is used to specify the effective address of the called subroutine. The return address is restored with the complementary RTS (Return from Subroutine) instruction. This zero-operand instruction pops the return address off the stack into the PC register.

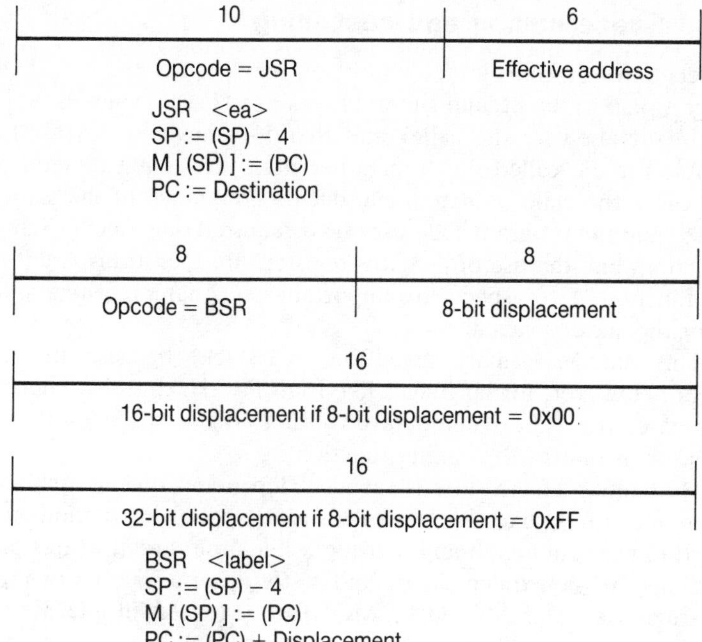

FIGURE 8.7
MC68020 JSR and BSR instructions.

8.3.3 Return address location

After the called function has been executed, the calling function or program should continue from the point where the call was made. Therefore, the called function must hold information about the point to which it must return. This can be done as follows:

- **In a register**: With this method, the return address is automatically stored in a register. This is a common solution for register-oriented architectures, because the call fits the instruction format of arithmetic and logical operations. These operations specify a register operand, which is then used to specify the return address, and a memory operand, which is then used to specify the subroutine address. The advantage is that read-only code is possible.

- **On the stack**: A call instruction that pushes the old PC on to the stack has the advantage of making recursive functions possible, provided parameters and local data are pushed on to the stack too. This is used by the JSR and BSR instructions of Example 8.2.

8.3.4 State saving and restoring

The execution of a subroutine or function may require the use of certain resources, such as the SP and general registers. These resources may have been already used by the caller and therefore have to be saved. It is preferable for the called function rather than the calling function to do this, because the called function can decide how much of the state must be saved, and the program code for this is required only once. Changes in the function, like the use of an extra register, are then transparent to the calling function. Two aspects are important here, namely *where* and *how much* of the state is saved.

The state is usually saved on the stack, because this allows recursion. However, for languages like FORTRAN, this is not necessary. In this case, the state can be saved either in the space of the called function or in that of the calling function.

How much of the state is saved is dependent on the architecture. Some architectures, like the MC68020, have special instructions to save and restore the contents of any register, while other architectures provide instructions for the explicit saving and restoring of a number of registers or all registers. The MC68020, MOVEM (Move Multiple Registers) instruction (see Example 6.2) has a mask in which every bit specifies a register, so any number of registers can be pushed on to the stack in one instruction. All registers and other parts of the state that have been saved must be restored when the called function returns. For the registers, this is done, if possible, by an MOVEM instruction in the opposite direction, or else by a series of POP instructions.

8.3.5 Reservation of space for local data

For function calls that require an activation record to be created, space for local data has to be reserved. Traditional instructions to support FPs and to reserve storage for local data are the LINK instructions (see Example 8.3) and its complement, the UNLNK instruction (described in Example 8.5).

□□EXAMPLE 8.3

Figure 8.8(a) shows the MC68020 LINK (Link and Allocate) instruction. Figure 8.8(b) shows its operation, which consists of the following steps:

- Save the current FP (specified to be the register An) on the stack.
- Create a new FP by copying the current value of the stack pointer into register An.

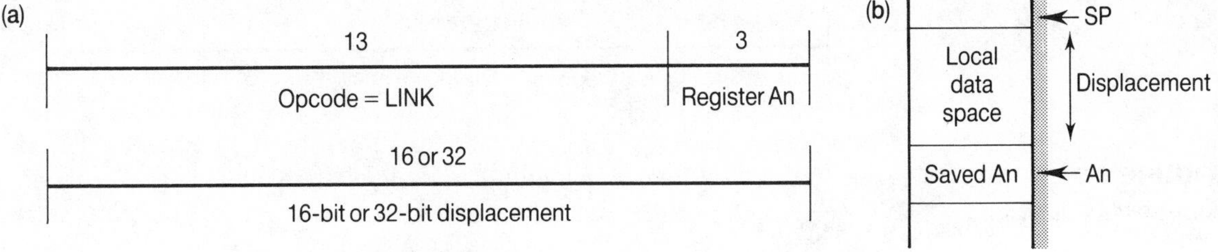


```
LINK   An, #<displacement>
SP := (SP) – 4
M [ (SP) ] := (An)
An := (SP)
SP := (SP) + Displacement
```

FIGURE 8.8

MC68020 LINK instruction.

- Reserve space on the stack by incrementing the SP. The size of the space to be reserved is specified in a negative 16- or 32-bit displacement, given as an argument of the instruction.

8.3.6 Returning storage space

When the called function returns, the storage space used for its activation record can be deallocated. In the case of a subroutine call, no activation record may have been created, but the parameters and local data still may have been placed on the stack. These parameters can be removed simply by adjusting the SP by means of adding a constant to it. This is done by one of the common arithmetic instructions (ADD #8, SP), or by a special return instruction. The MC68020 provides additional support by means of the RTD instruction (Example 8.4).

□□EXAMPLE 8.4

The MC68020 RTD (Return and Deallocate Parameters) instruction is a combination of an RTS instruction (see Example 8.2) and an instruction to adjust the stack in order to deallocate the storage space used for parameters. Functions with a variable number of parameters (most languages do not allow such constructs), or with local data structures, are not supported by the RTD instruction. The assembler syntax is RTD #<displacement>. The operation of RTD is as follows:

```
PC := (M[(SP)])
SP := (SP) + 4 + Displacement
```

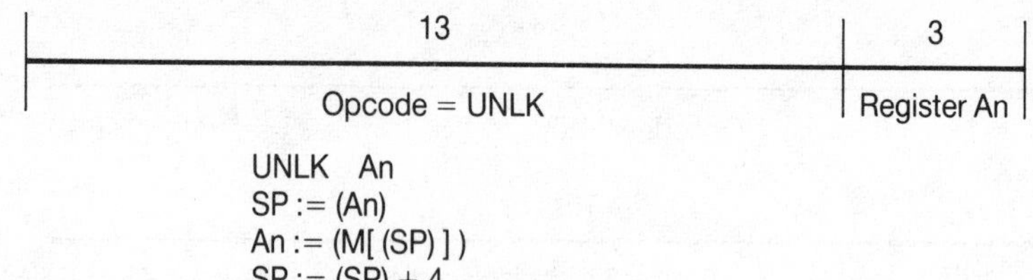


```
UNLK An
SP := (An)
An := (M[ (SP) ] )
SP := (SP) + 4
```

FIGURE 8.9
MC68020 UNLK instruction.

When a LINK instruction has been used to create a new environment for a function, an UNLK instruction can be used to unwind its actions (Example 8.5).

□□EXAMPLE 8.5

The UNLK (Unlink) instruction of the MC68020 (Figure 8.9) unwinds the actions of the MC68020 LINK instruction by copying the current FP (specified by An) to the SP and popping the old frame pointer from the stack (see also Figure 8.8(b)).

8.4 Function support by the MC68020

The support that commercial processors give to functions is described here using the MC68020 as an example. This support will be described in terms of the following aspects:

(1) Parameter passing.
(2) State saving and restoring.
(3) Reservation of space for local data.
(4) Returning storage space.
(5) Call mechanisms and return address location.

This order is slightly different from that of the preceding section because subroutine and function call instructions sometimes incorporate some of the other aspects in one instruction.

(1) **Parameter passing**: When parameters are passed via the stack, the following instructions can be used:

```
MOVE  par, -(SP)    ;For by value parameters
PEA   par           ;For by reference parameters (push
                    ;effective address)
```

The instruction PEA (Push Effective Address) is shown in Figure 8.10(a). It pushes the address of the operand, which is a long word,

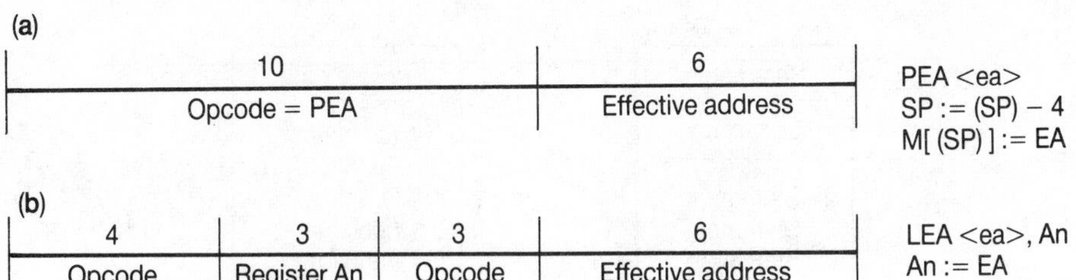

FIGURE 8.10

The MC68020 effective address instructions. (a) PEA (Push Effective Address). (b) LEA (Load Effective Address).

on the stack. When the effective address specifies immediate data or a Dn or An register, an illegal instruction trap will be generated. When parameters are passed via registers, the following constructions can be used:

```
MOVE  par, Dn     ;For by value parameters
LEA   par, An     ;For by reference parameters
```

The operation of the LEA (Load Effective Address) instruction (shown in Figure 8.10(b)) loads the address of the source operand into the address register An.

(2) **State saving and restoring**: The MOVEM instruction can be used to push/pop multiple registers on/off the stack (see Example 6.2).

(3) **Reservation of space for local data**: The LINK instruction can be used for this (see Example 8.3).

(4) **Returning storage space**: The RTD and UNLK instructions support this (see Examples 8.4 and 8.5).

(5) **Call mechanism and return address specification**: The MC68020 has the JSR and BSR subroutine call instructions, which specify the memory location of the called subroutine and push the return address on the stack (see Example 8.2). The RTS instruction hands control back to the calling function.

8.5 Modules

One of the methods used to control the complexity of a large program is modularization; that is, the division of a program into a number of independent modules. When this is done, each module is like a small program that can be implemented independently of the other modules. Each module can be debugged, understood and maintained independently.

With a large number of functions, it is desirable to group related functions and data together, and treat them as one object. Just as a

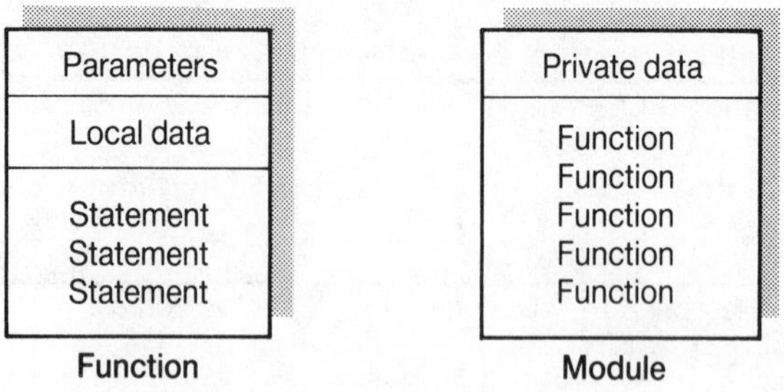

Parameters
Local data
Statement Statement Statement

Function

Private data
Function Function Function Function Function

Module

FIGURE 8.11

Functions and modules.

function is intended to collect and encapsulate a group of related statements and data, a module is intended to collect and encapsulate a group of related functions and data (Figure 8.11).

The term 'module' has been introduced in several programming languages under a number of different names, such as a module in Modula-2, a segment in ALGOL 68 and a package in Ada. A module not only provides facilities for 'bundling' program constructs (constants, types, variables and functions) but also to separate the properties of that module into a **public part** and a **private part**. The public part specifies the object, type and function names, which are accessible from outside. The private part contains the body of the module, which may consist of local data and functions. It is internal to the module and is hidden from the external world.

It is ensured that no function outside the module can change the data or use the functions of the module, if the module does not allow this. When functions or data are made accessible to other modules, they are **exported** (exported symbols) by the module that has declared (owns) them. On the other hand, a module can import functions and data (imported symbols) that have been exported by other modules.

8.6 Architectural support of modules

The code that is generated for a program written in a language that supports the module concept will not differ much from the code generated for a similar program written in a language without modules. The subroutine and function mechanisms used for function support can also be used for modules. Nevertheless, loading and linking a program consisting of modules is more complicated and architectures could provide the following support:

- **External address independence**: The code within a module should be independent of the addresses of the imported data and code; that is, the module need not be changed if the external addresses of the module are changed. This can be done by providing special tables, called **function descriptors**, to describe the import symbols of other modules. Consequently, when the addresses of imported data and code change, only the function descriptors have to be changed, while the code of the module remains unaffected. As a result, a module can even be stored in read-only memory (ROM) and used by other modules that have no fixed location.

- **Linking of modules**: The main problem with module support is that the modules must be linked to each other to form a complete program. Thus, the compiler (or a special linkage editor) must generate link modules that contain sufficient information to allow linking to other link modules, in order to create the final program. To enable this, a link module must contain a list of all imported symbols and a list of all exported symbols. A linkage editor takes a list of these modules and connects the exported symbols of a module to the imported symbols of other modules with the same name. It also checks to see whether the types of the linked symbols agree.
- **State saving/restoring**: When a function calls functions in other modules, it must first save the old environment, and then reload the new environment. This operation can be supported by special instructions that can save/restore the state, which is part of the environment.

8.7 Module support by the MC68020

The MC68020 support for modules will be described in this section on two levels. The first level gives a programming example in Pascal and its corresponding MC68020 assembler version. The second level shows the details of the module support of the MC68020. It describes the call and return instructions together with their run-time model.

8.7.1 Module programming example

The following program shows a rather simple Pascal program that adds the value of *S* to the by reference parameter *A*:

```
procedure Inc (var A : integer; S : integer);
var Nwa : integer;
begin
  Nwa := A + S;
  A := Nwa;
end;
```

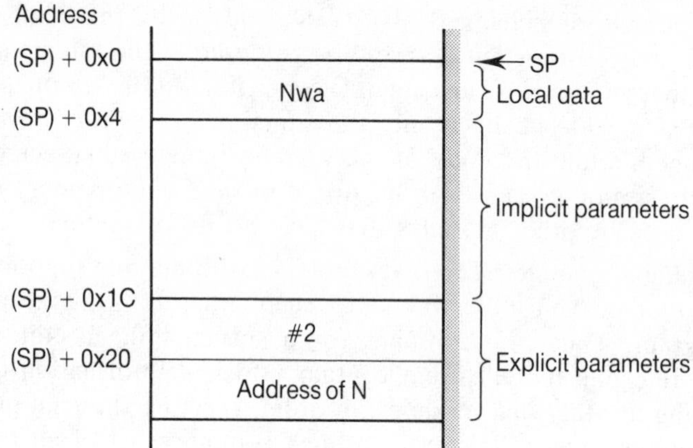

FIGURE 8.12

Activation record for *Inc*(*N*, 2)

The code generated for this program using the module support of the MC68020 is as follows. Figure 8.12 shows the activation record created as a consequence of the call. The first part of the code shows the call *Inc*(*N*, 2) together with the way it is translated: the parameters are passed via the stack and the call is effectuated by using the MC68020 CALLM instruction which has an operand to specify the number of bytes required by the parameters. Details of this instruction are given in Section 8.7.2.

The second part consists of the code generated for the body of the procedure *Inc*. It consists of the following three components (for details, see Section 8.7.2):

(1) The function descriptor of *Inc*: The precise format of a function descriptor is shown in Figure 8.13(d). This descriptor has a control word which is 0, indicating that no special facilities, such as parameter passing via an argument pointer, are required. The second word of the descriptor contains a pointer which points to the function entry word of the function *Inc*. The third word, which is 0, indicates that this function does not have global data.

(2) The function entry word: This word precedes the code for the body of the function. It specifies that no global data area pointer is needed, because the function does not have any global data.

(3) The code for the procedure body of *Inc*: Because of the simplicity of the function, the generated code is trivial. To understand the addressing modes, the reader is referred to Table 5.2 and Figure 8.12.

The Pascal procedure call

Inc(*N*, 2);

is translated into:

```
PEA       N              ;Push address of N
MOVE.L    #2, -(SP)      ;Push 2
CALLM     #8, Inc        ;Call Inc with 8 bytes of parameters
```

And the procedure body is translated into:

```
                                         ;1. Function descriptor of 'Inc'
Inc:  defl     0                         ;Control information
      defl     _inc                      ;Function entry word pointer
      defl     0                         ;Function global data pointer

_inc:                                    ;2. Function entry word for 'Inc'
      defw     0xF000                    ;No global data area pointer
                                         ;needed

                                         ;3. Code for procedure body of
                                         ;'Inc'
      SUBQ     #4, SP                    ;Claim work space for local
                                         ;variable 'Nwa'
      MOVE.L   (0x1C, SP), D0            ;Get value of parameter 'S'
      ADD.L    ([0x20, SP], 0, 0), D0    ;Add reference parameter 'A' to it
      MOVE.L   D0, (SP)                  ;Put local variable in Nwa
      MOVE.L   (SP), ([0x20, SP], 0, 0)  ;A := Nwa
      ADDQ     #4, SP                    ;Release local work space
      RTM                                ;Return from module
```

8.7.2 MC68020 module call and return instructions

This section describes the MC68020 CALLM (Call Module) and RTM (Return from Module) instructions, together with the function descriptors and the run-time model they support. To avoid obscuring the concepts, details have been deleted and the terminology used by Motorola has been adapted slightly to allow for consistency throughout the book.

The module support mechanism of the MC68020 is based on the run-time model described in Section 8.2. In addition it uses several descriptors to allow for calling external functions. These descriptors, together with a global view of a module, will be described first, using Figure 8.13. Figure 8.13(a) shows a module that consists of *F* functions. Each function is represented by a function entry word followed by the code for that function. Figure 8.13(c) shows the format of the function

(a) Module code

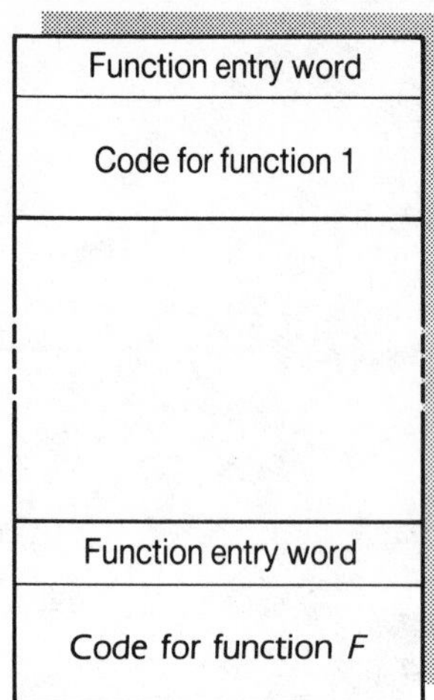

(b) Function descriptor table

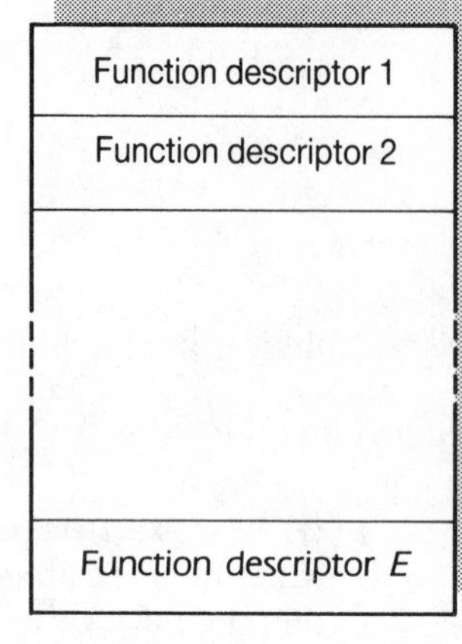

(c) Function entry word

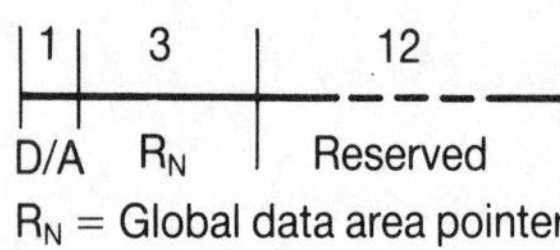

(d) Function descriptor

Function descriptor
Control
Function entry word ptr
Function global data ptr
User defined area

FIGURE 8.13

MC68020 module information.

entry word. It specifies the register used by the corresponding function to point to the global data area of that function.

The *F* functions of the module of Figure 8.13(a) can reference the *E* external functions specified in the function descriptor table (Figure 8.13(b)). These external functions have to be referenced indirectly via a function descriptor. The layout of the function descriptor for function *X* is shown in Figure 8.13(d). It consists of: control information, a function entry word pointer, which points to the function entry word of function *X*, a function global data pointer, which points to the global data of function *X*, and a user-defined area (which is optional).

Calling a function that is not local to the current module can be done with the CALLM instruction (Figure 8.14). The effective address of this instruction specifies the function descriptor of the function 'to be called'. The immediate 'data' value specifies the length (in bytes) of the area occupied by the explicit parameters. The control field of the function descriptor (see Figure 8.13(d)) has a flag which specifies whether parameters should be passed via the stack or via an argument pointer. When passed via the stack, the calling function is responsible for pushing the parameters on to the stack.

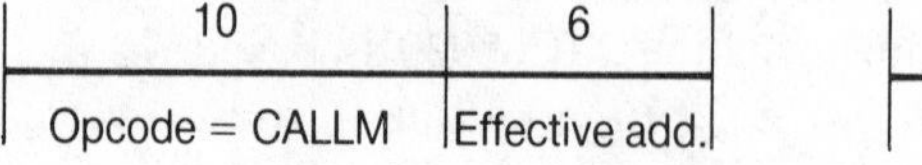

Syntax: CALLM #<data>, <ea>
#<data> describes the length (in bytes) of the area used for explicit parameters
<ea> specifies function descriptor of called function

Operation: Save stack of calling module
Create activation record for called module, specified by the effective address

FIGURE 8.14

MC68020 CALLM instruction.

Figure 8.15 shows the situation where function Fy, which had been called by function Fx, has just called function Fz at line L1 in the code for function Fy. The call instruction at line L1 'CALLM #Pz, Z' specifies the area occupied by the explicit parameters to be '#Pz' and 'Z' the function 'to be called'. Z points to the function descriptor of function Fz (dashed line A in Figure 8.15). Just before the CALLM instruction of Fy at L1, the stack contained the activation record of function Fy and the SP was pointing to location S1. The operation of the CALLM instruction (assuming that the parameters are passed on the stack in the area marked 'explicit parameters for Fz') is as follows:

(1) Set up global data area pointer: The effective address of the CALLM instruction specifies the function descriptor of Fz (dashed line A in Figure 8.15). The second entry of the function descriptor (see Figure 8.13(d)) is the function entry word pointer which points to the function entry word belonging to the code of Fz(B). This entry word (see Figure 8.13(c)) specifies that register Rn should be used as the global data area pointer. This register is set up as follows:

    (a) Push Rn on the stack (C). In Figure 8.15 it is assumed that Rn was used to point to the global data area of the caller Fy.

    (b) Load Rn with the third entry of the function descriptor of Fz, this is the global data area pointer for Fz(D). Rn now points to the global data area of Fz(E).

(2) Save PC: The value of the return address, which is the address of line L2 in the code for function Fy, is pushed on to the stack.

(3) The address of the function descriptor of Fz is saved on the stack (F).

(4) The length of the explicit parameter area of Fz is saved. This length is passed as a parameter by the CALLM instruction (see Figure 8.14).

(5) The condition code register of function Fy is saved.

(6) The control information of the first entry of the function descriptor of Fz (see Figure 8.13(d)) is pushed on to the stack. This completes the operation of the CALLM instruction, after which the code of Fz is executed until the RTM instruction is encountered at line L3 in the code for function Fz.

The execution of the RTM instruction essentially undoes the work of the CALLM instruction (Figure 8.16):

(1) It reloads the condition code register of Fy.

FIGURE 8.15
MC68020 function call.

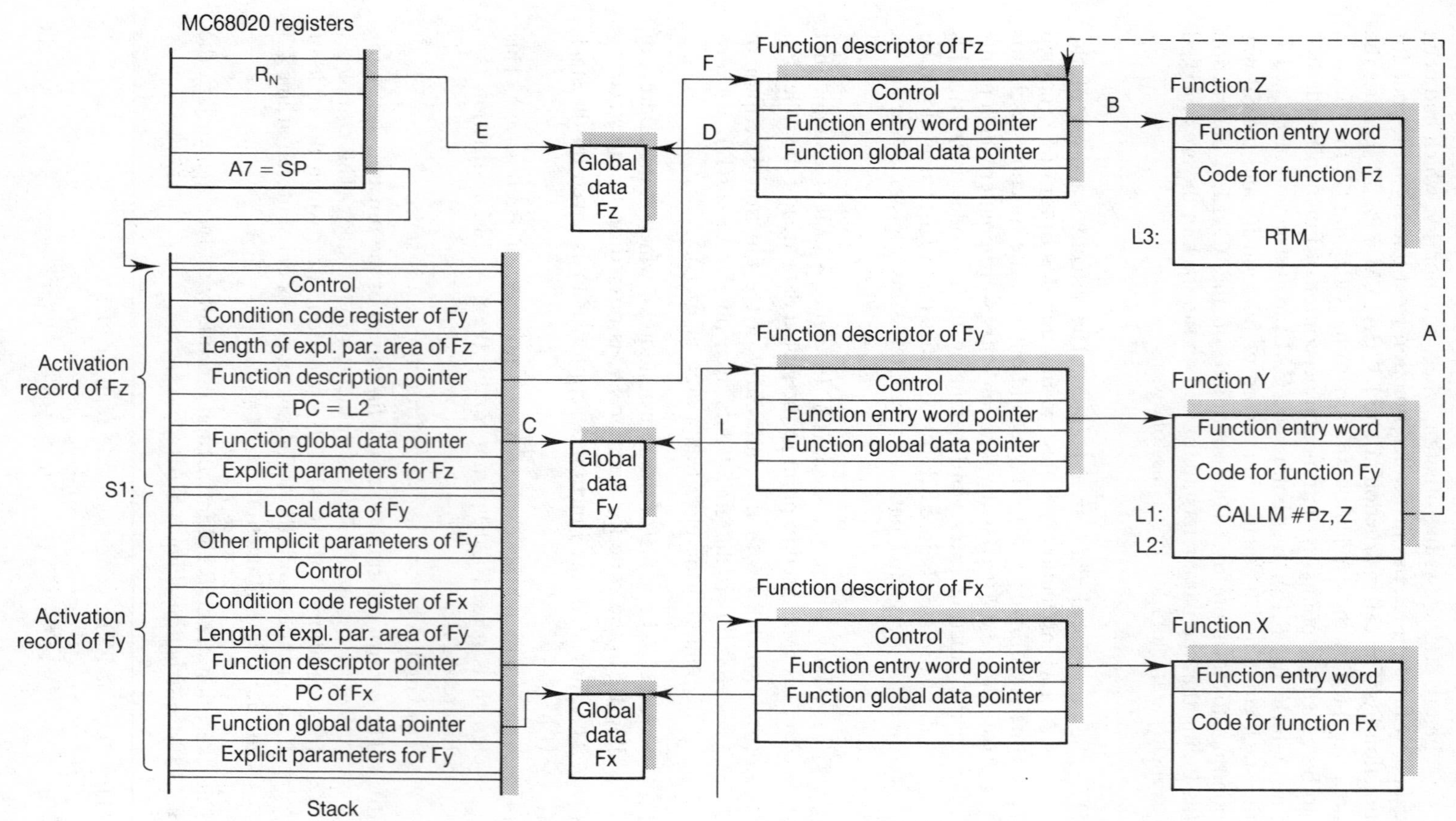

Syntax: RTM Rn
Rn specifies the register to be used to point to the global data area.
Operation: Restore saved state of the module to return to

FIGURE 8.16

MC68020 RTM instruction.

(2) It reloads the PC, which will now point to line L2 in the code for function Fy.

(3) It reloads Rn, specified as an operand of RTM (see Figure 8.16), to point to the global data of Fy.

(4) It deletes the area used for the explicit parameters for Fz. The length of this area was saved on the stack.

After this the RTM instruction has been completed. The SP points to label S1 again and instruction execution continues at line L2 of Fy.

SUMMARY

- The hierarchy in a program, in terms of levels of abstraction, consists of the following levels: module, function, instruction and machine cycle.
- Objects in a program may not be accessible everywhere. The scope of an object is that part of the program where the object is accessible. Shadowing means that a nested program defines an object with an already existing name, which makes the existing object inaccessible.
- Parameters can be passed by reference or by value.
- The binding mechanism used to bind actual parameters to formal parameters is usually based on positional correspondence. The actual parameters are either bound to a reference or a value.
- The local environment of a function contains the locally declared objects. References to objects that are not locally declared are called non-local references.
- Binding can be done before the program is executed (static or lexical binding) or during execution time (dynamic binding).
- A run-time model describes the structure of the environment required for the execution of functions. For ALGOL-like languages, this environment consists of a set of stack-based activation records.
- An activation record contains all the information required to support the execution of a function. It consists of explicit parameters (specified by the user), implicit parameters (required by the system) and local data.
- The implicit parameters may contain: a static link, which points to the activation record of the lexically enclosing program and is used for lexical addressing; a dynamic link, which points to the activation record of the calling program; the return address; and other implicit parameters such as registers to be saved.
- Parameters can be passed via the stack, a parameter list or via registers. The latter is the fastest but most difficult for the compiler.
- The architectural support for functions consists of the subroutine mechanism, when the function to be performed is simple and does not require a complete activation record. In addition, it may consist of a function call mechanism, which is more complex due to the partial support for allocating and deallocating activation records.
- Return addresses can be best saved in a register or on the stack, since this allows for re-entrant and recursive functions, which can be located in read-only memory.
- State saving and restoring can be best done by the called function, which knows how much should be saved/restored.
- The space required by an activation record can be best supplied by the system, to allow for re-entrancy and recursion.
- The addressing of local data and parameters can be done using base addressing, where the frame pointer should be used to contain the base address.

- The MC68020 has a LINK and UNLK instruction to support function calls and returns. It has a PEA and a LEA instruction to support passing by reference parameters, and an MOVEM instruction for saving/restoring registers.
- Modules make a program more manageable because they allow for independent development and compilation, and for information hiding.
- Objects that are allowed to be accessed by other modules are exported by the 'parent' module. Objects from other modules, required by a particular module, are imported.
- The public part of a module is visible outside the module, while the private part is only visible within the module.
- Access to functions in other modules is obtained via function descriptors. They allow for a level of indirection such that modules can be compiled separately and linked afterwards.
- The MC68020 has a CALLM and an RTM instruction to support the module concept.

EXERCISES

8.1 Which levels of abstraction can be recognized in a program?

8.2 What are the reasons for using functions?

8.3 Why is it important to provide architectural support for functions?

8.4 What is local data, non-local data and global data?

8.5 What is the most common way of passing a return value and why?

8.6 What is static binding?

8.7 What is an activation record and which elements does it consist of?

8.8 What is a run-time model?

8.9 What is the purpose of a static link and a dynamic link?

8.10 What is the purpose of a frame pointer? Does the run-time model for Pascal (which has data structures with static bounds) require a frame pointer?

8.11 What is the purpose of an argument pointer? Does the run-time model for Pascal require an argument pointer?

8.12 Which way of providing storage space for activation records is most flexible and why?

8.13 What is the most efficient place to pass parameters? What is the most flexible way to pass parameters?

8.14 What is the advantage of the MC68020 BSR instruction as compared to the JSR instruction?

8.15 Why is the specification of the return address in a memory location not used by the MC68020 architecture? Where is the return address stored in the MC68020 architecture?

8.16 Should the calling or the called function do the state saving/restoring? Which support does the MC68020 architecture have for this?

8.17 Which functions are performed by the MC68020 LINK instruction?

8.18 What is the purpose of the MC68020 PEA instruction? Why does PEA not have to specify a data type (such as byte, word or long word)?

8.19 Which MC68020 instructions support the module concept?

8.20 What is the purpose of a function descriptor. What does it consist of and where is it located?

8.21 How can a function in one module specify the address of a function in another module?

References

Knuth, D. E. (1971). An empirical study of Fortran programs. *Software Practice and Experience*, **1**(2), 105–33.

Motorola (1985). *MC68020, 32-bit Microprocessor User's Manual*. Prentice Hall Incorporated: Englewood Cliffs, NJ.

Shimasaki, M. *et al.* (1980). An analysis of Pascal programs in compiler writing. *Software Practice and Experience*, **10**(2), 149–57.

PART THREE

THE OPERATING SYSTEM INTERFACE

The operating system interface is that part of the architecture of interest only to the operating system designer. It consists of the architectural constructs that support operating system functions, such as process synchronization, I/O, memory management and exception handling. These constructs are used by the operating system and are not of interest, and usually not available, to the compiler designer.

Rather than cover all these subjects in one chapter, a chapter has been devoted to each subject, which can be read and studied in isolation. Sections 9.1 and 9.2 contain an overview of the complete area, showing how everything fits together.

9 Operating Systems

When one cannot find peace within oneself, it does not make sense to look for it elsewhere.
– La Rochefoucauld

The operating system presents the user with the equivalent of an extended or virtual machine which is much easier to program than the underlying architecture. The purpose of this virtual machine is to shield higher machine levels from detailed operations, such as those required for I/O, and to provide an orderly and controlled allocation of processor time, memory space and I/O devices.

In this chapter, only those functions of an operating system that require architectural support (for example, process synchronization) are discussed; the other functions (for example, file handling) are only mentioned to make the picture complete.

As with the use of high-level languages, operating systems introduce overhead. The aim of this chapter is to familiarize the reader with the basic mechanisms and present architectural alternatives to reduce this overhead.

The chapter begins by discussing operating system functions and various types of operating systems, followed by a model for dealing with parallelism – the process model. The protection of processes against undesired effects from other processes is the subject of the next section. This is followed by a discussion of the synchronization of processes, using shared data or resources, and process switching. The last section is devoted to interrupt handling.

9.1 Operating system functions and types

9.1.1 Operating system functions

Broadly speaking, the operating system performs two types of basically unrelated functions (Peterson, 1985): **user functions** and **system functions**.

User functions

These functions provide the user with an environment (virtual machine) for executing programs. The specific user functions will differ from one operating system to another; however, some common function classes can be identified:

- **Program control**: A user should be able to manipulate programs and data within the computer system; for example, the compilation and execution of a certain program, with a particular set of data values. The user is therefore presented with a command language, which allows him to control the virtual machine.
- **I/O operations**: Because the I/O functions, as supported at the architecture level (see Figure 2.2, interface I1) may be complicated and hard to use, the operating system provides a virtual machine with I/O operations that are simpler, more powerful and user friendly.
- **File system manipulation**: A file system may be used for the long-term storage of programs and data. The operating system allows the user to access and manipulate the stored information by symbolic names, rather than by its physical location on the storage medium (mostly tape or disk storage).

System functions

A number of system functions can be identified:

- **Memory management**: If the virtual machine is provided with a different (mostly larger) address space than the size of the physical memory of the underlying real machine, one of the operating system functions is to manage this virtual memory.
- **Protection**: Programs should be guaranteed a level of privacy and non-interference, while being able to communicate at the same time. Therefore, the interaction between user programs, and between user programs and the operating system program, should be controlled and guarded.

- **Resource allocation and scheduling**: When several programs are running concurrently, resources (such as CPU time, memory and I/O devices) must be allocated to each of them, to prevent conflicts. Furthermore, scheduling should be done to achieve optimal utilization of those resources.
- **Accounting**: The operating system should keep track of how much of certain computer resources a program uses, to charge the corresponding account.

9.1.2 Operating system types

General-purpose operating systems can be classified into serial batch, multiprogramming and time-sharing systems (Toy, 1986).

The **serial batch** system was the first general-purpose operating system, primarily designed to schedule input and output. Programs were read from a card reader, executed and the output data was written to a card punch or a printer. This operation was repeated for every program, without any overlap. Later versions allowed for some overlap by performing the following operations concurrently:

- Read programs from card reader to disk or drum.
- Read program from disk or drum, execute program and perform output to disk or drum.
- Write output data from disk or drum to card punch or printer.

This enabled the long card reader input and card punch or printer output time to be substituted with the shorter disk or drum read/write times.

This method of overlap, called **spooling**, still only executes one program at a time: from the initial reading of the program in memory (called **loading**) until final completion. Although spooling allows for the overlap of the very slow I/O devices, such as card readers and punches, disk access times are not overlapped.

Multiprogramming was introduced to allow for this overlap. When the CPU has to wait for some I/O operation (this may be a disk access or any other I/O operation), it switches to a different program which is not blocked due to I/O. This way a higher degree of CPU utilization can be obtained, because all I/O operations can be done in overlap, provided that enough programs can be resident in main memory such that at least one program is always ready to be executed.

Time sharing is a form of multiprogramming whereby a user can interact with a program (by means of a terminal) while it is being executed. This is accomplished by executing every user program for a short time period, after which another user program is executed. In this way, each user appears to be the sole user of the system. This interaction allows the user to have more direct control over a program. For example, data and/or program errors can be reacted to immediately, thereby saving precious user time.

Time sharing became of interest when the capacity of the CPU, main memory and peripherals was adequate to guarantee a reasonable short response time for multiple users. Time sharing, therefore, can be seen as a method for using both hardware (through multiprogramming) and human resources more efficiently.

Looking at the historical development of operating system types, it can be seen that this places increasing demands on the functionality of the operating system, in terms of resource allocation, scheduling and protection.

9.2 The process model

Modern computers can perform several tasks at the same time. For example, a time-sharing system can communicate with the user, by doing terminal I/O, while at the same time reading from or writing to disk. In the case of multiprogramming or time sharing, the CPU also has to switch from program to program several times per second. Because of the high execution speed of current CPUs, switching between programs and executing them for a short time gives the user the idea that those programs are executed in parallel; this is a form of **virtual parallelism**. The major task of the operating system is to control these virtual parallel activities, which is very complicated. Over the years, operating system designers have developed a model, called the **process model**, to deal with these complexities of parallelism.

9.2.1 Definition of processes

The process model is a structured way of describing the activities of an operating system (used, for example, in the UNIX operating system). All the software, including the operating system, is organized into a number of programs that can be executed in parallel. Each of these programs, when activated, forms a process. This means that processes are either in some active state or they can be removed from the system.

Conceptually, every process can be run on a separate processor. In practice, however, multiprogramming is used, meaning that multiple processes share a single processor. Consequently, scheduling must be performed by the operating system to determine when to stop executing one process and service a different one.

Operating systems based on the process model provide a way of creating and discarding processes. Initially, a single process starts

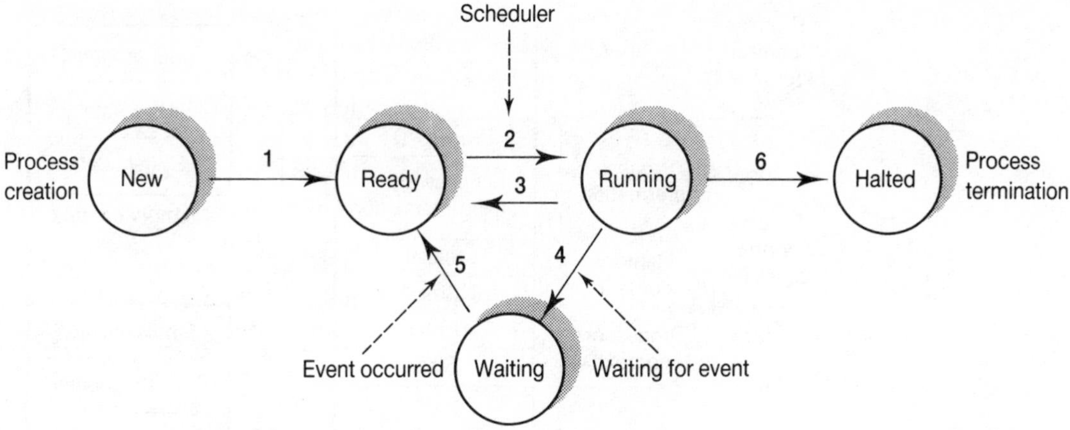

FIGURE 9.1
Process state diagram.

executing. This initial process may continue execution by itself, or may create new, independent, processes by means of a system call (see Section 9.5). When a process creates a new one, the original process (the *parent* process) may continue to execute or may be suspended, while the new process (the *child* process) starts executing concurrently, without any effect on one another, even when they happen to be executing the same piece of program code. This makes the process notion different from the usual notion of a program.

9.2.2 Process states

During execution, the level of activity of a process, called its **state**, changes. The state of a process is defined by its current activity. Process execution consists of an alternating sequence of CPU and I/O activities, beginning and ending with a CPU activity. Five process states and six state transitions can be distinguished as shown in Figure 9.1. Some operating systems include other states, such as a suspended state, used to temporarily stop a process (Comer, 1984).

9.2.3 Process context

The **context** of a process can be defined as the information needed to completely specify its current status. This includes all the information that has to be saved when a process leaves the running state and has to be restored on entering the running state. The process context information can be divided into the following parts (Figure 9.2), depending on when it has to be resident:

- **Process control block (PCB)**: This contains information that resides in main memory for the duration of the existence of the process (states New, Waiting, Ready and Running). The information

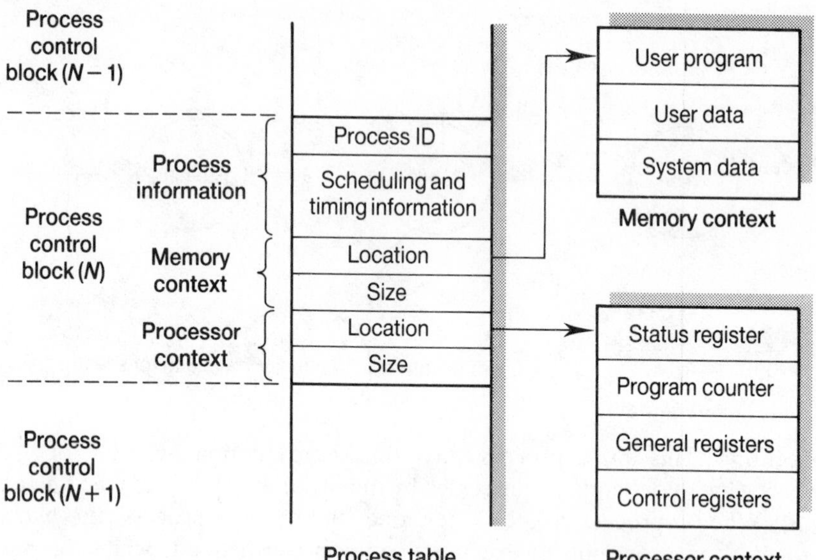

FIGURE 9.2
Process context.

stored in the PCB is required by the operating system for process management. This also applies to processes that are on disk, because these processes can receive events from other processes, which may cause the state of the process to change. The PCBs of all processes in the system are typically stored in a large table, called the **process table (PT)**. Each PCB has to contain at least the following information:

(a) Process identification number (process ID).

(b) Scheduling and timing information, which includes the state and priority of the process and how long it has been in this state.

(c) Location and size of the memory context and the processor context of the process (either in memory or on disk), which allows for memory allocation and loading of the process context when it is scheduled for execution.

- **Memory context**: This is the program and data parts of the process context. This information only has to be resident in the memory when the process is in the running state or in the ready state, to allow transition 2 to be very fast.
- **Processor context**: This is the part of the process context that is stored in the registers of the processor. These registers are an integral part of the CPU, allowing high-speed processing. Most CPUs, therefore, only have one set of such registers. For most

computers, the processor context consists of four parts:

(a) **Status register** (**SR**).

(b) **Program counter** (**PC**).

(c) **General registers** (accumulator and index registers).

(d) **Control registers** (special processor registers that control address translation and protection).

□□EXAMPLE 9.1

The processor context of the MC68020 is shown in Figure A.1. In addition to the SR and the PC, the processor context of the MC68020 consists of eight data registers (D0–D7) and eight address registers (A0–A7). Address register A7 is implicitly designated as stack pointer (SP). Because the MC68020 does not provide memory management support, the processor context does not require an area for memory management control registers. Memory management is left to off-processor hardware, implementable as a co-processor. Those memory management and co-processor registers may also be saved as an additional part of the processor context, however.

9.2.4 Process levels

Looking at the collection of processes forming an operating system, one may wish to structure this collection to allow for a better understanding. A commonly used structuring criterion is the **usage relationship**, whereby a process that uses (or depends on the results of) another process is placed on a hierarchically higher level. Similar processes are placed at the same level. Such a structured representation of a computer system is shown in Figure 9.3. Each level is built on top of the previous levels, which means that the services of the lower levels are available to processes executing at higher levels. Four process levels are distinguished:

(1) **User processes**: These perform the execution of the user programs, using the services of the supervisor processes. Because user processes are not of importance to the subject matter of this chapter, they will not be discussed any further.

(2) **Supervisor processes**: These perform the less time-critical functions of the operating system, such as file management, memory management and scheduling. Whenever time-critical functions have to be performed, the corresponding I/O handling process is activated.

L3	User process	User process	User process	User processes
L2	Booting process	Memory management process	File-handling process	Supervisor processes
L1	Disk process	Terminal process	Clock process	I/O handling processes
L0	Exception handling processes			Exception handling processes

FIGURE 9.3

Process levels in a computer system.

(3) **I/O handling processes**: These perform time-critical functions. They typically respond to interrupts and perform device driver functions, consisting of low-level I/O operations.

(4) **Exception handling processes**: These perform actions to maintain system integrity and allow for some degree of fault tolerance. Errors and exceptions detected during the execution of processes at higher levels are handled at this level. (Chapter 12 is devoted to exception handling.)

The operating system performs many functions, each of which may be performed by one or more processes (at levels L2, L1 and L0 of Figure 9.3). The most important supervisor functions are: process management, I/O handling and memory management.

Process management

The process management function consists of a collection of processes that can be found at several of the levels of Figure 9.3. It performs the following tasks:

- Creation and updating of process data structures.
- Process creation and deletion.
- Process protection (see Section 9.3).
- Process synchronization (see Section 9.4).
- Process scheduling.
- Process switching (see Section 9.5).

I/O handling

I/O handling, such as the handling of disks, terminals or the clock, should be part of the supervisor functions for the following reasons:

- The hardware of most I/O devices requires complex software to control and use them. The operating system hides these details in routines called **device drivers**, through which user processes can transfer data and control the devices.
- The operating system should provide the user with a consistent, uniform and flexible interface to all devices, hiding all device dependencies. This allows users to write programs that reference devices by name (for example, through a filing system) and perform high-level operations without any specific knowledge about the device.
- Because devices may be shared by several processes, they must be protected and allocated by the operating system, to provide a safe and fair access to them.

Chapter 11 is dedicated to the architectural support of I/O handling.

Memory management

Beside I/O devices, main memory is another important resource that the operating system must manage. Memory management keeps track of the location and size of available memory, allocates it to requesting processes and recovers it when necessary. Computer systems often provide a virtual memory space to every process. Therefore, the operating system must divide the real memory among those processes wanting to use it.

A well-defined memory management mechanism offers the operating system the possibility of dividing memory in such a way that the hardware protects the memory allocated to one process against accesses from other processes, while on the other hand controlled sharing of memory space between processes is made possible. Memory management is further discussed in Chapter 10.

9.3 Process protection

As stated before, a large number of processes (both user and supervisor) can be present in a computer system. Without some form of protection, system integrity cannot be guaranteed, since a user process could, for instance, have access to scheduling information, thereby preventing other processes from being executed. Protection of all processes (whether user or supervisor) is therefore required and should take care of the following:

- **Security**: The prevention of system crashes due to unintended or malicious actions or operations.
- **Privacy**: Preventing unauthorized users to access data and programs that should not be visible to them.

The issue of process protection is complicated by the fact that processes are not run in isolation; many processes perform functions for other processes, thereby requiring some form of communication. This requirement for communication demands some form of bypass of the protection mechanism. Communication can be implemented either by reference (called sharing) or by value (called message passing).

One method of protection, **prevention**, guarantees that a user, intentionally or unintentionally, cannot generate operations violating security and privacy requirements. This can be done at the high-level language level (at level L4 of Figure 2.2). A second method is based on **detection and resolution**: detect the undesired operations and nullify them. This must be done at run time by special provisions in the architecture of the computer (at level L1 of Figure 2.2).

9.3.1 Protection at the language level

The Burroughs B6000 series of computers provide protection at the language level (Burroughs, 1969). All programs are written in an ALGOL-like high-level language, which is secure in terms of operations, memory use and addressing (due to the absence of variables of the access type, such as pointers, see Section 3.4). Thus, processes are secure because the language does not contain any insecure constructs. This also guarantees privacy, because memory management is done for each object. The only security aspect that cannot be guaranteed at the language level (at compile time) is that array subscripts are within range. Therefore, the addressing mechanism of the B6000 is supported by hardware run-time checks (via descriptors), which guarantee that dynamically generated addresses (such as those needed for array subscription) stay within the bounds of the object. Because the high-level language used has no pointers or other insecure constructs, and the use of an assembly language is not possible, because it is not available to the user, sufficient protection can be guaranteed, provided that the computer hardware functions correctly.

Although protection by prevention is a very elegant method, it cannot be used in general, because many languages do have constructs that are deemed necessary but insecure – for example, pointers in Pascal.

9.3.2 Protection at the architectural level

Protection at the architectural level is performed by detecting illegal operations at run time and preventing them from being executed. The illegality may be caused by an illegal component in any of the three spaces of an instruction: opcode, operand and data space. Special hardware has to be available to detect illegal components in any of these spaces. When detected, the execution of the instruction to which this component belongs is prevented and the occurrence of this is signalled to the exception handler via an interrupt-like mechanism called **exception** (see Section 9.6).

Protection via opcode space

The execution of some instructions should only be allowed to operating system processes, and not to user processes, because they may violate protection requirements. These instructions are called **privileged instructions**. Examples of privileged instructions are interrupt and exception handling instructions, process-switching instructions, memory management instructions and I/O instructions. To determine when privileged instructions are allowed, computers must be able to operate in (at least) two modes: **supervisor mode** and **user mode**. Instructions that can only be executed in the supervisor mode are the privileged instructions. (Note that the fact that the instruction is privileged is determined by the opcode, rather than by the operand specification.) All other instructions can be executed in both modes. Usually, the current mode is indicated by a bit in the program status word (status register).

□□EXAMPLE 9.2

The MC68020 (Motorola, 1985) has a user and a supervisor mode, indicated by bit 13 of the SR (see Figure A.2). If S = 1, the system is in the supervisor mode, so execution of privileged instructions is allowed; if S = 0, the system is in the user mode. This bit further determines which of the stack pointers (SSP and USP) is designated by address register A7.

The privileged instructions of the MC68020 are listed in Table A.9. Four instructions (ANDI, ORI, EORI, #data,SR and MOVE Src,SR) are used to manipulate the system byte of the SR and are privileged, because otherwise the user is able to set the S bit. The MOVE USP,An and MOVE An, USP instructions allow the operating system to save the stack used by a user process and set up a new stack. These instructions are privileged in order to support the virtual machine monitor concept (Appendix B). The RESET instruction is used to reset all external devices, while STOP is used to stop the processor. Both instructions should not be executable by user mode processes for obvious reasons. The RTE (Return from Exception) instruction restores the PC and SR

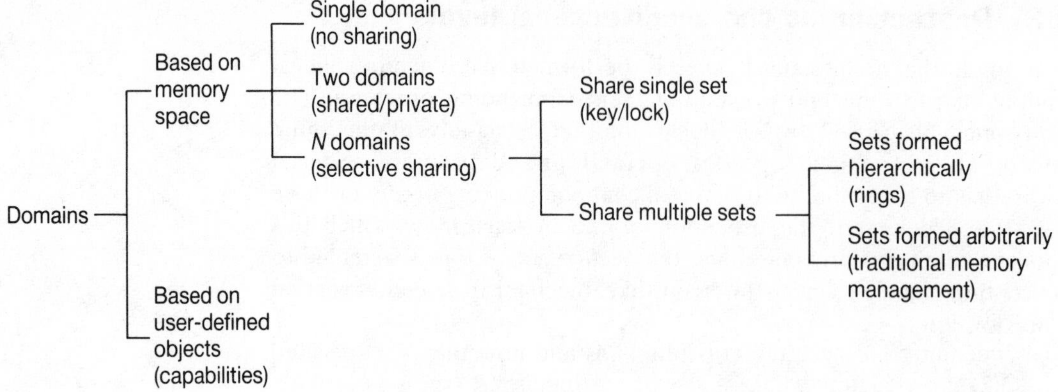

FIGURE 9.4
Memory protection alternatives.

from the stack after the handling of an exception. A user can push a pseudo stack frame with bit S = 1. This could be loaded in the SR by the RTE instruction. This undesirable switch to supervisor mode is prohibited by making the RTE a privileged instruction.

Protection via operand space

An operand can be illegal because it is a privileged operand, accessed in the user mode (for example, the specification of the SR as an instruction operand in user mode is illegal), or the operand address is out of domain. The latter may be the case when a subscript is out of bounds or when a pointer variable points to a wrong or a non-existing object. Memory management is the mechanism that has to guarantee the integrity of the operands. It protects a process against unwanted influences from other processes and potentially against itself, if more domains per process exist. A **domain** is the 'object' to be protected. It can consist of an area of memory such as a page or a user-defined object such as an array. Figure 9.4 shows the types of memory protection mechanisms, based on what determines a domain, the number of domains and the shareability of domains. Section 9.3.3 is devoted to the protection of domains based on memory space and Section 9.3.4 to domains based on user-defined objects.

Protection via the data space

Protection via the data space would require every data item to be equipped with a tag field which has to specify the domain the item belongs to. This is not of practical interest because of the memory required for the tag field.

9.3.3 Protection of domains based on memory space

This is the more traditional way of memory protection. The domains are specified in terms of address ranges, forming subspaces of the total address space. These domains have no direct relationship with the objects used or operated on by the processes. Groups of program and data objects are put in one domain, which makes the protection mechanism more coarse, because only groups of objects, rather than individual objects, can be protected or shared. The advantage of this scheme lies in its implementation, because fewer domains have to exist, requiring less hardware support.

Depending on the number of domains and how they are specified, the following protection schemes can be distinguished (see Figure 9.4):

- **Single domain (private)**: The simplest form of protection is to disallow the sharing of programs and data. Every process is given a single (virtual) memory address space, which cannot be referenced by any other process, so the single domain is always private with respect to the process. This is, of course, not a viable solution when processes need to share programs and data.
- **Two domains (shared/private)**: A slightly more complex protection scheme is to restrict the access of a process to its private domain or a single-shared domain, accessible by *all* processes. Public library routines (for mathematical computations, for example) may be placed in the shared domain. This method is still very crude as only two domains exist, although it does allow for sharing. The disadvantage is that the shared part is accessible by *all* processes.
- ***N* domains (selective sharing)**: This can be done in two ways: sharing a single set or multiple sets of domains.

  (a) Sharing a single set of domains: Assuming *N* domains, process *A* has access to a single set (*Sa*), which consists of an arbitrary number of the *N* domains. Another process *B* may have access to a different set (*Sb*). Sharing means that the intersection of *Sa* and *Sb* is not empty. A well-known implementation of this protection scheme is based on the key/lock mechanism (see Example 9.3). This method provides protection at the set level, because a single set of memory domains is given an identical lock. Although this scheme is more flexible than that of two domains, a process only has access to a single set, because it has only one key, and so does not allow selective sharing. Suppose that process *A* consists of domains *a*1 and *a*2, and process *B* of *b*1 and *b*2, and that process *A* wants to share *b*1. This means that domains *a*1, *a*2 and *b*1 form the set of domains for process *A* with the lock value La. The set of domains for process B consists of $b1$ and $b2$ with the lock value Lb. Because of the sharing requirement $La = Lb$, domain $b1$ can only have a single lock. This allows process A to have access to all domains of B and vice versa. The way to solve this problem is to update the locks between process switches, which is time consuming.

(b) Sharing multiple sets of domains: This protection mechanism allows a process to access several sets of domains. Selective sharing is possible because a separate set of domains is created for sharing with each group of (one or more) other processes. For example, if process A wants to share domain $b1$ with process B, the following sets should be formed: Sa, consisting of $a1$ and $a2$, Sab consisting of $b1$, and Sb consisting of $b2$. Process A will only have access to Sa and Sab, while process B will have access to Sab and Sb. Two implementations, based on the way the sets are formed, can be distinguished:

Hierarchically ordered sets (rings): An example of a protection mechanism based on hierarchically ordered sets is the method of rings. **Rings** are thought to be concentric such that rings with a lower number (which have a higher level of protection) are enclosed by the rings with higher numbers. Each ring is formed by a set of domains. These rings form a protection hierarchy such that a process executing at ring i has access to all domains at ring j if $i \leq j$ (to domains at its own and its outer rings). Access to inner rings is only allowed via a system call-like operation which bypasses the protection mechanism in a controlled way. It uses a special facility called a **gate**. This introduces an extra level of indirection, which enables verification of the access rights, which are defined per gate. In this way, accesses by processes with insufficient privilege can be prevented. A protection mechanism based on rings has been implemented in the iAPx286 (Intel, 1983).

Arbitrary number of sets of domains: This protection mechanism allows each process access to an arbitrary number of sets of domains, specified as part of the processor context via the translation table of the process (see Figure 9.5 and Section 10.4). Some sets may be shared while others may be private. When domains are shared, they are also a member of the set of some other process. Figure 9.5 shows process A with private domains $a1$ and $a2$, and a shared domain ab, and process B with a private domain $b2$ and a

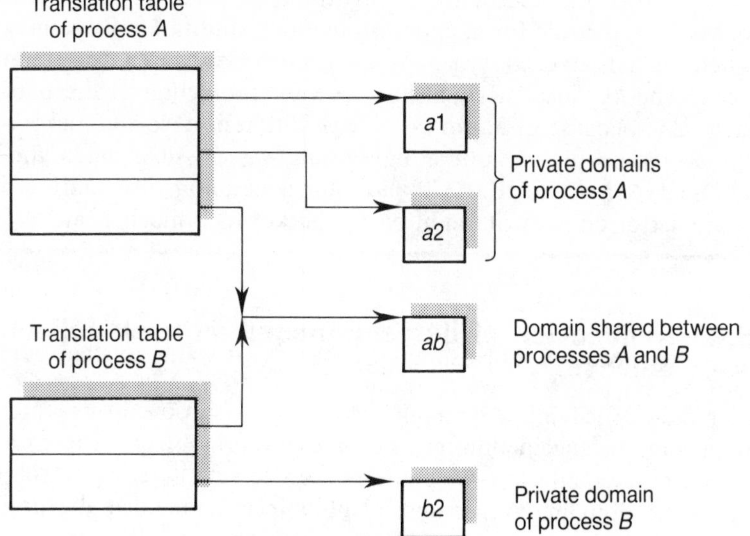

FIGURE 9.5
Sharing of domains using translation tables.

shared domain *ab*. The advantage of this scheme is its flexibility and the possibility of selective sharing. Traditional memory management schemes, based on segmentation (see Chapter 10), support this protection mechanism.

So far, protection mechanisms that either allow or disallow access to a certain domain have been discussed. However, the permission to access a certain domain may be more refined in terms of the operation to be performed – for example, allowing only an operand read or write operation. This kind of restriction, called **access right**, is part of the protection mechanism and is included in, say, segment and page tables of memory management systems (see Chapter 10).

□□EXAMPLE 9.3

Every process in the IBM/360 architecture is given a 4-bit key, stored in the PSW (IBM, 1970). The key identifies the single set of domains belonging to that process. Furthermore, memory is divided into domains of 2 kbytes. A 7-bit tag is associated with every domain, it contains a 4-bit lock, which is compared against the 4-bit key. (A set of domains (*Sa*, for example) is formed by giving the same lock value to each of the 2K memory areas belonging to that set.) On a match, access to that domain is allowed. (A match occurs if the key and lock value are equal or if the key value equals zero; the latter key value is used by the supervisor to allow access to all domains.)

The key/lock mechanism was initially used by the IBM/360 architecture to provide for memory protection. Multitasking systems were designed such that each task was assigned a fixed area (partition) of memory. The key/lock mechanism allows for protection of the partition of each task, because different tasks have different keys and locks, while communication with the operating system was possible when the key value equals zero. The IBM/370 and later generations use sharing of an arbitrary set of domains in addition to the key/lock mechanism.

9.3.4 Protection of domains based on user-defined objects

Rather than specifying a domain in terms of a subspace of memory, a domain could be specified in terms of one or more objects. These objects can be program objects (procedures or processes) and/or data objects. Because the domains are composed of objects defined at the program level, each program can specify its own domains with any level of granularity. A domain may consist of a single variable such that protection and/or sharing to this level of granularity is possible.

The identification of a domain is done via a descriptor object called **capability**. A capability consists of the address of the object and the access rights to that object (for example, read only, execute only). Because capabilities are objects, they can be treated like other objects; for instance, put in some domain and passed as a parameter such that a called process can have access to the domain of the capability. However, operations that modify capabilities are privileged. Corsini (1987) gives a description of an architecture with a protection mechanism based on capabilities. The disadvantage of this, more elegant, scheme is its implementation difficulty: the association of a domain with an address is non-trivial. The memory management schemes of sharing an arbitrary set of domains typically use a page or a segment to represent a domain, and a simple address translation table can be used to associate the domain with the operand address.

9.4 Process synchronization

As already shown, a computer system is composed of many processes. Processes can be executed in parallel (simultaneously) when several processors are available. If only one processor is available, the effect of parallel processing can be simulated by the processor running each process in turn for a short time. In other words, the processor can be shared among several processes. Even when parallel processing is simulated, it is useful to regard each process as having its own dedicated virtual processor. Many difficulties of true parallel processing also arise in the simulated case. These difficulties are illustrated in Example 9.4.

□□EXAMPLE 9.4

Consider the following two processes:

```
process Observer
  repeat
    Observe_an_event;
    Count := Count + 1;
  until false;

process Reporter
  repeat
    Print_count;
    Count := 0;
  until false;
```

The first process, *Observer*, is responsible for observing and counting events. The second process, *Reporter*, occasionally prints reports about the number of events and then clears the event counter. When both processes are executed concurrently, the following situation might occur. Suppose that the reporter just printed 10 and before it can set the count to zero, the observer increments the count to 11 (for example, when the reporter is interrupted and the observer is scheduled next). After that, the reporter is scheduled again and clears the count, meaning that at least one event remains unreported. In general, the reporter may fail to report any number of events because incrementing the variable count may occur between printing the value of count and setting it to zero.

Example 9.4 shows that the results are unpredictable because the processes are executed with unpredictable relative speeds. When the outcome of a computation depends on the relative speeds of processes, a **race condition** is said to exist. Race conditions occur when parallel processes share data or resources, like the variable *Count* in Example 9.4.

The solution to these race conditions is to control the order in which processes operate on shared data or resources. This is called **process synchronization**. A major synchronization problem is the **mutual exclusion** problem. Mutual exclusion guarantees that, at most, one process accesses shared data or resources. Processes accessing shared data or resources typically do this via small sections of program code, called **critical sections**.

When trying to solve the mutual exclusion problem, one must be aware of possible **deadlock** situations. Deadlocks occur when processes are waiting for an event that never takes place. For example, a deadlock may occur in the following situation. Assume two processes *P*1 and *P*2, and two resources *R*1 and *R*2. Further assume that both processes need both resources simultaneously to complete. When *R*1 is allocated to *P*1 and before *P*1 can request *R*2, *R*2 has already been allocated to *P*2; hence, a deadlock situation has occurred because both processes are blocked, waiting for a resource held by the other process. This shows that, although the mutual exclusion requirement avoids race conditions, it is not sufficient to have concurrent processes co-operate correctly and efficiently by using shared data. The following four conditions should hold for a proper solution:

(1) At any moment, there can be at most one process in a given critical section. This is a mutual exclusion requirement.

(2) No assumptions can be made about the relative speeds of the processes, to avoid race conditions.

(3) A process stopped outside a critical section should not block any other process, to avoid deadlocks.

(4) Processes about to enter a critical section should not block each other indefinitely, to avoid starvation. **Starvation** means that some process is never executed because other processes continuously take their turn in an unfair way.

A number of synchronization methods, at hardware, firmware as well as software level, can be utilized to solve the mutual exclusion problem.

9.4.1 Disabling interrupts

The simplest solution to the mutual exclusion problem is for a process to disable all interrupts upon entering its critical section and re-enable them just before leaving it. The processor (in a uniprocessor system) is switched between processes upon an interrupt (for example, from a timer); thus, by disabling further interrupts on entry to a critical section and enabling them on exit, mutual exclusion of the various competing processes can be guaranteed. This way, the operations that access shared variables or resources are made **indivisible** or **atomic**. An operation is indivisible or atomic if its execution cannot be interrupted. Most machine instructions are indivisible (assuming that a single memory reference is indivisible), but high-level language statements are not, because they may be translated into a sequence of machine instructions.

The advantage of solving the mutual exclusion problem by disabling interrupts is its simplicity. However, a number of disadvantages must be mentioned. First, the critical sections must be short, since otherwise interrupts could be lost or I/O devices may not get serviced in time. Second, this method is only suitable for uniprocessor systems, because for multiprocessor systems the disabling of interrupts on one processor does not stop processes on the other processors, so that they may still enter the critical section. One way of avoiding this problem is by designing the multiprocessor system such that only one processor handles all interrupts.

9.4.2 Busy waiting

As an alternative to disabling interrupts, a lock variable could be used to control access to the critical section. The following program shows the use of such a lock variable to simulate a test-and-set operation. The variable Lock controls access to the critical section as follows: if Lock = 0, the critical section may be entered; if Lock = 1, the critical section is blocked.

```
Loop : TST      Lock       ;Note: if Lock = 0 the
                           ;critical section is free
       BNE      Loop       ;Critical section blocked
       ADDQ.B   #1, Lock   ;Occupy critical section
```

The execution of this program could be interrupted – for example, after the execution of the TST instruction. The result would be unpredictable if the interrupting process would be allowed to enter the critical section. To prevent this, the program has to be executed with interrupts disabled as shown below, which is not desirable for reasons discussed in Section 9.4.1.

```
Loop : Disable interrupts
       TST      Lock
       BEQ      Free       ;Critical section may be entered
       Enable interrupts
       BRA      Loop       ;Critical section is blocked
Free : ADDQ.B   #1, Lock   ;Occupy critical section
       Enable interrupts
```

Alternatively, the instruction sequence of the program could be made indivisible. Such an indivisible sequence results in an atomic action because it behaves as a single action to the outside world. Most computers have special instructions to support atomic actions. The following will be discussed: TAS, CAS and the lock meta-instruction.

Test-and-set instruction

The operation of the test-and-set instruction has just been shown. Most current computer architectures have a single instruction to provide for an atomic execution of this operation (Example 9.5).

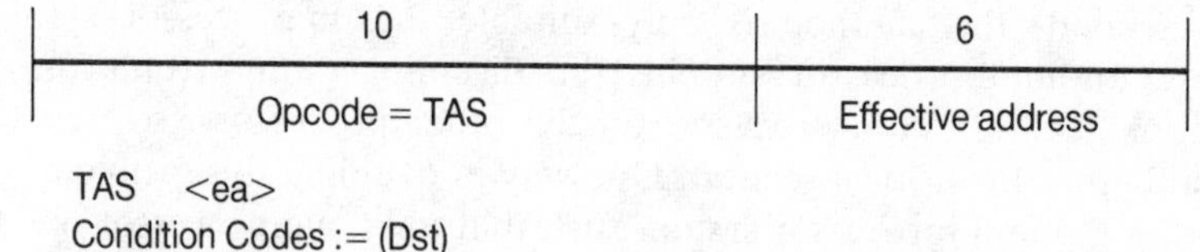

TAS <ea>
Condition Codes := (Dst)
Dst [7] := 1

FIGURE 9.6
MC68020 TAS instruction.

□□EXAMPLE 9.5

The MC68020 (Motorola, 1985) has a TAS (Test and Set) instruction, as shown in Figure 9.6. The byte operand, addressed by the effective address field, is tested, and the high-order bit (bit 7) of the operand is set to 1. The operation is made indivisible by making the instruction uninterruptible and using a read–modify–write memory cycle. During this memory cycle, the path to memory is blocked for other processors (these may be CPUs in a multiprocessing system, DMA channels or I/O processors). TAS may be used as follows to enforce mutual exclusion:

```
Wait : TAS      Lock    ;Test if critical section is free
       BMI      Wait    ;Wait because Lock[7] = 1
       Critical section ;Perform operation which has
                        ;to be serialized
       CLR.B    Lock    ;Free critical section
```

A process repeatedly tests the lock variable via the TAS instruction until it detects that the high-order bit of the lock variable has been reset. TAS sets this high-order bit by means of an indivisible operation, the process enters its critical section and clears the lock variable when it leaves the critical section.

As the processes attempting to enter critical sections are busy accessing and testing the lock variables, this technique is called **busy waiting** or **spin lock** and the processes are said to be **spinning**.

Compare-and-swap instruction

Another instruction used to enforce mutual exclusion is the CAS (Compare and Swap) instruction. The TAS instruction controls access to a critical section based on a Boolean lock variable. This makes TAS a rather simple instruction. The CAS instruction, in contrast, controls access to the critical section via an integer lock variable. The blocking of the critical section is done by an integer value specified in the instruction. This makes CAS more powerful, but also more complex. Example 9.6 shows the MC68020 CAS instruction and how it can be used to simulate TAS. Example 9.7 shows how CAS can be used to increment a common counter, shared by a set of concurrent processes.

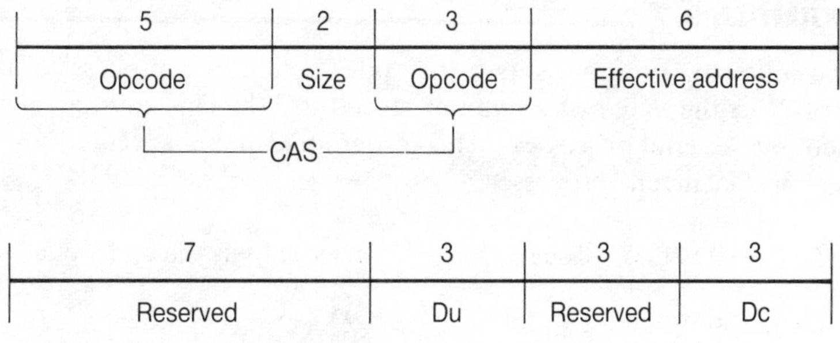


```
CAS    Dc, Du, <ea>
Condition Codes := (Dst) – (Dc)
If Z then Dst := (Du)
     else Dc  := (Dst)
```

FIGURE 9.7

MC68020 CAS instruction.

□□EXAMPLE 9.6

The MC68020 CAS instruction is shown in Figure 9.7. Three operands are specified in this instruction: data registers specify a compare operand (Dc) and an update operand (Du), and an effective address is used to specify the destination operand (Dst). The destination operand, which contains the lock, is compared with the compare operand and, if they are equal, the critical section is occupied by writing the update operand to the destination; otherwise, the compare operand is loaded with the destination operand, such that the blocked process knows the value of the lock. The size field specifies the length of the operands (byte, word or long word). The CAS operation is made indivisible by disallowing interrupts and using a read–modify–write memory cycle. The outcome of the compare operation is indicated in the Z condition code bit. CAS may be used to enforce mutual exclusion by simulating the operation of the TAS instruction, as follows:

```
       MOVEQ  #128, D2          ;Put blocking value in update
                                ;operand in D2, #128 for TAS
Loop : CLR.W   D1               ;Clear compare operand in D1
       CAS.W   D1, D2, Lock
       BNE     Loop             ;Critical section blocked
        Critical section        ;Operation to be serialized
       CLR.W   Lock             ;Free critical section
```

If Lock contains zero, which is the value of the compare operand in D1, the content of the update operand in D2 is stored in the Lock, indicating that this process is entering its critical section. Otherwise, if Lock contains a 1, the process loops back and tries again.

□□EXAMPLE 9.7

The following program shows the code section of a process to add a value of *N* to the value of a counter stored in D1. This counter may be updated by several processes. This program can be executed by any number of concurrent processes.

```
       MOVE.W  Count, D0         ;Get current value of Count
                                 ;in D0
Loop : MOVE.W  D0, D1            ;Make copy of Count
       ADD.W   #N, D1            ;Increment Count by N
       CAS.W   D0, D1, Count     ;If no other process changed
                                 ;the value of Count in the
                                 ;meantime, update it
       BNE     Loop              ;If the value of Count has
                                 ;been changed by another
                                 ;process, try again
```

Some architectures with a CAS instruction, such as the MC68020, also have a CAS2 instruction which is similar in operation but has more operands. CAS2 allows queue manipulation to be done automatically.

LOCK meta-instruction

The Intel 80X86 processor family has a special 1-byte LOCK prefix instruction. This can be used with any other instruction, called the locked instruction (Intel, 1983), by placing it in front of the instruction. This prefix makes the locked instruction indivisible. LOCK may be used to create a test-and-set primitive as shown in the following program:

```
Loop : MOV   AL, 1                ;Move 1 to general register
                                  ;AL
       LOCK  XCHG AL, Lockvar     ;Exchange AL with the lock
                                  ;variable, the critical section
                                  ;will be blocked now because
                                  ;Lockvar = 1
       CMP   AL, 0                ;Test if critical section was
                                  ;free initially, i.e.,
                                  ;Lockvar = 0
       JNE   Loop                 ;Critical section blocked,
                                  ;try again
       Critical section           ;Operation to be serialized
       MOV   Lockvar, 0           ;Free critical section
```

The XCHG instruction of the Intel iAPx286 and later versions implicitly causes a bus lock, thereby eliminating the need for the LOCK prefix for a test-and-set operation.

Table 9.1 Synchronization constructs and implementation primitives.

Concepts	Implementation Primitives
Monitors	Module mechanism
Events	Wait, signal
Semaphores	P and V
Locks	TAS, CAS, LOCK meta-instruction
Disabling	Interrupt enable/disable

9.4.3 High-level synchronization constructs

Until now, mutual exclusion has been implemented using busy waiting. Busy waiting causes a waste of CPU time; even when each process has a CPU dedicated to it, busy waiting may be impractical. The problem is that busy waiting can saturate the path to memory, which can slow down I/O and other CPUs (in the case of a multiprocessing system). Semaphores, introduced by Dijkstra (1956), avoid the busy-waiting problem by suspending (putting the blocked process in the waiting state) and then placing the process in the ready state when the critical section becomes free. They can be implemented using the TAS and/or CAS instructions. Other, higher-level, synchronization constructs, such as events and monitors (Comer, 1984; Toy, 1986), can also be implemented using the TAS and/or CAS instructions. These synchronization constructs show an increasing level of abstraction, where higher-level constructs use the lower-level constructs (Table 9.1). The computer architect should always make a tradeoff as regards the level of abstraction to which the architecture should support the synchronization primitives. In most computer architectures, support goes as far as disabling interrupts and provisions for lock operations.

9.5 Process switching

As stated before, user processes need to co-operate with lower-level processes to accomplish a certain task. Because all processes need to share the same CPU, this CPU must be **switched** between processes. The subject of process switching consists of process switch invocation, which deals with why and when a process switch takes place, and context switching, which deals with what context should be saved when and how.

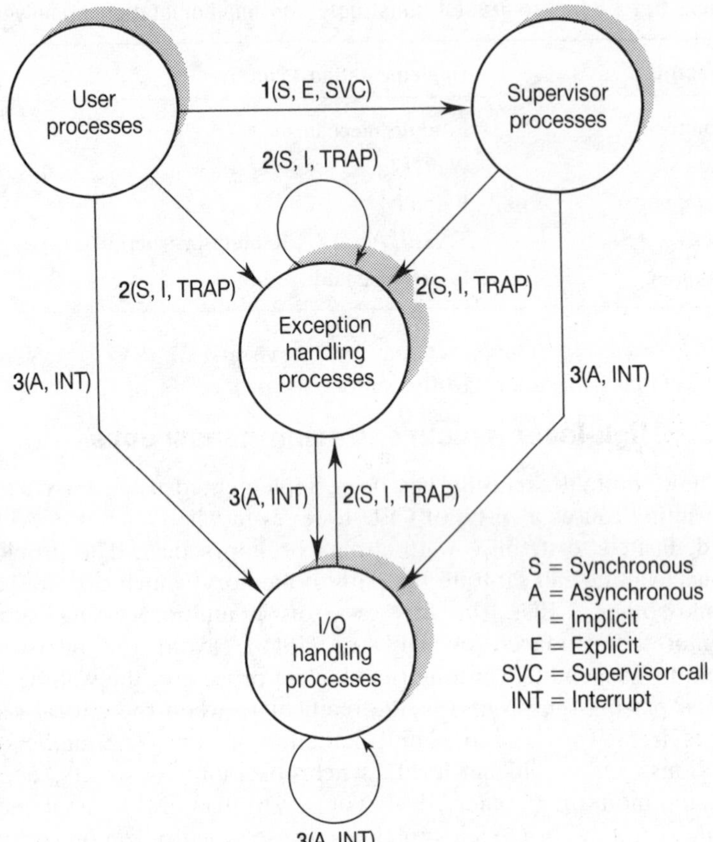

FIGURE 9.8

Process switching.

9.5.1 Process switch invocation

Process switches can be invoked in several ways, determined by the reason for the process switch. In Figure 9.8, switches between the processes of Figure 9.3 are indicated by arrows. The corresponding reverse arrows, indicating a return from the process switch, have been omitted to simplify the figure. Process switching may be done on behalf of the currently executing process or on behalf of another process.

Process switching on behalf of the currently executing process

This occurs when the current process, which is in the running state, needs the services of a lower-level process. This switch is done **synchronously**, which means that the invoked process can be considered to be executed serially with the invoking process. A synchronous exception is reproducible by re-executing the process that raised that exception. The invocation can be done in two ways, explicitly or implicitly.

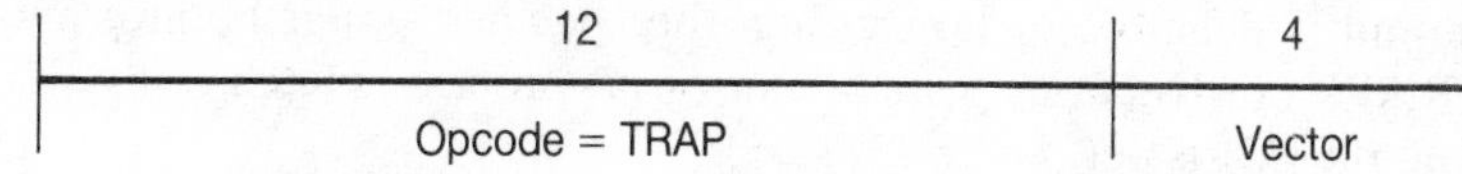


```
TRAP  #<Vector>
SSP := (SSP) – 2        ;  Decrement stack pointer
M[ (SSP) ] := Vector    ;  Save vector #
SSP := (SSP) – 4
M[ (SSP) ] := (PC)      ;  Save PC
SSP := (SSP) – 2
M[ (SSP) ] := (SR)      ;  Save SR
PC := (M[Vector] )      ;  Load PC with start address
```

FIGURE 9.9

MC68020 TRAP instruction.

Explicit invocation This is called a **supervisor call (SVC)**, which is a process switch from a user to the supervisor process (**1** of Figure 9.8). An SVC is issued by a user process when it requires an operating system function to be performed, or to indicate that it is ready (has finished). Most architectures have a special instruction to indicate such a supervisor call. (Subroutine or procedure calls cannot be used, because they allow any memory location to be specified as the entry point of the called routine, which would be insecure.) An advantage of a special supervisor call instruction is that it can include a parameter to indicate which operating system service is required (Example 9.8).

□□EXAMPLE 9.8

The MC68020 supports supervisor calls via the TRAP instruction. (Note that the MC68020 TRAP and TRAPV instructions should not be confused with the trap operation described later.) The TRAP instruction (Figure 9.9) has a 4-bit operand which is used to specify a vector number. The instruction first pushes the vector number, the PC and the SR on to the stack, then the PC is loaded with the start address of the called supervisor routine. This start address is determined by the vector field of the TRAP instruction, which allows 16 different supervisor calls to be implemented.

Implicit invocation This is called a **trap** or an **internal interrupt** (**2** in Figure 9.8), which is a process switch to the exception handler. It is invoked automatically by the hardware of the computer when an unusual or exceptional condition has been detected. Examples of such conditions are data errors (such as overflow, underflow or divide by zero), storage protection violation, undefined or privileged opcodes and stack overflow. Internal interrupts are considered to be **synchronous** process switches, because they transfer control to an exception handling process which is executed on behalf of, and serially with, the invoking process.

In the MC68020, internal interrupts are generated by the DIVU and DIVS instructions if the divisor is zero; by the CHK instruction when its operand is negative or larger than the specified upper bound; and by the TRAPV instruction, which causes a process switch only if the overflow bit (V) is set.

Internal interrupts can also be used to simulate supervisor calls. In this case, an invalid opcode is specified, which automatically causes a switch to an exception handling process. However, this method violates the principle of propriety (see Section 1.2.3).

Process switching on behalf of another process

While the hardware of the CPU is executing a process, other processes (obviously using different hardware) may also be active. These other processes may be I/O processes (disk or terminal I/O) or the clock process. When such other processes require service by a process that has to be run on the CPU, they indicate this via an **external interrupt** request. When this request is honoured, an external interrupt takes place and an I/O handling process is invoked (**3** in Figure 9.8). This is done **asynchronously** with the execution of the process that was interrupted, because the external interrupt was not requested by that process. The process switch may, therefore, occur at any point in time and does not have any relationship with the currently executing process.

Summarizing, process switching may take place because of the following reasons: a supervisor call, an internal interrrupt (also called a trap) and an external interrupt (often called interrupt). The CPU uses only a single hardware mechanism, the interrupt mechanism, to invoke the three classes of process switches, which can all be denoted as interrupts. The operation of the interrupt mechanism is covered in Section 9.6.

9.5.2 Context switching

On every process switch, the process context needs to be switched. This means that the status of the currently executing process must be saved, a new process must be selected and the context of that process must be restored. Context switching should be done fast, since the time spent on it does not benefit user programs. Moreover, external devices often require fast response to their interrupt, so little time should be wasted.

Context switching can be done in many ways (Figure 9.10). If only a single set of hardware resources (for example, processor registers) is available, this has to be shared between different contexts. Upon a context switch, the current values stored in those shared resources must be saved, so that they can be loaded with the values of the new process. On return to the original process, these resources can be restored to their old values. This saving and restoring can be done automatically as part of the context switching operation, or under program control.

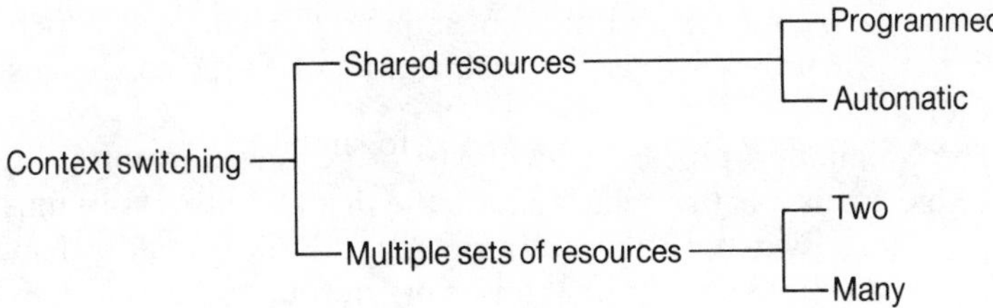

FIGURE 9.10

Context switching alternatives.

An alternative to shared resources is to provide multiple sets of resources, where each set can contain a context. This allows a context switch to consist merely of the selection of a different resource set.

The issue of context switching is discussed in the following sections, special attention being given to the switching of the different parts of the context (see Figure 9.2). It consists of the context switching performed by the interrupt operation, the context switching of memory and stack space, and the context switching of the remainder of the processor context.

Context switching performed by the interrupt operation

Switching between processes is initiated by an interrupt. Figure 9.11 shows the classification of interrupts, as discussed in the previous section, together with the terminology used throughout this book.

Interrupts for process invocation can be compared to subroutine and procedure calls for program invocation. The difference is in the amount of processor context. Procedures are run in the environment of a process; their context therefore is a subset of that of the containing process. The processor context of a procedure consists of the data and address registers of the CPU (and of possible co-processors) together with the program counter. The processor context of a process (see Figure 9.2) includes additionally the processor status word, which specifies the privilege and priority level of the process, as well as the memory management information (stored in the control registers of Figure 9.2), which specifies the memory context and the access information of the process. This determines the information to be saved/restored upon a process switch.

Interrupts, as well as subroutine and procedure calls, do not have to save/restore the complete processor context, because this would make

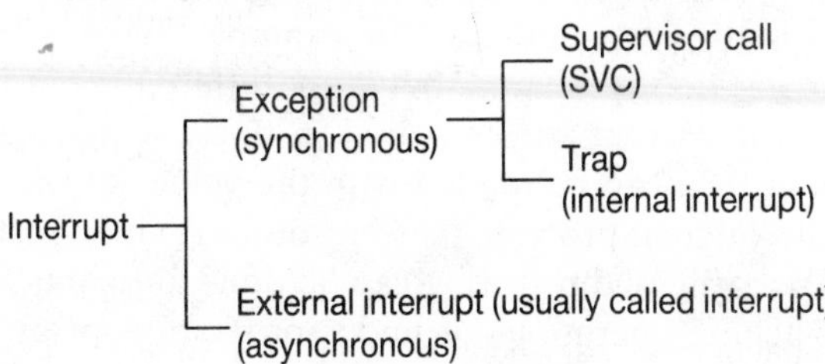

FIGURE 9.11

Interrupt classification.

the operation too complex and time consuming. Certain parts may be just as easily performed by instructions such as MOVEM, as has been shown in Chapter 8.

The minimum processor context to be saved/restored by the interrupt mechanism is that which allows the invoked process to finish the process context switch. The interrupt mechanism should, therefore, save/restore the contents of the following resources in an indivisible operation:

- The status register (because it is a single-shared resource).
- The program counter (because it is a single-shared resource).
- The stack pointer (because each process has its own stack).
- Memory management information (to switch the memory context).

Because the minimum processor context has to be switched as an atomic action, shared registers such as the SR and PC have to be saved automatically; or when multiple register sets are used, the selection of a different set has to be done automatically.

The handling of an interrupt, which means the invocation of a new process, is as follows:

- Save minimum processor context of the current process.
- Load minimum processor context of new process. The value of the SR is typically generated by the interrupt hardware. The value of the PC is obtained from a fixed location in memory, determined by an interrupt vector (IV), which specifies the process to be invoked.

□□EXAMPLE 9.9

The complete MC68020 interrupt operation consists of the following steps, executed as an atomic action (Figure 9.12):

```
;Save minimum processor context in an interrupt stack frame
;Use the MSP (master stack pointer) in case of an exception
;Use the ISP (interrupt stack pointer) in case of an external interrupt

MOVE.W   Extra word, -(SP)     ;The extra word is generated by the
                               ;interrupt hardware to specify the
                               ;stack frame format and the vector
                               ;offset

MOVE.L   PC, -(SP)
MOVE. W  SR, -(SP)

;Load minimum processor context of the new process
```

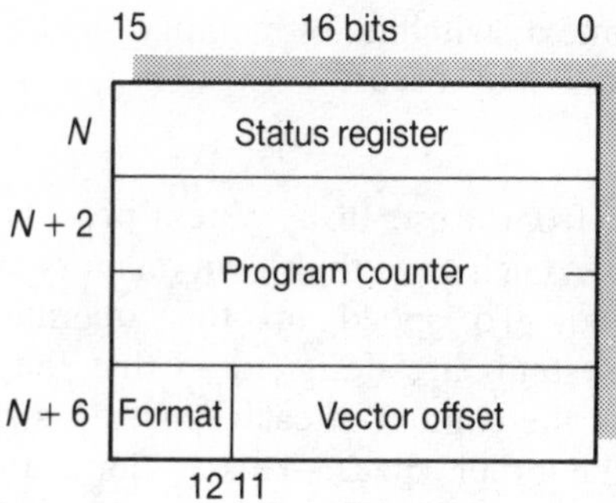

FIGURE 9.12

MC68020 normal interrupt stack frame.

```
MOVE.W   SRinfo, SR        ;The initial contents of the SR of the
                           ;invoked process SRinfo is generated
                           ;by the interrupt hardware
MOVE.L   InitialPC, PC     ;The InitialPC value is taken from M[IV]
```

When a process completes, it issues a return instruction to reinvoke the interrupted process. This privileged instruction restores the saved SR and PC and removes the stack frame. Example 9.10 shows the MC68020 return instruction.

□□EXAMPLE 9.10

The MC68020 RTE (Return from Exception) instruction has all its operands specified implicitly. It restores the SR (which automatically selects the correct set of memory management registers), the PC and pops the stack frame. In this stack frame, the format field determines the size of the stack frame, which is used by the RTE instruction to deallocate the correct number of words from the stack. Figure 9.12 shows the normal interrupt stack frame; other stack frames, such as those created due to an exception, may have a different length.

Context switching of the memory and stack space

Figure 9.8 showed the four classes of processes. From a memory protection point of view, these should be divided into two groups: the user processes and the system processes (formed by the supervisor, I/O and exception handling processes). The user processes consist of user programs which may contain errors or even code whereby one tries to violate the protection mechanism. The system processes, on the other hand, are considered to be trustworthy and well debugged. Therefore, memory management typically deals with two spaces: one for the user process and the other for the system processes. The memory space of the system processes may be further divided into subspaces for each of the system processes.

In terms of context switching of memory management information, the following situations may occur:

- Process switch from a user to a system process: Because user and system processes each have their own memory space, this space has to be switched. To speed up this operation, most memory management systems are designed so that they have two register sets, to contain the context of each space. A switch now means the selection of the other space. This is done under control of the supervisor/user state bit of the SR.
- Process switch from a system to a user process: Two situations can be recognized here. The first is a return from a system process to the user process that invoked the system process. This merely requires that the memory management context of the user space be selected again under control of the supervisor/user state bit of the SR. The other situation occurs when the system process switches to a different user process (because of an I/O wait or a time-out). To do this, a routine is invoked that saves the memory management context of the current user process and restores that of the user process to be switched to. After that, the supervisor/user state bit will automatically select the correct user context.
- Process switches between system processes: Because all system processes have the same memory management context, no special action is required.

Stack spaces are part of the process space. If different stack spaces exist for the user and system processes, the process switch also includes switching of stack spaces. Usually, this consists of selecting the appropriate stack pointer (Example 9.11).

□□EXAMPLE 9.11

The programmer's model of the MC68020 has three stack pointers which are selected under control of the M and S bits of the SR (Figure 9.13). User processes use the user stack pointer (USP). This stack is used only for operations *within* the user process, such as the creation of activation records for subroutines and procedures and for expression evaluation. I/O handling processes use the interrupt stack pointer (ISP). This stack is used for saving interrupt stack frames (due to external interrupts), allowing for nested interrupts. Supervisor and exception handling processes use the master stack pointer (MSP). This stack is used for saving exception stack frames.

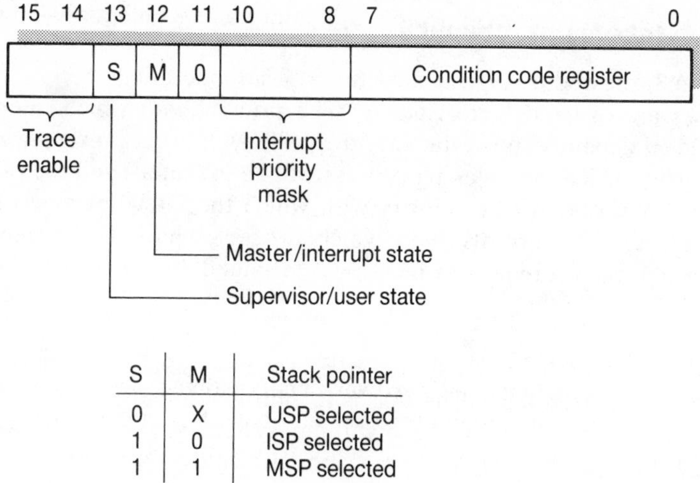

FIGURE 9.13
MC68020 status register.

Context switching of the remainder of the processor context

The minimum processor context has already been saved as part of the interrupt operation. The remainder of the processor context (for example, general-purpose registers, and registers of a numeric co-processor that may also be used by another process) has to be switched. (When registers are dedicated to a certain process, they do not have to be switched, since they are not used by other processes.) This context switching can be done automatically as a result of a process switch, in which case all registers are saved, or under program control by the newly selected process. In the latter case, only registers used by that process need to be saved, by using an MOVEM instruction, for example. The context is usually saved on a stack.

9.6 Interrupt handling

The requirement for process communication has been established. The desire for communication is indicated via an interrupt request; the invocation of this communication is an interrupt. In a computer system, many processes may have an interrupt request pending, since many processes may be executed in parallel. The selection of which interrupt to service requires some form of priority scheme based on the process hierarchy in the system. The moment at which the currently executing process is able to give up control may be restricted, for example, due to critical sections protected by disabling interrupts. Interrupts may be permitted at several points in the execution of an instruction. When the interrupt occurs, the source of the interrupt (the interrupting process) has to be identified.

9.6.1 Interrupt priority

Figure 9.3 showed a logical structure of an operating system where processes are ordered hierarchically. The priority with which interrupts are handled depends on two factors: the priority of process execution (the priority with which the invoking process will be executed) and the priority of process invocation (the priority with which the interrupt operation is taking place). The priority with which processes have to be executed depends on their urgency, which is determined by their function, as follows:

- **Security violations and hardware malfunctions**: These are handled by exception handling processes and have top priority. Only when they complete does it make sense to execute other processes.
- **Critical timing**: When messages from a data communication line are coming in, and interrupts from the communications interface are given on a per character basis, the interrupts should be serviced within a short time, to prevent loss of information.
- **Performance**: A particular user may have high priority for whatever reason. This means that processes running on behalf of this user should have a higher priority. Another reason for giving a higher priority to a process is that it may occupy a large percentage of the system resources, such as main memory, thereby making multiprogramming less optimal.

Example 9.12 shows how the processes of a UNIX system (System V) may be allocated to the interrupt levels of an MC68020 processor.

□□EXAMPLE 9.12

The MC68020 processor has eight priority levels, encoded in the interrupt priority mask, bits 10–8 of the SR (see Figure 9.13). The encoding is such that level 7 represents the highest and level 0 the lowest priority (Table 9.2). Exception and clock handling processes execute at the highest priority level; they are non-maskable because no process with a priority level higher than 7 can exist. Time-critical I/O (such as disk I/O) can be masked, but has a high priority because it has a great influence on the performance of the system. Non-time-critical I/O (such as I/O requests from a buffered printer) has been assigned priority level 4. Levels 3, 2 and 1 can be used by supervisor processes, while user processes run at the lowest priority level.

Table 9.2 Possible priority levels for a UNIX operating system.

Level	Process
7	Exception and clock handling (non-maskable)
6	Time-critical I/O
5	Terminal I/O processes
4	Non-time-critical I/O
3	Not used
2	Not used
1	Not used
0	User processes

When a process is run at some priority level and a request for a process to be run at a higher level is made, it is desirable for this request to be honoured, because of its higher urgency. This means that the servicing of interrupts will be nested, similar to the nesting of subroutine and procedure calls.

The invocation and execution priorities of a process are usually the same, as would be expected. The exception to this is the way traps (see Figure 9.11) are handled in most computers, because usually the number of status bits (in the SR) used to record the reason for the trap (overflow, invalid opcode, parity error, protection violation) is insufficient, and so the interrupt vector is used to distinguish between the different courses. To support a powerful exception handler, and to allow for better diagnostics (to facilitate repair), a precise reporting of the kind of exception, and a large variety of exception classes, is desirable.

An alternative to storing the information in the SR is to use the interrupt vector address to specify the cause of the trap implicitly, which obviously requires many vectors. This necessitates the instruction that caused the trap and the invocation of the trap handling process forming a single atomic action, because if other interrupts are allowed in between, the reason for the trap would be lost. This is accomplished by performing traps (invoking the exception handling process) at the highest priority level, essentially disabling interrupts.

9.6.2 Interrupt permission

Because of the necessity of allocating priorities to interrupts and disabling interrupts for process synchronization purposes, computers should be able to control when interrupts are permitted. Traps are always permitted and they cannot be **masked** (they are non-maskable). The fact that they have the highest invocation priority guarantees that instructions causing a trap and the invocation of the process to handle the trap form an atomic action. Other forms of interrupts may be masked. For example, floating-point underflow may be masked and so prevented from causing a trap, because the user may prefer to continue the computation with the computed result, which is almost zero, rather than invoking a time-consuming exception handling process.

Many peripherals also have an interrupt enable (IE) flag in their control register which determines whether or not interrupts are **disabled** – that is, ignored until a possible later time (see Chapter 11). The simplest priority-based interrupt handling system has two modes in which the CPU can run: with interrupts enabled, meaning that a requested interrupt will be invoked immediately after the completion of the current instruction, and with interrupts disabled, meaning that no interrupt requests are accepted. Normally, the interrupts are enabled.

More flexibility can be obtained by having several modes which are, for example, organized hierarchically, based on a priority structure (see the priority levels of Example 9.12). When the processor executes at a certain priority, the current and all lower levels are disabled, while all higher levels are enabled. An alternative scheme is to enable/disable each mode independently. In this scheme, a bit pattern in an interrupt mask register in the CPU specifies which interrupts are to be accepted. Each mask bit in this register corresponds to a particular interrupt condition or group of conditions, and only those conditions that have their mask bit set are enabled. All other conditions (corresponding to zeros in the mask register) are disabled.

9.6.3 Moment of interruption

Synchronous interrupts occur as a result of the currently executed instruction. Therefore, they can always be handled directly. The only problem is how the instruction is ended in the case of a trap. (A trap is generated due to an exceptional condition.) There are four alternatives:

(1) The instruction is completed, which means that all instruction actions are performed before the trap occurs. This is the case, for example, if overflow is detected.

(2) The instruction is suppressed; that is, it is regarded as if no operation had been specified. This is done, for example, if a protection violation is detected.

(3) The instruction is nullified; that is, the instruction is not executed and the PC is not incremented. This allows for a retry of the instruction execution, needed, for example, if a page fault is detected (see Chapter 10).

(4) The instruction is terminated, which means that none, a certain part or all, of the instruction actions have been performed.

The moment of interruption for asynchronous events is usually between instructions, because the processor state to be preserved at this point is minimal. Thus, if an external interrupt is received, the current instruction is first completed. However, for some instructions, such as string and vector instructions, completing their execution would take too long. This could make the **interrupt latency** (the time from the moment the interrupt is requested until the execution of the routine servicing the interrupt) unacceptably long. Therefore, these instructions are made interruptible, in which case the state of the interrupted instruction should be saved upon an interrupt, such that it can continue from the point where the interrupt occurred. Alternatively, instructions can be made restartable, so that they can be executed again upon completion of the interrupt. This can only apply to those instructions that do not change the initial conditions essential for the instruction – a block move operation that has overlap is not restartable, for example. A third possibility is to only allow interrupts at certain (program-controlled) moments. This can be used for time-critical routines and to keep the context to be saved relatively small.

9.6.4 Identifying the source of an interrupt

The process invoked due to an interrupt is executed on behalf of the interrupting process. In the case of an asynchronous interrupt, this may be any process. Servicing that interrupt usually means that the interrupting process has to be identified. Two methods for the identification of the interrupting process (also called the source of the interrupt) can be distinguished:

(1) **Polling**: A program called the interrupt handler has to identify the source of the interrupt. The simplest way to identify the interrupt source is for an interrupt request flag to be associated with every possible interrupt source. The interrupt handler executes a sequence of instructions, testing (or polling) each flag in turn, until a flag that has been set is encountered. Because polling is performed by the interrupt handler, which is not device specific, it is desirable for the checking of the interrupt request flag of each device to be done in a device-independent way. To do this, each device has to have a status register with a standard layout (see Chapter 11). If there are many potential interrupt sources, the polling process can be speeded up by reading all interrupt request flags simultaneously in an interrupt register, using a special I/O command. This register is then scanned for a bit set to one.

(2) **Vectored interrupt**: This allows the interrupting process to identify itself as part of the interrupt invocation operation. This eliminates the time-consuming polling operation but this is at the expense of extra hardware complexity in the interrupt source. A number, the interrupt vector, is associated with the interrupt source. This vector is used to modify the address of the entry point to the interrupt handling routine. The selection of a certain entry point of the interrupt handling routine identifies the interrupt source.

SUMMARY

- The function of an operating system is to provide a high-level virtual machine for the user and to provide protection and management of system resources.
- Processes are the abstraction level used by operating systems to deal with the problem of concurrency. A process has a state and a context.
- Process protection can be done at the language level or at the architectural level. Process protection at the architectural level involves privileged instructions and operands, requiring a CPU to have at least two modes of operation (supervisor and user).
- The protection of operands can be based on domains specified in terms of user-defined objects or memory space. Selective sharing is an important aspect in judging the quality of a protection mechanism. Protection mechanisms may be based on the key/lock mechanism, on rings or on segmentation and/or paging.
- Process synchronization is required to avoid race conditions. Architectural support is required to obtain indivisible operations. Disabling interrupts is the simplest mechanism, followed by test-and-set and compare-and-swap operations, which all use a form of busy waiting. Higher-level synchronization primitives are built out of the lower-level mechanisms.
- Process switching can be initiated on behalf of the currently executing process (via a supervisor call or a trap) or on behalf of another process (via an external interrupt).
- Process switching involves the switching of the context, which consists of the processor and the memory context. The minimum processor context is switched as part of the interrupt operation. Context switching can be done by the saving/restoring of shared resources, or the selection of an alternate resource set, if multiple sets are available.
- The handling of interrupts is usually based on priorities. Interrupt requests may be disregarded or disabled. Synchronous interrupts (SVCs and traps) may allow the execution of the current instruction to be completed, suppressed, nullified or terminated. Asynchronous interrupts are usually only allowed between instructions. Very long instructions are usually made interruptible in such a way that they can be continued later.
- The source of an interrupt can be determined via polling by the interrupt handler, or via a vector passed by the interrupting process.

EXERCISES

9.1 Which function types are performed by an operating system?

9.2 List the operating system types and their main characteristics.

9.3 Of which parts does the process context consist?

9.4 What is the purpose of a supervisor mode? Which privileged instructions does the MC68020 support?

9.5 What is an important aspect of protection of domains based on memory space?

9.6 What is the purpose of process synchronization? Which mutual exclusion mechanisms exist?

9.7 (a) Which process switches occur on behalf of the currently executing process?

(b) What is an asynchronous process switch?

9.8 Which part of a context switch has to be performed by the interrupt operation?

9.9 (a) Why are interrupt priority levels required?

(b) What is a non-maskable interrupt, and which interrupts are non-maskable?

(c) When are asynchronous events allowed to cause an interrupt, and why?

(d) Which is the most efficient way of identifying the interrupting process?

9.10 In a memory management system, based on segmentation, a domain is called a segment. Assume three processes: *Pa*, *Pb* and *Pc*. *Pa* has access to a private segment *Sa*, and shared segments *Sab* (shared with *Pb*) and *Sac* (with *Pc*). *Pb* has access to a private segment *Sb* and a shared segment *Sbc* (with *Pc*). *Pc* has access to a private segment *Sc*, and shared segments *Sac* and *Sbc*. The set of domains of a process is represented by a segment table, where each entry in the table represents a pointer to a domain. When a domain is shared, a pointer in the segment table of each sharing process points to the same shared domain. Which pointers do the segment tables of *Pa*, *Pb* and *Pc* contain?

9.11 Protect a critical section, using the CAS instruction, such that when the critical section is occupied the lock variable will contain a pointer to the PCB of the process in the critical section. When the critical section is free, the lock variable will contain the NIL pointer, which has the value 0.

9.12 A system with N servers uses the P operation to protect a critical section. The semaphore S is used to indicate the number of free servers ($0 \leqslant S \leqslant N$). The atomic operation P(S) is defined in the first two statements as follows:

Loop:	**If** $S = 0$ **then goto** *Loop*;	No free servers	P(S)
	$S := S - 1$;	Occupy a free server	
	Critical section;	There can be up to N processes in the N critical sections	
	$V(S)$:	Free server; Note: $V(S)$ means $S := S + 1$;	

Implement the operation P(S) using the CAS instruction.

References

Burroughs (1969). *Burroughs B6700 Information Processing Systems Reference Manual*. Burroughs Corporation: Detroit, MI.

Comer, D. (1984). *Operating System Design: the Xinu Approach*. Prentice Hall Incorporated: Englewood Cliffs, NJ.

Corsini, P. and Lopriore, L. (1987). The architecture of a capability-based microprocessor system. *IEEE Micro*, **7**(3), 35–51.

Dijkstra, E. W. (1965). *Cooperating Sequential Processes*. Technological University, Eindhoven, The Netherlands. Reprinted in *Programming Languages* (F. Genuys, ed.), 1968, pp. 43–112. Academic Press: New York.

IBM (1970). *IBM System/370, Principles of Operation*. Form No. GA22–7000. IBM Corporation: Armonk, NY.

Intel (1983). *iAPx286 Programmer's Reference Manual*. Intel Corporation: Santa Clara, CA.

Motorola (1985). *MC68020, 32-bit Microprocessor User's Manual*. Prentice Hall Incorporated: Englewood Cliffs, NJ.

Peterson, J. L. and Silberschatz, A. (1985). *Operating System Concepts* 2nd edn. Addison-Wesley: Reading, MA.

Toy, W. and Zee, B. (1986). *Computer Hardware/Software Architecture*. Prentice Hall Incorporated: Englewood Cliffs, NJ.

10 Memory Management

He who always puts things in place, is too lazy to look for them.
– Anonymous

The chapter begins by presenting the aims of a memory management system. The concept of virtual memory, which has been introduced to achieve these aims is discussed in the following section. Two aspects of memory management, protection and sharing, are then discussed. This section is followed by several implementation forms of address translation mechanisms – relocation, paging and segmentation. Address translation acceleration mechanisms are then presented, followed by a discussion of several memory management policies. The chapter concludes with an overview of the memory management system used with the MC68020.

10.1 Aims of a memory management system

During the evolution of computer architecture, the amount of main memory present in a computer has increased. However, the size of the programs has grown faster than the available memory. A first approach to overcome the limited memory size used a technique called **overlays**. An overlaid program is divided into several parts. One of these parts is always present in memory and controls the loading of other parts from secondary memory (drums, disks, tapes, and so on) into main memory. These other parts may be loaded into main memory such that they use the same memory region as a previously used part, thus overlaying this old part. Although used with much ingenuity, programmers spent much of their time dividing a program into overlays, instead of being able to simply write a large program. Furthermore, the necessity of offering several users a part of main memory reduced the amount of memory available for each user, and made it necessary to introduce some protection mechanism to shield the activities of one user from another.

Summarizing, therefore, the following aims for a memory management system can be distinguished:

- **Protection**: An important objective of memory management is protection. If several processes share main memory, it should be ensured that no process is able to change locations, not allocated to it. Although writing can have more devastating effects, reading is also not allowed, to provide a process with some privacy. As most languages allow the use of dynamic pointers and array subscripts, checking only at compile time is not sufficient; further checks must be made at run time by the memory management system. Protection can be applied at two levels: at one level, protection ensures that locations cannot be accessed by unauthorized users; at the other level, authorized accesses are further constrained by specific access rights (see Section 9.3).
- **Sharing**: The sharing objective appears to be in contradiction with protection. However, it is often necessary for users to be able to share and update information – for example, a database system. Furthermore, it is not necessary to have several copies of a single re-entrant routine, if all users are allowed to execute this single copy. Of course, protection against inadvertently changing this routine must be present, thus allowing the controlled access to shared portions of memory.
- **Relocation**: Multiprogramming requires several processes to be in memory at the same time. A process does not know in advance where it will be loaded, so it is not practical to use absolute memory addresses.

- **Physical memory organization**: The cost of fast main memory usually necessitates extending main memory with cheaper and slower secondary memory, often using magnetic storage devices such as disks and tapes. This memory hierarchy, which is present in most modern computers, makes it necessary to control the flow of data between these two levels of physical storage media. This burden can be left to the programmer (by using overlays, for example) but this is not feasible, as it is a time-consuming job for a programmer and, because of dynamic relocation, a programmer does not always know which and how much memory will be allocated. Thus, it is more convenient to leave this to the system, as will be seen later.
- **Logical memory organization**: Although most main memories are organized as a linear address space, with sequential addresses from 0 to some maximum, this hardly reflects the way programs are (or should be) written – that is, using some logical program and data structures such as modules, procedures and arrays. If a memory management system could provide several address spaces, each logical structure could be an independent entity (usually called a **segment**). This is advantageous for several reasons: segments can be compiled and loaded independently (with linking of segments done at run time), and each segment can have its own access rights (read only, read and execute, and so on). The simplest segmentation scheme could use two segments, one program segment (which can be read and executed) and one data segment (which can be read and written). The most sophisticated scheme could use a separate segment for every logical structure.

10.2 The virtual memory concept

The concept of virtual memory is covered in two parts. The first part covers address translation, which is the way addresses generated by the process being executed are translated into memory addresses. The second part covers the working set model, on which the memory management policies of Section 10.6 are based.

10.2.1 Address translation

Figure 10.1 shows the hierarchy of addresses as they may exist in a computer. In analogy to the virtual machines of Chapter 2, the addresses generated by an executing process are called **virtual addresses**, because they may differ from the address used to access main memory. The total address space available to an executing process is called the **virtual**

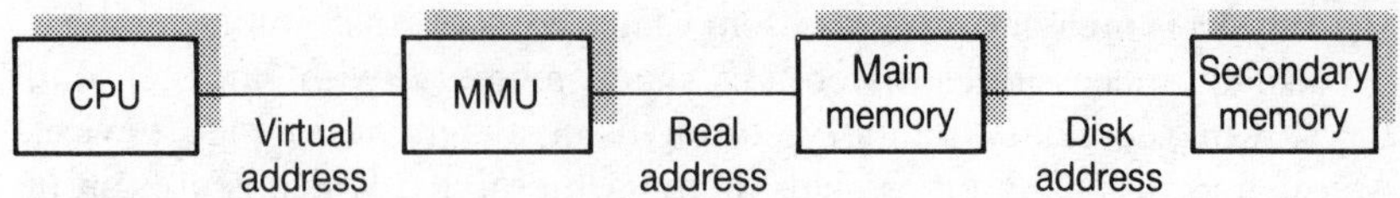

FIGURE 10.1
Memory address naming.

address space. The addresses used to access main memory are called **real addresses**, because for each such address a corresponding memory location really exists. In the absence of relocation, virtual addresses are identical to real addresses. In the case of relocation, however, they may not be the same, so that the virtual addresses have to be translated into the real addresses, which is called **address translation**. This translation is done by a hardware unit called the **memory management unit (MMU)**.

Due to the limited size of main memory, an object may not be in main memory but in secondary memory. This object then has to be brought in from secondary memory – for example, by specifying the disk address of that object. When this is done transparently to the process that is being executed, one speaks about a **virtual memory system**. The alternative would be to use an overlay technique, which is *not* transparent to the process being executed.

Sometimes the terms **logical address** and **logical address space** are used for systems that do not support a virtual memory system; while the terms virtual address and virtual address space are used for systems using a virtual memory system. To simplify the terminology, only the terms virtual address and virtual address space will be used in this book.

As mentioned earlier, when relocation is required, some form of address translation has to take place. This can be done at several stages during the generation and/or execution of a program. When the allocated area of memory is known at load time, the loader may be able to change the virtual addresses into real addresses such that when the program is executed real addresses are generated; this is called **static relocation**. When the allocated area of memory is not known at load time, the executing process will use virtual addresses, which have to be relocated during execution time; this is called **dynamic relocation**. Because dynamic relocation has to be performed during execution time for each address, special hardware (in the form of an MMU) is used, so that the translation can be done at a high speed.

The function of an MMU can be formally described as follows: the set of virtual addresses $V = \{0, 1, \ldots, v - 1\}$ is mapped on to the set of allocated real memory addresses $R = \{0, 1, \ldots, r - 1\}$ by using the function $f: V \rightarrow R$. The function f is defined as:

$$\begin{aligned} f(x) &= y \text{ if the data at virtual address } x \text{ is in } R \text{ at real address } y \\ &= \phi \text{ if the data at virtual address } x \text{ is missing from } R \end{aligned}$$

If $f(x) = \phi$, a **missing-item fault** occurs and the referenced item has to be

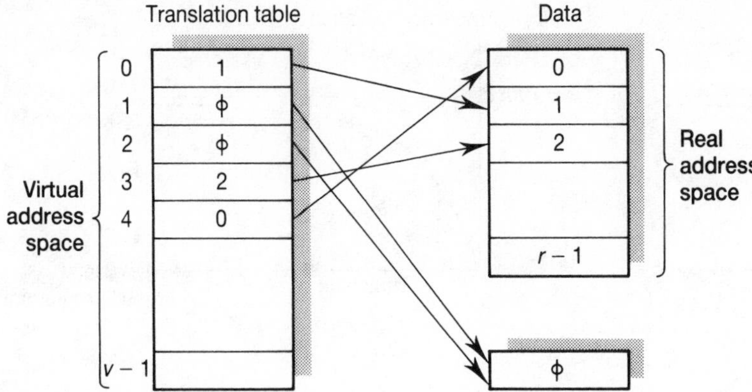

FIGURE 10.2
Example of a memory management unit.

brought into main memory, from secondary memory, by the **fault handler**.

A simplified example of an MMU is shown in Figure 10.2, using single addresses. The virtual address 4 is translated into real memory address 0 ($f(4) = 0$), while virtual address 3 translates into real address 2 ($f(3) = 2$). An access to virtual address 1 would produce a missing-item fault as the translation of this location is undefined ($f(1) = \phi$). The empty set in fact translates into secondary memory, but this is not shown in Figure 10.2.

A virtual memory address is usually split into two parts: a virtual block number and an offset. The virtual block number is mapped on to a real block address, while the offset is used to select a word inside this block. (Note that the terms offset and displacement are used interchangeably.) Blocking has the advantage that the size of the translation table is reduced significantly. If a 1 Mbyte virtual space is translated without blocking (that is, a block size of 1), the translation table would consist of 1M entries, whereas with a block size of 4096 bytes the number of entries is reduced to 256. The block size is often dictated by the access and transfer time of the secondary memory, as well as the size of main memory (see Chapter 11).

10.2.2 Working set model

If the dynamic behaviour of programs, and especially the sequence of memory references, is examined closely, it will appear that this sequence is not completely random; in fact, it is somewhat predictable. This led to the postulation of the **principle of locality**, which states that during some time interval, a program tends to group its references over a small portion of the total available address space (Denning, 1970). Within this locality,

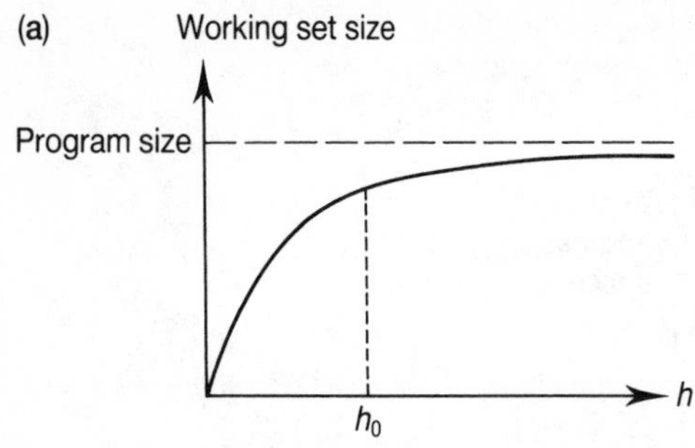

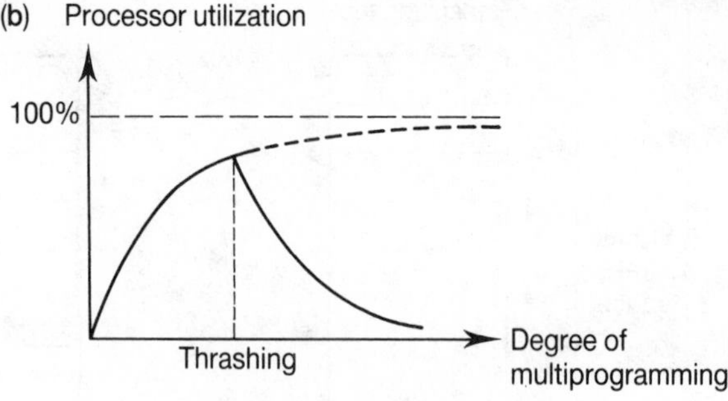

FIGURE 10.3

Working sets: (a) expected size; (b) thrashing.

two components can be distinguished: temporal and spatial locality. **Temporal locality** implies locality in time: in the near future, a program will reference those program and data objects that have been referenced in the recent past. This locality can be due to instruction references in program loops, or data references in activation records or working stacks. **Spatial locality** implies locality in space: in the near future, a program will reference those program and data objects that have addresses close to the last reference. This is caused by the sequential execution of program code and the traversal of data structures such as arrays. Of course, all programs show different degrees of locality, and both spatial and temporal locality can occur at the same time. The degree of spatial locality is an important factor in determining the block size.

During some time interval, a program only references a subset of its virtual address space (temporal locality). The set of blocks at time t, referenced during the last h references, is called the **working set** $W(t, h)$. Of course, h can also be expressed in units of time, instead of memory references. (Note that for multiprogrammed systems, h must measure process time rather than elapsed time.) The parameter h can be seen as a measure of the 'recentness' of the working set. A small value for h will produce a working set that includes only the most recent references, so h functions as a window on the reference sequence. The size of the working set at time t, $S(t, h)$, is equal to the number of blocks in $W(t, h)$.

Observing the working set during program execution reveals that it varies slowly with time, as could be expected from the available temporal locality. Denning (1968) has shown that the working set size $S(t, h)$ varies with h as shown in Figure 10.3(a). After a fast accumulation of several blocks, increasing h further will only result in a few blocks being added to the working set $W(t, h)$. If the window size h approaches the total execution time of the program, the working set size $S(t, h)$ will reach its upper limit, which is the total size of the program. Now, a value h_0 can be chosen such that the block fault rate is reasonable in relation to the amount of allocated memory.

The importance of working sets is that they link memory management and process management. The memory management unit and the scheduler should be governed by the following principle:

> Never replace a block that is part of the working set of an active process, and make a process active only if its entire working set is present in main memory.

The importance of this rule becomes apparent in multiprogrammed computers. If the degree of multiprogramming is increased (that is, more processes are allowed to be in memory at the same time), the utilization of a processor is expected to increase, because other processes can be executed when a process is waiting for an I/O request to complete. This is true to some extent, but at a given moment processor utilization sharply decreases (Figure 10.3(b)) because processes cannot be allocated enough memory to hold their working set. Thus, the block fault rate increases and most processes get blocked, awaiting block transfers that require an increasing service time due to the large number of outstanding requests and the latency of secondary memory. This phenomenon is called **thrashing** and should be avoided by applying the above rule to the memory management policies. Section 10.6 shows how the working set model can be implemented.

10.3 Protection and sharing

It is important to understand the exact meaning of the terms protection and sharing. In this context, protection means that an object is protected when a particular process is not allowed to perform read, write or execute operations on that object; others may be allowed to perform read, write or execute operations. Sharing implies the ability to access an object that is owned by another process. Protection and sharing are two important (but rather conflicting) objectives for memory management. To understand why they conflict, consider what would be the ideal situation for either of them. If protection would be supported optimally, a process would be allowed to access only its own objects and no others. On the contrary, the most ideal situation for sharing is when any process may access any object of any other process and no process would corrupt objects of the other processes. Unfortunately, this latter situation is rather unrealistic, whereas the former situation is hardly workable. Therefore, a compromise is needed between these two objectives, where controlled sharing is possible. Controlled means that one process can allow some other processes to access some or all of its objects, while others are inhibited from doing this. If access is allowed, it may even be further refined by distinguishing between different access rights (read, write, execute).

Sharing is an important issue in multiprogrammed and time-sharing systems. Suppose 20 users use a 100K compiler (which includes 20K for user data). Then, 2 Mbytes of memory are occupied. When the code is re-entrant (it does not modify itself), only one copy of the code needs to be present, and this is shared by all users. When each user has a private data space, the total size of memory needed is reduced to $80K + 20 \times 20K = 480K$, which is a significant reduction. To share this code, the translation table of each user has to translate the virtual addresses relating to the compiler code into real addresses, which are the same for all users. A difficulty arises when one user wants to remove a shared block from memory; the translation tables of the other users have to be searched to see if they contain this object so that the corresponding entries can be invalidated. This overhead can be reduced by having a single, shared translation table, used by all users of the shared objects. The disadvantage is, however, that the protection is all or nothing in such a case. If a shared object is protected as read–write, then all processes can read–write that object, while it may only be desirable for a single process to have write access.

From the foregoing, it is clear that sharing causes a problem when a shared object has to be removed from memory. Another problem arises when processes have their own virtual address space and want to share some program. Suppose process 1 allocates the virtual addresses 1000 to 2000 to its private data, and process 2 allocates (completely independent of process 1) virtual addresses 2000 to 3000 to its private data. When the shared program executes on behalf of process 1, it has to use virtual addresses 1000 to 2000 to access the data, while virtual addresses 2000 to 3000 are used when executing on behalf of process 2. One way to solve this problem is to have a single virtual address space for all processes (Fabry, 1974). Then, the data of each process would use the same virtual addresses (Figure 10.4), such that it is transparent for a program on behalf of which process it is executed. This solution requires that all virtual addresses are administered centrally. Other solutions exist, such as capabilities, using multiple segment tables or an extra level of indirection in the address translation process (Fabry, 1974).

10.4 Address translation mechanisms

Address translation, needed to perform dynamic relocation, can be done in various ways. The conventional address translation mechanisms are relocation, paging, segmentation and paged segmentation.

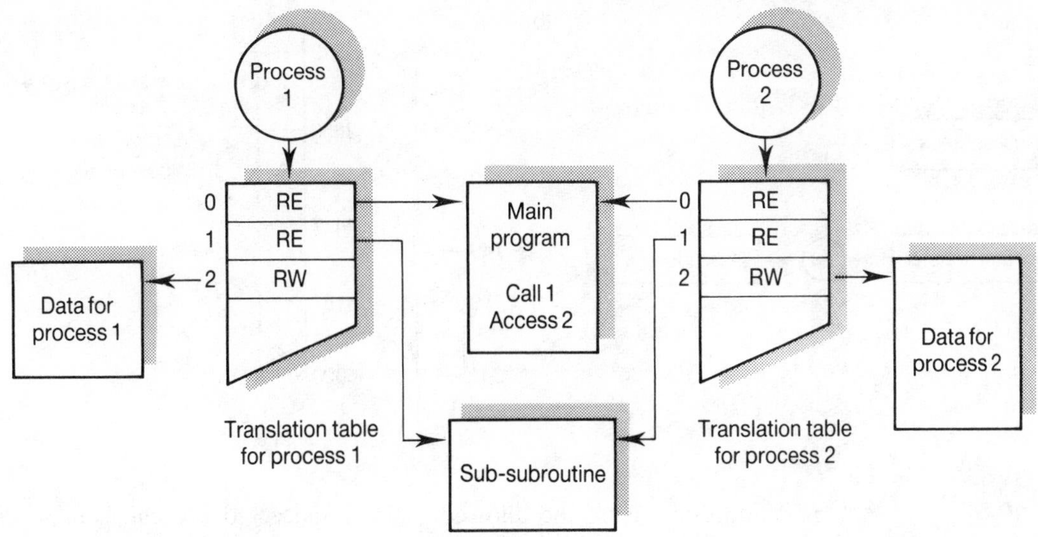

FIGURE 10.4

Sharing using a single virtual address space.

10.4.1 Relocation

In older computers, the objective of memory management for dynamic relocation is often fulfilled by using **relocation registers**. A process uses a virtual address space that is smaller than or equal to the real address space, starting at virtual address 0. If a process is loaded somewhere in memory, the real address of the first location is stored in the relocation register. Thereafter, for each memory reference, the virtual address is added to the relocation register to obtain the real address (Figure 10.5(a)). Now several processes can be in memory simultaneously, each starting at their virtual address 0. Every time the processor switches to another process, the relocation register is updated. Relocating a process only involves updating the relocation register. Figure 10.5(b) shows the situation where three processes are spread over main memory, together with their own virtual spaces. To reduce the size and the time required for the relocation addition, the low-order k bits of the relocation register could be stripped off, allowing programs to be loaded only at those locations that are a multiple of 2^k.

However, this scheme offers no protection: process C may change its virtual location 2500, such that process A may crash next time it executes the instruction at its virtual address 159. This can be prevented by pairing the relocation register with a corresponding **protection register** that contains the real address of the last location allocated to the process. If process C of Figure 10.5(b) was running, its protection register would contain the value 2853. For every memory reference, the virtual address is added to the relocation register and the result is checked against the protection register. (Note that a check for negative virtual addresses must be made as well, because adding -3 to the relocation register produces a

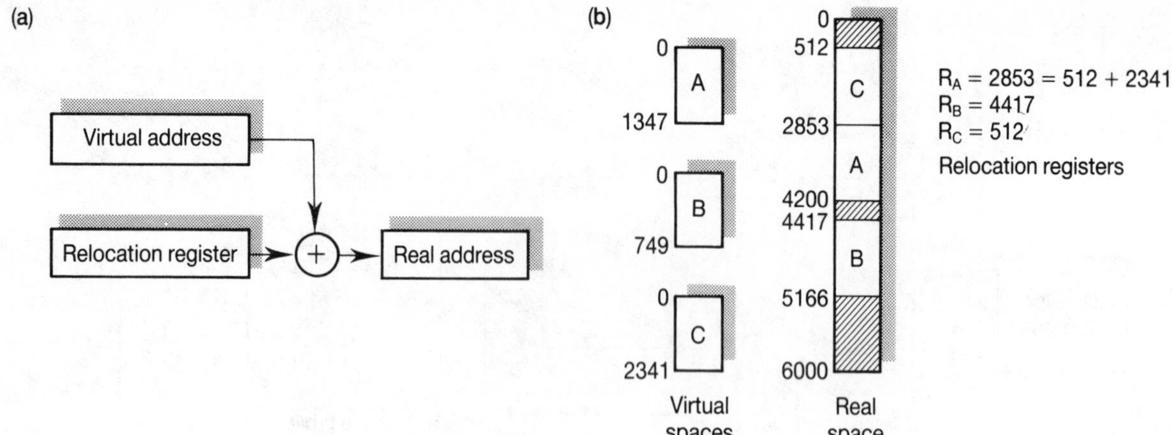

FIGURE 10.5

Relocation: (a) address calculation; (b) three resident processes.

real address outside the allowed address space.) If the check fails, the memory access is aborted and a fault is raised. This process can be speeded up if the protection register contains the length of the virtual address space, instead of the highest real address. Now, the checks for overflow and underflow (negative virtual addresses) can be done in parallel with the relocation-address addition. Even controlled sharing of information can be implemented to some extent.

10.4.2 Paging

The relocation–protection scheme suffers from the following problems:

- Each process must occupy a contiguous area of real memory.
- The virtual address space is not allowed to exceed the amount of available memory.

Paging can be used to solve these problems.

Paging divides the virtual address space into blocks, called **pages**, which all have the same size. Main memory, accessed via the real address space, is divided into blocks of the same size, called **page frames**. The translation of virtual to real addresses is done using a translation table, called the **page table**. Each process has its own page table, located somewhere in memory and addressed via a **page table register (PTR)**, as shown in Figure 10.6. Upon a process switch, the PTR is set up to point to the page table of the process to be activated.

The virtual address space is divided into blocks with the size of a page. A virtual address, therefore, consists of a virtual page number Vp and a displacement in the page Dp. An entry in the page table, a page table entry (PTE), consists of the real page address Rp, the access rights

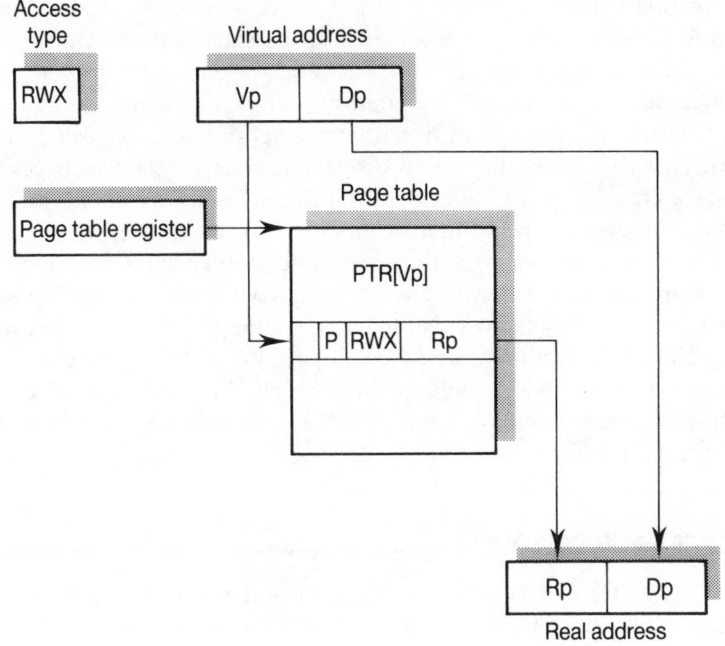

FIGURE 10.6

Address translation using paging.

this process has for that page and a presence flag P, to indicate if that page is in real memory. Address translation is performed as follows: the value of Vp is used as an index in the page table, pointed to by the PTR. Then the page table entry PTR[Vp] is accessed and the access rights (read, write or execute: RWX) are checked against the operation that is to be performed. Finally, the Rp field is extracted from the PTE and concatenated with the value in the Dp field of the virtual address to form the real address.

A simple paging system loads a process in its entirety. Thus, if the size of a process is *N* pages, *N* free page frames will be occupied. These page frames do not have to be contiguous, however, because the page table can relocate each page independently. This solves the problem of requiring a contiguous area of memory. A problem presents itself, called **superfluity**. This stems from the fact that a whole process is brought into main memory when only a small part may be needed for longer periods (remember the working set model), causing inefficiencies in memory use, because part of the unused (or at least not referenced) space could be used by other processes.

The second problem, stated at the beginning of this section, can be solved when the virtual address space of a process is allowed to exceed the size of main memory. A solution to this process size problem and to the superfluity problem is **demand paging**. This is based on the concept of the one-level store; that is, the address spaces of main memory and secondary memory form a single address space. Virtual addresses are translated into this one-level store space such that it is transparent to the process being executed irrespective of whether the object is in main memory or in secondary memory. Demand paging divides the pages constituting a process into two sets: a set of active pages (in steady state this set should be the working set) and a set of inactive pages, stored in secondary memory. When the process being executed references an inactive page, a **page fault** occurs. As a consequence of the demand to access the inactive page, the page fault handler loads the demanded page into main memory, whereby the page becomes active. The status of a page (active or inactive) is indicated by the presence flag (P) in the PTE of the corresponding page (see Figure 10.6). In the case of an inactive page (P = 0), the Rp field of the PTE can be used to specify the address in secondary memory. Example 10.1 gives some insight in to the size a page table may have.

□□EXAMPLE 10.1

The size of the page table is determined by the page size, which in turn depends on the transfer efficiency (block size) of the secondary memory. To get a feeling of the size of a page table, consider a system that has a 32-bit virtual address (4 Gbytes), 1 Mbyte (= 2^{20} bytes) of main memory and pages with a size of 4 kbytes (= 2^{12} bytes). Assuming an address resolution of a byte, the virtual page number field Vp consists of $32 - 12 = 20$ bits; thus, the page table has 2^{20} entries. The 1 Mbyte main memory has $2^{20}/2^{12} = 2^8$ different page frames, so the Rp field has a size of 1 byte (8 bits). Because, in addition to the Rp field, flags are needed for control and protection purposes, it is assumed that each page table entry occupies 2 bytes. This results in a page table size of 2.2^{20} = 2 Mbytes, which is rather large if only 1 Mbyte of main memory is available.

As this example shows, much of the area occupied by a large page table is not used and, therefore, is wasted, because the process being executed usually requires less than the total virtual address space. This waste is called **table superfluity**.

Another form of wastage, known as **internal fragmentation**, is caused by the fact that process sizes are hardly ever an integral number of pages, so part of the last page is wasted (with an average of one-half page per process, if *P* processes reside in memory, the internal fragmentation averages *P*/2 pages). Using smaller pages, to reduce the internal fragmentation, results in larger page tables, which increases the table fragmentation; thus, some compromise should be made.

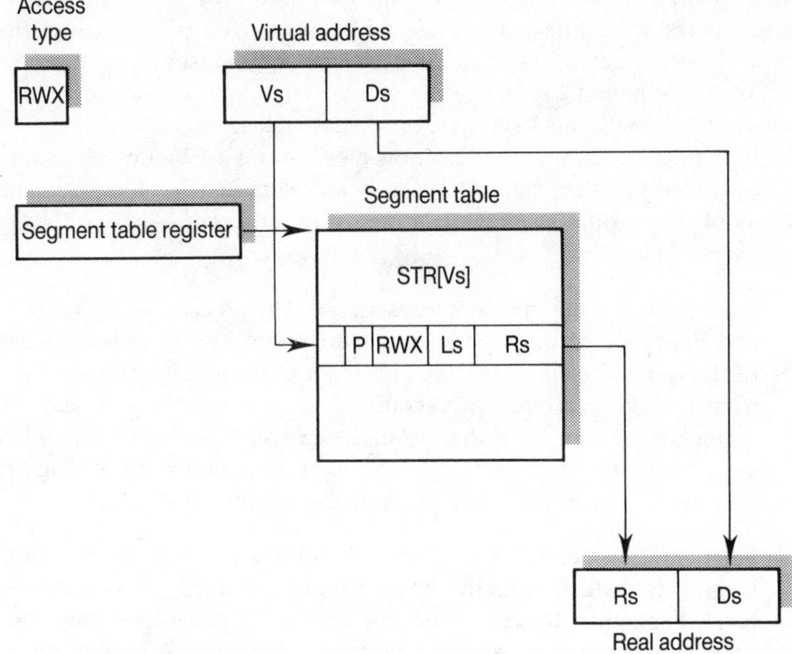

FIGURE 10.7
Address translation for segmented systems.

10.4.3 Segmentation

To achieve a logical organization of the virtual address space which resembles the user's view of memory, the concept of **segmentation** is introduced. Dividing a program into parts that have equal sizes is not natural. Normally, block-structured languages such as Pascal and C allow for the creation of logical entities such as procedures and modules with different sizes. Such a logical entity can be handled by the memory management mechanism by storing the information of the entity in a segment. Unlike a page, a segment can grow and shrink during its life time, as is the case for a stack segment.

A simple implementation could consist of several pairs of relocation–protection registers, one per segment. A disadvantage of this method is that the number of segments must be kept small (and fixed), because the number of available relocation–protection registers will be limited.

A more refined implementation of segmentation provides each process with a large number of segments. Figure 10.7 shows how this is realized. A virtual address is decomposed into a segment number Vs and a displacement Ds within that segment. Using a **segment table**, pointed to by the **segment table register** (STR), the segment number Vs selects a segment table entry (STE), also called a **segment descriptor**. This STE contains the real segment address Rs in addition to protection and control flags, comparable to those of a page table entry. However, because the space used by a segment has a variable size, an STE must also contain the length of that segment Ls. A process consists of a collection of segments, where each segment can have its own access rights.

Although the address translation mechanisms of Figures 10.6 and 10.7 appear to be the same (both can support virtual memory), the concepts of paging and segmentation are quite different.

- Paging divides the virtual address space, the physical address space and the space of the secondary memory into blocks (called pages) of the same size. It allows the contiguous virtual address space of a process to be scattered (non-contiguous) in real address space and secondary memory. Furthermore, a page relates to memory rather than to logical objects visible at the programming level. Paging, therefore, is transparent to the process being paged.

- Segmentation divides the virtual address space into blocks (segments) which directly relate to objects at the programming level. Segments, therefore, do not have a fixed size and may even vary in size during process execution. Protection and sharing is, therefore, possible at the object level, visible to the process being segmented.

A serious problem is caused by segmentation, called **external fragmentation**. This is illustrated by Figure 10.8, where the 64K main memory initially contains the four segments *A*, *B*, *C* and *D* (Figure 10.8(a)). After freeing the memory occupied by segments *B* and *C*, the checkerboard appearance of Figure 10.8(b) results. Upon allocation of segment *E* (Figure 10.8(c)), the total free memory space is 14K, but segment *F* (10K) cannot be allocated because the free space is divided over several holes, each of which cannot accommodate the new segment. The job of the memory management system is to keep the degree of external fragmentation as low as possible – it can never be eliminated. In the case of Figure 10.8(c), the segments could be moved to the beginning of the address space, producing one free memory area of 14K at the upper end, an operation called **compaction** (see Figure 10.8(d)). This is a time-consuming operation especially for large memories. Another possibility would be to delete as many segments as are needed to produce a large enough hole. Reconsidering Figure 10.8(c), freeing the space of segment *D* would result in a 16K hole, so segment *F* can then be loaded. The determination of which segments are replaced and where a new segment is placed is discussed in Section 10.6.

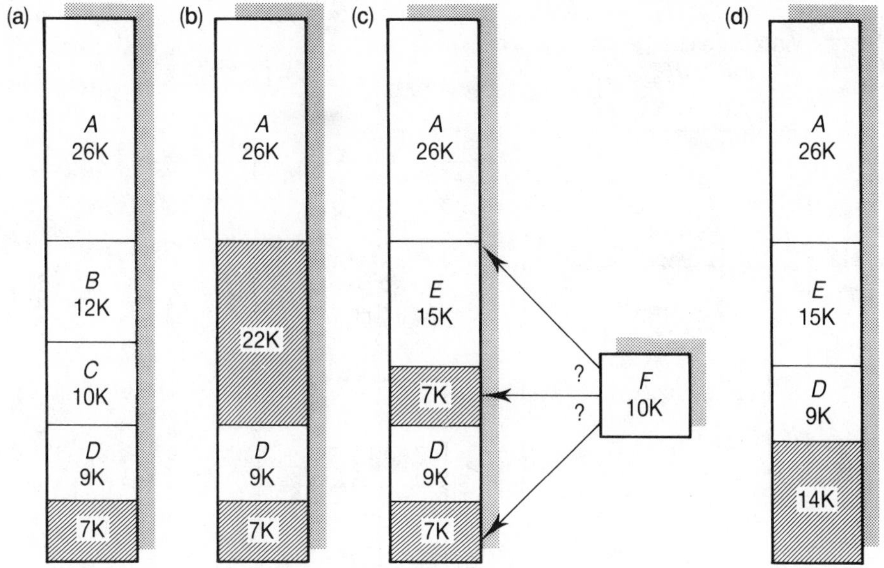

FIGURE 10.8
Checkerboard memory: (a) initial situation; (b) discard segments *B* and *C*; (c) load segment *E*; (d) compaction.

10.4.4 Paged segmentation

As segmentation also suffers from superfluity, it is often combined with (demand) paging to combine the advantages of both methods. Segments are divided into (equally sized) pages and each virtual address is decomposed into a triplet (Vs, Vp, Dp), where Vs denotes the segment number, Vp is the page number within that segment and Dp is the displacement within the page. Figure 10.9 shows the address translation mechanism, with the STR pointing to the segment table. Using Vs as first index, an STE is extracted that points to the page table of that segment. Then Vp is used to find the real page address Rp in the page table. Finally, Dp is used for the displacement in the page.

When a process is active, its segment table has to be present in main memory. Table superfluity is reduced by requiring that only the page tables of the segments, belonging to the working set of the process, be present in main memory. This is accomplished by the presence flag in the STE. External fragmentation is reduced by dividing a segment into pages and supporting virtual memory via demand paging.

In Figure 10.9, the access rights and the segment length are specified by the STEs, such that access is controlled on a segment basis. All pages of a segment, therefore, have the same access rights. This scheme, where segmentation is the dominating factor, is called **paged segmentation**.

If the access rights are moved to the page table entries and the STEs do not contain the length field, the scheme is simply an extended form of paging, where the notion 'segment' has no relation to a logical

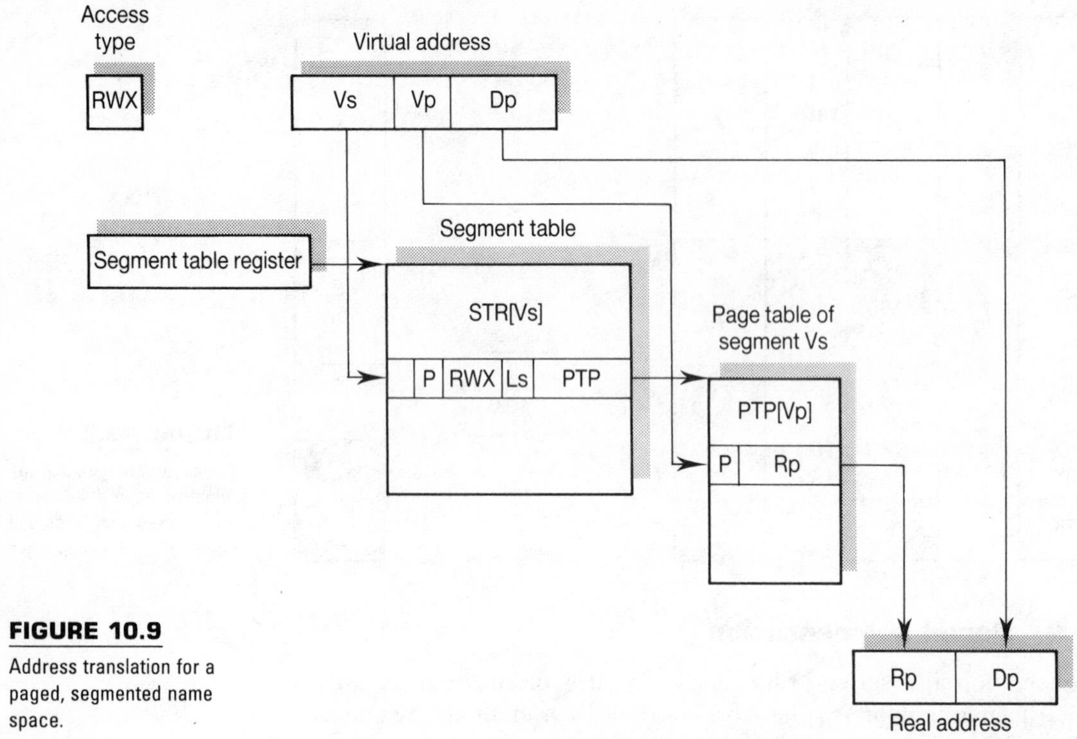

FIGURE 10.9

Address translation for a paged, segmented name space.

entity, leaving only the paging characteristics. This is called **two-level paging**. The advantage of two-level paging over one-level paging (see Figure 10.6) is that the degree of table fragmentation is decreased, as only the page tables of the processes that are currently in memory have to be in main memory, instead of a page table for the entire virtual address space.

10.5 Address translation acceleration mechanisms

The address translation technique shown thus far has assumed **direct mapping**. With direct mapping, the number of entries in the translation table, located in main memory, is equal to the number of blocks in the virtual address space (see Example 10.1); and every memory access requires this table to be interrogated, thereby incurring a delay of one memory cycle (in the case of one-level translation), or two or more memory cycles (in the case of two or more levels of translation, see Figure 10.9). Because memory accesses are done frequently, this form of address translation would introduce a considerable performance penalty.

In a system with a relatively small virtual address space – for example, 2^{24} bytes – and a relatively large block size – for example, 2^{12} bytes – only 2^{12} translation table entries are required. These could be stored in a fast memory (rather than main memory) to accelerate the address translation operation (Dekker, 1987). For systems with a large virtual address space, this is not a good solution, because the translation table would become too large (see Example 10.1), and therefore too slow (because of address decoding time) and expensive (because of the size of the table). Several mechanisms for accelerating the address translation operation exist: translation lookaside buffers, inverted page tables and multiple virtual spaces.

10.5.1 Translation lookaside buffers

The address translation acceleration mechanism using translation lookaside buffers (TLBs) is based on the principle of temporal locality. (A TLB can be considered to be a hardware cache (see Chapter 14) used to contain recently used virtual-to-real address translations.) An associative memory is used to contain the N most recently translated addresses. Figure 10.10 shows a translation lookaside buffer for the paged segmented system of Figure 10.9. Each TLB entry can be considered a combined STE/PTE of Figure 10.9. A TLB entry consists of a segment number Vs, a page number Vp, the access rights flags and the real page address Rp. Address translation is performed as follows: a parallel comparison of all N entries in the TLB is made with the type of access to be performed, the virtual segment number Vs and the virtual page number Vp of the virtual address. When a TLB entry matches, the real page address Rp of that entry is concatenated with the Dp to form the real address. In this parallel comparison, the contents of the TLB is compared with a data value (determined by the access type, Vs and Vp of the virtual address). The memory used to contain the TLB entries is therefore also called a **contents addressable memory**, or an **associative memory**, because the desired output Rp is found by associating its contents with input data. When no match is found, which is called a fault or a miss, the address translation mechanism of Figure 10.9 is used (where the segment table and some page tables are in main memory). The result of this translation is used to update the TLB.

Using TLBs, some problems arise because of TLB size restrictions and process switches. Because of the fixed TLB size, only a limited number of entries can be stored. Clark and Emer (1985) analyzed the performance of the VAX-11/780 TLB, to simulate several configurations. They found that, using a TLB with 128 entries, misses occurred for 0.5% to 3.0% of the instructions executed, depending on the behaviour of the particular program.

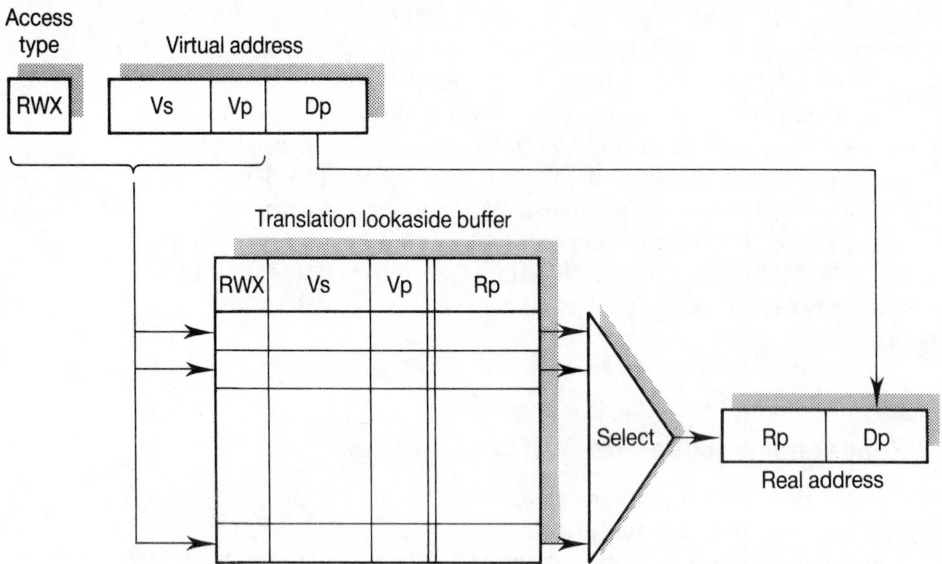

FIGURE 10.10
Translation lookaside buffer for paged segments.

Furthermore, a page fault or a segment fault (a reference to a segment that is not in memory) will cause the processor to stop the faulting process and switch to another process with its own virtual address space. To maintain system integrity, all TLB entries must be invalidated, which clearly degrades system performance as the TLB must be filled on behalf of the newly initiated process (remember each translation requires two memory accesses). While the TLB is being filled, this new process may again become interrupted, invalidating all entries once more.

10.5.2 Inverted page tables

An approach to reduce the size of the page table (that is, to reduce table superfluity) is to use an inverted page table (IPT), as used in the IBM PC–RT (Hester, 1986). An inverted page table has one entry for each *real* memory page, instead of one entry for each *virtual* page. This has the advantage that only a fixed (and limited) part of memory is occupied by the table, regardless of the size of the virtual address space used. This table may be implemented in a fast memory, thus accelerating the address translation operation.

Each entry of the IPT (Figure 10.11) consists of a link field (which forms a chain of IPT entries with the same hash value), a Vp field and an Rp field. Address translation may be performed by hashing (this is a form of scrambling) the page number of the virtual address such that it can be used to address an entry in the IPT. The contents of the Vp field of that entry is compared with the Vp number of the virtual address. Upon a match, the Rp value is taken to specify the real page address. On a miss,

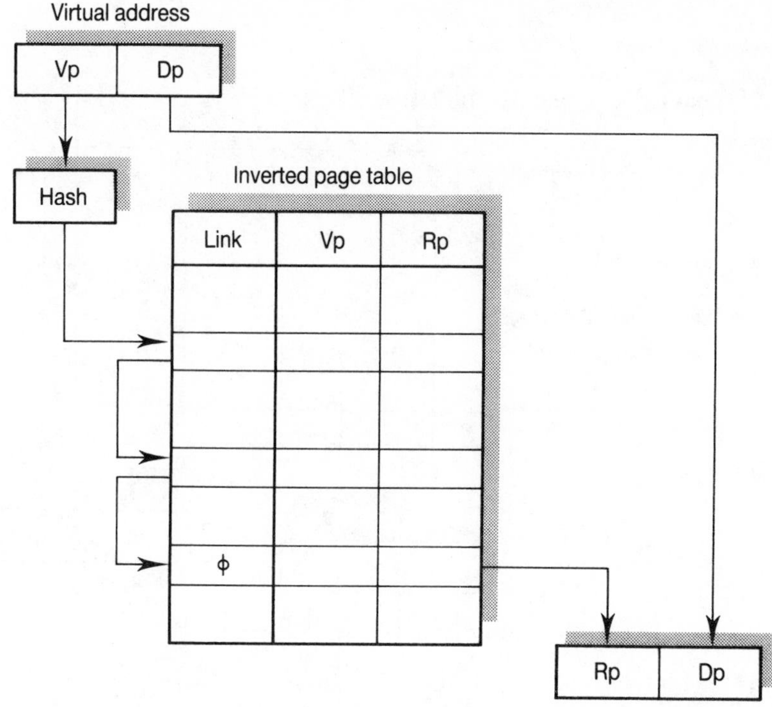

FIGURE 10.11
Address translation via an inverted page table.

the link field is used to check the next IPT entry, in the chain of IPT entries with the same hash value. If no match is found, the page is not present in memory, so a page fault occurs. Although long chains would imply long translation times, it is found that the average chain length is between one and two.

The address translation mechanism using an IPT could be implemented in hardware using a regular high-speed memory for storing the IPT. To speed up address translation, the IBM PC–RT uses a TLB that contains the most recently used translations. Upon a TLB miss, the TLB is updated using the IPT.

10.5.3 Multiple virtual spaces

The address translation acceleration mechanism described so far only allows one virtual address space to be translated. Upon a process switch, the translation tables have to be cleared and reloaded with translation information of the newly activated process. One way to prevent the clearing of the translation table (which may be a TLB or an IPT) is to extend the entries with a field containing the processes identification (PID). Figure 10.12 shows such a TLB for a paged virtual memory system. An associative search is done by which a match with the PID number is also required.

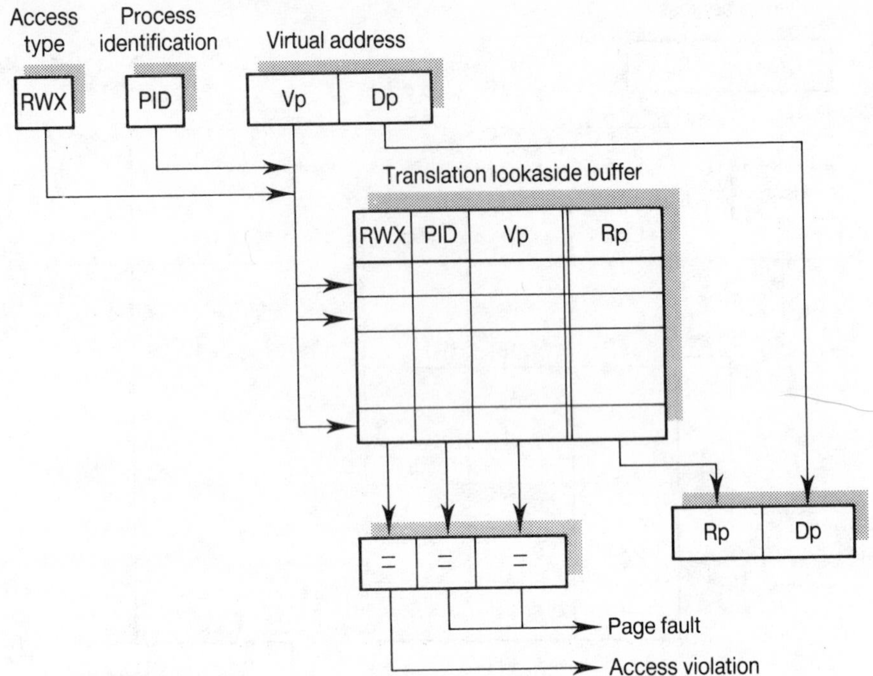

FIGURE 10.12

Address translation for paged systems with multiple virtual spaces.

Given a large TLB and frequent process switches, the PID concept may improve the address translation speed because many entries of a reactivated process may still be in the TLB, and so the miss rate is reduced.

10.6 Memory management policies

The previous sections have discussed address translation and translation acceleration mechanisms, not the policies by which these mechanisms are controlled. Figure 10.13 gives an overview of the memory management policies. These policies are dependent on the memory allocation policies and the scope of those policies, which determine which of the management policies are applicable in a particular situation.

The memory management policy determines the loading of information into main memory. This involves a decision as to when the loading should take place, which is controlled by the **fetch policy**. After information has been fetched from secondary memory, it must be stored in a free location in main memory, governed by the **placement policy**. Often, there is not enough free memory left to store the new information, so the **replacement policy** determines which information is removed from memory to create enough free locations.

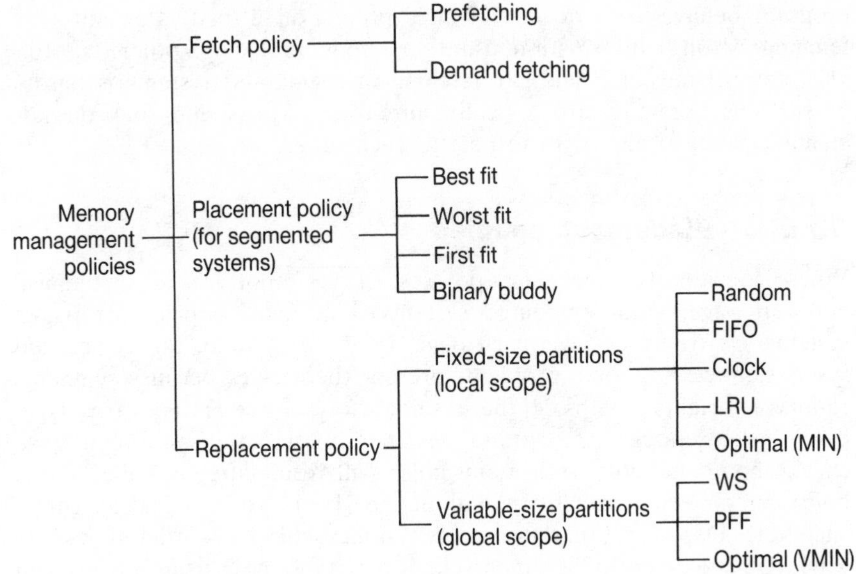

FIGURE 10.13
Overview of memory management policies.

For **memory allocation**, two overall policies can be distinguished (Denning, 1970). With the **fixed-size partitions policy**, the amount of allocated main memory remains the same during the life time of a process. The advantage of fixed partitions is its simple implementation. Due to the fixed size of allocated memory, this policy cannot cope efficiently with processes that exhibit a large variation in temporal locality during their life time. The **variable-size partitions policy**, however, permits this allocation to vary dynamically, according to the needs of the active process. Variable-size partitions offer a better memory utilization, because they are able to reallocate parts of memory to other processes.

The scope of a memory allocation policy can be constrained to the memory allocated to a single process. This is of interest when fixed-size partitions are used. The policy is said to have a local scope. A memory allocation policy that takes into account the memory allocated to all processes is said to have a global scope. This is of interest when variable-size partitions are used.

10.6.1 Fetch policies

The fetch policies are not influenced by memory allocation or scope policies. In principle, information can be fetched before it is needed, called **prefetching** (Smith, 1978), or when it is needed, referred to as **demand fetching**. Demand fetching is used most frequently because it is easy to implement: if a page or segment is missing from memory (a missing-item fault), a fetch request is issued to obtain that item. Prefetching is used less often, as some knowledge or prediction of future program behaviour is needed. If this prediction is bad, a penalty for fetching wrong information (and possibly replacing other, useful, information) must be paid. Prefetching in segmented systems is hardly possible as segments are logically unrelated objects and thus do not exhibit spatial locality with respect to each other.

10.6.2 Placement policies

When considering placement policies, it is important to distinguish between paged and segmented systems. Placement policies for paged systems are trivial because each page fits in every hole. For segmented systems, however, some problems present themselves because segments can have variable lengths, so there is not always a free area of memory (a hole) large enough to contain the new segment. Consequently, a checkerboard memory with many holes will result after a while. These holes are collected in a list containing the begin address and length of each hole. Depending on the placement policy, this list is ordered in some way. The placement policy then selects a suitable hole from this list and places the segment, updating the hole list with the newly created hole. If no hole can contain the entire segment, the placement policy (together with the replacement policy) moves (or removes) other segments to free as much memory as needed.

The best-known placement policies for segmented systems are:

- **Best fit**: The hole list is maintained in order of increasing size and the segment is placed in the first hole large enough to hold that segment.
- **Worst fit**: This maintains a list of holes in order of decreasing size. The segment is placed in the first available hole, while inserting the newly created hole at the correct place in the list.
- **First fit**: The list of holes is ordered according to increasing memory addresses. The segment is placed in the first hole large enough for the segment to fit into. However, after some time, many small holes are accumulated near the head of the list, resulting in longer delays to find a fit. This can be avoided by advancing the start position in the list of holes cyclically by one hole after each search.
- **Binary buddy**: In this algorithm, the segment size is rounded up to a power of 2. Furthermore, n hole lists are maintained, one for each hole size.

Although the best-fit and worst-fit policies adopt opposing strategies, they are both viable. Intuitively, one might choose the best-fit algorithm as this minimizes the amount of wasted memory, but, after a while, memory may become fragmented in many small and useless holes. The worst-fit policy, on the other hand, is based on the philosophy that choosing a large hole may leave another hole that is large enough to be used in the near future.

All policies in fact leave a fragmented memory that must be compacted once in a while. Compaction is most easily done when the holes are listed in order of increasing (or decreasing) base address, as in the first-fit algorithm. Altogether, the first-fit and binary buddy policies are the most efficient algorithms.

10.6.3 Replacement policies

In the discussion of replacement policies, the memory allocation policies are important. With fixed-size partitions, there is a need to replace a page on a page fault, once all allocated page frames of that partition have been used. With variable-size partitions, a decision can be made to increase the size of the partition, instead of replacing a page. Although these concerns are not pure replacement aspects, they will be discussed in this context.

Replacement policies for fixed-size partitions

The policies for fixed-size partitions have a local scope because they can only take into consideration the allocated memory of the faulting process. The well-known policies for fixed-size partitions are:

- **Random replacement**: This policy consists of choosing a random page for replacement, without looking at the number of references or the time of placement of the page. Because locality has no influence on the decision of this policy, it generally has a poor performance, except in environments where hardly any locality is present, such as database systems.
- **First-in, first-out (FIFO) replacement**: In this policy, a page that has been resident in memory the longest is replaced. This requires the placement sequence of pages to be recorded (in a FIFO queue). Although some temporal locality can be captured with this policy, it ignores the possibility that the oldest page to be replaced may also be the most frequently referenced page.
- **Clock replacement**: This policy, also called first-in, not-used, first-out (FINUFO), is an improvement over the FIFO policy in that it also checks if a page has been referenced, thereby making better use of the temporal locality. To implement this policy, the same queue as for the FIFO policy is maintained, only the queue is made circular with a pointer to the last replaced page, and each page has a used flag, which is set on a reference to that page.

- **Least recently used (LRU) replacement**: A disadvantage of the clock policy is that the 'recentness' of each reference is not taken into account. The LRU policy overcomes this by keeping the pages in some sort of stack, where a page is moved to the top of the stack on a reference, whereas the bottom page (the page that was referenced the longest time ago) is replaced on a page fault. This is a better method for capturing temporal locality. The implementation of this policy does not use a real stack, as this is time prohibitive. A possible realization could use a counter associated with every page, to indicate its relative stack position.
- **Optimal (MIN) replacement**: The best policy is not to replace the page that was referenced the longest time ago but the page that will not be referenced for the longest time to come (Belady, 1966). Although this policy has the least number of page faults (hence the name MIN policy), it cannot be realized in real time, as it would need to look into the future. However, it can be used as a theoretical policy for benchmarking other policies in an experimental environment.

Replacement policies for variable-size partitions

Several approaches can be taken for partitions with a variable size. One approach simply extends the scope of the replacement policies for fixed-size partitions from local to global, without identifying which page (or page fault) belongs to which process. Examples of this approach are global LRU and global clock. However, these policies, just as all fixed-size partitions policies, do not maintain the working set of each process, which can result in thrashing. Three other policies, which accommodate the varying memory requirements of an executing process, are:

- **Working set (WS) replacement**: This policy, which has received much attention, represents a practical approximation of the working set model (Denning, 1970).
- **Page fault frequency (PFF) replacement**: This policy was proposed by Chu (1972). It uses the page fault frequency, which is the reciprocal of the time between successive page faults, to determine the size of the partition. Upon a page fault, this frequency is compared with some threshold value and if the PFF is larger than this value, no replacement will be made but the size of the partition is increased instead. On the other hand, if the PFF is less than this threshold, all pages not referenced since the last page fault are removed. As this policy only acts upon a page fault, it is easier to implement. However, it shows anomalies for certain programs, as it does not satisfy the stack property (Franklin, 1978).

- **Optimal variable (VMIN) replacement**: Comparable to the MIN algorithm for fixed partitions, the VMIN algorithm for a variable-size partitions generates the lowest possible page fault frequency (Prieve, 1976). For each reference, the VMIN policy checks whether that page will be referenced again in the upcoming time window. If this happens, the page is kept, otherwise the page is immediately removed from the working set (freeing as much memory as possible). Similar to the LRU and MIN policies (LRU looking backwards and MIN forwards), the VMIN policy uses a forward scan window. This makes it impossible to realize this policy in practice and again it can only be used for benchmarking purposes.

Although WS and VMIN have (almost) comparable performances, the VMIN policy can better cope with a possible overshoot in the size of the working set that occurs at the transition of two locality phases. If the area of locality changes, the WS policy will keep the old pages during the upcoming window. At the same time, the partition gets larger, because pages of the new locality area are added. Thus, at a locality transition, the WS policy retains pages of both phases during the first window after the change. The VMIN algorithm is able to anticipate these transitions, as it uses a forward-looking window. Hence, it can see that pages of the previous locality are not needed any more, so they are removed immediately.

Figure 10.14(a) shows the performance (expressed in the number of generated page faults) for the fixed-size partitions LRU replacement policy, for pages sizes of 64, 128, 256 and 512 bytes. The horizontal axis shows the size of the partition in Kwords (whereby each word consists of 4 bytes). The results are derived from the execution behaviour of a FORTRAN compiler (Chu, 1974). Every program exhibits activity in several parts of its address space (for example, due to instruction fetches and data references in several areas) thereby requiring its working set to consist of several pages. If the working set consists of only a few pages, which will be the case for large pages and small size partitions (the left area of Figure 10.14(a)), a high page fault rate will result. When the working set is increased beyond a certain point, temporal locality is less important while spatial locality becomes the dominant factor, favouring larger page sizes.

Figure 10.14(b) shows the page fault rate for variable-size partitions, using the working set (WS) replacement policy. The horizontal axis shows the parameter h of $W(t, h)$, expressed in units of msec is 1000 page references. The page fault rate obviously decreases with increasing value of h (which represents temporal locality). Spatial locality is taken into account by the page size. Larger pages have a better spatial locality and therefore a lower page fault rate.

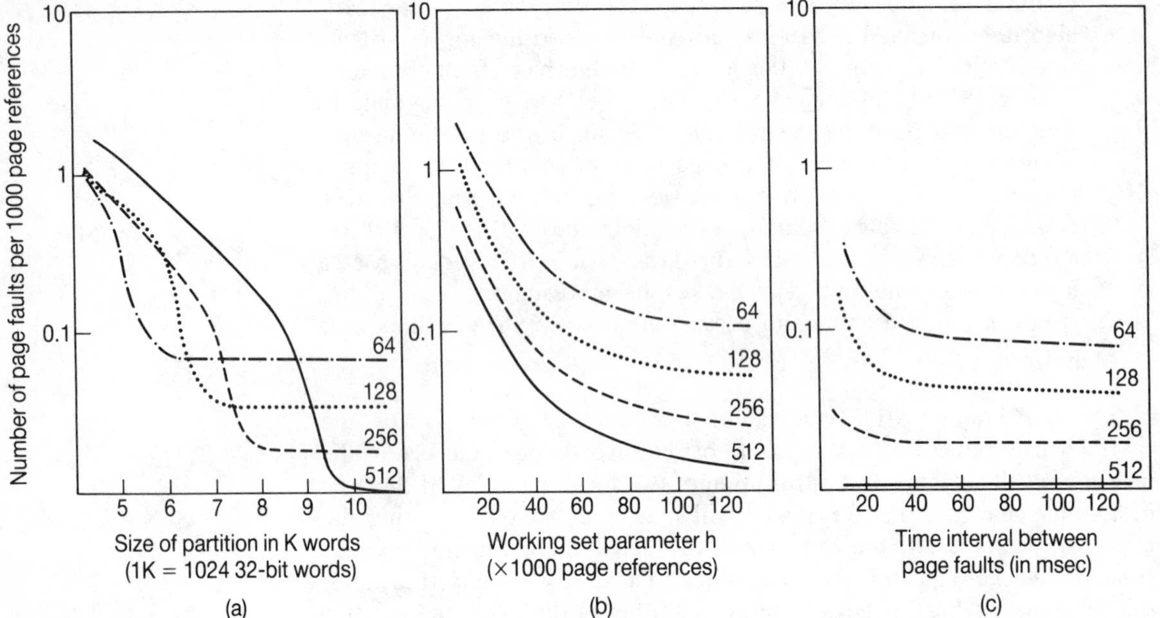

FIGURE 10.14

Page fault frequency for different page sizes: (a) LRU replacement; (b) WS replacement; (c) PFF replacement (Chu, IEEE Computer, 1974).

Figure 10.14(c) represents the page fault rate as a function of the time between successive page faults, using the page fault frequency (PFF) replacement policy. The horizontal axis shows the time interval between page faults, expressed in msec, where a time interval of 1 msec represents about 1000 page references.

10.7 The Motorola MC68851 paged memory management unit

The MC68551 paged memory management unit (PMMU), to be used in conjunction with the MC68020 processor, offers facilities for creating a demand-paged virtual memory environment. It is a very flexible MMU, as both the level of paging (see Section 10.4.4) and the page size are not fixed; they can be adjusted according to the user's needs. A short description can be found in Cohen (1986), while all details can be found in Motorola (1985).

An overview of memory management techniques used in other microprocessors (such as the Zilog Z80000 and the Intel 80386) and their support for virtual memory can be found in Furht (1987).

It is not appropriate to discuss all the details of the address translation of the PMMU, and therefore only the overall concept will be presented, as shown in Figure 10.15.

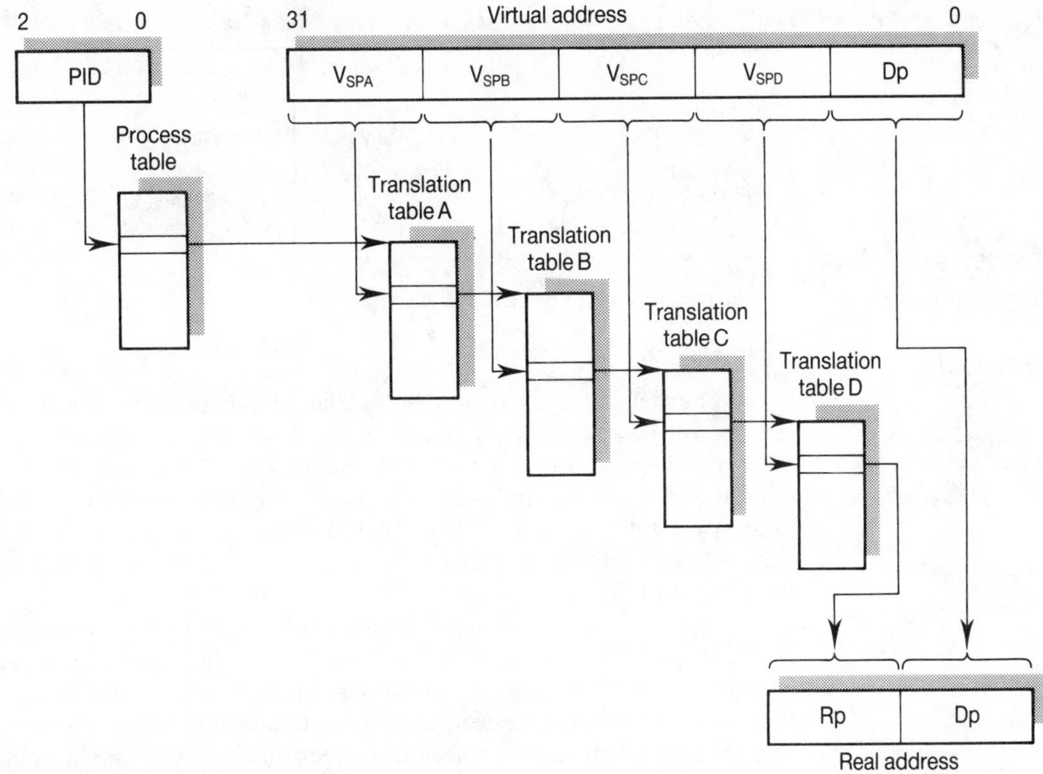

FIGURE 10.15

PMMU address translation.

The MC68851 PMMU allows the 32-bit virtual addresses to be split into several fields to allow for multi-level address translation. It supports up to eight virtual address spaces to allow for fast process switching (see Section 10.5.3). The currently active process is identified via the 3-bit PID field of Figure 10.15. The value of this field is used as an index in the process table to select a pointer to the tree of translation tables.

Each of the four virtual segment or page fields of the virtual address (denoted by V_{SPA} through V_{SPD}) are further used to translate the virtual address into a real page address R_p. The R_p field is concatenated with the page displacement D_p of the virtual address to form the final real address. Fast process switching is supported by having several virtual addresses, while table superfluity is prevented by having up to four levels of address translation.

The address translation operation is under control of the translation control register (TCR), shown in Figure 10.16. The page size field (PS) of the TCR specifies the page size (which is the width of the D_p field of Figure 10.15). Pages can be specified to have a size of 256 bytes to 32 kbytes, corresponding with a D_p field of 8–15 bits. The initial shift (IS) field determines the size of the virtual address space as follows: size $= 2^{32-IS}$, whereby $0 \leqslant IS \leqslant 15$.

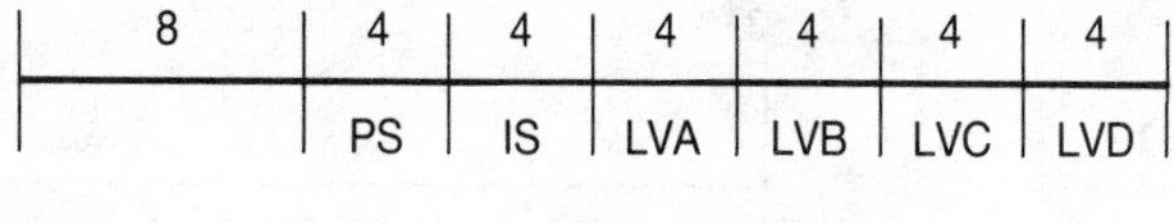

Field starting bit	Contents	Restrictions
LVA 31 – IS	1..15	LVA≥1
LVB 31 – IS – LVA	0..15	if LVB = 0 then LVC = LVD = 0
LVC 31 – IS – LVA – LVB	0..15	if LVC = 0 then LVD = 0
LVD 31 – IS – LVA – LVB – LVC	0..15	

PS + IS + LVA + LVB + LVC + LVD = 32

FIGURE 10.16

Translation control register.

The length of each of the translation tables, and therefore the lengths of the fields V_{SPA} through V_{SPD} of the virtual address, is determined by the four fields LVA through LVD. The values specified by these four fields is constrained, such that if LVB = 0 then LVC and LVD must also be 0 (see Figure 10.16). A last constraint is put on the sum of the contents of all fields, which is required to be 32 (which is the size of the virtual address).

The translation tables of Figure 10.15 contain flags that specify the format of the entries of their tables. This format can be specified to contain optionally a segment length field and an access rights field, such that both a segmented name space as well as a simple (one, two, three or four level) paging address translation mechanism may be supported.

The PMMU is an MC68020 co-processor, especially designed to *accelerate* the address translation function. The most important function of the PMMU is the translation of virtual addresses into real addresses. Furthermore, it has to check the user's permission to access the requested part of memory and take action if the user has no such permission. The PMMU consists of a TLB which has an on-chip, 64-entry, fully associative address-translation cache (ATC) that contains the 64 most recently translated addresses. When a virtual address is offered to the PMMU by the MC68020, the ATC is searched and, on a hit, the real address is presented to main memory. Otherwise, the translation is obtained by walking through the hierarchical table structure of Figure 10.15 (tablewalking) and the result is loaded into the ATC.

Each entry in the ATC has a lock bit, which enables the operating system to cause translations for commonly used (time-critical) system functions to be locked in the ATC. Locked entries are not removed until they are explicitly removed from the ATC by a PMMU instruction.

The PMMU contains an 8-entry process table which allows for eight processes to reside simultaneously in the translation cache, reducing the performance decrease which could arise from process switches. The ATC entries are extended with a 3-bit PID field, to identify the process they belong to.

SUMMARY

- Memory management is necessary for several purposes, such as relocation (making it possible for a program to be loaded anywhere in memory), protection, physical organization (controlling the memory hierarchy of secondary storage and main memory), logical organization (closely connected with the user's point of view of memory) and sharing.

- Virtual memory allows the address space of a process (called the virtual address space) to be larger than that of real memory (called the real address space).

- The concept of virtual memory is supported by the working set model, which in turn is based on the principle of locality. This states that, over a period of time, a program tends to reference a relatively small portion of its entire address space. Therefore, it is sufficient for this period to have only that referenced part of the program (the working set) in memory, while the rest of the program can remain in secondary memory.

- The principle of locality distinguishes temporal locality (locality in time) and spatial locality (locality in space).

- A first implementation of virtual memory uses register relocation. This has the restrictions that the size of a process cannot exceed the amount of available main memory, and a process has to occupy a contiguous area of real memory.

- With paging, both virtual and physical memory are divided into parts of equal sizes, called pages. Each page is relocated independently such that a process does not have to occupy a contiguous area of real memory. In addition, pages must be flagged to be not resident, resulting in a demand paging system to support virtual memory.

- Table superfluity occurs when a complete translation table has to be memory resident while only a small portion is needed.

- Segmentation divides memory into blocks of variable lengths. Each segment can hold one (or more) logically related object(s), thus matching the user's conceptual view of memory. Segmentation causes external fragmentation: main memory will contain free areas (called holes) after some time. The total size of these holes may be large, but each of them may not be able to accommodate a new segment.

- To solve some of the problems, paging and segmentation can be combined in two ways, one with paging as the dominant factor, the other with segmentation dominating.

- Direct mapping is a form of address translation where a table look-up is used to translate the virtual address into a real address.

- Pages and segments normally belong to one process and should be protected from others (either write or even read–write protection). On the other hand, it is sometimes useful, or necessary, to share information in pages or segments. The objectives of sharing and protection are hence contradictory and a compromise must be found between them.

- A translation lookaside buffer is a cache to hold the last translated addresses. It is used to accelerate the translation process.

- An inverted page table is a way of reducing table superfluity by having a translation table that has an entry for each block of real memory (rather than for each block of virtual memory).

- Multiple virtual spaces are used to accelerate the process switch operation.

- Memory management includes the fetch, placement and replacement policies.

- Memory allocation can be based on fixed-size or variable-size partitions for a process. The scope of a memory allocation policy may be local (only look at the current process) or global (look at the memory allocated to all processes).

- Pages can be fetched before they are needed by a process (prefetching) or they can be fetched only when they are needed (demand fetching).

- Pages and segments must be placed in memory. For pages, this is no problem, as each empty space has the correct size. Segments can be placed according to policies such as best fit, first fit or binary buddy.

- The amount of memory allocated to a process can be fixed (fixed-size partitions) or it can vary during execution (variable-size partitions). When the allocated memory fills up, pages and segments can be replaced according to non-usage-based policies such as random and first-in, first-out (FIFO) replacement; or usage-based policies such as Clock and least recently used (LRU) replacement. For variable-size partitions, the best-known replacement policies are working set (WS) replacement and page fault frequency (PFF) replacement. For both partitioning schemes, a theoretical optimum exists, called MIN and VMIN, respectively.

EXERCISES

10.1 (a) What are the main objectives of a memory management system?

(b) Which address spaces can be recognized?

10.2 What is dynamic relocation, and why is blocking used?

10.3 (a) What is temporal locality, and what is spatial locality?

(b) What is the working set model?

10.4 (a) Which are the main address translation mechanisms?

(b) What is the purpose of relocation, and what are the disadvantages?

(c) What is the advantage of demand paging?

10.5 What is segmentation and paged segmentation?

10.6 Which address translation acceleration mechanisms exist?

10.7 Which memory management policies exist?

10.8 (a) Which fetch policies can be distinguished?

(b) Why is the placement policy trivial for paged systems?

(c) Which are well-known replacement policies for segmented systems?

(d) Which are well-known replacement policies for fixed-size partitions?

(e) Why do the replacement policies for variable-size partitions differ from those with fixed-size partitions?

10.9 What is the most optimal replacement policy, and why is it impractical?

10.10 What is the purpose of multi-level address translation, as used in multi-level paging?

10.11 A system contains the following segments: *A*, a pure code segment, *B*, a code segment that also includes constants (for example, for table look-up), *C*, a segment with only constants, *D*, an I/O buffer segment, *E*, a normal data segment and *F*, a stack segment. Indicate the access rights (read, write, execute) each of these segments should have.

10.12 A paged segmented system has a virtual address space of 32 bits. The page size is 2 kbytes and a segment has a maximum size of 16 Mbytes (see Figure 10.9). Assume that the maximum amount of real memory the system is able to contain is 64 Mbytes.

(a) Determine the size of the Vs, Vp and Dp fields of the virtual address.

(b) Determine the layout of a PTE.

(c) What is the size of a page table, in bytes?

(d) Determine the layout of an STE.

References

Belady, L. A. (1966). A study of replacement algorithms for a virtual storage computer. *IBM Systems Journal*, **5**(2), 78–101.

Chu, W. W. and Opderbeck, H. (1972). The page fault frequency replacement algorithm. In *Proc. AFIPS FJCC*, **41**, pp. 597–609.

Chu, W. W. and Opderbeck, H. (1974). Performance of replacement algorithms with different page sizes. *Computer*, **7**(11), 14–21.

Clark, D. W. and Emer, J. S. (1985). Performance of the VAX-11/780 translation buffer: Simulation and measurement. *ACM Trans. on Computer Systems*, **3**(1), 31–62.

Cohen, B. and McGarity, R. (1986). The design and implementation of the MC68851 paged memory management unit. *IEEE Micro*, **6**(2), 13–28.

Dekker, G. J. and van de Goor, A. J. (1987). AMORE: Address mapping with overlapped rotating entries. *IEEE Micro*, **7**(3), 22–34.

Denning, P. J. (1968). The working set model for program behavior. *Comm. of the ACM*, **11**(5), 323–33.

Denning, P. J. (1970). Virtual memory. *Computing Surveys*, **2**(3), 153–89.

Denning, P. J. (1980). Working sets past and present. *IEEE Trans. on Software Engineering*, **SE–6**(1), 64–84.

Fabry, R. S. (1974). Capability-based addressing. *Comm. of the ACM*, **17**(7), 403–12.

Franklin, M. A. *et al.* (1978). Anomalies with variable partition paging algorithms. *Comm. of the ACM*, **21**(3), 232–36.

Furht, B. P. and Milutinovic, V. M. (1987). A survey of microprocessor architectures for memory management. *Computer*, **20**(3), 48–67.

Hester, P. D. *et al.* (1986). The IBM RT PC ROMP and memory management unit architecture. *IBM RT Personal Computer Technology*. IBM Publication No. SA 23–1057, pp. 48–56.

Motorola (1985). *MC68851 Paged Memory Management Unit User's Manual.* Motorola Incorporated.

Prieve, B. G. and Fabry, R. S. (1976). VMIN – An optimal variable-space page replacement algorithm. *Comm. of the ACM*, **19**(5), 295–97.

Smith, A. J. (1978). Sequential program prefetching in memory hierarchies. *Computer*, **11**(12), 7–21.

11 Input/Output

The difference between news and gossip lies in whether you raise your voice or lower it.
– Franklin P. Jones

The purpose of a computer system is to process information. In addition, a computer system must exchange information with its environment. This can be the input of information that must be processed by the computer system, or the output of the results of that processing.

In the early days, a computer system was dedicated to a single user, who used input/output (I/O) for direct communication with programs and for storage of data on secondary memory. But the function of I/O has been greatly expanded and has become increasingly complex. Multiprogramming and time-sharing techniques allow multiple users to access both private and shared program and data files simultaneously; users compete for computer resources; processes are broken up, interleaved and completed as time becomes available. Therefore, the user cannot be directly responsible for the I/O function any more; this has been taken over by the operating system.

In this chapter, first the structure of the I/O system is presented, followed by a description of I/O devices. Next, an overview of the functions of each of the layers of the I/O software is given. The section on the I/O process describes the different ways of performing I/O from a process point of view, in the order of an increasing degree of parallelism (that is, process independence). Architectural support for I/O is presented as a requirement to obtain the incréasing degree of parallelism. The chapter ends with a discussion of the realization alternatives of device controllers, including channels and I/O processors.

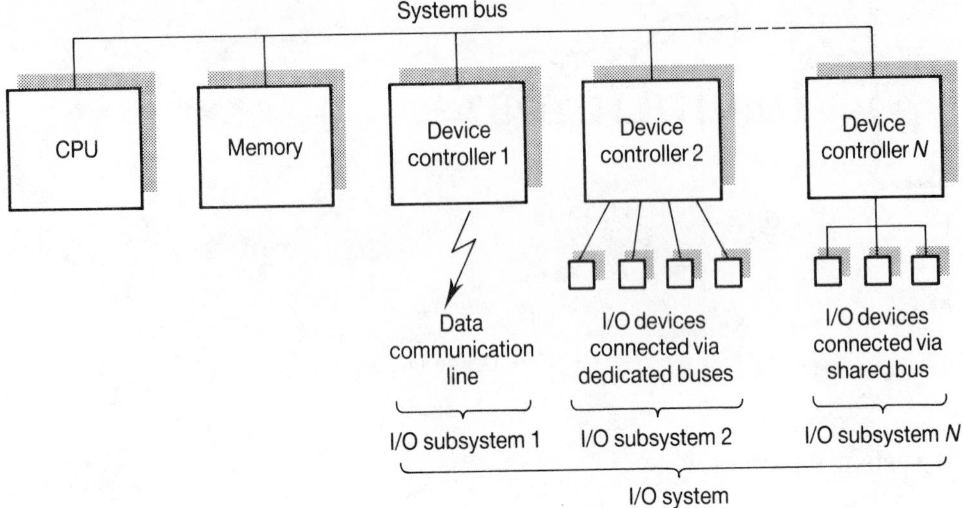

FIGURE 11.1
System configuration including I/O.

11.1 I/O system structure

Communication between the computer and its environment takes place via I/O devices. I/O devices are pieces of machinery that can store computer-readable information, convert inputs from the environment into computer-readable form, or convert computer data into outputs understandable by its environment. This environment can consist of humans, in addition to other computers, chemical processes, and so on.

The I/O devices connected to the CPU are collectively called the **I/O system**. A single device controller with its attached devices is called an **I/O subsystem** (Figure 11.1). A **device controller** can be a simple interface between the CPU and an I/O device or, in a more sophisticated form, can control several devices that are independent of the CPU. In all cases, the device controller provides the control and buffering functions necessary to operate the associated I/O devices. The device controller may be physically located in the I/O device, the CPU or packaged separately. Some device controllers may only control a single device, because only a single device of that type is needed in the system, or because of performance reasons. Often, however, the cost of the controller may be shared between devices of the same type, because most of the devices are inactive most of the time, so the device controller may be multiprogrammed.

The general structure of an I/O subsystem is shown in Figure 11.2. I/O devices are connected to the controller via a **device interface**. The device controller is connected to the (host) CPU via the **system bus**.

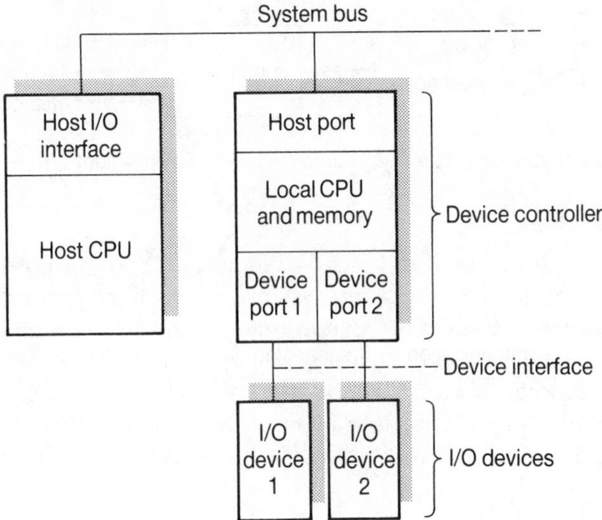

FIGURE 11.2
General structure of an I/O subsystem.

The simplest device controller always consists of two parts: the **host port** and the **device port**. Normally, there is one device port per attached device. The host port presents the status and control information to the CPU, and receives the commands and addresses from the CPU. In more intelligent device controllers, it may also contain local processing and memory to allow for direct memory access (DMA) and I/O processing, concurrent with CPU processing. The device port takes care of the control of, and the transfer of, data to and from the I/O device(s). An internal bus provides the connection between both ports.

11.2 I/O devices

I/O devices have many properties distinct from those of CPUs and memories. This is due to their mechanical nature (which makes them inherently less reliable and rather slow compared with electronic devices) and their large variety.

11.2.1 Classification of I/O devices

A general-purpose computer can be configured for a specific application by adding I/O devices suitable for that application. Those I/O devices, often just called devices, are classified as follows: **storage devices**, which are used by the system to store data for later retrieval, and **source/sink devices**, which are used by the system to communicate with its environment (Figure 11.3).

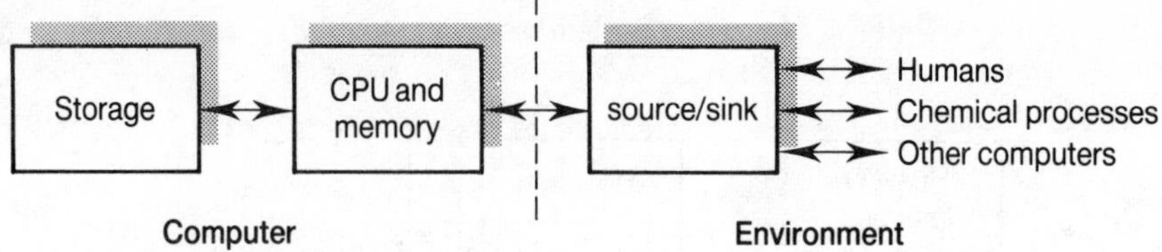

FIGURE 11.3
Classification of I/O devices.

Storage devices

Storage includes memory and auxiliary devices whose purpose is to hold data to be used later in the same system. Consequently, storage devices can be considered as memory extensions. Because electronic memory is relatively expensive and volatile, almost all systems also include mechanical storage devices. There is a variety of storage devices, each with their own storage capacity ranging from about 1 Mbyte for a floppy disk to 1 Gbyte for a hard disk to 50 Gbytes for an optical disk.

Source/sink devices

The purpose of source/sink devices is to allow communication between the computer and its environment. This can be done via source devices that allow input by humans (keyboard, voice analyzer, digitizer or mouse) or by equipment (modem, sensor or switch). Other devices serve as sink devices, providing output to humans (printer or graphics display) or to equipment (modem, actuator or chemical process). Data communication lines used for connections with other computers and networks are also regarded as source/sink devices.

11.2.2 Properties

Device properties that directly influence the computer system operation are access time (latency), data transfer time (bandwidth) and error rate.

Access time

Because many bits share a storage medium, which has a sequential rather than a random access, the requested data item cannot usually be read or written immediately; first, some mechanical motion has to be performed. This is called the **access time**. For example, for a moving head disk, the access time consists of the time required for positioning the head (the seek time) and the time until the right sector passes the head (the rotational delay).

The access times of I/O devices are significantly larger than the access times of main memory (about 25 ms for a moving head disk versus 0.5 μs for main memory, giving a ratio of 5×10^4). Furthermore, access times can vary considerably, not only for different devices (a disk access is much faster than a tape access), but also for different data items stored in one device. Finding an arbitrary word on a magnetic tape may take quite a long time, while finding the next word on that tape is much faster. Therefore, it is advisable for such storage devices to read and write data in blocks, so a single access provides many words of data.

Data transfer time

The data transfer time of an I/O device depends on the amount of data to be transferred (the block size) and the data transfer rate (the time between successive data elements). The block size is determined by the device type. Character-oriented devices (terminals) send their data on a byte-by-byte basis, whereas block-oriented devices (disks and tapes) only transfer blocks of data. The size of the block is determined by such factors as the access time, transfer time, the fragmentation of partly filled blocks, buffering requirements, and so on.

The data transfer rate is often slow compared to memory-to-memory transfers. For example, the transfer rate of a disk may be 1 Mbyte/s. Assuming disk sectors of 1 kbytes, this results in a data transfer time of 1 ms.

Error rate

Due to the mechanical nature of most storage devices, they have a much higher error rate than CPUs and memories. Because of the physical motion of the information-carrying medium and the high information density (in terms of bits/inch), dust particles, wear and mechanical tolerances are a major cause of errors. Data communication devices are error prone due to their often long, unshielded, lines, which are susceptible to radiation and power transients, for example. The detection and correction of these errors requires some form of **redundancy** in hardware as well as provisions to handle these errors in the software. This can be in the form of additional checking bits (using error-correcting codes), reverse transmission of the received message (echo) or retransmission of messages.

11.3 I/O software

A major function of the operating system is to control all I/O devices. This consists of issuing I/O commands and handling interrupts and errors. In addition, the operating system should provide a high-level device interface, which is consistent between all device types, and easy to use. To accomplish this, the I/O software is organized into layers, as shown in Figure 11.4. The lowest layer consists of the interrupt handler (see Section 9.6).

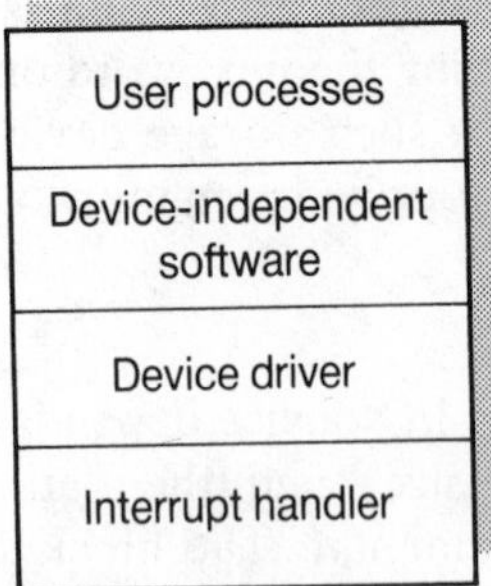

FIGURE 11.4
I/O software structure.

The device driver contains all device-dependent code. It is, presumably, the only part of the operating system that has knowledge of the attached device type, such as the type of I/O commands to be issued, the physical organization of the device, the mechanical properties of the device and the way device errors should be dealt with. The operating system requires one device driver per device type, of which more than one drive may be present. The function of the device driver is to translate the high-level logical commands into low-level physical commands (for example, read disk x, track y, sector z). For example, it may perform the following actions:

- Allow for queueing of logical commands.
- Translate the logical block number into a physical disk address.
- Reorder the sequence of disk requests to improve throughput.
- Communicate with the device controller.
- Error handling (I/O devices have a high error rate).

The device-independent software translates the high-level user interface using symbolic commands into the logical commands for the device driver. (Note that the boundary with the device driver is somewhat arbitrary because sometimes functions could be done at either layer, or are done at a particular layer because of performance reasons.)

(1) Translation of a symbolic device name in order to identify the corresponding driver. For example, the UNIX symbolic name */dev/tty*0 is translated into the name of a control block specifying the terminal device driver.

(2) Translation of a system-wide logical block size into the device's physical block size. This may include buffering to pack or unpack system level data into the physical blocks required by the device.

(3) Storage allocation and deallocation. Administrating the storage space for the devices can be done in a device-independent way.

11.4 I/O process

All operating system functions are performed by processes. The process notion has been introduced to allow for concurrency, synchronization and scheduling (see Chapter 9). An I/O process can be considered to consist of two parts (see Figure 11.2): the part executed by the CPU and the part executed by the device controller(s). The device controller part can form a single process with the CPU part (**direct I/O**) or it can form an independent process (such that multiple device controllers may be active simultaneously and in parallel with some CPU-based process). Depending on the degree of synchronization required with the CPU-based process, one can distinguish **overlapped I/O**, requiring a high degree of synchronization, or **autonomous I/O**, requiring a low degree of synchronization.

Synchronization between the CPU and the device controller part of the I/O process takes place in the form of communication, which exchanges two types of information:

(1) **Device control information**: This consists of control and status information. Control information is sent by the CPU to the device controller for control purposes; that is, it puts the I/O subsystem in some state. The part of the control information that determines the state of the I/O subsystem is stored in one or more control registers. Status information is sent by the device controller to the CPU, under control of a sense command, to inform the CPU about the state of the device controller and/or device. This information is stored in one or more status registers.

(2) **Device data**: This is the data read from or written to the device. Usually, it is passed via a special register, the data register, in the host port. A data output (write) operation is used to transfer data from the CPU to the device controller to be consumed by the device; a data input (read) operation is used to transfer data, produced by the device, from the device controller to the CPU.

The control and sense operations are performed by writing to a control register or by reading from a status register. In terms of control and status information, one can distinguish (see Figure 11.2):

- Host port control/status information: This is related to the communication with the host port. Since there is only one host port per group of connected devices, a single (set of) host port control/status register(s) is required.

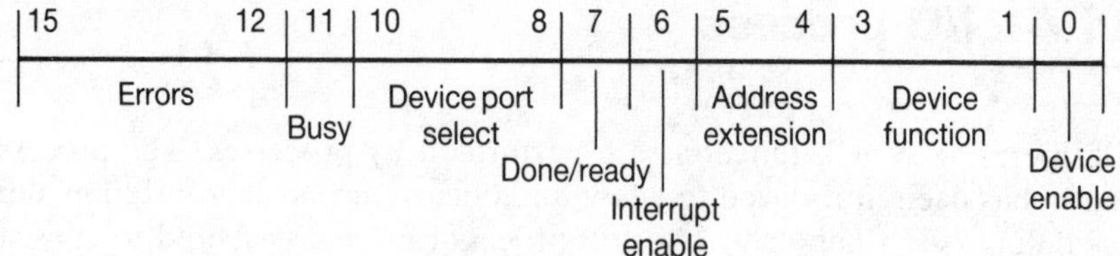

FIGURE 11.5

Unibus collective control/status register format.

- Device port control/status information: This is directly related to the attached device. When multiple devices are connected to a single device controller, multiple (sets of) device port control/status registers have to be present when these devices have to be active simultaneously.

Many computer architectures prescribe the format of one control/status register, which represents the collective control/status information of the device controller and all attached devices. This way, interrupt and exception handlers initially only have to deal with the collective control/status information. By prescribing a standard format of the collective control/status register, a major part of the interrupt and exception handlers can be device independent. It should be noted that for simple devices, such as a printer, the collective control/status register may be sufficient to include all host and device port control/status information. Example 11.1 shows the DEC collective control/status register format for Unibus peripherals. Note that a single 16-bit register is used, where control/status information is intermingled. In this way, the most significant bit of the high- and the low-order byte contain important status information which can be tested for with a Test Byte instruction. The sign bit of the byte will be reflected in the condition codes.

□□EXAMPLE 11.1

Unibus peripherals for the VAX family of computers require a collective control/status register with the layout of Figure 11.5 (DEC, 1976). Many peripherals use less than 16 bits, so that the collective control/status register is the only control/status register, while others may require additional control/status information. The format of the collective control/status register is as follows:

- Bits 15–12 (errors, status) are error flags. Generally, each bit is associated with a specific error, while bit 15 is the OR of all error flags. Thus, the testing of this single bit is sufficient to determine if an operation has been completed without errors.
- Bit 11 (busy flag, status).
- Bits 10–8 (device port select, control).

- Bit 7 (done or ready, status).
- Bit 6 (interrupt enable, control).
- Bits 5–4 (address extension, control) allow devices to use an additional 2 bits, to specify 18-bit addresses. (This is a peculiarity of the Unibus!)
- Bits 3–1 (device function, control) specify the operation that a device should perform.
- Bit 0 (enable, control).

In the following subsections, four ways of implementing the I/O process are presented, in the order of increasing degree of parallelism, together with the implications for CPU and host port support. This sequence also represents the way I/O has evolved historically.

11.4.1 Direct I/O

This is the simplest form of I/O, where the CPU and the device controller part form a single process, thereby disallowing any form of concurrency. The following program shows the sequence of steps required for an I/O write operation. Steps 1–3 form a loop in which the CPU interrogates (polls) the device. This is needed to synchronize the CPU part with the device controller part of the I/O process.

CPU	**Device**
(1) Read device status register.	
	(2) Send status.
(3) Inspect device status: if device not ready, go to 1.	
(4) Write data to device data register.	
	(5) Accept data and set status to 'Not Ready' until data has been written to device.
(6) If more data to send, go to 1.	

Each CPU step is programmed (direct I/O is therefore also called **programmed I/O**) in one or more CPU instructions, as illustrated in Example 11.2).

□□EXAMPLE 11.2

This example shows an MC68020 assembler program to output a character string of Count characters, located at the address Data_addr, to a printer that has an 8-bit wide interface (that is, control/status information and data can be transferred between the CPU and the device controller 8 bits at a time). The status register of the printer is located at memory location Printer_stat and the printer data register at location Printer_dat.

```
       MOVE.L  #Data_addr, A0          ;A0 points to the character
                                       ;string
       MOVE.B  #Count, D0              ;D0 contains length of the
                                       ;character string
Wait : BTST.B  #Rdy_bit, Printer_stat  ;Polling loop to wait until
                                       ;the printer is ready
       BPL     Wait
       MOVE.B  (A0)+, Printer_dat      ;Move a character to the
                                       ;data register of the printer
                                       ;and print
       DBNE    D0, Wait                ;Decrement D0, if (D0) ≠ 0
                                       ;loop until string is printed
```

The requirements for direct I/O, in terms of CPU and device controller support, are the availability of at least a collective control/status register (with an enable and a ready flag) and a data register. Furthermore, I/O instructions have to be available. These instructions allow the CPU to communicate with the device controller. They have to be able to specify the operation to be performed, the host and the device port (often collectively called the device address), and usually a CPU address (which is the source/destination of the I/O data). For the specification of each of these three components, several alternatives exist, as discussed in the following.

Specification of the I/O operation

The specification of the I/O operation can be done in the opcode or operand space. When the opcode space is used to specify the I/O operation, depending on the available opcode space and the desire to include I/O operations in the specification of the instruction set, several alternatives can be distinguished.

- The opcode space specifies that the instruction is an I/O instruction and the exact operation to be performed (which typically is device dependent) is specified in an opcode extension field.
- The opcode space specifies the I/O operation. This means that I/O operations are part of the CPU architecture and that all devices should handle all operations in a uniform way. The IBM/370 channel architecture uses this method (IBM, 1970). For operations

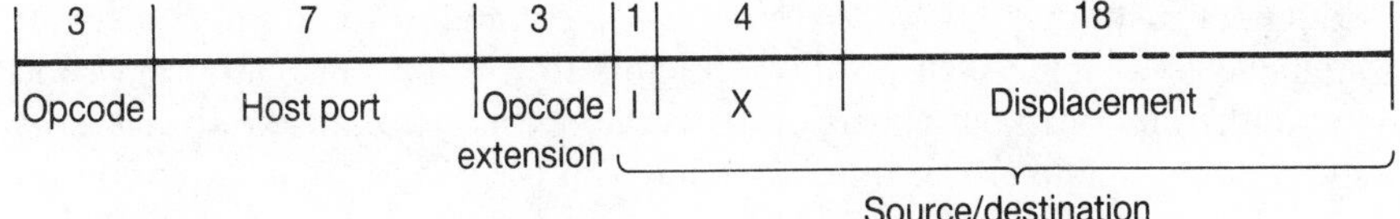

FIGURE 11.6

DEC PDP-10 I/O instruction format.

involving the transfer of data, the IBM/370 architecture requires an opcode extension field, located in the so-called channel command word (CCW).

Architectures with a limited address space have historically used the opcode space to specify the I/O instruction (and operation). I/O instructions should be privileged instructions.

□□EXAMPLE 11.3

This example shows the DEC PDP-10 I/O instruction format of Figure 11.6 (DEC, 1969). While the opcode extension field specifies the I/O operation, the 3-bit opcode field is used to specify that the instruction is an I/O instruction. The host port is specified via a 7-bit immediate field and device port selection is done via an implicit register. The CPU address is specified in the same way as the PDP-10 architecture specifies operand addresses located in memory (see Example 4.1). It consists of the I, X and displacement fields.

The operand space can be used to specify the I/O operation by reserving some part of this space for I/O. Memory addresses are used to access each of the control/status and data registers; that is, memory space is used to overlay these registers. This is called **memory-mapped I/O**. The advantage of memory-mapped I/O is that all instructions of the CPU can be used for I/O, at the expense of a small loss of address space available for main memory. I/O operations can be made privileged by protecting the area of memory assigned to I/O. Almost all newer architectures, which typically have 32-bit addresses, use memory-mapped I/O. The PDP-11 architecture, with only 64 kbytes of address space, specifies the top 8 kbytes to be reserved for I/O (DEC, 1975).

Specification of host and device port

The specification of the host port is not subject to any constraints imposed by the device drivers. It can be done using an immediate data field (see Example 11.3) or in the form of an operand address.

When a host port can control more than one device, I/O instructions have to be able to specify the device port, in order to access the device control/status registers. Device drivers (see Figure 11.4) are designed such that they can handle all devices of a particular type, attached to a single host port. To be able to use the same program code to handle any of the attached devices, the specification of the device port should be possible at run time; it should not be embedded in the program code (compile time selection). Device port specification can be done in the following ways:

- All ports accessible: The device port control/status registers of all devices (assuming the device controller has several devices attached) are accessible, because, for example, all are memory mapped. The device driver can set up a base register to point to the block of control/status registers of a particular device and use the base-displacement form of addressing to access a particular control/status register.
- One port accessible: The device port control/status registers of only one port are accessible at any time. The particular device port can be selected via a control register in the host port. The selection of a control/status register of a particular device port may be done via an opcode extension field, or via a memory address, when memory mapping is used. Memory mapping for only *one* set of control/status registers is then required, thus saving overlay space.

Specification of a CPU address

When transfer of information between the CPU and the I/O system has to take place, a CPU memory location has to be specified to act as source/destination. Usually, a register or a memory location can be specified for this, using the same addressing modes and instruction formats as used by other, non-I/O instructions (see Example 11.3).

Because of the low data transfer rates of I/O devices compared to the CPU instruction execution speed, the CPU is capable of executing many instructions in the time it takes for a single device access and data transfer. The CPU will, therefore, waste a lot of time in the polling loop, synchronizing with the device. This may be acceptable for single-user systems (for example, a personal computer executing MS-DOS), but will certainly not be acceptable for multiprogramming or time-sharing systems, which require CPU processing to overlap with (be in parallel with) I/O.

11.4.2 Overlapped I/O

Overlapped I/O is the most simple form of having the CPU and the device part of the I/O process behave as independent processes. The direct I/O polling synchronization mechanism, which is a form of busy waiting, is replaced with an interrupt mechanism. Instead of executing the polling loop, the CPU is freed to execute other processes, while the device process is performing its operation. When the device process needs to be synchronized with its counterpart CPU process for service (typically a transfer of data), it signals this via an interrupt. Thus, in addition to the facilities required for direct I/O, an interrupt mechanism is required. A host port can interrupt the CPU for several reasons:

- An I/O device is ready to transfer the next data item.
- The operation is completed, in which case a done interrupt is given.
- An exception is signalled, which could be an invalid command or parameter, a data error or a device error.

The advantage of overlapped I/O is that the CPU is not continuously bound to a single I/O process of a particular device, but only during the synchronization periods when a next data transfer is requested. This is a relatively short time, so other processes (including I/O processes) may be executed by the CPU. Many I/O devices may be operated concurrently this way. The disadvantage of overlapped I/O is that process synchronization is required for each data transfer and the CPU overhead due to interrupt handling can be considerable, because it involves a process switch, which may involve the execution of several hundred instructions.

11.4.3 Autonomous data transfers

The frequency of process synchronization, and therefore also the incurred overhead, can be reduced further by synchronizing the transfer of a block of data, rather than for each individual data item. Blocks typically vary in size from 80 bytes (for a matrix printer) to 512 or several kbytes for a disk. This results in a reduction of the synchronization overhead by two to three orders of magnitude. The mechanism required to support autonomous transfers of data by the I/O subsystem is called **direct memory access (DMA)**. Example 11.4 outlines an MC68020 assembler program to set up autonomous data transfers.

□□EXAMPLE 11.4

The following program prints a line of text using DMA. It does this by merely providing the DMA controller in the host port with the required parameters. These parameters consist of the values to be loaded into the Data_ar (the data address register used to contain the CPU address of the data transfers) and the Cnt_r (a counter register which specifies the block size).

```
MOVE.L   #Data_addr, Data_ar      ;Data_ar points to the character
                                  ;string
MOVE.B   #Count, Cnt_r            ;Cnt_r contains the length of the
                                  ;string
IOR.B    #Start, Printer_stat     ;Start printer and give interrupt
                                  ;when the string has been printed
```

The subject of DMA is discussed in the following subsections together with the concept of data chaining. Because DMA allows the I/O subsystem to access main memory for the transfer of data, conflicts may arise when the CPU makes use of a memory management mechanism. This is discussed in Appendix B.2.1. Another subject, devoted to the issue of data coherence, which is of interest when the CPU is provided with a cache mechanism, is presented in Appendix B.2.2.

Direct memory access

The DMA operation is analogous to a multiple data move instruction (see Section 6.2.2), the main difference being that DMA is executed by a host port, rather than by the CPU. The operands required for DMA are called the DMA parameters. These parameters are stored in the host port and are the same as those required for a block move (see Example 11.4):

- The CPU memory address is the address in main memory where the data has to be transferred to or from.
- The block length is a count, representing the size of the area in main memory the data has to be transferred to or from.
- The device data address is the address of the data on the I/O storage device. In the case of a disk drive, this address consists of a disk, track and sector number. In the case of a source/sink device (a printer), no device data address is required, because the data is not stored; it is a stream that leaves or enters the device controller via the data register.

The execution of the DMA operation for the printer of Example 11.4 is as follows:

(1) The DMA parameters are transferred to the host port and the printer is started.

(2) Because the printer data register is empty, the device port requests the data register to be filled with one character in order to start printing; this is done by the DMA channel (steps 3 and 4).

(3) The DMA channel in the host port requests control over the system bus (see Figure 11.2), and when this is granted by the CPU, it can start the DMA operation.

(4) The DMA operation, to fill the data register, consists of:

- Placing the memory address on the system bus.
- Performing a memory-read operation.
- Storing data read in the data register.
- Releasing the system bus.
- Incrementing the memory address to point to the next character.
- Decrementing count.

(5) On the next request for data from the device port, the action to be taken depends on the value of the count:

- If Count $\neq 0$, then proceed with step 3.
- If Count $= 0$, then stop printer and generate an interrupt to signal completion of the print operation.

Depending on the number of data transfers per DMA operation, two types of DMA can be distinguished:

(1) **Single-cycle DMA**: Only a single transfer takes place during one DMA operation (step 4). The advantage of this type of DMA is that the system bus is only taken away from the CPU for a very short time. The disadvantage is that, for every transfer, a bus arbitration has to take place, with its associated overhead (see Chapter 13).

(2) **Burst-mode DMA**: Multiple data transfers take place during one DMA operation. To do this, the device controller has to be able to buffer (temporarily store) the data. The advantage of burst-mode DMA is its higher speed and lower bus arbitration overhead. The disadvantages are a longer occupation of the system bus (thereby locking out the CPU and other DMA channels) and the cost of buffering facilities in the device controller.

Data chaining

Most memory management systems allocate/deallocate memory in blocks of some size (for example, 512 bytes or more) called pages (see Chapter 10). These pages may not be of the same size as the blocks of the storage devices. Tape drives, for example, tend to have large block sizes (called records) because of their relatively large start and stop times. During this time, the tape passing the read/write head cannot be read/written. This amount of tape is called the inter-record gap. Large records reduce the waste of tape due to these inter-record gaps. The size of sectors on a disk may also be different from that of a page for similar reasons.

In general, one wants to do memory (de)allocation in blocks with a size optimized for the particular technology. As a rule, pages tend to be smaller than sectors or records, because the size of the latter two is determined by mechanical factors such as the access time. Reading/writing data from/to a storage device has to be done in blocks of data determined by the storage device (a sector or a record), which typically has a size that is a multiple number of pages; for example, when writing a sector to a disk, P pages may have to be written. One way of implementing the writing of P pages is to write a page under DMA control and then generate an interrupt to set up the DMA parameters for the next page. If no buffering in the device controller is provided, the time allowed for the interrupt handling and the set up of the next DMA parameters would be the transfer time of a single data element, which is in the order of 1 μs and is far from sufficient. A solution to this problem would be to have a buffer with the size of a sector in the device driver such that the block size of the I/O operation is the block size of the device. The device driver copies P pages to/from this buffer, while the buffer can be written/read from/to disk. This copying operation causes CPU overhead. A variant of this solution is to locate the buffer in the device controller. The host port can then fill or empty the buffer under DMA control, one page at a time. This avoids the CPU copying overhead. A disadvantage of both these methods is that, for certain devices (for example, tapes), the record size, which determines the buffer size, can be very large, and so at least two buffers have to be present to sustain continuous operations (while one buffer is filled by the device, the other is emptied by the CPU).

A more elegant solution, which does not impose time-critical interrupt service times, CPU overhead or a buffer, is the use of **data chaining**. The basic idea is for the DMA channel itself to set up the DMA parameters, which imposes no restrictions on the sector or record size. In support of this, the device port is equipped with a data chain register (DCR), in addition to the registers required for the DMA parameters. The DCR points to a chain of P blocks of DMA parameters, located in main memory. Usually, a flag, the data chain flag (DCF), in the DMA parameter block indicates whether chaining should be continued. Most current architectures support data chaining, to allow for independence in the size of pages, disk sectors and tape records.

A DMA operation, using data chaining, is performed as follows:

(1) The DMA mechanism is used to transfer the DMA parameters. The DCR is used to access this DMA parameter block in main memory.

(2) The DMA mechanism is used to transfer a block of data to/from the I/O device. The Data_ar (see Example 11.4) is used to address that data in main memory.

(3) When the block of data has been transferred, one of the following actions is performed:

  (a) The data chain flag in the DMA parameter block is set, so another block of data has to be transferred: go to step 1.

  (b) The data chain flag is not set, so the DMA operation has been completed: an interrupt is generated.

When data chaining is used for a read operation, a single block of data of a storage device may be scattered over several pages in memory, which therefore is often referred to as a **scatter read operation**. Conversely, for a write operation, several pages are gathered to be written to a single block on the storage device, which is often referred to as a **gather write operation**.

11.4.4 Autonomous control transfers

The frequency of process synchronization can be further reduced, but even more important, the throughput and the level of autonomy of the I/O subsystem can be increased, by allowing the host port to fetch its own control information in the form of a control block. The fetching of the control block can be done under DMA control, using the mechanism used for fetching the DMA parameters for data chaining. This is called **command chaining**. In support of this, the DMA mechanism is extended with a command chain register (CCR), which points to the chain of commands, and a command chain flag (CCF), which indicates whether command chaining should be continued.

Using command chaining, the device driver merely has to append each new I/O command to the end of the command chain, which may consist of a linked list of control blocks which contain the required I/O commands. Rather than waiting until all I/O commands have been executed, a certain process may be able to proceed when its I/O command has been completed. I/O subsystems supporting command chaining therefore have a flag in their control block to indicate that an interrupt has to be generated when that command has been completed.

11.5 Device controller structure

This section discusses some implementation aspects of device controllers. It describes the functions of the host port and the levels of intelligence it may have, followed by a discussion of the functions of the device port.

11.5.1 Host port

The host port consists of hardware for I/O command decoding and device port selection, control/status registers and interrupt hardware. In addition, the host port may be equipped with facilities to support autoconfiguration of the system, which means that a program can determine the configuration of the system by interrogating all the host ports. Each host port needs, therefore, to contain (in an EPROM or via switches) identification of the I/O subsystem type, its version, its configuration (the number of attached devices) and its update status. To allow for flexibility in interrupt priority level allocation, the priority level should also be selectable, preferably under program control. When geographical addressing is used (see Chapter 13), a register must also be available to contain the logical address of the I/O subsystem. Figure 11.2 shows that the device controller may contain a local CPU and memory in order to make it more intelligent. This intelligence is considered part of the host port.

Buffering

Buffering is a function, performed at the implementation level, whereby the device controller is equipped with a buffer mechanism. This mechanism can be used to make the I/O process less time critical and to increase performance.

Storage devices such as disk drives typically have a fixed rate with which they transfer data. When a write operation is being performed, the device controller has to be able to supply this data at the requested rate. If, due to system load, this rate may not be obtained, an **under-run error** is considered to have occurred: the disk has to write data that is not available yet. The under-run error can be recovered by a retry. The opposite situation can occur in the case of a read I/O operation: if the data is not taken away sufficiently fast, an **over-run error** occurs, causing the data register to be overwritten before the previous data has been stored in memory. Disk data transfers are time critical, as are most communications links. Other I/O devices may not be time critical.

By introducing a buffer, consisting of a piece of memory in the device controller, information transfers become less time critical or non-time critical, because the sector can first be written into the local buffer. This reduces or eliminates critical timing requirements for all forms of I/O (direct I/O, overlapped I/O and autonomous data transfers). System performance may also be increased because, for example, in the case of overlapped I/O, a block of data may be transferred upon every interrupt (thus reducing the number of interrupts), or, in the case of DMA, burst-mode may be used.

Non-intelligent device controllers

Device controllers used for direct or overlapped I/O do not usually require local intelligence. The controller can be very simple: it may consist of a system bus interface, a collective control/status register (of which only a few bits have to be implemented) and a data register. All intelligence is located in the I/O software.

Intelligent device controllers

Intelligent device controllers contain processing power and generally a larger buffering capacity (local memory) than non-intelligent device controllers. With this processing power, device driver functions as well as some of the device-independent software functions may be performed, thereby off-loading the CPU and allowing for concurrent operation. The simplest form of concurrent operation is the provision of autonomous data transfers, using DMA. This requires little intelligence on the part of the device controller, because none of the functions of the device driver are taken over. However, it does reduce the CPU overhead, as shown before. More advanced device controllers are channels and I/O processors.

Channels Channels, as used by the IBM/370 architecture, allow for a higher level of I/O. Their level has been chosen such that they present a uniform interface to the CPU, in spite of the large variety of storage and source/sink devices. The I/O commands are included in the architecture of the CPU, because they are identical for, and apply to all, channels (rather than being I/O device specific).

Channels execute channel programs, which consist of a sequence of channel command words that allow chaining of data and commands. The channel programs and their buffering facilities are a major contribution to the reduction of I/O overhead and make I/O less time critical. Because of their uniform and consistent interface, channels also ease the implementation of device drivers. Depending on the capabilities for multiprogramming the host port (called channel by IBM) facilitates, two types of channels can be distinguished:

(1) **Selector channels** (the device controller is not multiprogrammed): These channels have the property that they stay logically connected to a device port (called subchannel by IBM) for the duration of the operation. They are typically used to connect devices with high data transfer rates (for example, disk drives and magnetic tape drives), and use burst-mode DMA. When a selector channel is logically connected to a device port, it is busy and not capable of accepting commands for any other device port connected to that host port. Other device ports may, however, be completing I/O

operations issued previously and which do not involve the host port (for example, a tape rewind or disk seek operation).

(2) **Multiplexor channels** (the device controller is multiprogrammed): These channels allow several I/O operations, which may involve the host port, to be performed simultaneously. This is a form of multiprogramming of the host port, which must have a set of device control/status and data registers for each device port. When one or more device ports and devices are executing I/O operations, other device ports and devices may be selected to start new operations. When several devices are transferring data, the DMA hardware of the host port is multiplexed at the expense of a reduced transfer rate per device. Therefore, devices with a lower data transfer rate are typically connected to a multiplexor channel. The IBM/370 architecture distinguishes two types of multiplexor channels, based on the DMA burst length.

Channels, when introduced as part of the concept of the IBM/360 architecture (in 1964) were a significant contribution to the architecture of I/O systems. They provided a device-independent, uniform, interface to the CPU, and reduced CPU overhead and critical CPU response time requirements, by using DMA for data transfers and allowing data and command chaining. They did not perform any of the functions of the device drivers and/or the device-independent software, because that would require I/O subsystems to have a local processor, which was not economically justified at that time.

I/O processors The availability of low-cost microprocessors opened the way to increase the intelligence (functionality) of the I/O subsystem. Rather than using the low-level physical I/O commands, higher-level logical and/or symbolic I/O commands could be used. Many of the functions of the device driver (error handling and optimization of access times) can be done by the microprocessor of the I/O subsystem, the I/O processor (IOP).

Error handling, when done by the IOP, may be a significant improvement over error handling by the device driver. The IOP has a much more device-specific interface with the device (compared with the device-independent CPU–host port interface), and therefore can monitor and control the device in a more accurate and direct way.

Functions of the device-independent software, such as storage allocation/deallocation and mapping of logical blocks into physical blocks and vice versa, can also be done by the IOP.

Currently, IOPs are performing functions even at the application level. For example, a file subsystem may itself be able to keep track of the directory of the attached devices and be able to execute search commands of the type 'Which employees are over 40 years of age, own their home and have 3 children'.

The trend of raising the functionality of IOPs has reached a level where the application-oriented I/O processes should be executable in overlap with on-going device operations. This closes the circle and brings us back to overlapped I/O and DMA (but now for the IOP!), introduced to off-load the CPU and allow for parallelism.

Technology has now progressed to the point where DMA, command and data chaining, together with many device port functions, can be integrated on to a single chip. The existence of disk controller chips and data communication chips helps to open the aforementioned, otherwise closed, circle.

11.5.2 Device port

A device port controls a device and transfers data to and from the device. Device ports are not shared or multiplexed, so there is always one device port per device (see Figure 11.2). The device–device port connection, the device interface, can consist of dedicated lines (see I/O subsystem 2 of Figure 11.1) or shared lines (see I/O subsystem *N*). Some device control functions, performed by the device port, are:

- Start and stop device.
- Device initialization.
- Environmental control.
- Electrical parameter conversion.
- Address recognition for data communication lines.

Some data transfer functions, performed by the device port, are:

- Serial/parallel conversions.
- Composition/decomposition of words and bytes.
- Data transfer protocol.
- Parity and cyclic redundancy check (CRC).

SUMMARY

- In the architecture of a computer system, I/O requires special attention because of the large diversity of I/O devices in terms of types, capacity, access times and data rates. They also differ in the way data can be addressed and how they should be controlled.

- I/O device processes are slow compared with CPU instruction execution times. I/O should, therefore, be done concurrently with CPU processing to allow for a higher system throughput.

- To facilitate interrupt and exception handling, I/O subsystems could/should have a collective control/status register with a standard bit layout.

- To have one device driver per I/O subsystem, the device port specification should be such that it can be a parameter for that device driver.

- The use of interrupts allows for concurrent I/O and CPU processing. The use of DMA relieves the CPU of the overhead of data transfers. Data chaining supports the independence of the block sizes of memory, disks, tapes, and so on. Command chaining allows the queueing of I/O commands at the CPU–host port interface. Buffering releases (or eliminates) real-time response requirements.

- Channels are device controllers supporting DMA, and data and command chaining.

- I/O processors allow for high-level I/O commands, thereby performing device driver and device-independent software functions, traditionally performed by the CPU. They also have improved error-handling capabilities.

EXERCISES

11.1 Which parts constitute an I/O subsystem?

11.2 Which I/O device classes exist?

11.3 What are the major properties of I/O devices?

11.4 (a) Which types of information are exchanged between the CPU and the device controller?

(b) What is the distinction between host port and device port control/status information?

(c) What is a collective control/status register?

11.5 (a) What is direct I/O?

(b) Which method of specifying the I/O operation is preferable?

(c) How should the device port be specifiable?

11.6 (a) What is the advantage of overlapped I/O?

(b) What is the advantage of DMA?

(c) What is data chaining?

(d) What is command chaining?

11.7 What is the purpose of buffering?

11.8 What is a channel?

11.9 What is the purpose of an I/O processor?

11.10 Given a typical PC moveable head disk drive with the following properties: 4 disks per drive (only one side per disk is used); each disk has its own head and only one head can be active at a time; 600 tracks/disk; 20 sectors/track; 512 bytes/sector; rotation at 3000 revolutions/minute.

(a) What is the capacity of the disk drive?

(b) What is the transfer rate of the drive?

(c) What is the time to transfer one sector?

(d) What is the average rotational delay?

11.11 What would be the total elapsed time when the information of two consecutive sectors on the disk of Exercise 11.10 have to be transferred?

(a) Using DMA only.

(b) Using data chaining.

References

DEC (1969). *PDP-10 Reference Handbook*. Digital Equipment Corporation: Maynard, MA.

DEC (1975). *PDP-11 Processor Handbook*. Digital Equipment Corporation: Maynard, MA.

DEC (1976). *PDP-11 Peripherals Handbook*. Digital Equipment Corporation: Maynard, MA.

IBM (1970). *IBM System/370 Principles of Operations*. Form No. GA22–7000. IBM Corporation: Armonk, NY.

12 Exception Handling

Success covers a multitude of blunders.
– Bernard Shaw

Exception handling is a major operating system task. The importance of this task can be derived from its purpose: the increase of system availability and reliability. This chapter, therefore, opens by defining these two terms as well as other important terms concerned with exception handling. This is followed by a discussion of the methods used to detect errors in hardware and software, respectively. Finally, architectural support for exception handling is covered – that is, the architecture of the interface (exception handler) between hardware and software to detect and invoke the handling of exceptions.

12.1 Availability and reliability

The **availability** of a system as a function of time, $A(t)$, is defined as the probability that the system is operational at time t (Siewiorek, 1982). Availability is typically used as a basis for the evaluation of systems in which service can be delayed or denied for short periods of time, without serious consequences.

The **reliability** of a system as a function of time, $R(t)$, is defined as the conditional probability that the system has survived the interval $[0, t]$, given that it was operational at time $t = 0$. Reliability is a measure used for systems in which 'on-line' repair is not possible (such as in satellite computers) or in which the computer is performing a critical function which cannot be interrupted, even for the duration of a repair. The reliability of a system is taken as the measure with which it meets its specifications with respect to service to its users, even when subjected to unexpected conditions.

In general, it is more expensive to build a highly reliable computer system than a highly available one, because of the more stringent requirements imposed by the reliability definition; namely, that the system is operational during the complete time interval 0 to t. A highly reliable system will continue to meet its specifications even in the case of hardware malfunctions.

In this context, the following terms have to be defined (Siewiorek, 1982) (see also Example 12.1):

- A **failure** occurs or is present when the service of the system differs from the specified service. This failure is caused by an error. The average time between successive failures is called the mean time between failures (MTBF).
- There is an **error** in the system (the system is in an erroneous state) when the system state differs from the state required to deliver the expected service. The error is caused by a fault.
- A **fault** is the cause of an error. Errors may be caused by a hardware malfunction, by user or operator actions, or by a bug in one of the (system) processes.
- **Damage** caused by the error is the amount of information that is corrupted as a result of the error. This damage can result in more faults, which can lead to further errors.

□□EXAMPLE 12.1

When a car cannot be used due to a flat tyre, this is called a failure. This failure is caused by an error; namely, the erroneous state of the air pressure in the tyre. The fault that caused the error was a puncture in the tyre, which is a physical difference between a good and an erroneous tyre. Note that in the case of a flat spare tyre, the error does not immediately result in a failure.

Two techniques are used to increase the reliability of computer systems: fault avoidance (based on prevention) and fault tolerance (based on detection and resolution). Traditionally, system reliability was mainly achieved using **fault avoidance** techniques, also called **fault intolerance** techniques (Avizienis, 1976). This means that highly reliable hardware components are used to build the computer system. Furthermore, both hardware and software components are thoroughly tested before use. Once the design has been completed, a quantitative prediction of the system reliability can be based upon the known or predicted failure rates of the components and interconnections. Occasional faults, unavoidable even with the most careful fault avoidance techniques, are accepted as a necessary evil.

An alternative approach to fault avoidance is **fault tolerance**. Fault tolerant computing allows for the correct execution of a process even in the presence of faults. Fault tolerance is always achieved by using **redundancy**; that is, the provision of extra hardware or software for the purpose of error detection and handling, without influencing the system availability. Four stages can be distinguished by which a redundant system responds to the occurrence of an error:

(1) **Error detection**: Errors should be detected as soon as possible to reduce the damage. Error detection can be done 'off line', which means that the system is not able to do useful work while under test, or 'on line', concurrently with useful work. The latter requires real-time error detection capabilities.

(2) **Fault treatment**: This relates to the identification of the cause of the fault and possible repair of that fault. An error may be due to several possible faults, both in hardware and software, and none of them may be apparent. Fault treatment can be supported by the computer system by producing a trace or log of its recent activities.

(3) **Damage assessment**: This deals with the determination of the amount of information in the system that is corrupted. This may be based entirely on *a priori* reasoning or may involve the system itself in performing a number of checks to determine what damage has occurred.

(4) **Error recovery**: This is closely related to damage assessment because the damage caused by the error must be eliminated. Recovery is defined as the continuation of system operation after

an error. It may mean that the level of operation is unchanged; the operation is restarted, degraded or terminated; or processes may have to be removed from the system, continued or re-run.

For the exception detection and handling methods discussed in this chapter, it is not always possible to make a clear distinction between these four stages. The order in which these stages is carried out can vary and there can be much interaction between them, but the starting point is always the detection of an error. Note that when the term **exception** is used in this chapter, it is intended to stand for the words **exception** (which is caused by an unusual condition, such as divide by zero) or **error** (which is caused by a hardware or software fault).

12.2 Hardware exceptions

Due to component aging and environmental conditions, a system cannot be guaranteed to be free of hardware exceptions (this even applies to fault-intolerant systems). Faults in a system, causing exceptions, can be categorized, in terms of their behaviour in time, as follows:

- **Permanent faults**: This class of faults affects the functional behaviour of the system permanently. Examples of permanent faults are incorrect connections (bad soldering), broken components and design errors.
- **Non-permanent faults**: These do not occur all the time. Depending on their cause, the following subdivision can be made:
    (a) **Transient faults**: These faults are caused by environmental conditions, such as cosmic rays, α-particles (important for dynamic RAMs), vibration and electrical discharges (lightning).
    (b) **Intermittent faults**: These faults are caused by non-environmental conditions and, over time, often result in permanent faults. Some causes are loose connections, aging components and critical timing.

Permanent faults cannot be recovered through a retry operation – that is, repeating the operation during which the fault occurred – and system operation can only proceed when the faulty component has been repaired or bypassed. Non-permanent faults can be recovered through a retry operation because of the time dependency of the fault. Siewiorek (1982) found that only 3% to 6% of all faults are permanent. This emphasizes the importance of retry operations.

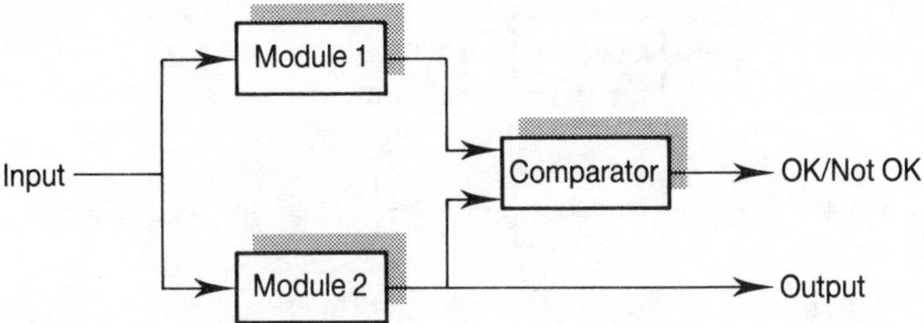

FIGURE 12.1
Duplication of hardware modules.

12.2.1 Hardware exception detection

As stated before, redundancy is the key to exception detection. This redundancy can consist of information redundancy or hardware redundancy, both of which enable on-line error detection.

Information redundancy

Information redundancy involves the use of error-detecting codes for the information in a computer system, for memories, for data paths and for units operating on the data. The redundant information allows valid and invalid data words to be distinguished. The simplest form of an error-detecting code is the single-bit parity check. With this method, a single bit is added to every byte, so that the resulting code word is forced to have either an odd or an even number of ones. By counting the number of ones in a code word, single-bit errors can be detected. Other error-detecting codes are the M-out-of-N code, which is used, for example, to encode instruction operands in the STAR (Self Testing And Repairing) computer (Avizienis, 1971), checksums, and arithmetic and cyclic codes (Johnson, 1984). Many computers use some form of error-correcting code (ECC code) for memories because, especially dynamic RAM chips, are very susceptible to radiation by α-particles, causing transient faults. ECC codes not only allow for the detection of errors but also allow for the correction of single- or multiple-bit errors.

Hardware redundancy

The most common hardware redundancy technique is the physical duplication of hardware modules, as illustrated in Figure 12.1. The results of two identical modules are compared and an error message is generated if their results disagree. Other hardware redundancy techniques include the addition of special hardware that tests for hardware errors. An example of hardware redundancy is the provision of watchdog timers. The operation of a data transfer may be monitored with such a timer. When the data transfer is initiated, the timer is started. If no response to the transfer request is received after a certain time (which is signalled by the timer), a time-out exception is generated.

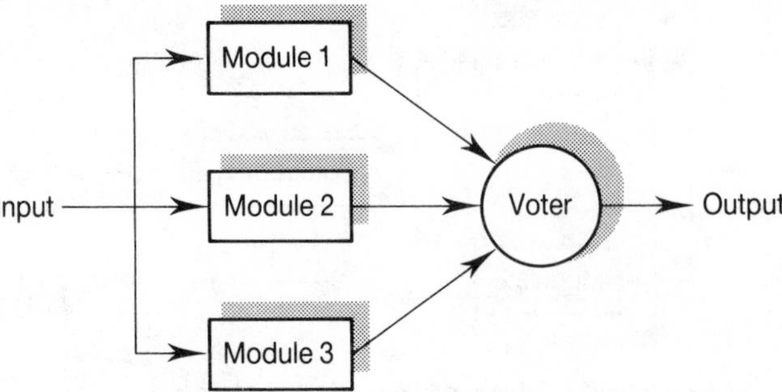

FIGURE 12.2
TMR with ideal voter.

12.2.2 Hardware exception handling

An approach to hardware exception handling is fault-tolerant computing, which tries to allow for the correct execution of a process even in the presence of certain hardware faults. Again, redundancy is the key word. The following types of redundancy can be distinguished: masking, dynamic redundancy and the retry operation.

Masking

Masking, also called **static redundancy**, tolerates faults: it masks them. For information (in memories and data paths), this could be done by information redundancy using, for example, error-correcting codes, such as Hamming codes (Hamming, 1950). With one of these codes, designed to perform single-bit error correction and double-bit error detection (SECDED), the occurrence of single-bit errors is masked; that is, they are not visible and correct execution is maintained.

A masking technique, based on hardware redundancy, is triple modular redundancy (TMR). The purpose of TMR is to mask single faults by triplicating hardware modules and voting for the result (Figure 12.2). The output is accepted if at least two of the modules agree. This scheme is based on the assumption that faults in a single module do not affect other modules and that the voter is always functioning correctly (ideal voter). Because the latter constraint is hard to guarantee, another, less constraining, configuration is shown in Figure 12.3. This configuration consists of two identical parts, each consisting of two modules and a comparator. The comparator is assumed to produce the signal 'OK' when its modules produce the same result and it is working correctly itself. The switch is controlled by the output of both comparators. In the event of a fault in one of the parts, the switch selects the result of the correct path. This method is used in fault-tolerant computers produced by the Stratus company.

The advantage of masking is that it can cope with all permanent as well as non-permanent faults, because the result of each operation is

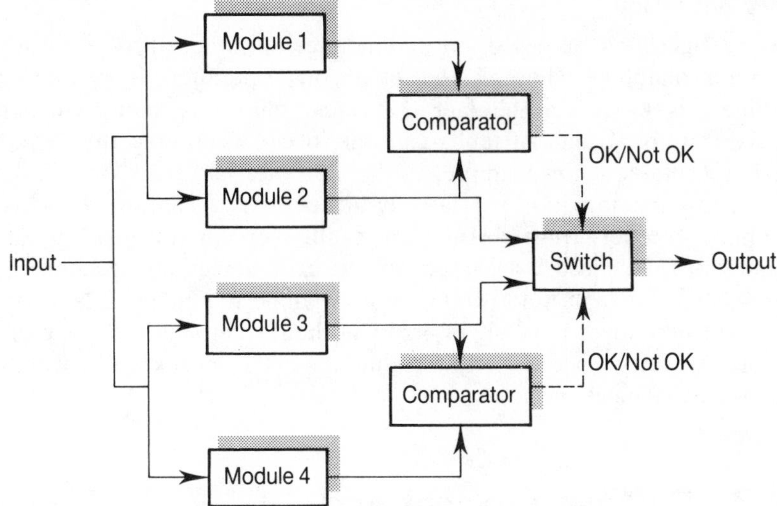

FIGURE 12.3
Stratus fault-tolerance concept.

checked for correctness. Because of the high cost of tripling (Figure 12.2) or quadrupling (Figure 12.3) the hardware, masking is only used in situations where the cost of a non-operational system is high.

Dynamic redundancy

With **dynamic redundancy**, the occurrence of a fault is not masked, but a recovery attempt is made which involves the reconfiguration of system modules in response to the detection of an error. One form of dynamic reconfiguration is **standby replacement**. In this case, one module is operational, while one or more other modules serve as a standby. If an error is detected in the operational module, this module is replaced by a standby module. This gives full operational capability after the occurrence of a fault, but processing might be interrupted for some time while replacing the faulty module. If this time loss cannot be tolerated, 'hot sparing' may be used, in which case the spare module(s) operate in synchrony with the operational module and can take over at any given moment. Another dynamic reconfiguration technique is **graceful degradation**, mostly used in multiprocessing systems. If one of the processors fails, it is disabled and processing can continue in a degraded fashion.

Dynamic redundancy enables recovery from permanent as well as non-permanent faults. Its cost is lower than that of masking because of each unit type – only a single standby unit is required. It is based on a good exception detection mechanism. Because of the cost involved, most exception detection mechanisms will not detect all exceptions – for example, parity will only detect exceptions with an odd number of bits. This means that the system cannot be guaranteed to be operating correctly when no exceptions are detected.

Retry operation

A **retry operation** is based on redundancy in time. It is a form of exception handling whereby the erroneous operation is retried. Its usefulness is based on the fact that most faults are non-permanent. Recovery from permanent faults can only occur when graceful degradation is acceptable – for example, in the case of a bad track on a disk.

The retry operation is relatively inexpensive to support. However, it cannot recover from permanent faults (except through graceful degradation). Because it is based on an error detection mechanism, it suffers from the same disadvantages as dynamic redundancy. Nevertheless, due to the low frequency of errors in the system, and the low cost to support the retry operation, this technique is the most commonly used error recovery mechanism.

12.3 Software exceptions

Much has been said and written about methods for writing reliable software. Management practices, programming methodologies such as top-down design, formal correctness proofs and systematic testing are well-known examples of software fault avoidance. However, as every programmer knows, software errors cannot be completely avoided. Therefore, detection and handling of software errors is an important issue, requiring architectural support. In addition to software errors, exceptions raised due to the execution of a program should be recoverable, preferably under control of the program that generated the exception.

12.3.1 Software exception detection

Errors can be detected and handled by software – for example, by application programs. The detection and handling of software errors may be done using recovery blocks. Validity checks are used to raise exceptions. Several programming languages allow for the specification and handling of exceptions raised as a consequence of a validity check.

Recovery blocks

The recovery block scheme (Randell, 1975) is based on the use of several alternative algorithms to solve the same problem. It is analogous to the hardware method of dynamic redundancy with standby replacement. Before a particular program module is executed, a copy is made of the data to which it has write access. This copy is called a **recovery block**. When program module *A* has completed, a check is made on the acceptability of the result. If this check fails, a copy of the recovery block is made and passed to program module *B*, which has the same functionality as module *A* but of a different design. Upon completion of module *B*, a check is made, and so on.

The recovery block concept allows for the detection and recovery of programming errors (assuming that at least one of the alternative modules is correct). It also allows for the detection of permanent and non-permanent hardware exceptions and the recovery from non-permanent faults.

Designing a program using recovery blocks multiplies the programming effort and causes extra execution overhead, because of the creation of the recovery blocks and the checks to be performed. Only systems requiring a very high level of (software) fault tolerance, such as the space shuttle programs, use this technique.

Validity checks

Validity checks are analogous to the hardware retry method. They allow for the detection of software errors by performing checks on the input data and the results of certain modules. The software errors are passed to a handler via user-defined exceptions. These exceptions may be used for validity checks, such as temperature variables that exceed a certain maximum (process control) or buffers that are overflowing.

Exceptions caused by the execution of an instruction, called **predefined exceptions**, can also be passed to a handler under program control. For predefined exceptions, one can think of divide-by-zero and end-of-file operations, overflow, underflow, and so on. When, during the execution of a process, a software exception is generated, the process is said to *raise* that exception. The response to the raised exception is called *handling* the exception (Goodenough, 1975). Programming languages require special provisions for this. For example, Ada (Ada, 1983) allows predefined and user-defined exceptions to be raised and handled under program control.

When an exception has been raised, it will be handled by an **exception handler**. The exception handler can be part of the process that raised the exception, in which case it may be user defined, or part of the underlying operating system, in which case the exception handler is system defined.

12.3.2 Software exception handling

The process of determining the possible cause of certain software exceptions is called **debugging**. Most computer architectures support debugging by means of single step, tracing or breakpoint facilities. These facilities can also be used to support monitoring of the execution of a program.

Single step

The single-step facility halts the processor after every program step or bus cycle, allowing examination of machine registers, variables, memory locations, and so on. For example, the MC68020 HALT input signal forces the processor to execute a single bus cycle and then halts execution. This allows a user to proceed and therefore debug a program one bus cycle at a time.

Tracing

Tracing the execution of a program means that a trap to a special routine, the trace monitor, is made after the execution of every instruction of a particular class of that program. This allows program execution to be monitored or statistics about the executed program to be collected – for example, to find the performance critical parts. Tracing requires the CPU to be in a specific mode, the trace mode, usually indicated by one or more bits in the status register. The class of instructions that activate the trace trap may be all instructions or only instructions that change the flow of control.

Breakpoints

A **breakpoint** is a location in a program where an instruction is replaced by a special breakpoint instruction. The execution of the breakpoint instruction will raise an exception. Consequently, a program can run at full speed until it reaches a particular address, at which the breakpoint instruction has been inserted. Handling a breakpoint exception involves restoring the original instruction at the breakpoint address. In principle, any illegal instruction that causes a trap can be used as a breakpoint instruction, although it is more proper to use a special instruction for this. When debugging programs, usually more than one breakpoint is required.

12.4 Architectural support for exception handling

The architectural support for exception handling is covered in the following subsections: exception detection, which shows a classification of exceptions detected at the architectural level; exception priorities and the moment of invocation of the exception handling process; and, finally, exception handling.

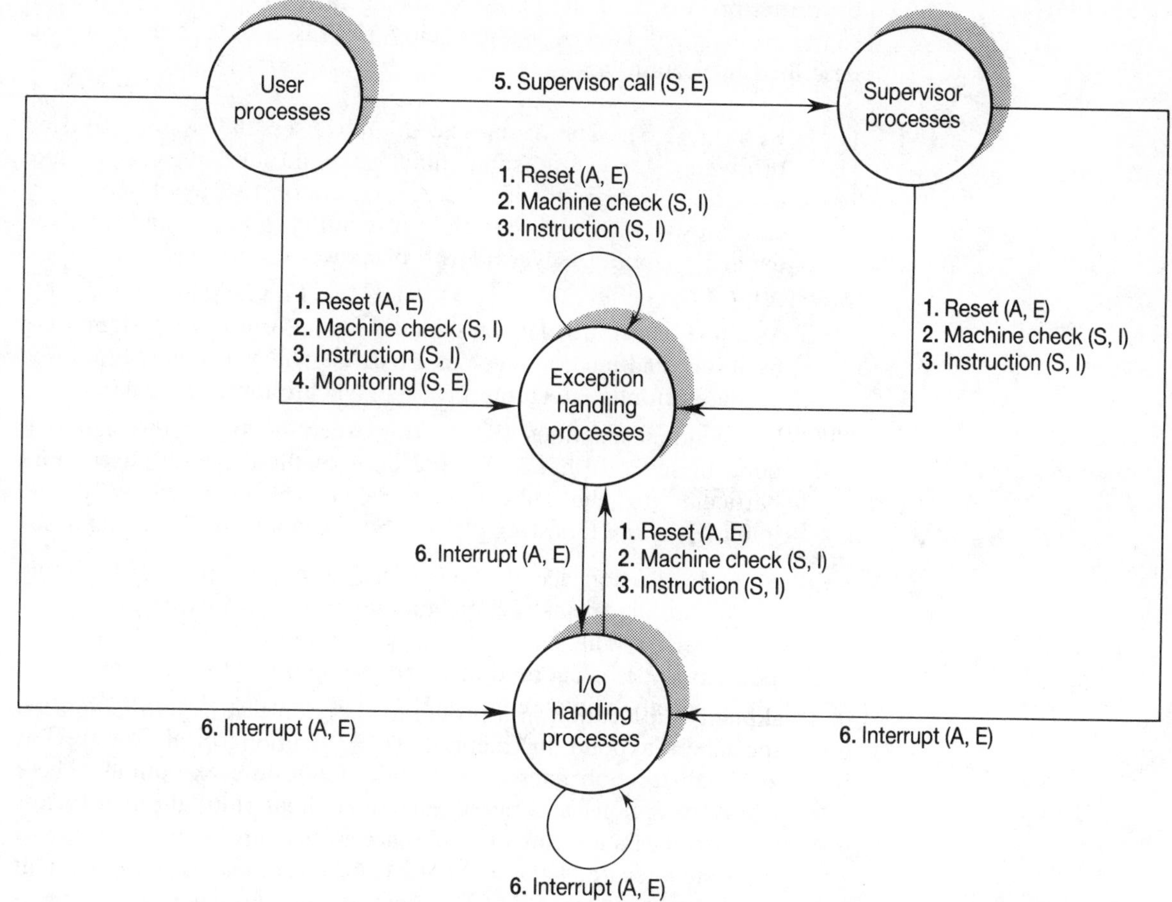

FIGURE 12.4

Exceptions and process switches.

12.4.1 Exception detection at the architectural level

In early computers (as well as fairly recent microprocessors), the detection of exceptions was poorly supported because the available hardware had to be used to support the functions required for regular program execution. In today's computers, exception detection and handling is provided, although no established standard exists.

Exceptions are used to cause a process switch. Figure 12.4, which is derived from Figure 9.8, shows the process switches caused by the exceptions in the following list. The corresponding reverse arrows, which should indicate a return from an exception, have been left out to simplify the figure. (Note that no standard currently exists for the terminology about and the classification of exceptions.) The notions of exceptions being raised synchronously (S) or asynchronously (A) with the currently executing process, and the exception being raised explicitly (E) (due to some pre-planned action) or implicitly (I) (as a side effect) are as described in Section 9.5.

(1) Reset (A, E): The reset exception causes the system to stop processing, forces it to some initial state and starts the execution of a booting program. The reset exception is generated asynchronously with the currently executing process and invoked explicitly upon a severe error or power-on. It has the highest priority.

(2) Machine check (S, I): This exception informs the system of a hardware malfunction (such as a parity error) which may be caused by the currently executing process (synchronous, implicit).

(3) Instruction exceptions (S, I): The execution of an instruction is done in several phases. During each of these phases, exceptions particular to that phase may be raised (synchronously and implicitly). The following phases and exceptions can be recognized:

- Instruction decode exceptions: During instruction decoding, the 'illegal instruction' or the 'privileged' exception can be raised. The illegal instruction exception is raised when the opcode or operand fields are not defined; that is, they do not specify implemented codes. The privileged exception indicates that a privileged operation is specified in user mode.
- Instruction fetch and operand fetch/store exceptions: These exceptions are raised due to address translation or access right faults. For example, access to non-existing memory or unallocated memory (which may cause a page or segment fault), or the use of improper access rights (writing to a read-only area).
- Execution exceptions: During the execution phase, three causes of exceptions can be recognized: domain exceptions, which are raised when the value of the input data does not satisfy the requirements for producing a correct result; range exceptions, which are raised when the value of the result of an operation is not considered a valid result; and significant result – in some architectures, the exception mechanism is used to indicate certain properties of the result of an operation, such as the overflow trap, invoked by the MC68020 TRAPV instruction when the V bit is set.

(4) Monitoring exceptions (S, E): This class of exceptions does not apply to the execution of the instruction (see class 3) but to the fact that an instruction to be monitored has been executed. Trace and breakpoint exceptions are typical for this class. They are raised

Table 12.1 Invocation and execution priorities of exceptions.

Exception	I	E	Priority
(1) Reset	0	0	Highest priority for I (invocation) and highest priority for E (execution)
(2) Machine check	1	1	Hardware malfunctions have second highest priority for I and E
(3) Instruction execution	2	CP	Executed at the priority level of the currently executing process
(4) Monitoring	3	CP	
(5) Supervisor call	4	CP	
(6) Interrupt	5	IP	Executed at the priority level with which the external interrupt was requested

synchronously and explicitly, and are considered an extension to the instruction raising the exception.

(5) Supervisor call exceptions (S, E): These exceptions (see Chapter 9) allow for a service request of user mode programs to the supervisor. They are raised explicitly by and synchronously with the process raising the exception.

(6) Interrupts (A, E): This class of exceptions allows concurrent processes, such as I/O processes, to request service from a CPU-based process. Interrupt exceptions are raised explicitly and are asynchronous with the currently executing process.

12.4.2 Exception priorities and the moment of invocation

This section starts with the relative priorities of the various exceptions, followed by the moment (related to the currently executing instruction) at which the exception handling process is invoked.

Exception priorities

Most architectures support a single interrupt mechanism for invoking an exception handling process (see Section 9.6). In dealing with exceptions, two phases can be distinguished, each of which may have its own priority. The **exception invocation phase** is the phase during which the interrupt operation is performed to cause a switch to the process that has to handle the exception. It can be seen as the *recording* of the exception. During the **exception execution phase**, the process, which handles the exception, is executed. The priorities of the two phases may not be the same for

Table 12.2 MC68020 exception groups.

Group	Priority	Exceptions
(0)	0.0	Reset (1)
(1)	1.0	Address error (3 – instruction fetch and operand fetch/store exception)
	1.1	Bus error (2 and 3)
(2)	2.0	BKPT #n (4), CALLM (3), CHK (3 – significant result) CHK2 (3 – significant result), Divide-by-zero (3 – significant result) RTE (3), RTM (3), TRAP #n (5), TRAPV (3 – significant result)
(3)	3.0	Illegal instruction (3 – instruction decode exception) Privilege violation (3)
(4)	4.0	Trace (4
	4.1	Interrupt (6)

each exception class. Table 12.1 shows the priorities of the exception classes of Section 12.4.1, where 0 is the highest priority, CP is the priority of the currently executing process, IP is the priority of the external interrupt request, I is the invocation priority and E is the execution priority. The processes handling the exceptions due to instruction execution, monitoring and supervisor calls are executed at the priority of the process raising the exception, 'CP', because they are handled on behalf of the process raising the exception (there is no need to handle these exceptions with a higher priority level). Processes handling interrupt exceptions are executed at the priority with which the interrupt exception is requested, 'IP', because the priority level with which the interrupt is requested reflected the urgency with which it should be serviced. IP has to be higher than the priority of the currently executing process for the interrupt request to be honoured.

□□EXAMPLE 12.2

Table 12.2 shows the invocation priorities for the MC68020 exceptions. They are divided into five groups. These groups do not map directly on to the classes of Table 12.1 (which are denoted in parentheses after the exception) as some groups have subpriorities, and exceptions of certain classes (such as operand fetch exceptions during instruction execution) are not uniquely identifiable (because of a lack of hardware support) and therefore indistinguishable from exceptions that may belong

Table 12.3 Moment of exception invocation.

Exception		Invocation
(1)	Reset	Immediately
(2)	Machine check	During instruction execution
(3)	Instruction execution	
	Instruction decode	Before instruction execution
	Instruction/operand fetch/store	During instruction execution
	Execution	After instruction execution
(4)	Monitoring	After instruction execution
(5)	Supervisor call	After instruction execution
(6)	Interrupt	Between instructions

to another class. The machine check group consists of address error (for example, a byte address used to fetch an instruction word) and bus error, which is a catch-all for hardware malfunctions. Because the memory management unit is implemented as a co-processor, the external bus error signal is also used to invoke instructions fetch and operand fetch/store exceptions.

When several exceptions are raised simultaneously (trap, trace, interrupt exception), the trap exception handler is invoked first, followed by the trace exception handler and only then the interrupt exception handler. The execution of the exception handling processes is in reverse order (because the invocation uses a LIFO stack): first the interrupt handling process is executed, followed by the execution of the process handling the trace exception, while the trap handling process is executed last.

Processes can be executed at any of the priority levels supported by the architecture; that is, $0 \leqslant CP \leqslant 7$. Interrupts can be honoured at priority levels $1 \leqslant IP \leqslant 7$; an interrupt with priority level 0 will never be honoured because the lowest level of priority of a process is 0. The machine check and reset essentially have an invocation priority higher than level 7. They are non-maskable, as they will always be honoured.

Moment of exception invocation

The moment at which the exception operation is invoked depends on the urgency of the exception and/or the fact that the exception has to be considered an integral part of the instruction (for example, in the case of a monitoring exception or a supervisor call). Table 12.3 lists the moment of exception invocation for the exceptions of Section 12.4.1.

12.4.3 Exception handling

In the discussion on exception handling, first the general case is covered, followed by the special cases (such as reset, trace and breakpoint exceptions).

General form of exception handling

Most architectures use a single mechanism (the interrupt mechanism) to invoke the exception handling process. In the MC68020, this invocation operation is done in four steps:

(1) An internal copy of the status register (SR) is made in SR*, after which the S bit of SR* is set (switch to supervisor mode) and the trace bits are cleared, disabling further tracing. For reset and interrupt exceptions, also the interrupt priority level of SR* is changed.

(2) An exception vector number is obtained. For internally generated exceptions, this number is determined by the exception type; for interrupts and co-processor exceptions, this number is provided by the interrupting device/co-processor.

(3) An exception stack frame is generated and saved on the supervisor stack, or on the interrupt stack (when the exception is an interrupt). This stack frame is used to save the minimum processor context, together with some additional information, depending on the exception type.

(4) The exception vector number is used to fetch an exception vector, which determines the starting address of the exception handling process, and the SR is loaded with the value of SR*.

The exception stack frame contains the minimum processor context. Depending on the moment the exception is invoked, internal state information of the processor may have to be saved as well (for example, to save the contents of internal pipeline registers when the exception was raised during the execution of an instruction). Additional information, such as the starting address of the instruction causing the exception, may be stored to facilitate exception handling. Example 12.3 shows the MC68020 exception stack frame and the assignment of exception vectors.

□□EXAMPLE 12.3

The general form of an MC68020 exception stack frame is shown in Figure 12.5. The SR and PC are always saved, together with the format field, which determines the size of the stack frame, and the vector offset, which determines the start address of the exception handler. The format

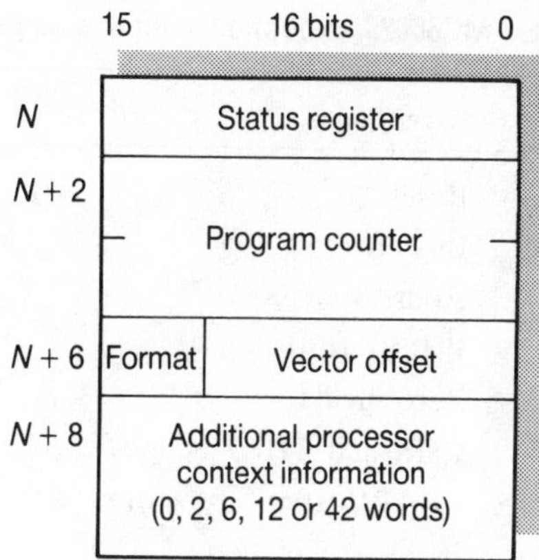

FIGURE 12.5
General form of an exception stack frame.

field is used by the RTE (Return from Exception) instruction to deallocate the proper amount of stack space. The additional processor context information can consist of 0, 2, 6, 12 or 42 words, depending on the exception type.

The size of the exception stack frame is determined by the exception class and the moment at which the exception occurs (because during instruction execution the internal state of the processor is larger than between instructions). The sizes of the MC68020 exception stack frames are as follows, where the numbers in parentheses refer to the exception classification of Section 12.4.1 and of Table 12.3:

(1) No exception stack frame: This will be the case for reset (1) exceptions.

(2) Regular exception stack frame (4 words): This is generated in the case of instruction decode (3), supervisor call (5) and interrupt (6) exceptions.

(3) Six-word exception stack frame (6 words): The additional word contains the address of the instruction causing the exception, because the PC already points to the next instruction to be executed. This exception stack frame will be generated for instruction execution (3) and monitoring (4) exceptions.

(4) Co-processor exception stack frame (10 words): This consists of 10 words and is generated for co-processor exceptions. The internal state of the processor is rather small during the execution of co-processor instructions.

(5) Short bus cycle fault stack frame (16 words): This is generated for machine check (2) and instruction or operand fetch/store (3) exceptions occurring at instruction boundaries.

(6) Long bus cycle fault stack frame (46 words): This is similar to (5), except it does not occur at an instruction boundary.

Table 12.4 MC68020 exception vector assignment.

Location	Exception
000	Reset
008	Bus error
00C	Address error
010	Illegal instruction
014	Zero divide
018	CHK and CHK2 bounds checking
01C	TRAPV, trap on overflow
020	Privilege violation
024	Trace
028	Unimplemented opcode class 1010
02C	Unimplemented opcode class 1111
⋮	
080–0BF	TRAP #0 . . F (supervisor calls)
⋮	
100–3FF	User interrupt vectors

Table 12.4 shows the assignment of exception vectors for the MC68020 architecture.

Special cases of exception handling

Not all exceptions are invoked the same way. Reset is handled differently, while the handling of trace and breakpoint exceptions may require further explanation. The moment of invocation of instruction/operand fetch exceptions needs further clarification, because several alternatives exist which have major architectural implications.

Reset exception The reset exception is a special case because it has to initialize a minimum process context in order to allow a booting process to be started. No return from that exception has to be done, which means that no exception stack frame has to be generated. The reset exception vector specifies the initial value of the PC (which specifies the address of the booting routine), as well as an initial value for the stack pointer.

Trace exception In general terms, a trace exception can be viewed as an extension to the function of any instruction. Thus, if a trace exception is generated by an instruction, the execution of that instruction is not complete until the trace exception processing associated with it is completed. If the instruction does not complete, due to some error or other exception, trace exception processing is deferred until the execution of the suspended instruction has been completed. If the instruction is executed and an interrupt is pending, trace exception processing is completed before the interrupt is allowed to take place. Example 12.4 shows how the MC68020 supports tracing.

□□EXAMPLE 12.4

The MC68020 supports instruction tracing for two classes of instructions, determined by the two most significant bits of the SR; SR[15] = T1 and SR[14] = T0. The trace bits T1 and T0 are interpreted as follows:

T1, T0 = 0 0 No tracing
T1, T0 = 0 1 Trace on change of flow (BRA, JMP, etc.)
T1, T0 = 1 0 Trace on any instruction
T1, T0 = 1 1 Reserved

The trace exception processing starts on completion of the traced instruction but before the start of the next instruction. The trace trap makes an internal copy of the SR (to preserve the values of T1 and T0) and a new SR is loaded (with the supervisor mode bit set and the T1 and T0 bits cleared, to prevent the trace monitor from being traced). Then, the address of the instruction that caused the trace trap is stored in the exception stack frame (in addition to the usual values of SR, PC and vector offset). Thereafter, control is transferred to the location specified by the trace trap vector.

Breakpoint exception The breakpoint exception, which is used for monitoring purposes, is raised when a breakpoint instruction is executed. This breakpoint instruction replaces an instruction of the original program. The handling of a breakpoint exception consists of inserting the original instruction back into the program. Often, the memory management unit, which already has the task of monitoring memory addresses, provides extra support for breakpoint operations. Example 12.5 shows the MC68020 breakpoint support facilities.

□□EXAMPLE 12.5

The MC68020 architecture has a breakpoint instruction with the following syntax: BKPT #<data>. The 3-bit <data> field specifies the breakpoint number, enabling eight different breakpoints to be specified.

The execution of a BKPT instruction causes a special bus cycle (breakpoint acknowledge bus cycle) with one of the following results, depending on whether a memory management co-processor (MMU) is installed:

- MMU installed: The MMU provides the instruction word which was replaced by the BKPT instruction, after which normal execution continues. The MMU contains eight registers to hold the replaced instructions, together with eight counters which are decremented each time the corresponding BKPT instruction has been replaced. When a counter becomes zero, an interrupt is generated.
- MMU not installed: An 'illegal instruction' trap is generated. The monitor has to replace the BKPT instruction with the replaced instruction. Another BKPT instruction is required at some other location to re-insert the previous BKPT instruction.

Instruction fetch and operand fetch/store exceptions These exceptions are raised during the execution of an instruction on behalf of that instruction. Therefore, decisions have to be made on how to continue this execution, which depends on the specific exception as well as on the operating system policies. In a system using virtual memory, operand fetch exceptions can occur because the referenced operand may not be in main memory (for example, in the case of a page fault, the page containing the operand is still on disk). These exceptions should be recoverable, since they occur as part of the normal operation of a virtual memory system. In the case of a page fault, the page should be brought in from disk such that the instruction causing the page fault may still be executed. Two methods exist for handling exceptions of this class (MacGregor, 1983):

(1) Instruction restart method: The instruction causing the exception is restarted from the beginning, after the exception handling process has completed all activities associated with the correction. This implies that the processor has to be able to reconstruct and restore the state of the machine to that at the beginning of the instruction: all modifications by the partly executed instructions (for example, an address autoincrement) have to be undone. This can be a problem for architectures with complex instruction sets which have instructions with several operands, where the address and/or the data value of each operand may have been changed. Another problem may occur with I/O instructions. They may have side effects that become effective *before* the execution of the I/O

instruction has been completed (for example, the device may have been started already, or the interrupt request may have been removed due to the initial phase of a write operation to a control register, or a read operation from a status register, respectively). Another problem may occur when data is transferred from memory to memory, while the operands overlap. The advantage of the restart method is that the state of the machine to be saved as part of the invocation operation is small, comparable to that of an interrupt.

(2) Instruction continuation method: This allows, on completion of the exception handling process, the instruction to continue execution from the point the exception occurred. This necessitates saving and restoring the entire state of the machine (user visible as well as non-visible, internal state). Architectures with complex instruction sets and an implementation using pipelining techniques tend to have a large internal state. The instruction continuation method does not have the disadvantages of the instruction restart method and may appear to be the ideal solution. However, it has its own disadvantages. Extra chip area is required (in the form of microcode and/or hard-wired control logic) to save/restore the internal state. The large internal state (for the MC68020 this can be up to 46 words, see Figure 12.5) requires a long time for the save/restore operation, thus increasing the interrupt latency. Furthermore, instructions that have to perform an indivisible operation (TAS and CAS) must remain indivisible. Naturally, this can be solved by making those instructions restartable, rather than using the continuation method.

SUMMARY

- A fault-intolerant system is designed such that the probability of occurrence of a fault is minimized. A fault-tolerant system allows the correct execution of a process in the presence of faults.

- Hardware faults can be permanent or non-permanent. Non-permanent faults can consist of transient or intermittent faults. Statistics show that most faults are non-permanent.

- Hardware error detection can be based on information redundancy or hardware redundancy. Hardware exception handling can be done by masking, dynamic redundancy or via retry operations (redundancy in time).

- Software error detection can be done using recovery blocks or validity checks. Validity checks enable the detection of software errors and the handling of exceptions under control of a higher-level language.

- Software error localization requires support in terms of single-step operation, tracing and breakpoints.

- Architectural support for exception handling enables exceptions, detected by the hardware, to be passed on to (software) exception handlers. Exceptions are divided into the following classes: reset, machine check, exceptions due to instruction execution, monitoring exceptions, supervisor calls and interrupts.

- An exception has a priority level with which it is invoked, and a priority level with which it is handled. Exception invocation is usually done in the same way for all exceptions, using the interrupt mechanism. The moment at which an exception is invoked may be immediately before, during or after execution of the instruction raising the exception, and between instructions.

- The handling of memory management faults requires special provisions by the exception handling mechanism, to allow for instruction restart or continuation.

EXERCISES

12.1 (a) What is fault avoidance?

(b) What is fault tolerance?

(c) What are the four stages that can be recognized in handling errors?

12.2 Which faults are more likely to occur: permanent or non-permanent?

12.3 (a) What is information redundancy?

(b) What is hardware redundancy?

12.4 (a) Which type of hardware error handling allows faults to be unnoticed, and which types of faults can it cope with?

(b) Why is the retry operation an effective error recovery method, and on what is it based (that is, what is required to trigger a retry operation)?

12.5 (a) Which classes of exceptions can be recognized?

(b) Which classes of instruction exceptions exist?

12.6 (a) Which mechanism is used for exception handling?

(b) Which two priorities can be recognized with exception handling?

(c) With which priority should the process that handles instruction execution exceptions be executed?

(d) At which moment should the reset exception be invoked?

(e) At which moment should an interrupt exception be invoked?

(f) What is the MC68020 name of the SVC instruction?

12.7 (a) Why is the reset exception a special case?

(b) For which classes of MC68020 instructions can trace exceptions be generated?

(c) What is the concept behind breakpoints?

12.8 (a) Which methods exist for handling instruction/operand fetch exceptions?

(b) Which method should be used for instructions that perform an indivisible operation such as TAS?

(c) Which instruction/operand fetch exception handling method is mainly used by the MC68020, and what are the consequences for the exception stack frame?

References

Ada (1983). *Reference Manual for the ADA Programming Language*. ANSI/ MIL–STD 1815A. US Department of Defense.

Avizienis, A. *et al*. (1971). The STAR (Self Testing And Repairing) computer: An investigation of the theory and practice of fault-tolerant computer design. *IEEE Trans. on Computers*, **C–20**(11), 1312–21.

Avizienis, A. (1976). Fault-tolerant systems. *IEEE Trans. on Computers*, **C–25**(12), 1304–12.

Goodenough, J. B. (1975). Exception handling: Issues and a proposed notation. *Comm. of the ACM*, **18**(12), 683–96.

Hamming, R. W. (1950). Error-detecting and error-correcting codes. *Bell System Technical Journal*, **26**(2), 147–60.

Johnson, B. W. (1984). Fault-tolerant microprocessor-based systems. *IEEE Micro*, **4**(6), 6–21.

MacGregor, D. and Mothersole, D. S. (1983). Virtual memory and the MC68010. *IEEE Micro*, **3**(3), 24–39.

Randell, B. (1975). System structure for software fault tolerance. *IEEE Trans. on Software Engineering*, **SE–1**(2), 220–32.

Siewiorek, D. P. and Swarz, R. S. (1982). *The Theory and Practice of Reliable System Design*. Digital Press: Bedford, MA.

PART FOUR

THE HARDWARE INTERFACE

CHAPTER 13 BUS SYSTEMS

The hardware interface describes that part of the computer architecture which is of interest to those who want to interface the computer to the external world. Usually, this interface is organized into some form of a bus.

13 Bus Systems

Strangers are friends that you have yet to meet.
– Roberta Lieberman

As technology advances, system complexity and communication requirements increase. Buses, which are being recognized as a primary architectural resource, can frequently be the limiting factor in system performance, modularity and reliability. This chapter begins with an overview of the classification of bus systems. It then goes on to describe the types of data transfer operations performed by buses, which is followed by a discussion of bus arbitration and interrupt mechanisms. Finally, some special topics relating to buses are covered – namely, multiplexing, error detection and handling, and utilities.

13.1 Classification of bus systems

Buses are used to connect two or more digital system elements (Borill, 1981). A bus is a set of lines that is shared by these system elements and which is used for communication between those system elements. The term 'bus' usually implies *parallel* related connections, where several signals are travelling together along approximately the same route at approximately the same time. This can, however, be simulated by a sequence of signals on a single connection, which is called a **serial bus**. Buses come in several shapes and sizes: to interconnect components on a board, to interconnect boards, peripherals, and so on. A **bus system** is a set of buses used to connect the various system elements in a computer system. The bus system is often regarded as the backbone of the computer system. A well-designed, fast and flexible bus system extracts the maximum power from the processor's architecture and enhances the generality of the complete system.

Bus systems consist of a hierarchy of buses at different levels (Figure 13.1). The following bus levels can be distinguished:

- **Board level**: Board level buses connect system elements consisting of components (for example, chips) placed on one or more printed circuit boards. They are called **local buses** (see the VMX bus of Figure 13.1) (VME, 1985). These buses are mostly shared between many components, to reduce the number of intercomponent connections. Another feature of board level buses is that they often provide so-called housekeeping signals, which are dedicated signals between particular components – for example, dynamic memory refresh signals between the refresh timer and the memory array.
- **Backplane level**: Backplane level buses provide the communication path between system elements, consisting of boards (see the VME bus of Figure 13.1). Recently, backplane bus standards have been developed, which are processor and manufacturer independent. Examples are the IEEE Standard 1014–1987, which is based on the VME bus (VME, 1985); the IEEE Standard 1296–1987, which is based on the Multibus II (Intel, 1984); and the IEEE Standard 1196–1987, which is based on the Nubus (Texas Instruments, 1983).
- **Interface level**: Interface level buses provide the common communication path between I/O devices (disk, printer, card reader) and the rest of the system (see the I/O channel of Figure 13.1). Some interface bus standards have been developed; for example, the Small Computer System Interconnect (SCSI) bus (SCSI, 1984). This bus shows a large resemblance to backplane buses.

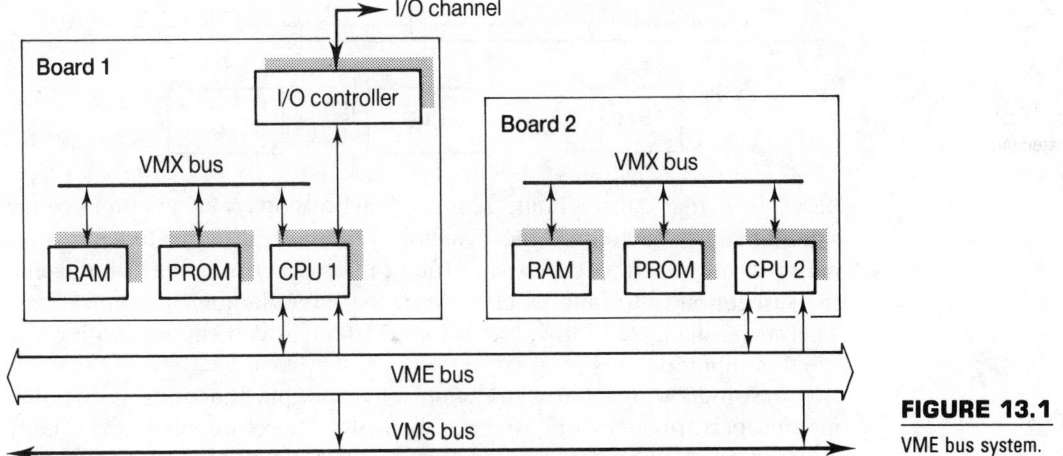

FIGURE 13.1
VME bus system.

The VME bus system of Figure 13.1 consists of the VMX board level bus, the VME backplane level bus and the VMS bus. The VMS bus is a backplane level serial bus, which may be used for initialization, testing and exception handling purposes.

This chapter focuses on backplane level buses, because they are general, often processor/device independent, and because their characteristics can be applied to the other bus levels. These characteristics include mechanical, electrical and logical properties. The emphasis here is on the logical properties of backplane buses.

13.1.1 Bus classification according to dedication

Buses can be either dedicated or non-dedicated. A dedicated bus performs only a single function, such as interconnecting the CPU with the I/O system in the case of an I/O bus. Because of the dedicated function, a computer system usually requires several different dedicated buses. Each of the boards of Figure 13.2 performs a particular function, and they are connected to the CPU via their own bus. The advantage of dedicated

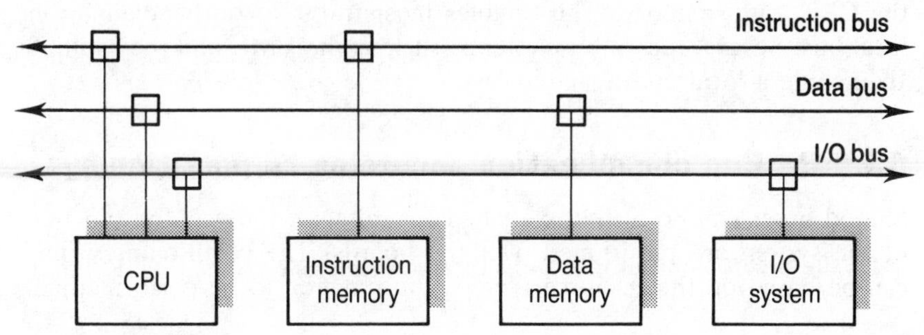

FIGURE 13.2
Dedicated bus.

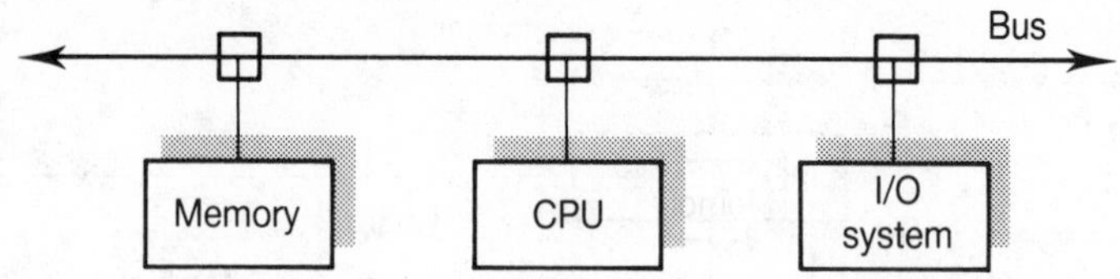

FIGURE 13.3
Non-dedicated bus.

buses is a high throughput; several functions may be communicating simultaneously, assuming the availability of several dedicated buses. A major disadvantage is the expense due to the larger number of buses and the susceptibility to failures because of the large number of connections. Therefore, dedicated buses are not used frequently at the system level in small computers.

Non-dedicated buses are *shared* by multiple functions (a function may be performed by one or more boards). Therefore, they are usually referred to as shared buses. In Figure 13.3, a CPU is connected to a number of other functions by means of a single, shared bus. Shared buses result in simpler, lower-cost systems, as compared with dedicated buses, but this is at the expense of a lower total data transfer capacity (the bus bandwidth) and the requirement for an arbitration mechanism, which has to prevent conflicts that can occur when two or more potential users request the bus simultaneously.

For computer systems with a relatively small number of low-performance boards, a bus system consisting of a single, shared bus gives a sufficient performance. When many boards are connected to this bus, however, as in the case of multiprocessing, a single, shared bus system is not suitable, because the heavy traffic on the bus becomes a major bottle neck in the system, and significantly lowers system performance. A solution to this can be to use multiple, shared, backplane buses. Then, boards can communicate via a number of alternative buses, so fewer conflicts occur. Further, failure of one bus may simply reduce the number of available buses, allowing the system to remain operational with reduced performance. Fault-tolerant computers adopt this approach. An alternative solution to the bandwidth problem of a single, shared bus, in the case of systems with multiple processors, is to connect each processor to two buses. One bus is the shared bus and one is a local bus, connecting the CPU with memory. This enables most traffic to be handled by the local bus. Several recent bus systems, such as the VME and the Multibus II, include a local and a shared bus.

13.1.2 Bus classification according to partitioning

Shared buses can be further classified according to the way the functions of the system are partitioned over the boards. The partitioning criteria can be based on the resource type or the function to be performed.

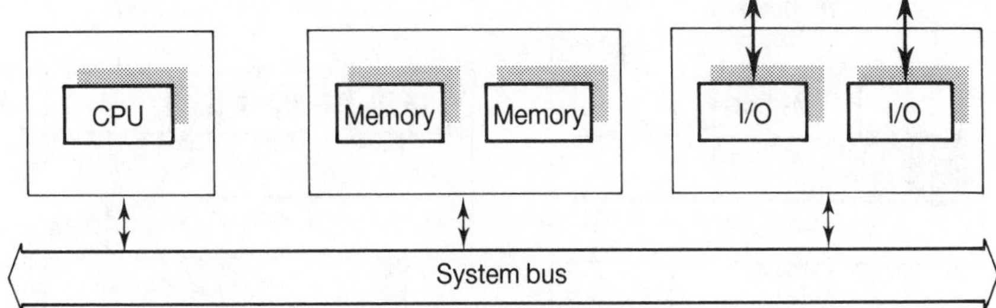

FIGURE 13.4
Resource partitioned bus.

Resource partitioned buses

Resources of the same type (for example, memory) are packaged together and connected via the bus (Figure 13.4). The bus is essentially a CPU–memory–I/O bus, connecting all resource types, thereby forming a single computer system. More established buses, such as the VME bus, belong to this class. They were conceived at a time when the level of integration was such that memories consisted of one or more boards (rather than a few chips) and I/O interfaces were not intelligent (that is, they did not have their own processor), so I/O was done under control of the CPU. The main characteristics of resource partitioned buses are:

- Single-processor oriented: This means that the bus usually has a default master (namely, the CPU), the bus is arbitrated centrally and all interrupts have a default destination (namely, the CPU).
- Memory bus oriented: CPU–memory traffic dominates the bus utilization. Because of this, the bus has the following characteristics:
  (a) Single data transfer: Most memory references by the CPU involve just a single data element (rather than a block of data).
  (b) Short bus cycle time: While the CPU is waiting for memory, it typically cannot do any processing. The bus is therefore designed such that the cycle time is short. This is accomplished by:
    — Separate paths for address and data such that they can be handled in parallel.
    — A simple bus protocol (the **bus protocol** is the method of signalling addresses, commands, data and status information).
    — No checking (for example, parity) because this would slow down the bus.

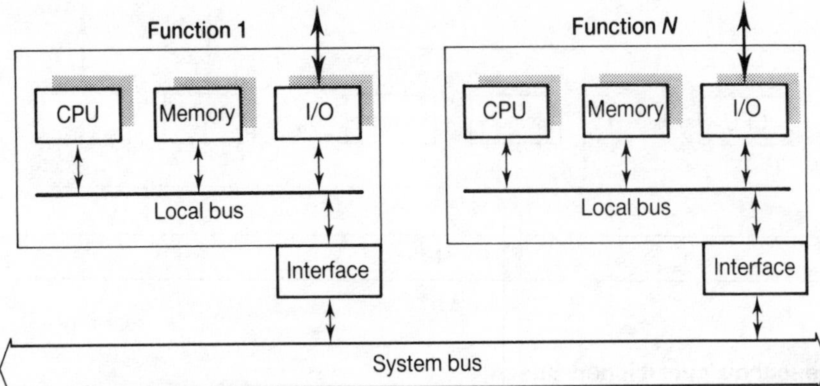

FIGURE 13.5

Functionally partitioned bus.

— Asynchronous operation to accommodate different CPU speeds (for example, 4.77, 8, 12 and 25 MHz processors) and different memory speeds.

- Optimal match of CPU and bus signals: This is due to the short cycle time, which makes this class of buses often dependent on the architecture of the processor.

Functionally partitioned buses

The functionally partitioned bus is used to connect boards that perform a semi-independent function (Figure 13.5). Each function is supposed to contain its local processing power, memory and I/O, connected via a local bus. More recent bus designs, such as the Multibus II (Intel, 1984) and the Futurebus (IEEE, 1986), belong to this class.

Technological progress has been such that a single board can contain a processor, memory and I/O interface circuitry (whenever required). This means that the high-speed CPU–memory traffic can be handled by a local bus, so the system bus only has to be used for communication between intelligent functions. The main characteristics of the functionally partitioned bus are:

- Multiprocessor oriented.
- Message oriented: Communication between the intelligent devices is typically done via messages. Transferring messages can proceed in parallel with local processing. Because of this, the bus has the following characteristics:
  - Blocks of data are transferred.
  - High message throughput rate: Requests to transfer messages may be queued and messages may be buffered. Therefore, only the bandwidth of the bus is important. A more complex

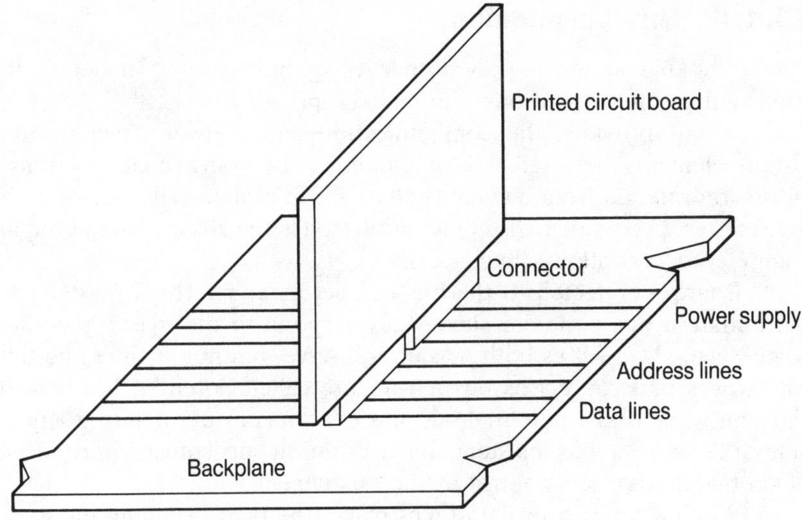

FIGURE 13.6
Backplane bus system realization.

bus protocol, using a high degree of multiplexing (for example, address and data lines), is acceptable and desirable, because it reduces the number of signal lines of the bus. Facilities for error detection (typically a parity mechanism) and error recovery are desirable, because they allow for a higher level of system integrity with only a marginal increase in hardware and protocol complexity. Furthermore, functionally partitioned buses are often synchronous, because synchronous buses can be faster and more reliable (less susceptible to noise) than asynchronous buses.

- Uncoupling of CPU and bus signals: Because of the fact that a CPU communicates via the system bus only indirectly, using a message mechanism that typically has its own hardware support, CPU properties in terms of signals and their timing relationships can be uncoupled from those of the system bus. Functionally partitioned buses therefore tend to be processor independent.

13.1.3 Mechanical bus properties

A typical realization of a computer system with a common backplane is shown in Figure 13.6. The backplane consists of copper-printed circuit traces in the form of parallel lines. These lines form the communication links between the boards connected to the bus. Separate lines can be used for power supply and other utilities (see Section 13.5.3). Industry standards have been developed for the connectors and the sizes of the boards (Dalrymple, 1984).

13.1.4 Bus terminology

Before looking at the logical properties of bus systems in detail, it is important to understand bus terminology.

A bus provides the communication path between two or more system elements between which data must be transferred. A transfer moves information from one data cell or group of data cells (memory cell, I/O register, processor register) to another. These cells are numbered and a unique address allows their access.

Boards connected to the bus can act as either (bus) **master** (they can initiate a bus cycle) or **slave** (they respond to the master's wishes). Some devices can act as both master and slave, but not at the same time. All devices that can act as bus master are called potential bus masters. Since only one of the potential bus masters can control the bus at any one time (the current bus master), an arbitration mechanism must decide which bus master gets control of the bus next.

When a transfer of data takes place, the board sending the data is called the **source**, while the board receiving the data is called the **destination**. A slave requiring service can signal this condition over the bus via an interrupt request; it would not be efficient for the master to continuously check for service requests of the slaves.

A complete sequence, from requesting the bus until the completion of the transfer of the data element(s), is termed a **bus transaction**. This may consist of several operations, each of which may require several **bus cycles**. The operations and cycles may overlap in time if parallel paths exist (for example, separate arbitration, address, data and interrupt paths).

The speed of a bus depends on many factors, such as the type of drivers and receivers that are used, its length, the number of boards that it may have to drive, and so on. Many current backplane buses have a cycle time of about 100 ns. This means that for a data path of 32 bits, a maximum bandwidth of 40 Mbyte/s can be obtained. The effective bandwidth is less because not all cycles are used (or can be used) for transferring data.

To perform a bus transfer, the following operations may take place:

- request operation;
- arbitration operation;
- addressing operation;
- data transfer operation;
- error detection and signalling operation.

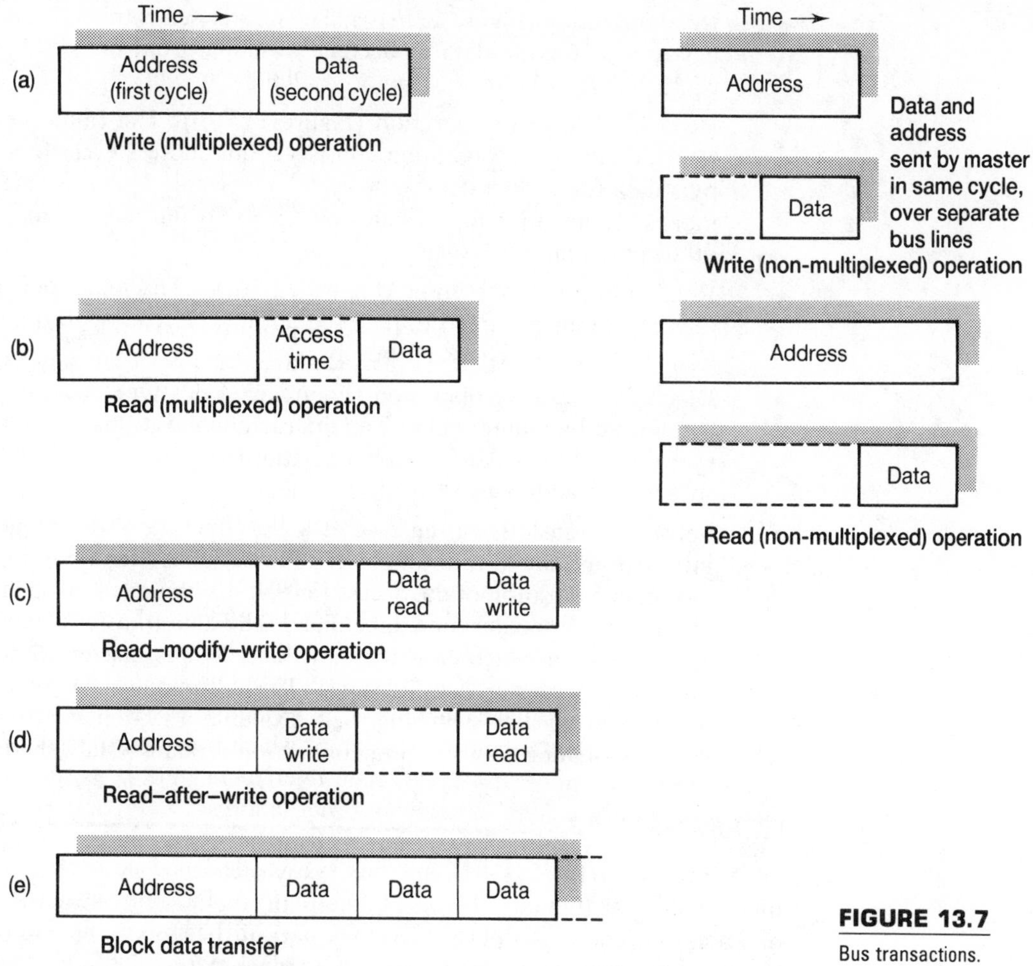

FIGURE 13.7
Bus transactions.

13.2 Data transfer

Data transfers on a bus consist of a set of control and data exchanges between the bus master and one or more slaves. Several types of data transfer operations are possible, as illustrated in Figure 13.7:

- Write operation (Figure 13.7(a)). The left figure shows the multiplexed case (see Section 13.5.1) where the master (the source unit) sends an address in the first cycle, followed by data in the second cycle. Note that the slave (the destination unit) must first recognize the address before it can receive the data. The right figure shows the non-multiplexed case where data and address are presented in the same cycle, over separate bus lines.

- Read operation (Figure 13.7(b)). The master sends the address and has to wait for the data to become available from the slave. This waiting time is known as the access time.
- Read–modify–write operation (Figure 13.7(c)). The (multiplexed) read–modify–write operation consists of an address cycle followed by a data read and a data write cycle. The whole operation may be indivisible in order to prevent any access to the data element by other potential bus masters.
- Read-after-write operation (Figure 13.7(d)). This operation consists of an indivisible write, read sequence. The read operation may be performed for checking purposes.
- Block data transfer operation (Figure 13.7(e)). One address cycle is followed by *n* data cycles. The first data item is transferred to the specified address, and following data items are transferred to subsequent addresses.
- Split data transfers. In the case of a read operation, the requested information may have a long access time. Rather than holding the bus for the duration of the access time, it may be released such that other bus transactions may take place. The data transfer is initiated again later, in which case the slave acts as bus master while the original bus master acts as slave. This technique is often called **message** or **packet switching** (see Example 13.1), in contrast to **circuit switching** in which the connection remains established.

□□EXAMPLE 13.1

Multibus II (Intel, 1984) is a bus system designed according to the functionally partitioned scheme of Figure 13.5. Passing messages from one board to another is performed by a part of the system bus interface, the message passing co-processor (MPC) (Muchmore, 1986). Multibus II offers, in addition to circuit switching, a message switching protocol for interprocessor communication, known as message passing. A message consists of a destination and source address (1 byte each), 2 bytes of qualifying information (such as priority) and up to 28 bytes of user data. The entire message is sent as one block of data via the system bus (iPSB bus). The following sequence of events takes place when a processor on one board (for example, CPU *i*) requests a block of data from a disk connected to another board (for example, disk *j*):

(1) CPU *i* requests the data block from I/O controller *j* using an interrupt message, containing the parameters needed to identify that data block.

(2) I/O controller *j* responds, after retrieving the block of data, with a message requesting that a memory buffer be made available.

(3) CPU i signals that it has made a memory buffer available in its local memory.

(4) I/O controller j sends the data, using 32-byte messages. Between these messages, other boards can use the bus.

In this way, data is sent at a very high speed, without using the bus longer than is strictly necessary.

13.2.1 Addressing

Once a bus master controls a bus, it must establish contact with one or more slaves in order to set up the data transfer. This is called **addressing**, which potentially consists of two parts: board addressing and the addressing of the data elements on that board. Often, the same mechanism is used for both. Each board is allocated a block of addresses such that the high-order address bits specify the board and the low-order bits of the same address specify the data element on the board. The subject of addressing is discussed here in terms of how a slave address can be specified and the number of slaves involved in a bus transaction.

Slave address specification

During a bus operation, the address of the slave to be involved in the operation is specified via the address lines of the bus. The address of the slave is usually the address of the slave's board. Each board, therefore, has a unique address. When this matches the address specified via the address lines, the board is said to be selected. Two methods can be distinguished for allocating board addresses: logical (location-independent) addressing and geographical (location-dependent) addressing.

Logical addressing means that each board is given a unique address or group of addresses by means of (manual) switches, for example; that is, this address can be given in a completely arbitrary way, it does not depend on, for example, the type of the board or its position in the backplane. This requires extra hardware and may also require human interaction to customize the board address. Traditional buses, such as VME and Unibus, use this concept (see Example 13.2).

Geographical addressing means that a board may be addressed by its physical location, which is where a board is inserted in the backplane. This location is called the **slot number** and is hard-wired into the backplane, rather than via customizable hardware, such as switches, on the board. Geographical addressing allows for location independence of the boards and for operating system-initiated reconfiguration of the system.

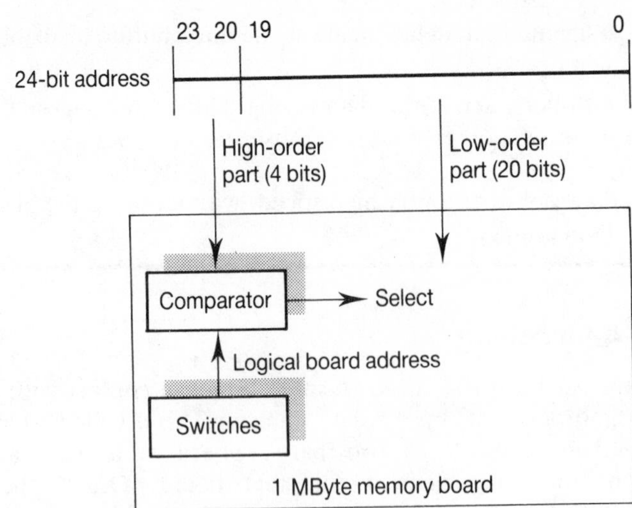

FIGURE 13.8
Logical addressing.

The operating system can use geographical addressing as part of its initialization sequence to set up logical addresses which are stored in an address register on the board, such that customizing the address is done completely under software control. The logical addresses are subsequently used by all bus transactions. Essentially, geographical addressing allows the allocation of logical board addresses under software control. Newer buses, such as the Multibus II, the Fastbus and the Nubus, use this concept (see Example 13.3).

□□EXAMPLE 13.2

The VME bus transfers a logical address at the beginning of each bus cycle. This may be a 16-, 24- or 32-bit address (respectively called short, standard and extended addresses), depending on the capabilities of the bus master and the slave. The address size, together with some additional information (data/program, user/supervisor, single or block data transfer), is specified via six address modifier (AM) lines, which form an extension of the address. Customizable hardware, in the form of switches or an EPROM, has to be used to specify the logical address of the board. For example, when the boards contain 1 Mbyte memories and 24-bit addresses are used, the four high-order address bits specify the board address (Figure 13.8).

Number of slaves involved in a bus transaction

Most bus transactions require only a single slave to be involved in the bus transaction. However, for certain bus transactions, such as reset, it may be desirable to involve all slaves or a group of slaves. Read and write

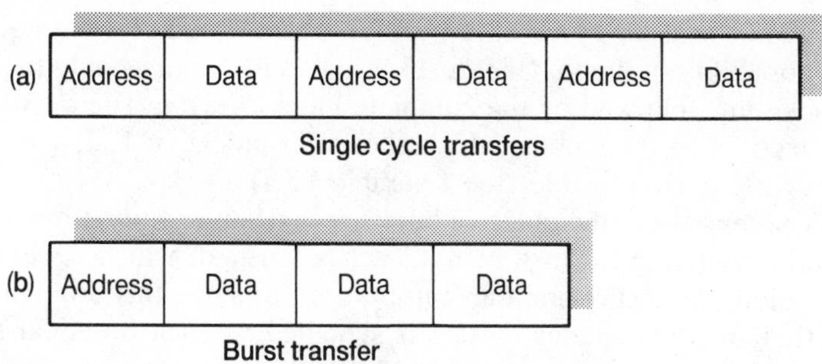

FIGURE 13.9
Block data transfer for a multiplexed bus.

operations that may involve more than one slave are called **broadcall** and **broadcast** operations, respectively. The concept of broadcast/broadcall addressing is orthogonal to logical/geographical addressing; it deals with the communication of a single master with multiple slaves.

Broadcall operations cause all selected slaves to place their data on the bus, which will result in the collective AND or OR of the data of the selected slaves. This restricts the use of broadcall addressing to special cases; for example, to identify the source of an interrupt where each potential interrupter is assigned a single-bit position to identify itself. A broadcall on a 32-bit bus can then be used to identify up to 32 interrupt sources.

Broadcast operations are important for performance reasons; for example, in the case of data consistency, when several caches in a multiprocessor system with distributed caches (see Chapter 16) have to be updated simultaneously. The reset operation, where each board is expected to assume its initial state, is also a form of broadcast operation.

Broadcast/broadcall operations can be indicated via a special address (for example, address 0) or via a special control line, in which case the address lines can be used to select a subset of all slaves.

□□EXAMPLE 13.3

The Fastbus (Gustavson, 1986) supports geographical, logical and broadcast addressing specified by control lines. Broadcast addressing is supported for all write operations, so that data can be written to several slaves simultaneously.

13.2.2 Block data transfers

When a block of data rather than a single data item must be transferred (for example, a cache block or a message of several words), normally every single bus cycle requires an address to be transferred followed by the datum, as shown in Figure 13.9(a). For block data transfers, this is clearly inefficient, since the block of data is stored at consecutive memory locations. For a faster block data transfer, therefore, buses are equipped for the possibility of **bursts** (Figure 13.9(b)). With a burst, only the initial address is sent, followed by the complete block of data. The burst length can be fixed, as in the Nubus, which allows for blocks of 1, 2, 4, 8 and 16 words, or it can be variable (see Example 13.4).

A potential disadvantage of bursts is that, once a burst has started, requesting masters have to wait until it has finished, which could take a relatively long time. **Pre-emption** can be used to solve this problem. This means that the current bus master is signalled when a potential master with a higher priority is requesting the bus (see Example 13.6). When the current master receives this signal, it stops its burst and releases the bus, to continue later on.

□□EXAMPLE 13.4

The VME bus allows for a fast block data transfer. The master initiates a bus operation in the standard way, except that it places a special code on the AM lines (see Example 13.2), indicating the burst mode. All slaves that allow for this type of data transfer (mostly memory units) latch the address into an on-board address register. The master sends the first data item and waits for an acknowledge of the addressed slave. Then, it sends the next data item. Every time data is sent, all slaves increment their address counter and check whether this address falls within that particular slave's address boundaries. This way, blocks can be transferred to different memory boards.

13.2.3 Bus timing protocols

Information transfers over a bus are subject to timing rules so that the source and destination can be synchronized. A typical timing sequence, where time progresses from step 1 to 11, for a source writing information to a destination is as follows:

Source	Destination
(1) Put information on bus lines.	
	(2) Received information stabilizes.
(3) Signal that information is stable.	
	(4) Know that information is stable, take information.
	(5) Acknowledge that information has been taken.
(6) Know that information has been taken.	

(7) Remove information.

(8) Acknowledge that information has been removed.

(9) Know that information is removed.

(10) Acknowledge transfer finished.

(11) Start next transfer.

When information is put on a bus in parallel (for example, 16 or 32 bits of data), all bits may not arrive at the destination at the same time due to timing variations in the source's line drivers, variations in the delay of the bus signal lines and variations in the destination's receivers. This total delay is called the **bus delay**. Typically, the source has to indicate when the data has stabilized. This is done with a special control signal (step 3). The time at which the destination needs to take the information from the bus and store it away internally may not be known to the source, so the destination may have to indicate this (step 5). When the source knows that the destination has taken the information, it can safely remove it from the bus, thus freeing the bus, and signal the destination that it should also free the bus – for example, by removing its timing signals (step 8). When the destination has acknowledged that it has freed the bus (step 10), another transfer may take place.

This sequence, or a subset thereof, can be implemented according to three timing concepts: **synchronous**, meaning that all events happen at fixed moments in time; **asynchronous**, meaning that the signals of the sequence can be generated at arbitrary moments in time; and **semi-synchronous**, which means that the signals can only be generated in a fixed relationship with a clock.

Synchronous bus timing

With synchronous bus timing the transfer of data is controlled by a common clock – for example, by a central oscillator broadcasting clock signals to all connected slaves. The moment at which the events 1 through 11 take place are fixed in time and do not depend on the source and/or destination. Data is presented by the source at a fixed moment in time under control of the data ready (DR) clock and accepted by the destination under control of the data accepted (DA) clock.

It is common practice to specify the transfer of data by means of a timing diagram, which shows the timing relationships that must exist between the control signals and the data. A timing event may be indicated by a rising edge (a transition from 0 to 1) or a falling edge (a transition from 1 to 0) of a control line. Figure 13.10 shows the timing diagram for a write operation, assuming a synchronous bus.

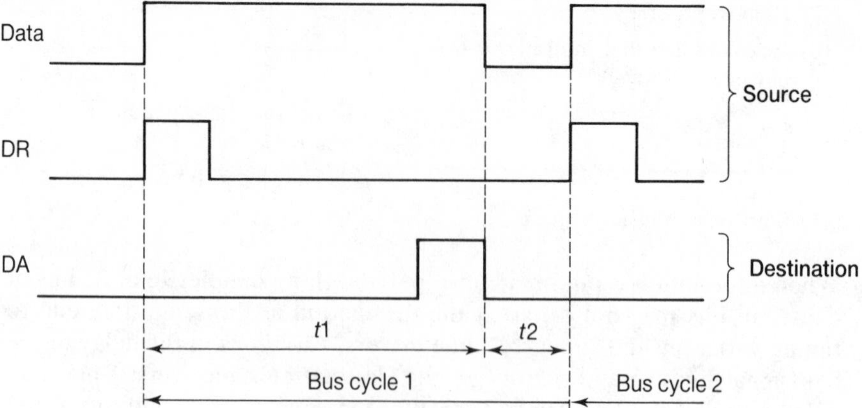

FIGURE 13.10
Synchronous bus timing (write operation).

Synchronous bus timing protocols have a theoretically higher throughput than asynchronous bus timing protocols, because no signalling between source and destination is required (steps 3, 5, 8 and 10 are not required). On the other hand, the length of the time slots *t*1 and *t*2 must be adapted to the slowest device connected to the bus. If this is not the case, buffers must be inserted in the devices for temporary storage of data.

A disadvantage of synchronous bus timing is that the source has no way of knowing whether the destination has actually received the data. Similarly, a destination that must receive data has no way of knowing whether the source has actually placed the data on the bus.

Asynchronous bus timing

The basic characteristic of asynchronous bus timing is the absence of a fixed clock. This means that each step of the timing sequence has to be indicated by a specific timing event, and that event has to be propagated down the bus to the communicating partner. The time required for the propagation of the event, the bus delay time, may be considerable – for example, 10 to 50 ns. Therefore, rather than signalling all events, at the expense of the bus delay time for each event, some protocols assume that the timing of certain events is done implicitly – that is, by assuming a long enough, fixed delay time for that event. They trade the variable time required for an internal delay plus a bus delay for a fixed delay time.

Depending on the number of implicit events, asynchronous bus timing distinguishes **non-interlocked**, **half-interlocked** and **fully interlocked** bus protocols.

The asynchronous, non-interlocked bus protocol is shown in Figure 13.11. It assumes fixed times for the duration of the DR and the DA/DE signals. Data is put on the bus by the source after a delay time *t*1, when the source drives DR high; that is, it makes the DR signal a logical 1. The

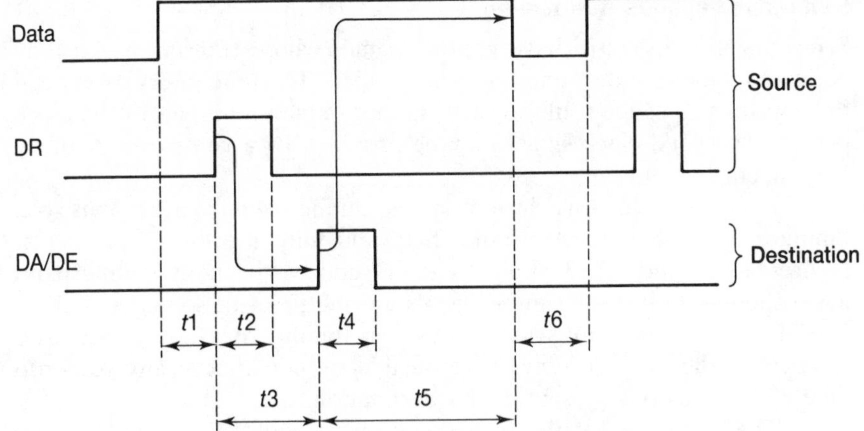

FIGURE 13.11
Asynchronous, non-interlocked bus timing.

DR signal is received by the destination, which then stores the data (assuming a write operation) and notifies the source (after a time period $t3$) by driving DA high. When the source receives DA, after a time period $t5$, it removes the data from the bus and waits for a time period $t6$ for the bus to stabilize, after which the next bus cycle may be started.

If an error is found – for example, due to bad parity – the destination may respond by driving the data error (DE) line high instead of the DA line. Note that this protocol assumes the control signals DR, DA and DE to have a fixed length.

From this timing diagram, it should be clear that the speed of the destination may be arbitrary, because the time interval $t3$, which is the response time of the destination (being the sum of the internal and the bus delay), is under complete control of the destination. Similarly, the response time of the source, determined by time interval $t5$, is under control of the source. This means that devices with arbitrary speeds can communicate. The penalty paid for this protocol, in terms of bus speed, is two propagation delays for control purposes, $t3$ and $t5$.

The problem with this protocol is that the time intervals $t2$ and $t4$ are fixed; that is, they do not depend on a timing event of the communicating partner. In the case of a fast source, which means a short time interval $t5$, the next bus cycle could start while the DA/DE signal is still high, violating the bus protocol. By driving the DR signal low in response to the rising edge of DA/DE, the time interval $t2$ is made variable, and the problem is partly solved. This is the half-interlocked protocol. The next cycle may still start too early, however, because the source does not know when the destination has driven the DA/DE signal low. The fully interlocked protocol of Section 13.2.4 solves both of these problems.

Semi-synchronous bus timing

Semi-synchronous buses have control signals whose transitions can only occur at moments determined by a fixed clock. The time interval between the control signals may still be variable, but only in multiples of the clock period. The fixed clock signal may be provided by a central clock or by the current bus master.

Analogous to asynchronous bus timing, semi-synchronous bus timing distinguishes between non-, half- and fully interlocked protocols. Figures 13.11 and 13.12 apply to their semi-synchronous counterparts when the duration of all timing signals are multiples of some fixed clock period. Also, with semi-synchronous bus timing, the fully interlocked protocol is the most flexible, because it does not impose any response time restrictions on the source and destination.

The advantage of the semi-synchronous protocol is that it is less susceptible to noise, because only noise signals on control lines occurring exactly at the moment of the leading or falling edge of the clock may be misinterpreted to be a timing signal. The disadvantage is that response times have to be rounded up to multiples of the clock period.

13.2.4 The asynchronous, fully interlocked bus protocol

This protocol is called fully interlocked because all transitions in the control signal levels only occur in response to transitions of the partner. Another term for this interlocking is **handshaking**.

The control signals in a fully interlocked protocol all have a variable length. To prevent hardware malfunctions from hanging the bus, a **time-out mechanism** is used. This time out assumes that all handshakes should be performed within a fixed, upper time limit. When this does not happen, the time-out circuitry drives an error signal high. This can be a special time-out (TO) signal or the DE signal could be used for this.

The fully interlocked, asynchronous bus protocol is widely used because each device can operate at its own speed: fast devices will have a short bus cycle time and slow devices will automatically cause a longer bus cycle time. The handshaking of every cycle requires four edges (Figure 13.12, which shows a write operation):

(1) The rising edge of DR, which indicates the presence of valid data.

(2) The rising edge of DA/DE, which indicates that the destination has accepted the data.

(3) The falling edge of DR, which indicates that the source has seen the acknowledge (DA/DE) signal of the destination, and so the source may remove the data from the bus to prepare for the next bus transaction.

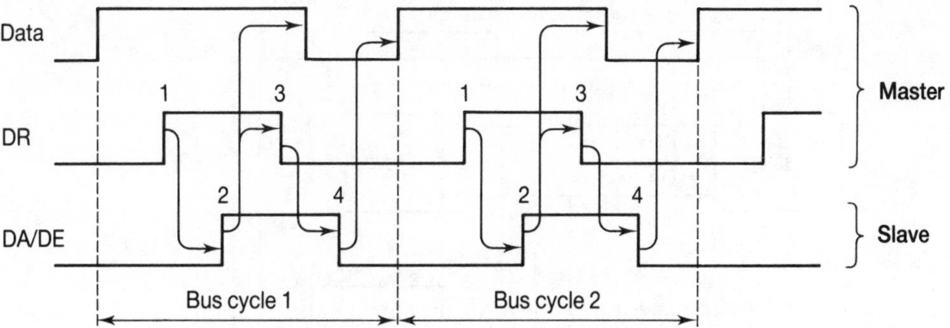

FIGURE 13.12
Asynchronous, fully interlocked, four-edge handshake, bus timing.

(4) The falling edge of DA/DE, which frees the bus for the next bus transaction.

A disadvantage of this protocol is that each event, indicated by an edge, has to be propagated down the bus. The four-edge handshake protocol, therefore, takes at least four bus delays. Another disadvantage of asynchronous buses is their susceptibility to noise on the control lines, because a transition on a control line is allowed to occur at any moment in time. The semi-synchronous bus protocol reduces this susceptibility for noise, because transitions in timing signals can only occur at fixed moments in time, determined by a clock. Only noise at those moments may influence the correct operation of the bus.

Two variants of the asynchronous, fully interlocked protocol should be mentioned at this point: the two-edge handshake, and the six-edge handshake, as described below (Figure 13.13).

Until now, only the situation of one source and a single destination has been considered. Situations do occur (for example, in broadcast or broadcall bus transactions) where a single source needs to communicate with multiple destinations, in which case the source must ensure that all destinations are ready for the transfer, and that every slave has accepted the data before it is removed from the bus. The IEEE Standard 488 (IEEE, 1975) has adopted a handshaking method with three control signals, allowing multiple slave units to respond to one master, resulting in a fully-interlocked, six-edge handshake (see Example 13.5).

□□EXAMPLE 13.5

The IEEE Standard 488 defines a bus system that contains 16 lines, of which eight lines are used for data transfer and eight lines for control. Three control lines are used for a six-edge handshake protocol (Figure 13.13(a)). Each slave can generate a ready (RDY) signal and a data-accepted (DA) signal. Each of these two control signals form a so-called wired-AND connection; that is, the master only receives a high signal

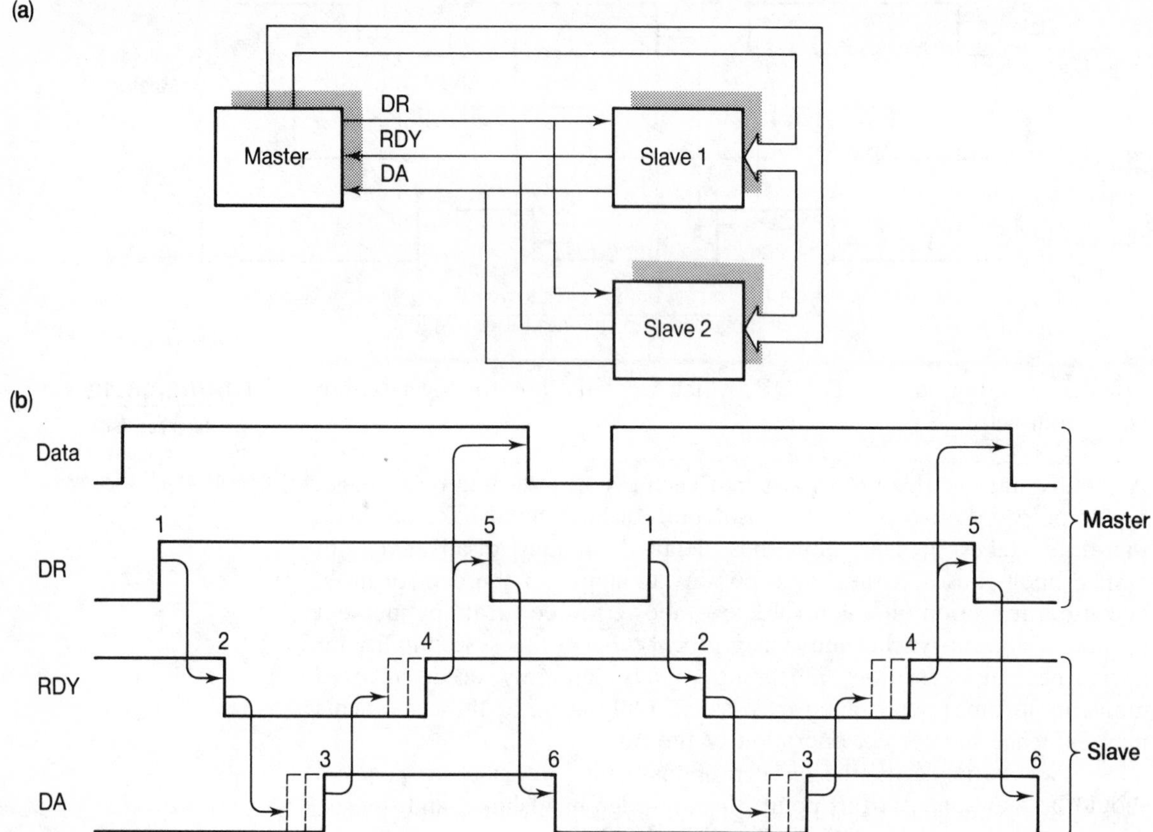

FIGURE 13.13

Asynchronous, six-edge handshake, bus timing.

level on its input if all slaves produce a high signal level. If one slave produces a low signal level because one slave is not ready to accept data, for example, the master also receives a low signal level. Figure 13.13(b) shows the timing diagram for a bus transaction where a master sends two bytes of data to n slaves. The operation is as follows:

(1) The master puts the data on the bus.

(2) The master checks whether all slaves are ready (RDY = high) and, if so, drives DR high (edge 1).

(3) The slaves respond to the rising edge of DR by becoming not ready and drive RDY low (edge 2). Because RDY is a wired-AND control line, RDY becomes low as soon as the fastest slave has driven its RDY line low.

(4) In response to the falling edge of RDY, all slaves start accepting the data. When a slave has accepted the data, he drives his DA high. Because DA is a wired-AND control line, DA will only

become high when *all* slaves have accepted the data. This will occur at the moment of edge 3 of Figure 13.13(b).

(5) In response to DA being high, all slaves release the bus. When the slowest slave has succeeded in doing so, RDY will become high (edge 4).

(6) The master senses the rising edge of RDY, indicating that all slaves are ready. He drives its DR line low (edge 5) and removes the data from the bus in preparation for the next bus cycle.

(7) In response to the falling edge of DR, all slaves drive their DA signal low (edge 6) in preparation for the next bus cycle.

13.3 Bus arbitration

In bus systems with more than one potential master, the bus can only be allocated to one of the potential masters at a time. The bus arbitration mechanism guarantees that this is done in such a way that conflicts are prevented; that is, one master controls the bus at a given time, while bus ownership can be transferred between potential masters. Bus arbitration can essentially be done in two ways: static and dynamic arbitration.

13.3.1 Static bus arbitration

Static bus arbitration consists of distributing the bus transactions over all potential masters in a predetermined way. For example, in a system with four potential masters, M1 through M4, M1 may be allocated bus transaction 1 (T1); M2, T2 and T3; M3, T4; and M4, T5 and T6. After that, M1 will be allocated T7, which is the T1 of the next round of allocations. This requires a bus system where a bus transaction takes place regardless of whether the master to which that transaction is allocated has anything to communicate (no-operation (NOP) transactions). Any bus timing protocol, synchronous, asynchronous or semi-synchronous, can be used. Most systems using static arbitration use a synchronous bus protocol, because then the number of bus transactions per unit of time (the **bus bandwidth**) can be guaranteed for each potential master.

The advantage of this scheme is its simplicity, resulting in low hardware cost and a guaranteed bus bandwidth. The disadvantage is that bus bandwidth is wasted when the current master has nothing to transfer. This is aggravated by the fact that the allocation policy should be such that the peak data rate of each potential master has to be accounted for, leading to a lot of wasted bandwidth and/or a shortage of total bus bandwidth. To solve this problem, dynamic bus arbitration can be employed.

13.3.2 Dynamic bus arbitration

Dynamic bus arbitration allows ownership of the bus to be transferred dynamically – that is, on demand. The arbitration uses bus allocation policies and bus deallocation policies.

Bus allocation policies

When a potential master wants to perform a bus transaction, it raises a request to do so. Similar requests may be raised by other potential masters. When the current bus master releases control of the bus, it must be decided to which of the requesting potential masters the bus should be allocated. The policy used to select a potential master is called the bus allocation policy. Three allocation policies can be recognized:

- Priority based: Each potential master has a unique, fixed priority. The bus will be allocated to the requesting master with the highest priority. I/O subsystems are an example of potential masters with a priority structure; their priority is determined by their urgency of service. Most bus systems, therefore, support several levels of priority (typically 8 or 16).
- Fairness: In situations where potential masters have the same priority, it must be guaranteed that the bus will be allocated to each requesting potential master before any of them has had a second turn. This policy is important for multiprocessor systems where processors may have the same priority, because they are performing similar functions. Giving a higher priority to one of the processors could imply that the service is not evenly distributed, or, even worse, one of several processors with higher priority could permanently prevent the bus from being allocated to lower-priority processors; this is called **starvation**. The fairness policy prevents starvation.
- Combined: The priority and fairness policies can be combined. Typically, higher-priority requests are allocated the bus on a priority basis, while low-priority requests are allocated the bus according to the fairness policy.

Multiprocessor systems typically use the combined policy; for I/O subsystems, the priority policy is used; while the other processors, which execute user and system programs, use the fairness policy.

Bus deallocation policies

Deallocation of the bus, in which a bus master releases the bus for use by other potential masters, can be based on the following policies:

- Release on request: The current bus master has access to the bus as long as no other requests are made, even if this current bus master is not using the bus. This policy is used in many single-processor systems, where, in principle, the CPU always has access to the bus, except when, say, a DMA transfer takes place. Because the CPU would be requesting the bus very frequently, the release-on-request policy saves the bus allocation time in all those cases where the bus has not been released.

- Release when done: With this policy, the bus is released after a bus transaction has been completed. Therefore, bus masters will have to request the bus for each transaction.
- Pre-emption: With this policy, a requesting bus master with a higher priority than the current bus master can force the current bus master to release the bus directly, without finishing its data transfer first. This can be used to interrupt transfers of large blocks of data.

13.3.3 Bus arbitration hardware mechanisms

The bus arbitration hardware mechanism implements the dynamic bus arbitration policy. The hardware can be implemented in a centralized or distributed way. **Centralized arbitration** means that the arbitration hardware is concentrated at one location. This hardware can be either located in one of the modules connected to the bus or in a separate hardware **bus arbiter**. **Distributed arbitration** means that the arbitration hardware is distributed over the potential bus masters.

Centralized arbitration

With centralized arbitration, one central arbiter decides which potential bus master actually gets control of the bus. For a master to use the bus, it must send a bus request to this central arbiter. That arbiter decides, in the case of multiple requests, which master gets control of the bus, based on the allocation policy used. Three mechanisms can be identified for requesting and granting use of the bus: shared requests with daisy-chained grant, independent requests and grants, and a combination of these two.

Shared requests with daisy-chained grant This method is illustrated in Figure 13.14. Every potential bus master can generate a request via the shared bus request (bus request*) line. (The * here indicates that the signal is active when it is low.) The bus request* lines of all bus masters form a wired-OR connection; this means that bus request* will be active (be driven low) when any number of potential bus masters has a bus request outstanding. When the central arbiter receives a bus request, it sends a bus grant signal to potential bus master 1. The bus grant line

(a)

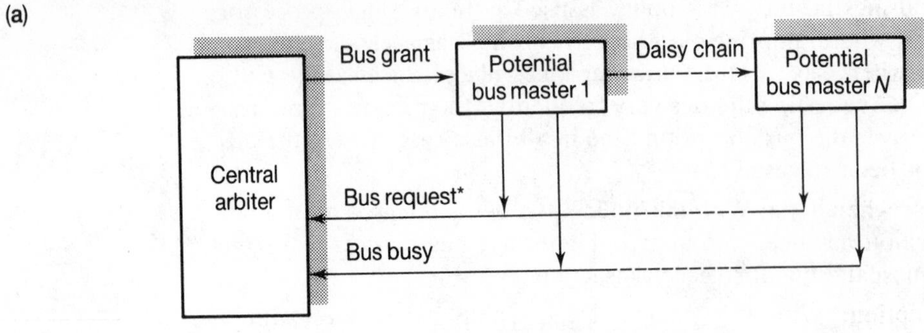

(b)

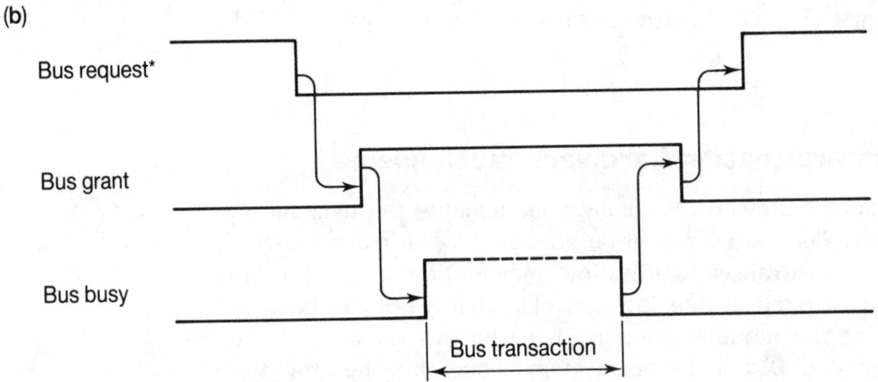

FIGURE 13.14

Centralized arbitration: Shared requests with daisy-chained grant.

connects all potential bus masters to form a chain, called a **daisy chain**, such that potential bus master 1 may send the bus grant signal to potential bus master 2, and so on. The allocation policy is priority based, where the priority is determined by the position of the requesting master in the daisy chain. If a potential bus master does not request the bus, it just passes the bus grant signal to the next potential bus master in the daisy chain until the requesting bus master has been reached. The requesting bus master does not pass the bus grant signal (it breaks the chain), but drives the bus busy line high (to indicate that the bus has been occupied) and removes its bus request* signal. When the current bus master releases control, it drives the bus busy line low, the bus grant line is driven low by the arbiter and the next arbitration cycle can begin.

The advantage of this mechanism is its simplicity. Very few control lines are required and their number is independent of the number of potential masters. The addition of a new potential master can be done simply by connecting it to the already present bus request* and bus busy lines, and inserting it somewhere in the daisy chain. A disadvantage is that the priority of the potential masters is determined by their position in the daisy chain, which is fixed. Potential bus masters 'closer' to the arbiter

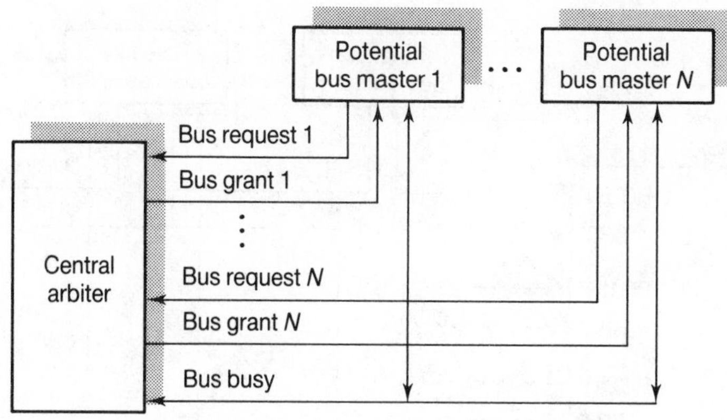

FIGURE 13.15
Centralized arbitration: Independent requests and grants.

are, therefore, more likely to get control of the bus, so fairness is not guaranteed. Another disadvantage is that bus allocation is quite slow, because of the sequential propagation of the bus grant signal. A third disadvantage is that a failing bus master could prevent bus masters with a lower priority ('further away' in the daisy chain) from getting control of the bus. However, because of its simplicity, many bus systems use daisy chaining. (Note that this is called **central arbitration** because a central arbiter is being used. The actual arbitration is done in the daisy chain, which is decentralized.)

Independent requests and grants This method is illustrated in Figure 13.15. Every potential bus master has a separate pair of bus request and bus grant lines, used for communication with the central arbiter. When a potential bus master wants to get control of the bus, it drives its private bus request line high. The arbiter selects the potential bus master that is allowed control of the bus and sends a bus grant signal to that master. The selected bus master removes its request and drives the bus busy line high, indicating to all other potential bus masters that the bus is currently being used. When the bus master wants to release the bus, it drives the bus busy line low, after which the arbiter removes the bus grant signal and allocates the bus to a new bus master. The timing sequence is identical to that of the shared request with daisy-chained grant.

The central arbiter can monitor the requests from each potential bus master such that any bus allocation policy may be implemented. Malfunctioning potential bus masters may be ignored by the arbiter, thus providing for some level of fault tolerance. Another advantage of this mechanism is the short arbitration time, because every bus master is connected directly to the arbiter. A major disadvantage, however, is the large number of control lines required when many potential bus masters are connected to the bus, as in multiprocessor systems.

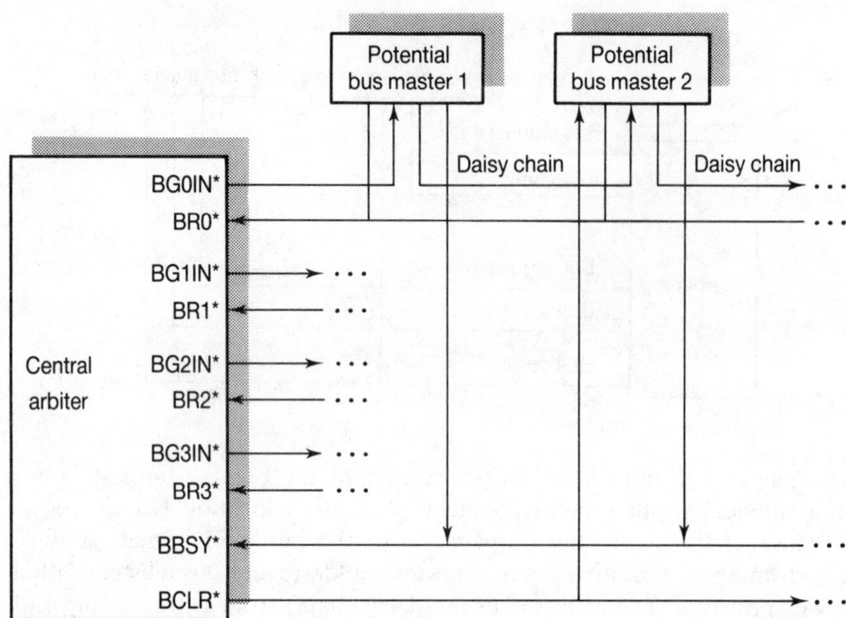

FIGURE 13.16
VME bus arbitration mechanism.

Combined mechanism The combined arbitration mechanism will be explained with an example taken from the VME bus. This system uses a combination of both arbitration mechanisms just described.

□□EXAMPLE 13.6

The VME bus arbitration mechanism is shown in Figure 13.16. It essentially uses the mechanism with independent requests and grants, consisting of four bus request lines (BR0*–BR3*), four bus grant lines (BG0IN*–BG3IN*) and a bus busy line (BBSY*). To allow for more potential masters, without increasing the number of bus lines, subpriorities per bus grant line are formed through daisy chaining (see potential master 1 and 2 of Figure 13.16). Three bus allocation policies can be used, allowing for flexibility (it should be noted that the allocation policy within a daisy chain is always based on priority):

- Priority-based allocation: The arbiter gives priority to the four bus request lines from BR0* (the lowest priority) to BR3* (the highest priority) and responds with BG0IN* to BG3IN* as appropriate.
- Round-robin allocation: If a potential bus master in daisy chain m (requesting via BRm*) is currently using the bus, then the arbiter assigns the highest priority for the next arbitration cycle to daisy chain $m - 1$ (BR($m - 1$)*), where priority 0 is followed by priority 3. This is a form of the fairness policy.

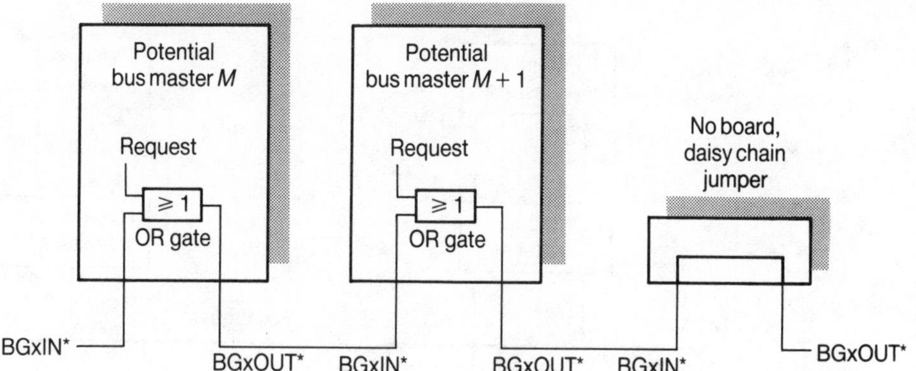

FIGURE 13.17
VME bus daisy chain.

- Single-level allocation: The arbiter only responds to requests on BR3* and so only a single daisy chain is available. A very simple bus arbiter can be built this way.

In most cases, a release-when-done policy is used for deallocation. For a prioritized allocation policy, however, the arbiter informs the master currently in control of the bus when a higher-level request is pending, by driving BCLR* low (bus clear). This may be used to implement pre-emption.

When a bus request is granted, the arbiter drives the BGxIN* daisy chain line low. This low level propagates down the daisy chain (Figure 13.17). If a potential master is not the requesting bus master, it just passes the signal. If a particular slot is not occupied on the backplane, a jumper wire is required to maintain the daisy chain (Heath, 1986).

Distributed arbitration

With distributed arbitration, the arbitration hardware is distributed over the potential bus masters. This is typically used in buses optimized for multiprocessor systems, because of the absence of a default master and the higher reliability requirements. Most implementations support a variant of the independent requests and grants mechanism, where the request and grant lines are shared and encoded, and every potential bus master is assigned a unique arbitration number.

The operation of the distributed arbitration mechanism is shown in Figure 13.18(a). A potential bus master requesting control of the bus indicates this by presenting its X bit arbitration priority number (AP#) to its distributed arbiter. This arbiter passes this AP# to the X-shared request/grant lines. All other requesters also pass their AP# to those request/grant lines by performing a logical OR operation between the X bits of their AP# and the X request/grant lines. Each distributed arbiter compares the resulting AP value on the shared request/grant lines with

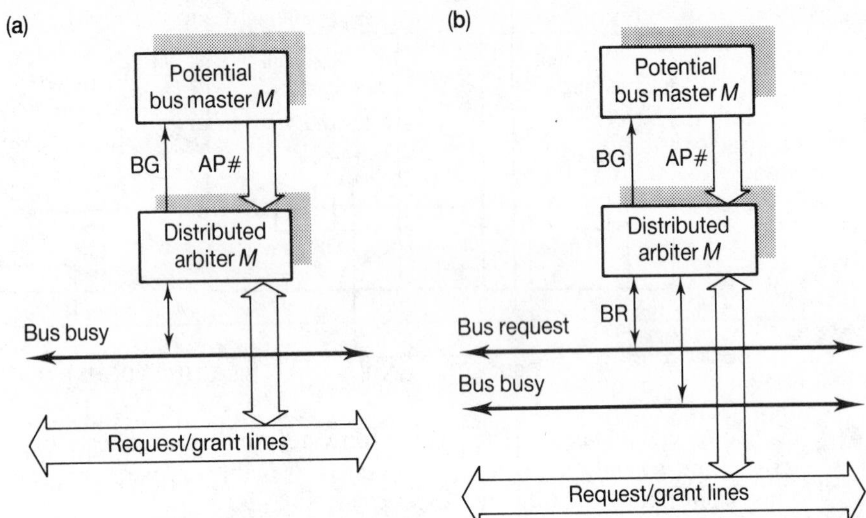

FIGURE 13.18
Distributed arbitration: (a) priority based; (b) fairness and priority based.

that of its requester. If the AP# of the requester is lower, that AP# is removed, because higher-priority requests are being made. After some time, the arbitration process has stabilized and the AP# of the requester with the highest priority (which has the highest AP#) can be found on the shared request/grant lines. The distributed arbiter of that requester then waits until the current bus transaction has been completed (indicated by the falling edge of bus busy), claims the bus (by raising bus busy) and notifies its requester via its local bus grant line. This gives a purely priority-based allocation policy.

The Multibus II, Futurebus (IEEE, 1976) and Nubus use an arbitration method based on this principle, where the allocation policy is based on a combination of prioritized arbitration and fairness.

□□EXAMPLE 13.7

The Nubus (Texas Instruments, 1983) uses distributed arbitration via a separate arbitration bus (Figure 13.18(a)). This scheme does not yet allow for fairness, since the bus master with the highest AP# gets control of the bus more frequently, and could even keep the bus occupied continuously, excluding other potential bus masters from using the bus. The fairness scheme is supported via the bus request line, on which the requests of each potential bus master can be ORed (see Figure 13.18(b)). At a given moment, many potential bus masters request the bus. The fairness policy requires each requester to be serviced in term. This is accomplished as follows. The arbitration takes place in the same way as just described, with the highest-priority requester being granted the bus. On being granted the bus, the shared bus request line is inspected, and if others are requesting the bus (when the bus request line is still high), this requester refrains from requesting the bus until all other requesters have been serviced (this will be when the bus request line is low). In this way, the fairness policy can be enforced. Those requesters that want to be serviced only on a priority basis (such as used for I/O) can do this by not listening to the request line.

13.4 Interrupt mechanisms

An interrupt is a request from some requester to a processor for service or attention. System elements capable of being interrupted contain some hardware, referred to as an **interrupt handler**, to take care of the interrupt requests. The interrupt mechanism, which is always priority based, can be implemented with a dedicated bus or time shared with bus resources already available.

13.4.1 Dedicated interrupt bus

The dedicated interrupt bus uses separate interrupt lines (consisting of interrupt request and grant lines). Requesting an interrupt can be done via separate lines to send interrupt requests to an interrupt handler. Each interrupt handler is the only destination of some of the interrupt request lines – that is, the interrupt destination is hard-wired.

The arbitration mechanisms of the interrupt bus (which always uses a priority-based allocation policy because interrupts are priority based) are the same as those used for centralized arbitration, with the same advantages and disadvantages. Because several interrupt requests may be made at the same priority level, serviced by the same handler, the handler does not necessarily know the source of the interrupt. The identification of the source of the interrupt can be done by vectored interrupts (see Section 9.6.4). Note that the grant part is only required when the interrupt source is identified via an interrupt vector; when polling is used, no grant has to be issued because the polling program has to find the requester and turn that request off, while other requests remain pending.

□□EXAMPLE 13.8

The VME bus uses seven dedicated interrupt request lines (Fischer, 1984) (IRQ1*–IRQ7*). From one to seven interrupt handlers can exist in the system, each taking care of one or more interrupt request lines (Figure 13.19). Each of the seven interrupt request lines may be shared by two or more devices; therefore, an interrupt acknowledge daisy chain

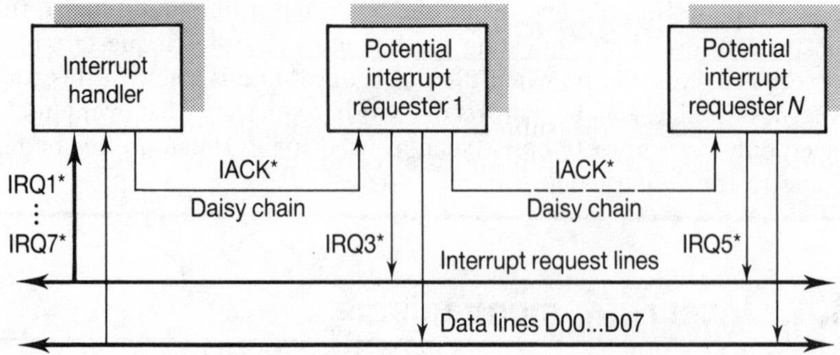

FIGURE 13.19

VME bus dedicated interrupts.

signal passes through every device connected to that particular interrupt request line. When the interrupt handler receives an interrupt request, it arbitrates for the use of the data bus and, if granted, it acknowledges the interrupt by means of the IACK* signal. The IACK* line is connected to the IACKIN* input of potential request 1 (start of the daisy chain). When a potential requester did not request an interrupt, it (and subsequent potential requesters) pass the IACK* signal via their IACKOUT* line until the requester has been reached. The requester sends an 8-bit identification (called the interrupt vector) to the interrupt handler via the data bus. Based on this interrupt vector, the handler invokes the appropriate I/O handling process.

13.4.2 Time-shared interrupt bus

Interrupt requests using a time-shared interrupt bus are usually made by sending a message of a certain length over the data bus (see Example 13.1). Due to the absence of a dedicated interrupt bus, these interrupts are often called **virtual interrupts**. The message contains a destination address as well as a source address and it may also contain other information. This means that any module may interrupt any other module. The bus arbitration hardware for data transfers is used to arbitrate the interrupt (using a priority-based policy), so no special arbitration hardware is required. The only extra requirement is that each device should have a number of addresses (equal to the number of priority levels of the interrupt handler) which when involved in a write operation will cause an interrupt as a side effect. Analogous to memory-mapped I/O, virtual interrupts can be considered memory-mapped interrupts. Buses introduced more recently support virtual interrupts so that a dedicated interrupt bus is not required. This mechanism supports the functional partitioning concept very well, since each module can potentially interrupt any other module at any of the priorities supported by the interrupt handler.

13.5 Special topics

In order to complete the subject of buses, the following special topics remain to be covered: multiplexing, error detection and handling, and utilities.

13.5.1 Multiplexing

The **bus width** (the number of lines of the bus) has a great impact on the cost, reliability and throughput of the system. Bus lines require drivers, receivers, cable, connectors and power, all of which tend to be costly compared to logic. Furthermore, connectors are among the least reliable components in a system, so using few connectors and connections increases reliability. Basically, the objective is to achieve the highest throughput with the smallest number of lines.

A commonly used method to reduce the bus width is time sharing, which is also called **time multiplexing**; that is, several signals from a device are sent over the same bus lines at different moments in time. Some common forms of multiplexing are: address/data lines, interrupts via address/data lines (virtual interrupts) and arbitration via address/data lines (embedded arbitration). By multiplexing the address and data lines, an (32-bit) address is sent over the same bus lines as the (32-bit) data, reducing the number of bus lines (by 32). The price paid for this is that some logic has to be added to the modules to demultiplex the multiplexed lines. Furthermore, multiplexing decreases the throughput, as the multiplexed signals cannot be transferred in parallel, only sequentially.

Arbitration via the address/data lines, also called **embedded arbitration**, is illustrated in Figure 13.20. Every bus transaction consists of three cycles:

- Command/address cycle: This cycle is the first cycle of every transaction. A code identifying the command type is sent, followed by an address used for the selection of the slave(s). Possible command types are read and write, interrupts, broadcast and broadcall.
- Embedded arbitration cycle: This cycle is the second cycle of every transaction. It uses the time needed by a module for address decoding to arbitrate the bus for the next transaction.
- Data cycle(s): All bus transactions are concluded by at least one data cycle.

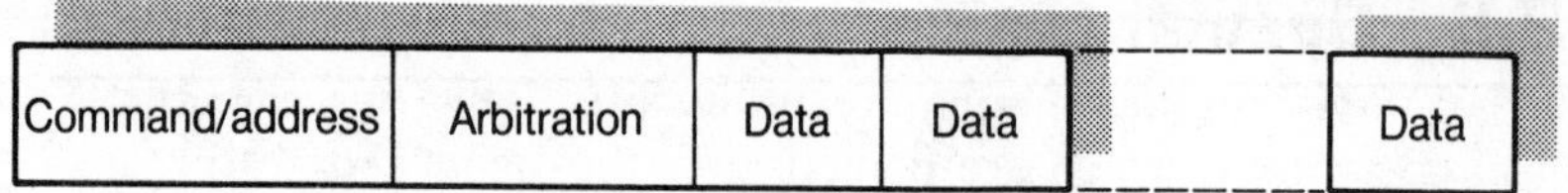

FIGURE 13.20
Multiplexing arbitration lines.

In general, non-multiplexed buses are faster, use more lines and more power, are less reliable and are cost effective for short connections. Message-oriented buses tend to be multiplexed (they use address/data line multiplexing) as the incurred time penalty is less (one bus cycle per message). Local buses do not tend to be multiplexed because they usually connect a CPU with memory, where data transfers of one data element are typical.

13.5.2 Error detection and signalling

Whenever an error occurs during a bus transaction, data is erroneous or can get lost, so errors should be detected, reported and, if possible, recovered. The following errors can be distinguished:

- Addressing errors: These errors include issuing non-implemented addresses and attempts to overwrite forbidden areas (for example, operating system code). On an asynchronous bus, addressing of non-present memory is detected by the absence of a slave response. The time-out mechanism can detect this and can generate a bus error signal. Further error handling should be done by the operating system (see Chapter 12).
- Data transfer errors: These errors can be due to noise, cross-talk and power fluctuations. The usual way to detect these errors is by using error-detecting codes, such as parity. If an error is detected, a retry of the transfer could be done upon a data error response.
- Arbitration errors: A potential error (especially in multiprocessing systems) is a failing arbitration mechanism (either the bus is not allocated upon a request or is allocated to two or more requesters). A possible recovery mechanism uses a time out such that a potential master that has waited a certain time removes its request in order to retry some time later.

13.5.3 Utilities

Most bus systems have some lines reserved for utility functions, such as power supply, system initialization and reset, system clocks, and so on. The utilities supplied are bus dependent. Therefore, as an example, the VME utility bus is discussed.

□□EXAMPLE 13.9

The VME bus has a separate utility bus. This bus consists of the following six lines, which are named after the signal they carry:

(1) System clock (SYSCLK): This signal is driven by an independent, fixed frequency (16 MHz) system clock, which may be used by any attached device (for example, to eliminate the requirement for a local clock). The bus timing is independent of this clock.

(2) Serial clock (SERCLK): The SERCLK and SERDAT* signal lines are used for serial communication and may be used as a diagnostic bus (see Figure 13.1).

(3) Serial data (SERDAT*).

(4) AC fail (ACFAIL*): The VME bus system can be equipped with a power monitor which monitors the AC power and gives an early warning via the ACFAIL* line in the event of a power failure. The time interval between ACFAIL* and the loss of power can be used to save the state of the system on disk.

(5) System reset (SYSRESET*): When power becomes available again, indicated by the SYSRESET* line, the system may reboot itself and continue from the point at which failure occurred.

(6) System failure (SYSFAIL*): This signal is used to indicate a detected system failure or to indicate that a VME board performs a self-test during system initialization. During this test, no normal bus operation is possible.

SUMMARY

- Buses are used to connect system elements. In a computer system, they are usually parallel, rather than serial, to allow for a higher bandwidth.

- Buses can be found at the board level, backplane level or at the interface level. A bus system is a collection of buses, typically one for each level. Standard buses allow for flexibility in system configuration.

- Buses can be classified to be dedicated versus non-dedicated (shared), or as resource partitioned versus functionally partitioned.

- A bus transaction consists of one or more operations, each of which consists of one or more cycles.

- A bus master controls the bus, while a slave responds to the master. Data is transferred from a source (which may be a master or a slave) to a destination.

- The addressing of a slave can be done using logical or geographical addressing. Broadcast/ broadcall addressing allows one master to communicate with multiple slaves.

- Three bus timing concepts can be distinguished: synchronous, asynchronous and semi-synchronous. The latter two concepts allow for three levels of interlocking: non- (two-edge), half- and fully (four edge) interlocked.

- Arbitration can be done statically or dynamically (on demand). Dynamic bus arbitration uses a bus allocation and a bus deallocation policy. Its implementation may be centralized or distributed.

- Two interrupt mechanisms can be distinguished: dedicated interrupts (using separate bus lines, each line representing an interrupt priority to be handled by a handler, hard-wired to that line) or virtual interrupts (where the data transfer path of the bus is used to simulate memory-mapped interrupts).

- Multiplexing is a technique for time sharing bus lines.

- Buses have to provide capabilities for the detection and signalling of errors.

EXERCISES

13.1 Given a resource partitioned and a functionally partitioned bus:

(a) Which bus is preferable for multiprocessor systems?

(b) Which bus is preferable for a CPU–memory bus?

(c) Which bus is more processor independent?

(d) Which bus tends to have a very short cycle time?

(e) Which bus does not multiplex address and data lines?

(f) Which bus has less support for error detection?

13.2 (a) Which operation is required when a CPU transfers data to memory?

(b) Which operation is required when a TAS instruction is being executed?

(c) For which operation (read or write) does a split data transfer make sense?

(d) What is the advantage of a block data transfer?

13.3 (a) How is the address of a system element determined for geographical addressing?

(b) What is a broadcast operation?

13.4 (a) For which bus timing protocol do all events occur at fixed moments in time?

(b) A handshake of how many edges is required for a fully interlocked protocol?

(c) Why does the IEEE-488 bus use a six-edge handshake?

(d) What is the difference between asynchronous and semi-synchronous bus timing?

(e) What is the advantage of semi-synchronous bus timing?

13.5 (a) Which bus arbitration method is very simple?

(b) Which bus arbitration method uses the available bus bandwidth more optimally?

(c) For which systems is a fairness-based bus allocation policy important?

(d) Which bus deallocation policy is preferred for a single-processor system, and which for a multiprocessor system?

(e) When does the use of the pre-emption bus deallocation mechanism make sense?

13.6 Which bus arbitration mechanism is preferred.

(a) In a multiprocessor system?

(b) In a single-processor system?

13.7 Is a daisy chain used for requesting or granting a bus?

13.8 What is a virtual interrupt and for which systems is it useful?

References

Borill, P. L. (1981). Microprocessor bus structures and standards. *IEEE Micro*, **1**(1), 84–95.

Dalrymple, R. (1984). Eurocard/DIN single-board computers signal era of international standards. *Mini-Micro Systems*, **17**(8), 171–8.

Fischer, W. and Roper, P. (1984). Versatile bus suits real-time processor applications. *Computer Design*, **23**(7), 137–42.

Gustavson, D. (1986). Introduction to the Fastbus. *Microprocessors and Microsystems*, **10**(2), 77–85.

Heath, S. (1986). Building up a system architecture using VME bus. *Microprocessors and Microsystems*, **10**(2), 86–90.

IEEE (1975). *Digital Interface for Programmable Instrumentation*. IEEE Standard 488–1975. IEEE Computer Society: New York, NY.

IEEE (1986). *Futurebus: A Backplane Bus Specification for Multiprocessor Architectures*. P896 Draft 7.4. IEEE Computer Society: New York, NY.

Intel (1984). *Multibus II Bus Architecture Specification Handbook*. Order number 146077–C. Intel Corporation: Santa Clara, CA.

Muchmore, S. (1986). Multibus II message passing. *Microprocessors and Microsystems*, **10**(2), 91–3.

SCSI (1984). *SCSI Small Computer System Interface*. ANSC X3 T9.2/84–40. Computer Business Equipment Manufacturers Association: Washington, DC.

Texas Instruments (1983). *NuBus Specification*. Texas Instruments Order No. TI–2242825–0001.

VME (1985). *VME Bus Specifications Manual*. Rev. C. IEEE P1014/D1.0. IEEE Computer Society: New York, NY.

PART FIVE

ACCELERATION

One way to express the quality of a computer is by its execution speed, often expressed in millions of instructions per second. To increase the speed of a computer, some form of acceleration is required. The concept of acceleration can be applied to each of the three levels in a computer system: the architectural, the implementation (also called organization) and the realization level. Chapter 14 describes the various acceleration mechanisms at these three levels.

One way to accelerate the execution of programs using a single processor is to have an architecture with simple instructions, which can be executed very fast. These architectures are called reduced instruction set computers and are the subject of Chapter 15.

The execution of programs can be further accelerated by using more than one processor. Network topologies, describing the way these processors can be interconnected, are of concern as well as the subject of data coherence, which is of particular interest in tightly coupled multiprocessor systems. These issues are covered in Chapter 16.

14 Acceleration Mechanisms

Nothing is more irrational than a life which is completely rational.
– Jacob Israel de Haan

Computer designers are always looking for mechanisms to improve the performance of computer systems. One way of doing this is to use mechanisms that increase the performance of a (conventional) single-processor system. Another approach uses parallelism to increase system performance – for example, via multiple processors. Acceleration mechanisms implemented at the various levels of the hierarchy of computer systems for both the single-processor and multiprocessor set-up are described in this chapter, some of which are explained in more detail in Chapters 15 and 16. For a classification of non-conventional architectures, designed to achieve a higher performance (most of which are currently in the research stage), the reader is referred to Chapter 17.

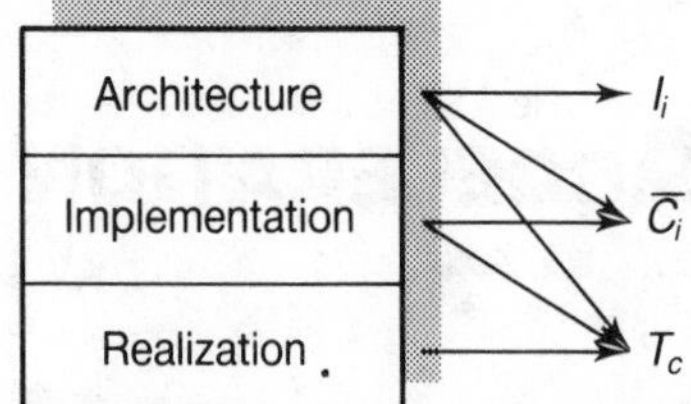

FIGURE 14.1
Program execution time components.

14.1 Introduction to acceleration mechanisms

Acceleration mechanisms can be applied to single-thread as well as multiple-thread systems, as discussed in the following subsections.

14.1.1 Acceleration mechanisms for single-thread systems

Computer systems that execute one program at a time are called **single-thread systems**. This means that the system has only one program counter, and therefore only one processor executing the program (other processors may be part of the system, but these are not involved in executing the program; they may perform dedicated functions such as I/O, thereby raising the level of program execution of the CPU). Mechanisms to speed up a single-thread system can be classified according to the level at which the mechanism can be found: at the realization level (technological), at the level of the implementation (often called organizational) or at the architectural level (Figure 14.1).

The execution time of a program can be expressed by the following equation:

$$\mathrm{T}_{\mathrm{prog}} = T_c * \sum_{i=1}^{\mathrm{N}} I_i * \overline{C}_i$$

where:

- T_c is the cycle time of the processor. It is determined by the architecture, because complex instructions usually cause the cycle time to be longer; the implementation, because, for example, a wider data path requires a longer cycle time due to carry propagation; and the realization, because faster circuits reduce the cycle time.
- $\overline{C}_i$ is the average number of cycles per instruction. It is determined by the architecture, because complex instructions require more cycles; and the implementation, because an operation can be implemented in parallel or serially.

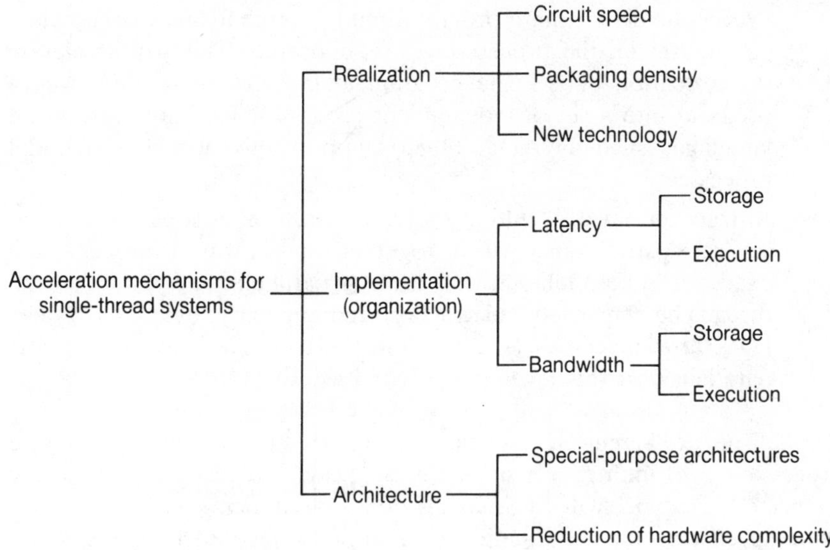

FIGURE 14.2
Acceleration mechanisms for single-thread systems.

- I_i is the number of times instruction i is executed. This depends on the program being executed and on the architecture of the machine.

An overview of acceleration mechanisms for single-thread systems is given in Figure 14.2. Many of these mechanisms can be applied equally well to processors that are used to build an array processor or a multiple-thread (multiprocessor) system.

14.1.2 Acceleration via multiple-thread systems

A **multiple-thread system** executes more than one program at the same time. This is accomplished through some form of parallelism. Multiple-thread systems can be implemented at any of the several levels of the software hierarchy in a computer system:

- Program level: Each of the threads represents a program which is executed in parallel with other threads. A multiprocessor system supporting multiple threads on this level does not improve the execution time of a single program, because parallelism below the program level is not supported. Programs can be written, compiled and run, independently of other programs, which makes it easy to migrate single-thread programs to this type of multiple-thread system.

- Process level: Within a program, multiple threads may occur when parallelism on the process level is supported. This will accelerate the execution of a single program at the cost of decomposing a program into a set of independent processes. Recently introduced languages such as ADA (1983) support this notion of parallel processes.
- Instruction level: Multiple threads, each consisting of one or several instructions, which together may form a process, are executed in parallel. This low level of parallelism requires that the threads be generated and synchronized implicitly, by the hardware. Data flow machines (see Section 17.3) are designed to support parallelism at this level.

Parallelism at higher levels can be realized by replicating entire processors. In multiprocessor systems, these processors are usually connected via some switching network to a shared memory. As this poses some specific problems, Chapter 16 is entirely devoted to this subject. Another approach for multiprocessor systems is to use simple processors that have on-chip communication facilities and that can be easily connected to each other. An example of this approach is the INMOS Transputer (Whitby-Strevens, 1985), which contains a simple processor, memory and four bit-serial communication links on a single chip.

14.2 Acceleration at the realization level

Acceleration at the realization level is determined by the technology used by the components of the system. The first computers were characterized by the use of electromechanical relays, such as the ENIAC introduced in 1946, which contained more than 1500 relays and 18 000 vacuum tubes. In later models, these relays were replaced by vacuum tubes (first-generation computers) and still later by transistors (second-generation computers). An example of such a development is the second-generation IBM 7090 computer, which was based on exactly the same architecture and implementation as the first generation IBM 709. However, the vacuum tubes of the 709 were replaced by transistors in the 7090, because the very tight schedule did not allow the engineers to complete a new implementation of the IBM 709. Using the new technology (which was adopted from the IBM Stretch computer), the IBM 7090 had a clock frequency six times that of the 709. In later computers, the transistors were packaged into small-scale integrated (SSI) and medium-scale integrated (MSI) circuits, which could be used as building blocks.

Furthermore, the core memory was replaced by solid-state memory, which improved the system performance.

Due to these technological improvements, the implementation has also been affected. For example, as a result of the price drop of hardware, functions could be implemented bit parallel (such as the addition of two words) in contrast to the older CPUs, where the cost of hardware forced arithmetic to be performed bit serially.

The increase in packaging density has resulted in large-scale integration (LSI) and eventually very-large-scale integration (VLSI) chips which are being used in most current computers. Chips fabricated with modern VLSI techniques can contain tens of thousands to hundreds of thousands of transistors and operate at clock speeds as fast as 25 MHz or more. The 16 MHz Intel 80386 CPU contains over 275 000 transistors, occupying about 100 mm^2 of silicon (El-Ayat, 1985). Another example of using this higher packaging density is the MC68030 CPU, which integrates the functions of the MC68020 CPU and the MC68851 memory management unit, and a data cache on a single chip. The latest trend in achieving a higher density is wafer-scale integration (WSI) where chips, produced on a single wafer, are not separated from each other and packaged in separate chips, but they are interconnected on the wafer to form, for example, a processor array. WSI requires that each individual processor must be tested and that the faulty processors are masked off so that only the good ones are used. At this moment in time, WSI still presents many practical problems such as testing, routing around a faulty processor, power consumption and synchronization.

The use of new, higher-speed, circuits (due to new device designs) and of higher packaging densities (which results in less propagation delays and fewer chip boundary crossings) is only an *evolutionary* step in improving processing speed. Due to physical limitations, this will only show gradual improvements (illustrated by the flattening trend of the curve of Figure 14.3) and not the revolutionary improvements needed for the fifth (and sixth?) generation of computers, unless new technologies are employed. Examples of such new technologies are the use of gallium–arsenide (GaAs) circuits instead of silicon, and cryogenic-based techniques using Josephson tunnelling. GaAs offers a speed advantage over silicon and can withstand more severe environmental conditions, such as temperature and radiation. Furthermore, it can interface directly with optical circuits, which is particularly useful for telecommunication applications. However, in two areas, GaAs chips are currently inferior to silicon: cost and packaging density (Milutinovic, 1986). Josephson junction tunnelling is based on superconducting properties of materials that are kept at a few degrees Kelvin (Anacker, 1980). Due to recent breakthroughs in the field of superconductivity (claiming to have reached superconductivity at 240K or even 300K), this area will again attract much interest in forthcoming research efforts. However, at present, VLSI

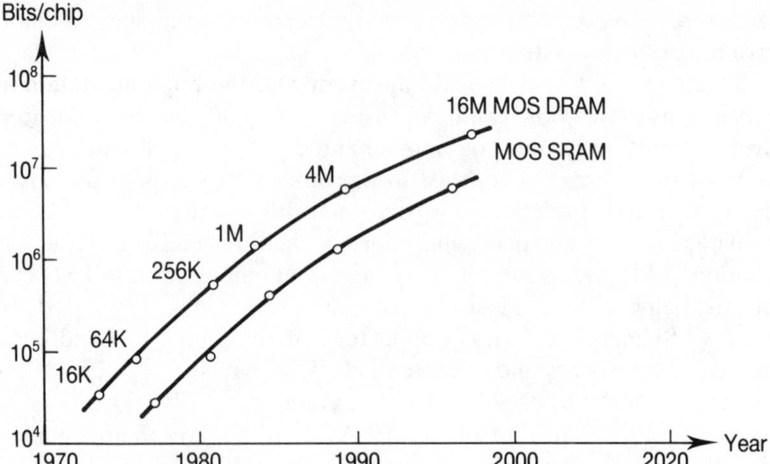

FIGURE 14.3

Expected trend of memory capacity of bipolar and MOS memories.

silicon circuits are used in the main and are not likely to disappear for many years to come, despite some of their shortcomings. Therefore, acceleration mechanisms other than those at the realization level (technological) are sought.

In conclusion, the possibilities for acceleration at the realization level are limited by the used technology. Performance improvements are evolutionary and will have an upper bound, dictated by the properties of the used technology, such as minimum line widths and minimum component spacing.

14.3 Acceleration at the implementation level

Before further elaborating Figure 14.2, it is useful to reconsider the conceptual model of a processor. Examining a traditional processor, at least three sections can be distinguished: the instruction unit (I unit), the execution unit (E unit) and main memory (Figure 14.4). The I unit fetches instructions from memory and, after decoding, passes them to the E unit. This E unit contains adders, multipliers, shifters, and so on, and performs the required operations. Often, a memory control unit (or storage control unit, S unit) is also included in the processor. This S unit is the interface between the I unit and the E unit on the one side, and main memory on the other; it may map virtual addresses into real addresses, for example. In fact, this model is already a form of acceleration, as older machines only had one combined I/E unit.

Examining the implementation level acceleration mechanisms of Figure 14.2, two new notions are identified: latency and bandwidth.

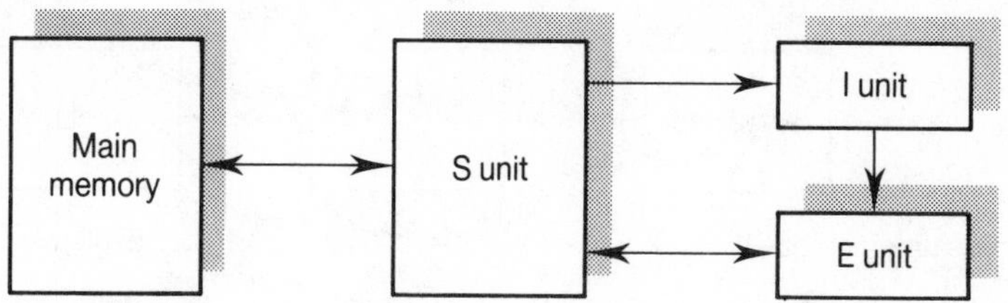

FIGURE 14.4
Conceptual model of a processor.

Latency is defined as the total time between the start of an operation and the availability of the result. In this context, an operation can vary from 'read memory location 1234' to 'compute arctan(4)'. **Bandwidth**, on the other hand, is concerned with the number of operations performed per second; it is an expression of frequency of occurrence, such as a transfer rate of 40 Mbytes per second for a bus or 2 million floating-point operations per second (2 MFlops) for a processor. Bandwidth is made up of two components: the width of the operation (32-bit data path or 64-bit multiply) and the rate of the operation (one memory word transferred per 100 ns or one multiply per 500 ns). Note that although both latency and bandwidth are related to time, there is a difference. Bandwidth or *throughput* is a measure of the time rate (in sec^{-1}), while latency (comparable to delay time) is a measure of the time period (in seconds). Again referring to Figure 14.2, it can be seen that both latency and bandwidth have two aspects, related to memory and execution. This results in the following four notions:

(1) Memory latency: This is the time period needed to respond to a memory request. This latency depends heavily on the type of memory used (the latency for a register access is orders of magnitude lower than the latency for a disk drive access).

(2) Memory bandwidth: This is the amount of data (both instructions and operands) that can be transferred per second from and to memory.

(3) Execution latency: This is the time between issuing, say, a multiply instruction and the time the result is available.

(4) Execution bandwidth: This is the amount of data, processed per second, or, equivalently, processed per clock cycle. This measure is often referred to as throughput.

14.3.1 Memory latency

If methods are to be devised to reduce memory latency, it is important to consider the normal memory hierarchy. Figure 14.5 shows this hierarchy with typical access times for modern computers. The reason for this

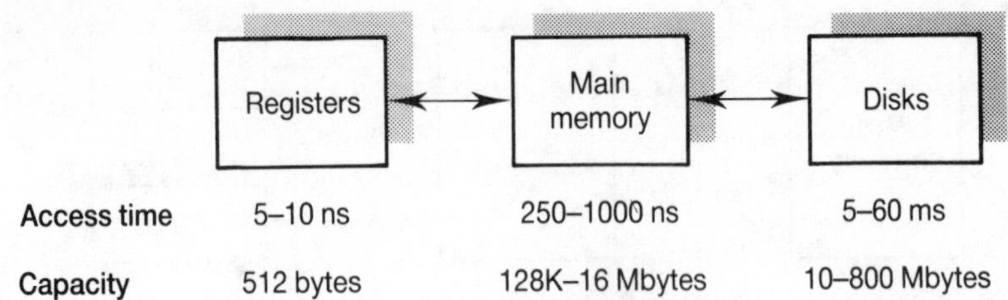

FIGURE 14.5
Memory hierarchy in conventional computers.

hierarchy is that, although disk drives are slower than main memory, the cost per bit of storage decreases towards the end of the hierarchy, while the storage capacities increase. This hierarchy can even be extended with archival storage and off-line storage, such as tape units. For tape units, the access time varies greatly because of its serial access – the time for finding a block on a tape can vary from one second to possibly several minutes. It is clear that there is a gap of about two orders of magnitude between the access time of a register file (normally located inside the processor) and main memory.

One way of ensuring that enough data is supplied to a processor is to increase the number of registers, so the most frequently used operands (that must be stored in those registers) can be accessed with a small latency. Instead of simply implementing a larger number of registers, multiple register sets that can hold the data of different procedures can be used, reducing the overhead of procedure calling, because much less data has to be transferred from and to memory (see Chapter 15). However, because registers consume a large chip area, this solution is not always realizable, as chip area is expensive and limited.

Another way of filling the access time gap in the memory hierarchy is to use high-speed memories – for example, with a typical access time of 50 ns. These memories are called **caches** and are placed between the processor (containing the register file) and main memory. Of course, it would be beneficial to replace all of main memory with these fast memories, but this is very costly, as caches are more expensive than normal memories. Therefore, a tradeoff has to be made between cost and performance: larger caches allow more data to be accessed faster (in 50 rather than 250 ns), but a user should consider if this performance increase is worth the cost. Currently, most mainframes and minicomputers possess cache memories, while some microprocessors even have a cache on-chip; the MC68020 has an on-chip 256-byte instruction cache. Because of the importance of caches (and the problems that come with these caches), a separate section (Section 14.6) is devoted to this subject. Some cache problems that arise in multiprocessor systems (coherence between data elements that reside in different caches) and solutions to these problems are discussed in connection with other multiprocessor aspects (see Chapter 16).

14.3.2 Memory bandwidth

For memories, not only the latency, but also the bandwidth is important. It would be ideal if main memory could provide a single byte in 100 ns, but it would be more useful to have a memory that, after an initial latency of 200 ns, could transfer 2 bytes every 50 ns. In the first case, a request for 8 bytes would be completed after 800 ns; in the second case, the total time required to transfer 8 bytes is 350 ns. This illustrates the two basic approaches for increasing the bandwidth: **pipelining** (normally referred to as interleaving for memories) and **parallelism**.

If memory is divided into several modules, each module can process a memory request independently of other modules. This interleaving technique is used in most larger computers, because it is an easy (and inexpensive) method of increasing the memory bandwidth without using very fast (and expensive) memories with a small latency.

Parallelism in this context can imply the use of wider memory data paths or the use of multiple paths. Using a 32-bit data path to memory is more efficient than an 8-bit path, as more information can be transferred in the same amount of time. The use of multiple memory paths is mostly based on the division of memory into an instruction and a data part. If one memory path is dedicated to the transfer of instructions, and the second path only transfers data, the memory bandwidth is effectively doubled. The concept of multiple memory paths can also be used for I/O processors, where both the CPU and the I/O processor can have their own memory path. However, interleaving and multiple memory paths also create some problems. A more extensive discussion of both techniques and their problems can be found in Section 14.5.

14.3.3 Execution latency

Execution latency is often associated with arithmetic operations, as these operations require the longest time to complete. Therefore, most mechanisms that accelerate the execution of instructions focus on integer multiply and divide, and floating-point operations. This is obvious because these complex operations require many clock cycles to complete; a reduction of the number of cycles is a direct improvement of the execution latency. The only way to accelerate instructions that already execute in one clock cycle is to shorten this cycle, a technological acceleration mechanism.

Implementing algorithms for arithmetic operations directly in hardware normally requires many levels of gates, each introducing an extra delay (possibly lengthening the cycle time). Using specialized arithmetic units will decrease the latency because an add operation can be executed faster in a dedicated add unit than in a multifunctional arithmetic unit. This dedicated unit may also use some optimized

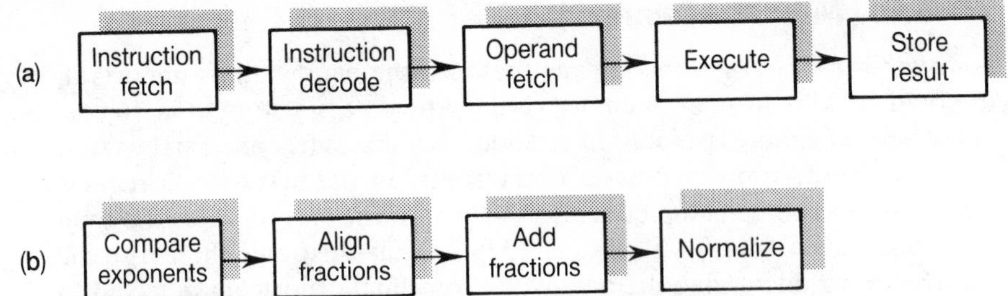

FIGURE 14.6

Pipelining: (a) I unit; (b) floating-point add unit.

algorithm that requires less hardware (and thus fewer delay stages). An example of this for multiplication is the Wallace tree multiplier (Wallace, 1964) or variations on it.

Another, more recent, approach to improve the execution latency is the development of so-called **co-processors**, which are attached to the main processor and optimized for specific operations. They are similar to special arithmetic units, except they are usually located externally because of the lack of sufficient silicon area on the CPU chip. A well-known example is the floating-point co-processor (such as the MC68882, the Intel 80387 or the NS321000), but one can imagine the use of a co-processor that, say, efficiently executes decimal arithmetic operations in an administrative environment (see Appendix B.4).

14.3.4 Execution bandwidth

Methods for improving the execution bandwidth (the number of instructions executed per second) can also be classified into the classes pipelining and parallelism. Recalling Figure 14.4, only the I and the E units are concerned with the execution bandwidth (the S unit and main memory are only concerned with the memory bandwidth and latency). Both the I unit and the E unit can be pipelined. Pipelining can be compared to assembly lines in a car factory. The process of assembling a complete car is split into several stages, which are performed sequentially. However, all stages can be active simultaneously, operating on different cars. Comparable to the contribution of assembly lines to the success of mass production in modern industry, pipelined processors and arithmetic units have provided an enormous increase in system performance.

Transferring this concept to computer organization, a pipelined I unit (including a normal E unit) might look as shown in Figure 14.6(a), while a pipelined E unit (or at least a floating-point add unit) could resemble Figure 14.6(b). The improved bandwidth stems from the fact that several independent operations or instructions are being processed simultaneously (making better use of the available hardware), whereas in

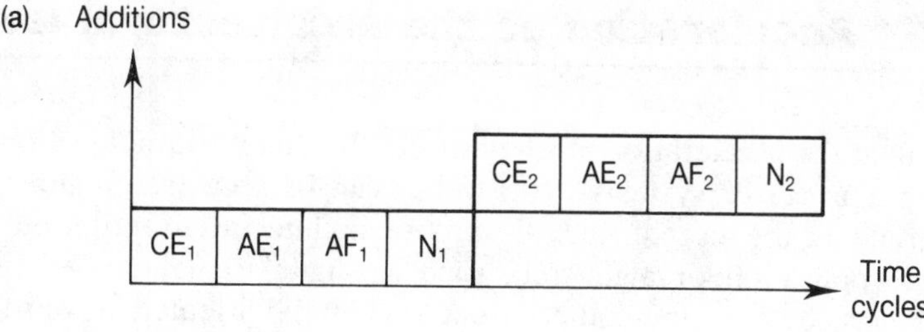

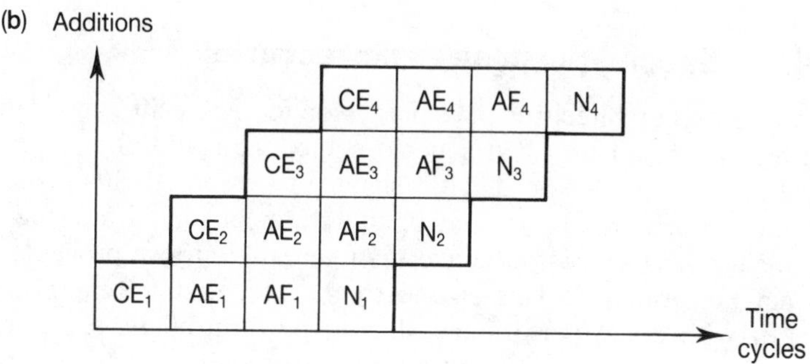

FIGURE 14.7

Timing diagram of floating-point add operation: (a) non-pipelined; (b) pipelined.

the other case (executing one instruction at a time and starting the next when the previous instruction has finished), not all hardware is used efficiently.

As an illustration, consider the floating-point add of Figure 14.6(b). The timing diagram of Figure 14.7(a) shows the result of two floating-point add operations for a non-pipelined execution; the operations are performed without any overlap in time. Pipelining allows the next instruction to start when the previous instruction can leave the first stage of the pipeline. Figure 14.7(b) shows how four floating-point add operations can be performed simultaneously, because of a pipeline with four stages.

More details on arithmetic pipelines can be found in Hwang (1984), Stone (1987) or Kogge (1981). A discussion of pipelined instruction execution and some of the related problems is given in Section 14.8.

Another method for improving the execution bandwidth is parallelism; parallelism within the I unit leads to multiprocessing (see Chapter 16) or data flow machines (see Chapter 17).

In conclusion, most acceleration mechanisms at the implementation (organization) level have been exploited. Further improvements are limited when programs consist of single-instruction streams, which have to be executed sequentially. Only gradual improvements can be expected, by using larger caches, for example.

14.4 Acceleration at the architectural level

Looking at the acceleration mechanisms at the architectural level (at least for single-processor systems), two trends can be seen (see Figure 14.2). One trend is the use of special-purpose architectures optimized for a specific application or algorithm, such as digital signal processors and display processors; the other trend is more oriented towards the performance enhancement of general-purpose architectures and involves the reduction of the hardware complexity.

14.4.1 Special-purpose architectures

Optimizing the architecture of a processor for a specific application or algorithm will result in a better performance than that obtained using a general-purpose processor. Digital signal processors (DSPs) computing fast-Fourier transformations, matrix operations or digital filtering operations are much more cost effective than general-purpose processors with an equal performance. This is due to the fact that a general-purpose processor with equal performance has to perform all its functions at a high speed, while a special-purpose processor only has to perform one particular function very fast. Usually, special-purpose processors are single-chip devices with an ALU, multiplier and/or barrel shifter, some address calculators, a program sequencer and local memory. They are often used as replacement for bit slices.

Performance improvements are being made because older implementations, such as the Texas Instruments TMS32010 or the NEC uPD7720, suffered from architectural and implementation limitations. Architectural limitations were due to a primitive (and therefore hard to use) instruction set, a limited addressing range for off-chip addressing, few operand addressing modes and only 16-bit integers. Examples of implementation limitations were a restricted I/O capability, a limited number of on-chip registers and low speed. Improvements in newer machines, such as the NEC uPD77230 (Eichen, 1986) and the Motorola DSP56000 (Kloker, 1986), include faster instruction execution speed, off-chip addressing, floating-point and high-level language support, all of which make it easier to program (and reprogram) special-purpose architectures and offer a higher throughput. Of course, special-purpose architectures are not only used for signal processing, but also for display control, data communication and disk control.

14.4.2 Reduction of hardware complexity

Speed improvements can be obtained by reducing the delay (the number of gates) in the critical data path. A reduction in the number of instructions, addressing modes and data types eliminates the need for a

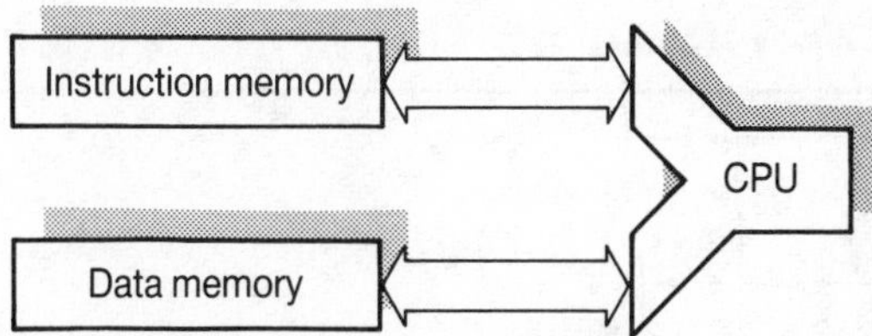

FIGURE 14.8
Harvard architecture.

large (in terms of chip area) microprogrammed control area in favour of the faster hard-wired control. The migration of functions from execution to compile time also contributes to simpler instructions and shorter cycle times. These are the basic concepts behind the RISC (reduced instruction set computers) approach, which is receiving much attention these days. Significant improvements have been claimed by RISC designers and several reputed firms are now marketing computers based on the RISC philosophy, including the Hewlett-Packard Spectrum and the IBM PC–RT (Gimarc, 1987). Because of this current interest and the importance of this concept, a complete chapter (Chapter 15) is devoted to this subject.

In conclusion, although architectural limitations are less severe and many research efforts result in architectures that are better and faster than their predecessors (the RISC philosophy, in particular, offers improvements), retaining a single processor in tomorrow's computer will not be sufficient to keep up with the increasing user's requirements and needs. To improve system performance significantly, it is necessary to perform more operations in parallel; that is, systems should have a higher degree of parallelism (see Chapter 16).

14.5 Acceleration of main memory

Because of the increasing speed of processors, the demand rate for operands and instructions has increased accordingly. To cope with this increased demand for memory bandwidth, two organizational methods have been devised: multiple memory paths (a form of parallelism) and memory interleaving (a form of pipelining).

14.5.1 Multiple memory paths

Currently, most computers follow the von Neumann concept where instructions and data are mixed, using the same memory. It is obvious that the amount of instructions and data, transferred in one memory cycle, is limited by the available memory bandwidth. If this bandwidth is not sufficient, the processor cannot operate at its maximum speed. A possible method for increasing the memory bandwidth is to introduce two separate memories: one for instructions and one for data. This allows for two memory paths (Figure 14.8), which is a form of parallelism.

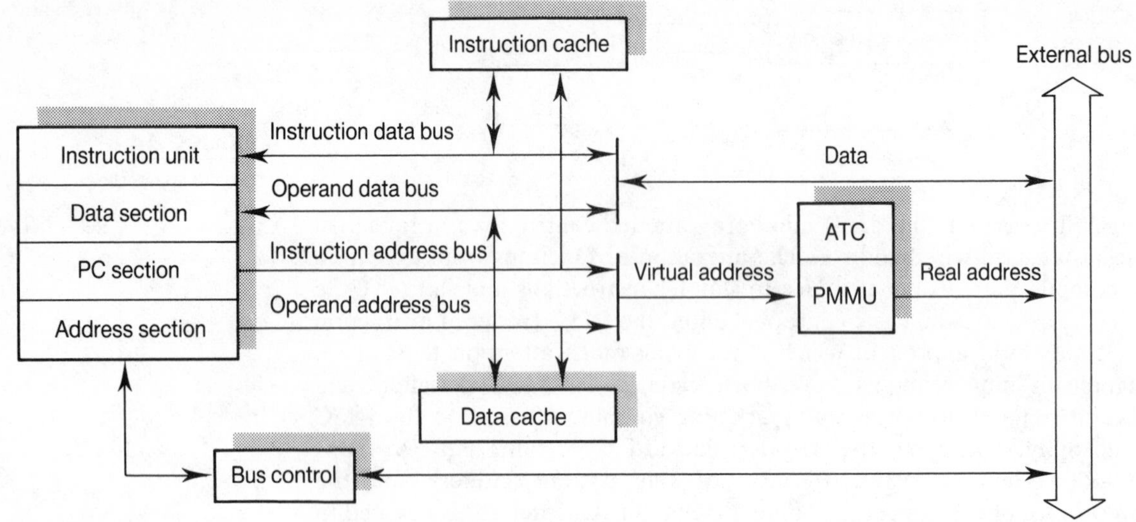

FIGURE 14.9
MC68030 block diagram.

Computer architectures with such a memory organization are called **Harvard architectures**. The Harvard architecture requires that programs do not change themselves, because operations on data apply to the data memory only. This is not much of a problem because self-modifying programs are considered bad practice (LISP implementations, however, require program and data to be indistinguishable). Furthermore, this restriction makes it easier to include instruction prefetch units in a computer, because no instructions that have already been prefetched can be modified.

□□EXAMPLE 14.1

An example of a processor that partly uses the Harvard architecture is the MC68030 (Figure 14.9). The MC68030 integrates the functions of the MC68020 CPU and the MC68851 memory management unit on a single chip (Scales, 1986; Motorola, 1987). This CPU can be subdivided into an instruction unit and an execution unit consisting of three separate sections – the address section, the data section and the program counter section – which are capable of operating independently. Furthermore, the MC68030 contains two 256-byte on-chip caches, one for data and one for instructions that, together with the instruction and the execution unit, implement a Harvard architecture. Externally, the MC68030 has a single 32-bit bus that accesses a single address space, so the MC68030 is (upwards) compatible with all other members of the MC68000 family. However, internally, the MC68030 contains two separate 32-bit buses that support the Harvard architecture: an instruction bus, which consists of a data and an address part, and an operand bus, which consists of a data and an address part. If both caches have a hit, the MC68030 uses its

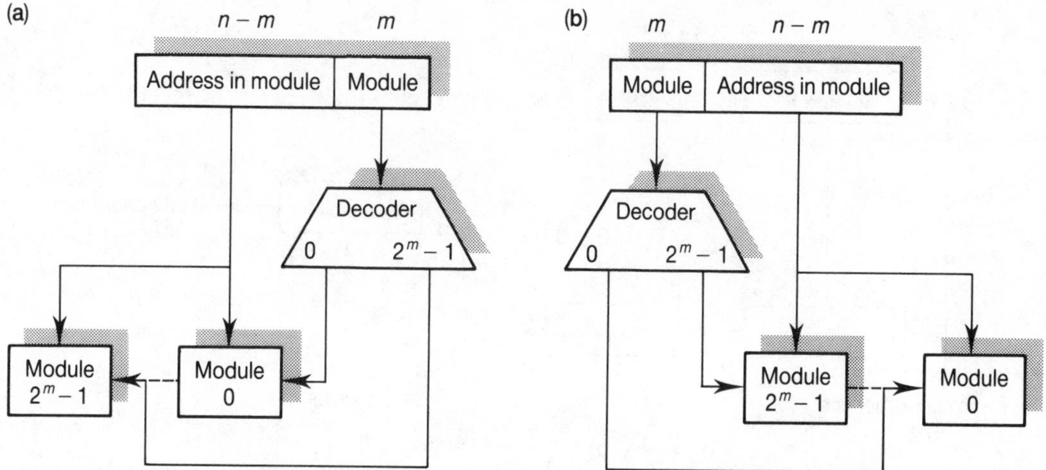

FIGURE 14.10
Interleaving: (a) low order; (b) high order.

Harvard architecture optimally and has a performance more than three times that of an MC68020. When neither cache hits, the MC68030 is a simple von Neumann processor with a performance comparable to that of the MC68020.

14.5.2 Memory interleaving

An increase in processing power results in a requirement for a larger and faster memory. Larger memories require a longer address decoding time, while technological improvements alone cannot cope with the larger address decoding time and allow the memory to be faster at the same time. One solution to this problem could be the use of multiple memory paths of a Harvard architecture. However, a more general approach for achieving a higher memory bandwidth is to retain a single memory path but partition the memory into multiple, physically independent, modules, instead of only two for the Harvard architecture; this is called interleaving. When main memory is partitioned into M modules, $m = \log_2(M)$ bits are needed to specify which module is addressed, and the remaining $n - m$ bits (assuming n-bit addresses) are used to select a word in the addressed module.

There are two approaches to interleaving. The first approach is called *low-order* interleaving (Figure 14.10(a)) where the m low-order address bits are used to select the required module. The consequence of this is that consecutive addresses are found in consecutive modules. This makes such an organization well suited for accessing vector elements or instructions that are executed sequentially; that is, it supports spatial locality. On the other hand, a failure of one module will almost certainly have catastrophic effects on the system. Consider an eight-way inter-

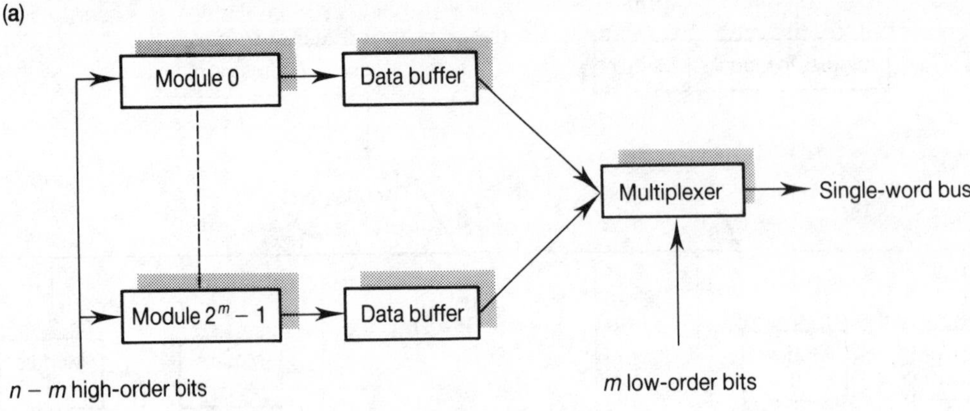

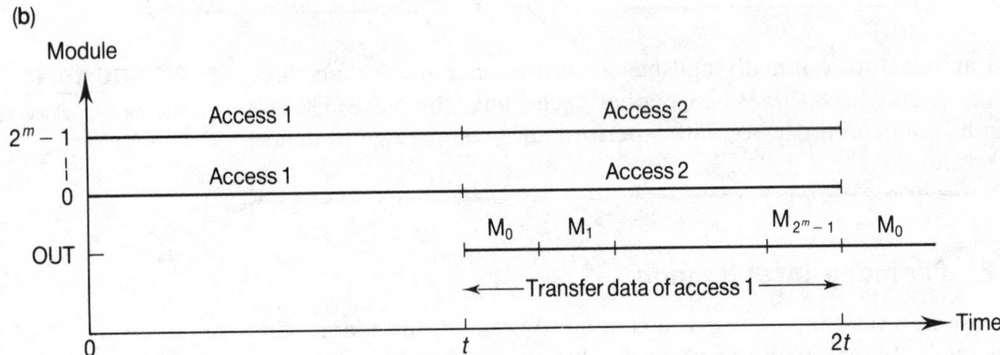

FIGURE 14.11

Low-order interleaving: (a) simultaneous access; (b) timing diagram.

leaved memory; if module 3 fails, the addresses 3, 11, 19, 27, . . . , $8i + 3$, . . . cannot be used any more.

With the other approach, called *high-order* interleaving, the m high-order address bits are used to select the desired memory module (Figure 14.10(b)). Using high-order interleaving, the address space is split into M contiguous parts, where each part is contained within one module, so consecutive addresses can be found in one module. The disadvantage of this type of interleaving is that it does not support spatial locality; all data has to come from one single module, which does not improve the available bandwidth. However, with high-order interleaving, it is easy to expand memory; it also allows for fault tolerance. If one module fails, only a specific area of the address space needs to be disabled.

As low-order interleaving supports spatial locality in a natural way, it is therefore used more frequently.

The memory organizations of Figure 14.10 still do not speed up memory access. However, if instead of one module at a time, all modules are processing memory requests simultaneously, a significant speed-up can be achieved. Using low-order interleaving, two possible organizations are possible. In the first, called **simultaneous access**, the $n - m$ high-order bits are presented to all memory modules at the same time (Figure 14.11(a)). Each module stores the addressed memory word in a buffer and a multiplexer selects each buffer in turn, in such a way that all M words are transferred in overlap with the next access (Figure 14.11(b)). In this way, the memory access time is incurred only once per M memory accesses, assuming all M words can be used. However, for non-sequential memory accesses, the performance of this method sharply decreases, because every memory access still has to endure the full memory latency (there is a lack of spatial locality).

To overcome the low efficiency of the simultaneous access for non-sequential memory accesses, concurrent access may be used. With **concurrent access**, the modules are offered different addresses, which are processed at the same time. The buffers that were used to hold the data with simultaneous access are now used to hold the memory address. Because all modules operate independently of each other, a memory control unit must be included to keep track of which modules are busy and which have completed their memory request. Again, a maximum speed-up factor of M may be achieved. A major advantage of this method is that the memory modules do not have to be accessed sequentially; an arbitrary order is allowed.

14.6 Cache memories

Cache memories are high-speed buffer memories that are placed between the processor and main memory (see Figure 14.5). The success of cache memories can be explained by considering the principle of locality, which states that over a short interval of time, a program tends to favour a restricted part of the address space (see Section 10.2.2). This locality consists of spatial and temporal locality. If it is possible to put the complete working set of a program in the cache, then most memory references by the processor can be supplied by the cache, thereby substantially increasing the system performance.

To measure the effectiveness of a cache in capturing memory references, the **hit ratio** is introduced: this is the probability of finding the requested information in the cache. If a processor references an item that is contained in the cache, this is called a hit. On the other hand, if the referenced data is not present in the cache, a miss occurs. The hit ratio h for a given sequence of memory references is defined as the number of hits divided by the total number of memory references. Similarly, the miss ratio m is the number of misses divided by the total number of memory references. Because each reference is either a hit or a miss, $m = (1 - h)$. Example 14.2 shows the effectiveness of a cache memory.

□□EXAMPLE 14.2

The effectiveness of a cache memory will be shown, with the following computation. Assume a memory access time of 500 ns (T_{MA} = 500 ns) and a cache access time of 50 ns (T_{CA} = 50 ns) with a hit ratio of 99% (P_{HIT} = 0.99), which are all very common numbers. A system without a cache has an average access time of:

$$T_{ACC} = T_{MA} = 500 \text{ ns}$$

A system with a cache has an average access time of:

$$\begin{aligned} T_{ACC} &= T_{CA} * P_{HIT} + T_{MA} * (1 - P_{HIT}) \\ &= 50 * 0.99 + 500 * 0.01 = 54.5 \text{ ns} \end{aligned}$$

This is an improvement of almost an order of magnitude.

A cache design involves a tradeoff between the following (sometimes contradictory) aspects:

- the hit ratio;
- the access time on a hit;
- the delay time on a miss;
- the cost.

To obtain a low miss ratio, the cache size should be large. However, as a large cache is costly and has a long address decoding time, a balance between the performance and the cost must be found.

14.6.1 Cache operation

Figure 14.12(a) shows a simplified block diagram of a cache memory. When a memory access is to be performed, the address is presented to the cache memory. This memory determines whether it contains data associated with that address; if so, it delivers that data; if not, it signals a cache miss.

One way of implementing a cache memory is by using an *associative* memory, as shown in Figure 14.12(b). This memory consists of two parts: a tag memory and a data memory containing lines of data. Each entry in the tag memory is paired with a corresponding entry in the data memory. When a requested tag (which in this case consists of the address of Figure 14.12(a)) is presented to the tag memory, it is necessary to determine whether the cache contains data belonging to that tag. Each entry of the tag memory consists of memory to store a particular tag

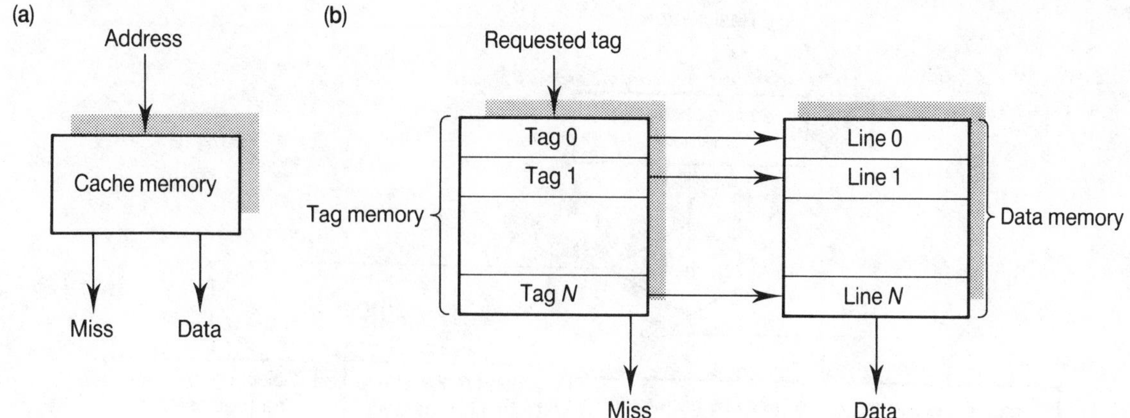

FIGURE 14.12
Cache memory basics.

(which will be a memory address in this case) and a comparator to compare that tag with the requested tag. Because each tag memory entry contains a comparator, the comparison with the requested tag can be done for all entries in parallel. Upon a hit by entry i (tag_i = requested tag), line i in the data memory will be accessed. When none of the entries produces a hit, a miss is signalled.

Each entry in the data memory consists of a **line of data**, which may be several memory words. For example, when an M-way interleaved memory is used, a cache line may consist of M words (or $2 * M$ or $4 * M$ words, or even more).

The operation of a cache is as follows. After offering the real address to the cache, it searches its tag memory for a matching address tag (Figure 14.13). On a hit, the cache selects the correct byte(s) from the corresponding line. Furthermore, the status bits of the referenced line are updated (for example, to reflect which line was referenced last and whether a write has been performed). On a miss, the real address is sent to main memory, which supplies the line to the cache. During the read operation from main memory, the cache (if all entries are occupied) selects a line to be replaced using a replacement algorithm. The received line is stored in the cache, and the requested byte(s) are selected and transferred to the processor.

Computer systems that use virtual memory techniques (see Chapter 10) have a memory management unit (MMU) to perform the address translation operation. When a cache memory is also used, the sequence of operations for each memory reference consists of an address translation, followed by a cache or memory access. This sequence can be performed serially (Figure 14.14(a)) or in parallel (Figure 14.14(b)).

The serial way implies that each cache access is preceded with an address translation operation performed by the MMU. The time required for this is about the same as that required for a cache access, because

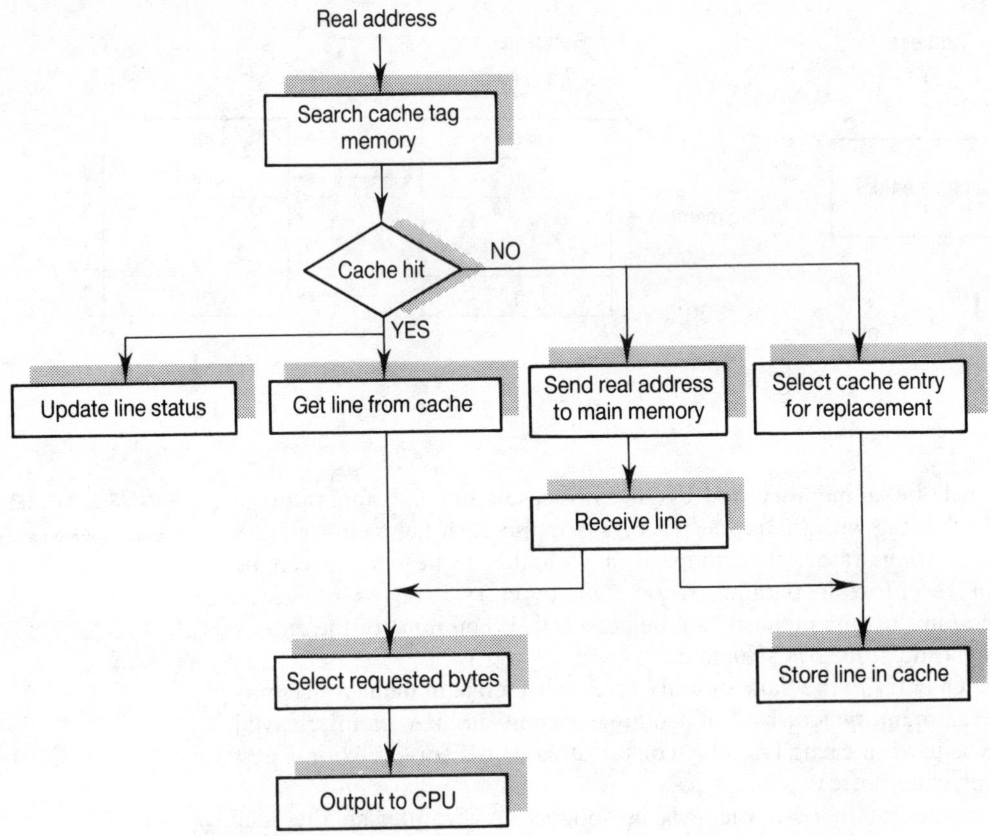

FIGURE 14.13
Cache operation flowchart.

the MMU translation lookaside buffers (TLBs) use the same associative memory technology as the cache of Figure 14.12(b).

The solution of Figure 14.14(b), where address translation and cache access are done in parallel, is preferable because of its higher speed. The operation is as follows. The virtual address (VA) is split into two fields: a displacement field (of D bits), which does not participate in the address translation operation, and a field (consisting of the high-order VBA address bits) that specifies the virtual address of the block, which has to be translated. Because the displacement does not have to be translated, the D bits are passed to the cache memory. Upon a hit, the corresponding line of data may be accessed under the condition that the line of data belongs to the block specified by the VBA. This is checked by comparing the translated virtual block address (which is the real block address RBA) with the real block address of the line that produced the hit. Each cache line now has, in addition to data, a field specifying its real block address.

The schemes of Figure 14.14 both assume that the cache is located in the real address space. This is the most common solution, because a

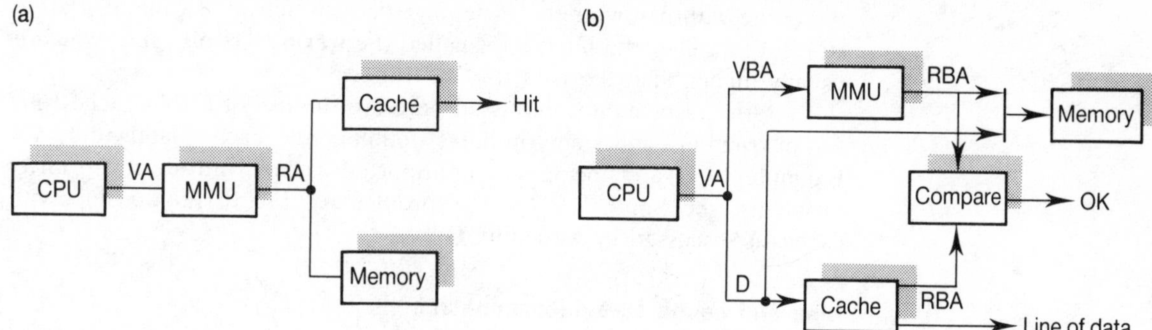

FIGURE 14.14

Address translation and cache access: (a) serial implementation; (b) parallel implementation.

system has only a single real address space, simplifying the implementation. The scheme where a cache is located in the virtual address space is presented in Appendix B.3. This requires a solution to the problem of the non-uniqueness of the virtual address space, because each process is allowed to have its own virtual address space.

14.6.2 Cache design aspects

When designing caches, many tradeoffs and decisions have to be made. One of the first decisions will be about the line and cache size. Other important aspects that have to be determined are the memory fetch policy, the placement policy, the replacement policy and the main memory update policy. The fetch policy decides when to fetch an item (on demand or beforehand). Prefetch algorithms try to have information already in the cache before it is explicitly requested by the processor. The placement policy establishes the positional relation between lines in the cache and in main memory. Policies that are discussed here are direct mapping, fully associative and set associative. The replacement policy determines which line must be replaced on a miss, when the cache is full. This can be based on random, first-in, first-out (FIFO) and least recently used (LRU) replacement (see Section 10.6). Finally, the updating of main memory is considered, when cache data has been modified. This can be done on each write (write-through) or when a modified line is replaced (copy-back), each method having its own advantages and disadvantages.

Another aspect that should be kept in mind is the effect of multiprogramming on a cache. This affects the cache hit ratio because on every context switch the activated process requires its own data, which is probably not in the cache due to its previous activation. The hit ratio of an initially empty cache (or at least empty with regards to the new process) is called the **cold-start** hit ratio. This hit ratio can be improved by allowing several contexts to reside in the cache simultaneously, using a process identification tag to identify the corresponding process.

Apart from caches with multiple contexts, it is also possible to increase the time slice of each process, offering a process the chance to fill the cache with its own data. When a process is activated while its data is still in the cache, the hit ratio is called the **warm-start** hit ratio, which is usually higher than the cold-start hit ratio.

Other aspects not discussed here are the use of a split cache (one for instructions and one for data, doubling the cache bandwidth, see Example 14.1) and the use of multiported caches (introducing priority problems, see Smith, 1982). The problem of I/O in relationship with caches is discussed in Appendix B.2.

Line and cache size determination

The most important factors determining the cache hit ratio are the line size and the cache size. Increasing the line size results in a better hit ratio due to the spatial locality (longer lines cover more of the spatial locality). There are, however, a few disadvantages of long lines. Moving long lines from memory to the cache takes more time than moving small lines, and an increased line size reduces the number of lines in a cache, assuming a fixed cache size, and thus the cache will have less temporal locality. For a given line size, an increase in the cache size will cover a larger part of the temporal locality while maintaining the same coverage of spatial locality, so larger caches have a higher hit ratio (as could logically be expected). It is obvious that for a given cache size and a specific work load, an optimal line size exists (although it may not always be easy to determine). Figure 14.15 shows the effect of the cache size and the line size on the miss ratio for a set of PDP-11 traces (Smith, 1982). Temporal locality can be accounted for by the number of lines in a cache. A program only addresses a limited number of memory areas during some time interval, represented by the working set $W(t, h)$. Having more cache lines will, therefore, not decrease the miss ratio. This is shown by the horizontal lines of Figure 14.15. The miss ratio can then only be decreased by increasing the line size. Smith (1987) found that a line size between 16 and 64 bytes offers the best tradeoff for high-performance microprocessors, as shorter line sizes have a lower spatial locality, causing a higher miss ratio and therefore a higher access time due to memory latency (although they reduce memory traffic). Larger line sizes are suitable for systems with larger caches and a higher memory bandwidth.

Memory fetch policies

Two memory fetch policies exist: demand fetch and prefetch. With demand fetch, a line is only fetched when it is needed and it is not already in the cache (a miss). Prefetching anticipates which lines may be required in the immediate future and fetches these lines.

The question 'what is prefetched' is simple to answer for caches, because of the high speed of caches (which requires a simple hardware implementation), it has to be the immediately following line. Thus, if a

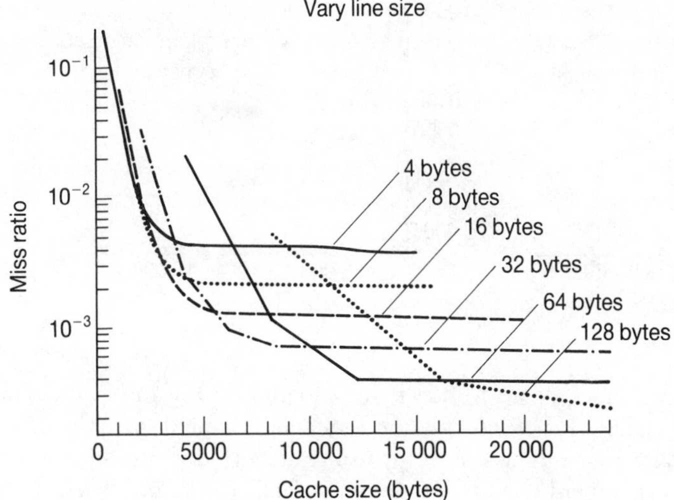

FIGURE 14.15

Miss ratios as a function of the line and cache size.

reference to line i initiates a fetch, then line $i + 1$ will be prefetched. This type of prefetching is known as **one block lookahead (OBL)**.

Several policies on when to initiate a prefetch exist: always prefetch, which offers the best increase in the hit ratio but also significantly increases memory traffic, which may be unfavourable in multiprocessor systems, for example; prefetch on miss, which improves the hit ratio, although this increase is not as large as for always prefetch, and reduces the increase in memory traffic; and the more complicated tagged prefetch policy where, apart from prefetch on misses, also initiates a prefetch on the first reference to a prefetched line – the tags are extended with flags to indicate if a line has already been referenced. Figure 14.16 shows the miss ratio for some fetch policies (Smith, 1982). The prefetch on misses (see open circles) has almost the same miss ratio as the no prefetch policy, while the tagged prefetch policy (see closed circles) approaches the miss ratio for the prefetch always policy. Smith (1978) found that prefetching always reduces the miss ratio by about 75% (for larger caches), while prefetching on misses was about one-half as effective. Tagged prefetch is always found to be equally effective as prefetching, but, where always prefetching increases the memory traffic by as much as 20% to 80%, tagged prefetch and prefetch on misses increases it by only 10% to 20%.

When prefetching is used, demand fetching remains necessary because no prefetch policy can always predict the future, but a well-chosen prefetch policy may reduce the number of demand fetches (and thus the number of misses). Prefetching too many lines would replace other cache lines that might be useful in the near future. An important factor to determine if prefetching is useful is the line size. Smith (1978)

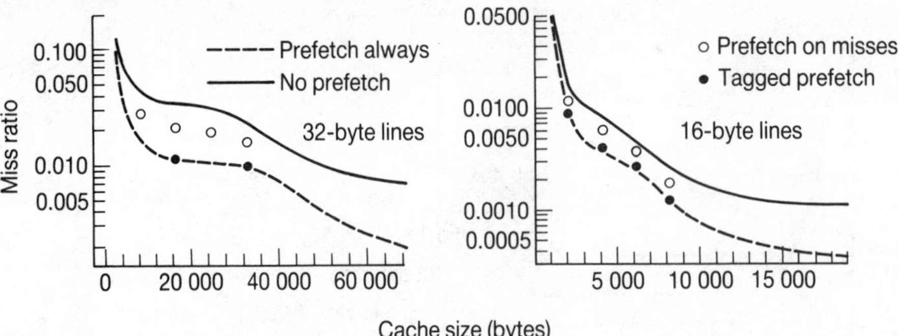

FIGURE 14.16

Miss ratios for several fetch policies.

found that lines of up to 256 bytes can reduce the miss ratio, but larger lines transfer a lot of information that is not needed, meanwhile replacing other data that might still be of use. Furthermore, prefetching also uses memory bandwidth and if a demand fetch (on a miss) has to wait for memory that is processing a prefetch request, then prefetching could have an adversary effect on the system performance.

Placement policies

One of the most important design aspects of a cache is the placement of lines of main memory in cache memory; that is, where to place a line from main memory in cache so it can be easily retrieved. This is a problem because, for reasons of economy, a cache is smaller than main memory, so several memory lines map on to the same cache line.

The most frequently used placement policies are direct, fully associative and set associative. In the following discussion, an example computer is assumed with 1 Mbyte of main memory (addressable with 20 bits) and a 16-kbyte cache. Each line contains 16 bytes, so main memory consists of 64K lines and the cache can hold 1024 lines.

Direct mapping This is the simplest placement policy (Figure 14.17(a)). In this scheme, line *i* in main memory is placed in line (*i* modulo 1024) in the cache. Figure 14.17(b) shows how the real address is broken down into three fields: the 10-bit line field is used to access an entry in the cache; the 6-bit tag field is used to check whether the addressed entry in the cache contains the requested line; and the 4-bit byte field is used to address part of a line. No associative comparison is needed and the replacement policy is trivial, both simplifying hardware implementation. However, a cache entry can only contain one line of the 64 (= 2^6) main memory lines that map on to a single cache line. Therefore, if two main memory lines that are used alternatively map on to the same cache line, the hit ratio will sharply drop, even when the cache is not full.

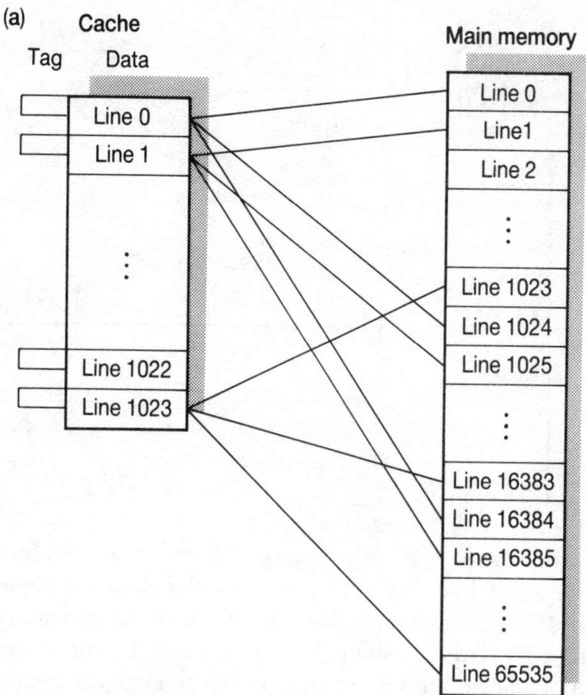

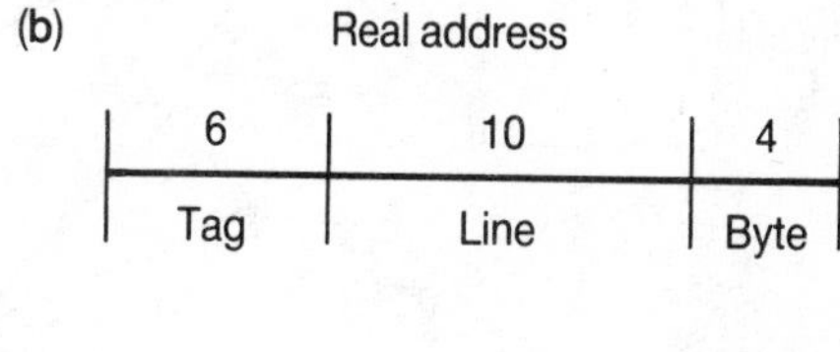

FIGURE 14.17
Direct mapping cache.

Fully associative cache This scheme represents the other extreme in that *any* memory line can reside in *any* cache location. The placement of Figure 14.18(a) requires an (expensive) associative memory, because any cache entry may contain the required data. Figure 14.18(b) shows a 16-bit tag field, which is required to identify a cache line, because memory contains 64K lines. Although this method obviously has the highest hit ratio, it may be slower than direct mapping because associative searching is not as fast as direct access; however, this may change in the future with the appearance of VLSI associative memories.

Set-associative cache This method combines the advantage of direct with fully associative placement policies. With this policy, the cache is divided into S sets, each containing L lines. If M is the number of lines in the cache, then $L = M/S$, giving the set size or set associativity. As an example, a four-way, set-associative cache ($L = 4$) has been chosen, so there are $S = M/L = 1024/4 = 256$ sets. A line can now be found by using the eight middle bits of the address (Figure 14.19) to select a set (line i of main memory is placed in set i modulo S = i modulo 256) and then associatively comparing the tags. The advantage of this method over the fully associative policy is that the associative search only extends over L elements instead of over M elements ($M = 1024$), so the cost is much lower (fewer comparators are needed).

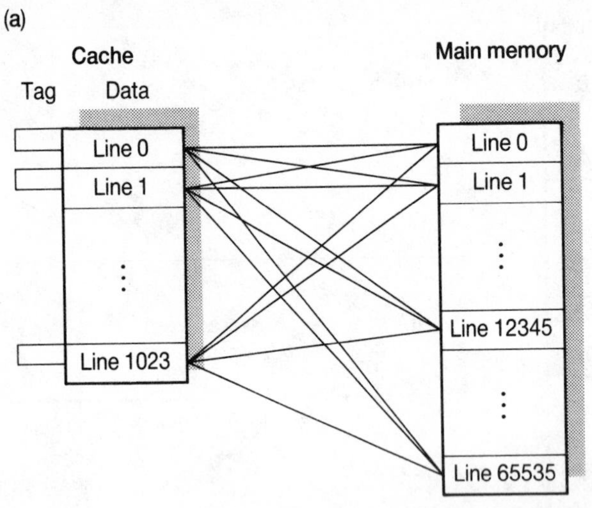

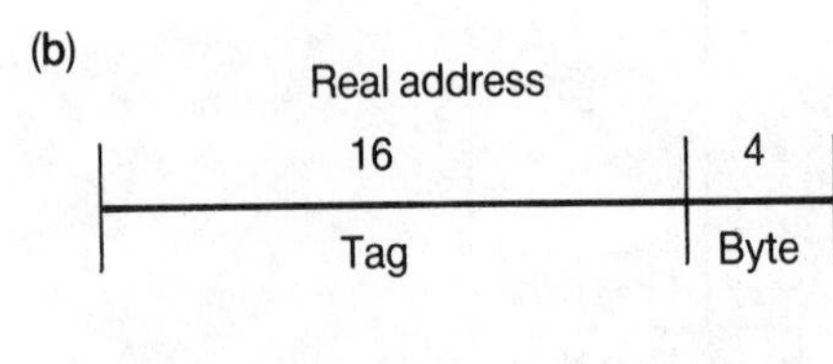

FIGURE 14.18

Fully associative cache.

If $S = 1$ (only one set), the fully associative cache is obtained, whereas setting $L = 1$ (one line per set) produces the direct mapping cache. Therefore, for a given cache size M, a tradeoff between S and L has to be made because $S * L$ is constant. It will be clear that increasing the associativity L (more lines per set) results in a better hit ratio and a higher cost. Experimental results show that an associativity of 2 to 16 provides the best performance, considering both the hit ratio and the cost (Smith, 1982). This is the reason why most commercial machines use a

FIGURE 14.19

Set-associative cache.

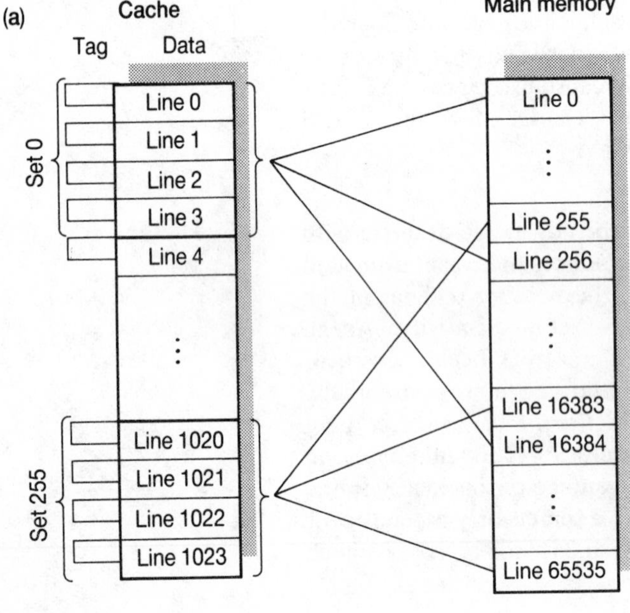

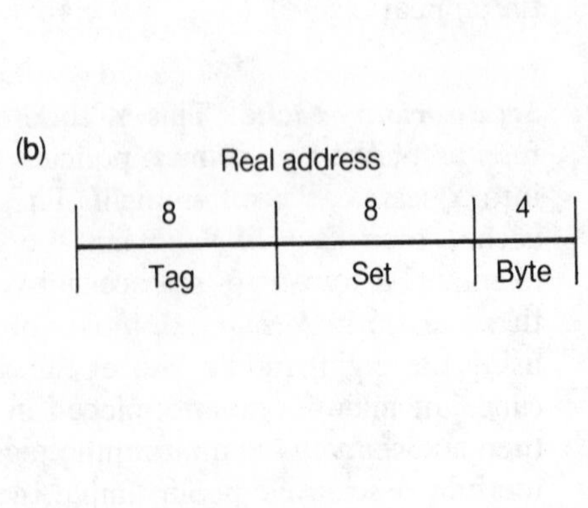

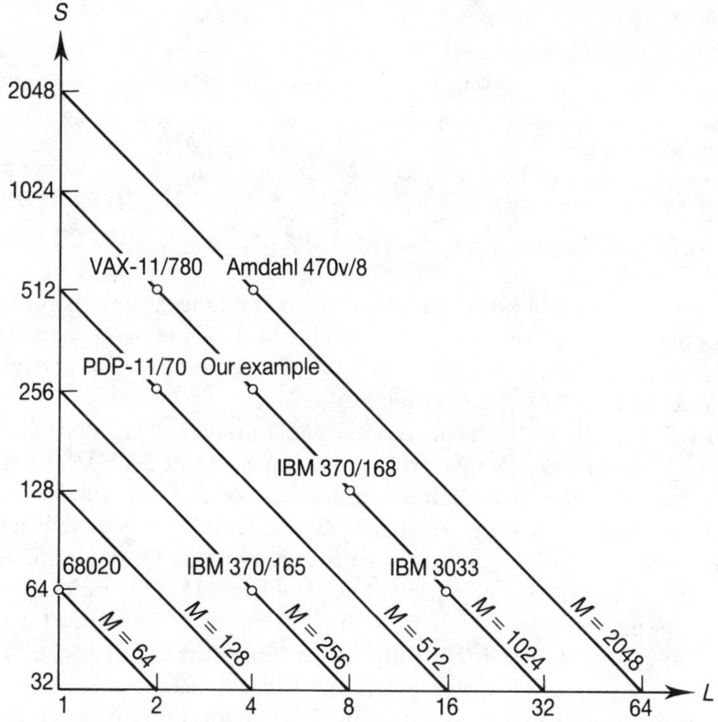

FIGURE 14.20

Some values of S and L in existing computer systems.

set-associative cache. Some values for L and S are shown in Figure 14.20 where the straight lines indicate a constant product of S and L (that is, an equally sized cache).

Replacement policies

It is often necessary to replace a line in a cache because the cache is full, or because a line from memory maps on to an occupied line in the cache. Because of this, it is necessary to decide which line is to be replaced. The replacement policies of paged main memory can apply to caches, with the additional constraint that a cache replacement policy must be implemented entirely in hardware, due to speed considerations. Therefore, not all replacement policies available for paging (see Section 10.6) can be used for caches. Variable-size partitions (where the amount of cache memory allocated to a process can vary dynamically) are not attractive because of implementation complexities, which therefore leaves only fixed-size partitions (a process is allocated a fixed area, usually all of cache memory). Two approaches are possible: usage based and non-usage based. Usage-based replacement policies take into account when a line was last referenced. An example is the LRU (least recently used) policy. Non-usage-based policies are random replacement and FIFO (first-in, first-out). These methods can be compared to the MIN (minimal) policy

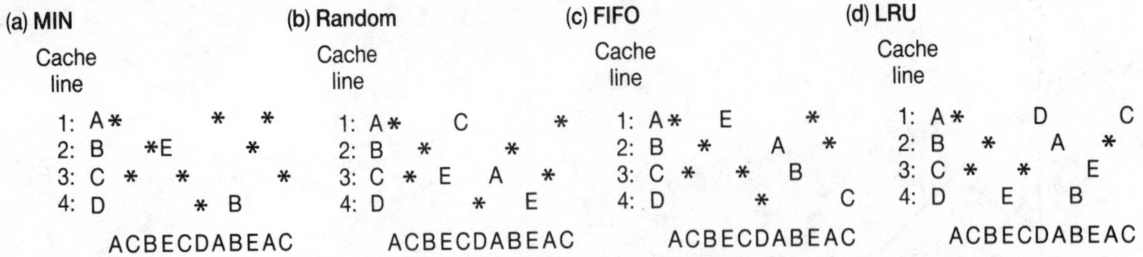

(a) MIN

```
Cache
line

1: A*           *   *
2: B    *E         *
3: C  *     *          *
4: D           * B

   ACBECDABEAC
```

(b) Random

```
Cache
line

1: A*     C         *
2: B    *       *
3: C  * E    A    *
4: D           *   E

   ACBECDABEAC
```

(c) FIFO

```
Cache
line

1: A*    E         *
2: B    *      A     *
3: C  *     *    B
4: D            *      C

   ACBECDABEAC
```

(d) LRU

```
Cache
line

1: A*        D          C
2: B    *        A    *
3: C  *    *          E
4: D        E      B

   ACBECDABEAC
```

FIGURE 14.21

Cache behaviour with different replacement policies.

where the line that will not be referenced for the longest time is replaced. This policy, of course, only has theoretical value and cannot be implemented in a cache (unless hardware is equipped with a crystal ball or a deck of cards to predict the future!)

In Figure 14.21, a cache (containing four lines) is filled with the lines A, B, C and D (in this order). For each method (MIN, random, FIFO and LRU), the cache behaviour is given for the reference sequence ACBECDABEAC. A letter in this figure indicates a miss, whereas a * indicates a hit. Of course, no conclusions can be made from Figure 14.21. Smith (1982) found that non-usage-based policies (FIFO, random) have comparable hit ratios, whereas LRU has a 10% to 15% higher hit ratio. Smith (1985) found that for a fully associative instruction cache, FIFO and LRU have equal hit ratios, while random replacement is better than FIFO and LRU, because of small loops that do not quite fit in the cache.

Although LRU has the highest hit ratio, it may also be costly to implement. In our example cache with a fully associative mapping, an LRU policy must decide which of the 1024 lines was the last to be referenced, so a 10-bit counter must be associated with each line. In set-associative caches, the set associativity is often kept low because of the marginal performance increase for larger set sizes, and because of the hardware required (an associativity $L = 2$ only requires one bit to indicate which line was last referenced).

Statistics have shown that the influence of the placement policy on the cache performance is much larger than that of the replacement policy, although the latter varies with the placement policy used. For direct mapping, the replacement policy is trivial; for a fully associative cache, it is most difficult; and for a set-associative cache, where the replacement policy determines which line within one set is replaced, the difficulty level is in between. Smith (1985) found that, for small instruction caches and programs with many simple loops, a direct-mapped cache can outperform a fully associative cache with LRU replacement, but this does not hold for larger caches and the occurrence of large complex loops (composed out of non-contiguous code sequences). Furthermore, a fully associative cache with random replacement is better than a direct-mapped cache, while for some cache sizes (not too large), a random replacement, set-associative cache gives the best performance.

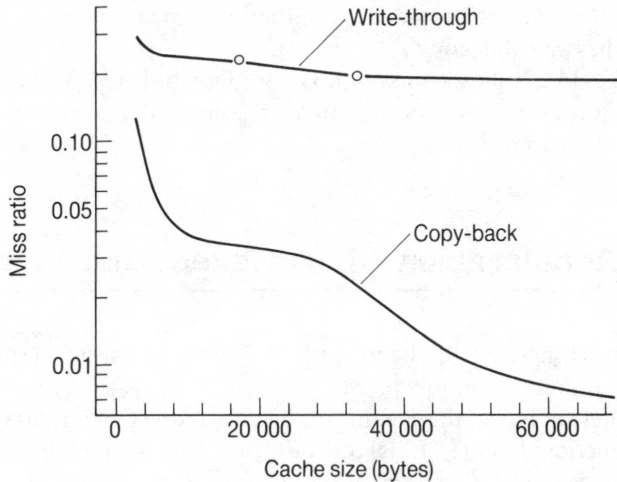

FIGURE 14.22

Miss ratios for write-through and copy-back policies.

Main memory update policies

If a line in the cache is replaced, information may be lost if the line is modified and the cache hardware does not take care to ensure data coherence between the cache and main memory. There are two policies to solve this problem. In the first, write operations always transmit changes to both the cache and main memory. This policy is called **write-through**. It has the advantage that main memory *always* has a valid copy of each line in the cache, which simplifies data coherence in multiprocessor systems with multiple caches. However, memory traffic is also high because each write-hit still generates a memory access. On a write-miss, the missing line may or may not be allocated to the cache, depending on the update policy.

The other policy, called **copy-back**, only transmits a cache line to memory if it has to be replaced in the cache, thus reducing memory traffic. In this case, a line can always be updated in memory, regardless of whether or not it was modified (called *always* copy-back), or only when it has been modified, which is indicated by an associated 'dirty' flag. This last policy, called *flagged* copy-back, clearly reduces the number of transfers to main memory. Although the write-through policy does not specify whether or not to allocate a cache location on a write-miss, with the copy-back policies one usually allocates a line in the cache to the written line.

A disadvantage of the copy-back policies is that main memory sometimes has a stale copy of data, so that when a processor or a cache fails, it is not always possible to restore the contents of main memory. Also, if another cache or an I/O device requests some data, care must be taken that the data is provided by either the cache or main memory, whichever has a valid copy.

Figure 14.22 shows miss ratios for both policies. For the write-through policy, no line is allocated on a write-miss; that is, writes are then only done to memory.

14.7 Acceleration of the execution unit

Mechanisms to increase the bandwidth of the execution unit (E unit) are based on parallelism or pipelining.

Parallelism inside the E unit can be realized via wider data paths or multiple functional units. It is obvious that the data path width is a determining factor for the performance of a processor. If a 32-bit multiplication has to be performed, multiplying 32 bits in parallel is faster than the repeated multiplication of 8 bits. A natural limitation will be reached when the data path can contain most application-defined scalars (such as integers and addresses), which is currently achieved by most 32-bit architectures (MC68020, VAX-11, NS32000, iAPX80386). It is therefore questionable whether 64-bit microprocessors will provide a substantial performance improvement over their 32-bit counterparts.

Another approach to accelerate the E unit via parallelism is to have several execution units. As the first computers only had one arithmetic and logic unit (ALU), this E unit was only capable of performing one function at a time. It is possible, however, to distribute functions to specialized functional units, such as co-processors, so these units can operate in parallel. However, most microprocessors that use co-processors only allow co-processor operations to be performed synchronously with (in line with) regular operations. This is for ease of implementation – no synchronization is needed and exceptions can be easily attributed to the only operation being performed.

14.8 Acceleration of the instruction unit

In this section, the emphasis is put on instruction pipelining; that is, pipelining of the I unit; the effect of pipelining the execution unit has already been covered in Section 14.3 where it was shown to be only of interest to complex operations. Parallelism in the I unit would imply the handling of several instructions simultaneously, which is only applicable to very long instruction word (VLIW) machines (Colwell, 1988).

Paying closer attention to instruction execution, the following stages may be found (see Figure 14.6(a)):

- Instruction fetch (IF): The instruction is fetched from memory and stored in some register.
- Instruction decode (ID): The previously fetched instruction is decoded.
- Operand fetch (OF): The operand address is computed and the data is fetched.
- Execution (E): The operands and the operation to be performed are passed to an E unit, where the result is calculated.
- Store result (S): The result from the operation is stored.

Relating the above stages to Figure 14.4, it is not always obvious which unit performs which function. Of course, instruction fetching and decoding normally takes place in the I unit and the execute stage will normally be performed by the E unit. The operand address can be computed in the I unit, requiring extra adders for indexing, and so on; or it can be done in the E unit, which already possesses one or more adders.

Note that pipelining is not the same as parallelism: with pipelining, the hardware to accomplish a single operation is split in stages; with parallelism, the hardware is replicated, so several operations can be executed simultaneously. The throughput increase with pipelining is limited to the maximum number of stages, while, in principle, the increase with parallelism is unbounded. This is illustrated in Figure 14.23 in which a five-stage ADD instruction is executed serially, via pipelining and via parallelism (Hockney, 1981). In the serial add, the first addition must be completed before the second addition can start, so one result is produced every five cycles, assuming one cycle per pipeline stage. In the pipelined case, the second addition can start when the first addition has completed its first stage. If the pipeline is full (after five cycles), there are five additions at various stages of completion within the pipeline. Ideally, one result is produced per cycle. With N-way parallelism, N additions can be started simultaneously, but results are only produced every five cycles. As N results are produced in the same time as one result for the serial case, the increase is N-fold (ideally) over a serial add.

In theory, the maximum speed-up with pipelining could be achieved if the CPU is composed of five different specialized hardware units, one for each pipeline stage. (Note that the number of pipeline stages in a computer is implementation dependent, and may therefore vary for different computers and different implementations of the same architecture.) However, in practice, when these five units are operating concurrently, severe problems can arise. If instruction i is in its execute phase (E), instructions $i + 1$, $i + 2$, . . ., have already been started in

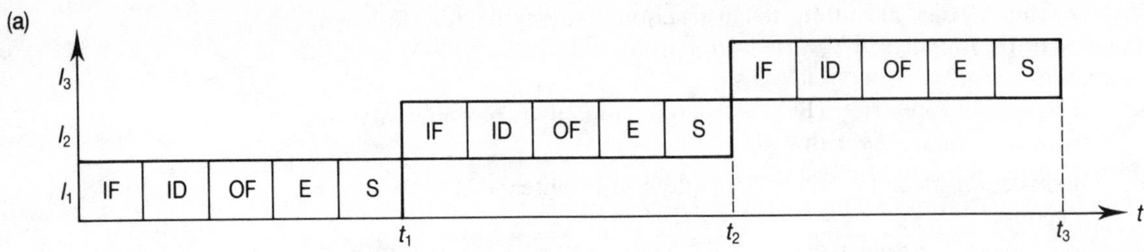

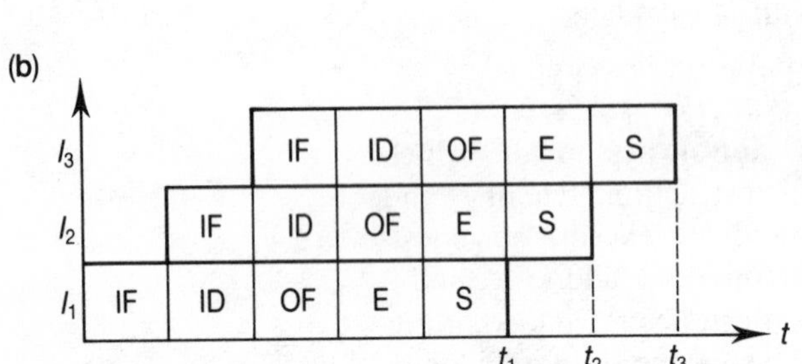

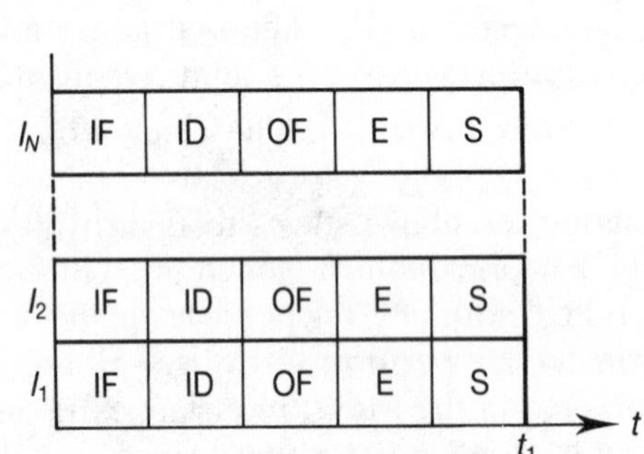

FIGURE 14.23

Comparison of serialism, pipelining and parallelism.

other pipeline stages (IF, ID, . . .). The problem is that often one of the instructions $i + 1$, $i + 2$, . . ., depends on the result of instruction i, which has not yet been produced. Pipelining the I unit therefore does have some problems, because of dependencies in the pipeline stages of different instructions. Several such dependencies exist:

- data dependencies;
- run-ons;
- branch dependencies.

14.8.1 Data dependencies

Data dependencies occur when two instructions share a resource. In such a situation, instruction i (I_i) updates the value of that shared resource, but that value is accessed by I_j before I_i has delivered the result. This problem is analogous to that of process synchronization (see Section 9.4).

Three classes of data dependencies can be identified (Ramamoorthy, 1977), as illustrated by the following example program:

```
        ⋮
MOVE.W  #17, D0
MULS.W  (A1), D0
CLR.W   (A1)
MOVE.W  #1, (A1)+
```

Data dependency can exist between I_i and I_{i+k} if at least k pipeline stages are present. However, for the sake of clarity, I_i and I_{i+1} will be used in the description of the three classes.

The read-after-write (RAW) dependency can occur when I_{i+1} wants to read a data object that is modified by I_i. If the write operation has not been completed before the read takes place, instruction I_{i+1} uses a value that is 'too old'. This situation may occur between instructions 1 and 2 of our example program, if the MULS instruction reads the contents of D0 before 17 has been moved to it.

A write-after-read (WAR) data dependency occurs when the write operation of I_{i+1} is completed before I_i can perform its read operation. Looking at the program, a WAR data dependency may exist between instructions 2 and 3. If the CLR instruction clears the location specified by A1 before the MULS instruction reads this location, it will multiply the contents of D0 by zero, instead of the desired value. That is, the MULS instruction has used a 'too new' value.

The third data dependency, write-after-write (WAW), occurs when the order of two write operations is not properly retained: the write of I_i is done after I_{i+1} is completed. Now the destination is left with the value of I_i, instead of the final value, produced by I_{i+1}. A WAW data dependency may occur between instructions 3 and 4, when the second MOVE is performed before the CLR operation. The result will be that the location specified by A1 contains 0, instead of 1.

There are several approaches for solving the data dependency problem, which are, in fact, similar to those used to solve the problem of process protection (see Section 9.3): data dependencies may be prevented or detected and resolved.

Prevention

The dependence of I_j on a shared resource in pipeline stage x (P_{jx}), produced in P_{iy}, can be prevented by delaying the execution of I_j with $y - x + 1$ pipeline stages. This can be accomplished by inserting $y - x + 1$ instructions between I_i and I_j. This means that the compiler has to rearrange the program and find $y - x + 1$ instructions which can be executed following I_i and before I_j. If $y - x + 1$ instructions cannot be found, then NOP (no-operation) instructions should be inserted. The advantage of this approach is that no hardware is required, but this is at the expense of a more complex compiler and a time loss due to the execution of NOP instructions (when no useful instructions can be found).

Detection and resolution

This method requires extra hardware to detect the data dependencies during execution time and to resolve these dependencies. This can be done in several ways:

- Stall the pipeline: As soon as a potential data dependency is detected for I_j, instructions I_j, I_{j+1}, . . ., are prevented from entering the pipeline, until all instructions in the pipeline have been completed. Alternatively, when I_j depends on a shared resource in pipeline stage x (P_{jx}), while this shared resource will be produced in P_{iy}, the pipeline can be stalled for $y - x + 1$ cycles, which may be more optimal. This approach is comparable to the disabling of interrupts (see Section 9.4.1) and requires the detection of the data dependency before the instructions enter the pipeline.
- Flush the pipeline: If I_j depends on a shared resource in pipeline stage x (P_{jx}), the pipeline stages 1 through x are flushed; that is, the contents of these stages is discarded and the instructions I_j, . . ., I_{j+x-1} have to be executed again. The hardware required in this case is less complicated, because a data dependency is only signalled at the moment it occurs. This approach is comparable to the busy waiting for a critical section (see Section 9.4.2): all processes are allowed to proceed until the critical section; when the critical section is blocked, they have to try again later.
- Data forwarding: In the case of a read-after-write data dependency, I_j may need an operand during its OF stage, which is produced in the same cycle by the E stage of I_i (see Figure 14.23(b)). By forwarding the result of the E stage of I_i directly to the input of the E unit, the effect of the OF stage of I_j is obtained. In terms of our example program, data forwarding occurs when the value 17 of the MOVE.W instruction is forwarded to the MULS.W operation, in parallel with storing the value in D0. A well-known implementation of register forwarding is the register-tagging scheme of the IBM 360/91 (Tomasulo, 1967). This processor has a common data bus (CDB), controlled by the use of tags, which allows data, produced as the result of any operation, to be forwarded directly to the next E unit without first going through a floating-point register, thereby reducing the overhead caused by read-after-write data dependencies.

14.8.2 Run-ons

In the pipeline of Figure 14.23, it is assumed that the execute stage (P_E), during which the acutal operation of the instruction (such as ADD or XOR) is performed, takes the same amount of time for each instruction. More complex operations, such as multiply and divide, may require a longer time to complete, thus causing pipeline dependencies. There are two solutions to this problem:

(1) Synchronous: The time allocated to all pipeline stages is made equal to the time required for the execution of the more complex operation (P_E). This can be done *statically* (all pipeline stages always assume the cycle time of the more complex operation) or *dynamically* (all pipeline stages take on the longer cycle time of the complex operation for only the P_E of the complex operation). The advantage of the synchronous solution is that no new data dependencies are created, but this is at the expense of a more complicated timing scheme.

(2) Asynchronous: This solution assumes the availability of more than one E unit. Many processors have special hardware for multiply, divide and floating-point operations. Complex operations are performed by such a special E unit, while the regular pipeline may proceed. This allows for a higher performance than the synchronous solution because the pipeline is not delayed; in addition, the special hardware can perform the complex operation much faster. However, the data dependency problem becomes more severe, as it also has to take into account the special hardware units.

14.8.3 Branch dependencies

Branches constitute from 15% to 30% of the instructions executed. In pipelined machines, these instructions consume a large fraction of the total execution time of a program, as branches cause a discontinuity in the pipeline, disrupting the throughput of one instruction per cycle. The pipeline disruption will be explained using the five-stage machine model of Figure 14.23(b).

When a branch instruction is executed in the execute (which is the fourth) stage of the pipeline, the three instructions already partly completed must be stalled or flushed. This means that the branch in question causes a waste in time of three cycles; this is called the **branch problem**. The three wasted pipeline stages are called **delay slots**, because this is the delay incurred before the pipeline is filled again. The implication of the branch penalty for the machine throughput is shown in Example 14.3 (for a survey, see Lilja (1988)).

Again, several approaches are available for solving the branch problem; they can be based on preventing the occurrence of a penalty or reducing this penalty when it occurs, by detecting the occurrence of a taken branch.

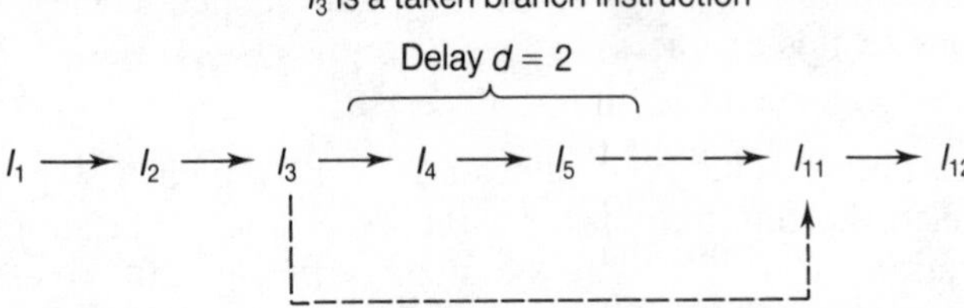

FIGURE 14.24

Execution of delayed branch with $d = 2$.

□□EXAMPLE 14.3

Assume that 25% of all instructions executed are branch instructions. Further assume that two-thirds of these branches are taken (Clark, 1984; McFarling, 1986). Due to the taken branches, the throughput of one instruction per cycle will now change to one instruction per $0.75 * 1 + 0.25 * (1/3 * 1 + 2/3 *(3 + 1)) = 1.5$ cycles. This is a performance degradation of 33%. Note that a taken branch takes one cycle, while a not-taken branch takes one cycle but in addition causes a waste of three cycles.

Prevention

Prevention is based on filling the delay slots with useful instructions. Given that a taken branch causes d delay slots (for the machine of Figure 14.23(b), $d = 3$), the execution of branch instructions should be modified such that an additional d instructions, after the branch has been taken, are executed; this is called a **delayed branch**. For example, consider Figure 14.24, where branch instruction 3 (I_3) is taken. Normal execution would produce the sequence $I_1, I_2, I_3, I_{11}, I_{12}, \ldots$. If a delayed branch is used (with a delay $d = 2$), the resulting sequence is $I_1, I_2, I_3, I_4, I_5, I_{11}, I_{12}, \ldots$, where the instructions filling the delay slots are either useful instructions or NOPs. It is the task of the compiler to find useful instructions to fill the d slots.

For unconditional branches, it is easy to fill the d delay slots, but for conditional branches, this is more of a problem. Patterson and Piepho (1982) claim that an optimizing compiler can fill 78% to 96% of the slots with useful instructions. Hennessy (1982) states that almost 20% of all executed MIPS instructions are executed during a branch delay slot.

As this method is not transparent for the architecture, it cannot be used to speed up existing architectures. Only new architectures (having a compiler that knows about the delayed branch scheme) can implement this technique. As there was no need for compatibility with existing architectures, nearly all RISC architectures use this method. The Hewlett-Packard precision architecture (Mahon, 1986) includes a nullification feature which allows the instruction lexically following the branch instruction to be forced into an NOP instruction, depending on whether the branch is taken. This can be useful for loop control branches where the instruction following the loop control branch has to be executed when the branch is taken, and nullified otherwise.

Another method used to prevent a branch penalty is to prefetch both potential target instructions and throw away the incorrect one. If the pipeline can contain more than one unresolved branch ($d > 1$), then 2^d target instructions may have to be prefetched (to cover the case that the pipeline is filled with d branch instructions). This approach is called **branch by-pass** or **multiple prefetch**.

Reduction

When a branch occurs, the penalty (in terms of the number of delay slots wasted) can be reduced. One method uses prediction, such that the pipeline is filled with d instructions which are most likely to be useful. The other methods reduce the branch penalty by either eliminating the instruction fetch (IF) stage of the target instruction or the execute stage (E) of the branch instruction.

Branch prediction If it can be predicted whether a branch will be taken or not, the correct sequence of instructions can be fetched such that the branch penalty will be zero. Branch prediction can be done statically or dynamically.

The easiest way to implement static branch prediction is to assume that a branch is never taken because no provisions have to be made in the machine as the normal instruction sequence is maintained. McFarling (1986) found that 37% of all branches are not taken, resulting in a cost of a branch instruction of $0.37 * 1 + (1 - 0.37) * (1 - d) = 1 + 0.63 * d$ cycles. The other alternative is to assume that the branch will always be taken; according to McFarling (1986), this will be correct for 63% of the branches. When the implementation of the computer is such that a branch instruction and the address it branches to can be determined in the IF stage, the branch target instruction can be fetched without delay. The cost of a branch instruction will then be $0.63 * 1 + (1 - 0.63) * (1 + d) = 1 + 0.37 * d$ cycles. The process of predicting whether a branch will be taken can be made more refined by taking the opcode and the branch condition into account; for example, a loop branch, such as the MC68020 DBcc instruction, will have a higher 'always taken' probability than a BVS (Branch on Overflow Set) instruction, while the BRA (Branch Always) instruction has a 100% 'always taken' probability. Lee (1984) found that, for the PDP-11, the prediction 'always taken' has a probability of 73.8% of being correct, while taking the opcode and branch condition into account this probability rises to 80%. Another method of static branch prediction requires conditional branch instructions to be extended with a likely taken bit, which has to be set by the

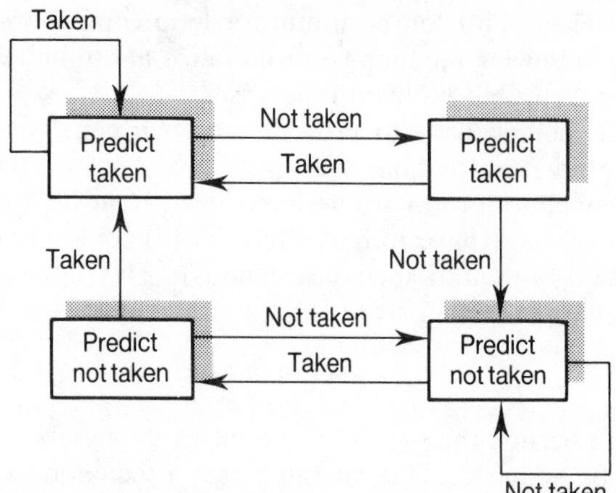

FIGURE 14.25

Branch prediction state diagram.

compiler. Ditzel (1987) reports prediction accuracies using this method of 74% to 94% (depending on the benchmark program being used).

To further reduce the branch cost, the process of predicting whether a branch is taken can be done dynamically, by taking the branch history into account. Lee (1984) found that, for the PDP-11, using a branch history consisting of only the result of the previous execution of that branch, an accuracy of 96.5% was obtainable, while with the result of the two previous executions, the accuracy was improved to 97.5%. A longer branch history did not improve the accuracy significantly. McFarling (1986) found a prediction accuracy of 83% for RISC-type architectures, using a branch history of two. A simple implementation of the prediction method, using a direct-mapped cache with 128 entries, where the eight low-order bits of the address of the branch instruction are used as an index into this cache, gives adequate performance. A larger number of entries did not improve the performance significantly (McFarling, 1986).

Using the state diagram of Figure 14.25, a branch history of two can be maintained, using only two bits per branch instruction. The states in the diagram specify the prediction to be made, and they are updated whenever a branch instruction is executed. The state diagram shows that if the last two branches occur in a different direction, that direction will be predicted; otherwise the original direction will be predicted.

Saving the delay of the instruction fetch stage A simple method that saves the IF delay uses a buffer to store (sequentially) prefetched instructions and keeps these instructions in the buffer after they have been used. As small loops often fit entirely in this loop, instructions in this loop no longer have to be fetched from memory; hence the name **loop buffer**. A different method only stores targets of the branch instructions, in a **branch target buffer**.

Loop buffers normally contain a contiguous block of instructions. If a branch instruction has its target inside the loop buffer (usually implying a backward branch), the target instruction can be provided without accessing main memory, and a complete loop may be executed without instruction fetches. Examples of machines with a loop buffer are the IBM 360/195, which can store eight double words (8 bytes each), the ICL DAP, which can save up to 60 (32-bit) instructions, and the MC68010, with a three-word loop buffer. It is also possible to have multiple loop buffers, rather than a single one. In this case, each buffer can contain a block of sequential instructions, but the contents of the buffers do not have to be contiguous. The effectively executed sequences of a loop can be contained in the multiple buffers, while the complete loop (including the parts skipped by the branches) would be too large to fit in a single loop buffer. This concept was used in the Cray-1, which has four loop buffers, each capable of holding 128 bytes.

A branch target buffer (BTB) acts as a cache for branch targets: given the address of a taken branch instruction, it returns the actual target instruction, thus saving the IF stage of that instruction. The BTB may be organized in the same way as caches; using direct mapping or (set)-associative placement policies, and LRU or FIFO replacement policies. It can be considered a selective instruction cache (only for branch target instructions). Example 14.4 shows the effectiveness of a BTB.

□□EXAMPLE 14.4

The Advanced Micro Devices AMD29000 microprocessor uses a BTB with 32 branch targets, implemented as a two-way, set-associative cache, using a random replacement strategy (Johnson, 1987). McFarling (1986) found hit ratios of 47% for a direct-mapped cache with 16 entries (branch targets), 83% for 64 entries and 93% for 256 entries. Using a different work load mix and a two-way, set-associative BTB, Lee (1984) found hit ratios of 27% for a BTB with 16 entries, 47% for 64 entries and 72% for 256 entries.

Saving the delay of the execution stage The execution of a branch instruction ends with the execution stage (a store stage is not needed), see Figure 14.23(b)). When the conditional operation is a compare-and-branch instruction, being a single instruction that performs the testing, selection and condition use functions of Section 7.3 (alternative D of Table 7.2), the execution stage of the compare-and-branch instruction may be avoided in certain cases, thereby reducing the number of delay slots by one. Hennessy (1982) found that 98.9% of the branch instructions were preceded by a compare or a test instruction, but only in

1.1% of these cases was the setting of the condition code for free (that is, done by some other instruction as a side effect). Combining the compare/test function with the conditional branch function into a compare-and-branch instruction enables the elimination of the Z and N condition code bits, at the expense of an instruction overhead of 1.1%. McFarling (1986) found the following statistics for the compare/test part of the combined instruction: compare for equal/not equal – 36%; compare against 0 – 56%; and full compare – 8%. Only the full compare involves a subtraction of two operands with a (time-consuming) carry propagation, which requires the time allocated to the execute stage of the pipeline. In 36 + 56 = 92% of the cases, the comparison does not involve a carry propagation, so that this may be done much faster. By properly designing the pipeline, these comparisons may be performed during the operand fetch (OF) stage, thereby saving the delay of the execution stage. This method is called **fast comparison**.

Combination of prevention and reduction

Many of the techniques to prevent and reduce the branch delay may be combined. Many combinations are easy to visualize and are therefore not covered any further at this point.

14.9 Acceleration mechanisms in the MC68000 family

Looking at some members of the MC68000 family, several of the previously discussed acceleration mechanisms can be identified. The MC68000 uses a simple prefetching mechanism, which is extended to a loop buffer in the MC68010. The MC68020 uses a three-stage instruction pipeline and possesses a 256-byte on-chip cache, whereas the MC68030 has two caches, one for instructions and one for data.

14.9.1 MC68000 instruction prefetching

In the MC68000, a simple prefetching mechanism of two words is used (Motorola, 1982b). When instruction execution starts, both the basic instruction part and the next word have already been fetched. A new word is fetched when the first word has been used. When the first word causes a branch, the second word was fetched in vain and must be discarded, while interrupts and exceptions cause both words to be discarded.

14.9.2 MC68010 loop buffer

The MC68010 contains a loop buffer that can contain three words to execute a simple loop without instruction fetches, offering the full memory bandwidth to data accesses and other possible bus masters, such as DMA controllers. For the loop mode to be entered, two conditions must be satisfied. First, a DBcc instruction (see Example 7.9) must be executed with both branch conditions true (that is, the 'cc' is false and the contents of the register, containing the loop count, is not equal to −1) and the displacement must be −4 (that is, one instruction before the DBcc instruction). Second, the processor checks whether the instruction fetched from the branch address is one of the allowed loop instructions, because only the simple arithmetic and logical instructions are allowed here, such as MOVE, ADD, CMP, AND, NOT, TST, ASL, SBCD, and so on, and not instructions such as TRAP, JSR or RTE. For a complete list, see Motorola (1982a).

14.9.3 MC68020 instruction pipeline

In the MC68020 the instruction fetch and decode phases are pipelined in three stages, called stage B, C and D (Motorola, 1985). Stage B fetches instructions from cache or main memory and sequences them via stage C to D, which offers a completely decoded and validated instruction to the execution unit. If immediate data or extension words are present, these can be found in previous stages (B and C) and they can then be immediately offered to the control and execution units.

14.9.4 MC68020 instruction cache

The MC68020 contains a 256-byte direct-mapped cache that is used to store instructions only (prohibiting the use of self-modifying code). A virtual address is composed of 32 address bits and three bits (FC2–FC0) that specify the address space.

The cache contains 64 lines, each containing two words, a 25-bit tag and one valid bit (see Figure 14.26). It uses a direct-mapped organization and a cache entry is selected via bits 7–2 of the virtual address, while bit 1 selects the desired word within a line. The corresponding tags consist of bit FC2 (because it distinguishes between user and supervisor space) and the 24 most significant address bits. Because addresses have a byte resolution (whereas the addressable entity inside a cache entry is a word), the least significant bit (bit 0) is not used.

Because of the direct-mapped organization, the replacement policy is trivial, while on a miss, both words of a line are fetched simultaneously. For explicit cache control, the MC68020 offers possibilities to enable or disable the functioning of the cache, to clear or freeze (that is, not replace) selected lines in the cache, and to invalidate all cache lines.

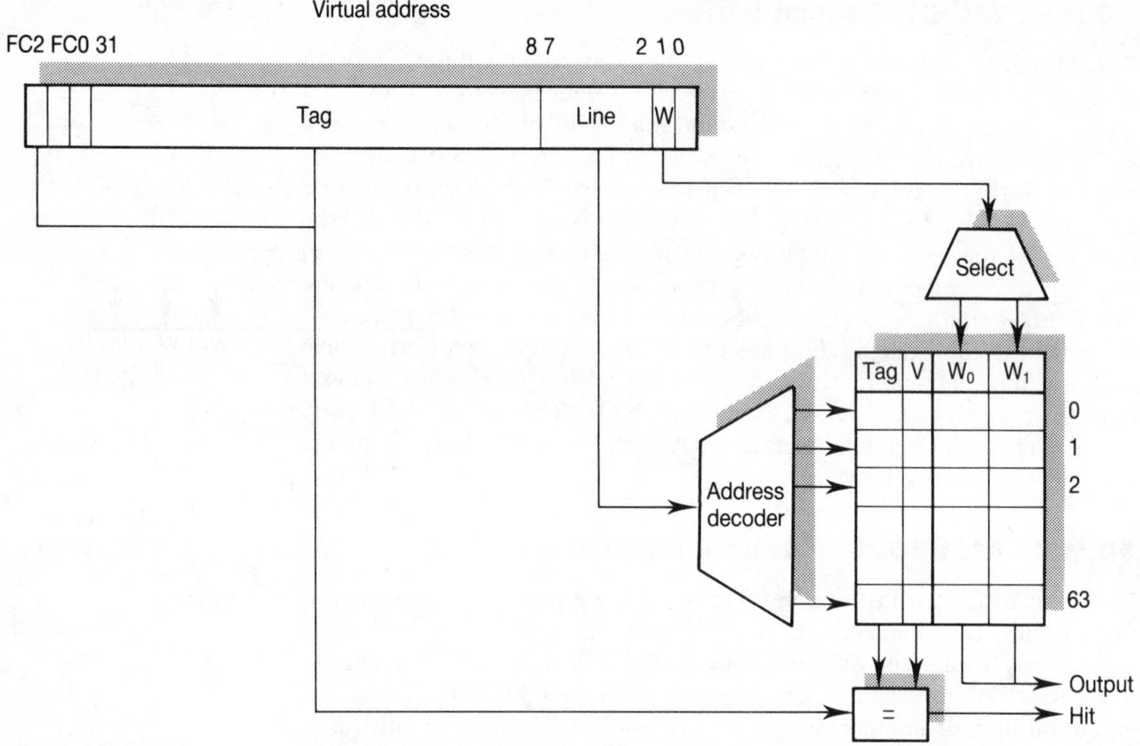

FIGURE 14.26
MC68020 cache organization.

14.9.5 MC68030 instruction and data caches

The MC68030 contains two separate caches (see Example 14.1), one for instructions (that is, no modification allowed) and one data cache that will be considered in more detail (Scales, 1986). Again, each cache is capable of storing 256 bytes, but the organization is slightly different from that of the MC68020 (see Figure 14.27). A cache is divided into 16 direct-mapped lines, but each line now contains four long words (that is, 16 bytes/line), four valid bits and a 27-bit tag. A line is selected by bits 7–4, and the long word within each line by bits 3–2 (the cache address resolution is 'long word', so bits 1 and 0 are not used in this context). The tag is composed of the function code bits FC2–FC0 and the 24 high-order address bits.

On a miss, the cache fetches an entire line (16 bytes) from main memory using the so-called 'burst mode', when the line was empty. Otherwise a single long word (while setting its associated valid bit) will be fetched.

The replacement policy is again trivial and for updating main memory, the write-through policy is used. On a write-hit, the replacement status of that entry is updated and the change is immediately

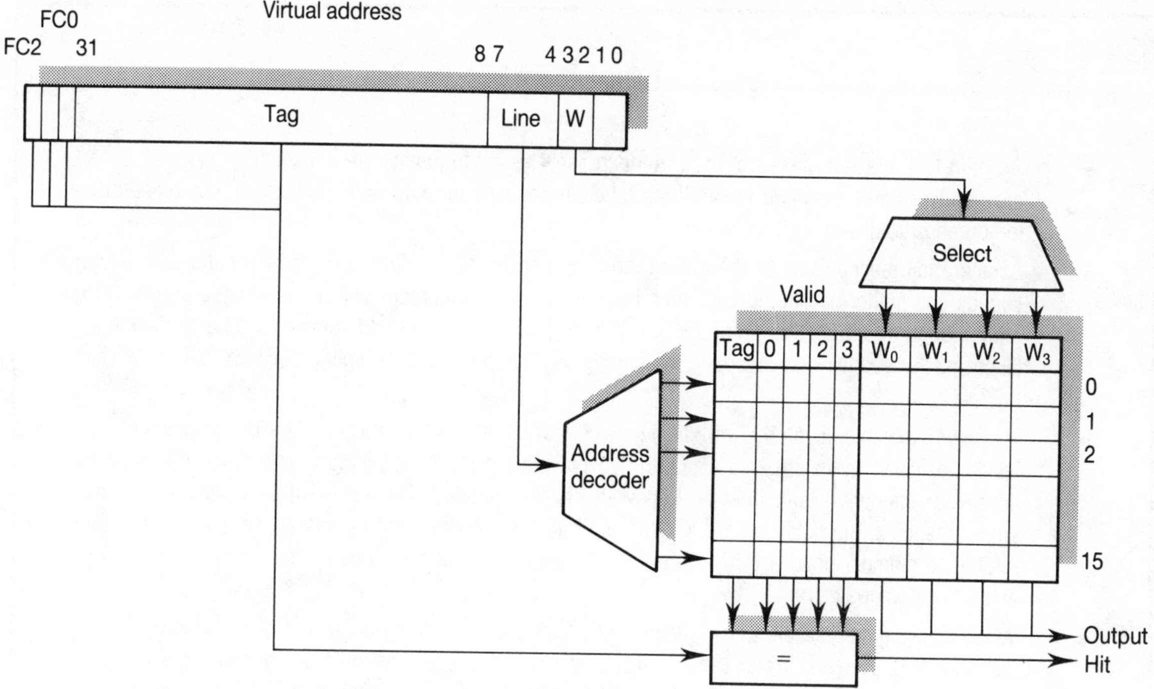

FIGURE 14.27

MC68030 data cache organization.

transferred to memory, using the write-through memory update policy. On a write-miss, no cache entry is allocated; the data is written to main memory only. This of course does not hold for the instruction cache, as no modifications take place there, resulting in the absence of write-misses.

SUMMARY

- Acceleration mechanisms are used to increase the performance of a computer system. These mechanisms can be applied at the three levels introduced in Chapter 1: realization, implementation (or organization) and architecture.
- Acceleration mechanisms at the realization level consist of the development of circuits with higher speeds and higher packaging densities. However, this development will not produce a performance high enough to satisfy the needs for future computers. Also, new technologies are being developed (such as GaAs chips and cryogenic technologies), but these technologies still have a long way to go.
- The most feasible level for introducing acceleration mechanisms is usually the implementation level. Basically, there are two aspects of a component (such as memory or a CPU) that must be improved: bandwidth and latency. Bandwidth is the amount of work, performed per unit of time, while latency is the delay before a result is produced. Methods to improve these quantities (either related to memory or to a CPU) are pipelining, replication of functional units, memory interleaving or cache memories.
- When looking at acceleration mechanisms at the architectural level, two trends can be distinguished. The first trend uses architectures that are specially tailored for their specific jobs, thus offering an optimal cost/performance ratio. The other visible trend is the reduction of hardware complexity in favour of a higher performance. These so-called RISC processors are discussed in Chapter 15.
- The use of multiple-thread (multiprocessor) systems usually results in a higher performance, as compared with that of single-thread systems.
- Organizational acceleration mechanisms, discussed in this chapter, are related to storage latency, storage bandwidth and execution bandwidth. The corresponding mechanisms are caches, memory interleaving and instruction pipelining.
- Cache memories are fast memories placed between main memory and the CPU. Because the access times for caches are lower than for main memory, it is important that the most useful information is contained in the cache. The ratio of successful cache references to all memory references (for a period of time) is called the hit ratio.
- Caches can be filled using demand fetching or prefetching. The mapping of lines of main memory on to cache lines can be done using direct mapping, associativity or set associativity. Main

memory can be updated on each write to the cache (write-through) or only when a (modified) line is replaced (copy-back).

- To increase the memory bandwidth, it is possible to use two memories, one for instructions and one for data, thus doubling the bandwidth. This is called a Harvard architecture. Another method is to partition memory into separate modules, and access these modules simultaneously. This is called interleaving and, depending on the division of the memory address space over the modules, is classified as low-order interleaving (successive addresses in successive modules) or high-order interleaving (memory is split into contiguous blocks).
- Instruction pipelining is used to increase the number of instructions processed per cycle. The execution of an instruction is split into separate phases, where each phase has its own dedicated hardware and can execute in parallel with other phases. Problems encountered with pipelining are data dependencies, run-ons and branch dependencies.
- Data dependencies may be classified as read-after-write, write-after-read and write-after-write. Solutions to the problem of data dependency can be based on prevention or detection, where the pipeline is stalled or flushed, or data is forwarded.
- Run-ons are caused by complex operations that require a longer execution time.
- A branch causes instructions that are partly executed at the moment of the branch to be lost. The pipeline stages these partly executed instructions occupy are called the delay slots. Several methods are available for eliminating or reducing the number of delay slots: prevention or reduction.
- A delayed branch is a solution to the branch problem, where delay slots are prevented from occurring. A compiler has to find useful instructions or NOPs to keep the pipeline filled.
- Branch prediction can be used to reduce the time loss due to branches, by predicting which direction the branch will take and prefetching the instructions located at the branch target.
- The delay slots can be reduced with the instruction fetch slot, when the instruction specified by the branch target is already fetched and stored in a buffer. This concept can be applied to the branch targets only (branch target buffer), or to all instructions in a loop (loop buffer).
- The branch operation can be accelerated in certain cases by deleting the execution stage of the branch instructions. This can be done when a compare-and-branch instruction is being used (fast comparison).

EXERCISES

14.1 What is a single-thread system?

14.2 (a) At which levels in a computer system can acceleration mechanisms be found?

(b) What acceleration mechanisms exist at the implementation level?

14.3 A processor has a memory cycle time of 200 ns and can execute 3 MIPS. Which figure relates to latency and which figure to bandwidth (which is the same as throughput)?

14.4 Which method is commonly used to increase the execution bandwidth?

14.5 Why is pipelining usually more often applied to the instruction unit rather than to the execution unit?

14.6 What is the purpose of a Harvard architecture?

14.7 (a) What is the purpose of interleaving?

(b) Which form of interleaving (low or high order) provides spatial locality?

(c) Which form of interleaving is often used with caches?

14.8 (a) What is the hit ratio?

(b) What is a cache line?

(c) The total size of a cache memory is determined by the line size and the number of lines. Which quantity determines the temporal and which the spatial locality?

14.9 Which fetch policy has almost the same hit rate as the always prefetch policy, while the memory traffic is lowest?

14.10 (a) Which placement policy is easiest to implement?

(b) Which placement policy has a good cost/performance?

14.11 Given a byte-addressable main memory of 16 Mbytes, and a two-way, set-associative cache with lines of 16 bytes and a total size of 8 kbytes, determine the size of the following fields of the real address: tag, set and byte (see Figure 14.19(b)).

14.12 (a) Which replacement policy should be used for a direct-mapped cache?

(b) Which replacement policy allows for the highest temporal locality?

14.13 (a) What is the advantage of the flagged copy-back main memory update policy?

(b) What is the disadvantage?

14.14 Which dependencies can be caused by pipelining?

14.15 (a) How can data dependencies be solved?

(b) Which solution has the least implication for the hardware?

(c) Which solution has the lowest performance impact?

14.16 What is the most efficient solution to the branch penalty problem?

14.17 Why is branch prediction a useful method to reduce branch delay problems?

14.18 How can the instruction fetch delay of the branch target instruction be eliminated?

14.19 What is the purpose of a compare-and-branch instruction?

References

ADA (1983). *Reference Manual for the ADA Programming Language*. ANSI/MIL–STD 1815A. US Department of Defense.

Anacker, W. (1980). Josephson computer technology: An IBM Research Project. *IBM Journal of Research and Development*, **24**(2), 107–12.

Clark, D. and Emer, J. (1984). A characterization of processor performance on the VAX-11/780. In *Proc. 11th Annual Symposium on Computer Architecture*, pp. 301–11.

Colwell, R. P. *et al*. (1988). A VLIW architecture for a trace scheduling compiler. *IEEE Trans. Computers*, **37**(8), 967–79.

Ditzel, D. R. and McLellan, H. R. (1987). Branch folding in the CRISP microprocessor: Reducing branch delay to zero. In *Proc. 14th Annual Symposium on Computer Architecture*, pp. 2–9.

Eichen, B. (1986). NEC's uPD77230 digital signal processor. *IEEE Micro*, **6**(6), 60–9.

El-Ayat, K. A. and Agarwal, R. K. (1985). The Intel 80386 – Architecture and implementation. *IEEE Micro*, **5**(6), 4–22.

Gimarc, C. E. and Milutinovic, V. M. (1987). A survey of RISC processors and computers of the mid-1980s. *Computer*, **20**(9), 59–69.

Hennessy, J. *et al.* (1982). Hardware/software tradeoffs for increased performance. In *Proc. of the Symposium on Architectural Support for Programming Languages and Operating Systems*, pp. 2–11.

Hockney, R. W. and Jesshope, C. R. (1981). *Parallel Computers: Architecture, Programming and Algorithms*. Adam Hilger Ltd: Bristol, England.

Hwang, K. and Briggs, F. A. (1984). *Computer Architecture and Parallel Processing*. McGraw-Hill: New York, NY.

Johnson, M. (1987). *Am29000 User's Manual*. Advanced Micro Devices: Sunnyville, CA.

Kloker, K. L. (1986). The Motorola DSP56000 digital signal processor. *IEEE Micro*, **6**(6), 29–48.

Kogge, P. M. (1981). *The Architecture of Pipelined Computers*. McGraw-Hill: New York, NY.

Lee, J. K. and Smith, A. J. (1984). Branch prediction strategies and branch target buffer design. *Computer*, **17**(1), 6–22.

Lilja, D. L. (1988). Reducing the branch penalty in pipelined processors. *Computer*, **21**(7), 47–55.

Mahon, M. J. *et al.* (1986). Hewlett-Packard precision architecture: The processor. *Hewlett-Packard Journal*, **37**(8), 4–21.

McFarling, S. and Hennessy, J. (1986). Reducing the cost of branches. In *Proc. 13th Annual Symposium on Computer Architecture*, pp. 396–403.

Milutinovic, V. M. and Fura, D. (1986). An introduction to GaAs microprocessor architecture for VLSI. *Computer*, **19**(3), 30–42.

Motorola (1982a). *MC68010, 16-bit Virtual Memory Microprocessor*. Motorola Incorporated: Austin, TX.

Motorola (1982b). *MC68000, 16-bit Microprocessor User's Manual*. Prentice Hall Incorporated: Englewood Cliffs, NJ.

Motorola (1985). *MC68020, 32-bit Microprocessor User's Manual*. Prentice Hall Incorporated: Englewood Cliffs, NJ.

Motorola (1987). *MC68030, Enhanced 32-bit Microprocessor User's Manual*. Motorola Incorporated: Austin, TX.

Patterson, D. A. and Piepho, R. S. (1982). Assessing RISCs in high-level language support. *IEEE Micro*, **2**(4), 9–18.

Patterson, D. A. (1985). Reduced instruction set computers. *Comm. of the ACM*, **28**(1), 8–21.

Ramamoorthy, C. V. and Li, H. F. (1977). Pipeline architecture. *Computer Surveys*, **9**(1), 61–101.

Scales, H. (1986). MC68030 manages memory. *Digital Design*, 129–31.

Smith, A. J. (1978). Sequential program prefetching in memory hierarchies. *Computer*, **11**(12), 7–21.

Smith, A. J. (1982). Cache memories. *Computing Surveys*, **14**(3), 473–530.

Smith, J. E. and Goodman, J. R. (1985). Instruction cache replacement policies and organizations. *IEEE Trans. on Computers*, **C–34**(3), 234–41.

Smith, A. J. (1987). Line (block) size choice for CPU cache memories. *IEEE Trans. on Computers*, **C–36**(9), 1062–75.

Stone, H. S. (1987). *High-Performance Computer Architecture*. Addison-Wesley: Reading, MA.

Tomasulo, R. M. (1967). An efficient algorithm for exploiting multiple arithmetic units. *IBM Journal of Research and Development*, **11**(1), 25–33.

Wallace, C. S. (1964). A suggestion for a fast multiplier. *IEEE Trans. on Elec. Computers*, **EC–13**(1), 14–17.

Whitby-Strevens, C. (1985). The transputer. In *Proc. 12th Annual Symposium on Computer Architecture*, pp. 292–300.

15 Reduced Instruction Set Computers

Everything should be made as simple as possible, but not simpler.
– Albert Einstein

The evolution of computer architecture has shown a trend towards an increasing complexity. However, as early as 1975, computer architects questioned this increasing complexity as the ideal way to achieve a higher cost/performance ratio. Investigations on this subject resulted in the current surge of reduced instruction set computers (RISCs), as opposed to the complex instruction set computers (CISCs).

To understand the reasons for the increased complexity of some architectures, the chapter begins by considering the history and evolution of CISC computers. From an implementation point of view, a CISC computer is optimized to reduce the number of instructions executed by having complex instructions. This forms the framework for the main section on RISC principles and characteristics. RISC computers are optimized to reduce the number of cycles per instruction and to keep the cycle time short at the same time. Several controversial issues between RISC and CISC architectures are discussed next, followed by a presentation of the RISC II architecture, which has served as a base for the SPARC microprocessor, as used by SUN.

15.1 History and evolution of complex instruction set computers

In the early days of computing, memory was a very costly resource. This gave rise to the line of thought that the best architecture was the one with the shortest programs (in terms of memory). Other factors used as a measure of the quality of an architecture were the number of bits per instruction, or the amount of program and data bits fetched during program execution. After the introduction of microprogramming (using read-only memories which allowed the complex random control logic to be replaced by more structured microprograms), it became cost effective to move functions that were previously executed by a series of instructions to microcode, thereby improving the code density. In this way, the slow fetching of instructions from memory was avoided, thus increasing the execution efficiency. As more and more functions were moved to microcode, its size increased. Because the microcode could not be shown to be fault free, it was stored in writable (rather than read-only) memory, the so-called writable control stores (WCS). This made it possible for the microcode to be adapted to the used programming language or application, offering each user an optimal vehicle for his goal. The use of virtual control memory was also suggested, despite the problems that it introduces, such as virtual micro-instruction page faults.

Another argument for implementing functions in microcode was that these functions were better suited for supporting compilers. If a high-level language (HLL) statement could be translated into a single machine language instruction, writing compilers seemed much easier. Furthermore, including instructions in the machine language, which closely resemble HLL statements, closes the semantic gap that had risen between the machine languages and the HLLs. Examples of instructions that were added for a better HLL support are the VAX-11 INDEX, CASE and CALL instructions, and the MC68020 CHK instruction. Even more complex instructions, such as the VAX-11 POLY and CRC instructions, or the iAPX–432 SEND instruction, were included.

This enrichment of the instruction set was paralleled by an equally fast increase in the number of addressing modes. For example, where the MC68000 already had 12 addressing modes, the MC68020 increased this number to 18, which includes some esoteric new modes. Also, the need for upwards compatibility has caused many computer firms to constantly increase the size of their instruction sets in newer and more powerful models.

The quest for code density and many instructions made it necessary to use instruction formats with a variable length; that is, the opcode and operand specifier fields of the instructions have variable lengths. In the

Table 15.1 Characteristics of some CISCs.

Characteristic	IBM 370/168	VAX-11/780	iAPX-432
Year of introduction	1973	1978	1982
Number of instructions	208	303	222
Microcode memory size	420 kbytes	480 kbytes	64 kbytes
Instruction size (bits)	16–48	16–456	6–321

VAX-11, it is not possible to tell where the second operand specifier starts until the first operand specifier has been decoded. The variable lengths of instructions can cause instructions to start at arbitrary bytes and, in some architectures, even on arbitrary bit boundaries, which does not improve the efficiency of instruction fetch units or memory data transfers. Furthermore, the nature of the operands makes it possible for access to an operand to cause a page fault (if that operand is not in main memory), while some irreversible action has already taken place. An example is the MC68020 instruction MOVE −(A1), −(A2): if the indirect access via the (decremented) register A2 causes a page fault, the instruction cannot be simply restarted after the page has been loaded, because both A1 and A2 have already been changed. An extreme example of such an instruction is the IBM/370 MVC (Move Characters) instruction. This can cause as many as eight page faults during execution, due to unaligned instruction placement and access of operands crossing page boundaries. Table 15.1 shows the characteristics of some well-known CISC architectures.

15.2 Evaluation of program execution characteristics

Several researchers have investigated the characteristics of compiler-generated code to determine whether the complex CISC instructions and addressing modes were actually used (Lunde, 1977; Tanenbaum, 1978; Patterson, 1982). Some findings have already been discussed in Chapter 4, and these are summarized here for completeness. These characteristics have several aspects, each with their own area of influence: the operations performed influence the design of the CPU; the operands used influence the memory organization and addressing modes; and the control flow operations have an impact on the control organization and the instruction pipeline. These characteristics are discussed here under the following headings: simple and fast instructions; procedure calls; and compiler aspects.

Table 15.2 Frequency distribution (%) of MC68000 instructions.

Instruction Class		Dynamic Frequency	
Move	32.85		
Branch/jump	15.58		
Decrement and branch	8.37		8.37
Compare/test	10.95		
Arithmetic/logical	16.31		
Add, Subtract, AND, OR		11.47	
Multiply		0.58	0.58
Divide		0.13	0.13
Shift and rotate		3.25	
Extend sign		0.88	
Subroutine	6.14		
Branch/jump to subroutine		1.69	
Return from subroutine		1.69	
Link/unlink		2.76	2.76
Miscellaneous	7.53		
Bit operation		0.22	0.22
Clear		2.69	
Load and push effective address		4.25	
Set conditional		0.37	
Total	100.00		12.06

15.2.1 Simple and fast instructions

The importance of simple instructions, which can be executed very fast because they require only one cycle to execute and keep the cycle time short, is the key to the RISC concept (see Example 15.1, p. 449). The arguments for simple instructions can be derived from many statistics.

Simple operations

Table 15.2 shows the dynamic frequency distribution of MC68000 instructions (MacGregor, 1985). The figures in the extreme right-hand column are for instructions that involve an operation that could be considered more complex, such as DBcc, MUL, DIV, LINK, UNLINK and bit operations. They only constitute 12% of the instructions executed.

Table 15.3 Frequency distribution (%) of MC68020 addressing modes.

Addressing Mode	Source EA Frequency		Destination EA Frequency	
None	35.10		17.28	
Register direct	12.50		49.48	
Register indirect	30.71		25.44	
(An)		4.08		1.50
(An)+, −(An)		4.16*		13.00*
Displ + (An)		20.10		9.13
Displ + (An) + (Xn)		2.37*		1.81*
Absolute	0.54*		0.00*	
Program relative	0.42			
Displ + (PC)		0.32		
Displ + (PC) + (Xn)		0.10*		
Immediate	7.77			
#xxx		6.57*		
Quick		1.20		
Implied stack	3.08*		4.93*	
Total	90.12		97.13	
Total complex addressing mode		16.82*		19.74*

*Addressing mode is considered complex.

Simple addressing modes

The complexity of an instruction is also determined by the addressing modes used to specify the operands. Table 15.3 shows the dynamic frequency of the addressing modes used in the MC68020 (MacGregor, 1985). From this table (for an explanation, see Section 4.1), it can be concluded that the complex addressing modes constitute 16.82% of the source and 19.74% of the destination addresses. A complex addressing mode is defined to be a mode where the address may not be computable in one cycle, because it requires several additions and/or extra extension words.

Small constants as immediate data, and small displacements

The statistics given so far apply to the MC68000 architecture; it will be obvious that for a different architecture these numbers will differ. For example, constants can be specified by the MC68020 to be 'quick', consisting of 3 (ADDQ, SUBQ) or 8 (MOVEQ) bits, so that they fit into

Table 15.4 Dynamic frequency (%) of 8- and 32-bit integers.

Data Type and Operation	Frequency
8-bit loads	2.6
32-bit loads	68.6
8-bit stores	2.6
32-bit stores	26.2
Total	100.0

the basic part of the instruction (the first word). For 32-bit fixed-length instruction sets, as used by several RISC architectures, larger constants can be included as an immediate field of the instructions. For example, MIPS (Hennessy, 1982) allows for 8-bit immediate values, which allows 95.5% of all constants to be specified as an immediate value (see Table 4.4). Similar arguments also hold for the size of the displacement field; 8 to 16 bits cover the majority of the cases (see Table 5.5).

Few data types

One way of reducing the number of operations is to reduce the number of data types. It may be questioned whether all integer data types are required. Hennessy (1982) analyzed the frequency of occurrence of 8-bit integers, used for manipulating characters and Boolean values (Table 15.4). The statistics were obtained from several large Pascal programs. Only load and store operations are considered, as all other operations (such as ADDB or ADDW) are performed on 32-bit registers. The table shows that only 5.2% of the load/store operations use 8-bit integers. An optimizing compiler may be able to reduce this number further by allowing operations on four 8-bit integers simultaneously. For the remaining cases, the 8-bit load operation can be replaced by a 32-bit load, followed by an extract byte operation; the 8-bit store can be replaced by a 32-bit load, an insert byte and a 32-bit store operation. By not having the 8-bit load and store operations, Hennessy claims that the data path to memory can be simplified so that 32-bit load/store operations are 20% faster, which is at the expense of a rather low overhead caused by the emulation of the 8-bit load/store operations.

Few instruction formats

Figure A.4 shows the MC68020 instruction formats. The 10 formats shown do not even include the special formats of the co-processor instructions or the format of the TRAP instruction (they have been left out consciously, for simplification reasons). A large number of instruction formats means that a given bit field has different interpretations, depending on other fields, such as the opcode field. Consequently, instruction decoding takes longer, because more gate delays are required. This may increase the cycle time of the processor and require more hardware for instruction decoding.

□□EXAMPLE 15.1

Assume a program with an execution profile where 80% of the instructions executed are simple instructions (such as AND, XOR, ADD and BRANCH) and the remaining 20% are complex instructions (such as MUL, DIV and POLY). Further assume that the simple instructions take four cycles and the complex instructions take eight cycles on a CISC machine, with a cycle time of 100 ns ($= 10^{-7}$ s). On a RISC machine, in contrast, the simple instructions are executed in one cycle, while the complex instructions have to be interpreted via subroutines, taking an average of 14 cycles per complex instruction. Because of the simplicity of the RISC instructions, their cycle time is 75 ns ($= 0.75 * 10^{-7}$ s). Assuming that the program executes one million instructions, this will require the following execution times:

CISC: $10^6 * (0.80 * 4 + 0.20 * 8) * 10^{-7}$ s $= 0.48$ s
RISC: $10^6 * (0.80 * 1 + 0.20 * 14) * 0.75 * 10^{-7}$ s $= 0.27$ s

Note that RISC is 48/27 = 1.78 times faster than CISC.

15.2.2 Procedure calls

Table 15.5 shows the frequency of operations for several Pascal and C programs (Patterson, 1982). The first subtable presents the dynamic frequency of the HLL statements, while in the second and third subtable these frequencies are weighted according to the number of machine instructions and the number of memory references for the RISC I architecture, respectively. It is clear from the table that although the assignment statement is the most frequently executed HLL statement, with a frequency of about 40%, this is not the case when considering which HLL statements use the longest execution time: the procedure CALL and RETURN sequences are very demanding both in terms of the required number of machine instructions and memory references, so it is worth providing some support for these functions.

Due to their importance, procedure calls have been studied in detail. Tanenbaum (1978) found that only 1.25% of the called procedures had more than six parameters, while only 6.7% of them had more than six local scalar variables. These figures, which are supported by other studies, show that the size of a procedure activation record is not large.

Table 15.5 Dynamic frequencies of HLL statements.

Procedure Call	Percentage of Total Number of Statements		Percentage of Total Number of Machine Instructions		Percentage of Total Number of Memory References	
	Pascal	C	Pascal	C	Pascal	C
ASSIGN	45	38	13	13	14	15
IF	29	43	11	21	7	13
CALL/RETURN	15	12	31	33	44	45
LOOP	5	3	42	32	33	26
Other	6	4	2	1	2	1
Total	100	100	99	100	100	100

Tamir (1983) found that the 'call depth' is limited; that is, programs where procedures call subsequent procedures to a great depth are very rare. Also, when a certain call depth has been reached, the variation in depth tends to be small; that is, many procedures are executed with about the same depth. This is a natural consequence of the way programs are structured; in some procedure in some program at call depth CD a procedure is called to perform a function. This called procedure may 'use' other procedures to perform that function, thus causing several procedure calls around the call depth CD. This means that a mechanism for fast procedure calls only has to take into account a depth of a few calls.

The following arguments support the idea of using registers to contain parameters and locally declared scalars in procedures, such that part of the activation record should be contained in registers.

When measuring the nature of the operands used, Lunde (1977) found that, for the DEC System-10, each instruction, on average, referenced 0.5 operands in memory and 1.4 operands in registers, which already indicates the importance of registers (for speed reasons) to hold frequently accessed operands. This figure of $0.5 + 1.4 = 1.9$ operands per instruction for System-10 can be considered typical; for example, it compares very well with the average number of 1.8 operands per instruction for the VAX-11 (see Section 5.4).

Table 15.6 shows the dynamic percentage of operand types in Pascal and C programs, as found by Patterson (1982), and in the Pascal-like language SAL (Tanenbaum, 1978). Only 20% to 26% of the operands cannot be contained in registers, because they are of the array/structure type, and of these over 90% are global variables. From 16% to 33% of the operands are constants, which can be specified as immediate values in the instruction. Of the remaining scalar operands, over 80% are local variables, which can be stored in registers. Excluding

Table 15.6 Dynamic frequency of operands.

Operand	Language		
	Pascal	C	SAL
Scalar	58	53	42
Integer constant	16	23	33
Array/structure	26	24	20
Other	—	—	5

integer constants, because they can be specified with a zero-component operand (see Section 5.2), about two-thirds of all operands are scalars, of which 80% are local variables. So, 2/3 * 80% = 53% of all operand references can use the very fast register-direct addressing mode.

15.2.3 Compiler aspects

Statistics have supported the beliefs of many researchers that compilers only subset instruction sets; that is, they do not use the full power of an instruction set. This may arise for several reasons. One reason is that, although some machine instructions resemble HLL statements, their semantics is slightly different, so they cannot be used in all cases, or only for one language. A good example of such a statement is the FOR statement that differs between several languages. In some languages, the count variable is undefined at the end of the loop; in others, it is equal to the final loop value; and in yet others, it is larger than the final loop value. Therefore, it is not possible to equip a processor with a single FOR instruction that can cope with all these languages. As a consequence, compilers use a sequence of simple instructions or primitives with which the desired function can be composed, instead of the single FOR instruction.

Another reason why compilers do not use the complete instruction set is that it would be very time consuming to do a case analysis of which instruction or which instruction sequence is the fastest or the shortest. As Wulf (1981) has pointed out, compiling is 'just a large case analysis'. He stated that an instruction set should provide only *one* way of accomplishing a task (no choice) or *all* ways should be possible (again no extensive case analysis). In many contemporary architectures, it is possible to carry out an operation in many different ways, and many exceptions must be dealt with. To make an instruction set a good target for compilation, it should show regularity and orthogonality. Furthermore, it should provide *primitives* rather than *solutions*, thus giving the compiler the opportunity to compose the optimal sequence of primitive instructions, instead of having no alternative but to use an inefficient complex instruction. An illustration of this is the VAX-11 INDEX instruction. The INDEX instruction is used to calculate the address of an element in a one-dimensional array, while simultaneously checking the index against the array bounds. When replacing the INDEX instruction by a sequence of simple instructions (Compare, Branch, Add, Multiply), Patterson (1980) reported a 45% speed gain. A nasty side effect of the inclusion of complex instructions is that the simple instructions (which are executed most frequently) are slowed down because of the increased data path length and the increased control complexity.

The steadily declining price of memory has made the need for compactly coded programs less urgent while the increased speed of memory has allowed for a higher memory bandwidth, so the amount of data that is transferred to and from memory has become somewhat less important.

All in all, the reduction of the semantic gap, which was achieved by using a machine instruction set that was closer to the HLL, has turned out to introduce a performance gap.

15.3 RISC principles and characteristics

The evaluation of program execution characteristics has led to the RISC approach, which involves making tradeoffs between architecture and implementation, hardware and software, and compile time and run time, to achieve an optimal performance. These tradeoffs have led to a computer architecture with fewer instructions which execute faster (preferably as fast as or faster than a CISC micro-instruction). The architecture also has a better compiler interface, instead of a user friendly interface. As most applications are written in high-level languages, the user need not be bothered with implementation details that are only known to the compiler. Because of the small number of instructions, the Berkeley group has coined the acronym RISC (reduced instruction set computer), but, as the RISC philosophy comprises more than just a reduced number of instructions, the adjective *streamlined* is more appropriate (Hennessy, 1984).

Many computer firms are nowadays marketing computers partly or entirely based on the RISC philosophy. Examples are the IBM RT-PC, the HP Spectrum, the Pyramid 90X, the Acorn ARM, the Fairchild Clipper, the AMD29000, the SPARC, the MC88000 and the Intel i860 and i960, although there are some disputes as to whether some of these computers are RISCs or not. These were preceded by the experimental IBM 801, the Berkeley RISC I and II, and the Stanford MIPS processors. A survey of many commercially available RISC processors can be found in Gimarc (1987).

The RISC philosophy is based on the following observations and principles (Patterson, 1985; Radin, 1983):

Observations:

- Simple operations: Complex operations, such as multiply, should be interpreted.
- Simple addressing modes: More complex operand specifications can be replaced by in-line address computations, which often can be optimized or eliminated by the compiler.
- Small constant and displacement values: An 8- to 16-bit field can cover the majority of cases.
- A small number of data types: Missing data types can be emulated.
- Procedure calls (and returns) occur very frequently.
- The number of parameters in a procedure call tends to be small.
- The number of locally declared data objects in a procedure tends to be small.
- Compilers cannot easily exploit complex instructions.
- Replacing a complex instruction with a number of simple instructions often turns out to be faster.

Principles:

- Simple instructions to allow for fast execution, typically one cycle per instruction.
- The cycle time should be short, which means that the data path has to be simple, banning complex operations.
- Instructions operating on data should be of the reg-reg type, thereby allowing for the shortest operand fetch time.
- A large number of registers should be used to contain as much of an activation record as is possible.
- Only load/store instructions should access main memory.
- Fixed-length instructions are used which are aligned, which speeds up the instruction fetch operation.
- Instructions have a simple layout and only a few different formats, which speeds up the instruction decoding operation.
- Simple addressing modes should be used, thereby allowing for a fast operand address computation.
- Harvard architecture should be used to allow for more memory bandwidth; access to memory has to be optimized to sustain the execution bandwidth.

Table 15.7 Characteristics of some microprocessors.

	CISC		RISC	
Characteristic	**MC68000**	**Z8000**	**RISC II**	**MIPS**
Year of introduction	1980	1979	1983	1983
Basic instructions	56	110	39	55
General registers	15	14	137	16
Addressing modes	14	12	3	4
Transistor count	68K	18K	41K	25K

- Use pipelining to accelerate the instruction execution process.
- Use compiler technology to resolve pipeline dependencies, which means that the implementation will be visible at the architectural level.

The result of these principles and observations is shown in Table 15.7, highlighting some characteristics of CISC and RISC microprocessors.

15.3.1 RISC architecture characteristics

RISC architectures can be considered to be designed so that they exploit compiler technology in order to simplify the architecture and accelerate the implementation. Several of the implementation acceleration mechanisms are not unique to RISC architectures and are (or could be) used to accelerate CISC architectures as well. The advantage of RISC architectures is that they have been designed with these mechanisms in mind.

Several architectural characteristics have already been mentioned. Here, the compare-and-branch instruction and register windows will be discussed. Note that because the implementation is visible at the architectural level (to simplify the implementation), the distinction as to whether certain concepts belong to the architecture or to the implementation becomes less meaningful.

Compare-and-branch instruction

Assuming 32-bit instructions, it is possible to incorporate a compare and a branch function into a single instruction. This leads to compare-and-branch instructions that do not require condition code bits (Z and N) and can be implemented to execute in one cycle. Hennessy (1982) found that 98.9% of the branches were preceded by a compare (or test) operation, which means that, in those cases, program execution is accelerated by one instruction. Also, the hardware is simplified due to the absence of the condition code bits.

Register windows

The most debated feature of the RISC I and RISC II processors is the large register file used to accelerate the procedure-calling mechanism (Patterson, 1982). The implementation of a large register file was made possible by the small size of the chip area required to implement the instruction set. Because of the hard-wired implementation and the simplicity of the instruction set, the control area of RISC-type processors is about 6% of the chip area, as compared to about 50% for conventional microprocessors (see Table 15.10). Figure 15.1 shows the RISC II register file, which consists of 138 registers. (Note that the register R0 is not really a register because it is hard-wired to zero. Therefore, RISC II is sometimes claimed to have a register file consisting of 137 registers.) At any given moment, 32 registers are accessible by the procedure being executed. This set of 32 registers is divided into two parts:

(1) The global registers (R0 through R9): RISC II uses 10 registers, which are accessible to all procedures. They are used to contain global data.

(2) The window (R10 through R31): This is used to accelerate the procedure mechanism. It consists of a part with 22 registers, which are located somewhere in the register file. An active procedure has access to this part which consists of the following three subparts:

- Incoming parameter registers (R10 through R15): These registers contain the parameters of the calling procedure.
- Local registers (R16 through R25): These registers can be considered to be the working registers of the active procedure.
- Outgoing parameter registers (R26 through R31): These registers contain the parameters of the procedure to be called.

When a procedure is called, parameter passing and the reserving of space for local scalars is done simply by moving the window, which is essentially a relocation operation (see Section 10.4.1) in register space. This relocation operation consists of relocating the window to the next position, which has a distance of 16 registers to the previous position (Figure 15.1(b)). This is done such that R10 of the called procedure becomes R26 of the calling procedure. The effect is that the outgoing parameter registers of the calling procedure become the incoming parameter registers of the called procedure. At the same time, the called procedure gets a free set of local registers and registers for outgoing parameters. Upon a return, the window is relocated to its previous position; this allows return values to be automatically passed, while the local registers of the returned-to procedure become accessible again.

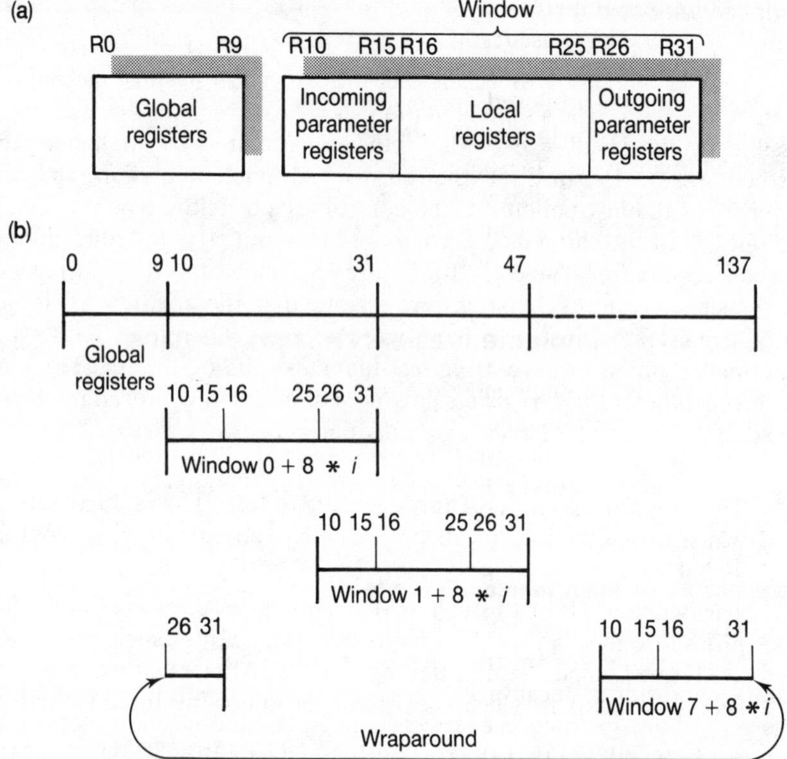

FIGURE 15.1

Register windowing: (a) registers accessible by a procedure; (b) window concept.

The windows are organized as a circular buffer, with the last window overlapping the first. When the register file is exceeded, because no free windows are available (an overflow), the contents of a window must be transferred to main memory, thereby freeing one window. Similar steps must be taken upon underflow. Tamir (1983) found that moving only one window contents from and to main memory upon an overflow or underflow is generally the best approach for the RISC I and II register files.

Disadvantages of the register window scheme are that it uses more chip area, it has a larger register access time, because of the large number of registers, and a considerable increase in the process context. On a context switch, the complete register file (or minimally the global registers and the registers of the windows that have been used) must be saved in memory, which is a time-consuming operation. Because all windows have a fixed length, they are not all fully used; for example, it would be a coincidence if all procedures had exactly 10 local variables. This causes the processor to save many unused registers on a context switch. Huguet (1985) found that using a register file of 32 registers together with variable-size windows gives the same performance as the register file of the RISC II, while the processor state is kept small and the register utilization is increased. While, in the RISC processor, an average of 10.9 registers is unused; this is decreased to 0.74 in the variable window size scheme. Because this scheme may be more difficult to implement, Huguet proposed another scheme, which uses a register file of 64 registers and a window that can assume three sizes (8, 12 and 16, including the overlap). In some aspects, this scheme performs slightly worse than the variable-size window scheme (in terms of the number of registers transferred on a context switch), but it is easier to implement.

15.3.2 RISC implementation characteristics

Several of the RISC implementation characteristics have already been mentioned; for example, the single-cycle execution of instructions that operate on data, where the cycle time is kept as short as possible. Several acceleration mechanisms are considered to be 'standard' for RISC architectures and are summarized here.

Acceleration of main memory

Most RISC implementations use a Harvard architecture to allow for independent paths for instructions and data, thereby doubling the memory bandwidth. Because of the short cycle time and the execution speed goal of one instruction every cycle, main memory cannot supply the required bandwidth, so that the use of cache memories is a requirement. The Harvard architecture may be at the CPU–cache interface, so that there are two cache memories. When the Harvard architecture is extended to main memory, a separate data and instruction memory exist. In the other case, when the Harvard architecture only applies to the CPU–cache interface, a single main memory is present, containing both program and data. This obviously has a lower bandwidth, but is less costly to implement (see Example 14.1).

Acceleration of the instruction unit

Pipelining is the most common method used to accelerate the instruction unit (see Section 14.8). Because of the simplicity of the instructions, RISC pipelines tend to contain fewer stages than comparable CISC processors. This reduces the severity of the pipeline dependency problems.

A unique characteristic of RISC architectures is that the implementation of the pipeline is visible at the architectural level. This allows pipeline dependencies to be resolved by software, rather than hardware, which again simplifies the implementation. Section 14.8 gave solutions to pipeline dependencies in general; here, the solutions adopted by most RISC implementations are highlighted.

Table 15.8 Branch: traditional, delayed and optimized.

Address	Traditional Branch		Delayed Branch		Optimized, Delayed Branch	
100	LOAD	X, R1	LOAD	X, R1	LOAD	X, R1
101	ADD	1, R1	ADD	1, R1	BRANCH	L
102	BRANCH	L	BRANCH	L	ADD	1, R1
103	ADD	R1, R2	NOP		ADD	R1, R2
104	SUB	R3, R2	ADD	R1, R2	SUB	R3, R2
105	L: STORE	R1, Y	SUB	R3, R2	L: STORE	R1, Y
106			L: STORE	R1, Y		

- Data dependencies: A data dependency occurs when a shared resource between two instructions, I_i and I_j, exists such that the shared resource will be accessed by I_j before I_i has delivered its result. Load instructions, which usually require two cycles to execute (because of the extra access to data memory), are, for example, more likely to cause a data dependency.

  Prevention, which is the most efficient solution because it does not require hardware support and does not waste any cycles, has been adopted by many RISC designs. It requires the implementation to be visible at the architectural level.

  Prevention is based on the capability of the compiler to be able to rearrange the instruction sequence such that the dependency does not exist any more. It essentially consists of inserting other useful (or NOP) instructions in the instruction stream, before the instruction with the data dependency.

  The relatively large number of registers in a RISC computer (typically 32) makes it easier for the compiler to solve the data dependency problem by finding an operation on registers which have no dependencies.
- Run-ons: Because all instructions execute in one cycle, run-ons cannot occur.
- Branch dependencies: These are solved by preventing their occurrence, using delayed branches. This again is the most efficient solution, because it has the potential of having a penalty of zero cycles. The large number of registers is also an advantage here. The delayed branch requires the branch instruction to be followed by *d* instructions (where *d* is the branch delay), which are executed before the branch is effectuated. According to Patterson (1982), this will be possible for 78% to 96% of the branch delay slots; in the remaining cases an NOP has to be inserted. Table 15.8 shows

the delayed branch concept. When a compare-and-branch instruction is available, the fast-comparison method may be used to reduce the branch delay by one stage (this is the execution stage of the compare-and-branch instruction). The fast-compare method is applicable in 98.9% of the conditional branches (McFarling, 1986). As the branch delay is reduced by one delay slot, it is easier to fill the remaining branch delay slots.

15.3.3 Compiler requirements

Because of the register-oriented instruction set, efficient algorithms have to be used for register allocation. In the IBM 801, and also in the MIPS compiler, a graph-colouring algorithm was used to maximize the use of registers (Chaitin, 1982; Chow, 1984). This algorithm has to minimize spill code, which is the code inserted into a program to move variables, which cannot be allocated to a register, to and from memory. The algorithm considers the cost and saving involved in allocating variables to registers – cost refers to the memory–register transfer operations for loading and freeing registers.

Another aspect considered in the MIPS compiler was the prevention of pipeline dependencies. As the instruction pipeline has no hardware interlocks (hence the name Microprocessor without Interlocked Pipeline Stages), the compiler must solve these pipeline dependencies by re-organizing code and eventually inserting NOPs in the program code.

Furthermore, the MIPS compiler tries to pack multiple instructions in one word, if they can be executed simultaneously (for example, an ALU operation and a LOAD operation). The MIPS processor always fetches a 32-bit instruction word. This word may contain a single 32-bit instruction, a 16-bit instruction together with a 16-bit NOP instruction, or a 16-bit ALU and a 16-bit LOAD instruction (which is executed in the execution stage of the ALU instruction).

15.4 The RISC/CISC controversy

The introduction of the RISC philosophy has led to many discussions about its merits. One of the key aspects is its performance, since RISC processors are considered to outperform conventional (CISC) processors.

Table 15.9 shows the execution time of benchmarks, written in C, using Johnson's Portable C Compiler (Johnson, 1978), and written in assembly language. The results are normalized so that the execution time of the C programs on the 8 MHz RISC II is equal to one. The third line shows the ratio As/C, which is the execution time for the benchmarks in assembly language divided by the execution time in C (Patterson, 1982a).

Table 15.9 Normalized execution times of benchmarks.

Benchmark	RISC II (8 MHz)	RISC II (12 MHz)	VAX-11/780 (5 MHz)	MC68000 (10 MHz)	Z8002 (6 MHz)	PDP-11/70 (7.5 MHz)
C	1.0	0.7	2.1	2.8	3.5	2.7
Assembly	0.9	0.6	0.9	0.7	1.4	1.2
Ratio As/C	0.9	0.86	0.45	0.34	0.46	0.53
Program size	1.0	1.0	0.8	0.9	1.2	0.9

The published figures for the 7.5 MHz RISC I processor have been adjusted to the 8 and 12 MHz versions of the newer RISC II processor. The results show that RISC II is slightly faster in executing programs written in assembly language and substantially faster in executing programs written in C. The ratio As/C shows that a user of C on the RISC II processor is penalized less for using this high-level language than on a CISC, whose compilers apparently are not able to generate efficient code. To evaluate these benchmarks without the large register file influencing the results, Heath (1984) rewrote the benchmarks to remove this advantage. His conclusion was that the RISC II processor executed at a rate comparable to that of the MC68000 and Z8000. He also signalled the discrepancy (both in program size and speed of execution) between compiled C code and hand-coded assembly language programs for the MC68000 and the Z8000.

Another figure of interest is the relative code size. As might be expected, the RISC code is larger, because the instructions are simpler and less oriented to a high-level language. However, studies have found that RISC I programs are, at worst, a factor of two larger than programs for the other machines (Patterson, 1982), and typically 10% to 20% larger (Table 15.9). The advantage of CISC instruction sets in terms of reduction of code size should not be over-estimated, because compilers tend to use only a subset of the large number of available instructions and addressing modes.

An argument against RISC is that it is optimally tailored for the language C. This is true to some extent, but the run-time characteristics of C and other high-level languages are comparable, with simple operations being highly favourable. Patterson (1982) states that, for languages with unusual data types or operations, such as decimal in COBOL, a designer should find the most frequently used data types and operations and support them in a RISC processor. This way, other languages can certainly be executed efficiently. However, it should be noted that a specially tailored RISC processor for each group of languages would be required, while most CISC architectures try to

Table 15.10 VLSI design metrics.

Characteristic	RISC I	MC68000	Z8000
Total number of devices	44K	68K	17.5K
Regularity factor	25	12.1	50
Control area in percentage of total chip	6	50	53
Design time in months	19	30	30
Design effort in man.months	15	100	60
Layout effort in man.months	12	70	70

support several languages at the same time. This clearly reduces the performance for any single language.

On the implementation side, several facts favour the RISC approach, as shown in Table 15.10 (Patterson, 1982). This table shows the following design metrics:

- Total number of devices: This is a measure of the complexity of the chip.
- Regularity factor: This is the ratio of the number of hand-designed devices (transistors, and so on) to the number of standard devices that could be extracted from a library. Because of its simplicity, the RISC approach does not need many hand-designed devices. This saves design effort and time, and reduces the chance of mistakes.
- Control area: This is the percentage of the chip area used for control (rather than the data path). Simple instructions need less control.
- Design time: A short design time is very important, particularly for competitive reasons – the economical life of a product is determined by technological obsolence, which happens when the same function can be implemented in a new technology (which is faster and can integrate more functions on the chip). Assuming a new technology every three years, the RISC approach has a life time that is $30 - 19 = 11$ months, or almost one year, longer than a CISC design.
- Design and layout effort: These can be translated into one-time cost. From this, it can be concluded that RISC designs become economically attractive with lower volumes, at a lower cost.

The main debate of the RISC philosophy is often focused on the large register file in the RISC I processor, particularly its organization with multiple overlapped windows (Colwell, 1985). It is indeed debatable whether this feature is a characteristic of RISC. The point in favour of RISC is that the reduction of the control area has made it possible to implement such a register file on the chip, which was not possible on processors such as the MC68000 and the VAX-11. To investigate whether CISC architectures would profit equally well from multiple register sets, Hitchcock (1985) added multiple overlapped register sets to the VAX-11 and the MC68000, and simulated the RISC I processor with a single register set. In addition, the effect of multiple, non-overlapping, windows was investigated. Hitchcock concluded that the performance gains due to multiple (overlapping) register sets are independent of the type of architecture.

Although the RISC philosophy has made it possible to incorporate such a register file on the chip, the process context has increased as well. Further studies are necessary to determine whether it is not more useful to dedicate this chip area to multiple register sets or to support, say, floating-point operations. An evaluation of several types of register file organization (and of RISC versus non-RISC instruction sets) can be found in Flynn (1987).

At present, most debates on the RISC/CISC controversy have quietened down somewhat and the main outcome is that designers do best if they use ideas from both worlds, thereby making the tradeoff that is best suited to their design and applications.

15.5 An example: The RISC II architecture

The best-documented RISC processors are the RISC I and RISC II processors, developed at the University of Berkeley (Katevenis, 1985). In this example, the RISC II processor is described, because its architecture has been implemented commercially as the SPARC processor (used by SUN and others). Its most outstanding (and most debated) characteristic is the register file organization, consisting of eight overlapped windows, for a total of 138 registers (Figure 15.1). Each procedure has access to logical registers 0 through 31, divided into 10 global registers, and 22 window registers shared with the calling (parent) procedure and a called (child) procedure. As a special feature, register R0 always contains zero and cannot be modified (although it may be used as destination register). The other characteristics of the RISC II architecture are described in the following.

15.5.1 Instruction formats

Figure 15.2 shows the instruction formats of RISC II. Being a RISC architecture, only a few (in this case only three) formats are present. The SCC (Set Condition Code) bit determines whether the condition codes

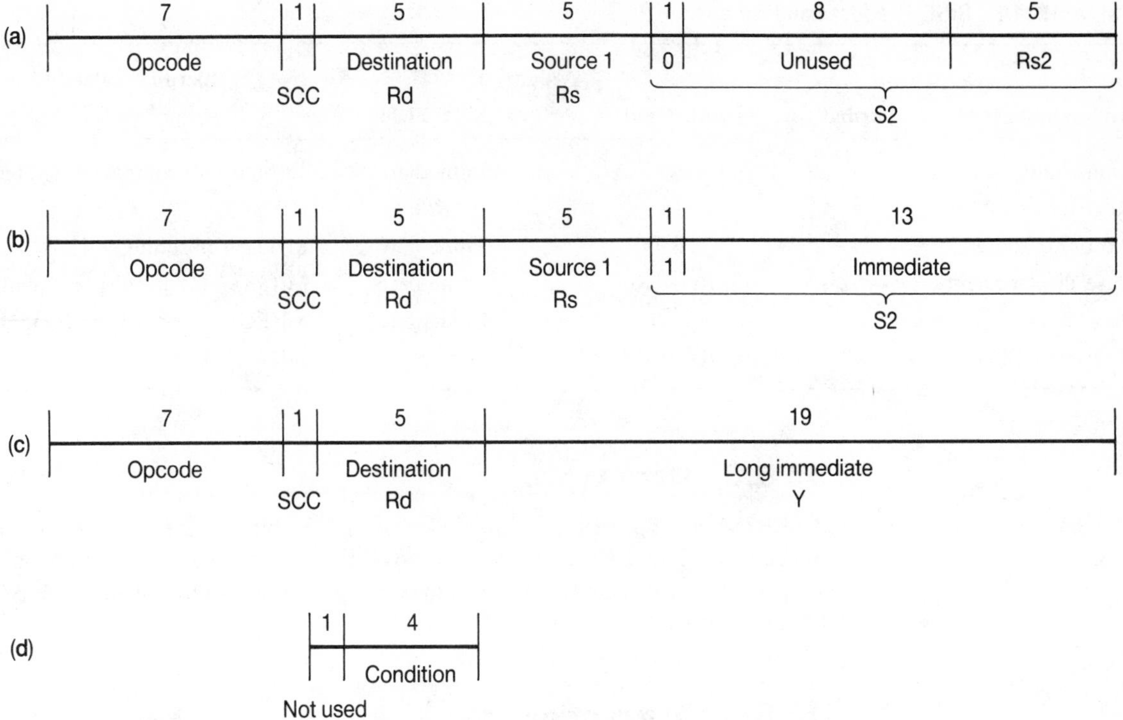

FIGURE 15.2
RISC II instruction formats.

should be affected as a result of the operation. In format *a*, Rd specifies a register destination operand, while Rs and Rs2 specify register source operands. In format *b*, Rd specifies a register destination operand, Rs specifies a register source operand and the 13-bit immediate field (S2) specifies a two's complement immediate value or a displacement, which is sign extended before being used. In format *c*, Rd specifies a register destination operand and the 19-bit immediate field (Y) specifies a two's complement displacement. In the case of conditional operations, the destination field specifies the condition (Figure 15.2(d)). When register R0 is specified by Rd, Rs or Rs2, a zero value will be returned on a read, while a write to R0 means that the data will be lost.

15.5.2 Addressing modes

The available addressing modes are such that the operand address can be computed in a single cycle. Only a few addressing modes are supported; however, in combination with R0 (which produces the value zero when read), several different modes can be synthesized (Table 15.11). For example, absolute addresses can be generated using format *b* and specifying Rs = R0; the sign-extended, 13-bit immediate field will then be considered as the (absolute) address.

Table 15.11 RISC II addressing modes.

Addressing Mode	Format	Value RS Field	Value S2/Y Field	Operand Value
Immediate	*b*	RS	Immediate	13-bit, two's complement value
Register	*a*	Rs	Rs2	(Rs2)
Absolute address	*b*	R0	Immediate	M[13-bit absolute address]
Base displacement	*b*	Rs ≠ R0	Immediate	M[(Rs) + 13-bit displacement]
PC relative	*c*		Immediate	M[(PC) + 19-bit displacement]
Register indirect	*b*	Rs ≠ R0	0	M[(Rs)]

15.5.3 Data types

The RISC II architecture allows 8-, 16- and 32-bit integer load and store operations. This is in contrast to many other RISC machines which only support 32-bit integers. The instructions operating on data always use 32-bit operands in registers.

15.5.4 Instruction set

RISC II has 39 instructions (Table 15.12). This 'reduced' number should be compared with the 303 instructions of the VAX-11/780 and the 208 instructions of the IBM 370/168. However, this comparison is not quite fair because the VAX and the IBM 370 also have instructions to support decimal and floating-point data types (which have been omitted in the RISC II architecture). From the instruction set of Table 15.12, it will be clear that none of the instructions are complex. Except for the memory-referencing instructions, they are all executed in one cycle. Because of this, instructions such as multiply and divide are not supported; they have to be simulated by a series of add-shift and subtract-shift instructions, using the condition codes (which consist of the traditional Z, N, C and V bits). Note that, in contrast to the MIPS, RISC II does not have a compare-and-branch instruction; however, this would have been possible using format *b*. The RISC II instructions are as follows.

Data move operations

This class consists of the load and store operations. Only these instructions reference memory. In contrast to some other RISC architectures, such as the MIPS, RISC II supports byte, half-word and word load/store operations. The result of a load instruction is always a 32-bit integer; in the case of a byte or half-word load operation this value may be loaded unsigned (high-order bits of the destination register will be cleared) or sign extended.

Load instructions use formats *a*, *b* and *c* of Figure 15.2. Format *c* is used to specify a PC-relative operand. Store instructions use formats *b* and *c*. Format *a* is not allowed because this would involve reading three registers (Rd, Rs and Rs2) in the operand fetch stage of the pipeline, and the register file only supports the reading of two registers simultaneously. Note that this is one of the implementation limitations visible at the architectural level.

Format transformation operations

These are performed by the SLL, SRL and SRA instructions. They use formats *a* and *b*, thereby allowing for the shift count to be computable as well as being specified as an immediate value. Here, RISC II deviates from the minimal RISC concept, because a barrel shifter (which allows a shift over any number of bit positions in a single cycle) is required. This requires much hardware. A more minimal approach would allow shifting only over a few places (one and two typically).

Fixed-point arithmetic operations

These are performed by the ADD and SUB instructions, using formats *a* and *b*. The 'with carry' versions have been included to support extended-precision arithmetic.

The arithmetic, as well as the logic, instructions operate on three operands (Rd := (Rs) + S2) so that one of the source operands is not destroyed. The reverse subtract instructions allow the two source operands to be exchanged. Several 'common' instructions are not present, but they can be easily synthesized with other instructions, as illustrated in Table 15.13.

Logical operations

The traditional AND, OR and XOR instructions are provided, using formats *a* and *b*.

Conditional operations

The condition is specified by the four low-order bits of the destination field (Figure 15.2(d)). The JMPR (Jump Relative) instruction uses format *c* and allows for PC-relative jumps; the JMP instruction uses formats *a* and *b* to support, for example, the CASE statement.

Subroutine call/return

The subroutine call instructions CALL and CALLR use formats *a*, *b* and *c*, similar to the jump instructions. The return address is stored in Rd. As

Table 15.12 RISC II instruction set.

Instruction	Operands	Operation	Description
LDXW	(Rs)S2, Rd	Rd := (M[(Rs) + S2])	Load word
LDXHU	(Rs)S2, Rd	Rd := (M[(Rs) + S2])	Load half-word unsigned
LDXHS	(Rs)S2, Rd	Rd := (M[(Rs) + S2])	Load half-word signed
LDXBU	(Rs)S2, Rd	Rd := (M[(Rs) + S2])	Load half-word unsigned
LDXBS	(Rs)S2, Rd	Rd := (M[(Rs) + S2])	Load half-word signed
STXW	Rd, (Rs) S2	M[(Rs) + S2] := Rd	Store word
STXH	Rd, (Rs) S2	M[(Rs) + S2] := Rd	Store half-word
STXB	Rd, (Rs) S2	M[(Rs) + S2] := Rd	Store byte
LDRW	S2, Rd	Rd := (M[(PC) + S2])	Load word relative
LDRHU	S2, Rd	Rd := (M[(PC) + S2])	Load half-word unsigned relative
LDRHS	S2, Rd	Rd := (M[(PC) + S2])	Load half-word signed relative
LDRBU	S2, Rd	Rd := (M[(PC) + S2])	Load half-byte unsigned relative
LDRBS	S2, Rd	Rd := (M[(PC) + S2])	Load half-byte signed relative
STRW	Rd, S2	M[(PC) + S2] := Rd	Store word relative
STRH	Rd, S2	M[(PC) + S2] := Rd	Store half-word relative
STRB	Rd, S2	M[(PC) + S2] := Rd	Store byte relative
SLL	Rs, S2, Rd	Rd := (Rs) shifted by S2	Shift left logical
SRL	Rs, S2, Rd	Rd := (Rs) shifted by S2	Shift right logical
SRA	Rs, S2, Rd	Rd := (Rs) shifted by S2	Shift right arithmetic
ADD	Rs, S2, Rd	Rd := (Rs) + S2	Integer add
ADDC	Rs, S2, Rd	Rd := (Rs) + S2 + carry	Add with carry
SUB	Rs, S2, Rd	Rd := (Rs) − S2	Integer subtract

Instruction	Operands	Operation	Description
SUBC	Rs, S2, Rd	Rd := (Rs) − S2 − borrow	Subtract with borrow
SUBR	Rs, S2, Rd	Rd := S2 − (Rs)	Reverse integer subtract
SUBRC	Rs, S2, Rd	Rd := S2 − (Rs) − borrow	Reverse subtract with borrow
AND	Rs, S2, Rd	Rd := (Rs) AND S2	Bit-wise AND
OR	Rs, S2, Rd	Rd := (Rs) OR S2	Bit-wise OR
XOR	Rs, S2, Rd	Rd := (Rs) XOR S2	Bit-wise EOR
JMP	COND, (Rs) S2	PC := (Rs) + S2	Conditional jump
JMPR	COND, S2	PC := (PC) + Y	Conditional relative jump
CALL	Rd, (Rs) S2	Rd := (PC) + 4	Call indexed
		PC := (Rs) + S2; CWP := (CWP) − 1	and change window
CALLR	Rd, Y	Rd := (PC) + 4	Call relative
		PC := (PC) + Y; CWP := (CWP) − 1	and change window
RET	Rd, S2	PC := (Rd) + S2; CWP := (CWP) + 1	Return and change window
CALLI	Rd	Rd := (PC); CWP := (CWP) − 1	Call an interrupt
RETI	Rd, S2	PC := (Rd) + S2; CWP := (CWP) + 1	Return from interrupt
LDHI	Rd, Y	Rd[31 : 13] := Y; Rd[12 : 0] := 0	Load immediate high
GTLPC	Rd	Rd := (PC)	Save PC for restarting the pipeline
GETPSW	Rd	Rd := (PSW)	Load status word
PUTPSW	Rd	PSW := (Rd)	Set status word

S2 may be: the contents of the register Rs2 in Figure 15.2(a); the value of the immediate field of Figure 15.2(b); or only a displacement, in the case of a store instruction. Y is the value of the immediate field of Figure 15.2(c). In the case of store instructions, S2 may only specify an immediate value.

Table 15.13 Synthesis of frequently occurring instructions.

Instruction		RISC II Equivalent		Operation	Description
MOVE	Rs, Rd	ADD	Rs, R0, Rd	Rd := (Rs) + 0	Register move
CLR	Rd	ADD	R0, R0, Rd	Rd := 0 + 0	Clear register
NOP		ADD	R0, R0, R0	R0 := 0 + 0	No operation
CMP	Rs, S2	SUB	Rs, S2, R0, {cc}	R0 := (Rs) − S2	Compare registers
TST	Rs	SUB	Rs, R0, R0, {cc}	R0 := (Rs) − 0	Test register

a side effect of the call, the register window is moved one position down by subtracting one from the CWP (Current Window Pointer) register.

The return instruction uses formats *a* and *b*, and moves the register window one position up again.

Interrupt handling instructions

CALLI and RETI are special instructions to call and return from an interrupt service routine.

Special instructions

LDHI allows the high-order part of a register to be loaded with an immediate value.

GETLPC allows access to the internal state of the processor for handling traps. It is used as the first instruction of every interrupt handler to save the address of the interrupted instruction.

The GETPSW and PUTPSW instructions allow the PSW to be accessed.

The instructions CALLI, RETI, GETLPC and PUTPSW are privileged and may only be executed in supervisor mode.

SUMMARY

- The development of complex instruction set computers (CISCs) was motivated by the desire to have a low memory bandwidth (because memory was slow and expensive), and the desire to offer high-level (complex) instructions to a compiler to reduce the semantic gap and facilitate compilation.
- The development of reduced instruction set computers (RISCs) was motivated by the idea that an architecture should provide low-level primitive operations to a compiler. The compiler can perform more complex operations by combining primitive operations.
- Primitive operations can be designed so that they can be executed in a single cycle, with a short cycle time.
- Because of the low number of simple operations, the control section of the processor can be hard-wired, rather than microprogrammed.
- Many implementation problems, such as pipeline dependencies, are solved by CISC architectures at the implementation level, and are transparent to the architecture, at the expense of hardware complexity and often also execution speed.
- RISC designs make pipeline dependencies visible at the architectural level, which simplifies the implementation. At the same time, the data dependency and branch delay problems may be solved without incurring extra delays.
- Program execution statistics have shown that: the most frequently performed operations are simple; only a few addressing modes are used frequently; small constants occur frequently; and only a few data types are required.
- Reg-reg instructions can be executed very fast.
- A large number of registers makes it more likely that data dependencies and branch delay problems can be solved by re-arranging the instruction sequence (by the compiler), without using NOP instructions.
- The number of procedure parameters and scalars declared in a procedure is such that they often can be contained in the register set of a RISC computer.
- RISC programs tend to require 10% to 20% more program memory due to the use of less powerful instructions.
- Compilers can generate code more easily, and also more efficient code, for RISC-type instruction sets.
- Because of their simplicity, RISC microprocessors can be implemented in a shorter time, and require less silicon area than their CISC counterparts.

EXERCISES

15.1 What was the main motivation behind CISC architectures?

15.2 What are the main ideas behind RISC architectures?

15.3 Is a large number of integer data types very important?

15.4 Why do many RISC architectures have three-address instructions – for example, of the form ADD Rs1, Rs2, Rd?

15.5 The register set of many RISC architectures is such that an instruction can access any of 32 registers, as compared with 8 or 16 registers of many CICS architectures. What is the motivation behind this?

15.6 Consider a RISC architecture that supports the compare-and-branch instruction. This eliminates the requirement for the Z and N condition code bits. Describe an instruction, which can be executed in one cycle, and with which a 32-bit multiply operation can be synthesized.

15.7 Which functions are performed by the RISC II window concept?

15.8 Can the value of a by-reference parameter be located in a register, using the window concept?

15.9 What problem is encountered when accessing a non-local variable, which is also not global, when this variable is stored in a local register and the window concept is used?

15.10 What is the usefulness of the SCC (Set Condition Codes) bit of the RISC II?

15.11 Show how the NOT function (the logical complement) of a value in register Rd can be computed using the RISC II instruction set.

References

Chaitin, G. J. (1982). Register allocation and spilling via graph coloring. *SIGPLAN Notices*, **17**(6), 98–105.

Chow, F. C. and Hennessy, J. L. (1984). Register allocation by priority-based coloring. *SIGPLAN Notices*, **19**(6), 222–32.

Colwell, R. P. *et al.* (1985). Computers, complexity and controversy. *Computer*, **18**(9), 8–19.

Flynn, M. J. *et al.* (1987). And now a case for more complex instruction sets. *Computer*, **20**(9), 71–83.

Gimarc, C. E. and Milutinovic, V. M. (1987). A survey of RISC processors and computers of the mid-1980s. *Computer*, **20**(9), 59–69.

Heath, J. L. (1984). Re-evaluation of the RISC I. *Computer Architecture News*, **12**(1), 3–10.

Hennessy, J. *et al.* (1982). Hardware/software tradeoffs for increased performance. In *Proc. of the Symposium on Architectural Support for Programming Languages and Operating Systems*, pp. 2–11.

Hennessy, J. L. (1984). VLSI processor architecture. *IEEE Trans. on Computers*, **C–33**(12), 1221–46.

Hitchcock, C. Y, and Sprunt, H. M. B. (1985). Analyzing multiple register sets. In *Proc. 12th Annual Symposium on Computer Architecture*, pp. 55–63.

Huguet, M. and Lang, T. (1985). A reduced register file for RISC architectures. *Computer Architecture News*, **13**(4), 22–31.

Johnson, S. C. (1978). A portable compiler: Theory and practice. In *Proc. 5th Annual Symposium on Computer Architecture*, pp. 97–104.

Katevenis, M. G. H. (1985). *Reduced Instruction Set Computer Architectures for VLSI*. MIT Press: Cambridge, MA.

Lunde, A. (1977). Empirical evaluation of some features of instruction set processor architectures. *Comm. of the ACM*, **20**(3), 143–53.

MacGregor, D. and Rubinstein, J. (1985). A performance analysis of MC68020-based systems. *IEEE Micro*, **5**(6), 50–70.

McFarling, S. and Hennessy, J. (1986). Reducing the cost of branches. In *Proc. 13th Annual Symposium on Computer Architecture*, pp. 396–403.

Patterson, D. A. and Ditzel, D. R. (1980). The case for the reduced instruction set computer. *Computer Architecture News*, **8**(6), 25–33.

Patterson, D. A. and Sequin, C. H. (1982). A VLSI RISC. *Computer*, **15**(9), 8–21.

Patterson, D. A. and Piepho, R. S. (1982a). Assessing RISCs in high-level language support. *IEEE Micro*, **2**(4), 9–18.

Patterson, D. A. (1985). Reduced instruction set computers. *Comm. of the ACM*, **28**(1), 8–21.

Radin, G. (1983). The 801 minicomputer. *IBM Journal of Research and Development*, **27**(3), 237–46.

Tamir, Y. and Sequin, C. H. (1983). Strategies for managing the register file in RISC. *IEEE Trans. on Computers*, **C–32**(11), 977–88.

Tanenbaum, A. S. (1978). Implications of structured programming for machine architecture. *Comm. of the ACM*, **21**(3), 237–46.

Wulf, W. A. (1981). Compilers and computer architecture. *Computer*, **14**(7), 41–7.

16 Multiprocessor Systems

The best way to learn to be modest is by correcting a book which is shortly going to be published.
– Paul Leautaud

With the rapid advances in technology, it is now possible to build systems consisting of many processors. These systems may be classified according to how they are used. When the processors are used to obtain acceleration at the program level, where each processor executes its own independent thread (program), one speaks about multiple-thread systems. They are designed to improve the overall system throughput, rather than the overall execution time of a single program. When the overall execution time of a single program (a single thread) has to be improved, that program has to be divided into co-operating tasks (processes). Several such tasks may be executed in parallel due to the availability of a number of processors. Such systems are known as multitasking or multithreading systems.

This chapter opens by describing the types of multiprocessor systems, according to the way they are constructed, and lists the characteristics of interconnection networks used to connect the processors of multiprocessing systems. The following two sections describe the interconnection networks typical for multicomputer and multiprocessor systems. The last two sections deal with the description of the data coherence (data consistency) problem and its solutions.

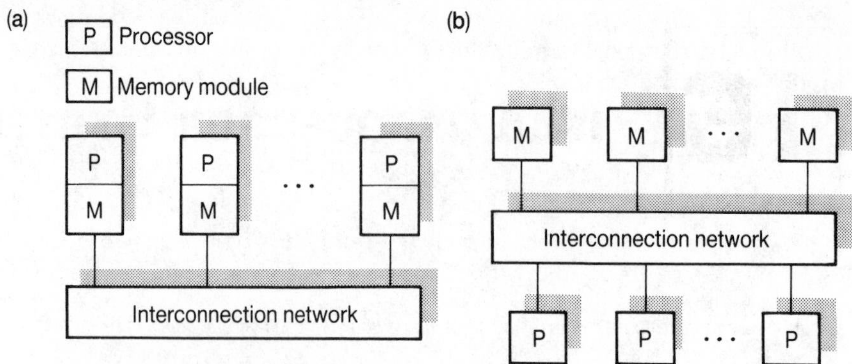

FIGURE 16.1

System types: (a) multicomputer system, loosely coupled; (b) multiprocessor system, tightly coupled.

16.1 Types of multiprocessor systems and interconnection network characteristics

When a large number of processors are connected to form a single system, the processors may spend a considerable portion of their time communicating among themselves. This will be more so for multithreading than for multiple-thread systems. The processors are connected via an **interconnection network (IN)**, which may be generally implemented at two levels in a computer system (Figure 16.1):

(1) At the system level: Processors have their own memory and the IN is only used for interprocessor communication. These systems are called **multicomputer systems**.

(2) At the processor–memory interface level: The processors share a common memory, which may consist of several modules. The IN is used for processor–memory traffic which requires a high communication bandwidth. Such systems are called **multiprocessor systems**.

(Note that the commonly used term 'multiprocessor system' has been used as the title of this chapter to denote both multicomputer and multiprocessor systems. From here on, these two names will be used distinctively.)

As already stated, the main purpose of most systems is to produce an increase in system performance. However, multiple processors are sometimes used because of reliability rather than performance reasons, but this subject will not be discussed in this text.

Multicomputer and multiprocessor systems can at best achieve an increase in system performance that is linearly related to the number of processors. This means that N processors can at best execute a single program N times as fast as a uniprocessor system. When a system is operating at this peak rate, all processors are contributing towards the execution of that program; no processor is executing instructions that would not have been executed if that program was executed on a uniprocessor system. However, several factors inhibit multicomputer and multiprocessor systems from operating at this peak rate:

- Synchronization: The activities of the independently executing processors must be occasionally co-ordinated. This may cause some processors to be idle while others continue to execute to catch up with these processors.
- Contention: As several processors may compete for some shared resource, contention will cause some processors to wait while a competing request is being completed; for example, delays are often introduced by the IN due to contention and routing time.
- Algorithms: Not every algorithm is suited to be executed efficiently on a multicomputer or multiprocessor system. In some algorithms, there is not enough parallelism to keep all processors busy, while sometimes a parallel algorithm may need more steps than a serial one, causing extra overhead.

16.1.1 Multicomputer systems

Multicomputer systems consist of several autonomous computers which may be geographically dispersed; therefore, they are sometimes also referred to as **loosely coupled systems**. These computers communicate according to a strict communication protocol and interface, often using (high-speed) serial lines. A well-known example of a multicomputer system is the Advanced Research Project Agency Network (ARPANET), which connects over 50 major computing centres in the United States (McQuillan, 1977).

Each processor in a multicomputer system has its own set of I/O devices and local memory (Figure 16.1(a)). These systems are well suited for problems that exhibit *coarse-grain* parallelism; that is, programs are split into relatively independent tasks that are executed without too much communication.

A processor, together with its memory and I/O devices, is called a **computer module** or **node**. Communication between nodes is done by exchanging messages via some IN. Multicomputer systems are efficient when the interaction between tasks, executing in different nodes, is low. If the interaction becomes too high, a performance loss arises, because the computer modules must spend too much time communicating with each other via an IN that may not be optimally suited for a heavy inter-node traffic.

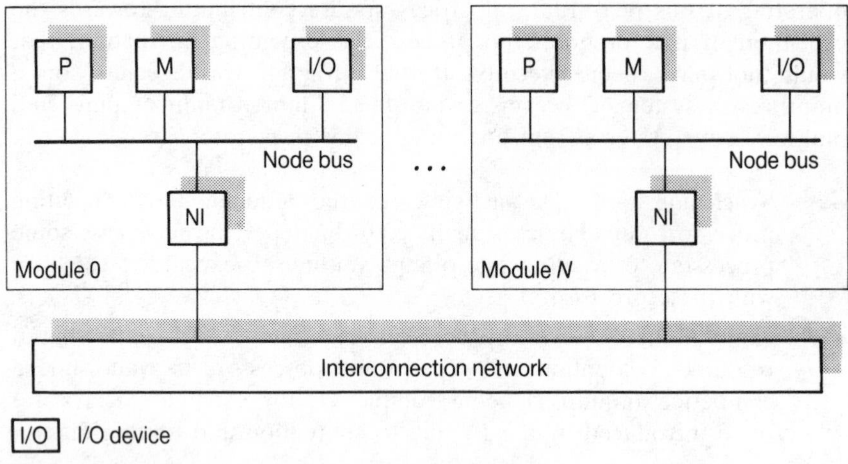

FIGURE 16.2

Multicomputer system.

A single node consists of a processor, local memory, a node interface and possibly local I/O devices connected via a (local) node bus (Figure 16.2). With the present VLSI technology, an entire node can often be implemented on a single chip, connected via the IN. Of course, it is possible to repeat the process of connecting nodes on a higher level, thereby creating a hierarchically structured multicomputer system.

16.1.2 Multiprocessor systems

The processors in a multiprocessor system are usually used to execute a single task together. To accomplish this, multiprocessor systems usually have a *common* memory for all processors with a single, *system-wide* address space available to all processors. Because of the intimate connection, these systems are also called **tightly coupled systems**. The processors may be used to execute a single program (a **multitasking** system) or several programs simultaneously (a **multithreading** system). For *fine-grain* parallelism, the degree of interaction between processors is too high for a multicomputer system, so multiprocessor systems may be used.

Figure 16.3 shows a general model of a multiprocessor system. Such a system contains p processors (P_1 through P_p), which are connected to a shared memory via a **processor memory interconnection network (PMIN)**. The processors can communicate via this shared memory and, in addition, often via a **processor-to-processor interconnection network (PPIN)**. Furthermore, the processors are connected to the I/O devices via another network: the **processor I/O interconnection network (PIOIN)**.

It may happen that two (or more) processors issue a request to the same memory module, resulting in a conflict at that module. This contention must be resolved by the PMIN. The number of conflicts can

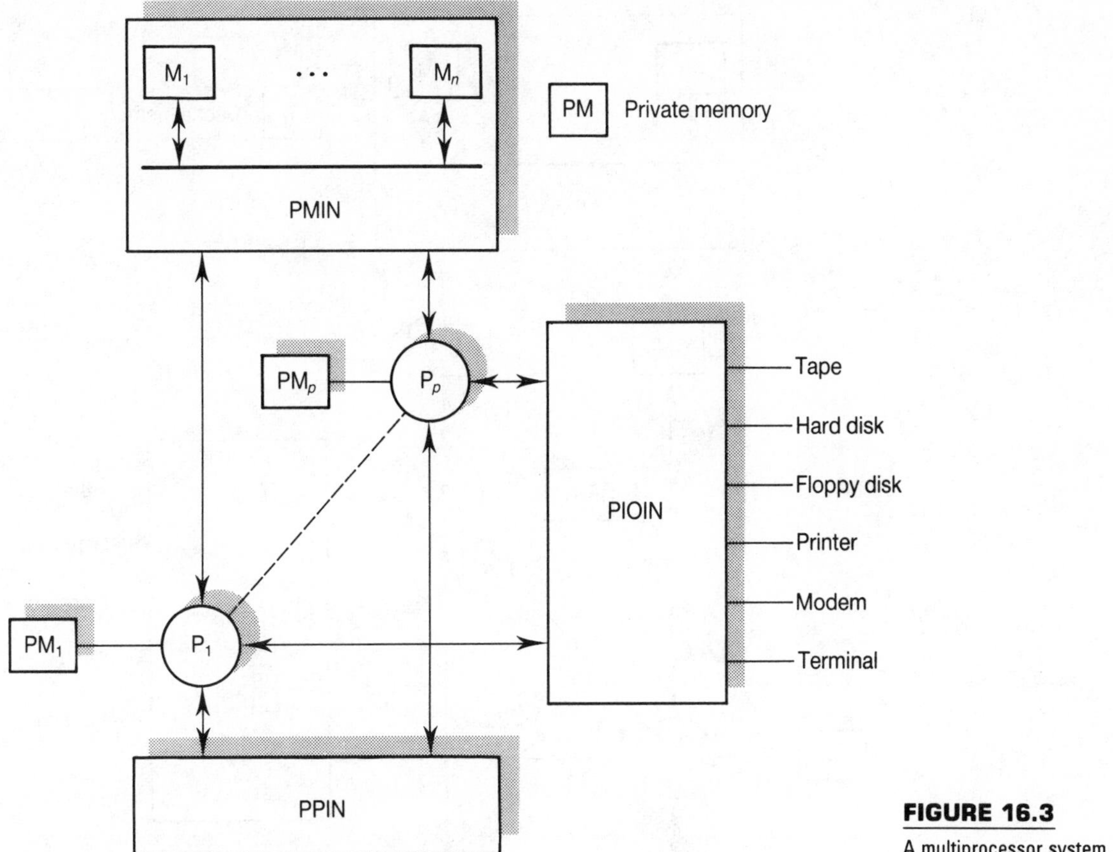

FIGURE 16.3

A multiprocessor system.

be reduced by providing every processor with some private memory. This memory may be used for storing operating system code that is used frequently, or saving the state of a blocked or interrupted process. Note, however, that processors cannot access the private memories of other processors efficiently, so processes that are blocked (and whose state is saved in a private memory) cannot be transferred to other processors without increased overhead. Despite the use of private memory, memory contention still arises, since processors always reference main memory, and these references encounter delays, either due to contention for memory modules or due to the switching time of the PMIN. Eventually, given enough processors, these delays cause a considerable decrease in system throughput. A solution to this problem may be the placement of a cache memory between each processor and the PMIN (Figure 16.4) to reduce the number of references to main memory (and thus alleviating the contention for the memory modules). Unfortunately, this solution also has its disadvantages because multiple copies of data can exist; there can be inconsistency between these copies if the data in one cache is

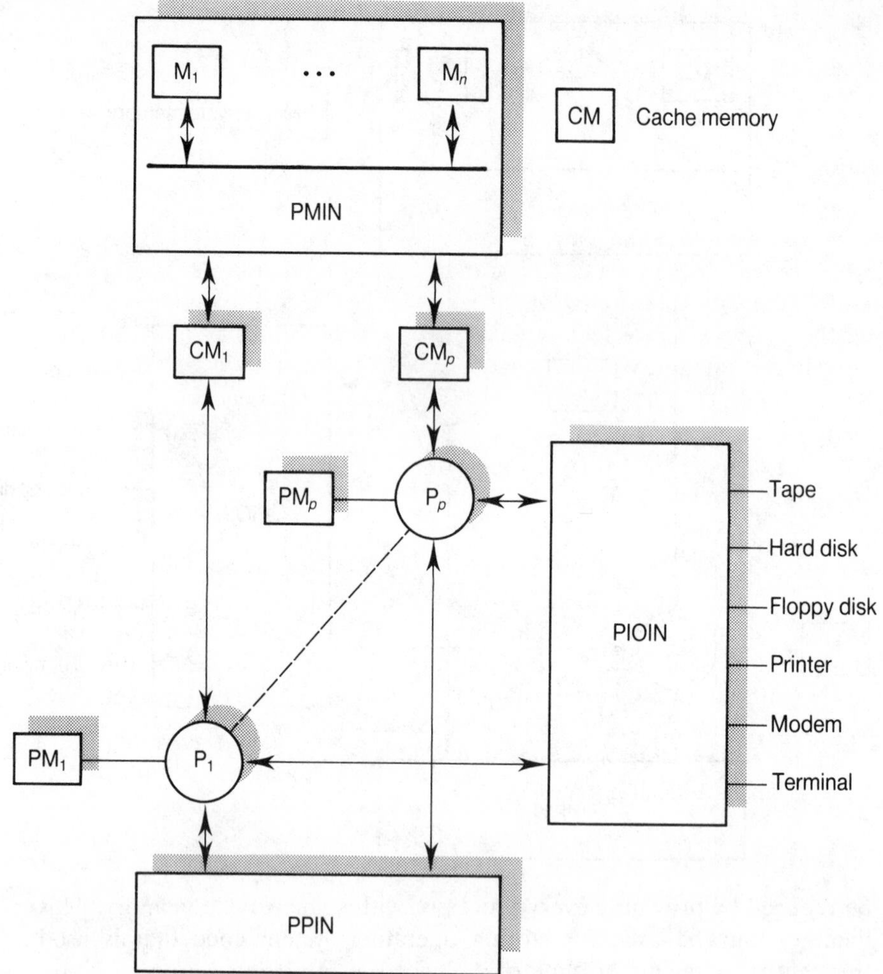

FIGURE 16.4

A multiprocessor system with cache memories.

modified without invalidating or updating the copies of this data in other caches and main memory. The data is then said to be incoherent (see Sections 16.4 and 16.5).

In Figures 16.3 and 16.4, the peripherals are connected to the processors via the PIOIN. To simplify the system, all peripherals may be connected to a single processor (which will be the I/O processor of the system), or to a few of the processors.

The PPIN is usually used for sending interrupts from one processor to another, for process synchronization purposes. This interrupt mechanism may also be implemented in a memory-mapped way (see Section 13.4), using PMIN, thus saving the PPIN.

It is clear from the foregoing that multiprocessor systems may be implemented using a single IN – namely, the PMIN.

16.1.3 Interconnection network characteristics

Generally, an IN has four distinguishing characteristics (Feng, 1981; Bhuyan, 1987).

Timing

Timing may be *synchronous* or *asynchronous*. Synchronous systems are used, for example, in an array processor to broadcast data to all processor nodes, or to cause all nodes to communicate with one of their neighbours simultaneously. A central global clock is used, causing communication in the IN to operate in a lock-step fashion. Asynchronous systems, on the other hand, operate without a global clock and can be used in systems where requests for connections are issued independently by the processors.

Switching method

The switching method used in an IN can be *circuit* switching or *packet* switching. In circuit switching, a physical path for the connection between the source and destination node is established, and this path is maintained for the duration of the data transfer. With packet switching, the information is split into packets and these are sent individually through the IN, without actually establishing a physical path (different packets can be routed along different paths). Normally, packet switching is more suited for many short messages while circuit switching better accommodates fewer but larger messages.

Control strategy

The control strategy of an IN can be based on *centralized* or *distributed* control. With centralized control, a global controller receives all communication requests and grants the IN by setting the switches of the IN. With distributed control, the handling of communication requests and the setting of the switches is handled by the IN itself in a distributed manner (see Section 13.3.3).

Topology

The topology determines which source nodes are connected to which destination nodes. It can be represented by a graph in which the nodes represent the switching points and the edges represent the communication links. Only regular topologies, which are easier for message-routing algorithms to deal with, will be considered in this text. These topologies can be classified as either *static* or *dynamic*. A static topology has dedicated links between the nodes, and these links cannot be reconfigured. In a dynamic topology, these links can be reconfigured by setting the switches of the network.

16.2 Multicomputer interconnection networks

Several structures for INs for multicomputer systems have been suggested (Feng, 1981). These networks usually have a static topology, adopt asynchronous timing, use packet switching and are based on a distributed control mechanism. Dedicated links exist between nodes and a message, generated by a source, may be divided into a number of smaller parts, or packets. Each packet is transferred over several links to reach its destination. Different packets may take different routes. Usually, the intermediate nodes store such a packet and route it to the next node, according to some routing algorithm. A message is divided into packets to reduce the memory requirements of the intermediate nodes for storing the packets, and to limit the time during which a link is busy.

To characterize a network with a static topology, two criteria are usually distinguished: the *degree* of a node and the *diameter* of the network. The degree of a node is the number of links connected to that node. It reflects the cost associated with the network. The diameter of a network is defined as the maximum number of links a message has to pass from any source to reach any destination node, along the shortest path. It places a lower bound on the delay required to propagate information through the network. Clearly, a low diameter (thus a short communication delay) requires a high degree for every node, which increases the cost. The research goal for multicomputer INs is to design a system where the performance of the algorithm is balanced against the network topology, in terms of its degree and diameter.

Figure 16.5 shows some static IN topologies. The classification used here is based on the number of dimensions required to draw them such that links do not intersect. Figure 16.5(a) shows a one-dimensional topology, the linear array. It is the simplest topology and may be useful for pipelined systems. Figures 16.5(b), (c) and (d) show two-dimensional topologies. By closing the linear array of Figure 16.5(a) to form a ring, the diameter is reduced from $(N - 1)$ to $(N/2)$ truncated (integer value obtained by truncating the result – that is, deleting the fraction part), while the degree remains two. The tree topology of Figure 16.5(c) is a regular topology, but is *asymmetric*. In a *symmetric* topology, all nodes possess the same view of the network. All topologies of Figure 16.5, except for the tree, are symmetric. Such topologies have the advantage that the load on the links and nodes, due to inter-node message traffic, is likely to be more evenly distributed; for example, in a tree topology, the root nodes, and the links to the root node, are more likely to exhibit a larger load and become the performance bottleneck of the system. Figures 16.5(e) and (f) show three-dimensional topologies. The fully

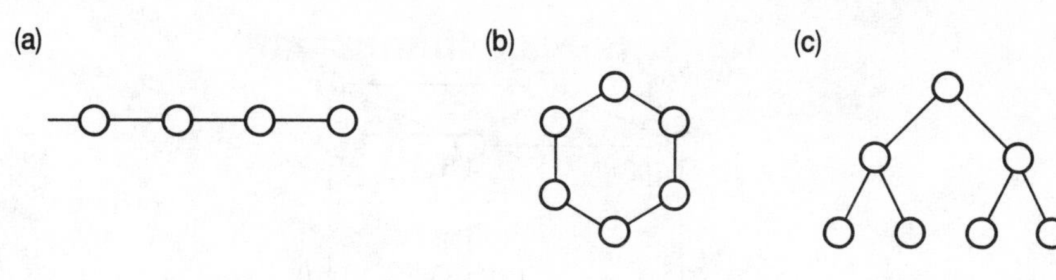

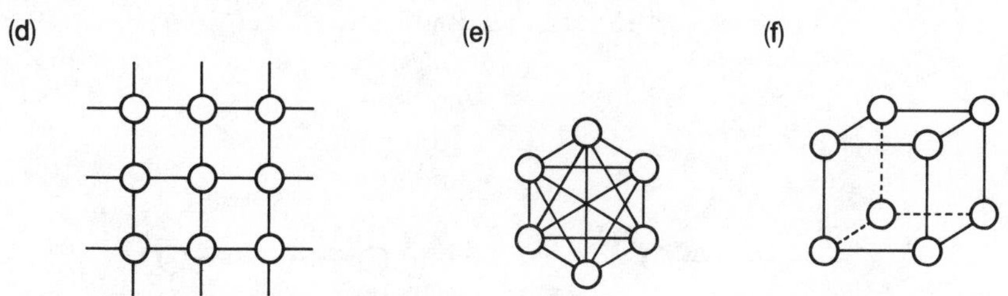

FIGURE 16.5

Some static multicomputer IN topologies: (a) linear array; (b) ring; (c) tree; (d) mesh; (e) fully connected; (f) 3-cube.

connected network is the most complex, with each node being connected to each other node. It has a diameter of one, but at the cost of degree $(N - 1)$.

An interesting topology is the Boolean n-cube or *hypercube* network (Figures 16.6(a) and (b)). A hypercube network is an n-dimensional network with $N = 2^n$ nodes. The diameter of an n-cube is n, as is the degree; this is a reasonable compromise between the linear and fully connected topologies. However, this degree may become cost prohibitive for larger values of N.

An interesting characteristic is that when the nodes are numbered with binary addresses, adjacent node numbers differ in only a single bit. Further, the distance between two nodes is equal to the number of bits by which both binary node representations differ. As an example, consider the 3-cube of Figure 16.6(a). Node 000 is connected to nodes 001, 010 and 100; that is, to those nodes that have an address that differs by one bit. Routing a message is simple, as a message is passed over a link for which a bit in the destination differs from the current node. For example, a message that resides in node 001 and whose destination is 111, can be routed first to node 101 (negating the first bit) or to node 011 (negating the second bit). It will not be routed to 000, as the third bit of the current node is already correct. An advantage of this topology is that n disjunct paths always exist between two nodes, making this topology highly fault tolerant. For example, from node 001 to node 111, which is a distance of two, we have:

001 → 011 → 111
001 → 101 → 111
001 → 000 → 100 → 110 → 111

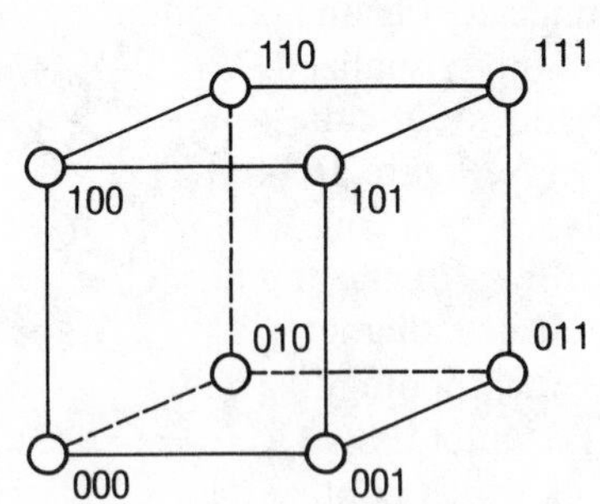

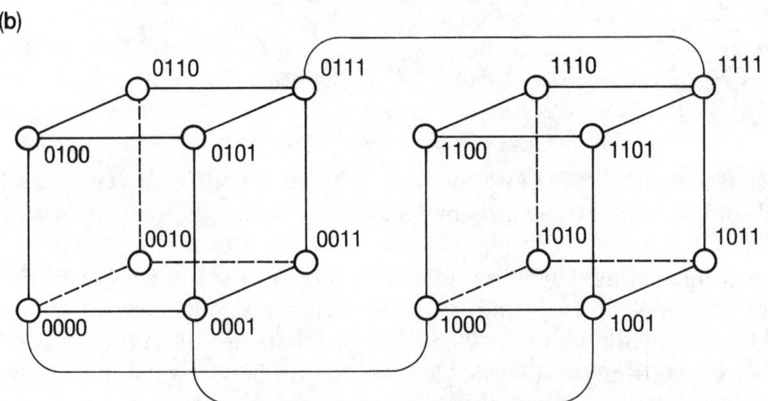

(c)

FIGURE 16.6

Some cube topologies: (a) 3-cube; (b) 4-cube (five links not shown); (c) 3-cube connected cycles.

This example shows that, for nodes with a distance less than n, not all disjunct paths have equal lengths.

It is easy to extend an n-cube to an $(n + 1)$-cube, as shown in Figure 16.6(b). A 4-cube is constructed by linking two 3-cubes via 2^3 links between the corresponding nodes at both 3-cubes. Figure 16.6(b) shows only three of the eight links for simplicity. For example, the nodes 0001 and 1001 are connected (again, only a single bit difference). The other five links can be easily visualized.

A variation on the n-cube topology is the *n-cube connected cycles* topology, as shown in Figure 16.6(c) for $n = 3$. Each of the nodes of the hypercube is replaced by a ring with n nodes, such that all nodes have a degree of 3, regardless of the dimension of the network. This topology has $N = n * 2^n$ nodes, a diameter of n + trunc ($n/2$) and a degree of 3.

The hypercube topology is being used in commercially available systems, such as the Intel iPSC (Rattner, 1985). The iPSC contains up to 128 nodes, each of which contain 512 kbytes of memory (which can be extended to 4.5 Mbytes), an Intel 80286 microprocessor, an Intel 80287 floating-point co-processor and seven Ethernet transceiver chips (one for each of the seven links connected to a node).

Although the hypercube network fits very well with the communication requirements of many algorithms, it has the disadvantage that the degree increases with $\log_2 N$. The limited I/O capabilities of VLSI chips, and the hardware required to provide this I/O capability, make the hypercube topology less attractive for systems with a large number of nodes. Other topologies, such as the tree (Figure 16.5(c)), the mesh (Figure 16.5(d)) and the n-cube connected cycles, can be used, each with their own advantages and disadvantages. Several of these have a fixed degree, independent of the size of the network.

Because of the high latency for message transmission (see Section 13.1.2), the optimization of message traffic, and a tradeoff between the cost of the interconnection and the execution time of the used algorithms, is essential, and is strongly application dependent. An analysis of the performance of static interconnection networks can be found in Reed (1987).

16.3 Multiprocessor interconnection networks

Interconnection networks for multiprocessor systems are usually based on a *dynamic* topology; that is, the connections between the nodes are established on demand, at program execution time. These INs range from a simple time-shared bus to a fully connective cross-bar switch. The complexity and cost of a time-shared bus are the lowest of all INs, being of the order $O(p)$, but its bandwidth is also the lowest. On the other hand, a cross-bar switch has the highest connectivity, at a cost of $O(p^2)$, assuming p processors and p memory modules. Multiple-bus systems and multiport memories (which allow multiple paths to a memory node) present an in-between solution. Another compromise between complexity (cost) and connectivity is found in INs using shuffle exchanges.

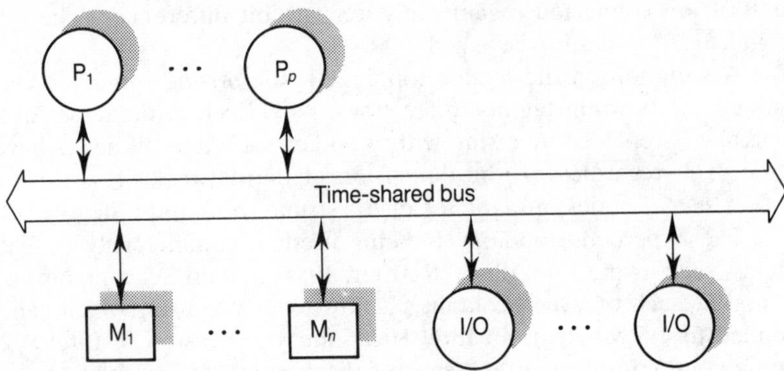

FIGURE 16.7
Time-shared bus IN.

16.3.1 Bus-based interconnection networks

This section discusses the following dynamic topologies: the time-shared bus, the cross-bar switch and the multiport memory.

Time-shared or common bus

The simplest interconnection network is to have all resources connected to one common data path, or bus (Figure 16.7). The bus is the interconnection network with the lowest cost, due to its simplicity, but it has a great disadvantage. System performance is limited by the bus bandwidth. However, this can be improved by equipping each processor with a cache or local memory. In addition, a bus is not fault tolerant, since a bus failure makes all resources inaccessible, resulting in a system crash. A solution to this could be to use more than one bus, as shown in Figure 16.8 (Mudge, 1987). This increases the bus arbitration logic, but allows more processors to access memory or I/O devices simultaneously, providing that processors do not access the same memory module or device. It also makes the network more fault tolerant, as redundant paths exist.

Cross-bar switch

The number of buses can be extended until eventually there is a bus for every memory module. At this limit, the interconnection network (Figure 16.9) is called a **cross-bar switch**, and a complete connectivity exists between all processors and memory modules. A cross-bar switch has great flexibility; however, its size grows with the product of the number of processors and memory modules. If there are p processors and n memory modules, the cross-bar requires $p * n$ switches; thus, if p is about equal to n, the number of cross-points grows as p^2. A cross-bar offers the possibility of simultaneous data transfers for all memory modules. To resolve contention for a memory module, each switch must be equipped

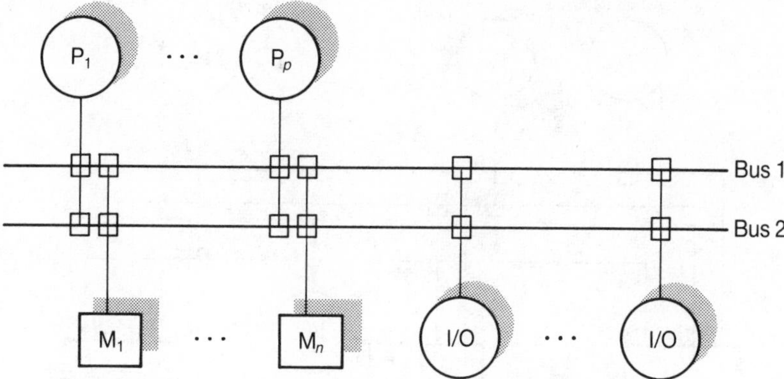

FIGURE 16.8
Multiple bus IN.

with extra hardware, which can become quite large and costly. Furthermore, a switch must be capable of switching as many lines as the width of the transmission path. Therefore, the cost of a cross-bar switch can become the dominant factor for a multiprocessor system, in spite of the fact that VLSI technology can reduce the size of the logic required for the switching function, because the requirement of a large number of I/O pins makes the cross-bar switch incompatible with VLSI packaging practices.

Multiport memory

When the arbitration logic and the switch function of every switch in a cross-bar connected to a single memory module is moved into the memory module, a **multiport memory** system results (Figure 16.10, which shows a p-port memory system). This is a compromise solution between a cross-bar switch and a single bus.

The multiport memory reduces interference between processors, as compared with a single bus system, because a processor only has to wait when accessing a resource used by another processor. In contrast, a

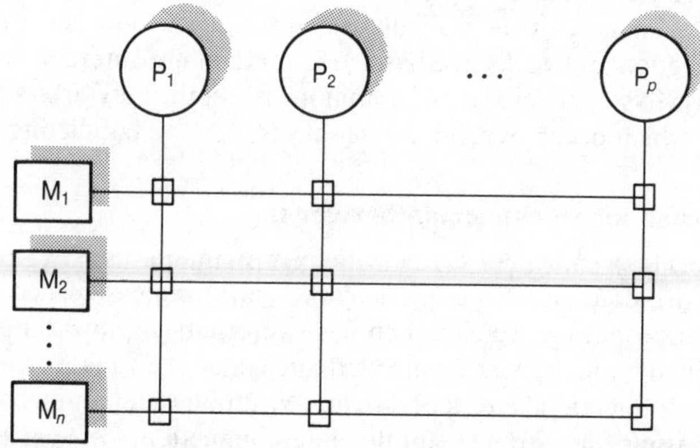

FIGURE 16.9
Cross-bar switch as IN.

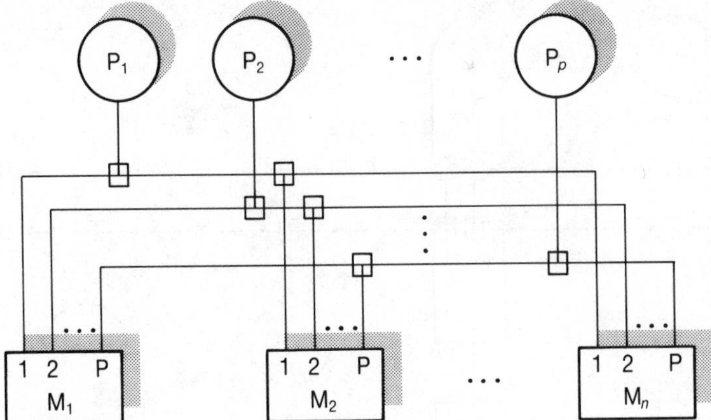

FIGURE 16.10

Multiport memory organization.

processor in a bus system always has to wait when an arbitrary resource is accessed by another processor (because the bus is in use). The cost of a multiport memory system is higher than that of a bus, because each memory resource must have logic to resolve contention and perform the switching function between the memory ports. Due to the cost caused by the high number of lines in the transmission paths, multiport memories are not often used in systems with many processors; most multiport memories only have two or three ports. An example of a multiprocessor system using a multiport memory is the PDP-10 (Model KL-10), which has two processors and up to 16 two-port memory modules (Bell, 1978).

16.3.2 Interconnection networks using shuffle exchanges

These networks can be considered to have N inputs and N outputs, which can be connected to memories and processors. They allow for a dynamic topology because switches are used to connect the inputs with the outputs. These switches are grouped into stages and, depending on the number of stages, it is possible to distinguish between single-stage interconnection networks (SSINs) and multi-stage interconnection networks (MSINs). A problem, common to both networks, is that of blocking, which occurs when a switch has to take on conflicting positions.

Single-stage interconnection networks

Figure 16.11(a) shows an SSIN with $N = 8$ inputs and $N = 8$ outputs. The network consists of a single stage of four switches, which determine the network topology. Each switch has two inputs and two outputs (it is a 2×2 switch), and can be controlled such that it forms a *straight* or an *exchange* connection internally. The N inputs are connected to the switches using a perfect shuffle interconnection. A **perfect shuffle**

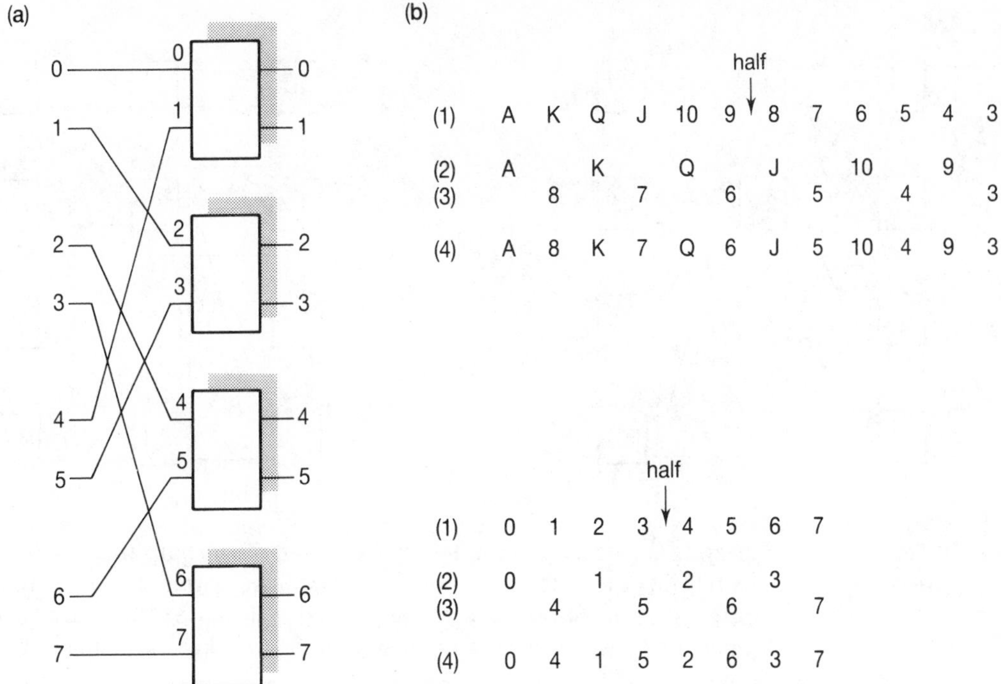

FIGURE 16.11

Shuffle exchange networks: (a) SSIN; (b) perfect shuffle.

interconnection is made as follows. A system with N inputs, labelled I[0] through I[$2^n - 1$], has a single stage of $N/2$ 2×2 switches. The inputs to these switches are labelled consecutively from S[0] through S[$2^n - 1$]. Figure 16.11(a) shows such an SSIN for $n = 3$. A perfect shuffle requires I[x] (input x) to be connected to switch input $2 * x$ modulo $(2^n - 1)$; that is, I[x] is connected to S[$2 * x$ modulo $(2^n - 1)$].

A perfect shuffle can be visualized using a deck of cards (because an even number is required, the sequence Ace through 3 will be used). First, the sequence is put in the normal order (Figure 16.11(b), line 1). This sequence is then divided into two halves, after which the first half is taken and put down, leaving a space between each card (line 2). Thereafter, the second half is put down in the spaces left by the first half (line 3). Line 4 shows the perfect shuffle when both halves are merged. The bottom part of Figure 16.11(b) shows how the perfect shuffle of Figure 16.11(a) is obtained.

SSINs require the outputs to be connected to the inputs with the same number, via a buffer. This is because the transmission of a data item from an arbitrary input to an arbitrary output cannot be done in one cycle through the network. The data item may have to be *recirculated* up to n times. For example, when input 0 wants to send a data item to output 2 (Figure 16.11(a)), two cycles are required: in cycle 1, the data item is sent from input 0 to output 1 by setting the switch in the 'exchange' position;

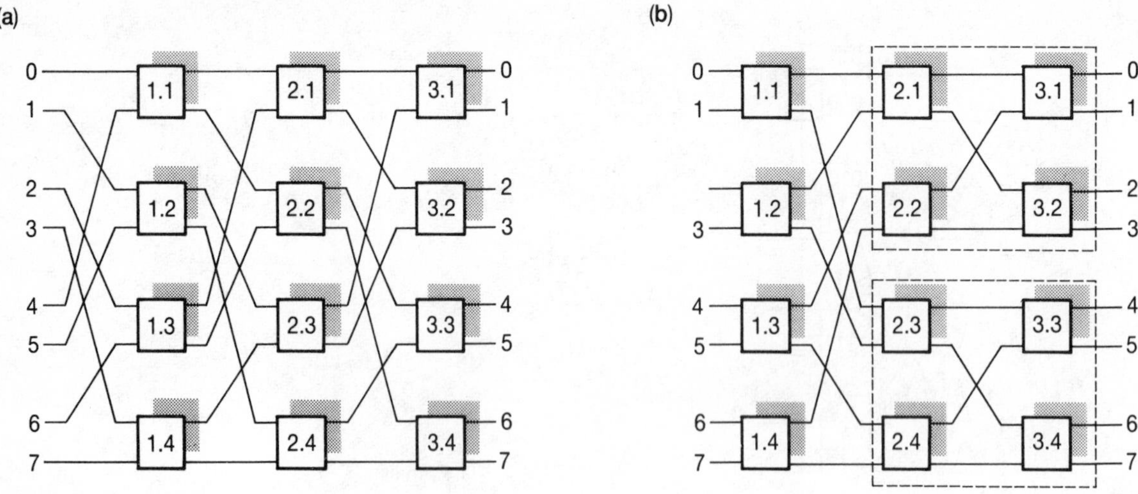

FIGURE 16.12

Multi-stage INs: (a) 8 × 8 Omega network; (b) 8 × 8 baseline network.

in cycle 2, the data item is sent from input 1 to output 2, by setting the switch in the 'straight' position. Because corresponding inputs and outputs of an SSIN have to be interconnected, SSINs are also termed 'one sided', which makes them suitable for packet-switching applications only.

Multi-stage interconnection networks

A class of MSINs, known as **Delta networks** (Patel, 1979), is designed to connect $N = m^n$ inputs to N outputs. They contain n stages of N/m cross-bar switches of size $m \times m$. The switches in adjacent stages are connected such that a path can be found from any input to any output. The discussion here will be restricted to MSINs with n or more stages, and m being a power of 2. Figure 16.12(a) shows an MSIN with $N = 2^3 = 8$ inputs ($m = 2$ and $n = 3$), $N = 8$ outputs, and three stages of $8/2 = 4$ cross-bar switches of size 2×2. This MSIN, which is called an 8×8 **Omega network**, has the property that it can be constructed by concatenating n shuffle exchange stages. The Omega network can be converted into a **baseline network** (Figure 16.12(b)) by relabelling the input lines (that is, deleting the perfect shuffle from the input lines in front of the first stage) and exchanging switches 2.2 and 2.3 (check this for yourself). The baseline network has the advantage that the second and third stages can be divided into two identical subnetworks, with all connections between the switches of each subnetwork internal to that network (see dashed boxes), which is of importance for VLSI implementation.

Of course, switches larger than 2×2 can be used. When 4×4 switches are used, the number of stages in an MSIN is reduced to $\log_4 N$,

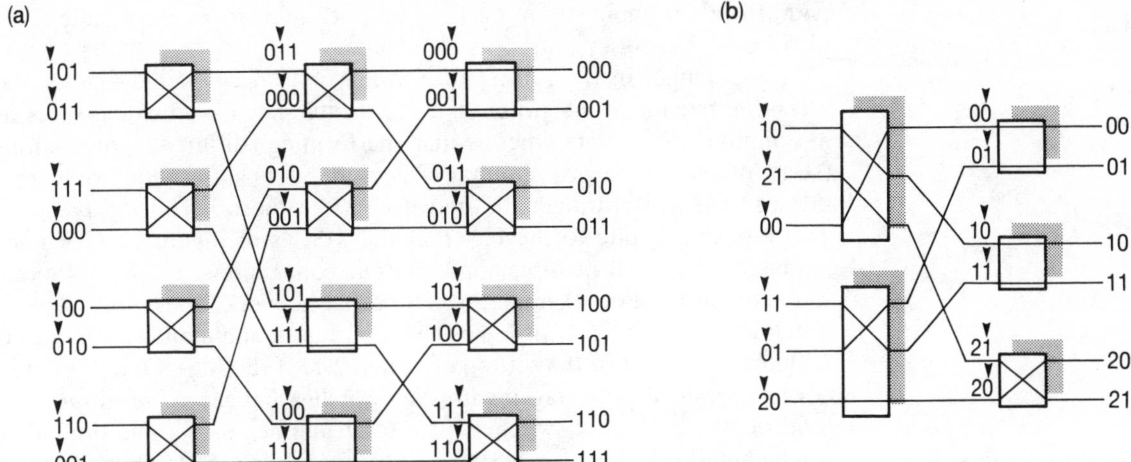

FIGURE 16.13
Illustration of the radix-sort algorithm: (a) IN with radix (2, 2, 2); (b) IN with radix (3, 2).

with $N/4$ switches per stage. Bhuyan (1983) has shown that MSINs with 4×4, instead of 2×2, switches can be more cost effective in larger systems.

MSINs can be designed so that they allow any input to be connected to any output simultaneously, at the expense of a more complex IN and control algorithm. The latter has to determine the setting of the switches such that the desired input–output connections are established. For the multi-stage shuffle exchange networks, a form of the *radix-sort* algorithm (Gear, 1974; Chen, 1981) is utilized. This uses a representation of keys to do the sorting, where the keys, represented in some radix system, indicate the desired setting of the switch. For example, the key 14 (base 10) is represented in the binary radix system (2, 2, 2, 2) as 1110, in the radix system (3, 2, 3) as 202 and in the radix system (3, 3, 3) as 112. The idea of the radix-sort algorithm is to perform sorting *locally*: in each stage of the MSIN, the corresponding digit of the key is taken to determine the setting of the switch. Figure 16.13(a) shows how the first digit of the key is used to determine the setting of switches of the first stage of the MSIN; note that a 0 on the upper input and a 1 on the lower input of the switch means a straight switch setting, while the reverse indicates an exchange switch setting. The second digit of the key is used to determine the setting of the switches of the second stage, and so on. Figure 16.13(b) shows the algorithm applied using an IN with radix system (3, 2), which requires 3×3 switches in the first and 2×2 switches in the second stage.

The advantage of MSINs with $\log_2 N$ stages (the MSIN of Figure 16.12(a) has $3 = \log_2 8$ stages) is that a unique path exists from any input to any output. This can be exploited for routing control. When the message to be routed is preceded by a tag, specifying the key of the output, this is called tag routing. Tag routing will automatically set up a path from an input to a desired output, and so is well suited for distributed control systems.

A conflict in the setting of a switch may occur if the tags of the messages arriving at the switch (a 2×2 switch may have two messages at its inputs) necessitate the switch performing different connections (straight and exchange) simultaneously. In such a situation, only one message can pass through the network, while the other(s) are *blocked*. This blocking is due to the fact that the MSINs of Figure 16.12 cannot always establish all possible input–output connections, or permutations simultaneously. For example, the Omega network does not allow a simultaneous connection of input 0 with output 0, and input 4 with output 2, due to a conflict in the setting of switch 2.1. If the MSIN has N inputs, it will contain $\log_2 N$ stages with $N/2$ switches per stage, resulting in a total of $(N/2) * \log_2 N$ switches. The total number of permutations that can be handled by such an MSIN is $2^{((N/2)*\log_2 N)} = (\sqrt{N})^N$, while the total number of potential permutations is $N!$ (N factorial). This means that, for the 8×8 INs of Figure 16.12, only $(\sqrt{8})^8/8! = 4096/40320 = 0.1016$ (about 10%) of all permutations are realizable; all others will cause blocking, resulting in a loss of system performance.

MSINs have several properties, however, which make them of interest for multiprocessor systems: $O(N \log_2 N)$ hardware cost in terms of gate count and $N^2/\log_2 N$ in terms of VLSI chip area (Kleitman, 1981) as compared with $O(N^2)$ for cross-bar switches; $O(\log_2 N)$ path length; and the ability to allow for up to N simultaneous connections. In addition, MSINs can be based on either the circuit-switching or the packet-switching method.

Solutions to the blocking problem

The blocking problem, as just described, is caused by the fact that, for a given input–output pair, only a single path is available in the Omega and baseline network. Several solutions are available for eliminating the possibility of blocks or to reduce the performance loss (Chen, 1981).

Queues allow the performance loss due to blocking to be reduced. The basic idea is that when a conflict arises at a switch, one of the messages is queued at the input of that switch. The advantage of such a queue is that the message can pass through several stages of the MSIN, until it reaches the stage containing the blocking switch, so that the message delay through that part of the network does not have to be re-incurred. This obviously requires packet switching, rather than circuit switching to be used.

A way to solve the blocking problem by elimination is to redesign the MSIN, forming a different type of network, called the **Benes network**. Figure 16.14 shows an 8×8 Benes network, which can be constructed from the 8×8 baseline network by mirroring the baseline network

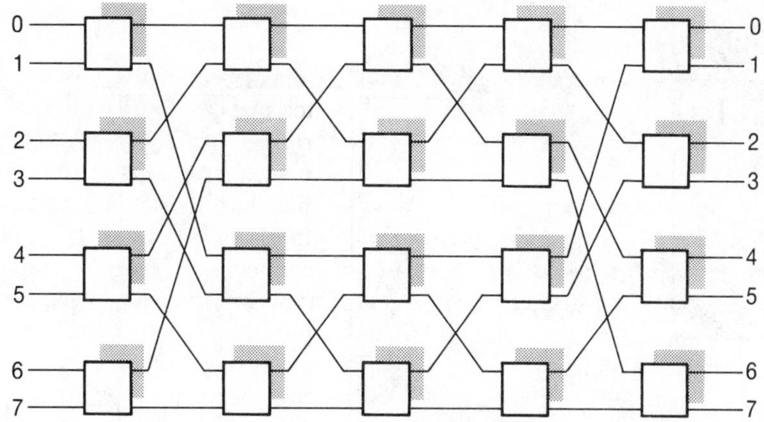

FIGURE 16.14

An 8 × 8 Benes network.

around its last stage. It consists, therefore, of $2 * n - 1$ stages. The 8×8 network allows $2^{4*5} = 2^{20}$ permutations, while only 8! are required; this gives a redundancy in switching paths of $2^{20}/8! = 26$.

From the construction of the Benes network, it can be concluded that two passes through the baseline network result in the same number of possible permutations as that of the Benes network. Similarly, it can be shown that three passes through the Omega network result in the same number of possible permutations as the Benes network (Parker, 1981). The Benes network is *re-arrangeable* because a potential blocking situation can be avoided by re-arranging the switch settings. The control algorithm for the Benes network is based on the *looping* algorithm, as explained in the following (Feng, 1981).

The particular permutation of a network to allow N inputs to be connected to N outputs can be represented by a two-dimensional array P[Input . . Output, 0 . . $(N - 1)$]. For example, the requirement that input 0 be connected to output 3, input 1 to output 7, and so on, may be represented by the following permutation array:

$$P = \begin{pmatrix} 0 & 1 & 2 & 3 & 4 & 5 & 6 & 7 \\ 3 & 7 & 4 & 0 & 2 & 6 & 1 & 5 \end{pmatrix}$$

The looping algorithm records matrix P in a two-dimensional diagram, where the X-axis represents the inputs and the Y-axis the outputs. The diagram is partitioned in rows, formed by pairs of inputs and outputs (because 2×2 switches are assumed to be used), and an X indicates a desired input–output connection (Figure 16.15(a)). Loops are made by selecting an arbitrary mark (mark 3–0), then looking for a mark in the same row (mark 6–1), then looking for a mark in the same column (mark 7–5), and finally looking for a mark in the same row again (mark 2–4), such that we are in the same column of the first mark of the loop. The four

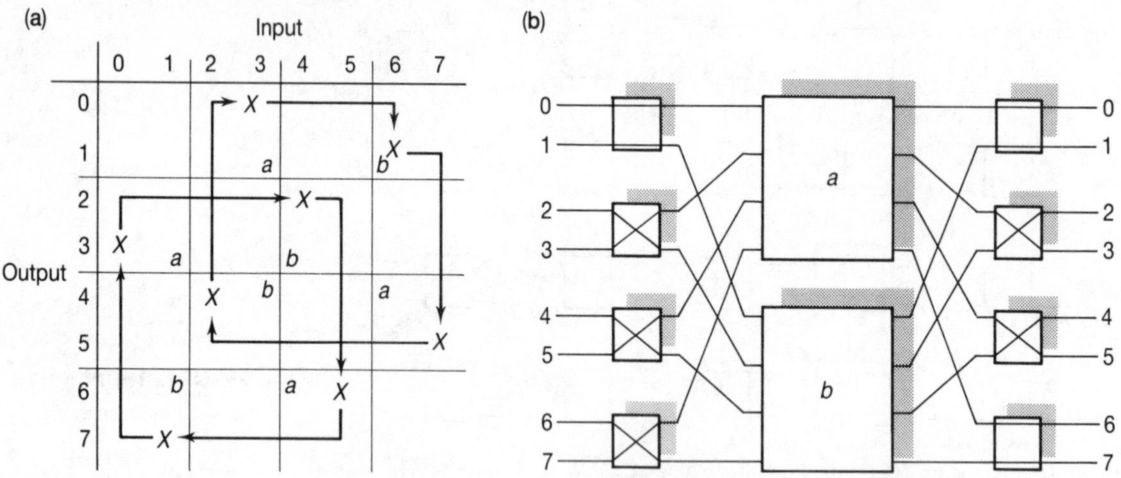

FIGURE 16.15

Illustration of the looping algorithm: (a) looping diagram; (b) control setting due to the first iteration of the looping algorithm.

marks found are then connected to form a loop. This process is repeated until all marks are part of a loop. The next step labels all marks in a loop alternatively *a* and *b*. Next, the input and output lines labelled *a* are connected to subnetwork *a*, and those labelled *b* to subnetwork *b* (Figure 16.15(b)). This determines the setting of the switches as follows: input 0 goes to *a* and starts with a straight connection; input 1 goes to *b* and therefore also requires a straight connection; input 2 (which is the next even input) goes to *b* and therefore requires an exchange connection; output 0 is connected to *a* and starts using a straight connection; output 2 (which is the next even output) is connected to *b* and therefore uses an exchange connection; output 6 is connected to *a* and therefore uses a straight connection. The looping algorithm is thereafter applied recursively to the subnetworks *a* and *b*. Obviously, the looping algorithm is only applicable in systems using central control.

16.4 The data coherence problem

Many commercially available multiprocessor systems are based on a single-shared bus because standard buses, such as the VME bus and Multibus II, are designed to support more than one processor. Hence, a natural way to increase the system performance is to add more processors to the system. To prevent the bus from becoming the performance bottleneck of the system too quickly, bus traffic is reduced by providing each processor with a private cache (Figure 16.16). Such systems can typically accommodate 8 to 32 processors. In such multiprocessor systems, data coherence problems may occur because of the existence of *multiple copies of data* (that are modified locally) or because there are

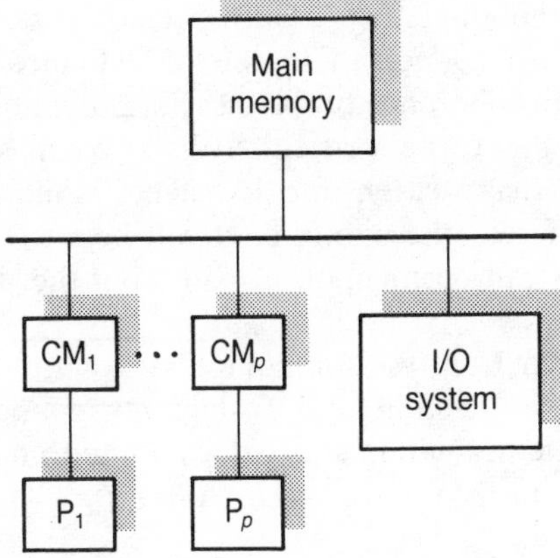

FIGURE 16.16

Single bus, shared memory, multiprocessor system.

several paths to a single data item. Data incoherence (contradictory information) is particularly imminent if the processors are equipped with private caches. Multicomputer systems do not usually share memory and therefore do not have this data coherence problem.

The data coherence problem in a system with caches can have any of the following causes:

- Sharing of writable data: Consider a tightly coupled multiprocessor system with private caches (Figure 16.16). Let A be a line of data located in main memory and possibly shared among multiple processors. Assume a copy of line A resides in cache memory i (CM_i). If a process running on processor P_i modifies the contents of line A in CM_i, two forms of data incoherence may exist: between CM_i and main memory, if main memory is not updated as well; or between CM_i and CM_j ($i \neq j$), if CM_j contained a valid copy of line A and is neither updated nor invalidated. Consequently, if two processes, running on distinct processors P_i and P_j have access to different copies of line A, and one process modifies its copy of A, the other process will read obsolete data if the modification has not been noticed, regardless of whether the data is read from main memory or from its cache.

- Process migration: The data coherence problem is not confined to data shared between multiple processes. If a process, running on processor P_i, is migrated to another processor P_j, for example, for load-balancing reasons, a data coherence problem may occur. When the process on processor P_i is migrated to processor P_j, after modifying line A in CM_i and before memory has been updated, it will read obsolete data from line A in main memory when running on P_j.

- I/O: In the single-bus multiprocessor systems, the I/O system is usually also connected to the bus (Figure 16.16). This can also cause data coherence problems. Suppose a block of data from main memory has to be written to disk. When some process on some processor has written into its cache, while main memory has not been updated, the wrong data will be written to the disk. Similar problems can occur upon a read from the disk.

It should be clear from the foregoing that a write-through main memory update policy (see Section 14.6.2) does not guarantee data consistency, because the write to main memory does not automatically update possible copies of the data in other caches.

16.4.1 Aspects of the data coherence problem

Censier (1978) states that data coherence (or data consistency) is guaranteed if the following requirement is satisfied:

> 'A memory scheme is coherent if the value returned on a LOAD instruction is always the value of the latest STORE instruction to the same address.'

This definition is not sufficient to guarantee data coherence for the class of multiprocessor systems of Figure 16.16, as will be shown in the following. To illustrate this, the data coherence problem will be analyzed for the single-access and the multiple-access operation.

Single-access operation

Instructions performing a single-access operation are concerned with data coherence for the duration of a *single* memory cycle. Load and store instructions belong to this class. If the condition of Censier is satisfied, single-access operations do not produce a data coherence problem.

Multiple-access operation

Instructions performing a multiple-access operation require that the caches and main memory be consistent for the duration of multiple accesses (multiple memory cycles). Lock instructions, such as TAS and CAS, have such a requirement. They operate on lock variables and are used for process synchronization purposes (see Section 9.4). Their implementation requires the use of a read–modify–write operation, which requires multiple memory accesses (a load and a store) to be performed. This read–modify–write operation should be atomic (indivisible), which may be a problem. Consider a system configuration, as depicted in Figure 16.16, where processor P_i can only read data from CM_i and from main

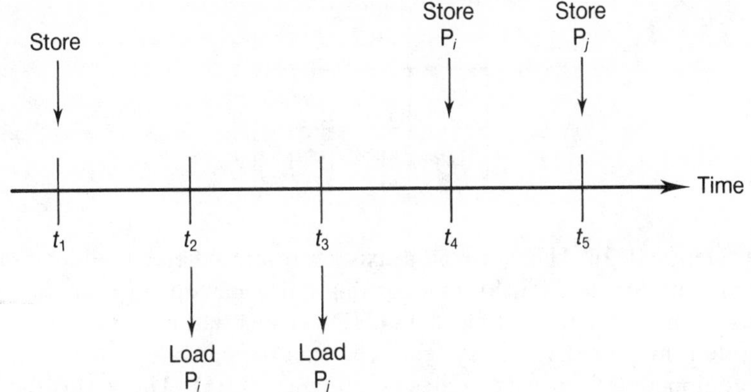

FIGURE 16.17
Timing sequence for two TAS instructions.

memory. Further suppose that CM_i contains a lock variable that is coherent with that variable in main memory; that is, the line contained in CM_i is an exact copy of the line in main memory. When two processors, P_i and P_j, both execute a TAS instruction on the same lock variable (because the processes running on them want to enter the same critical section), the timing sequence of Figure 16.17 may result. In the time period t_2–t_4, when P_i executes its TAS instruction, P_j does the Load part of its TAS instruction at time t_3. The data obtained during the Load part of the instruction determines whether a processor is allowed to pass the lock (enter the critical section). Because this data is the same for P_i and P_j (the value of the Store instruction at time t_1), both will pass the lock. This shows that, although Censier's requirement is satisfied, multiple-access problems can occur. Hence, this requirement is too weak to cover the multiple-access problem and must be redefined to the following condition:

> 'A memory scheme is coherent if the value, returned on a LOAD instruction, is always the value of the latest STORE instruction to the same address; and a multiple-access operation has to be executed atomically – that is, excluding any other operation to the same address.'

This redefinition can be translated into the following system requirement. Data coherence can be assured if the following two conditions are met:

(1) There is a single data path to every data item.

(2) There is a single copy of every data item.

16.4.2 Multiprocessor system classification

From a data coherence point of view, tightly coupled multiprocessor systems can be classified according to Figure 16.18 (van de Goor, 1986). This classification is analogous to Flynn's taxonomy for computer systems

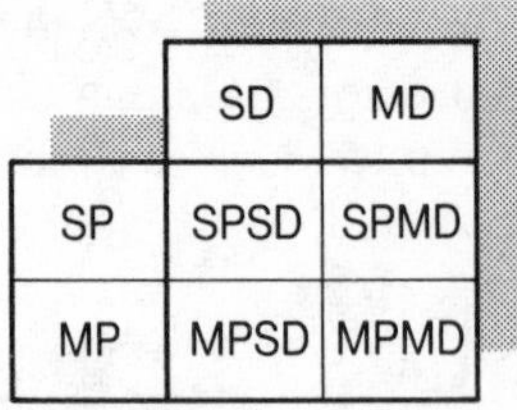

FIGURE 16.18

Multiprocessor system classes.

(see Section 1.3). The horizontal axis represents the redundancy in the stored data. Single data (SD) means that only one copy of each data item exists in the system. Multiple data (MD) means that multiple copies of a data item may exist in the system. This can happen when the processors are equipped with private caches (see Figure 16.16). The vertical axis of Figure 16.18 represents the multiplicity in the access paths to a given data item. Single-access path (SP) means that only a single path to a stored data item exists. Multiple-access paths (MP) means that multiple paths to the same data item exist – for example, in a multiprocessor system with a multiport memory. The classification according to Figure 16.18 results in four classes of multiprocessor systems. The classes SPSD, MPSD and MPMD exist, and are discussed in the following subsections. The class SPMD, however, does not have any real significance; it can be considered as an anomaly of this classification method, comparable to MISD computer systems in Flynn's taxonomy (see Section 1.3).

Single-path, single-data multiprocessor systems

The class of SPSD systems includes multiprocessor systems using a single time-shared bus (see Figure 16.7), multiple buses (see Figure 16.8) or a cross-bar switch (see Figure 16.9) as the IN. In these systems, the processors do not have private caches.

Looking at the data coherence problem of an SPSD system, it can be stated that both the single-access and the multiple-access situation do not cause a problem as both conditions, necessary to guarantee data coherence, are satisfied (only a single path to a data item exists at any moment in time, and a single copy of each data item exists).

Although no private caches may exist, the central memory subsystem can be implemented with performance enhancement features, such as a shared cache or the interleaving of memory modules, which logically present themselves to the processors as a single memory. (Data incoherence between the shared cache and main memory may occur when the copy-back policy is used; this is transparent to the processors using that shared cache however.) The UNIVAC 1100/80 is an example of a system that uses a shared cache: it has two processors and one cache. In general, this solution is not attractive, because the bandwidth of a single cache is not sufficient to support a large number of processors. Also, long cache time delays may be incurred, because the shared caches cannot be physically close to all processors. Consequently, the introduction of shared caches does not live up to the expectations of a high performance. An extensive analysis of shared cache systems can be found in Yeh (1983).

Multiple-path, single-data multiprocessor systems

Multiprocessor systems of the MPSD class can be implemented via multiport memories (see Figure 16.10). Each processor has its own bus, while the switching is implemented as part of the memory subsystem. This may consist of several independent modules to improve the memory bandwidth, using interleaving. It is assumed that memory requests are served sequentially, because a memory module can only service one request at a time. The Burroughs B7700 and the DEC KL-10 multiprocessor systems are examples of systems based on multiport memories (Satyanarayanan, 1980). The data coherence problem for MPSD systems can be analyzed for the two classes of operations:

(1) Single-access operation: Because memory requests are serialized (served sequentially), only a single path to a data item exists (and only a single copy of each data item exists) at any time. Therefore, data coherence (for instructions performing a single-access operation) is guaranteed.

(2) Multiple-access operations: In traditional uniprocessor systems, multiple-access operations are made atomic (indivisible) by the processor, which locks the bus or issues a special lock signal for the duration of the multiple-access operation, thereby guaranteeing a single-access path for the duration of the multiple access operation. In MPSD systems, data coherence can be guaranteed via one of the following mechanisms:

- Lock path to data item: This can be done via a lock signal generated by the processor P_i for the duration of the multiple-access operation, which forces the switch in the memory module not to change. So, processor P_j ($j \neq i$) will be denied access to that memory module; the memory subsystem is effectively mapped into an SPSD system for the duration of the lock signal.
- Lock data item: A block of main memory, containing the data item on which the multiple-access operation is to be performed, is made private to one processor P_i by setting a lock flag belonging to that block. During the multiple-access operation, other processors may still access memory, except for the block that is protected by the lock flag. This solution

essentially maps a block of memory into an SPSD system for the duration that the lock flag is set. The implementation requires two special memory operations: RDL (Read and Lock) and WRU (Write and Unlock). RDL is comparable to a normal memory read operation, but in addition the lock flag is set. Any subsequent RDL operations that access a block of memory, protected by a set lock flag, will be signalled as invalid. WRU, apart from writing data to memory, also resets the lock flag that protected the memory block. The size of a memory block, which is protected by a lock flag, can vary from all of memory to a single lock variable (semaphore). In the former case, only one lock flag is required, which allows only one process to be in any critical section. Other processes may still perform normal single-access operations. This has been implemented on the VAX-11/780 (DEC, 1979). In the latter case, one lock flag is required for each lock in main memory (for example, 1 bit per 32-bit word). It allows each critical section to be protected independently.

Multiple-path, multiple-data multiprocessor systems

Distributed cache systems, as shown in Figure 16.16, are an example of MPMD systems. They are usually designed with a shared memory and distributed caches, without private memories, because the use of private memories makes the address space of the processes inhomogeneous, while the presence of distributed caches already provides the performance advantages that private memories can offer. To further reduce the load on the bus, some form of copy-back is used, rather than a write-through main memory update policy (see Section 14.6.2). These systems have a potential data coherence problem because more than one path to a data item and more than one copy of that data item may exist. Section 16.5 presents solutions to the data coherence problem for MPMD systems.

16.5 Solutions to the data coherence problem

Solutions to the data coherence problem in MPMD systems can be static or dynamic. A *static* solution is performed at compile time and uses software to maintain data coherence by way of prevention. *Dynamic* solutions are performed at run time, requiring hardware for detecting and resolving the data coherence problem. Dynamic solutions can be implemented in a *centralized* or a *distributed* way.

16.5.1 Solutions based on prevention

The data coherence problem can be prevented if the operating system designates *all* writable data to be shared as non-cacheable, making this information accessible only in main memory. Then, only non-shared data may be cached, while shared data always resides in main memory. This shared data consists of locks and shared data structures.

To alleviate the problem of the substantial increase in memory access time for all shared data, shared data structures may be cached. The access to this data is only allowed in critical sections, which are protected by non-cacheable locks. Within the critical sections, the code is responsible for restoring all modified data to main memory, before releasing the lock. Therefore, each processor has to be equipped with commands to purge data from its cache. The Honeywell Series 66 (Satyanarayanan, 1980) uses this technique, as well as the C.mmp (Jones, 1980), where the caches have been implemented with write-through to main memory, but not to other caches. This technique necessitates the software (compiler) deciding which pages are allowed to be cached, and all pages must have a non-cacheable flag. Shared writable pages can only reside in main memory.

The disadvantages of the solutions based on prevention are the need for specialized system software, and the requirement for user assistance to declare data items shared or not shared, or for a compiler capable of determining this. In addition, a reduced cache hit ratio results, because part of the data is not cached. Special precautions have to be taken for I/O: either caches must be flushed before I/O is to proceed, or all I/O data has to be tagged as non-cacheable. In the case of process migration, caches have to be flushed before migration takes place, or migration has to be disallowed.

16.5.2 Centralized solutions based on detection and resolution

The advantage of solutions to the data coherence problem based on detection and resolution is that they are transparent to the user, although this is at the expense of extra hardware, because data coherence is maintained at program execution time. In this section, a centralized solution to the data coherence problem in MPMD systems based on the presence flag technique is presented. Other closely related schemes are the LSCS (logical semi-critical section) scheme of Yen (1982) and the scheme implemented in the S-1 (Widdoes, 1980).

Censier (1978) has proposed a scheme where the state of a data line in cache is stored: (1) in a tag associated with the cache line in cache; and (2) in a tag associated with the corresponding line in main memory (Figure 16.19). This scheme has been implemented on the IBM 3081

Line	Tag: P_0	P_1	P_2	P_3	M	Data
0	0	1	0	1	0	33
1	0	0	1	0	1	47
2	0	0	0	0	0	27
3	1	0	0	0	1	10
4	0	0	1	0	1	8

Main memory

P_i Presence flag
M Modified flag

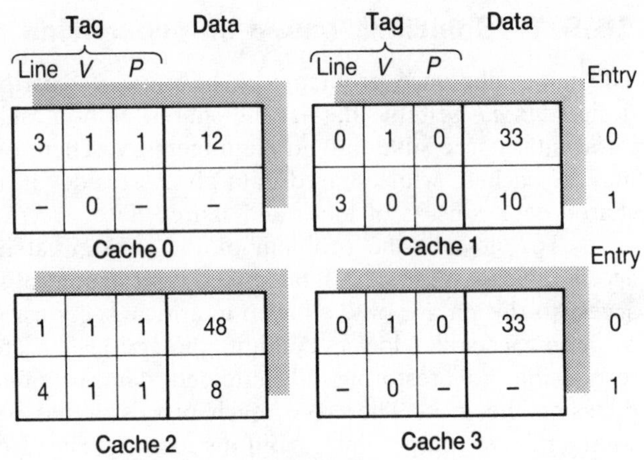

FIGURE 16.19
Example of presence flag coherence scheme.

(Gustafson, 1982). To illustrate this scheme, consider Figure 16.19, which pictures a multiprocessor system with a shared main memory (for this purpose, divided into five lines, line 0 through line 4) and four caches (cache 0 through cache 3), consisting of two entries each (labelled entry 0 and 1). Each line in main memory is provided with a tag that contains a presence flag P_i for each cache in the system and a modified flag M. $P_i = 1$ indicates that cache i contains a copy of the corresponding line of data in main memory. $M = 1$ indicates that a copy of a data line in some cache j has been modified. A processor P_j is only allowed to modify a line of data in its cache if it owns that line of data; this means that P_j holds the only valid copy. So, if $M = 1$, only one, and exactly one, of the presence flags will be set – namely, the flag of the processor owning the line of data.

Each cache line is provided with a tag that contains a private flag P, a valid flag V and a line number. The V flag indicates whether the corresponding cache line contains valid information; the P flag indicates that the corresponding cache owns the line of data (it is a private line); and the line number indicates which line of main memory is stored in the cache entry.

An inspection of the actual contents of the tag fields of Figure 16.19 reveals the following. Line 0 is shared by main memory, cache 1 and cache 3, as indicated by the presence flags P_1 and P_3 of this line in main memory. Looking at the flags of line 1, it can be seen, from $M = 1$ and $P_2 = 1$, that cache 2 contains a modified copy of this line, so the value 47, stored in main memory, is invalid. Line 2 can only be found in main memory, as indicated by the four presence flags being zero. The flags of line 3 show that cache 0 contains a modified copy of it, so the value 10 in main memory is invalid. When looking at cache 1, it can be seen that it has a copy of line 3, which is now invalid ($V = 0$). Line 4 can be found in main memory and cache 2, but cache 2 may write to this line as its private flag is set.

The operation of this scheme requires the following commands between the cache controller and the memory controller:

- Shared read (from cache to memory controller): This command is used when a cache miss occurs due to a processor read operation. The requested line is transferred to the cache, and the cache flags are set to shared ($V = 1$ and $P = 0$). The flags of the line in main memory record that the requesting cache contains the line as a shared line (flag $P_i = 1$ and $M = 0$). If, however, the line is owned by another cache (indicated by $M = 1$), this cache is forced to transfer the line back to main memory, after which that line is transferred to the requesting cache, and both caches mark this line as shared.
- Private read (from cache to memory controller): On a cache miss, this command is issued when a processor wants to perform a write operation. The line is transferred to the cache and marked as private ($V = 1$ and $P = 1$). If this line is already present in one or more other caches (private or shared), the memory controller invalidates these copies, because only one copy of a private line may exist.
- Declare private (from cache to memory controller): When the processor wants to perform a write operation to a line contained in its cache marked shared, the line must be declared private to ensure that no other caches contain copies of this line. On receiving this command, the memory controller must invalidate all other copies of the requested line. For this command, no transfer of data is needed.
- Invalidate (from memory to cache controller): This command forces the state of a cache entry to change from valid to invalid ($V = 0$). Two versions of this command are required, depending on whether the line is owned by the cache. If the cache does not own the line, the cache entry containing the line is marked invalid ($V = 0$); in the case where the cache owns the line (indicated by $P = 1$), it transfers the line of data to main memory and marks its entry as invalid ($P = 0$ and $V = 0$).
- Share (from memory to cache controller): This command causes the addressed cache to send its private line of data to main memory and change the status of that line to shared ($P = 0$).

The advantage of this scheme is that no unnecessary invalidation requests are sent and that the whereabouts of the most recent copy of a data line can be determined easily by the memory controller. Disadvantages include its cost (duplication of cache tags in the memory controller) and the fact that standard, off-the-shelf, memories cannot be used (a memory controller has to be inserted in the memory data path). In addition, every line in memory needs $p + 1$ flags; in large multiprocessor systems, this can become costly. In addition, a performance loss is incurred due to extra bus traffic (and bus load) required for correct maintenance of the states of the lines in the caches. This extra traffic is caused by such commands as 'declare private' and 'invalidate'.

The two-bit scheme of Archibald (1984) reduces the implementation cost. This scheme only stores the cache state for each memory line ('present' and 'modified'), not the whereabouts of a line (it does not know which cache has a copy of a line). The number of bits per memory line is now independent of the number of processors. The drawback is that it is not known which caches contain a specific line, so all caches must be polled causing extra delay and bus load.

16.5.3 Distributed solutions based on detection and resolution

With distributed solutions, the responsibility for maintaining data coherence belongs to the cache controllers, rather than to a central controller. This has the advantage that the amount of bus traffic for maintaining the state of the lines in the caches is reduced. This is important because, in a shared bus multiprocessor system, the bus is the most performance-constraining system resource; maximizing system performance requires the bus utilization of each individual processor to be minimized.

In a scheme based on a distributed solution, each cache controller must continuously monitor all data transfers and, in the case of an address match, take action (such as invalidating a line in a cache), according to the type of bus request. Such a cache controller is called a **snoopy cache controller**. Again, there are many distributed hardware approaches for the solution of the data coherence problem. It is not possible to discuss them all, so only three methods are discussed: the dedicated broadcast bus, the write-once scheme and the ownership scheme. A discussion of several other distributed hardware-based solutions to the cache coherence problem in shared-bus multiprocessor systems can be found in Papamarcos (1984), Katz (1985), Bitar (1986) and Archibald (1986).

Dedicated broadcast bus

This solution connects every cache to a special, high-speed broadcast bus. Each write to a cache is propagated to main memory (write-through) and, in addition, the address of each write is sent on the special bus, which is permanently monitored by each cache. If an address matches a cache tag (a cache hit), the copy of the line in that cache is invalidated. This dedicated broadcast bus protocol, used in the dual-processor versions of the IBM 370/168, the IBM 3033 and the more recent multiprocessor system Sequent (Fielland, 1984), has several disadvantages (Censier, 1978):

- A high traffic on the bus, because each write is propagated to memory.
- The cache may spend most of its time monitoring the broadcast bus if no precautionary measures are taken.
- A small buffer is needed in the cache to accommodate peak invalidation traffic.

Because of these disadvantages, this scheme can only be applied to multiprocessor systems with a few (typically two) processors.

Write-once scheme

In this scheme, proposed by Goodman (1983), a write-through method is used to claim the exclusive use of a line of data, instead of using commands like 'read private' or 'declare private'. This reduces the bus load since, when claiming a line and invalidating other copies of it, the line is also updated in memory without additional cost. After this first write, main memory is updated using a copy-back policy; only those blocks having a state 'dirty' have to be copied-back to main memory. Goodman, therefore, called his scheme write-once. In this scheme, a cache line can have four states (Archibald, 1986):

(1) Invalid: No data is found in the cache.

(2) Valid: The line has been read from main memory and has not been modified.

(3) Reserved: The line has been locally modified exactly once since being read from memory and the change has been transmitted to main memory.

(4) Dirty: A line has been modified more than once, whereas memory has not yet been updated.

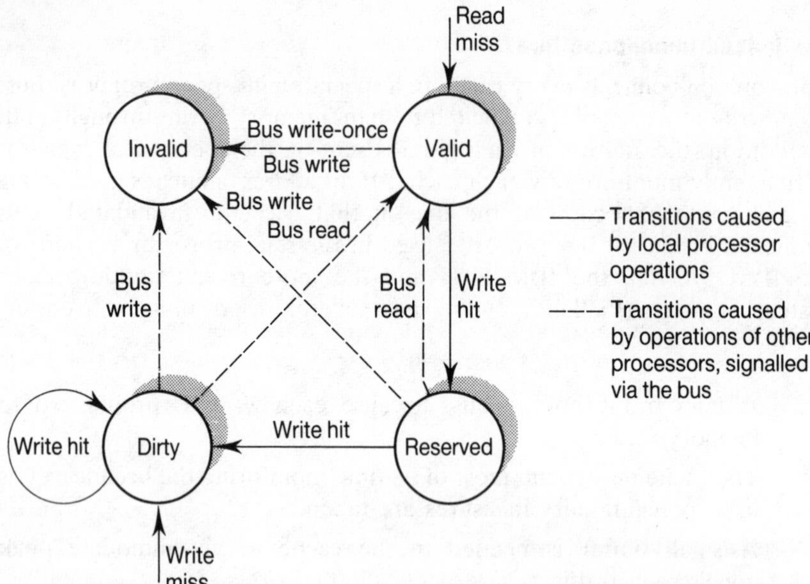

FIGURE 16.20

Write-once state-transition diagram.

The operation of the write-once scheme is as follows (Figure 16.20):

- Read miss: A read miss occurs when the processor wants to read a line from cache that is not present; a bus read operation will result. If some cache holds the requested line in state 'dirty', it will supply the data to the requesting cache and to main memory, while inhibiting main memory from supplying the data. If no cache holds a copy in state 'dirty', main memory will supply the data. All caches with a copy of that line will set the state of that line to 'valid' (dashed line marked 'bus read').
- Write hit: If the line is already in state 'dirty', the write can proceed (solid line marked 'write hit' leaving and entering state 'dirty'). If the line is in state 'reserved', the write proceeds and the state of the line is changed to 'dirty'. If the line is in state 'valid', a write-through is performed to main memory, the local cache line is also updated, the state of the line is set to 'reserved', and other caches with a copy of that line will notice the bus write-once operation (to update main memory) and set the state of that line to 'invalid'. Note that in the case of a write hit, other caches can only have a copy of that line in state 'valid'.
- Write miss: A bus write operation will be performed. When another cache contains the requested block in state 'dirty', it will supply the data; otherwise main memory will supply the requested line. The state of the requested line is set to 'dirty', while all other caches containing a copy of the requested line set the state to 'invalid'.

The disadvantage of the write-one scheme is that it requires special provisions of the bus. Upon a bus read operation, a valid copy of the requested line has to be supplied to the requesting cache controller. When main memory contains the valid copy, it should supply the data; when some cache contains the requested line in state 'reserved' or 'dirty', it should supply the data. Main memory does not know whether its line contains valid data (because it does not have any state information associated with the lines it holds); so, when a cache supplies the requested data, the involved cache controller has to inhibit main memory from supplying its invalid data. This inhibit operation requires a special line on the bus, but many standard buses have not been designed with this requirement in mind.

Ownership scheme

The ownership scheme is described by Frank (1984) for the Synapse computer system. It has the property that each line in main memory is provided with a 1-bit tag, which indicates whether main memory or a cache should provide the data during a bus read operation. The advantage of this scheme is that it does not impose any special requirements on the bus, such as an 'inhibit' line. In this scheme, ownership of a line has to be claimed before writing to it. To claim ownership, a cache controller issues a 'private read' or 'declare private' command. Each line can be either 'public' or 'private', indicated by a flag in main memory and in the caches. If a line is 'public', the main memory holds ownership of the line and caches may only contain read-only copies of this line (fetched with a 'shared read' command). If the status of a line is 'private', then the owner of the line (a cache) holds the only valid copy and has exclusive access to it.

If a 'shared read' command is issued by some cache controller while the line in main memory is marked 'private', the cache owning that line has to supply the data. This data will be supplied to the requesting cache controller and to main memory; the line will be marked 'public' (that is, the ownership of the line is transferred to main memory). If a 'shared read' command is issued while the requested line in main memory is marked 'public', main memory will supply the data. If, however, a 'private read' command is issued by a cache controller, the ownership and the data line are directly transferred to the other cache. Main memory ignores this 'private read' request (and subsequent data transfers) because it does not own the line.

Compared to the dedicated broadcast bus scheme, the traffic load on the Synapse bus is lower, because activities on the bus are now only caused by cache misses and by processors that want to modify a public

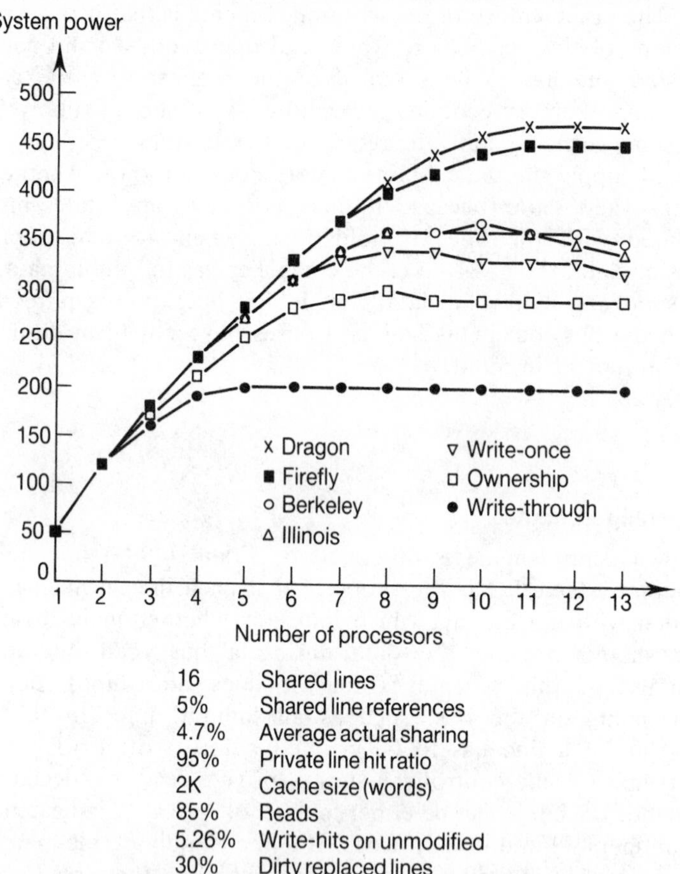

FIGURE 16.21

Performance of multiprocessor data coherence schemes.

line. Thus, this scheme allows more processors to operate concurrently while sharing a single bus.

Archibald (1986) describes, in addition, several other schemes that further reduce the load on the bus, and therefore allow the processors to be utilized more effectively (their performance is less constrained due to a lower bus load) and/or a higher number of processors to be employed. Figure 16.21 shows the system power (processor utilization multiplied by the number of processors) as a function of the number of processors for seven schemes: write-through, ownership, write-once and four more advanced schemes (which cause a lower bus load) that are not discussed here. The results obviously depend very heavily on cache and line sizes, miss rates, and so on, as indicated in the figure. The write-through scheme has been included for comparison purposes; however, it cannot be considered a serious candidate for a tightly coupled multiprocessor system.

SUMMARY

- The commonly used term 'multiprocessor system' stands for multiprocessor as well as multicomputer systems.
- A multicomputer system is a system where each processor has its own memory, and the interconnection network is used only for interprocessor communication. These systems are also referred to as loosely coupled systems.
- In a multiprocessor system, the processors share memory, and the interconnection network acts as a processor–memory bus.
- Interconnection networks can be characterized according to the timing (synchronous or asynchronous), the switching method (circuit or packet switching), the control strategy (centralized or distributed) and the topology (static or dynamic). Topologies for multicomputer systems vary from a simple ring to fully connected networks and cube networks. For multiprocessor systems, a bus, a cross-bar switch, multiport memories or interconnection networks using shuffle exchanges can be used.
- Multicomputer interconnection networks usually have a static topology which can be characterized by the diameter of the network and the degree of each node. One can distinguish the following two-dimensional topologies: ring, mesh and tree. Hypercubes and *n*-cube connected cycles are examples of *n*-dimensional topologies.
- Multiprocessor interconnection networks can be based on buses (single bus, cross-bar switch and multiport memory) or on shuffle exchange interconnection networks.
- A single-stage interconnection network (SSIN) consists of one stage of switches which are connected to perform a perfect shuffle. The outputs are connected to the corresponding inputs to allow data to be circulated through the network, to arrive at an arbitrary destination.
- Multi-stage interconnection networks (MSINs) consist of several stages of switches, to allow an arbitrary input to be connected to an arbitrary output.
- Blocking occurs in SSINs and MSINs when more than one path through the network is required simultaneously such that a switch has to take on conflicting positions. The Benes network allows blocking to be prevented.
- A data coherence problem may occur in systems with caches due to sharing of writable data, process migration and I/O.
- Solutions to the data coherence problem can be based on prevention (a static solution that requires software support) or detection and resolution (a dynamic solution that requires special hardware support).
- The solutions to the data coherence problem, based on detection and resolution, can be based on centralized or distributed schemes. The distributed schemes, such as write-once and ownership, typically cause a lower bus load than the centralized schemes and are therefore more suited for multiprocessor systems with a larger number of processors.

EXERCISES

16.1 When a single process has to be executed faster, is it preferable to use a multithreading or multiple-thread system?

16.2 In which system do processors have their own memory and is the interconnection network used for interprocessor communication? Is this a tightly or a loosely coupled system?

16.3 What are the distinguishing characteristics of an interconnection network?

16.4 Which topology is typically used for multicomputer interconnection networks, and which two properties characterize such an interconnection network?

16.5 What is the diameter and the degree of:

(a) A hypercube.

(b) An *n*-cube connected cycles?

16.6 What are the routing properties of a hypercube network?

16.7 Which two classes of interconnection networks can be distinguished for multiprocessor systems?

16.8 (a) Does an SSIN use packet or circuit switching?

(b) Do MSINs use packet or circuit switching?

16.9 Why are baseline interconnection networks useful and do they require centralized or distributed control?

16.10 Which two conditions have to be met to assure data coherence?

16.11 What is the advantage and disadvantage of the solution to the data coherence problem based on prevention?

16.12 What is the purpose of a 'private read' command from a cache controller to a central memory controller?

16.13 What is the disadvantage of using a write-through main memory update policy in a multiprocessor system? Does this guarantee data consistency?

16.14 What is the advantage and disadvantage of the ownership scheme?

References

Archibald, J. and Baer, J. L. (1984). An economical solution to the cache coherency problem. In *Proc. 11th Annual Symposium on Computer Architecture*, pp. 355–62.

Archibald, J. and Baer, J. L. (1986). Cache coherence protocols: Evaluation using a multiprocessor simulation model. *ACM Trans. on Computer Systems*, **4**(4), 273–98.

Bell, C. G. *et al.* (1978). The evolution of the DEC System 10. *Comm. of the ACM*, **21**(1), 44–63.

Bhuyan, L. N. and Agrawal, D. P. (1983). Design and performance of generalized interconnection networks. *IEEE Trans. on Computers*, **C–32**(12), 1081–90.

Bhuyan, L. N. (1987). Interconnection networks for parallel and distributed processing. *Computer*, **20**(6), 9–12.

Bitar, P. and Despain, A. M. (1986). Multiprocessor cache synchronization: Issues, innovations, evolution. In *Proc. 13th Annual Symposium on Computer Architecture*, pp. 424–33.

Censier, L. M. and Feautrier, P. (1978). A new solution to coherence problems in multicache systems. *IEEE Trans. on Computers*, **C–27**(12), 1112–18.

Chen, P. Y. *et al.* (1981). Interconnection networks using shuffles. *Computer*, **14**(12), 55–64.

DEC (1979). *VAX-11/780 Hardware Handbook*. Digital Equipment Corporation: Maynard, MA.

Feng, T. (1981). A survey of interconnection networks. *Computer*, **14**(12), 12–27.

Fielland, G. and Rogers, D. (1984). 32-bit computer system shares load equally among up to 12 processors. *Electronic Design*, **32**(3), 153–68.

Frank, S. and Inselberg, A. (1984). Synapse tightly coupled multiprocessors: A new approach to solve old problems. *AFIPS Proc. of the NCC*, **53**, 41–50.

Gear, G. W. (1974). *Computer Organization and Programming*, 2nd edn. McGraw-Hill: Hightstown, NJ, pp. 388–92.

Goodman, J. R. (1983). Using cache memory to reduce processor–memory traffic. In *Proc. 10th Annual Symposium on Computer Architecture*, pp. 124–31.

Gustafson, R. N. and Sparacio, F. J. (1982). IBM 3081 processor unit: Design considerations and design process. *IBM Journal of Research and Development*, **26**(1), 12–21.

Jones, A. K. and Schwarz, P. (1980). Experience using multiprocessor systems – A status report. *Computing Surveys*, **12**(2), 121–65.

Katz, R. H. *et al.* (1985). Implementing a cache consistency protocol. In *Proc. 12th Annual Symposium on Computer Architecture*, pp. 276–83.

Kleitman, D. *et al.* (1981). New layouts for the shuffle exchange graph. In *Proc. ACM Annual Symposium on Theory of Computation*.

McQuillan, J. M. and Walden, D. C. (1977). The ARPA network design decisions. *Computer Networks*, **1**(5), 243–89.

Mudge, T. N. *et al.* (1987). Multiple bus architectures. *Computer*, **20**(6), 42–8.

Papamarcos, M. S. and Patel, J. H. (1984). A low-overhead coherence solution for multiprocessors with private cache memories. In *Proc. 11th Annual Symposium on Computer Architecture*, pp. 348–54.

Parker, D. S. (1981). New points of view on 3-stage rearrangeable switching networks. In *Proc. Workshop on Interconnection Networks*, Lafayette, IN, pp. 56–63.

Patel, J. H. (1979). Processor–memory interconnection for multiprocessors. In *Proc. 6th Annual Symposium on Computer Architecture*, pp. 168–77.

Rattner, J. (1985). Concurrent processing: A new direction in scientific computing. *AFIPS Proc. of the NCC*, **54**, 157–66.

Reed, D. A. and Grunwald, D. C. (1987). The performance of multicomputer interconnection networks. *Computer*, **20**(6), 63–73.

Satyanarayanan, M. (1980). *Multiprocessors – A Comparative Study*. Prentice Hall Incorporated: Englewood Cliffs, NJ.

van de Goor, A. J. (1986). Multiprocessor cache systems. In *Proc. NGI–SION Symposium*, Utrecht, The Netherlands, pp. 167–82.

Widdoes, L. C. (1980). The S–1 project: Developing high-performance digital computers. In *Proc. of the COMPCON 80*, pp. 282–91.

Yeh, P. C. C. *et al.* (1983). Shared cache for multiple stream computer systems. *IEEE Trans. on Computers*, **C–32**(1), pp. 38–47.

Yen, W. C. and Fu, K. S. (1982). Coherence problem in a multicache system. In *Proc. Int. Conference on Parallel Processing*, pp. 332–9.

PART SIX

TRENDS

CHAPTER 17 ARCHITECTURAL TRENDS

The emphasis of this book has been on the architecture and design of conventional computers, based on the von Neumann model. To allow for more parallelism, new architectures are being developed, many of which are still in their research stage. These new architectures are based on computational models that differ from the classic von Neumann model. The final part of this book is intended to give the reader an overview and a classification of computational models, some of which may be of importance for future generations of computers. A short description of some architectures based on these new computational models, completed with many references, has been included to give the reader a feel for the direction these new developments are taking.

17 Architectural Trends

The future isn't what it used to be.
– Arthur C. Clarke

This chapter presents a classification of the trends in computer architecture. It should give the reader a feel of what is important in future architectures, together with the type of architectures that may be expected. A computer architecture is considered an embodiment (a particular implementation) of a computational model. A computational model is a conceptual method of how a computation can be performed.

The chapter opens with a discussion of the computational model (the von Neumann model) on which traditional computer architectures are based and highlights the major reasons why parallelism (which allows for high performance) is in conflict with this model. The following section presents a classification of computational models (taxonomy). This taxonomy distinguishes eight computational models, several of which can support parallelism. Each of these models is described briefly in the last section.

17.1 Traditional computer architectures

Currently, most computer architectures are based on the concepts that date back to one of the first computers ever built. This computer is referred to as the IAS, after Princeton Institute for Advanced Studies, and is described in a paper by Burks, Goldstine and von Neumann in 1946 (von Neumann, 1946). This paper is remarkable in the thoroughness and insight the authors displayed. Their concepts were brilliant solutions to the most important problems of that time. Almost every computer designed and constructed in the following decades embodied these 'von Neumann concepts'. An architecture, based on the IAS concepts, is often called a **von Neumann architecture**, to stress the contributions of John von Neumann to its development.

This section is entirely devoted to the von Neumann model. It first presents this model, then the extensions made in the last forty years are surveyed. The last section gives a critique on the von Neumann model and presents its two main problems: the semantic gap and the von Neumann bottleneck.

17.1.1 Classical von Neumann model

In its simplest form, the von Neumann architecture consists of three parts: a central processing unit (CPU), a memory and a connecting device that can transmit data between these two. The memory has the following properties:

- It is sequential and consists of words: The memory of the von Neumann computer is linear and appears as a vector of cells, called words, referenced with sequential addresses: $0, 1, 2, \ldots, N - 1$.
- It does not distinguish between instructions and data: The von Neumann model allows the instructions to be stored in the same memory as data. Instructions are indistinguishable from data and they can be manipulated in the same way as data. The interpretation of a word in memory only depends on the state of the machine at the moment the word is fetched from memory. Computers with this property are called **stored-program computers**.
- Meaning is not an inherent part of data: There is nothing that distinguishes a word representing an integer from a word representing a character string. For example, the memory word in Figure 17.1 (consisting of two bytes of 8 bits) may represent an integer, an ASCII string or an MC68020 instruction. The meaning of data only depends on the program logic. A memory word, which

The memory word

0	1	0	0	0	0	0	1	0	0	1	0	0	0	1	0

FIGURE 17.1

A memory word with different interpretations.

is addressed by an integer ADD instruction, is assumed to be an integer number. However, it is possible to perform an integer multiplication on two operands, which represent character strings or addresses.

The main task of a program is to process data located in memory; that is, to change the contents of the memory. The program can only change the contents of memory by moving words from and to it. Instructions read their operands from memory, process them and then write the results back to memory. There are instructions operating on internal processor registers, whose main aim is to optimize the traffic between the CPU and the memory, not to fight the general rule. The source of data is generally the memory, and the same memory is the ultimate destination of the results.

17.1.2 Extensions to the von Neumann model

Although the basic concepts of the von Neumann model have remained the same throughout the forty years of its existence, several of its parts have been changed or improved. This section lists the main extensions to the von Neumann model, some of which are within the model, while others are in conflict with the model.

Extensions within the model

Extensions within the von Neumann model are intended to support high-level languages and structured data types, and to speed up processing.

Modifications and additions aimed at supporting high-level languages are the following:

- New data types: These include floating-point numbers, strings and decimal numbers.
- Stacks: Stacks have been added to support procedure calls, recursion, expression evaluation, and so on.
- Virtual memory: High-level programming languages do not impose restrictions on memory size and many applications require a large memory. Virtual memory organization gives the illusion of having much more memory than the system physically contains.

When an operand is an element of a higher-level data structure, such as an array or a linked list, the operand address usually has to be determined at run time. To facilitate the computation of operand addresses, without requiring that the program modify itself, the following architectural extensions have been made:

- Index registers: To support such concepts as array indexing.
- Indirect addressing: To support dynamic data objects.

A number of extensions aim at increasing the performance of the computer:

- Internal processor registers and cache memories: To reduce the memory traffic.
- Memory interleaving: To increase the memory bandwidth.
- Instruction pipelining: To increase the effective instruction execution speed.
- Multiple execution units: The idea of multiple execution units is that a single instruction operates on several data elements. This reduces the overhead of instruction fetch and decode.
- Supporting processors (for example, co-processors and I/O processors): To free the central CPU from some time-consuming tasks.

Extensions in conflict with the model

These extensions aim at a higher semantic model of the data, thereby reducing the semantic gap (see Section 17.1.3) and/or improving the memory bandwidth. They include the following:

- Self-defining data: The von Neumann model does not make a distinction between memory cells. In contrast, some computers combine the data with their meaning, providing self-defining data. This is implemented by adding an identification field (a tag) to each data item (Feustel, 1973). The advantages of tagging are questionable for general-purpose applications (Gehringer, 1985); however, for the class of languages using late binding (such as LISP), tagging is usually a requirement.
- Separation of program and data spaces: A number of architectures, such as the MC68020, separate the program space from the data space. Instructions are always fetched from the program space, and instructions always fetch their operands from the data space. This is advantageous in systems using virtual memory (read-only

program pages) and in higher-performance systems, where two separate memories (one for data, one for programs) allow for a higher memory bandwidth.

17.1.3 Critique of the von Neumann model

Two aspects of the von Neumann model are subject to strong criticism: the semantic gap between the architecture and high-level programming languages, and the von Neumann bottleneck.

The von Neumann semantic gap

There is a significant semantic difference between a von Neumann architecture and high-level programming languages. This difference is due to the organization of the storage medium (that is, the memory), and is often referred to as the semantic gap. The concept of memory in high-level languages differs from that of the von Neumann model. Consider again the von Neumann memory characteristics presented in Section 17.1.1, compared to the memory presented in a high-level language, which consists of a set of named variables. There is very little correspondence to the linear space of the von Neumann model. Modern programming languages allow for multi-dimensional data structures, such as arrays and lists. The following legal Pascal declaration includes the definition of a three-dimensional array of three-dimensional arrays of integers:

```
var A: array[3 . . 10, 1 . . 17, 0 . . 100] of
        array[123 . . 156, −14 . . 2, 1 . . 100] of integer;
    I, J: integer;
    S: string;
```

The declarations in this Pascal program segment do not guarantee that the variable *I* is located next to the variable *J*, which is further located next to variable *S*. Further, they could be located in different memory modules – one just does not care. Referencing variables is done by calling their names without having to know the underlying access method.

In most programming languages, there is a sharp distinction between data and instructions. There are no concepts of executing data or referencing instructions as if they were data. Also, it is necessary to know if the program is located in the same memory as the data.

High-level languages have generic operations, operating on any data type. The meaning of data is associated with the data itself. For example, in Pascal it is possible to write:

```
var A, B: integer;
    ⋮
A := A + B;
```

rather than:

```
var A, B: word;
    ⋮
A := A "integer add" B;
```

To translate a high-level language program to a von Neumann architecture, excessive mapping is required, which is mostly done by compilers. The amount of code generated by the compiler to map the language concepts of storage and data to the underlying architecture outweighs the code required for problem solving. This code requires memory for its storage and decreases the performance, due to the time required for loading and execution.

Many programming languages are very strict and forbid a number of possible operations – for example, assignment between different types of data, violating array bounds, modifying the program code, access to any memory location, and so on. The execution of high-level language programs requires these constraints to be enforced. It is usually the case that the underlying architecture is more general than the high-level programming language and allows for more operations. (This is caused by the fact that most computers are designed for several applications. Besides, they must support system software, where these restrictions are not welcome.) This generality has to be hidden or removed, when mapping the high-level language programs on such an architecture.

The von Neumann bottleneck

The von Neumann computer consists of three parts: a CPU, a memory and a connecting tube that can transmit a single word between the CPU and the memory (send an address to the memory and receive/send a data word from/to memory). Backus has proposed calling this tube the **von Neumann bottleneck** (Backus, 1978).

Physical bottleneck The task of a program is to change the contents of the memory by moving words from and to it through the tube connecting it to the CPU. A large part of the traffic in the tube is not useful data but merely names of data, as well as operations and data used to compute such names (addresses, and operations and data to compute addresses). This traffic causes the tube to quickly become the bottleneck for the speed of the computation. No matter how fast the CPU or the memory device is, the total performance is restricted by the speed of the tube.

Computer architects became aware of this problem early on and, in addition to the technological improvements that result in faster memories and CPUs, proposed several techniques for speeding up the communication. Although developments in technology have resulted in memories with access times of about 10 ns, computers are based on electronic circuits, whose speed is restricted by the speed of electromagnetic waves (about 300 000 km per second). Producing memory devices with access times of 0.1 ns means approaching the limits, because 1 ns is the time needed for electromagnetic waves to cross the distance of 30 cm! Consequently, having reached this limit, it will soon not be possible to make conventional computers faster, and this is the reason why the computer science community is increasingly aware of the von Neumann bottleneck. The main way in which the physical von Neumann bottleneck can be overcome is to devise architectures based on new computational models.

Conceptual bottleneck Conventional languages, developed when the von Neumann model was the only model known, are in some sense high-level, complex versions of the von Neumann model. They use variables to imitate the computer storage cells, control statements to elaborate its jump and test instructions, and assignment statements to imitate its fetching, storing and arithmetic. Solving complicated problems is done in terms of low-level, rather than high-level, operations. The style of the conventional von Neumann programming languages resembles the word-at-a-time traffic through the bottleneck, rather than larger conceptual units of problems.

> 'The assignment statement is the von Neumann bottleneck of programming languages and keeps us thinking in word-at-a-time terms in much the same way the computer's bottleneck does.'
>
> (Backus, 1978)

The conceptual bottleneck is effectively fought by inventing new programming styles. Backus proposes the functional programming style, where solutions for problems are described at a high functional level. Another alternative is offered by logic programming, where the programmer describes what has to be solved and not how it has to be solved.

17.2 Classification of computational models

The purpose of this section is to present a classification of computational models. This classification uses as its basis two mechanisms existing in every computer: the control mechanism and the data mechanism. A combination of these mechanisms is defined to be a computational model.

17.2.1 Control and data mechanisms

Analogous to Flynn's approach (see Section 1.3), the foundations for the classification of computational models are program and data. However, instead of instructions, computational units are considered:

> Computational units are abstract functional blocks performing operations on their arguments and producing some results.

In the case of conventional computers, these computational units are program instructions, but in the case of data flow computers, for example, they are nodes of a data flow graph. The introduction of computational units, instead of instructions, gives a more general view of computer architecture and the way computation is carried out. It allows for the classification of different novel architectures, which do not operate at the instruction level.

Instead of Flynn's instruction and data streams, Treleaven's approach is followed, and control and data mechanisms are considered (Treleaven, 1984).

Control mechanisms

For any computer architecture, it is possible to speak of computational units as being abstract functional blocks performing operations on their arguments and producing some results. Computer programs, written in a human-readable form, are translated into sets of computational units. These sets are executed by the computer. The control mechanism is an important aspect of this execution and is defined as follows:

> The control mechanism is the mechanism that determines how the computation will proceed; that is, which computational units execute next and when they start executing.

Four possible control mechanisms are described here: control driven, data driven, demand driven and pattern driven.

Control driven A control-driven control mechanism is one where every computational unit appoints itself its unique successor. A problem is decomposed into a specific sequence of directives (instructions), which are encoded and stored in the memory. These directives are sequentially read and executed, causing data to be modified.

A variety of control constructs, such as branches, loops and procedures, are used to build sequences of instructions. Using these constructs, instructions determine their successors explicitly.

The contents of a central sequence control device, usually called a program counter, determines implicitly the flow of the computational units; that is, if a unit does not choose its successor explicitly, a default successor is chosen by the sequence control device.

The control-driven control mechanism is used in conventional computers. Program instructions are computational units. They are active agents transforming passive data.

Data driven This denotes a computational organization where computational units passively wait for some combination of their arguments to become available. In a data-driven computational organization, the key factor driving the execution is the availability of data. For this reason, data driven is the same as availability driven.

Every computational unit in a computer working according to the data-driven control mechanism is by default chosen to be executed. Every unit expects a strictly specified number of arguments. If and only if they are all available, the unit executes. The execution produces some results that are passed to strictly specified consuming units. Programs in the data-driven computation are specifications of the paths data have to take, together with the operations that must be performed on them.

The data-driven computation is parallel in nature. Its parallelism is inhibited only by direct data dependencies. This offers great opportunities, but also gives rise to problems. Potential problems are:

- Too much parallelism may be generated. Memory may be swamped with partial results, which are not yet used, causing deadlock. Decisions about suspending processes are difficult because there is no centralized control mechanism. Control passes from bottom up in a distributed fashion, only as a direct result of availability of data.
- In a purely data-driven system, all subexpressions of conditional statements are evaluated in parallel, causing unnecessary computations to be performed.

Demand driven This originates from the fact that a computational unit is executed only when the result it produces is needed; that is, when its execution is demanded by another, already active, unit. In other words, the requirement for a result triggers the execution of the computational unit that will generate it. This is also known as 'lazy evaluation'. A demand-driven execution is thought of as performing precisely those computations that are required to produce the output of the program. Typically, a request for printing the value of some variable in a program is considered to be a demand for the value of that variable. The computation of this value will require, in general, the values of other variables in the program. The process of identifying those variables is commonly known as demand propagation.

The main advantage of demand-driven evaluation is the potential for eliminating a vast amount of computation. In a demand-driven evaluation, only those computations are performed which are required to produce the demanded output. Therefore, demand-driven evaluation will, in general, require less computation that data-driven evaluation.

The disadvantage is that in the case of a multiprocessing system, processors may be idle while they could be used to do some useful work, which is not directly demanded, but needed in the near future (for example, pre-evaluation of parameters, or evaluation of the possibly needed parts of a conditional expression).

Pattern driven Computational units in pattern-driven computation are executed when some enabling patterns or conditions are matched. The occurrence and matching of an enabling target pattern causes a computational unit to execute. The execution of a unit results again in the generation of result patterns. These patterns take part in further matching or are the final results. The pattern-driven control mechanism contains a high potential for parallelism, because many patterns may be matched in parallel.

Data mechanisms

> The data mechanism defines the way computational units exchange data between them.

Two data mechanisms can be distinguished: shared data and message passing.

Shared data Shared data assumes that one single copy of the argument is placed in memory, which is accessible to each computational unit. This way of communicating data is the most popular and is widely accepted as the simplest. Shared, common, memory was one of the main concepts of conventional computers and was for many years the only known way of passing data between instructions. For the machine instructions of a conventional computer, it is the only way of communicating data. High-level programming languages, such as FORTRAN or ALGOL, allow many of the details of this to be hidden, but they implement the same mechanism. The programmer is not concerned with memory directly, but with many small symbolic pieces of memory, called variables. Constructs such as global variables, 'call by name', 'call by reference' and pointers are extensions of the shared data mechanism. Computational units are equipped with a mechanism to refer to the data, so they know their names or their locations (memory addresses).

The shared data mechanism causes many problems in parallel systems. Access to data has to be synchronized by an arbitration mechanism, as each of the computational units working in parallel is capable of modifying it.

Message passing Message passing assumes one copy of the argument for each computational unit. Whenever an argument must be passed to another unit, it is copied, and this copy is passed as a message to the destination units. Although this mechanism is less obvious, it is known in the world of conventional computers. It is encountered mostly at higher levels, such as procedures or processes. A typical example of message passing is the call-by-value mechanism of high-level programming languages such as FORTRAN, ALGOL and Pascal. A procedure parameter, passed by value, is only a copy of the original data and is local to the called routine.

17.2.2 Taxonomy of computational models

This section gives a classification of computational models in terms of the control and the data mechanism, which are orthogonal to each other; each type of control mechanism can be combined with each type of data mechanism. This combination describes an execution scheme, also called a computational model (Treleaven, 1984):

> A computational model is the execution scheme prescribing the execution order of computational units and the way data is passed between them.

There are eight different types of computational models: COSH, COME, DASH, DAME, DESH, DEME, PASH and PAME (Figure 17.2). The

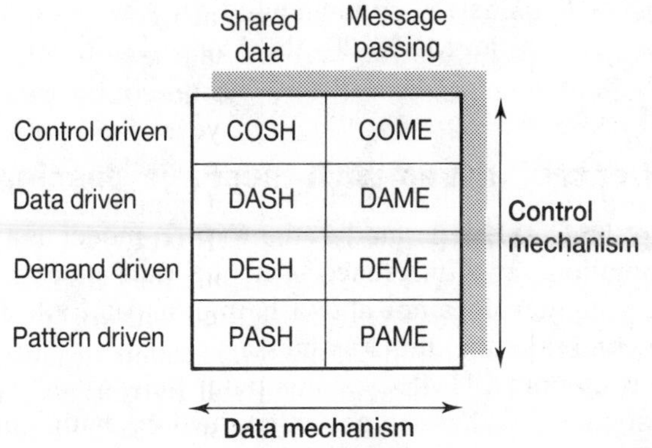

FIGURE 17.2
Taxonomy of computational models.

computational model on which the von Neumann architecture is based is classified as COSH. Architectures described by other models belong to so-called non-conventional or non-von Neumann computer architectures.

The proposed classification of computer architectures does not pretend to order all existing and future architectures. A number of architectures use mixed control or data mechanisms and do not fit well into a single cell of the proposed taxonomy. Every computer, however, has a control and a data mechanism, so it is always possible to determine the appropriate class in Figure 17.2, even if the class crosses boundaries between cells.

17.3 Description of computational models

This section describes the computational models of Figure 17.2. As the issue of parallelism is of increasing importance for computer architectures, special attention is paid to the ability of the different computational models to support parallelism. Examples of, or references to, architectures of each type are given.

17.3.1 Control driven with shared data

The COSH computational model combines the features of the control-driven control mechanism and shared data mechanism. A centralized control mechanism and code acting as an active agent transforming passive shared data are the main characteristics of COSH.

It is inherently difficult to express parallelism in a language working according to a COSH-type model. The first problem is that the control mechanism is based on the concept of a single sequence of operations. The second problem is the shared data mechanism. Access to data needs synchronizing, as each of the parallel computational units is capable of modifying the data.

The COSH model is implemented by conventional computer architectures, such as the MC68020, the VAX-11, the IBM/360 and the NS32000.

17.3.2 Control driven with message passing

Analogous to the COSH-type model, the COME model assumes control-driven computation. The difference is in the data mechanism. A pure COME-type computer does not allow sharing of data. All data is passed between the computational units as messages.

There is no pure COME-type computer built so far. However, one can speak about a COME type when dealing with communicating processes. Each process is considered a computational unit, which passes data to other units by means of messages. Messages consist of copies of data, which are further processed by the receiving process.

17.3.3 Data driven with shared data

The DASH computational model assumes data-driven computation and shared data. Data-driven computers imply a high degree of relatively fine-grain parallelism and consist mostly of a large number of computational units. Synchronization problems related to the shared memory mechanism inhibit fine-grain parallelism, as the synchronization overhead outweighs the parallelism benefits. Fine-grain parallelism is parallelism at the instruction level, whereas coarse-grain parallelism is at the level of groups of instructions – for example, at the subroutine level.

No computational models of the DASH type have as yet been invented. Some implementations of data structures in data flow computers, such as I-structures, implement the DASH model (Arvind, 1980; Nikhil, 1986). Synchronization of access to the data is indeed organized at the level of single memory cells.

17.3.4 Data driven with message passing

In computational units of the DAME class, the arrival of a message causes the computational units to execute. Each computational unit expects a certain combination of operands and after execution it produces one or more results, which are passed to the consuming units. This may cause their execution, thus the computation is data driven. Operands (also called tokens) consist of data together with the identification of the computational unit for which they are destined.

A DAME-type computer is inherently parallel, as it consists of a number of independent computational units, executing in parallel if there is no data dependency between their operands. If many computational units have their operands available, then these units may execute concurrently.

The DAME-type architectures are widely used and are called **data flow architectures** (Ackerman, 1982). A single-chip, data flow machine is available from NEC (1985).

□□EXAMPLE 17.1

A data flow graph is a form of symbolic representation of a solution to a problem embodying all operations on data and dependencies between them. Data flow graphs describe the parallelism of problems at a very low level. A problem is portrayed in a graph, in which operations are represented by vertices (the square boxes of Figure 17.3) and the data

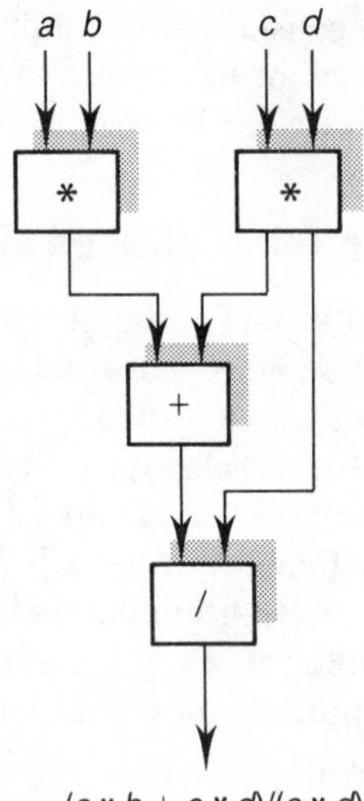

FIGURE 17.3
Example of a data flow graph.

dependencies between the operations by directed arcs. Figure 17.3 shows a data flow graph representing the computation of the expression $(a * b + c * d)/(c * d)$.

Data flow graphs describe the way a computation takes place. Data flows through the graph via the arcs, while the vertices perform operations on the data. The vertices producing results send these to the proper consuming vertices by attaching the proper addresses to the result. The execution of any computational unit (vertex) is only dependent on the arrival of the operands.

17.3.5 Demand driven with shared data

The DESH computational model assumes demand-driven execution of computational units operating on shared data. The computation starts with the evaluation of an initial query (initial demand). This evaluation proceeds as long as all arguments are available. When an argument is needed, a subquery (a demand) for its evaluation is formulated and the computation proceeds with evaluating that subquery. When the argument is finally evaluated, the computation continues with the original query.

Initial query and subqueries are located in a shared memory. This combination allows for an optimization in argument evaluation. Once an argument has been evaluated, it does not need to be computed again, although it may be used many times.

Parallel evaluation of a DESH model architecture is possible, if a good synchronization mechanism for the shared data is provided.

Example 17.2 shows the general concept of a reduction machine. The evaluation process is one of substitution of subexpressions in the expression to be evaluated. Reducible subexpressions are successively replaced by their simpler in-form equivalents. The evaluation process ends when a constant expression, representing the result of the computation, is reached.

An example of the DESH class of computers is the **graph-reduction** computers, such as SKIM (Clarke, 1980; Stoye, 1984) and ALICE (Darlington, 1981). The evaluation process is shown in Example 17.2, where subgraphs may be shared, and therefore only need to be evaluated once – for example, in the expression (+ (∗ *a* (+ *b c*))(/ *d* (+ *b c*))), the subgraph (+ *b c*) will be evaluated once.

□□EXAMPLE 17.2

Assuming the following definitions:

$a = 5$ **(17.1)**

$b = 3$ **(17.2)**

$c = (+\ a\ b)$ **(17.3)**

$d = (-\ a\ b)$ **(17.4)**

+, −, ∗

The expression (∗ *c d*) is evaluated as follows (assuming serially demand-driven evaluation):

Applied Definition	Resulting Expression
	(∗ *c d*)
(17.3)	(∗ (+ *a b*) *d*)
(17.1)	(∗ (+ 5 *b*) *d*)
(17.2)	(∗ (+ 5 3) *d*)
+	(∗ 8 *d*)
(17.4)	(∗ 8 (− *a b*))
(17.1)	(∗ 8 (− 5 *b*))
(17.2)	(∗ 8 (− 5 3))
−	(∗ 8 2)
∗	16

From this example, it can be seen that a sub(expression) is reducible when either the name of a definition is encountered or built-in reduction rules can be applied (in this case the operators +, − and * applied to numbers).

In the case of a parallel evaluation process, the evaluation of the expression will take the following form:

Applied Definition	**Resulting Expression**
	(* *c* *d*)
(17.3), (17.4)	(* (+ *a* *b*) (− *a* *b*))
(17.1), (17.2), (17.1), (17.2)	(* (+ 5 3) (− 5 3))
+, −	(* 8 2)
*	16

17.3.6 Demand driven with message passing

The DEME computational model assumes demand-driven evaluation with message passing. Just as in DESH, computation is driven by demand. An initial query starts the evaluation, which proceeds as long as all arguments are available. When an argument is needed, a subquery for its evaluation is formulated and the computation proceeds with evaluating that subquery. When the argument is finally evaluated, the computation continues with the original query.

Logically, there is no shared memory. The advantage of this model is that it offers good opportunities for parallel evaluation. Almost no synchronization is necessary, as there is no danger of modifying the same data by different computational units during parallel evaluation. A disadvantage is the need to evaluate the same subexpression several times, if the need for it occurs at different places, as there is no way to share expressions already evaluated. This may introduce a fair amount of overhead. In practical implementations, this problem is often solved by introducing an impurity in the model, consisting of an additional shared memory area for storing results of evaluated expressions. When an argument is demanded, it is first determined whether it has already been evaluated. If so, the result of the previous evaluation is used; if not, the argument is evaluated and the result of this evaluation is placed in the shared memory. This causes problems in a multiprocessor environment, as several computational units working in parallel may simultaneously demand the same data to be evaluated. In such cases, synchronization of access to the shared memory area is required, as one of the processors may want to write it.

An example of the DEME class of computers is the **string-reduction** computers, as described in Berkling (1975) and Kluge (1986). Example 17.2 shows the evaluation process of a string-reduction computer. Because of the message-passing data mechanism, subgraphs cannot be shared, and therefore will be evaluated independently – for example, the expression (+ (* *a* (+ *b c*))(/ *d* (+ *b c*))) will contain two copies of the subgraph (+ *b c*) and both will be evaluated, unless shared memory is added.

17.3.7 Pattern driven with shared data

The PASH computational model combines pattern-driven evaluation with the shared data mechanism. The execution is driven by goal statements (patterns), located in shared memory. Computational units are equipped with pattern-matching devices, which cause these units to execute when a matching pattern is found. An initial goal pattern is used to start the execution. This pattern is compared with the patterns already present in the shared memory of the computer. When a suitable match is found, subgoal patterns are generated, which are then satisfied in the same manner, until a solution is found or further matching fails. Alternative solutions to the problem are generated by means of parallelism or backtracking.

The PASH model offers good possibilities for parallel execution, as many goal patterns can be matched in parallel. A good synchronization mechanism is necessary for the newly generated patterns (hence they are shared by a number of computational units).

Examples of architectures based on the PASH computational model are **logic** architectures, such as the Parallel Inference Engine (Moto-Oka, 1984) and the Personal Sequential Inference Machine (Hertzberger, 1984).

□□EXAMPLE 17.3

Logic programming in languages such as PROLOG is based on Horn clauses, which are a subset of the predicate calculus (Kowalski, 1979). Consider the following example clauses, where variables start with an upper-case letter, and constants or atoms start with a lower-case letter:

```
son(Parent, Child) :- child(Child, Parent),
                      male(Child).
son(Parent, Child) :- brother(Child, Brother),
                      child(Brother, Parent).
```

The first clause expresses the fact that the son **(Child)** of somebody **(Parent)** is a male child of the **Parent**. The second clause states that the son **(Child)** of somebody is a brother of one of the children of the **Parent**.

A clause without a body is used to express explicit facts and is called an assertion. The following assertions express three relationships between Adam, Kain and Abel:

```
male(kain).
child(kain, adam).
child(abel, adam).
brother(abel, kain).
```

All clauses of a program form a database of clauses. This database is often called a knowledge base.

A clause with an empty head is interpreted as a query or goal. The query:

```
?- son(adam, Who).
```

asks for a suitable value of the variable **Who**, or, in other words, asks the question 'Who is the son of Adam?' The task of the system is to try to answer this question by investigating the knowledge base. For a further and more detailed explanation of PROLOG, refer to Clocksin (1984).

17.3.8 Pattern driven with message passing

The PAME model combines pattern-driven evaluation with the message-passing mechanism. The execution is driven by messages, consisting of data patterns. Computational units are equipped in pattern-matching devices, which cause these units to react on the received pattern messages. An initial pattern message is used to start the execution. The pattern contained in that message is matched against patterns present in the receiving computational unit. When a match is found, the unit reacts on the message, generating possibly new pattern messages and sending them to other computational units. These messages are then treated in the same manner until the solution is found.

The PAME model offers good possibilities for parallel execution, as many computational units may work in parallel. As there is no shared data, there is nothing to restrict parallelism, except for the parallelism of the computed problem. The PAME computational model is strongly related to the concept of object-oriented programming.

Examples of architectures based on the PAME computational model are **actor** architectures, such as the Apiary machine (Hewitt, 1980; Hewitt, 1984).

□□EXAMPLE 17.4

Computation in object-oriented programming is performed by sending a message pattern to an object. For example, an expression to take the square root of X looks like this:

```
X : sqrt
```

Strictly speaking, it means that X is asked to perform the operation sqrt on itself. X is said to be the receiver of the message sqrt.

A message may also include parameters. In the following example, the matrix X is asked to add matrix Y to itself:

```
X : matrixadd Y
```

Typically, an object sends messages to other objects, which invoke other objects, until the point is reached where a primitive object is invoked. Here the chain of messages ends. matrixadd would probably send messages to add the elements of the matrix X with elements of the matrix Y as parameters.

Object-oriented languages also contain the concept of assignment. The following assigns the result of matrixadd to the matrix object Z:

```
Z ← X :matrixadd Y
```

SUMMARY

- A computational model is a conceptual method according to which a computation can be performed.
- An architecture is a concrete embodiment of a computational model.
- A von Neumann architecture is based on the computational model used by von Neumann for the first computer ever built.
- The von Neumann computational model is based on a computer consisting of a CPU, a memory and a connecting tube. A single-instruction stream is executed on data stored in memory.
- The semantic gap is the difference in the execution model used by higher-level languages and the von Neumann computer.
- The von Neumann bottleneck is the restriction in processing speed due to the connecting tube (physical bottleneck) or the restriction placed on the design of the higher-level languages because of the von Neumann model (conceptual bottleneck).
- The control mechanism is the mechanism that determines how a computation will proceed. It can be control driven, data driven, demand driven or pattern driven.
- The data mechanism defines the way computational units exchange data. This can be via shared data or via message passing.
- Traditional architectures are based on the control-driven with shared data computational model.
- Data flow architectures are based on the data-driven with message-passing computational model.
- Graph-reduction architectures are based on the demand-driven with shared data computational model.
- String-reduction architectures are based on the demand-driven with message-passing computational model.
- Logic architectures, which support logic programming languages such as PROLOG, are based on the pattern-driven with shared data computational model.
- Actor architectures, to support object-oriented programming, are based on the pattern-driven with message-passing computational model.

EXERCISES

17.1 What is a computational model and what is an architecture?

17.2 Which parts constitute a von Neumann computer?

17.3 What are the properties of the memory in the von Neumann model?

17.4 Which extensions to the von Neumann model are in conflict with the model?

17.5 What is the critique on the von Neumann model?

17.6 Give definitions of the two mechanisms used for the classification of computational models, together with the forms each mechanism can have.

17.7 Which control and data mechanisms allow for the most parallelism?

17.8 To which of the computational models do the following architectures belong:

(a) Conventional architectures?
(b) Data flow architectures?
(c) Graph-reduction machines?
(d) String-reduction machines?
(e) Architectures for logic programming?
(f) Architectures for object-oriented languages?

17.9 What is a potential disadvantage of the following computational models?

(a) Data driven with message passing.
(b) Demand driven with message passing.

References

Ackerman, W. B. (1982). Data flow languages. *Computer*, **15**(2), 15–25.

Arvind, T. R. E. (1980). I-structures: An efficient data type for functional languages. *Technical Memo 178*. MIT, Laboratory for Computer Science: Cambridge, MA.

Backus, J. (1978). Can programming be liberated from the von Neumann style? A functional style and its algebra of programs. *Comm. of the ACM*, **21**(8), 613–41.

Berkling, K. J. (1975). Reduction languages for reduction machines. In *Proc. 2nd Annual Symposium on Computer Architecture*, pp. 133–40.

Clarke, T. J. W. *et al.* (1980). SKIM – The S, K, I reduction machine. In *Proc. 1980 Lisp Conference*, Stanford, CA, pp. 128–35.

Clocksin, W. F. and Mellish, C. S. (1984). *Programming in Prolog*. Spring-Verlag: Berlin.

Darlington, J. and Reeve, M. (1981). ALICE, A multi-processor reduction machine for the parallel evaluation of applicative languages. In *Proc. International Symposium on Functional Programming and Computer Architecture*, pp. 32–62.

Feustel, E. A. (1973). On the advantages of tagged architectures. *IEEE Trans. on Computers*, **C–22**(7), 644–56.

Gehringer, E. F. and Keedy, J. L. (1985). Tagged architectures: How compelling are its advantages. In *Proc. 12th Annual Symposium on Computer Architecture*, pp. 162–70.

Hertzberger, L. O. (1984). The architecture of fifth generation inference computers. *Future Generation Computer Systems*, **1**(1), 9–21.

Hewitt, C. (1980). The Apiary network architecture for knowledgeable systems. In *Proc. 1980 Lisp Conference*, Stanford, CA, pp. 107–17.

Hewitt, C. and Lieberman, H. (1984). Design issues in parallel architectures for artificial intelligence. In *Proc. of the COMPCON 84*, pp. 418–23.

Kluge, W. E. (1986). Reduction machines and functional languages. *Lecture Notes of the Esprit Summer School on Future Parallel Computers*, Pisa, Italy.

Kowalski, R. (1979). *Logic for Problem Solving*. North-Holland Publishing Company: New York, NY.

Moto-Oka, T. *et al.* (1984). The architecture of parallel inference engine – PIE. In *Proc. International Conference on Fifth Generation Computer Systems*, Tokyo, Japan, pp. 479–88.

NEC (1985). *User's Manual of the uPD7281*. NEC Electronics: Europe.

Nikhil, R. S. *et al.* (1986). ID nouveau. *Technical Memo 265*. MIT Laboratory for Computer Science, Computer Structures Group: Cambridge, MA.

Stoye, W. R. *et al.* (1984). Some practical methods for rapid combinator reduction. In *Proc. 1984 ACM Symposium on LISP and Functional Programming*, Austin, Texas, pp. 159–66.

Treleaven, P. C. and Lima, G. I. (1984). Future computers: Logic, data flow, . . ., control flow? *Computer*, **17**(3), 47–57.

von Neumann, J. *et al.* (1946). Preliminary discussions of the logical design of an electronic computing instrument. *US Army Ordnance Department Report*. Reprinted in Bell, C. G. and Newell, A. (eds.) (1971). *Computer Structures: Readings and Examples*. McGraw-Hill: New York, pp. 92–119.

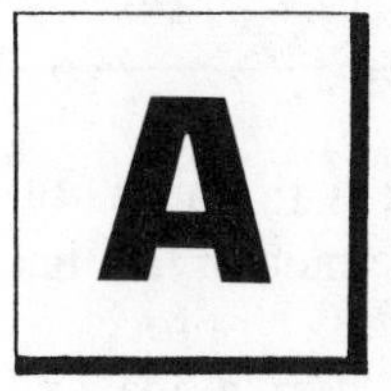

An Example: MC68020 Architecture

In science we resemble children collecting a few pebbles at the beach of knowledge, while the wide ocean of the unknown unfolds itself in front of us.

– Sir Isaac Newton

Because the notion 'architecture' is very abstract, it will be clarified by briefly describing the architecture of an existing microprocessor. This will give the reader a total view of an architecture and a frame of reference for the chapters of Part Two in which a detailed analysis of the different architectural aspects is presented. The material in this appendix is therefore presented in the same sequence as the topics of Part Two, but without the more extensive discussion, given in those chapters.

The Motorola MC68020 processor is chosen as an example because of its widespread use. Motorola has defined a complete and extensive architecture, the 68000 family, which is still being extended. The MC68000 was the first real embodiment of this family, containing only a subset of the complete architecture, due to technological constraints. Since 1979, more implementations have been introduced, such as the MC68010, the MC68020 and the MC68030, and yet others have been announced (MC68040, MC68070). Unless stated otherwise, this chapter will discuss the architecture of the MC68020 CPU. Rather than discussing every detail, the main characteristics of the MC68020 architecture are emphasized. More detailed information can be found in the manual (Motorola, 1985a) and the chapters of this book.

A.1 Main characteristics

The MC68020 is a true 32-bit architecture with a 32-bit data and 32-bit address bus, which allows for the addressing of a 4 Gbyte memory. It has a 256-byte, on-chip instruction cache and a general co-processor interface. The MC68020 has two modes of operation, user mode and supervisor mode, with the supervisor mode being the more privileged one.

A.1.1 Programming model

For both modes of operation (user and supervisor), the MC68020 has a different programming model. The user programming model consists of four parts whereas the supervisor programming model extends the user programming model with several parts.

User programming model

Data and address registers The general-purpose registers (see Figure A.1(a)) are somewhat different from many other processors, because the register file is divided into two sets: eight data registers (D0–D7) and eight address registers (A0–A7), all 32 bits wide. These two sets were probably created because there was insufficient operand space (the space used for binary encoding the operands) to specify one of the 16 registers for both the source and destination operand, as this would require 2 * 4 bits. The implemented solution only requires 2 * 3 bits at the expense of a non-consistent treatment of the data and address registers.

The data registers, used for manipulating data, can be addressed as bit, byte, word or long word operands (1, 8, 16 or 32 bits, respectively). Byte and word operations only use the low-order byte or word of the register, as shown in Figure A.1 by the broken lines. For addressing, registers D0–D7 can only be used as index registers.

The address registers are used to hold operand addresses; operations on them will not affect the status register, which is in contrast to operations on data registers. Furthermore, byte operations on address registers are not supported, and words that are moved to address registers are sign extended to 32 bits (again in contrast with data registers).

Stack pointer A7 is implicitly designated as a system stack pointer (SP) for subroutine calls and interrupts. This stack pointer is only used in the user mode of operation.

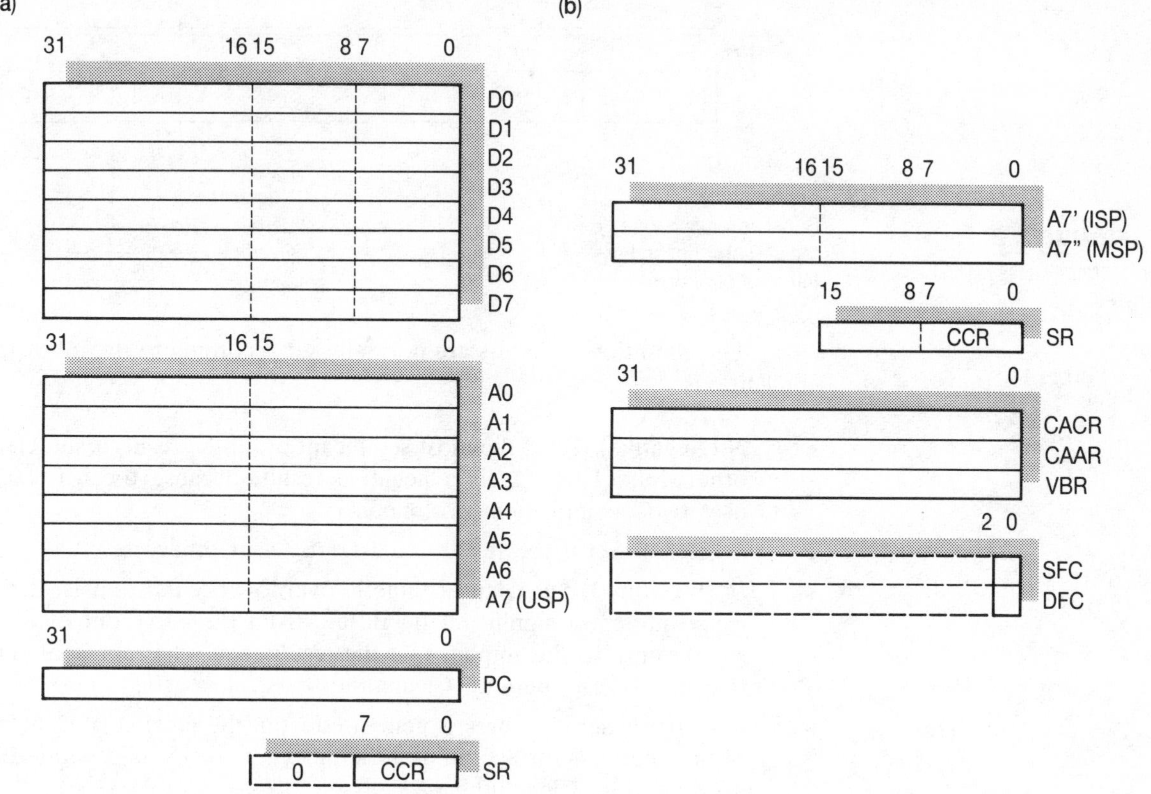

FIGURE A.1

MC68020 programming model: (a) user model; (b) supervisor extensions.

Program counter The MC68020 contains a 32-bit program counter (PC), which is used to access the next instruction to be executed.

Condition code register The MC68020 has a 16-bit status register (SR), composed of a **system byte** and a **user byte** (see Figure A.2). In the user mode of operation, only the user byte can be accessed, while the system byte is always read as zero.

The user byte, the low-order byte of the status register, contains the condition flags; therefore, it is normally called the condition code register (CCR). The CCR contains four condition code bits, Zero (Z), Negative (N), Overflow (V) and Carry (C), which reflect the processor status after an operation. In addition, the CCR contains the extend bit (X), which can be used as an operand (carry) in extended-precision operations (see Section 6.6). It is set in the same way as the normal carry flag (C), although it is left unchanged by data move operations, whereas the carry is cleared on a MOVE. The three other bits of the CCR are reserved and cannot be used.

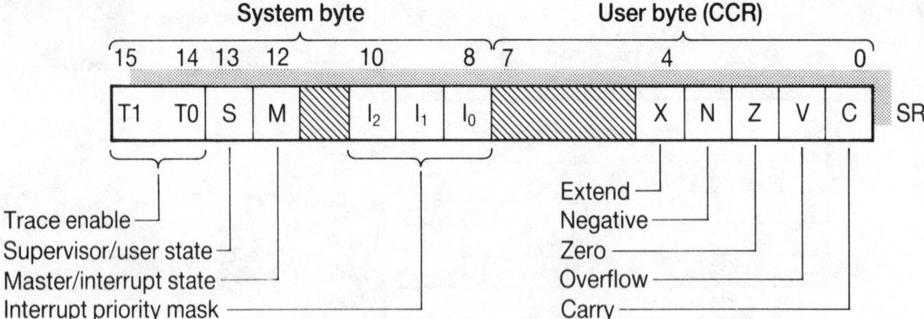

FIGURE A.2
MC68020 status register.

The condition code bits are normally set according to the following conventions:

- N (Negative): Set if the most significant bit of the result is set, clear otherwise. (This signals a negative result, because the MC68020 uses two's complement arithmetic.)
- Z (Zero): Set if the result equals zero, clear otherwise.
- V (Overflow): Set if an arithmetic overflow occurs; that is, if the carry into most significant bit differs from the carry out of most significant bit. This implies that the result cannot be represented in the destination operand. Clear otherwise.
- C (Carry): Set if a carry is generated from the most significant bit of the operands for an addition. Set also if a borrow is generated in a subtraction. Clear otherwise.
- X (Extend): Transparent to data movement. When affected, it is set the same as the C bit.

For the exact rules, the reader is referred to the Motorola manual (1985a).

Supervisor programming model

Several extra control registers can be accessed in the supervisor mode of operation (see Figure A.1(b)). These are the cache control register (CACR) and the cache address register (CAAR) to control the on-chip instruction cache, and vector base register (VBR), pointing to the start of the exception vector table, and the source and destination function code register (SFC and DFC, respectively) to provide the source and destination space identifiers for the MOVE instruction.

Stack pointers In addition to the user stack pointer A7 (USP), the supervisor programming model has two extra stack pointers: the interrupt stack pointer A7 (ISP) and the master stack pointer A7 (MSP). The

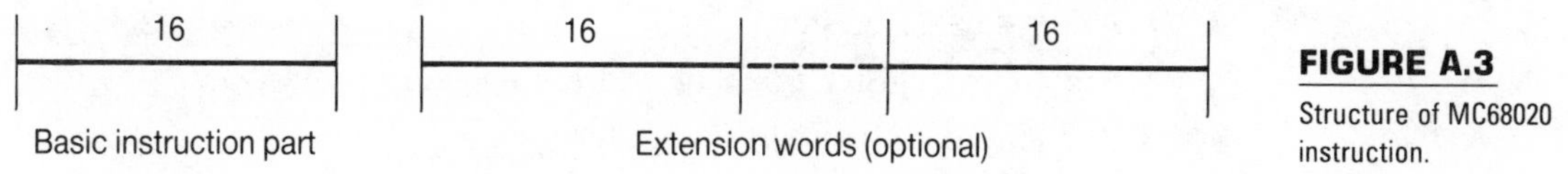

FIGURE A.3
Structure of MC68020 instruction.

register accessed as stack pointer depends on a bit in the status register. The general term supervisor stack pointer (SSP) refers to the MSP or ISP, depending on this bit.

Status register The system byte, the high-order byte of the status register (see Figure A.2), can only be changed in supervisor mode, and contains bits for processor control. The trace bits (T0, T1) are used to enable on-line debugging. Three trace states are defined: no tracing, trace on instruction execution and trace on change of flow. The interrupt mask bits (I_2, I_1, I_0) are used to indicate the current interrupt priority level. Only interrupts with a level higher than the current level are accepted; all others are masked. The supervisor bit (S) is used to indicate the mode of operation (S = 1: supervisor mode; S = 0: user mode). Supervisor mode is important in multi-user environments (for example, for memory management and protection purposes). When S = 0, the USP is selected as stack pointer; when S = 1, the Master bit (M) is used to select a stack pointer (M = 1: MSP; M = 0: ISP). The MSP is used in the stacking of process-related exceptions only.

A.1.2 Instruction formats

The MC68020 architecture supports instructions having a length of 2 bytes (called a word) or multiples thereof; that is, the address resolution for instructions is a word. The basic part of the instruction requires one word, while, depending on the opcode or the operand specification, a total of up to 10 extension words may be required (see Figure A.3). The architecture has been designed so that frequently used operand specifications require the fewest number of words for instruction specification (typically a single word).

In the remainder of this section, the formats of both the basic instruction part and the extension words are discussed. Throughout this book the following notation will be used:

- Src: A source operand. The set of allowed source addressing modes is instruction dependent.
- Dst: A destination operand. The set of allowed destination addressing modes is instruction dependent.

- Dn: Data register.
- An: Address register.
- Xn: Index register (data or address register).
- Rn: Any data or address register.
- Data: Immediate data contained in the instruction stream.
- Cnt: Data used for rotate and shift instructions.
- Bnum: Specification of bit number.
- Disp: 8, 16 or 32-bit displacement.
- d_{16}: 16-bit displacement.
- d_8: 8-bit displacement.
- List: List of selected registers.
- N: Operand size in bytes (1, 2 or 4).
- ( ): contents of.
- ea: Effective address.
- M: Memory.
- [ ]: Subscripting.
- #: Immediate value.
- 0x: Value expressed in hexadecimal notation.
- 0b: Value expressed in binary (two's complement) notation.
- blank: Value expressed in decimal notation.

□□EXAMPLES

(a) 61, 0x3D and 0B00111101 represent the same value.
(b) M[3] = memory location 3.
(c) M[(A0)] = memory location specified by (A0).
(d) D3[3] = bit 3 of data register D3.
(e) D3[10 . . 7] = bits 10 through 7 of data register D3.
(f) M[3][2] = bit 2 of M[3].

Basic instruction formats

The MC68020 instruction set contains 101 instruction types, which use many different instruction formats. These formats can be categorized according to the number of operands for each instruction (see Figure A.4).

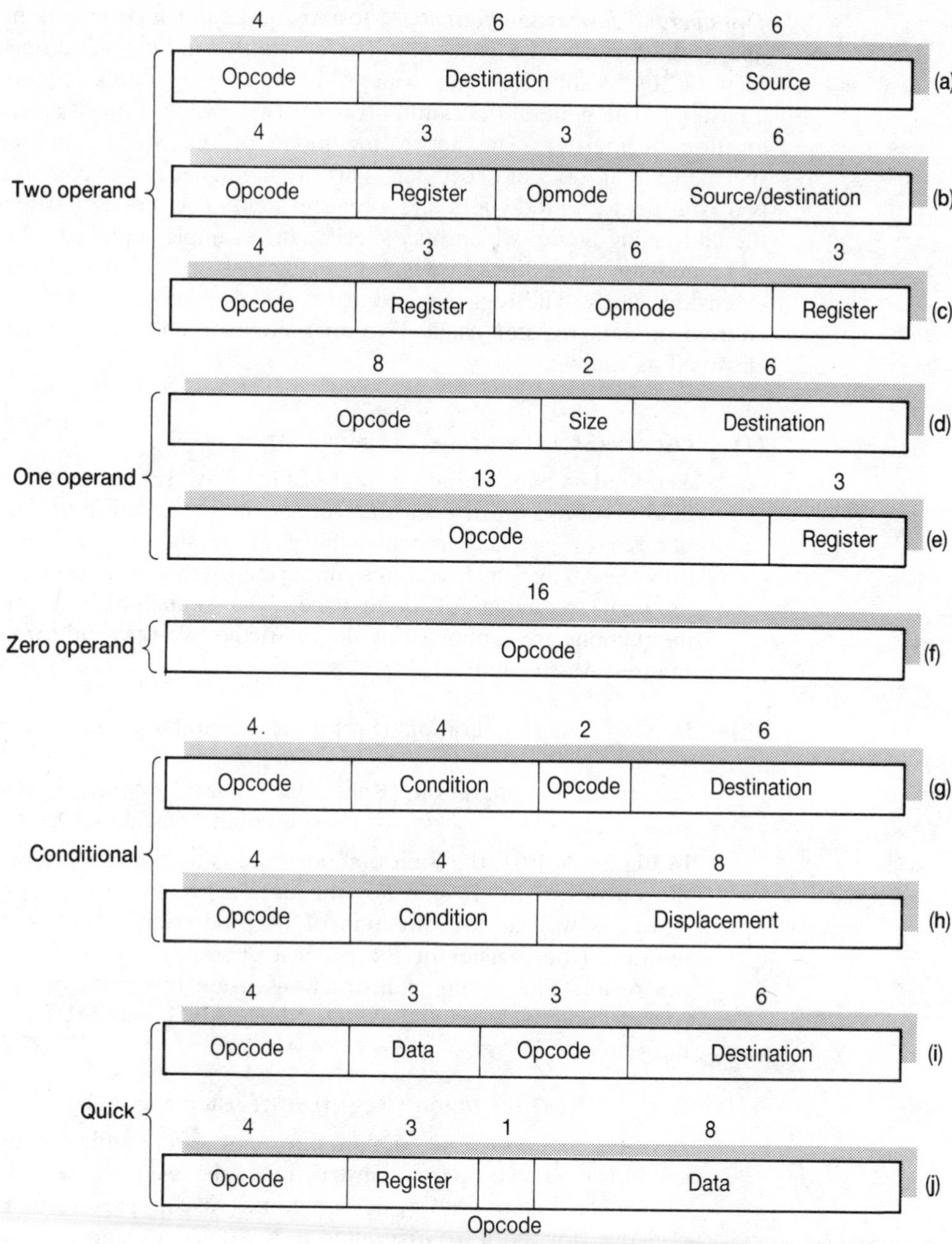

FIGURE A.4

MC68020 instruction formats.

Two-operand instruction formats Most two-operand instructions fit into one of the formats of Figure A.4. The operands can be **general operands** (denoted by 'destination' and 'source') or **register operands** (denoted by 'register'). The general operand allows for the specification of a memory location or register. The addressing mode of the Src/Dst operand is specified via an operand specifier. This operand specifier is composed of two 3-bit fields, a mode field and a register field. The mode field specifies the addressing mode, which may specify, for example, indexed, absolute or immediate addressing, in which case the instruction is extended with extension words. The register field normally specifies the number of the address or data register used. Two-operand instruction formats can be classified as follows:

(1) Dst := (Src) (two general operands).

The Src/Dst two-operand format of Figure A.4(a) leaves an opcode field of 4 bits, which is insufficient for the specification of the large number of instructions which have to be supported. Therefore, only the MOVE instruction is supported by this format, because of its high frequency of occurrence. The remaining two-operand instructions are supported by the restricted two-operand formats of Figures A.4(b) and (c).

(2) Reg := (Reg) operation (Src) (one general operand, acting as source).

Dst := (Dst) operation (Reg) (one general operand, acting as source and destination).

In Figure A.4(b), the 3-bit opmode field is used as an extension to the opcode field. It specifies the data type (byte, word or long word) as well as the direction of the operation – that is, which operand (the register or the general operand) is used for storing the result. The group of instructions using this form of operand specification includes the ADD, SUB, AND and MUL instructions.

(3) Reg := (Reg) operation (Reg) (two register operands).

Because the above restriction does not offer sufficient opcode space for all two-operand instructions, the even more restricted format of Figure A.4(c) is sometimes used. This format uses registers for both source and destination operands. The 6-bit opmode field now specifies not only the data type of the operands, but also whether data or address registers (or both) are used. Instructions in this class include EXG (exchange two registers) and SUBX (Subtract with Extend).

One-operand instruction formats Two formats for one-operand instructions are shown in Figures A.4(d) and (e). The first format is used for instructions requiring a Dst operand specification, such as CLR (Clear) and NEG (Negate, that is, perform the two's complement). The second form is used for one-operand instructions that only use one data register, such as EXT (sign extend the contents of a register) and SWAP (swap the two halves of a register).

Zero-operand instruction formats Figure A.4(f) shows the zero-operand instruction format for instructions that have no operand at all. Examples of these instructions are NOP, RESET and RTS (Return from Subroutine).

Conditional instruction formats Figures A.4(g) and (h) show the formats of some conditional instructions. The Scc (Set Conditionally) instruction format, shown in Figure A.4(g), uses a Dst operand, and the Bcc (Branch Conditionally) instruction format (see Figure A.4(h)) uses an 8-bit displacement field. If the coding of the condition is considered to be part of the opcode, these instructions use an 8 or 10-bit opcode, and the Scc instruction, for example, could be classified as a one-operand instruction (with a Dst operand).

Quick instruction formats Special instruction formats, shown in Figures A.4(i) and (j), are used for the ADDQ, SUBQ and MOVEQ instructions. These instructions use a small constant (immediate value) that is coded within the basic instruction part, so no extension words are needed. The ADDQ and SUBQ instructions of Figure A.4(i) contain a 3-bit constant, representing a range from 1 to 8 (8 is coded as 0; adding zero is not useful). The MOVEQ instruction, which uses the format of Figure A.4(j), is used to move 8-bit constants to a data register. The data is sign extended to a long word operand and all 32 bits are transferred to the data register. The 8 bits allow constants between −128 and +127 to be specified.

Extension word formats

As stated before, the length of the basic part of an instruction is always 16 bits, with a maximum of 6 bits per operand specifier. Because these 6 bits are not always sufficient to exactly specify the desired operand or operand address, the use of extension words is sometimes necessary.

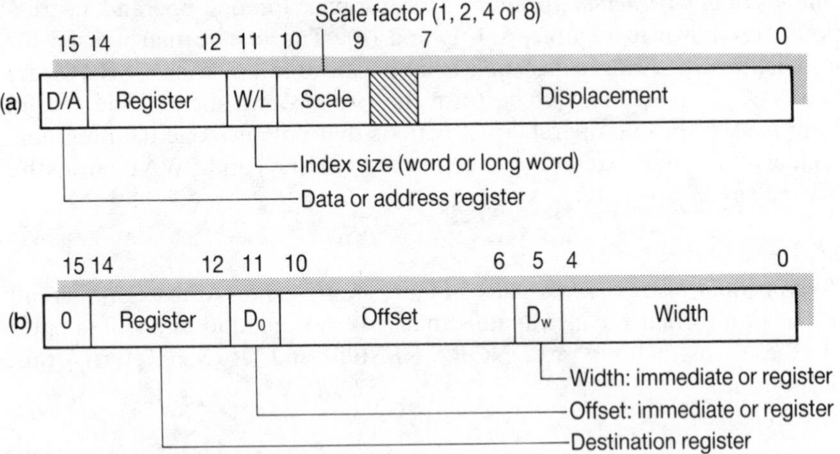

FIGURE A.5

Extension word format for indexed addressing mode.

Depending on the information in an extension word, the following classification of extension word formats can be made:

(1) A displacement in the MC68020 is a 16 or 32-bit two's complement integer, contained in one or two extension word(s), and it is sign extended and added to the program counter (PC) to form the destination address. These extension words are optional for branch instructions, where only one word is present if the 8-bit displacement contained within the basic part of the instruction is zero, or two words are present if the 8-bit displacement equals 0xFF (see Figure 7.7).

(2) Immediate data can be considered as a constant, specified inside the instruction stream. It can be 8, 16 or 32 bits in length, but, because the MC68020 only allows instruction lengths that are multiples of 16 bits, an 8-bit constant is stored in the lower byte of a word, while the upper byte contains zeros.

(3) If the absolute addressing mode is used, the instruction is followed by one or two extension words, containing the absolute memory address.

(4) In the indexed addressing mode, the MC68020 computes its operand address by adding the contents of a base (address) register to the contents of an index register and an 8-bit displacement. To specify all components, one extension word is needed, as shown in Figure A.5(a). For the memory indirect addressing modes, a more extensive extension word is necessary (see Motorola, 1985a).

The operand specifier contains the number of the base register, which is always an address register. The extension word specifies whether a data or address register is used as the index register, the register number, the size of the index value (the sign-extended, low-order word or the entire index register) and the (sign-extended) 8-bit displacement.

(5) The instruction MOVEM loads or stores a list of up to 16 registers from or to a specified memory address. To specify which registers are transferred, a list mask in the form of an extension word is used. If a bit in the mask is set, the corresponding register is transferred. A more detailed explanation of this list mask can be found in Example 6.2.

(6) The bit field instructions use an extension word (see Figure A.5(b)) to specify an optional destination register, the field offset (either immediate or contained in a data register) and the field width (either immediate or contained in a data register). Example 6.5 explains the MC68020 bit field extract instructions BFEXTS and BFEXTU.

The presence of an extension word can be specified by the opcode (in the case of the MOVEM instruction), the operand specifier (by an addressing mode that uses extension words) or the operand value (in branch instructions). Considering the extension word specifications, it appears that the presence of a register list mask is determined by the opcode, and that the presence of absolute addresses or index extension words is determined by operand specifiers. The presence of extension words containing immediate data and displacements can be determined by both the opcode and the operand specifiers, whereas the operand value can sometimes determine the necessity of a displacement extension word, as is the case with branch displacements.

A.1.3 Data types

The data types supported by the MC68020 can be divided into the following categories (see also Chapter 3):

(1) Booleans: To support high-level language Boolean variables there is an instruction, Scc, which can use the same conditions as the conditional branch instruction and which assigns a value of TRUE (all ones) or FALSE (all zeros) to a destination operand, depending on the condition specified.

(2) Integers: Integers can be divided into fixed-length and variable-length integers. The fixed-length integers have a length of 8, 16 or 32 bits (byte (B), word (W) and long word (L), respectively) and are considered to be in two's complement representation. Furthermore, the instructions MUL and DIV use 64-bit (quad word (Q))

integers, stored in two data registers, to hold a double-length product (the product of two long word integers). If 32 bits do not offer enough precision, the programmer can use extended-precision integers (integers with variable lengths), which are supported by a special bit in the condition code register (extend flag X) and special instructions, such as ADDX (Add with Extend), NEGX (Negate with Extend) and MULU (Multiply Unsigned). The MC68020 has no special support for characters, so they must be processed as 8-bit integers.

(3) Decimals: The MC68020 supports binary-coded decimal (BCD) numbers in a limited way. Two BCD digits are contained in one byte. All BCD instructions (ABCD (Add BCD), SBCD (Subtract BCD) and NBCD (Negate BCD)) operate on only byte operands. With the X bit (as was done with multi-precision integers), a program can use variable-sized decimal numbers, although the length must be controlled by software. Furthermore, the MC68020 contains the instructions PACK and UNPK to convert to and from unpacked BCD decimals.

Although they are not a complete data type, single bits can be manipulated by four special instructions that clear, set, complement or simply test a bit. Single bits cannot be considered to represent the Boolean data type completely because of the absence of support for such operations as AND and OR.

Bit fields are supported, where a bit field is from 1 to 32 bits in length and can start at any bit location in memory. A bit field is specified via an effective address operand, a bit offset with respect to the base address and a field width. Instruction support includes bit-field clear, set, complement or test (similar to single-bit instructions), in addition to instructions to extract, insert or search a bit field.

Addresses can be considered as a special kind of integer (unsigned, 32-bit integers). They are supported by several instructions that only operate on these addresses in address registers, such as MOVEA (Move Address) and CMPA (Compare Address).

A.1.4 Memory data organization

The MC68020 memory organization is shown in Figure A.6. The basic addressable data unit is a byte; that is, each byte can be addressed separately. A word consists of two bytes and the address of a word is determined by the byte address of the high-order byte. The address of a long word also corresponds to the address of the high-order byte. Instructions are accessed only on word boundaries (that is, on even byte addresses).

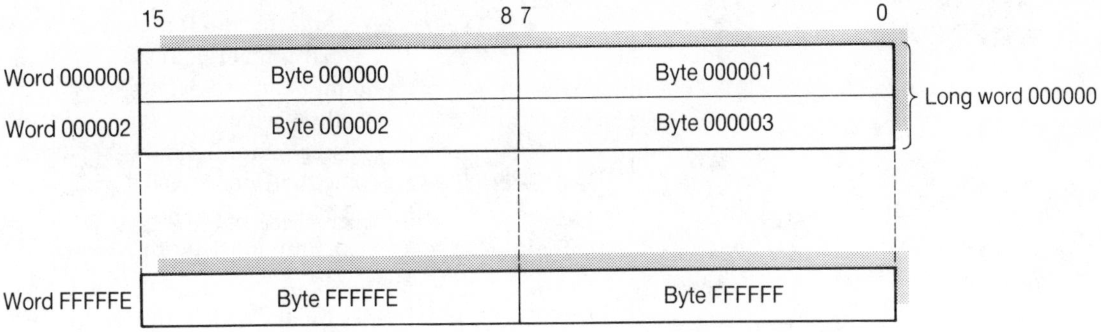

FIGURE A.6
MC68020 memory organization.

For data, the MC68020 has an address resolution of a byte; that is, a byte can be accessed. Words and long words do not have to be aligned on even byte boundaries, but the most efficient data transfer is only possible when data is aligned on the same boundary as its operand size (such as long words on long word boundaries). However, a problem arises when byte operands are popped off the stack (or pushed on to it) using the auto-increment/decrement addressing mode (see Section A.2) with the stack pointer. To keep the stack aligned, for maximum efficiency, the stack is decremented or incremented by two rather than by one, when byte data is pushed on or popped off the stack.

A.2 Addressing modes

The addressing modes of the MC68020 are modelled after the PDP-11 (DEC, 1975). The general operand specifier of the MC68020 consists of a 3-bit mode field and a 3-bit register field, which allows for the specification of 12 different addressing modes (see Table A.1). For modes 0 through 6, the register field specifies the register number used. Mode 0 designates the use of a data register, whereas modes 1 through 6 always use an address register. In mode 7, the register field is used for a more precise addressing mode specification.

The addressing modes of the MC68020 are summarized in Table A.1, together with the name given in the MC68020 manuals (note that these names are not consistent), the assembler syntax and the way in which the effective address (ea) is computed. The addressing modes are usually classified according to the number of components, where a component can be a register, displacement or absolute address (see Figure A.7).

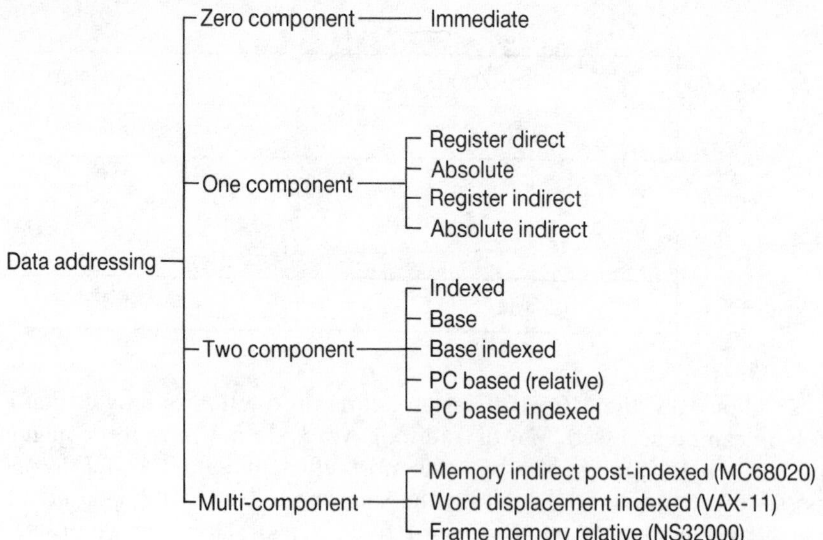

FIGURE A.7
Classification of addressing modes.

A.2.1 Zero-component addressing modes

The zero-component addressing mode of the MC68020 is called immediate addressing, as in most architectures. With the immediate addressing mode (mode 7.4 of Table A.1), the value of the operand is normally contained in one or two extension words, depending on the operand size. For example, in the instruction ADD.W #0x7AE2, D2 the source operand specifies the immediate value 0x7AE2; in the instruction ADD.L #0x700AB123, D2 the source operand specifies the immediate value 0x700AB123.

A.2.2 One-component addressing modes

Both data and address registers can be accessed directly, but for indirect addressing modes, only address registers can be used.

Data register direct

In the data register direct addressing mode (mode 0), the operand is contained in a data register. If a byte or word operation is performed on a data register, the high-order bits are not affected. The only word or byte instructions that read or write these bits are EXT and SWAP. For example, in the instruction ADD.W D0, D1 the operation performed is as follows: D1[15 . . 0] := (D1[15 . . 0]) + (D0[15 . . 0]); that is, the low-order word of D0 is added to the low-order word of D1.

Table A.1 MC68020 addressing modes.

Mode	Register	MC68020 Name	Syntax	Effective Address Computation
0	reg#	Data register direct	Dn	ea = Dn
1	reg#	Address register direct	An	ea = An
2	reg#	Address register indirect	(An)	ea = (An)
3	reg#	Address register indirect post-increment	(An)+	ea = (An), An = (An) + N
4	reg#	Address register indirect pre-decrement	−(An)	An = An − N, ea = (An)
5	reg#	Address register indirect displacement	(d_{16}, An)	ea = d_{16} + (An)
6	reg#	Address register indirect indexed	(d_8, An, Xn)	ea = d_8 + (An) + (Xn)
6	reg#	Memory indirect post-indexed	([bd, An], Xn, od)	ea = (M[(An) + bd]) + (Xn) + od
6	reg#	Memory indirect pre-indexed	([bd, An, Xn], od)	ea = (M[(An) + bd + (Xn)]) + od
7	0	Absolute short	xxx.W	ea = (next word)
7	1	Absolute long	xxx.L	ea = (next 2 words)
7	2	Program counter relative	(d_{16}, PC)	ea = d_{16} + (PC)
7	3	Program counter indexed	(d_8, PC, Xn)	ea = d_8 + (PC) + (Xn)
7	3	PC memory indirect post-indexed	([bd, PC], Xn, od)	ea = (M[(PC) + bd]) + (Xn) + od
7	3	PC memory indirect pre-indexed	([bd, PC, Xn], od)	ea = (M[(PC) + bd + (Xn)]) + od
7	4	Immediate	#xxx	data = (next word(s))

Note that the term Xn stands for the complete index operand Xn.SIZE * SCALE, where Xn selects any data or address register, SIZE specifies the index size (word or long word) and SCALE allows the index register to be multiplied by 1 (no scaling), 2, 4 or 8.

Address register direct

In the address register direct addressing mode (mode 1), the operand is contained in an address register. If the destination is the low-order word of an address register, all 32 bits are affected, because the word result is sign extended to 32 bits (that is, bit 15 is copied into bits 16 through 31).

Absolute

With absolute addressing (modes 7.0 and 7.1), the memory address is contained in one or two extension words, following the instruction. The MC68020 has two absolute addressing modes: a short and a long form. For 'absolute short' addressing, the instruction is followed by one 16-bit extension word that is sign extended to form the absolute memory address. This results in an address in either the bottom 32K (MSB = 0) or the top 32K (MSB = 1) of the 16-Mbyte address space. The 'absolute long' addressing mode uses two extension words (high-order word of the address first), which are concatenated to form the absolute memory address. For example, in the instruction ADD.W 0x76F1.W, D2 the source operand specifies the short absolute address 0x76F1, in the bottom 32 kbytes of memory, while in the instruction ADD.W 0xA6F1, D2 the short absolute address 0xA6F1 refers to memory location 0xFFFFA6F1.

Address register indirect

When the address register indirect addressing mode is used, the address of the operand can be found in the specified address register (modes 2, 3 and 4). Two variants of this addressing mode are supported: pre-decrement and post-increment. When the pre-decrement mode is used, the address register is first decremented by the size (in bytes) of the operand (1 for byte, 2 for word and 4 for long word operands) and then used as a pointer to the operand. For post-increment mode, the address register is incremented after it has been used. The post-increment and pre-decrement modes can be used for stepping through arrays, strings and other data structures, as well as for implementing stacks. For example, in the instruction ADD.W (A3)+, D2 the source operand specifies the address register indirect mode. Afterwards, the contents of register A3 is incremented by 2 (because the operation specified word operands).

A.2.3 Two-component addressing modes

The MC68020 does not have the indexed addressing mode of Figure 5.6 (using only two address components), but has the base addressing mode. A special PC-based addressing mode also exists.

Address register indirect with displacement

This addressing mode (mode 5), normally called based or base relative, requires one extension word to specify the 16-bit displacement. The (sign-extended) displacement added to the contents of the address register denotes the effective address used to fetch the operand. The displacement is considered to be signed, so the displacement ranges from −32768 to +32767. An example instruction is ADD.W 16(A3), D2, where the address of the source operand is computed as follows: ea = (A3) + 16.

Program counter indirect with displacement

This mode (mode 7.2), also normally called based or base relative, uses the PC as base register and adds a 16-bit sign-extended displacement to it to form the effective address. It differs from base addressing using address registers in that PC addressing modes may not be used for the specification of the destination operand, because this would allow self-modifying code, something the architects of the MC68020 have prevented.

This mode is useful for producing relocatable code, because the destination of, say, a jump instruction is then independent of the position of the program in memory. An example instruction is ADD.W 16(PC), D2.

A.2.4 Multi-component addressing modes

The MC68020 offers a slightly extended form of the base-indexed addressing mode of Figure A.7, because an 8-bit displacement is added to a base (address) register and an index register. Again, both an address register indexed and a program counter indexed mode exist, the difference being that the PC-indexed mode may not be used for destination operand address specification. A special mode, not depicted in Figure A.7, is used for addressing single bits.

Address register indirect with index and displacement

In this addressing mode (mode 6), the extension word (see Figure A.5(a)) specifies the index register (data or address register), the size of the index register (the sign-extended, low-order word or the entire register), a scale factor and an 8-bit displacement. Instead of the 8-bit displacement, a 16- or 32-bit displacement may be used as well, requiring one or two extra extension words. Instructions take the form ADD.L 8(A3, D1.W * 4), D2, where A3 is the base and D1 the index register (W specifies that the low-order word is used and the scale factor 4 specifies long word operands), resulting in the following source address: ea = 8 + (A3) + 4 * (D1).

Program counter indirect with index and displacement

This mode (mode 7.3), analogous to the address register indirect with index and displacement mode, can be used to access a nearby table of constants or jump targets. The displacement specifies the distance from the current instruction to this table and the index register can be used to select an element from this table. Again, either a short or long index may be used. In the instruction ADD.W 8(PC, A3.L * 2), D0 the effective address of the source is computed as follows: ea = 8 + (PC) + 2 * (A3), where both the high and low word of the index register A3 are used.

Memory indirect

The MC68020 includes memory indirect addressing modes by expanding the index addressing mode to include memory indirection, a full range of base and outer displacements, index scaling, pre-indexing and post-indexing. These extensions are available in both the data and program address space (see Table A.1, mode 6 and mode 7.3). Any one of the components can be suppressed (using a value of 0) in the calculation. The index register can be either a data or an address register and can specify a word or long word index value, scaled by 1, 2, 4 or 8. Memory indirection is indicated by [ ], which means that the address within the brackets is used to fetch a long word address, which is then used in the rest of the effective address calculation. There are two displacements available when memory indirection is used, although these can be suppressed if desired. Example 5.6 shows the use of addressing mode 6 of Table A.1.

Bit addressing

For bit-manipulation instructions, an operand (a memory byte or a data register) is addressed, using a general operand. The individual bit is addressed by its bit number in that byte or register, where bit zero always refers to the least significant bit. This bit number can be specified statically as immediate data or dynamically in a data register. However, there are some restrictions. If the general operand specifies a data register, a long word is assumed and the bit numbering is modulo 32. If the general operand specifies a memory location, a byte is assumed and the bit numbering is modulo 8. The instruction BSET D1, D0 sets bit D0[(D1) modulo 32] while the instruction BSET #3, D0 sets bit D0[3].

Bit-field addressing

A bit field is specified by a base address (selecting a byte in memory), a bit field offset (indicating the leftmost bit of the bit field in relation to the most significant bit of the base byte) and a bit field width (determining the number of bits in the bit field). The offset can be in the range of

-2^{31} to $2^{31} - 1$ and the field width may vary between 1 and 32. There are no restrictions as to how a bit field is aligned in memory; for example, a bit field of 26 bits can occupy up to 5 bytes in memory. The processor is capable of recognizing this condition in order to fetch the appropriate bytes.

A.3 Operations

This section contains an overview of the MC68020 instruction set. Only the most important variations for every instruction are discussed here. For a complete list of the instructions, the reader is referred to the Motorola manual (1985a). In accordance with Chapters 6 to 9, the following classes of instructions can be distinguished:

(1) data operations;
(2) sequencing operations;
(3) subroutine operations;
(4) supervisor operations;
(5) floating-point operations.

A.3.1 Data operations

The MC68020 data operations are grouped according to the classification given in Chapter 6, although it should be noted that the MC68020 does not have code transformation operations.

Data move operations

The MC68020 provides a full set of data move operations (see Table A.2). The MOVE instruction is the most flexible instruction since it can use all addressing modes for both source and destination operands. This flexibility, which is at the expense of opcode space, is desirable because move operations are executed frequently. Several variations of this MOVE instruction exist for special cases. For example, the SWAP instruction exchanges the low-order word of a register with its high-order word.

Format transformations

This class of instructions covers the shift and rotate operations. The MC68020 has a comprehensive set of shift and rotate instructions, as shown in Table A.3. The various instructions operate as described in Section 6.3.1.

Table A.2 Data move instructions.

Instruction	Operand Syntax	Operation
MOVE	Src, Dst	Move source to destination
MOVE	Src, CCR	Move source to condition code register
MOVEA	Src, An	Move source to register An
MOVEM	List, Dst	Move multiple registers
MOVEM	Src, List	
MOVEQ	#Data, Dn	Move 8-bit constant to register Dn
EXG	Rx, Ry	Exchange two registers
SWAP	Dn	Swap two halves of register Dn
CLR	Dst	Move zero to destination

All shift and rotate instructions allow three different addressing modes (as shown for the ASL instruction), showing that the shift count can be specified dynamically (in a register), statically (as an immediate value) or implied (for memory destinations):

- ASL Dm, Dn: Data register Dn is shifted by a number of positions specified in the 6 low-order bits of Dm.
- ASL #Cnt, Dn: Data register Dn is shifted Cnt positions, where Cnt ranges from 1 to 8.
- ASL Dst: A memory word, specified by the Dst operand, is shifted by one position.

Table A.3 Shift and rotate instructions.

Instruction	Operand Syntax	Operation
ASL	Cnt, Dst	Arithmetic shift left
ASR	Cnt, Dst	Arithmetic shift right
LSL	Cnt, Dst	Logical shift left
LSR	Cnt, Dst	Logical shift right
ROL	Cnt, Dst	Rotate left
ROR	Cnt, Dst	Rotate right
ROXL	Cnt, Dst	Rotate left with extend
ROXR	Cnt, Dst	Rotate right with extend
PACK	Src, Dst, #Data	Pack BCD decimal and adjust
UNPK	Src, Dst, #Data	Unpack BCD decimal and adjust

Table A.4 Bit manipulation and logical instructions.

Instruction	Operand Syntax	Operation
Logical, single bit		
BSET	Bnum, Dst	Test and set bit Bnum of Dst
BCLR	Bnum, Dst	Test and clear bit Bnum of Dst
BCHG	Bnum, Dst	Test and complement bit Bnum of Dst
BTST	Bnum, Dst	Test bit Bnum of Dst
Logical, bit vector		
AND	Src, Dst	AND Src to Dst
OR	Src, Dst	OR Src to Dst
EOR	Dn, Dst	Exclusive OR Dn to Dst
NOT	Dst	Complement Dst (one's complement)
Logical, bit field		
BFCHG	Src{offs : width}	Test bit field and complement
BFCLR	Src{offs : width}	Test bit field and clear
BFEXTS	Src{offs : width}, Dn	Extract (sign-extended) bit field
BFEXTU	Src{offs : width}, Dn	Extract (unsigned) bit field
BFFFO	Src{offs : width}, Dn	Find first one in bit field
BFINS	Dn, Dst{offs : width}	Insert bit field
BFSET	Src{offs : width}	Test bit field and set
BFTST	Src{offs : width}	Test bit field

To convert between the packed and unpacked decimal formats, the MC68020 has the instruction PACK and UNPK, which are character-set independent because the immediate operand #Data is added to the converted source operand (see Example 6.8).

Logical operations

The logical operations (see Table A.4) include instructions that operate on single bits as well as those that operate on bit vectors and bit fields.

The MC68020 instruction set contains four instructions that are used for manipulating single bits. With these operations, it is possible to test, invert, set or clear a bit in an operand. Analogous to the shift and rotate instructions of Table A.3, the logical, single-bit operations allow Bnum (the bit involved in the operation) to be specified dynamically (in a register) or statically (as an immediate value).

For bit-vector operations (that is, those operating on all bits of a byte, word or long word simultaneously), each bit in the result is

Table A.5 Integer and BCD arithmetic instructions.

Instruction	Operand Syntax	Operation
Integer arithmetic		
ADD	Src, Dst	Add source to destination
SUB	Src, Dst	Subtract source from destination
MULS	Src, Dn	Multiply Dn by Src (signed)
MULU	Src, Dn	Multiply Dn by Src (unsigned)
DIVS	Src, Dn	Divide Dn by Src (signed)
DIVU	Src, Dn	Divide Dn by Src (unsigned)
NEG	Dst	Negate Dst (two's complement)
EXT	Dn	Extend sign of byte or word in Dn
BCD arithmetic		
ABCD	Src, Dst	Add BCD Src and X to Dst
SBCD	Src, Dst	Subtract BCD Src and X from Dst
NBCD	Dst	Negate BCD Dst and subtract X

calculated from the corresponding bits in the operand(s), according to the specified operation. The four instructions that operate on bit vectors are shown in Table A.4. The instructions AND and OR must have a data register as one of their operands, but they can operate in both directions (Src → Dn or Dn → Dst). EOR, however, has only one possible direction (Dn → Dst).

Bit-field instructions allow for operations on bit fields, where the width of the bit field can be specified. Again, the width and offset of a bit field can be specified statically (as an immediate value) or dynamically (in a register). Bit-field operations are useful for manipulating packed data, in communications applications and in graphics applications.

Arithmetic operations

According to Chapter 6, arithmetic operations can be divided into those for fixed-point and floating-point arithmetic. As the MC68020 does not use floating-point arithmetic, only the class of fixed-point operations is discussed here. This class can be further split into fixed data length and variable data length arithmetic. Fixed data length arithmetic comprises the normal integer operations, whereas variable data length arithmetic is used with BCD numbers.

The MC68020 supports the usual set of integer arithmetic operations: add, subtract, multiply and divide (see Table A.5). Furthermore, it has instructions to sign extend (EXT) a byte or word to a word or long word, respectively, and to negate (NEG) a number (subtract a

Table A.6 Variants of the ADD instruction.

Instruction	Operand Syntax	Operation
ADD	Src, Dn	Dn := (Dn) + (Src)
ADD	Dn, Dst	Dst := (Dst) + (Dn)
ADDA	Src, An	An := (An) + (Src)
ADDI	#Data, Dst	Dst := (Dst) + data
ADDQ	#Data, Dst	Dst := (Dst) + data
ADDX	Dy, Dx	Dx := (Dx) + (Dy) + (X)
ADDX	−(Ay), −(Ax)	(Ax) := M[(Ax)] + M[(Ay)] + (X)

number from zero). For extended-precision arithmetic, the MC68020 has the instruction NEGX, which subtracts its operand and the current value of the X flag from 0, stores the result and sets the C and X flags to 1 if a borrow was generated.

The ADD and SUB instructions have several variations (see Table A.6). The normal ADD instruction operates on a data register and a general operand; however, an ADDA instruction also exists to operate on address registers. ADDQ is used to add a constant, with a value from 1 to 8, to a general operand; ADDI is used for adding larger (immediate) constants to an operand in memory (this is not possible with the normal ADD instruction, since one of its operands must be a data register). The ADDX instruction uses a carry from the previous stage (stored in the X flag) to achieve extended-precision arithmetic. After the operation, the X flag is set for the next stage.

The set of subtract instructions is similar to the ADD instructions (SUB, SUBA, SUBQ, SUBI and SUBX).

Multiply and divide both have two versions, a signed and an unsigned one. Each multiply instruction has three formats and the operand sizes: $16 * 16 \rightarrow 32$, $32 * 32 \rightarrow 32$ and $32 * 32 \rightarrow 64$. Both the signed and unsigned divide instructions have versions complementary to those of the multiply instructions. Normal operations will use signed arithmetic, while extended-precision arithmetic also uses the unsigned multiply and divide.

To support BCD arithmetic, the MC68020 has the instructions of Table A.5. They make use of the extend bit (X) to operate on BCD numbers longer than two digits (that is, one byte); for example, ABCD Dy, Dx is executed as follows: Dx := (Dx) + (Dy) + (X). Both ABCD and SBCD instructions can use the following two address formats (shown for the instruction ABCD):

- ABCD Dy, Dx: The operands are contained in the specified data registers.

Table A.7 Compare, test and program control instructions.

Instruction	Operand Syntax	Operation
Compare and test		
CMP	Src, Dn	Compare Src to Dn and set condition codes
CMP2	Src, Rn	Compare register Rn against bounds
TST	Src	Compare Src to 0 and set condition codes
CHK	Src, Dn	Check register against bounds
CHK2	Src, Rn	Check register Rn against bounds
Scc	Dst	Set Dst to all 0s or all 1s, according to cc
Program control		
JMP	Dst	Jump to Dst
BRA	Disp	Branch to (PC) + Disp
Bcc	Disp	Branch to (PC) + Disp if cc is true
DBcc	Dn, Disp	Conditional loop primitive

- ABCD −(Ay), −(Ax): The operands are addressed with the pre-decrement addressing mode, using the address registers specified in the instruction.

The pre-decrement addressing mode was chosen because of the fact that BCD numbers are normally stored in memory with their most significant digits first (that is, in the lower-numbered memory locations). However, as extended-precision computations, such as add and subtract, operate on the less significant digits first, they must be accessed first, followed by the digits in the lower-numbered memory locations.

A.3.2 Sequencing operations

Chapter 7 shows that, in order to control and change the instruction sequence of a program, special classes of instructions are required. These classes include instructions to test some specified condition and accordingly change the control flow of a program.

To explicitly generate some condition, the MC68020 has several instructions, as shown in Table A.7. The CMP instruction can be seen as a special subtract instruction, because while (Dn) − (Src) is computed, the result is discarded; only the condition codes are set. The TST instruction computes (Src) − 0 and sets the condition codes accordingly. The CMP2 instruction is an extended compare instruction, as it compares the contents of register Rn with two bounds. These bounds are specified by the single Src operand, where the lower bound is at the specified address and the upper bound is at the specified address plus the operand length. The CHK instruction checks whether the specified data register is not less than zero and not larger than the upper bound specified by the source operand. If the register is not within these bounds, a trap occurs via the CHK instruction exception vector. The CHK2 instruction is comparable to the CMP2 instruction, but with the difference that it generates a trap if the value is out of bounds. The instruction Scc tests for the specified condition and moves TRUE (all ones) or FALSE (all zeros) to the destination.

The program control instructions, also shown in Table A.7, are able to change the instruction sequence of a program. This means that after such an instruction, the program counter (PC) does not point to the next sequential instruction, but to a new address, specified by the instruction (except for a conditional branch instruction with a false condition, as the branch is not taken). JMP (Jump) and BRA (Branch) are unconditional jump instructions, where JMP uses a general operand to specify the destination address and BRA uses an 8-, 16- or 32-bit displacement. The Bcc instruction (Branch Conditionally) first tests whether the specified condition is true, and, if so, takes the branch, otherwise execution continues with the next instruction. The instruction DBcc (Decrement and Branch According to Condition) can be used as a loop control primitive, with two possible termination conditions: a condition or an iteration count. The exact working of the DBcc instruction is explained in Example 7.9. For DBcc and Scc, cc may specify one of the conditions listed in Table 7.1. The instruction Bcc may use these conditions, except for F (false) and T (true).

A.3.3 Subroutine operations

To call a subroutine, the MC68020 has two instructions, JSR and BSR (see Table A.8). They are similar to JMP and BRA, except that they first push the current value of PC on the stack, which is later used as a return address. To return from a subroutine, RTS can be used. RTR is equal to RTS, but it first pops a word off the stack and stores it in the conditional code register (the system byte of the status register remains unaffected); only then can the return address be popped off the stack. This is useful for subroutines that save the condition codes of the caller.

Other instructions in this class include LINK and UNLK, which can be used to maintain a linked list of local variables or activation records on the stack for nested subroutine calls. LEA can be used to compute the base address of a data structure at run time and to store this address in an address register, so it can be used later in the program via address register indirect addressing. PEA can be used, for example, to calculate the address of a variable and push it on to the stack for parameter passing (parameters by reference). The instruction CALLM and RTM support modular programming. For details about the subroutine operations of Table A.8, see Chapter 8 or the Motorola manual (1985a).

Table A.8 Subroutine instructions.

Instruction	Operand Syntax	Operation
JSR	Dst	Jump to subroutine at address Dst
BSR	Disp	Branch to subroutine at address (PC) + Disp
RTS		Return from subroutine
RTR		Restore CCR, then return
LEA	Src, An	Load source address into register An
PEA	Src	Push source address on to the stack
LINK	An, #Data	Create subroutine linkage
UNLK	An	Undo subroutine linkage
CALLM	#Data, Dst	Call module
RTM	Rn	Return from module

A.3.4 Supervisor operations

The supervisor instructions can be divided into three groups: privileged instructions, trap-generating instructions and instructions for process synchronization, as shown in Table A.9.

The privileged instructions (that is, those that may only be executed when the processor is in the supervisor mode) consist of instructions for changing the upper byte of the status register and some dangerous instructions such as RESET (resetting all external devices) and STOP (halting the processor). RTE (Return from Exception) loads an exception frame from the stack into the processor. This frame specifies the exact amount of information to be restored. Because an exception always causes the processor to switch to the supervisor mode, the RTE instruction should only occur in supervisor mode. It is, therefore, made a privileged instruction.

When an attempt is made to execute a privileged instruction in user mode, a trap occurs, causing the processor to switch to supervisor mode. The TRAP and TRAPV instructions are provided to allow programs running in user mode to request supervisor service. The TRAP instruction pushes the program counter and the status register on to the stack and loads the PC with the specified vector address. (Note that the vector address is specified in the instruction by the #Data operand.) The BKPT instructions can be used to support the program breakpoint function for debugging purposes.

The TAS instruction can be used for process synchronization or for implementing semaphores because it uses an indivisible read–modify–write memory cycle (see Chapter 9). This instruction first tests its operand and then sets the most significant bit. The CAS and CAS2 instructions are

Table A.9 Supervisor instructions.

Instruction	Operand Syntax	Operation
Privileged		
ANDI	#Data, SR	AND data to status register
EORI	#Data, SR	Exclusive OR data to status register
ORI	#Data, SR	OR data to status register
MOVE	Src, SR	Load new status register
MOVE	USP, An	Store user stack pointer in An
MOVE	An, USP	Load user stack pointer from An
MOVEC	Rm, Rn	Move control register
RESET		Reset external devices
STOP	#Data	Stop program execution
RTE		Return from exception
Trap generating		
TRAPV		Trap on overflow
TRAP	#Data	Trap via vector, specified by data
BKPT	#Data	Breakpoint
Synchronization		
TAS	Dst	Test and set MSB of Dst to 1
CAS	Dm, Dn, Dst	Compare and swap with operand
CAS2	Dm1 : Dm2, Dn1 : Dn2, (Rd1) : (Rd2)	Compare and swap, double operands

more complex process synchronization instructions. They allow for locked manipulation of byte, word and long word operands, to efficiently support system queue and stack functions.

A.3.5 Floating-point operations

Although floating-point instructions do not belong to the architecture of the MC68020, they are implemented as co-processor instructions executed on a dedicated floating-point co-processor (FPP). This FPP fully supports the IEEE floating-point format. Table A.10 summarizes the traditional floating-point operations while Table A.11 summarizes the more complex floating-point operations supported by the same co-processor. For a detailed description, the reader is referred to the Motorola manual (1985b).

The floating-point co-processor arithmetic operations can be divided into monadic and dyadic operations. With **monadic** operations, the operation is performed on one operand. This can be on a floating-point register (special register type in the FPP), on a memory operand or

Table A.10 MC68881 FPP arithmetic operations.

Instruction	Operation
Dyadic arithmetic operations	
FADD	Add
FDIV	Divide
FMOD	Modulo
FMUL	Multiply
FREM	IEEE remainder
FSUB	Subtract
Monadic arithmetic operations	
FABS	Absolute value
FGETEXP	Get exponent
FGETMAN	Get fraction
FINT	Integer part
FNEG	Negate
FNSCALE	Scale exponent
FSGLDIV	Single-precision divide
FSGLMUL	Single-precision multiply

on an MC68020 data register. The result is always stored in a floating-point data register.

Dyadic operations always have two source operands. One source operand can be a general operand and the second source operand (which is simultaneously the destination operand) is always a floating-point register. Examples are:

```
FMUL.X   Src, FPn
FMUL.P   FPm, FPn
```

The single-precision divide and multiply operations are provided for speed-critical applications requiring only single-precision accuracy.

The MC68881 FPP also supports several complex operations. They consist of the trigonometric and logarithmic functions shown in Table A.11. The instruction FSINCOS is worth paying attention to because, being a monadic instruction, it uses only one source operand but two destination operands (registers). The source operand is a general operand of which the sine and the cosine are computed, and the results are stored in two destination floating-point registers:

```
FSINCOS.F   #3.1415, FP0 : FP1     ;Computes the sine and cosine of
                                   ;3.1415 and stores the result of the
                                   ;sine in FP1 and the cosine in FP0
```

Table A.11 Complex arithmetic operations.

Instruction	Operation
FACOS	Arc cosine
FASIN	Arc sine
FATAN	Arc tangent
FATANH	Hyperbolic arc tangent
FCOS	Cosine
FCOSH	Hyperbolic cosine
FETOX	e to the x power
FETOXM1	e to the x power $-$ 1
FLOG2	Log base 2
FLOG10	Log base 10
FLOGN	Log base e
FLOGNP1	Log base e of $x + 1$
FSIN	Sine
FSINCOS	Sine and cosine
FSINH	Hyperbolic sine
FSQRT	Square root
FTAN	Tangent
FTANH	Hyperbolic tangent
FTENTOX	10 to the x power
FTWOTOX	2 to the x power

A.4 Exceptions

Exceptions are used to indicate that some special condition has occurred. They can be generated externally by interrupts, bus errors and reset requests, or internally by instructions or unusual conditions, arising during the execution of an instruction. Exceptions may also be used to request service from the operating system by programs running in user mode – for example, to print a file. An exception-handling mechanism is provided for efficient handling of such conditions. Each exception is identified by a vector number, identifying its corresponding vector. An exception vector is a memory location containing a pointer to a routine that has to handle that particular exception. A vector number has a length of 8 bits and is multiplied by 4 to obtain the vector address.

The MC68020 has a vector table consisting of 256 long word entries (in fact, this amounts to 255, because the reset vector occupies 2 long words). These 255 entries consist of 63 vectors used by system exceptions and 192 vectors reserved for user interrupt vectors. The MC68020 uses a special vector base register, allowing the vector table to be placed anywhere in memory.

The exception types supported by the MC68020 are summarized below:

- Reset: A reset is a special exception, caused by some external signal, to put the processor in a known state at start-up or after some irrecoverable crash. The vector number (vector 0) is generated internally to reference the reset vector. Because nothing is known about the validity of the register contents, the supervisor stack pointer must be initialized. Therefore, the stack pointer is loaded with the first long word of the reset vector, and the address in the following long word is loaded into the program counter. After this, execution starts with the power-up or restart routine.

- Interrupts: The MC68020 has seven levels of interrupt priorities, encoded in 3 bits. The processor contains an interrupt priority mask in the status register (see Figure A.2), and only interrupts with a higher level than the current processor priority level are accepted. The highest level (level 7) can never be inhibited and is thus a non-maskable interrupt level.

- Traps: A trap is an exception brought about by the appearance of abnormal conditions due to instruction execution (for example, divide by zero) or by the use of instructions that explicitly cause trapping (for example, TRAPV) in order to request service from the operating system. The MC68020 provides 16 different traps, Trap #0 through Trap #15, which are useful for implementing system calls, such as 'read a byte from keyboard' or 'ring bell and annoy operator'. This enables programs to be more portable, because only these system-dependent trap routines have to be rewritten if the software is moved to another system.

- Illegal and unimplemented instructions: If an instruction is fetched and the first word does not have a legal bit pattern, the 'illegal instruction' exception is generated. A special case of illegal instructions is when the most significant four bits equal 1010 or 1111. These two classes (called 'line A' and 'line F') are given separate exception vectors, because they correspond to instructions that are not implemented in all members of the 68000 family, and so, for example, the MC68000 can emulate these instructions. The 'line F' instructions are used for co-processor instructions. If no co-processor responds to these instructions, the 'illegal instruction' exception is raised and the instruction can be emulated.

- Privilege violation: To maintain system integrity, various instructions are made privileged. If these are encountered in user mode, the 'privilege violation' exception is generated.
- Trace: For debugging a program, it is desirable to operate in a trace mode, in which the state of the machine may be examined after each instruction or after a change of flow (for example, after executing a BRA or JMP instruction). For this, the MC68020 provides a trace facility, activated by setting one of the T bits in the status register. The 'trace exception' handling routine is called after a traced program instruction is executed, to offer a programmer the required debugging support.
- Bus error: A bus error is generated by external logic. The bus cycle that led to the bus error is aborted, because the processor cannot complete the operation. This error is provided to enable the processor to cope with hardware faults; for example, indicating faulty memory or access to a non-existent memory address. This exception also saves the address of the currently executing instruction and the memory address of the 'faulty' access in the exception stack frame, to facilitate recovery.
- Address error: An 'address error' exception occurs when a word or long word operand or an instruction is accessed at an odd byte address. The effeect of an address error is comparable to a bus error, so that once again the bus cycle is aborted.

SUMMARY

- The MC68020 is a 32-bit architecture because the data and address registers are 32 bits.
- The register set is divided into two parts (to save bits in the operand specifiers): 8 data registers (used to store data) and 8 address registers (used to hold operand addresses).
- The stack pointer is one of the address registers.
- The program counter is an address register which is not contained in the set of address registers.
- Instructions have a length of one word (2 bytes) or multiples thereof.
- The basic instruction format allows for two-operand instructions. These operands are specified via an operand specifier which consists of a 3-bit mode and a 3-bit register field. Because the basic instruction format is constrained to be one word, many instructions do not have two operands, or the operand specifier of one or both operands only allows for a subset of the addressing modes to be specified (for example, register only).
- The extension words allow for the specification of displacements, immediate data, absolute addresses, a register list or to further specify the index addressing mode.
- The data types supported by the MC68020 architecture are Booleans, integers (two's complement) of 8, 16 and 32 bits, unsigned integers for address arithmetic and binary-coded decimals.
- Data is byte addressable, whereby the location of the most significant byte of an item is considered to be its address.
- The operations and the addressing modes of the MC68020 are not orthogonal, due to the lack of sufficient opcode space.
- The MC68020 supports two modes of operation (user and supervisor) to support a protection mechanism (required for multi-user systems).
- Exceptions are detected and specified as part of the architecture to facilitate the implementation of exception handlers.

References

DEC (1975). *PDP-11 Processor Handbook*. Digital Equipment Corporation: Maynard, MA.

Motorola (1985a). *MC68020, 32-bit Microprocessor User's Manual*. Prentice Hall Incorporated: Englewood Cliffs, NJ.

Motorola (1985b). *MC68881 Floating-point Co-processor User's Manual*. Prentice Hall Incorporated: Englewood Cliffs, NJ.

B Special Topics

Compact writing requires a large vocabulary.
– Otto Weiss

This appendix contains a collection of special topics that were considered too detailed to be part of the main body of the text, but important enough to be included. Each of the topics can be considered as an extension to one of the chapters.

B.1 Virtual machine monitors

Chapter 9 discussed operating systems running directly on the computer hardware, from which user programs are shielded. A disadvantage of such an operating system is that user programs requiring a different operating system cannot be run; they should be run on separate hardware with a different operating system or should be converted, which generally is a difficult task. To solve this problem, virtual machine monitors (VMMs) have been introduced.

The concept of virtual memory, which allows addresses generated by a program to be different from those used to access physical memory, can be extended to that of VMMs. A **virtual machine monitor** is a computing system in which instructions issued by a program may be different from those actually executed by the computer hardware (Parmalee, 1972).

B.1.1 The virtual machine monitor concept

Figure B.1 illustrates the virtual machine monitor concept. In this figure, a new level (L1V) is introduced, which consists of the virtual machine monitor (VMM) and its virtual machine extension (VME). (Refer to Figure 2.2 for the notation.) The function of the VMM is to create, together with a particular VME, a virtual machine (VM) for a user. This is done in such a way that each VM user is given the impression of executing his program on a real machine of a specified type and configuration (amount of memory, number and type of disk drives, and so on). The specific properties of the machine of a particular user, say user *x*, are specified by VMEx. The VMs created by the VMM may not therefore be all the same, because types and configurations of the virtualized real machines may be different. VM users can be existing operating systems, user programs running on a 'bare' machine or other VMMs (when this is possible, the VMM is said to be **self-virtualizable**).

The function of a VMM is to generate multiple VMs, where a VM can be defined as *an efficient, isolated duplicate of the real machine* (Popek, 1974). This implies the following:

- The VMM has to provide an environment to the VM users which is identical to the original machine, except for differences caused by the availability of resources and differences in execution time.
- The execution time of programs in the VM environment (running at level L2 or higher, see Figure B.1) should only show a minor increase due to the presence of a VM. This implies that the majority of the VM instructions should be executable by the host machine directly, ruling out emulators and interpreters.

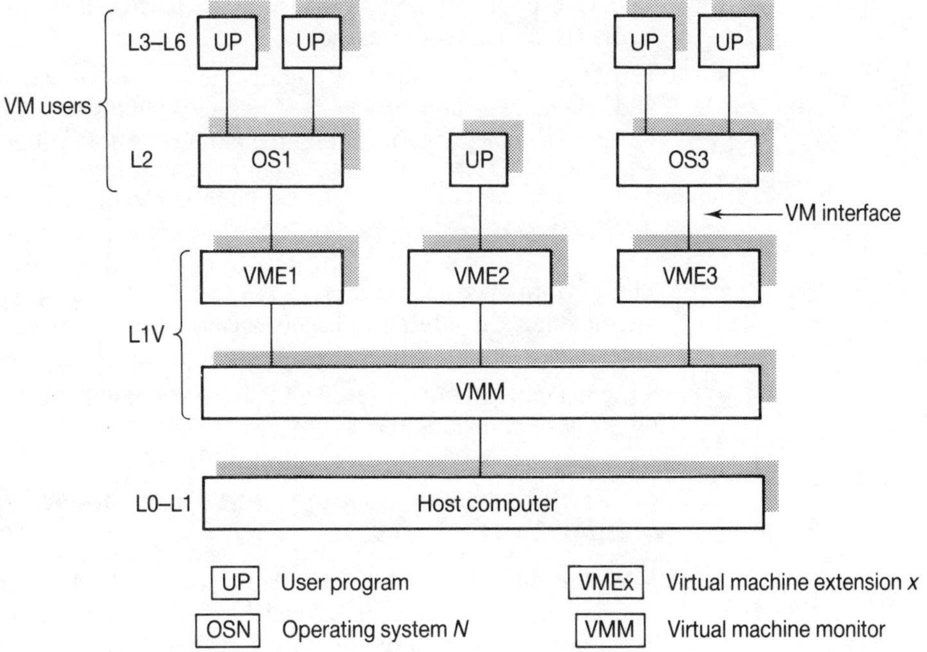

FIGURE B.1

A virtual machine system.

- The VMM has to be in complete control of all system resources (memory and peripherals). This means that VMMs can only access resources allocated to them and that the VMM may regain control over the allocated resources.

As the VMM runs directly on the hardware of the host computer, it greatly resembles a traditional operating system. Both provide a fair allocation of resources and an efficient protection of different processes. The main difference is that an operating system shields certain low-level processes, such as disk I/O, from the users, while the VMM makes all levels available to the VMs.

Some advantages of VMMs are:

- They allow for the concurrent running of dissimilar operating systems, which is a form of porting operating systems. This enables new versions of operating systems to be developed concurrently with the execution of other operating systems.
- System and application programs may be developed for machine configurations different from the host machine, while these configurations may not even be available yet.
- VMs are completely shielded from the effects, such as software failures, of other VMs.

- The VMM can be used to measure the performance (in terms of hardware and software usage) of the VMs.
- Hardware changes, such as adding a disk, can be simulated first and, then, say, networking facilities can be tested by using two virtual machines, without the demand for more than one real machine.

Some disadvantages are:

- The performance of the system is degraded, because part of the instruction set is interpreted, and because the virtual machines are time shared on a single real machine.
- System management at level L1V is complicated, because of the diversity of functions the VMM has to perform.

B.1.2 Architectural requirements for virtual machine monitors

The VMM concept of Figure B.1 requires the provision of special support by the host machine. This support will be derived from the way user programs communicate with the operating system. The traditional way in which user programs communicate with an operating system is shown in Figure B.2(a). It consists of two communication paths:

(1) Service requests by the user program (which is running in user mode) are passed to the operating system (which is running in supervisor mode) via a supervisor call (SVC).

(2) When the operating system has completed the SVC, it returns to the user program with the RETURN instruction, thereby switching back to user mode.

Figure B.2(b) shows the way in which user programs communicate with their operating system in a VM environment. The VMM is designed so that the user program and the operating system do not have to be modified; that is, the VM concept is transparent to them. The user program is executed in user mode, as is the operating system, but for the operating system this is called **virtual supervisor mode**, since the operating system is made to think that it runs in supervisor mode. The VMM is executed in supervisor mode. Figure B.2(b) shows six communication paths:

(1) A request for service by the user program is made via an SVC instruction. This causes control to transfer to the VMM (because the VMM runs in supervisor mode, to which control is transferred when SVCs are trapped).

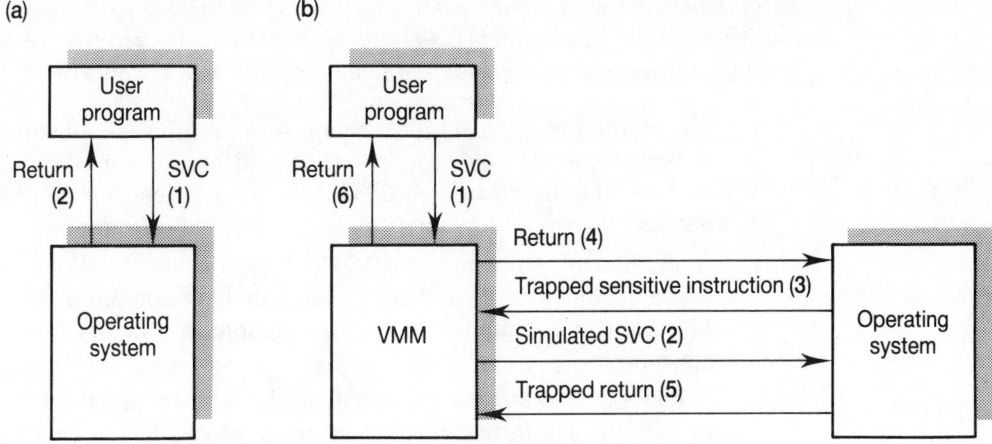

FIGURE B.2

Handling of supervisor calls: (a) traditional operating system; (b) operating system running under a VMM.

(2) The VMM simulates the effect of the SVC for the operating system. This consists of simulating the trap operation, which otherwise would have been caused by the SVC. Upon completing the simulation of the trap operation, the operating system is in control, servicing the SVC in virtual supervisor mode. This servicing typically involves the execution of one or more privileged instructions and/or access to privileged areas in memory (for example, I/O locations), collectively called **sensitive instructions**.

(3) The execution of each sensitive instruction by the operating system in virtual supervisor mode is trapped to the VMM. The VMM simulates these instructions using the simulated memory allocated to that VM and the simulated peripherals of that VM, specified in the VMEx.

(4) When the VMM has completed the simulation of the sensitive instruction, it returns to the operating system via the RETURN instruction.

(5) When the operating system has completed the SVC, after the execution of several instructions, some of which may be sensitive causing paths 3 and 4 to be used again, it returns via the RETURN instruction. This is a privileged instruction and therefore will be trapped to the VMM.

(6) The VMM re-issues the RETURN instruction after which the SVC is serviced and the user program is in control again. This completes the execution of the SVC instruction.

The model of Figure B.2(b) is based on so-called **software mapping**. This means that only the VMM runs in supervisor mode while the virtual machines always run in user mode. This model can only be used when the architecture of the host computer (L0–L1 of Figure B.1) satisfies certain requirements. Goldberg (1972) has derived the following architectural requirements for implementing the VMM concept:

(1) The method of instruction execution for non-privileged instructions in both supervisor and user mode should be the same for a large part of the instruction set. This is an efficiency requirement, because then only few instructions have to be interpreted.

(2) A method of protecting the VMM from the active VM must be available, as well as sufficient isolation between different VMs. This can be accomplished by, for example, a memory-protection mechanism.

(3) A method of automatically signalling the VMM when the VM tries to execute a sensitive instruction must be available. This signal, usually a trap, may not cause unrecoverable errors. Furthermore, the VMM must be able to simulate the effect of the sensitive instruction.

    Sensitive instructions include:

    (a) Instructions changing the mode of the CPU and instructions indicating the CPU mode, because the virtual supervisor mode is simulated by the VMM.

    (b) Instructions that alter or query the state of the machine and the reserved register and memory locations.

    (c) Instructions referring to the protection and memory management mechanisms.

    (d) Any I/O instruction.

Sensitive instructions are formed by two groups of instructions:

(1) Instructions that may alter the mode and the state of the machine, specified by the resources of 3(a), 3(b), 3(c) and 3(d). These are the traditional privileged instructions, required by the traditional operating system of Figure B.2(a).

(2) Instructions that sense the state of the resources of 3(a), 3(b), 3(c) and 3(d). This is an extra requirement imposed by the VMM concept of Figure B.2(b). The operating system, which is running in virtual supervisor mode, should not be able to find out, by using some sort of sense instruction (for example, the MC68000 instruction MOVE SR, <ea>), that it is actually not running in supervisor mode. These sense instructions should be trapped and simulated by the VMM.

Example B.1 shows the shortcomings of the MC68000 in complying with these three requirements.

□□EXAMPLE B.1

Inspecting the MC68000 architecture reveals that it violates the foregoing requirements on two points:

(1) Requirement 3a: The MOVE SR, <ea> instruction has to be considered a sensitive instruction because it allows the processor mode bit to be read. The execution of this instruction in user mode does not cause a trap on the MC68000. This has been corrected in the MC68010 and later models.

(2) Requirement 3: On the MC68000, traps caused by a bus or address error are not recoverable, because the value of the PC stored in the interrupt stack frame is not predictable. This has been corrected in the MC68010 and later models.

B.2 I/O memory management and data coherence aspects

This section discusses some aspects of input/output (see Chapter 11) which were considered too detailed for the main text. They have been included to show the consequences of design decisions related to the I/O system for the rest of the system. Two topics are covered: memory management aspects related to I/O and data coherence related to I/O.

B.2.1 I/O memory management aspects

With the introduction of direct memory access (DMA), more than one process in the system may access main memory. When a memory management unit is used (see Chapter 10), addresses may be classified as virtual (these are generated by the programs executed on the CPU) or real (used to address main memory). Figure B.3 shows the memory space alternatives for I/O: I/O using virtual addresses and I/O using real addresses.

The use of virtual addresses by I/O processes, executed by the device controllers, may seem to be advantageous because a CPU-based process requesting I/O to be performed also uses virtual addresses. In a system that does not use multiprogramming, this would be a valid conclusion.

In a system using multiprogramming, where I/O processes are executed concurrently with other processes, an I/O subsystem may be executing an I/O process on behalf of a CPU-based process that is not active at that moment (because, for example, it is waiting for I/O). The memory management unit (MMU) may be set up only to translate the

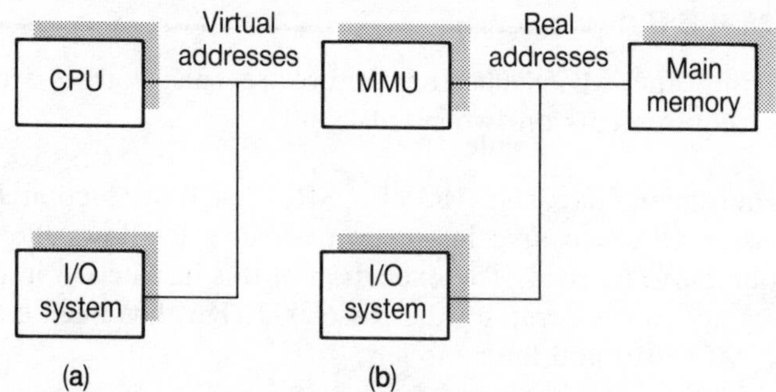

FIGURE B.3

Alternative I/O address spaces: (a) using virtual addresses; (b) using real addresses.

virtual addresses of the currently executing CPU-based process. The I/O process cannot, therefore, use the MMU, unless the MMU is extended so that it has separate translation facilities for each I/O process. This could be very costly and would require connecting the I/O devices to the CPU–MMU bus, which typically is a very short, high-speed bus, not suitable for the long connections to the I/O systems. I/O processes do not, therefore, usually use virtual addresses. The use of real addresses by the I/O processes is, therefore, the preferred way, the advantage being that all devices work in the same address space and that the MMU–memory bus, which is usually longer and less fast, is available for the connection of the I/O system. The use of real addresses for I/O, however, puts the following requirements on the device-independent software of the operating system:

- Address translation: The virtual addresses generated by a CPU-based process have to be translated to real addresses for the I/O processes. This is usually done by software, using the address translation tables of the process requesting the I/O service.
- Check for accessibility of data area: In a system using virtual memory techniques, a process is able to specify a data object to be read from or written to memory, while the memory space for that object is not accessible (because the object is still on disk or the block of memory to be used is occupied by another object). In the case of I/O, it is necessary to guarantee that the information to be written to a device is available in memory (rather than on disk), and that, for information to be read from a device, the addressed block in memory has been allocated for this data, such that other data does not get overwritten due to the I/O read operation.

  In the alternative case, where I/O uses virtual addresses, the MMU could be used to check the accessibility while data is being transferred. The handling of inaccessible pages may involve a disk operation, however, which is very time consuming. Therefore, when using virtual addresses, the check for accessibility is usually also done explicitly by the CPU.

The check for accessibility is usually done by the device-independent software (see Figure 11.4) which has to probe memory so that it can guarantee that the memory area, required for the I/O operation, is accessible. Most memory management systems control accessibility to the level of a page (smaller pieces of memory are not recognized). The probing operation has, therefore, to establish the accessibility of each of the P pages involved in the transfer of an I/O data block (for example, a disk sector).

In the case of an I/O write operation (which means writing data to an I/O device), the probing consists of executing P memory read instructions. The virtual addresses of these P instructions are such that they access the P pages of the required memory area.

In the case of an I/O read, memory write instructions have to be used for the probing operation, because an I/O read operation implies the writing of memory locations. Memory should, therefore, be accessible and write operations should be allowed (for example, the area should not be read only). If the required memory is not accessible, a memory management exception is generated. Some architectures, like the VAX-11, have architectural support for this in the form of a probe instruction.

- Locking physical pages: When the required memory area has proven to be accessible, it must remain accessible until the I/O operation has been completed. In support of this, a lock flag is included in the control information of every memory page. Page-replacement algorithms will skip pages with their lock flag set, because these pages are then not under control of memory management.
- Unlocking physical pages: Upon completion of the I/O operation, the pages of the required physical memory area have to be unlocked, so that they are brought back under control of memory management.

B.2.2 I/O data coherence aspects

In computer systems that have a cache memory to accelerate memory accesses (see Chapter 14), the I/O system may be connected to the MMU–cache interface or the cache–memory interface.

Transferring I/O data through the cache (Figure B.4(a)) means that the I/O data will be written to the cache (which will automatically perform write operations to memory) in the case of an I/O read operation, and I/O data will be read from the cache (which will automatically be refilled with memory data) in the case of an I/O write operation. The advantage of this alternative is that the data in the cache and main memory will be the same; in other words, the data in cache and

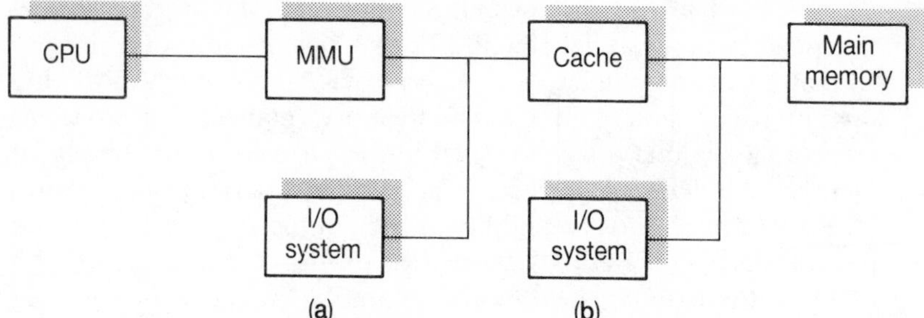

FIGURE B.4

Alternative I/O–cache configurations: (a) through cache; (b) to main memory.

main memory will be **coherent** (see Section 16.4). The disadvantage is that, because of the relatively high speed of DMA data transfers, the cache will be filled up with I/O data rather than CPU data, for which purpose the cache was not introduced. Another disadvantage is that the MMU–cache interface must be very fast and so, therefore, is not suited to direct connection to the I/O system (which requires long connection lines).

Transferring I/O data directly to main memory (Figure B.4(b)) is, therefore, the preferred alternative, despite the difficulties of potential data coherence. **Data incoherence** may arise when data is transferred by an I/O device to memory, while the cache (which is not updated during the I/O data transfer) holds a copy of the previous contents of that memory area. The CPU has to be prevented from using invalid data in the cache (see Chapter 14). Two methods exist for solving this problem:

(1) Prevention: This method is based on software that has to make the I/O memory area non-cacheable. Assuming a memory divided into pages, each page has to be equipped with a cacheability flag to indicate whether or not its data should be cached. The device-independent software of the operating system may set the flags of the pages involved in an I/O operation to non-cacheable before the start of the I/O operation, and reset those flags upon completion of the I/O operation. If pages to be used for I/O have to be made non-cacheable while some of the data in those pages has already been cached, the cache blocks containing that data have to be written to main memory under software control, requiring special instructions for cache control.

(2) Detection and resolution: This method uses hardware to guarantee cache data coherence. The cache controller may be equipped with extra hardware, called a **snoopy cache controller** (see Section 16.5.3), to monitor the memory addresses used during I/O transfers. When they match those of a data block in the cache, the hardware can either invalidate the cache block or update it with the new data from the I/O device.

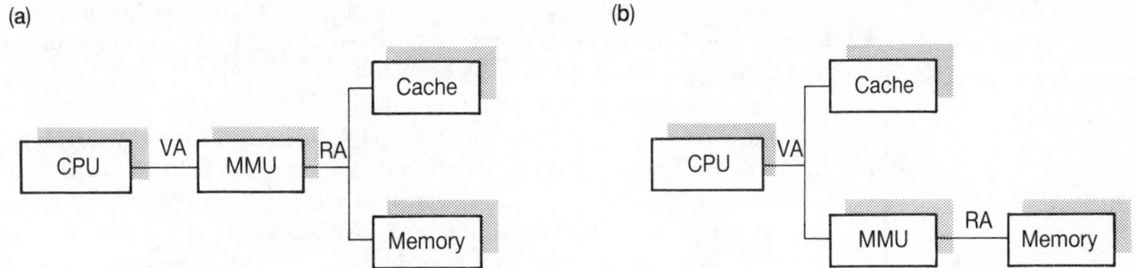

FIGURE B.5

Cache spaces: (a) in real address space; (b) in virtual address space.

B.3 Caches in the virtual address space

In Section 14.6, it was assumed that caches are usually addressed with real addresses (see Figure B.5(a)). The motivation for this is simplicity, while the address translation operation of the MMU can, in general, be overlapped with accessing the data in the cache. The virtual address of Figure 14.14(b) is split into two parts: a virtual block address (VBA), which is translated by the MMU into a real block address (RBA), and a displacement (D) in the block, which does not have to be translated by the MMU. While the VBA is being translated by the MMU, the displacement part of the virtual address (D) can be used to access data in the cache. This, however, generally restricts the size of the cache to that of a block (which usually is a page), unless a set-associative cache is used (see Figure 14.19), then the size of each set is restricted to that of a block.

A potentially large performance gain can be obtained when a cache can have an arbitrary size (considering the large size and low cost of currently available static RAM chips, caches with a size of, say, 128 kbytes are economically feasible) and the cache is addressed with virtual (rather than real) addresses, to save the address translation delay of the MMU. Figure B.5 illustrates both alternatives. The address translation of Figure B.5(b) need not be very fast, as it is only required on a cache miss (which should occur in only a few percent of the memory references). This is in contrast with the address translation of Figure B.5(a), which is needed on every memory reference.

The advantages of a cache in the virtual address space is that it can be accessed faster than a cache in the real address space and that there are no size restrictions. This is attractive as larger caches have a better performance and are economically feasible. Furthermore, caches in the virtual address space can be implemented on-chip, without requiring a translation mechanism to be present on-chip. However, there are three serious problems. The first problem is related to the fact that each process may have its own virtual address space and that virtual addresses are only relevant within their specific virtual address space; so, a given virtual address can have a different meaning (designate a different real address) in a different virtual address space. This causes a problem with process switches, but this can be solved by invalidating the cache contents on a process switch. This clearly reduces performance, especially for large caches, so a better solution is to attach an extra tag field to each cache entry that uniquely identifies the virtual address space that that cache entry belongs to. The disadvantage of this method is that cache control becomes more costly and complex because of the increased tag size. Another possibility is to use a single, global virtual address space that is shared by all processes and remains unchanged on a process switch (see Figure 10.4). This again increases the tag size (the virtual addresses are wider), but it has the advantage of sharing without synonyms, as described in the following.

The second problem is the converse of the first; that is, several virtual addresses map onto the same real address. These virtual addresses are called **synonyms** or **aliases**. With regards to cache consistency, it is not desirable to have multiple cache copies of a single memory line, since modification of one copy would leave the other copies with an incorrect value, causing data incoherence. Because the location of the cache line depends on the virtual address with which it is accessed, a problem occurs if another processor or, say, an I/O controller uses another virtual address. One solution would be to prevent synonyms from occurring by using a single, global virtual address space, where information is shared by putting it in a shared segment (that it, it always has the same global virtual address). The solution based on detection and resolution requires that synonyms must be detected, which is done by translating the virtual address and then checking that no other virtual address in the cache maps into the same real address. For this, the inverse mapping of every line in the cache must be available, which can be achieved by a **reverse translation buffer** (RTB), which is the opposite of a TLB. On a miss, the translated address is simultaneously offered to the RTB and main memory. If the line is already in the cache under another name, it must be renamed (get another virtual address) and moved to its new location. Otherwise, it is normally fetched from memory.

The third problem is caused by the fact that I/O devices normally use real addresses, rather than virtual addresses (see Section B.2.2). In such a case, care must be taken to ensure that information that is overwritten in memory by an I/O device is invalidated in the cache. This can be accomplished by doing I/O with virtual addresses, but as all I/O controllers and devices should be modified, the problem of synonyms still exists. The other solution is to do I/O with real addresses and have an RTB check these addresses and invalidate matching entries. It is also possible for the operating system to ensure that active I/O areas (areas that are being written) are made non-cacheable.

All in all, it should be carefully checked that the hit ratio is high enough to ensure that the advantage of fast access on a hit (no translation) is not nullified by the cost of a miss (a slower translation and a memory fetch). Currently, architectures have been proposed and/or implemented using caches in virtual space (Wood, 1986; Goodman, 1987).

B.4 Co-processors

Most microprocessors have been designed for a wide range of applications; consequently, they use a set of general-purpose instructions. As their design is constrained by the area of silicon they require, additional instructions are expensive in terms of design and debug time, and the required silicon area. To avoid limiting the instruction set, while still conserving silicon area, **co-processors** have been introduced. Co-processors extend the instruction set of the main processor by using a separate chip. This allows for flexibility in the system configuration and modularity in performance.

A co-processor is assumed to have the following properties:

- It is a piece of hardware dedicated to perform a certain class of operations with a performance that is significantly higher than that of a general-purpose processor.
- It cannot perform its operations in isolation; the presence of at least one other processor is required. This processor, the CPU, is capable of performing its operations in isolation, without the assistance of any other processor(s).
- It incorporates some form of local storage for operands and/or results (for example, in the form of a set of registers). For any co-processor operation, the result and/or one or more of the operands will be located in local storage. The requirement for local storage distinguishes co-processors from **special function units** (**SFU**s) (Birnbaum, 1985). SFUs can only operate on operands located in CPU registers, and so can be considered as an extension of the ALU of the CPU.
- Every co-processor implements a specific instruction set; object programs consist of a mixture of CPU and co-processor instructions. Fetching CPU and co-processor instructions from a single instruction stream implies that only one of the processors (the CPU) issues instruction addresses and takes care of control transfers. The single-instruction stream (single-thread) requirement distinguishes co-processors from **attached processors**, which have a

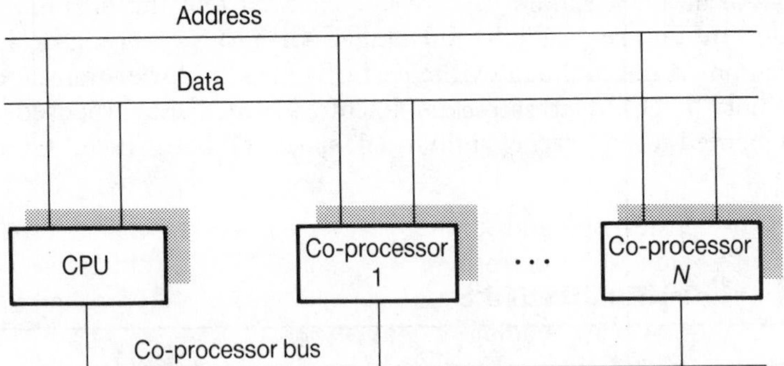

FIGURE B.6

Co-processor hardware interface.

significant amount of instruction and data storage. Vector processors, which can perform their operations almost completely independently of the host CPU, are an example of attached processors. This section will restrict itself to the discussion of co-processors because of their significance in relationship to current microprocessor architectures.

Co-processors cannot only be categorized according to the class of operations they perform (for example, floating point versus decimal arithmetic). They also differ widely in terms of the way they interface to the CPU and their autonomy of operation. This will be the subject of the next two subsections. The last two subsections are devoted to concurrency and synchronization, followed by a description of the MC68020 co-processor interface.

B.4.1 Co-processor interface

At the implementation level, a co-processor may be integrated into a system as shown in Figure B.6. Each co-processor in the system may be connected to the system address and data lines, as well as to a dedicated bus which connects the CPU with all co-processors. In the extreme case, all co-processors are only connected to the co-processor bus, which requires all information transfers to be passed via the CPU; this allows for co-processors with a low pin count. In the other extreme, the co-processors are connected to the address and data lines as well as to the co-processor bus, which gives them a high communication bandwidth.

At the architectural level, a distinction can be made in terms of the visibility of the instruction set of the co-processor.

- The co-processor architecture may be invisible (transparent) to the CPU. This will be the case when CPU–co-processor communication is performed using a subset of the CPU instruction set. For example, load and store type instructions may be used by the CPU

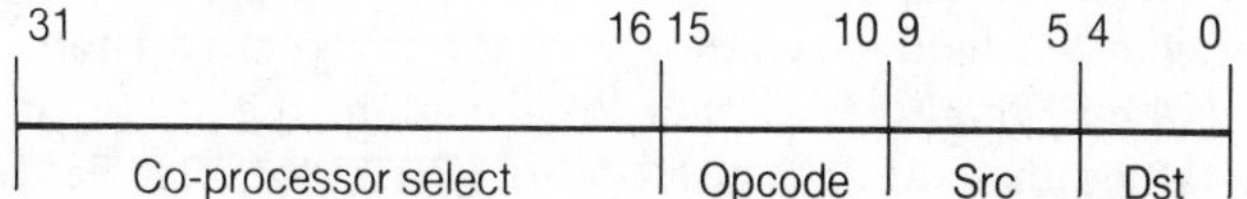

FIGURE B.7
Memory-mapped co-processor interface.

to transfer operands from/to the co-processor and to specify the operation to be performed (for example, by writing into a control register of the co-processor) as well as sense the status of the co-processor (by reading a status register). This necessitates the mapping of the registers of the co-processor on to the memory space of the CPU (see Example B.2).

- The co-processor architecture is partly visible to the CPU, which usually means that the CPU can only identify the instruction as being a co-processor instruction; the CPU cannot identify the particular operation to be performed, which has to be specified in some other part (not the opcode space) of the instruction. Such an instruction can be considered to be a **generic co-processor instruction**. The advantage of this approach is that, although the CPU is aware of the fact that a co-processor instruction has to be executed, which may require information transfer over the co-processor bus, the instruction formats and operations of the co-processor are transparent to the CPU (except for the field specifying the generic co-processor operation). This introduces the possibility of adding co-processors, possibly at a later date, with arbitrary functionality. (Note that the former approach also has this advantage.)
- The co-processor architecture is completely visible to the CPU. In this case, all co-processor instructions are included in the instruction set of the CPU; no new instructions can be added at a later date without modifying the CPU. Because all co-processor instructions are known to the CPU, the CPU can automatically perform certain stages of the execution of co-processor instructions, such as operand address calculation and data fetch/store.

□□EXAMPLE B.2

The Weitek 1167 floating-point co-processor, which contains a register file of 32 × 32-bit registers (R0 through R31), has been used as a co-processor for the iAPX80386 using memory mapping (Bonomi, 1988). The processor is connected to the address and data lines of the iAPX80386, and memory mapping is performed as shown in Figure B.7. A 32-bit address is interpreted by the co-processor as follows: the high-order 16 address bits are used to select a particular co-processor; the next

6 bits determine the particular operation to be performed by the co-processor; the Src field specifies one of the 32 local registers as a source operand (when Src = 0, the data lines contain the value of the source operand rather than local register zero (R0)); the Dst field specifies a local register, which acts as the second source and destination operands (when Dst = 0, the data is put on the data lines rather than in R0). The floating-point expression $A := B * C + D$ can be executed as follows (the mnemonic after the MOV specifies the operation to be performed by the co-processor):

```
MOV.WRITEF  B, R1    ;Write B into co-processor register 1
MOV.MULF    C, R1    ;R1 := (R1) * C
MOV.ADDF    D, R1    ;R1 := (R1) + D
MOV.READF   R1, A    ;A := (R1)
```

B.4.2 Co-processor autonomy

Co-processors receive their instructions from the same instruction stream as the CPU. The CPU is responsible for keeping track of the instruction address, causing the co-processor to be dependent on the CPU. A co-processor can be autonomous in terms of the way it fetches instructions and the way operand addresses are evaluated and operand data is fetched/stored.

Co-processor instruction fetch

Co-processors can fetch their instructions via **instruction tracking** or **instruction dispatching**. With instruction tracking, the CPU issues the instruction addresses, while all (co)processors examine the data lines in order to recognize and fetch an instruction intended for them. It is possible for more than one (co)processor to react to a single instruction – for example, to perform a data transfer between two (co)processors. This requires the co-processor architecture to be, at least, partially visible to the CPU (because the CPU has to ignore those instructions not intended for it) and allows for a large degree of autonomy of the co-processors.

With instruction dispatching, only the CPU examines the instructions, and when a co-processor instruction is fetched, it will be passed to the appropriate co-processor. When the co-processor architecture is invisible to the CPU, memory move type instructions have to be used, while the co-processor has to be connected to the address and data lines. When the co-processor architecture is (partly) visible to the CPU, the CPU may be involved in the execution of certain stages of the co-processor instruction and may exchange information with the co-processor via the co-processor bus.

Co-processor operand address evaluation and data fetch/store

Analogous to CPU operands, co-processor operands can be specified as immediate operands (being part of the instruction), and they can be located in a register local to the co-processor or in some memory location. In the latter case, some form of operand address calculation may be required (for example, when indexed addressing is being used). In this situation, several alternatives, in terms of co-processor autonomy, exist:

- The co-processor does operand address evaluation and data fetch/store. The co-processor has to be connected to the address and data lines and must have a local set of address (index) registers. This allows for a large degree of autonomy at the expense of a complete operand fetch unit in the co-processor.
- The co-processor only evaluates the operand address(es). The evaluated operand address has to be passed to the CPU, which fetches/stores the data. This requires that the co-processor contains most of the hardware of an operand fetch unit. A lot of communication with the CPU also has to take place. It will be no surprise that this alternative has not been implemented commercially.
- The CPU evaluates the operand address. The co-processor fetches/stores the data, using the data lines of the system. This requires that the operand formats of the co-processor instructions are visible to the CPU or else the co-processor has to pass information to the CPU as to how to perform the evaluation of the operand address. Because the CPU already has an operand fetch unit and a set of address registers, this is a natural and often-used alternative.
- The CPU does both operand address evaluation and data fetch/store. This is similar to the foregoing alternative but, in addition, the co-processor bus is used to pass data between the co-processor and the CPU.

B.4.3 Concurrency and synchronization

When a co-processor can execute instructions concurrently with the execution of CPU instructions, the CPU–co-processor interface is called **asynchronous**. When co-processor instructions can only be executed non-concurrently with the execution of CPU instructions (that is, the CPU has to wait until the co-processor instruction has completed before executing another instruction), the CPU–co-processor interface is called **synchronous**. Complete concurrency is not possible because, in a system with co-processors, only a single thread (a single instruction stream) may be executed; this facilitates exception handling. Synchronization with the CPU will therefore be required during instruction execution as well as for exception handling.

Synchronization during the execution of co-processor instructions

Every time the CPU wants to issue a new co-processor instruction, synchronization has to take place. The same type of synchronization is required when operands have to be transferred to the co-processor and results have to be passed to main memory (assuming that the autonomy of the co-processor is such that it cannot evaluate its operands and/or fetch/store the data), and when a data transfer has to take place between the CPU and a co-processor (for example, to pass the condition codes of the co-processor). This synchronization can be done in two ways:

(1) Using the busy form of waiting: The CPU is kept waiting by the co-processor until it has completed its current instruction.

(2) Using the non-busy form of waiting: The CPU checks whether the co-processor is busy; if so, it may execute other instructions (rather than wait) and try again later. This allows for a higher degree of concurrency but is harder to implement programmatically.

Note that co-processors may be implemented in such a way that local registers (not involved in the execution of the current instruction) may be read/written by the CPU concurrently.

Synchronization on exceptions

During the execution of co-processor instructions, exceptions (such as a divide by zero or a data parity error) may be raised. If the co-processor cannot cope with this exception, it will need CPU assistance. Again, here, the busy form (the co-processor waits until the CPU checks the status of the co-processor) or non-busy form (the co-processor signals the exception to the CPU immediately, via an interrupt, for example) of waiting can be used.

B.4.4 MC68020 co-processor interface

MC68020 co-processors are connected to the system via the data lines, a few address lines (used to select a control, status or data register in the co-processor), and a co-processor bus (consisting of only a few lines) for handshaking purposes and specifying the bus operation type (read/write). Because the co-processors are connected to the data lines, they use instruction tracking (this is more efficient than instruction dispatching because the instructions are directly fetched from the data lines, rather

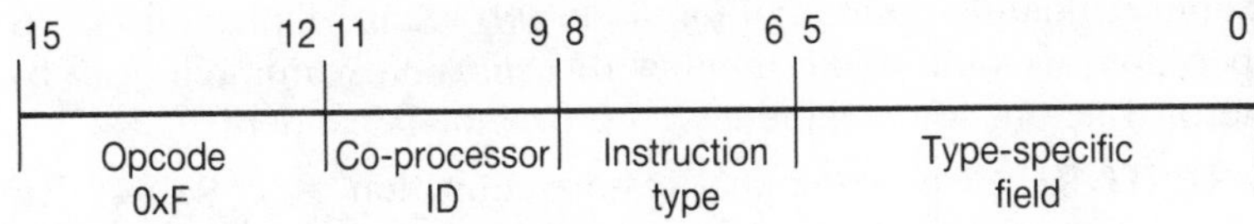

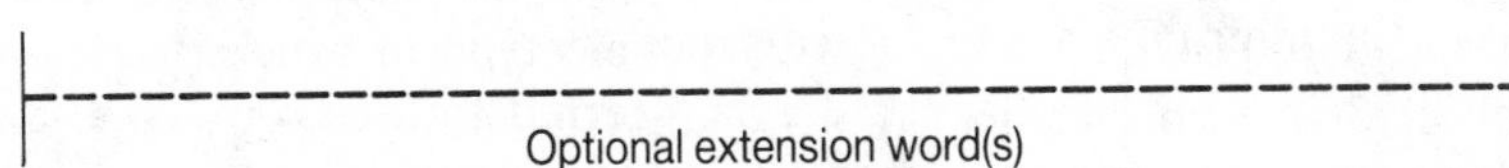

FIGURE B.8
Format of MC68020 co-processor instructions.

than passed via the CPU): the CPU performs the operand address evaluation (the way this should be done – that is, the addressing mode to be used – is specified in a co-processor control register which is read by the CPU) while data is taken from or put on the data lines by the co-processor.

The co-processor architecture of the MC68020 is partly visible to the CPU (see Figure B.8).

The opcode field specifies the generic co-processor instruction (using opcode 0b1111 which is 0xF).

In the case of a co-processor instruction, the next field (co-processor ID) specifies the particular co-processor involved in the execution of this instruction. When that particular co-processor is not implemented in the system, it will not respond to a CPU handshake operation, resulting in an 'F-line emulator exception'. This allows the co-processor instruction to be emulated by software. One of the eight co-processor ID codes specifies the MC68881 floating-point co-processor, another specifies the MC68851 paged memory management unit, four are reserved for use by Motorola and two are user definable (such that the user may implement his own co-processor).

The instruction type field is also visible to the CPU. It specifies the type of co-processor instruction. The following instruction types have been defined:

- cpBcc: Branch on Co-processor Condition – cpBcc <label>. The type-specific field specifies the condition to be selected, while one or more extension words specify the branch displacement. It allows the CPU to perform a conditional branch operation, depending on a co-processor condition.
- cpDBcc: Test Co-processor Condition Decrement and Branch – cpDBcc Dn, <label>. The type-specific field specifies the CPU data register Dn, while extension words specify the condition to be selected and the branch displacement.
- cpGEN: Co-processor General Function – cpGEN <parameters as defined by co-processor>. This instruction is used to perform, for

example, floating-point addition and subtraction. The details of its operation, as well as the number of extension words required by the instruction, are completely co-processor dependent.

- cpRESTORE: Co-processor Restore Function – cpRESTORE <ea>. This restores the internal state of the co-processor.
- cpSAVE: Co-processor Save Function – cpSAVE <ea>. This saves the internal state of the co-processor.
- cpScc: Set According to Co-processor Condition – cpScc <ea>. This is the co-processor equivalent of the Scc instruction.
- cpTRAPcc: Trap on Co-processor Condition – cpTRAPcc #<data>. This is the co-processor equivalent of the TRAPcc (Trap on Condition, rather than Branch on Condition) instruction.

SUMMARY

- Virtual machine monitors allow multiple users (which may be traditional user programs or operating systems) to have the impression of being the only user of a real machine. Each of these real machines may have its own configuration (in terms of amount of memory, types of peripherals, and so on). Virtual machine monitors allow for portability at the operating system level.
- The architectural support for virtual machine monitors requires sensitive instructions to be trapped. Sensitive instructions are privileged instructions, or instructions sensing the mode the CPU runs in or the state of privileged resources (such as memory management registers).
- Operating systems that run in a virtual machine monitor environment are run in user mode. Because they are given the impression of being run in supervisor mode, this is also called virtual supervisor mode.
- It is generally preferable to have I/O that uses real, rather than virtual, addresses because of speed considerations.
- When I/O uses real addresses, and virtual memory management techniques are used, it has to be guaranteed that the area of main memory is accessible to, and remains accessible, during the I/O operation.
- I/O data incoherence can occur when main memory is written with I/O data and a cache containing a copy of the old contents of that main memory data is not updated.
- Solutions to the I/O data coherence problem consist of: making the area of main memory used for I/O non-cacheable; or having the cache controller monitor (snoop) the I/O traffic in order to invalidate or update cache blocks that have become inconsistent.
- Caches are usually addressed with real addresses, for reasons of simplicity (no aliasing problems), and the address translation operation can usually be overlapped with a cache access.
- When the address translation time of a cache in real address space is overlapped, the size of the cache is limited to that of a page, or multiples thereof in case of a set-associative cache.
- Caches in virtual address space can have any size and only require address translation upon a cache miss. They have a potential aliasing problem, which occurs when more than one virtual address maps on to the same real address.
- Co-processors extend the instruction set of the main processor. They contain local operand storage, while the instruction sequencing is performed by the host processor.
- In general, it is preferable for the architecture of the co-processor instruction set to be transparent to the host or partially transparent to allow for the incorporation of co-processors at a later date.
- The MC68020 co-processor interface is partly visible to the host. Instruction tracking is used for instruction fetching, while the host evaluates the operand addresses.

References

Birnbaum, J. S. and Worley, W. S. (1985). Beyond RISC: High-precision architecture. *Hewlett-Packard Journal*, **36**(8), 4–10.

Bonomi, M. (1988). Avoiding coprocessor bottlenecks. *Byte*, **13**(3), 197–205.

Goldberg, R. P. (1972). *Architectural Principles for Virtual Computer Systems*, PhD Thesis, Harvard University: Cambridge, MA.

Goodman, J. R. (1987). Coherency for multiprocessor virtual address caches. In *Proc. 2nd Int. Conf. on Architectural Support for Programming Languages and Operating Systems*, pp. 72–80.

Parmalee, R. P. *et al.* (1972). Virtual storage and virtual machine concepts. *IBM Systems Journal*, **11**(2), 99–130.

Popek, G. J. and Goldberg, R. P. (1974). Formal requirements for virtualizable third generation architectures. *Comm. of the ACM*, **17**(7), 412–21.

Wood, D. A. *et al.* (1986). An in-cache address translation mechanism. In *Proc. 13th Annual Symposium on Computer Architecture*, pp. 358–65.

Glossary

Absolute addressing (5.2.2) A one-component address specified as part of the instruction in such a way that the address is fixed during program execution. It is used to address interrupt and trap vectors, and I/O devices.

Access data type (3.4) An access data type can be implemented via a pointer and is used to construct dynamic data structures.

Activation record (8.2.1) A block of consecutive memory locations, allocated upon the activation of a block.

Address resolution (5.1.1) The smallest possible amount of information that can be addressed (usually a byte or a word).

Address translation (10.2.1) The translation of virtual to real addresses. This is done by special hardware called a memory management unit (MMU).

Addressing mode (4.2) This defines the way in which an operand is specified.

Alignment (5.1.1) Alignment is the requirement that the address of an object should be divisible by the length of the object, for performance reasons.

Arbitration (13.1.4, 13.3) The process of transferring the bus from the current bus master to another bus master. This may be done using one of the following policies: priority, fairness or a combination of priority and fairness.

Architecture (1.1.1, 2.1, 17) The architecture of a computer is the way a user experiences the functionality of the computer. It can also be defined as the interface between the hardware and the software or an embodiment of a computational model.

Argument pointer (8.2.2) The argument pointer points to the block of explicit parameters, which allows this block to be placed anywhere in memory.

Associative memory (10.5.1) *See* Contents addressable memory.

Asynchronous bus (13.2.3) A bus whose timing is determined by the source and destination of the bus transaction, such that each may respond at its own speed.

Atomic operation (9.4.1) An operation that is indivisible; its parts cannot be interleaved with those of another operation.

Availability (12.1) The availability of a system is defined as the probability that the system is operational at a time *t*.

Bandwidth (14.3) Bandwidth, also called throughput, is the number of operations per second.

Base addressing (5.2.3) The corollary to indexed addressing: to a computable base address (usually stored in an address register), a fixed displacement is added. Scalar elements in an (activation) record may be addressed using base addressing.

Basic instruction part (4.2) This is the first word of an instruction. It usually specifies the opcode, the number of operands and (part of) the operand specifiers.

Binding mechanism (8.1.3) This determines how a correspondence between symbolic names and values is made.

Binding time (8.1.3) This determines when a name is made to correspond with a certain value. This can be before program execution (static binding) or during program execution (dynamic binding).

Block (8.1.2) A block consists of a sequence of statements and possibly declarations of data. Data declared in a block is called local data; data declared elsewhere is called non-local data. Within a block, other blocks may be declared. This is called nesting.

Block data transfer (13.2.2) A bus transaction during which more than one data element (a block of data elements) is transferred.

Blocking (16.3.2) This situation may occur in shuffle exchange networks when paths through the network cannot be set up because switches are required to take on conflicting positions.

Branch bypass (14.7.4) In the case of a branch instruction, the instruction fetch unit will prefetch both potential target instructions. When the branch instruction has been executed, the instruction fetch unit throws away the incorrectly prefetched instruction.

Branch dependency (14.8.3) The disruption of the pipelined operation of a computer due to branch instructions; partially executed instructions have to be discarded.

Branch target buffer (14.7.4) A memory containing target instructions (a branch target instruction is an instruction that is fetched after executing a branch). This buffer is used to save the delay of the instruction fetch stage of the pipeline in the case of a branch.

Breakpoints (12.3.2) This is a method to debug software. At certain locations in a program an instruction is replaced by a breakpoint instruction, the execution of which causes a trap to a monitor. At this point, the program may be checked and program execution statistics may be gathered. The execution of the program proceeds by re-inserting the replaced instruction at the location where the trap occurred.

Broadcall (13.2.1) A master performs a read operation from more than one slave simultaneously.

Broadcast (13.2.1) A master performs a write operation to more than one slave simultaneously.

Buffering (11.5) Buffering allows data to be temporarily stored in a device controller so that data transfers become less time critical and cause less overhead (because data may be transferred using DMA burst mode).

Bus (13) A bus consists of a set of lines used to connect two or more digital system elements. When more than one data bit is transferred over the bus in parallel, it is called a parallel bus; otherwise one speaks of a serial bus.

Bus master (13.1.4) The system element currently in control of the bus.

Bus system (13) A set of buses, usually with different functions and characteristics.

Bus transaction (13.1.4) A bus transaction consists of a complete sequence of bus operations; requesting the bus, transferring the data and releasing the bus.

Channel (11.6) A device controller that allows DMA data transfers, data chaining and command chaining.

Circuit switching (16.1.3) The transfer of data takes place along a physical path (connection), which remains established for the duration of the data transfer.

CISC (15) Complex instruction set computer. A computer architecture optimized to reduce the number of instructions executed, by having high-level (complex) instructions.

Code transformation operation (6.4) This changes the coding of the data.

Column-major ordering (3.3.2) The allocation of an array in memory such that columns are placed in contiguous memory locations; A[I + 1, J] is next to A[I, J].

Command chaining (11.4.4) This allows several I/O commands to be issued and outstanding to a single I/O subsystem.

Compilation (2.2.1) The process of replacing each source program statement by a series of lower-level statements (instructions), resulting in an object program that can be loaded and executed.

Completeness (1.2.4) A system is complete when all functions of a certain class are included.

Computational model (17) A conceptual method according to which a computation can be performed.

Computational unit (17.2.1) Abstract functional blocks that perform operations on their arguments and produce some result.

Consistency (1.2.1) This means that, with partial knowledge, the remainder of a system can be predicted.

Contents addressable memory (10.5.1) A memory where a value, rather than an address, is used to select a data item. All memory locations are searched in parallel for this value, and the matching entry will output its data. These memories are also called associative memories.

Context switching (9.5.2) This is part of the process-switching operation. It consists of saving the process context of the interrupted process and loading the context of the interrupting process.

Control mechanism (17.2.1) The mechanism that determines how the computation will proceed. This can be: control, data, demand or pattern driven.

Control space (5.1.3) The address space that contains control registers such as the program status word, the memory management registers and interrupt vectors.

Co-processor (B.4) A processor that is optimized to perform certain functions under control of a host processor to which it is attached.

Cross-bar switch (16.3.1) A switch that can connect p processors to n memory modules simultaneously.

Cube-connected cycles (16.2) A hypercube-like architecture where each node of the hypercube is replaced by a ring.

Daisy chain (13.3.3) When a bus or interrupt grant signal passes serially from one potential requestor to the next one, until a requestor has been found; this serial path is called the daisy chain.

Data chaining (11.4.3) Allows several pages of main memory data to be read from/written to a disk sector or a tape record, while only one I/O command (to read/write a sector or record) has been issued.

Data coherence (16.4) The consistency of data in a computer system.

Data dependency (14.8.1) Data dependencies occur in pipelined implementations when shared resources between instructions exist. The value of that shared resource is accessed before a previous operation has delivered its result. This dependency can be a read-after-write, a write-after-read or a write-after-write dependency.

Data flow (17.3) Data flow computers are based on the DAME computational model; data driven with message passing. A computational unit performs its operation when its arguments are available.

Data-handling operation (6.1) A data operation that can be a data move, a format or a code transformation operation.

Data mechanism (17.2.1) Defines the way computational units exchange data. This can be via: shared data or message passing.

Data move operation (6.2) Makes a copy of a data value and stores it under a different name (which means a different location).

Data space (4.3.3) Used to contain the values of the data. The location at which the data may be found in the data space is usually specified through an operand in operand space.

Data structure (4.3.2) This is the way structured data types are organized. A data structure may be a vector, an array, a record or a record of arrays.

Data type (4.3.2) The type of the data which may be integer, floating point or Boolean. The data type is usually specified in the opcode space.

Deallocation (13.3) The way a bus master gives up control over the bus. Deallocation can be done according to the following policies: release on request, release when done and pre-emption.

Debugging (12.3.2) The process of locating a programming error.

Dedicated bus (13.1.1) Performs only a single function and is used to connect two types of functional units.

Delayed branch (14.8.3) A branch instruction that, when taken, will additionally cause a number of instructions lexically following that branch instruction to be executed; after that, instruction execution proceeds at the branch target address.

Derived result (6.1) The result derived from an operation (such as overflow or carry) or from the result of an operation (such as zero or negative).

Descriptor (4.3.2) Descriptors are constructs, supported by the architecture of a computer, used to access data elements in a data structure. They contain information that describes the data structure, such that operations involved in accessing a data element of a structure (such as subscript checking) can be done implicitly.

Descriptor-based addressing (5.3.1) A descriptor is used to access a data element from a data structure (usually a vector). Since the descriptor describes all properties of the data structure, all computations required to access a data element can be done implicitly.

Device controller (11.1) The interface between a CPU and an I/O device. A device controller consists of a host port, which takes care of the communication with the host, and one or more device ports, which take care of communication with one or more devices.

Device driver (11.3) The device type specific software of an operating system, used to communicate with an I/O device.

Direct I/O (11.4.1) This is I/O, completely taken care of by a program executed on the host. During direct I/O, only that single I/O process is being executed by the host. Direct I/O is also called programmed I/O.

Direct mapping (10.5) This means that the number of entries in a translation table (used for translating virtual to real addresses) is determined by the size of the virtual address space, and every memory reference uses this translation table.

Direct memory access (11.4.3) Allows data to be transferred to/from an I/O device, in parallel with CPU processing, under control of dedicated hardware in the device controller.

Domain (3.2.5) The collection of all values that are representable in a particular data format. It consists of a range and a precision.

Dynamic binding (8.1.3) Dynamic binding uses the value of the variable found in the most recent activation of a block containing the declaration of the variable name.

Dynamic instruction frequency (4.1) The number of times an instruction is executed. It can be used to optimize the execution time of a program by having a fast implementation for instructions with a high dynamic frequency of occurrence.

Dynamic link (8.2.2) An implicit parameter, stored in the activation record, used to point to the activation record of the calling function.

Dynamic redundancy (12.2.2) This requires facilities to detect and locate faulty modules, and replaces those with spare modules.

Dynamic relocation (10.2.1) Address translation done at execution time.

Emulation (2.5) When a new interface is presented at the architectural level, implemented using microprogramming techniques, one speaks of emulation.

Environment (8.1.3) The set of constants and variable names that are visible while executing a particular block. The local environment of a block consists of all locally declared objects, including formal parameters.

Exception invocation (12.4.2) The recording of the exception, by causing a process switch (to invoke the process that has to handle the exception) via an interrupt.

Explicit parameters (8.2.2) The actual parameters passed as part of a call to a function. They are usually stored in registers or in the 'explicit parameter area' of the activation record.

Extended precision (6.6.1) The possibility of performing operations on numbers with arbitrary length. The two's complement representation for integers is preferred, because it facilitates extended-precision operations.

External fragmentation (10.4.3) This is caused by the fact that main memory is allocated in blocks with different sizes such that after some time, when some of these blocks have been de-allocated, main memory contains unused areas, each of which may not be large enough to contain the next block.

Fault avoidance (12.1) A way to design and implement systems such that faults are very unlikely to occur.

Fault tolerance (12.1) This enables correct results in the presence of faults, via redundancy.

Fetch policies (10.6.1, 14.6.2) Policies that determine when a block of data has to be loaded into main or cache memory; this can be on demand or based on prefetching.

Format transformation operation (6.3) This changes the format of the operand; that is, the bit assignment is changed. Shift and bit-field instructions are used for this.

Frame pointer (8.2.2) This is used to point to the area in the activation record containing the local data.

Functional dependency (7.1.1) When the way an instruction is executed depends on one or more other instructions, one speaks about functional dependency.

Functionally partitioned bus (13.1.2) This bus connects system elements that contain their own processing power and can perform their function almost autonomously. The bus is typically used to allow for communication between those system elements. This communication has a message-oriented nature.

Generality (1.2.4) Making functions such that they contain as few restrictions as possible, such that they can be used most widely. Generality is enhanced by completeness and open-endedness.

Generic operation (4.3.2) Specifies the operation to be performed, regardless of the data type. This means that the data type has to be specified elsewhere.

Geographical addressing (13.2.1) The bus master specifies the address of a slave via the physical position of the slave's board on the backplane.

Global data (8.1.2) The data declared in the outermost block, which is usually the main program.

Guard digit (6.7.1) A digit used to increase the accuracy of floating-point ADD and SUBTRACT operations.

Hardware redundancy (12.2.1) The duplication of hardware to allow two or more answers to be produced, which can be compared for equality; when equal, the answers are assumed to be correct.

Harvard architecture (14.5.1) An architecture with separate paths to main memory for instructions and data, to allow for a higher memory bandwidth.

Hidden bit (3.2.5) A normalized number using radix 2 will have a 1 as its most significant digit. When this digit is not stored, because it does not contain any information, it is called a hidden bit.

Hit ratio (14.6) The probability of finding the requested information in a cache.

Hypercube network (16.2) This is a multicomputer interconnection network which is n-dimensional ($n > 3$) with $N = 2^n$ nodes, where the degree of a node and the diameter of the network is n.

I/O (11) *See* Input/output.

I/O processor (11.6) Adds intelligence to a device controller such that functions performed by the host may be done by the I/O subsystem, therefore off-loading the host. This allows for a higher level of the host interface, and for better error detection and recovery.

I/O space (5.1.3) The address space used for I/O.

Implementation (1.1.1) The logic structure that describes how the functions described by the architecture are carried out. It includes the data path and control of the computer.

Implicit parameters (8.2.2) Parameters needed for internal use. They may consist of the dynamic link and the static link, and are stored in the 'implicit parameter area' of the activation record.

Indexed addressing (5.2.3) This addressing mode uses a base address to which a computable displacement (the index) is added.

Indirect addressing (5.2.2) A form of address specification where the operand contains a value that is the address of the data involved in the operation.

Indivisible operation (9.4) An operation that is considered to be executed at a single moment in time, used for process synchronization.

Information redundancy (12.2.1) Redundancy in the way the information is encoded, usually in the form of some error-correcting code.

Input/output (11) The mechanism a computer uses to communicate with its environment. This environment can be a storage device (used to extend main memory with lower cost memory) or a source/sink device (used to communicate with the external world).

Instruction (4.2) The amount of work that can be done by a computer at a time. Instructions consist of a basic part and optional extension words.

Interleaving (14.5.2) A method to increase the memory bandwidth by dividing memory into independent modules which can be accessed in parallel.

Internal fragmentation (10.4.2) The waste of memory space due to the fact that main memory is allocated in whole pages, while only part of a page may be needed.

Interpretation (2.2.1) The execution of a source program by analyzing each higher-level language statement, causing the execution of a set of lower-level statements (instructions). This process is repeated each time a source statement has to be executed.

Interrupt (9.5) An interrupt request is the indication of a process that it wants to be serviced by the processor. An interrupt operation is that part of the context switch where the minimum processor context is switched as an indivisible operation; the remainder of the process context can be switched by the invoked process.

Interrupt priority (9.6.1) The priority with which a process requests an interrupt.

Inverted page table (10.5.2) An address translation table whose size is determined by the amount of real memory.

Latency (14.3) The total time between the start of an operation and the availability of the result.

Line (14.6.1) The amount of information transferred between main memory and a cache.

Local data (8.1.2) Data declared in the block currently being executed.

Location dependency (7.1.2) When the position of an instruction is dependent on that of another instruction. Chained and sequential are two forms of location dependency.

Logical addressing (13.2.1) The way a bus master selects a slave; the address of the slave can be specified in a completely unconstrained (arbitrary) way.

Loop buffer (14.7.4) A buffer that contains instructions such that the instruction fetch stage of a pipeline can be skipped for those instructions.

Masking redundancy (12.2.2) The use of extra hardware so that, in spite of errors, a correct result will be produced. Error-correcting codes and triple modular redundancy allow for masking of errors.

Memory allocation policy (10.6) Determines the size of the area allocated to a process. This can be based on fixed-size partitions or variable-size partitions.

Memory management (10.1) Allows for protection, sharing and relocation of blocks of main memory.

Memory management policy (10.6) This policy determines the loading of information into main memory upon a page fault. It involves a fetch policy, a placement policy and a replacement policy.

Multicomputer system (16.1) Each processor in a multicomputer system has its own local memory; the interconnection network is only used for interprocessor communication.

Multiport memory (16.3.1) A memory having multiple ports (buses) with built-in logic to arbitrate between the ports.

Multiprocessor system (16.1) The processors in a multiprocessor system share a common memory. The interconnection network is used to connect the processors with this shared common memory.

Multiprogramming (9.1.2) A type of operating system where I/O can be done in overlap with program execution. When a program has to wait for I/O, the processor will be allocated to another program which is ready to be executed.

Mutual exclusion (9.4) The mechanism used to guarantee that, at most, one process can be in a given critical section at any one time.

Non-dedicated bus (13.1.1) A bus that is used by functional units of several different types. A non-dedicated bus is usually shared between those functional units.

Non-local data (8.1.2) Data not declared in the block currently being executed.

Normalization (3.2.5) This applies to floating-point numbers which, when represented in normalized form, have the highest precision.

One-component addressing mode (5.2.2) A single component specifies a register number or an absolute address.

Opcode space (4.3) Usually used to specify the operation to be performed, together with the number of operands and the data type involved.

Open-endedness (1.2.4) A system should provide room for growth, to accommodate unforeseen requirements. Room for extra instructions, and sufficient address bits, are typical precautionary measures used to satisfy the open-endedness requirement.

Operand extension (4.2) Operand extensions, also called extension words, are optional words that, together with the basic part, specify an instruction. Operand extension words are usually used to further specify operands. They may specify displacements, immediate values or absolute addresses.

Operand space (4.3) This usually specifies the location of an operand, which can be in main memory or in a register. It can also be used to specify immediate values.

Operating system (9) A virtual machine that provides for high-level I/O commands, protection and resource allocation.

Orthogonality (1.2.2) Conceptually separate functions are kept separate in their specifications.

Overflow (6.1, 6.7.4) This occurs when a result is produced which exceeds the range of the representable values, due to a value that is too large.

Overlapped I/O (11.4.2) With overlapped I/O, interrupts are generated by the device controller to request transfers of data to/from the device. Between interrupts, the host may execute other processes.

Overlay (5.1.3) A technique that allows one space to contain another space. A logical overlay is not visible at the architectural level, since at that level only a single space exists. A physical overlay means that, at the architectural level, separate logical spaces exist, which are implemented in a single physical space.

Ownership scheme (16.5.3) A data consistency scheme where a tag is used with every line in main memory to determine whether main memory owns a valid copy of the line, rather than some cache.

Packet switching (16.1.3) The data to be transferred is divided into equally sized packets, which are transferred individually, possibly along different routes.

Page fault (10.4.2) This occurs when the page addressed in the virtual address space is not present in real memory space.

Page frame (10.4.2) A block of main memory with the size of a page.

Paged segmentation (10.4.4) This is a memory management system based on segmentation, where the segments are paged.

Paging (10.4.2) A form of address translation where a program is divided into equally sized blocks, called pages, which are relocated individually. Demand paging allows for a virtual memory, where transfers of pages are done to and from secondary memory on demand and transparently to the executing process.

Parsimony (1.2.3) Relates to the economy of not including functions that are not essential for the purpose of a system.

Pipelining (14.3.2) Analogous to the assembly line concept: an operation is carried out in several stages by special hardware for each stage. A number of operations, equal to the number of stages, can be carried out simultaneously.

Placement policies (10.6.2, 14.6.2) Policies that determine where a block of data has to be loaded into main memory, to minimize the internal fragmentation for segmented systems. For caches, the placement policy determines where a line of data from main memory will be loaded; this policy can be: direct, fully associative or set associative.

Post-indexed addressing (5.2.3) A form of indirect, indexed addressing where the indirection takes place first, followed by an index operation.

Pre-indexed addressing (5.2.3) A form of indexed, indirect addressing where indirection takes place after the index operation.

Precision (3.2.5) The smallest difference between two successive representable numbers.

Privileged instructions (9.3) Instructions that are only allowed to be executed in supervisor mode. Instructions are privileged when they relate to process switching, exception handling, memory management and I/O.

Procedural extension (2.3) Extending the functionality of a language by using the procedure mechanism.

Process (9.2) The abstraction level used by operating systems to deal with the problem of concurrency; it is the smallest program unit that can be scheduled and run.

Process context (9.2.3) The information to specify the complete status of a process. It can be divided into a processor context (which consists of the information stored in the processor registers) and the memory context (which consists of the information usually stored in main memory).

Process switching (9.5) The operation of switching the processor from executing one process to executing another process. It is initiated by an interrupt operation.

Process synchronization (9.4) Guarantees that only one process can be in a critical section at any time, to access a shared resource.

Program counter relative addressing (5.2.3) A form of base addressing where the program counter is used to specify the base address.

Propriety (1.2.3) Only those functions that are required for functionality should be part of an architecture. The opposite to propriety is extraneousness, which means adding something that is alien to the purpose of the system.

Protection (9.3) Guarantees the security and privacy of processes.

Queue (3.5.2) A first-in, first-out (FIFO) buffer.

Range (3.2.5) The interval between the largest and the smallest representable number.

Real address (10.2.1) The address used to access main memory. The real address space is the total of all real addresses. It is directly related to the size of main memory.

Realization (1.1.1) A concrete version of an implementation. It involves component selection, reliability, packaging, cooling, and so on.

Register space (5.1.3) The address space that contains the general (address and data) registers.

Register window (15.3.1) A mechanism that relocates, in register space, the current working registers of a processor. A called procedure is automatically issued a free set of registers by relocating the current working registers to a new, unused area in register space.

Reliability (12.1) The reliability of a system is defined as the probability that the system has been operational during the time interval 0 to t.

Relocation (10.4.1) A form of address translation where a program, written to start at virtual address 0, can be located anywhere in memory.

Replacement policies (10.6.3, 14.6.2) The policies used for memory management to determine which block of data has to be removed such that the freed memory area can be used to contain another block of data. Ideally that block is selected for replacement which is not part of the current working set. For caches, the replacement policy is used to determine which line of cache data has to be moved to main memory. Some replacement policies are: least recently used (LRU), FIFO and random.

Resource-partitioned bus (13.1.2) A bus used to connect system elements, where each system element performs part of the function of a computer.

Retry operation (12.2.2) A form of exception handling where the fault causing the exception is assumed to be non-permanent, such that upon a retry the operation will succeed.

RISC (15) Reduced instruction set computer. A computer architecture optimized to reduce the number of cycles per instruction and to keep the cycle time short.

Rounding (6.6, 6.7.4) A precision operation. It makes a non-representable number (due to the lack of sufficient precision bits) representable by selecting the closest representable number.

Row-major ordering (3.3.2) The allocation of an array in memory such that rows are placed in contiguous memory locations.

Run-time model (8.2) The way environments, created due to the activation of different blocks, are allocated and de-allocated.

Run-on (14.8.2) A timing problem in a pipelined implementation of a computer.

Scalar data type (3.2) An atomic data type.

Scaling (5.3.1) An operation that may be used with the indexed addressing mode; the index value is multiplied with the length (in addressable units) of the data element to be accessed.

Segmentation (10.4.3) A form of address translation where the virtual address space is divided into blocks, called segments, which contain a program-defined object. Segmentation is therefore not transparent to the process being segmented.

Semantic gap (17.1.3) The distance between concepts and levels used in higher-level languages and the architecture of a computer.

Semi-synchronous bus (13.2.3) A bus where the timing is determined by the source and the destination involved in the bus transaction. This timing is constrained so that events may only happen at moments determined by a fixed clock.

Set associative (14.6.2) A placement policy used for caches. It can be considered a direct-mapped placement policy where the direct-mapped entries consist of several lines selected associatively.

Shuffle exchange (16.3.2) A concept used for interconnection networks for multiprocessor systems where interconnections are made in a shuffled way.

Simulation (2.5) Presenting a new interface on some existing system. At the architectural level, this can be done by: interpretation, emulation or a combined approach.

Snoopy cache controller (16.5.3) A cache controller that monitors data requests from its processor, as well as data requests and transfers on the memory bus. They are used in multiprocessor systems to solve the data coherence problem dynamically.

Software portability (2.5) Executing software from one computer system on a different computer system. The level at which porting can take place (this is also the level at which both computer systems should have identical interfaces) varies from the application to the machine language level.

Source/sink device (11.2) An I/O device used to communicate with the external world.

Spatial locality (10.2.2) Locality is space: in the near future a program will reference those programs and data objects having addresses close to the last references.

Stack (3.5.1) A last-in, first-out (LIFO) buffer used by the operating system to store activation records, and by compilers for expression evaluation and to store intermediate results.

Stack space (5.1.3) The space containing the stack. A stack is usually used to contain activation records and to hold temporary results.

Static binding (8.1.3) The correspondence of a name used in a program with the declaration of that name made at compile time by analyzing the program text. This is also called lexical binding, because after the local block, the textually enclosing blocks are searched for the symbolic name.

Static instruction frequency (4.1) The number of times an instruction occurs in the program text. It can be used to optimize the program size by giving shorter encodings to the instructions with a high static frequency of occurrence.

Static link (8.2.2) An implicit parameter, stored in the activation record, used to point to the activation record of the textually enclosing block, to support lexical addressing.

Static relocation (10.2.1) A form of address translation performed before the program is executed.

Storage device (11.2) An I/O device used to extend main storage.

Structured data type (3.3) A data type composed of other (structured or scalar) data types.

Subroutine (8.3.2) A simplified form of a function or procedure, supported by the architecture.

Superfluity (10.4.2) The waste of main memory due to the requirement that a process has to be memory resident in its entirety.

Supervisor mode (9.3) The mode in which a processor runs so that privileged instructions are allowed; the corollary is user mode.

Synchronous bus (13.2.3) A bus where data transfers take place under control of, and at a moment determined by, a fixed (system-defined) clock.

Table superfluity (10.4.2) The waste of memory due to the requirement that a complete translation table has to be memory resident.

Tag (4.3.2) A set of bits, added to every word in memory, used to specify the data type of the corresponding word. An architecture that uses tags is called a tagged architecture and may allow generic operations.

Temporal locality (10.2.2) Locality in time: in the near future a program will reference those program and data objects that have been referenced in the recent past.

Thread (14.1, 16) An instruction stream. A single-thread system executes a single instruction stream; a multiple-thread system executes multiple instruction streams.

Time sharing (9.1.2) A form of multiprogramming, where each program is executed in turn for a period of time.

Tracing (12.3.2) A method to debug software. After the execution of every instruction of a particular class, a trace-trap is made to a monitor, so that the program can be checked for correctness, or statistics about the execution of the program may be collected.

Translation lookaside buffer (10.5.1) An address translation acceleration mechanism, using a contents addressable memory.

Transparency (1.2.3) The definition of a function should be such that it is not influenced by lower design levels.

Truncation (6.6, 6.7.4) A precision operation. It makes a non-representable number (due to the lack of sufficient precision bits) representable by deleting the non-representable part.

Two-component addressing mode (5.2.3) An addressing mode where the address is composed of two components.

Two-level paging (10.4.4) A paging system where the page tables are paged, to reduce table superfluity.

Underflow (6.1, 6.7.4) Occurs when a result is produced which exceeds the range of the representable values, due to a value that is too small.

Update policy (14.6.2) A policy used to determine when information in a cache has to be written back to main memory. Well-known policies are write-through, copy-back and flagged copy-back.

User mode (9.3) The mode in which privileged instructions are not allowed to be executed.

Virtual address (10.2.1) The address generated by the process being executed. It may be different from the real address. The virtual address space is the total address space available to a process.

Virtual interrupt (13.4) A virtual interrupt mechanism does not use a dedicated interrupt bus, but uses that part of the bus used for transferring data; a side effect of the data transfer is the interrupt.

Virtual machine monitor (2.5, B.1) Allows many, possibly different, operating systems to coexist on the same machine. It allows for software portability at the operating system level. The virtual machine monitor gives each operating system the illusion of being the sole user of the machine.

Virtual memory (10.2.1) The possibility of having a virtual address space that is larger than the amount of main memory. This is made transparent to the user by the operating system.

Virtual supervisor mode (B.1.2) When an operating system in a virtual machine monitor environment is made to run in user mode, while to that operating system it appears to be running in supervisor mode, that operating system is said to be running in virtual supervisor mode.

Von Neumann bottleneck (17.1.3) This is the performance restriction of a von Neumann computer due to the CPU–memory interface (physical bottleneck) or the way of thinking, induced by the von Neumann model (conceptual bottleneck).

Von Neumann model (17.1) The von Neumann computational model is based on a CPU, a memory and a connecting tube. The memory is sequential, consists of words and does not distinguish between instructions and data, while meaning is not an inherent part of the data.

Working set (10.2.2) The set of memory blocks, at time t, referenced during the last h references, is called the working set $W(t, h)$.

Write-once scheme (16.5.3) A data consistency scheme where, upon a first write to a line in cache, a write-through is performed to update main memory and to invalidate other lines in the cache.

Zero-component addressing mode (5.2.1) An addressing mode that does not specify an address (it is an anomaly) but data. This data is called immediate data. This form of addressing is also called immediate addressing.

SOLUTIONS TO EXERCISES

Chapter 1

1.1 (a) Architecture; (b) implementation; (c) realization; (d) architecture; (e) implementation; (f) implementation.

1.2 (a) False; (b) true.

1.3 (a) True; (b) false; (c) false.

1.4 (a) Consistency; (b) completeness; (c) generality; (d) open-endedness; (e) consistency; (f) completeness; (g) consistency and completeness; (h) parsimony.

1.5 Flynn used the notions of instruction and data streams which could have the values single or multiple. The MC68020 belongs to the class SISD because a single instruction stream is executed, operating on a single data stream. The ILLIAC-IV belongs to the SIMD class.

Chapter 2

2.1 High-level language, because it allows for a higher productivity and maintainability.

2.2 Interpretation is slower because every high-level language statement has to be analyzed and replaced with equivalent machine language instructions. This has to be repeated every time the high-level language statement has to be executed (for example, upon each iteration of a loop).

2.3 Compilation, because of the resulting efficiency in execution time. Also, compilers are better in finding program errors.

2.4 Interpretation. The microprogram analyzes and decodes each instruction, every time it has to be executed.

2.5 A new function can be added at any level. For a high execution speed, the hardware level (L0 or L1) is preferred. At level L3, or higher, the user can specify the function to be added, using the procedural extension mechanism.

2.6 (a) emulation, using the mode concept; (b) emulation; (c) interpretation.

2.7 Emulation, because interpretation is performed on the assembly language level. The mode bit allows for the support of two architectures at the microprogramming level.

2.8 By porting the operating system as well. This can be done using the virtual machine monitor concept.

2.9 In languages such as APL the data types are not statically defined, but can vary from statement to statement. At execution time, data types have to be interrogated to generate the correct instruction (or sequences of instructions) – for example, to generate an 'ADD.W, add 16-bit integer word' or an 'ADD.F, add a 32-bit floating point number'. In addition, the amount of data may vary from statement to statement, which may require memory allocation on a per statement basis.

2.10 A virtual machine is a machine as experienced by the user – it may not be physically there. For example, at interface I4 of Figure 2.2 the user may have the illusion of having a Pascal machine.

2.11 A virtual machine monitor is a program that allows many, possibly different, operating systems to use a single machine simultaneously. This is done such that each operating system gets the idea of being the sole user of the machine.

Chapter 3

3.1 Integers, Booleans and characters.

3.2 Ease of implementing operations, symmetry in range of positive and negative values, and unique representation for the value zero.

3.3 A = 100 0001; 9 = 011 1001 and ! = 010 0001.

3.4 (a) 23; (b) 32 33; (c) 32 33.

3.5 (a) 0 and 255; (b) −127 and +127; (c) −127 and +127; (d) −128 and +127; (e) 0 and 99; (f) −9 and +9.

3.6 (a) False; (b) true; (c) false.

3.7 A denormalized number does not have to be normalized; it allows the fraction to be represented with leading zeros. Denormalized numbers are important because they allow small numbers to be handled with greater precision.

3.8 (a) −28 (don't forget the hidden bit); (b) +13/16; (c) +2.

3.9 (a) S = 0, E = 100 0001 and F = 0001 0000 0000 0000 0000 0000;

(b) S = 0, E = 100 0100 and F = 1111 1111 1111 1111 0000 0000.

3.10 (a) S, E, F (first the sign, then the exponent and then the fraction field);

(b) Zero means S = 0, E = 0 and F = 0 (as for integers);

(c) The exponent should be in excess notation, such that positive exponent values denote numbers with an absolute value bigger than zero.

3.11 As a bit vector:

(7	6	5	4	3	2	1	0)
–	–	–	Mon	5	March	10	1990

3.12 (a) The total amount of memory required is: 2 ∗ (25 − 5 + 1) ∗ (20 − 10 + 1) = 462 bytes;

(b) 1000 + 2 ∗ ((10 − 5) ∗ (20 − 10 + 1) + (15 − 10)) = 1120;

(c) 1000 + 2 ∗ ((15 − 10) ∗ (25 − 5 + 1) + (10 − 5)) = 1220.

3.13 The relative position of element day is 0; that of element year is 2.

Chapter 4

4.1 (a) False – static instruction frequency analysis is used to optimize the use of memory;

(b) False – dynamic instruction frequency analysis is used to optimize execution speed;

(c) False – most statements are very simple;

(d) True.

4.2 (a) The assignment statement;

(b) The form $A := B$ is most frequent;

(c) Constants and simple variables – together they account for about 75%;

(d) About 65%.

4.3 (a) Move, because it is used in assignment statements and for parameter passing;

(b) Bcc and DBcc, because they are used in **if . . . then . . . else** and loop statements;

(c) Arithmetic/logical, because the shift/rotate class does not have a direct higher-level language counterpart.

4.4 (a) Because on-chip registers are fast and instructions using the register-direct mode for the specification of an operand are shorter. This saves memory and the time needed to fetch a possible extension word.

(b) The register-direct mode is used more frequently to specify a destination operand, because expressions with several operands need a location in which to store the temporary result. A data register, rather than some memory location, is a more efficient choice for the location of the temporary result.

(c) The immediate mode is used to specify constants that have a high frequency of occurrence in high-level language programs.

4.5 (a) MC68020 belongs to class 2;

(b) 1, because it allows for the simplest instruction set, which is easier and faster to implement;

(c) 4, because it has least restrictions;

(d) Inefficiency in memory use, because reg-reg instructions can be encoded in fewer bits than memory-referencing instructions using a displacement.

4.6 (a) True, because each operand needs to specify its own data type;

(b) False, because the instructions can be generic;

(c) False, because mixed-mode arithmetic does not occur frequently;

(d) False, because tags also allow for the specification of the data type (in the data space).

4.7 (a) False, because every word has to have the extra tag bits;

(b) True, because when the data type changes, its tag must also be changed to guarantee that the correct operation will be performed automatically;

(c) True, because the opcode does not have to specify the data type;

(d) False, because tag checking slows down the machine;

(e) True, because operations on operands with different data types can be performed automatically;

(f) False, because a tag can only specify one data type – a floating-point data format may be designed such that integers are a subset of floating-point numbers.

4.8 (a) In the opcode space. This saves the specification of an operand. It is of interest in the frequent cases where an operand is compared with zero (**if** $A > 0$ **then**) or when an operand needs to be cleared or initialized. One operand instructions, such as TST or CLR, can then be used.

(b) In the operand space, preferably in that part of the operand specifier which is still in the basic instruction part.

(c) In the operand extension word or in the data space.

4.9 (a) Vectors.

(b) To support accessing an element in a data structure.

(c) Yes, usually a description contains a specification for the upper and the lower bound of a vector such that subscript checking can be performed.

(d) The size of the data elements.

(e) No, because usually the size of the data elements, and not their data type, is specified by the descriptor.

Chapter 5

5.1 Address resolution is the smallest amount of data that can be addressed. The address resolution for data and instructions does not have to be the same; for example, the MC68020 has an address resolution of one byte for data and one word (two bytes) for instructions (because instructions have a length that is one or more words). An address resolution of one bit is not often used because of the increase in the number of address bits and the extra alignment time required for instructions and/or data.

5.2 The numbering should be done consistently, either from least significant to most significant or in reverse order.

5.3 (a) True; (b) false; (c) false; (d) true.

5.4 Because immediate addressing, which specifies the value of constants, does not require an address. Immediate addressing is used frequently because constants have a high frequency of occurrence.

5.5 Register-direct addressing is important because the specification of register addresses requires only a few bits (which results in short, and therefore fast-to-fetch instructions) and registers are very fast (as compared with memory locations) such that operand fetches/stores are faster.

Absolute addressing means that the operand address is fixed (bound before execution time). It is used to address I/O, vectors and control registers.

5.6 Due to the TOS concept, the addressing modes (A_n), $(A_n)+$ and $-(A_n)$ are no longer needed for stack operations.

5.7 (a) No, because the Src operand specifies the SP rather than the stack;

(b) No, because modification of the (SP) should take place between the fetching of the Src and Dst operand;

(c) Yes, towards infinity;

(d) No, see B;

(e) No, see B;

(f) No, because the stack pointer is incremented twice, which means that the result is thrown away;

(g) Yes, towards zero.

5.8 (a) False, as read-only code has nothing to do with absolute addressing;

(b) True;

(c) False, because the program counter is not one of the address registers and the addressing mode $@(A_n)-$ is not available;

(d) True, as absolute addresses are specified via the addressing mode @(PC)+ and immediate data via the mode (PC)+.

5.9 Pre-indexing means that the operand address is formed by an index operation followed by indirection, as follows: address = M[base + index]. Post-indexing means that the operand address is formed by an indirection followed by an index operation, as follows: address = (M[base]) + index.

Scaling can be used as part of the index operation. The index value is then multiplied with the length of the data element to be accessed.

5.10 (a) True, because the descriptor has all information describing the data structure;

(b) False, because the upper and lower bound are assigned to the descriptor when the corresponding data structure is allocated;

(c) False, because the concept of tags is orthogonal to that of descriptors.

5.11 The specification of operands should require few bits because every instruction has, on average, about 1.8 operands, which is rather high. Short operands allow for shorter instructions, which require fewer bits and are faster to fetch. The methods available for achieving short operands are: the use of implicit operands, registers, relative addressing and pooling.

Chapter 6

6.1 The derived results consist of: results produced by the operation (such as overflow and carry); and results produced by the result of an operation (such as zero and negative).

6.2 With a multiple data move the source and destination may overlap. This problem can be handled by beginning the move operation with the first or the last source data element, depending on whether the source address is lower than the destination address.

6.3 Format transformation operations consist of shift and bit-field operations. Arithmetic shift operations do not really belong to this class of operations, as they are a special case of multiply and divide operations. Their operation, result and derived results should be consistent with multiply and divide.

6.4 The purpose of code transformation operations is to change the coding of the data. Two methods exist: using table lookup, used to perform character set transformation operations; and algorithmic, used to transform one number representation into another – for example, from integer to floating point.

6.5 Two's complement operation. Multiply has to be able to produce a double-length result. Divide should be able to accept a double-length dividend.

6.6 The 'ADDX $-(A_y)$, $-(A_x)$' instruction allows meta-numbers with an arbitrary number of meta-digits to be added, using the addressing mode $-(A_n)$. This is the correct addressing mode because the addition should begin with the least significant meta-digits. The Z condition code bit has to be treated differently because it should reflect that all meta-digits, processed at that moment, are zero. The correct setting of the Z bit is done as follows: Z = 1 **if** current result = 0 **and** previous value of Z = 1, **else** Z = 0.

6.7 The MC68020 architecture does not support a TSTX (Test Extended) instruction. When the TST instruction is used, special provisions have to be made to guarantee that Z = 1 means that all meta-digits are equal to zero. Another way of solving this problem may be to use the SUBX D_y, D_x instruction, whereby the (Dy) should be zero and the meta-digits have to be moved to Dx.

6.8 The routine whereby the MULU and/or MULS instructions are used should be much shorter and faster.

6.9 Only one guard digit is required. This digit takes 4 bits because radix 16 is used.

6.10 Floating-point numbers are stored almost exclusively in normalized form to allow for maximum precision. With extended precision, all but the most significant meta-digit are not allowed to be normalized. Because normalizaton is done implicitly as a side effect of all single-precision operations, the less significant meta-digits cannot be handled using the single-precision instructions.

6.11 The overflow and underflow exceptions can occur when the result of a floating-point operation is out of range. Truncation and rounding are two precision treatment methods. Rounding is more accurate because it is symmetrical with respect to zero and introduces the smallest error ($\leqslant 0.5*$ least significant digit).

Chapter 7

7.1 Functional dependence means that the way an instruction is executed is dependent on other instructions. The repeat instruction is not found in many architectures because of the extra hardware support it requires, and because of the many exceptions (such as one cannot repeat a HALT or a REPEAT instruction) this instruction introduces, which make repeat a conceptually difficult instruction.

7.2 The chained form of location dependency requires every instruction to specify its successor. This increases the instruction length with one extra operand while most of the time the next sequential instruction will be executed.

7.3 $A < B$: LT; $A \geqslant B$: GE; $A \leqslant B$: LE; $A > B$: GT; $A = B$: EQ; $A \neq B$: NE.

7.4 The introduction of a new instruction is useful when:

- It will have a high frequency of use – this may mean large savings in memory (due to better encoding) and/or savings in execution time (due to faster execution).
- No other instructions can simulate the function.
- It fits into the architecture.

7.5 2 answers : $A \leqslant X \leqslant B$; $X < A$ or $X > B$.

3 answers: $A \leqslant X \leqslant B$; $X < A$; $X > B$.

5 answers: $A < X < B$; $X = A$; $X = B$; $X < A$; $X > B$.

For array subscript checking the '2 answers' result is sufficient.

7.6 A conditional operation consists of the parts: testing, selection and condition use. The test part is often done implicitly through the derived results of an operation. The selection part has to check whether the test space (usually formed by the condition code bits) contains certain values.

7.7 There are two reasons why a conditional operation is usually not implemented as one instruction. Firstly, most architectures do not allow for instructions with four operands (because two comparison operands, a condition selector and usually some branch address have to be specified). Secondly, the testing part often does not have to be done explicitly; the derived results of other instructions perform an implicit test. For register-oriented architectures, the testing part should be a separate instruction (because it is not always needed due to the derived results of a previous instruction), and the selection and condition use part should be an instruction. The reason for this is that this instruction fits the one-and-a-half operand instruction format of register-oriented architectures.

7.8 Condition use can be done as follows:

- Store the condition. The MC68020 Scc instruction has been introduced for this purpose.
- Use the condition to change the flow of control. The MC68020 Bcc instruction has been designed for this purpose.

7.9 Absolute, implicit branches are used when a pre-determined function has to be activated, such as an exception handler. Implicit activation is used with absolute, implicit branches.

7.10 The **for** loop has many variants which are allowed in a particular high-level language. In addition, different high-level languages have different versions of the **for** loop. The result would be a very complex instruction, which would be inefficient.

Chapter 8

8.1 The levels of abstraction in a program are: module, function (or procedure), instruction and machine cycle.

8.2 Functions are used to reduce the code length, to allow for information hiding and to create new levels of abstraction.

8.3 Because functions have a high frequency of use.

8.4 Local data is declared local to the block that is currently being executed; non-local data is declared outside that block; and global data is declared in the outermost block, usually the main program.

8.5 A return value is usually passed in a register, rather than the stack, because it is the most simple and efficient way. Languages usually restrict the data type of the return value such that it can be contained in a register.

8.6 With static binding the correspondence between a name used in a program and the declaration of that name is determined statically (at compile time) by searching the local block, followed by the lexically enclosing blocks, until the declaration has been found.

8.7 An activation record is a block of data created and allocated upon the activation of a function. It consists of the following parts: explicit parameters, implicit parameters and the local data area.

8.8 A run-time model is the way activation records are built and chained together to support the function call and return, as well as the addressing of local and non-local data.

8.9 A static link (SL) is a pointer, which is part of an activation record, that is used to point to the lexically enclosing block. It is used to access non-local data. A dynamic link (DL) is a pointer, which is part of the activation record, that is used to point to the activation record of the caller. This supports the return operation.

8.10 A frame pointer (FP) is used to point to the beginning of the local data area of an activation record. It is used to access local data. The run-time model for Pascal does not need a FP because the SP may be used (the distance of all local data objects relative to the SP can be determined at compile time).

8.11 The argument pointer (AP) is used to point to the beginning of the explicit parameter block, which is of interest when parameters are not passed on the stack as part of the activation record. Pascal does not need an AP because, in order to allow for recursion, parameters are passed on the stack.

8.12 Storage space provided by the system is most flexible because it allows for recursion.

8.13 The most efficient place for passing parameters is in registers; the most flexible place is on the stack.

8.14 The BSR instruction can often be specified in one word. It is therefore usually shorter and faster than the more flexible JSR instruction.

8.15 Because it only allows for serially re-usable code, which cannot be stored in read-only memory. The MC68020 architecture stores its return address on the stack.

8.16 State saving/restoring should be done by the called function because it has knowledge of the resources it needs and it only has to be done in one place (the called function rather than in every calling function). The MC68020 architecture has the MOVEM instruction for saving/restoring multiple registers.

8.17 The LINK instruction saves the FP of the calling function, sets the FP to point to the beginning of the local data space and reserves the required memory for the local data.

8.18 The PEA instruction is used to pass parameters 'by reference'. PEA does not have to specify the data type because the MC68020 architecture requires the addresses of all data objects to be specified as the address of the most significant byte (regardless of the length of the data object).

8.19 The CALLM and RTM instructions are provided to support the module concept.

8.20 A function descriptor enables the calling of functions in a different module. It contains, in addition to control information, a pointer to the code of the function and a pointer to the global data area of the function. The descriptor is located in a table belonging to the calling module.

8.21 A function Fa in module Ma can call a function Fb in module Mb by specifying the function descriptor of Fb. The relative position of this descriptor can be determined at compile time, because the compiler creates the table with function descriptors. The function descriptor of Fb has pointers to the code and global data of Fb, and these pointers can be initialized when module Fb is loaded.

Chapter 9

9.1 An operating system has to perform user functions (such as program control, I/O and file handling) and system functions (such as memory management, protection, resource allocation and scheduling, and accounting).

9.2 Serial batch (no overlap of I/O with CPU processing).

Spooling (data I/O, such as printing, in overlap with CPU processing).

Multiprogramming (data I/O and disk I/O in overlap with CPU processing, which requires several executable processes to be memory resident).

Time sharing (user I/O concurrent and interactive with the execution of user processes).

9.3 The process context consists of a process control block (used by the operating system for managing the process), the memory context (this consists of the program and data parts of the context) and the processor context (this consists of the registers of the processor).

9.4 In supervisor mode, privileged instructions are allowed to be executed. These privileged instructions perform process protection functions. The MC68020 privileged instructions consist of instructions dealing with the status register (ANDI, ORI, EORI and MOVE with the SR as operand), and the RESET, STOP and RTE instructions.

9.5 Important aspects are: the number of domains (this represents the granularity of the protection mechanism) and the possibility for selective sharing.

9.6 Process synchronization allows for communication between processes. This is done by allowing only one process to be in a critical program section at a time (mutual exclusion). The following mutual exclusion mechanisms exist: disabling interrupts, busy waiting (test-and-set, compare-and-swap and the lock meta-instruction) and high-level constructs that are built out of the mechanisms already mentioned.

9.7 (a) A supervisor call (SVC) and a trap.

(b) This is a process switch on behalf of another process (for example, indicated by an external interrupt), because the process switch has no relationship with the currently executing process.

9.8 The interrupt operation should only perform a context switch of the minimum processor context, for speed reasons. This minimum processor context is such that the invoked process is able to perform the remainder of the process switching under program control. The minimum processor context usually consists of the SR, the PC, the SP and memory management information.

9.9 (a) Because different interrupt requests have different levels of urgency.

(b) A non-maskable interrupt is an interrupt request with the highest priority. It will, therefore, always be honoured. Traps are non-maskable interrupts because they signal some exceptional condition.

(c) Asynchronous events are usually allowed to cause an interrupt between instructions, because the processor context is minimal then.

(d) Vectored interrupts, because the interrupting process then identifies itself.

9.10 The segment table of *Pa* contains pointers to segments *Sa*, *Sab* and *Sac*; *Pb* contains pointers to *Sb*, *Sab* and *Sbc*; and *Pc* contains pointers to *Sc*, *Sac* and *Sbc*.

9.11 The program is:

```
       MOVE.L  PCBptr, D1      ;Load ptr to PCB in D1
Loop : CLR.L   D0              ;Load NIL ptr in D0
       CAS.L   D0, D1, Lock
       BNE     Loop            ;Critical section blocked
                    CRITICAL SECTION
       CLR.L   Lock            ;Free critical section
```

9.12 The program is:

```
Loop : MOVE.W  S, D0           ;Get value of S
       BEQ     Loop            ;If S = 0 then wait
       MOVE.W  D0, D1          ;Make copy of S
       SUBQ.W  #1, D1          ;Decrement D1
       CAS     D0, D1, S       ;If S still the same, update it
       BNE     Loop            ;If not, try again
```

Chapter 10

10.1 (a) Protection, sharing and relocation.

(b) Virtual, real and disk address space.

10.2 Dynamic relocation is address translation done at program execution time. Because of performance reasons, it requires special hardware. Blocking is used to reduce the size of the translation table.

10.3 (a) Temporal locality means locality in time: future references are likely to reference objects that have been referenced in the past. Spatial locality means locality in space: future references are likely to be to addresses close to those used in the past.

(b) The working set $W(t, h)$ is the set of blocks at time t, referenced during the last h references. Because of temporal locality, this set will only be a small part of all blocks constituting the program and data of the executing process.

10.4 (a) Relocation, paging and segmentation.

(b) Relocation allows a program, which starts at virtual address 0, to be located anywhere in main memory. Its disadvantage is that a process has to occupy a contiguous area of main memory; and the size of a process is not allowed to exceed the size of main memory.

(c) Demand paging divides the virtual and real address space into blocks of equal size, called pages. A process does not have to occupy a contiguous area of main memory, and the virtual address space may be larger than the allocated real address space.

10.5 Segmentation allows the virtual address space to be divided into blocks of different sizes (called segments), where the size of these segments may vary during execution time. These segments may relate to objects at the programming level (for example, a stack segment), rather than to memory space (as with paging).

Paged segmentation is segmentation where the segments are divided into equally sized pages, to reduce external fragmentation. When the paging system supports demand paging, segments do not have to be present as a whole.

10.6 Translation lookaside buffers, inverted page tables and multiple virtual spaces.

10.7 The fetch policy, the placement policy and the replacement policy.

10.8 (a) Prefetching and demand fetching.

(b) Because all pages are of equal size.

(c) Best fit, worst fit, first fit and binary buddy.

(d) Random, FIFO, Clock, LRU and MIN.

(e) Because with variable-size partitions the working sets of all memory-resident processes have to be taken into account.

10.9 MIN and VMIN. It cannot be realized in practice because it requires the future behaviour of a program to be known.

10.10 To reduce table fragmentation.

10.11 *A*: −X; *B*: R−X; *C*: R−; *D*: RW−; *E*: RW−; *F*: RW−.

10.12 (a) Vs = 11 bits, Vp = 13 bits and Dp = 11 bits.

(b) A PTE consists of a one-bit Presence flag and an Rp field of 15 bits. (*Note*: Main memory can at most contain 2^{15} pages.)

(c) The size of a page table is: # of PTEs * length of a PTE in bytes = $2^{Vp} * 2 = 2^{14}$ = 4 kbytes.

(d) An STE consists of a one-bit Presence flag, a 3-bit RWX field, a 13-bit Ls field and a 15-bit PTP field. Total: 1 + 3 + 13 + 15 = 32 bits per STE.

Chapter 11

11.1 A device controller, consisting of a host port and one or more device ports, and one or more I/O devices.

11.2 Storage devices (a disk) and source/sink devices (a keyboard and a display).

11.3 Their long access time, their low data transfer rate and their relatively high error rate.

11.4 (a) Device control information, consisting of control information to the controller and status information from the controller, and device data.

(b) Host port control/status information relates to the host port; device port control/status information relates to a device (attached via the device port). If the device controller has several devices attached, several device port control/status registers may be present.

(c) The collective control/status register is located in the host port and reflects the overall control/status information of the device controller. It is important for interrupt and exception handlers.

11.5 (a) Direct I/O means that the CPU part and the device controller part of the I/O process form a single I/O process. The CPU does all I/O operations in a programmed way and cannot perform any other operation while doing I/O.

(b) Memory-mapped I/O is preferred because it does not require special I/O instructions, and all memory-referencing instructions can be used for I/O.

(c) The device port should be specifiable as a parameter (for example, in a register) such that device drivers can use the same code for different attached devices.

11.6 (a) Overlapped I/O eliminates the busy form of waiting; the device does not have to be polled by the CPU to determine when it is ready to start the next transfer of data; instead, the device reports its ready status itself via an interrupt.

(b) The advantage of DMA is that CPU involvement in transferring data is reduced to a per block basis, thus considerably reducing the CPU overhead due to I/O.

(c) Data chaining means that the set of parameters required to control a DMA I/O operation are fetched by the device controller under DMA control. The data to be transferred to/from the host in a single I/O operation may now be split over several blocks of main memory, allowing for gather write and scatter read operations.

(d) Command chaining allows the device controller to fetch its set of control words, which specify an I/O operation, under DMA control. This allows the device controller to execute chains of I/O commands without intervention from the host.

11.7 Buffering allows synchronization between the CPU part and the device controller part of the I/O process to become less time critical, or non-time critical.

11.8 A channel is a device controller that supports DMA for data transfers, and which supports data as well as command chaining.

11.9 I/O processors allow device controllers to off-load the host by performing part or all of the device driver and/or device-independent software functions. They also allow for better exception handling, because of the more intimate device interface.

11.10 (a) The capacity of the drive is: # of disks * # of tracks/disk * # of sectors/track * 0.5 Kb = 4 × 600 * 20 × 0.5 Kb = 24 000 Kb.

(b) 3000 rev/min = 3000/60 rev/s = 50 rev/s. One revolution takes 20 ms. During this time 20 × 0.5 kbytes = 10 kbytes is transferred. The transfer rate is 50 * 10 kbytes/s = 0.5 Mbytes/s.

(c) The time to transfer 1 sector is: 0.5 kbytes/(0.5 * 10^3 kbytes/s) = 1 ms.

(d) The average rotational delay = 20 ms/2 = 10 ms.

11.11 (a) With DMA only, an interrupt has to be given upon the completion of the transfer of the first sector, after which the DMA parameters for the next sector can be set up. The total elapsed time would be: average rotational delay + transfer time of one sector + rotational delay + transfer of second sector = 10 + 1 + 20 + 1 = 32 ms average.

(b) The total elapsed time would be: 10 + 1 + 1 = 12 ms average.

Chapter 12

12.1 (a) A way to design and implement computers such that errors are very unlikely.

(b) Guaranteeing a correct result, in spite of the presence of errors, by using redundancy.

(c) Error detection, fault treatment, damage assessment and error recovery.

12.2 Non-permanent faults are more likely; they constitute 94% to 97% of all faults.

12.3 (a) Redundancy in the coding of the information – for example, ECC and parity.

(b) Duplication of hardware.

12.4 (a) Masking. It can cope with permanent and non-permanent faults.

(b) Because most faults are non-permanent. A good error-detection mechanism is required.

12.5 (a) Reset, machine check, instruction exceptions, monitoring exceptions, supervisor call exceptions and interrupts.

(b) Instruction decode, instruction/operand fetch and execution exceptions.

12.6 (a) The interrupt mechanism.

(b) The priority with which the exception-handling process is invoked (that is, with which the interrupt operation is taking place) and the priority with which the exception handling process is being executed.

(c) With the same priority as the process causing the exception is being executed.

(d) Immediately.

(e) Between instructions.

(f) TRAP.

12.7 (a) Because an initial value for the SP also has to be loaded and no exception stack frame has to be created (because a return from a reset exception is not meaningful).

(b) For instructions that change the program flow (BRA, JMP and Bcc), or for any instruction.

(c) An instruction in the program is replaced by a breakpoint instruction, which causes a trap when executed. The execution of the program can be continued by inserting the original instruction in the program.

12.8 (a) The instruction restart method and the instruction continuation method.

(b) The instruction restart method.

(c) The MC68020 mainly uses the instruction continuation method. This means that the internal state of the machine, which may be very large, has to be saved in the exception stack frame.

Chapter 13

13.1 (a) FP; (b) RP; (c) FP; (d) RP; (e) RP; (f) RP.

13.2 (a) A write operation.

(b) A read–modify–write operation.

(c) A read operation.

(d) The address has to be transferred only once.

13.3 (a) By the slot number in the backplane.

(b) A write operation to more than one slave.

13.4 (a) Synchronous bus timing.

(b) Four.

(c) Because multiple slaves may be involved.

(d) Semi-synchronous bus timing is identical to asynchronous bus timing, except for the fact that events in the semi-synchronous protocol are required to occur at fixed timing intervals, determined by a clock.

(e) The semi-synchronous protocol is less susceptible to noise.

13.5 (a) Static bus arbitration.

(b) Dynamic bus arbitration.

(c) For multiprocessor systems, to prevent starvation.

(d) Release on request for single-processor systems, and release when done for multiprocessor systems.

(e) When large blocks of data are transferred over the bus, to shorten the bus access time.

13.6 (a) Distributed arbitration.

(b) Centralized arbitration.

13.7 A daisy chain is used to propagate the bus grant signal, such that a single requester may be selected as the next bus master.

13.8 A virtual interrupt can be considered as a memory-mapped interrupt: as a side effect of a data transfer an interrupt takes place. This is important for multiprocessor systems, because interrupts have to have a source and a destination.

Chapter 14

14.1 In a single-thread system only a single instruction stream is executed.

14.2 (a) At the realization, implementation and the architectural level.

(b) Improvement of latency and bandwidth.

14.3 200 ns is a latency figure; 3 MIPS is a measure of throughput.

14.4 Pipelining.

14.5 The execution unit can perform most operations (such as ADD and AND) in a single cycle; only complex operations (such as MUL and DIV) or operations on floating-point data could be performed in several stages, and therefore be pipelined.

14.6 A Harvard architecture effectively doubles the memory bandwidth.

14.7 (a) Interleaving improves the memory bandwidth.

(b) Low-order interleaving.

(c) Low-order interleaving.

14.8 (a) The probability of finding the requested information in the cache.

(b) The amount of information transferred between main memory and cache.

(c) The line size determines the spatial locality; the number of lines determines the temporal locality.

14.9 Tagged prefetch.

14.10 (a) Direct mapping; (b) set associative.

14.11 Tag = 12, Set = 8 and Byte = 4 bits.

14.12 (a) With a direct-mapped cache there is only one line that can be replaced, so there is no choice.

(b) Least recently used.

14.13 (a) It has the lowest number of transfers to main memory.

(b) The contents of a line in main memory may not be the same as that of a line in cache; thus, special precautions have to be taken in systems where other processes may have access to that line of storage.

14.14 Data dependencies, run-ons and branch dependencies.

14.15 (a) By prevention: extra instructions are inserted between the two instructions exhibiting the data dependency. By detection and resolution: this can be done by stalling or flushing the pipeline, or by forwarding data.

(b) Prevention, because it is done by the compiler.

(c) Prevention, because the instruction stream is filled with instructions to prevent cycles from being wasted.

14.16 Using delayed branch instructions, because the delay slots may be filled with instructions.

14.17 Because it aims at prefetching those instructions that will be executed after having executed the branch instructions.

14.18 By a loop buffer or a branch target buffer.

14.19 In a compare-and-branch instruction, the comparison and the branch operation are done in a single instruction. Because many comparison operations compare for equal/not equal or against zero, they may be executed very fast (no carry propagation in the compare unit) such that the execute delay may be eliminated for those compare operations. This accelerates the branch operation.

Chapter 15

15.1 High-level, compact instructions to reduce the amount of memory required for storing programs and to reduce the required memory bandwidth.

15.2 RISC architectures are optimized to reduce the number of cycles per instruction and the cycle time. This results in fewer and simpler instructions with fewer instruction formats.

15.3 Statistics show that only a few data types are used frequently. Using only 32-bit integers to simulate all other integer data types reduces the number of different instructions, and may allow the load and store instructions to be faster, resulting in an overall speed gain.

15.4 Three-address instructions allow the source operands of an operation to be non-destructive. This may reduce data dependencies.

15.5 The register set represents the working set of active variables. A larger register set allows for a larger working set, resulting in less spill code. Also, pipeline dependencies become easier to solve by the compiler, because the chance of finding an instruction that can perform an operation on data that does not have a dependency is larger.

15.6 This can be done by using an MULS instruction, which requires special hardware support. An example will be given for the three-operand MULS instruction, MULS Rs1, Rs2, Rd, where Rd will specify a register pair, which is assumed to contain the double-length result Rd := (Rs1) * Rs2.

MULS Rs1, Rs2, Rd.
If least significant bit of Rs1 = 1, then Rd := (Rs2) + (Rd).
Shift right one (Rs1) and (Rd).

15.7 Upon a procedure call, a new set of local registers is allocated automatically, and the caller's outgoing parameters are passed and become the incoming parameter registers of the called procedure. Upon a return, the local registers of the returned procedure are accessible again and procedure results can be returned via the incoming parameter registers.

15.8 When the value of a by-reference parameter is passed in a register, Pr, using the window concept, the register Pr could be accessible by having the register space overlay memory space. The by-reference formal parameter in the called procedure then has to be set up with a memory address specifying the location of Pr. A problem arises, however, when the register space has been overflowed, due to a long chain of procedure calls, and in such a case Pr will be saved in some area of memory. Because the save/restore operation is transparent to the contents of the registers, the formal parameter will access the value that overlays Pr, rather than Pr. Therefore, by-reference parameters should be passed in memory (as part of the activation record).

15.9 Similar to 15.8. This variable should be stored in memory rather than in a register.

15.10 The SCC bit can inhibit the condition codes to be affected so that instructions can be placed out of sequence. Also, before a conditional jump instruction.

15.11
```
LDXW  (R0)−1, R1    ;Load −1 into R1
SUB   R1, Rd, Rd    ;Subtract Rd from −1 to form the one's
                     complement
```

Chapter 16

16.1 A multi-threading system should be used.

16.2 This is a multicomputer system, which is also called a loosely coupled system.

16.3 The timing (asynchronous or synchronous), the switching method (circuit or packet switching), the control strategy (centralized or distributed) and the topology (static or dynamic).

16.4 A static topology, characterized by the diameter of the network and the degree of a node.

16.5 (a) n, n; (b) n, $n + 1$.

16.6 Routing can be based on the difference in bit representation of the address of the source and destination node. Furthermore, for an n-dimensional hypercube, n distinct paths can be distinguished.

16.7 Bus based and INs using shuffle exchanges.

16.8 (a) Packet switching. (b) Either can be used.

16.9 Baseline networks allow blocking to be prevented. They require centralized control.

16.10 A single data path to every data item and a single copy of every data item has to exist.

16.11 The advantage is that little hardware support is required. The disadvantage is the lower performance, because not all data is allowed to be cacheable, and so special software (compiler) is required.

16.12 To obtain a private copy of a cache line.

16.13 The write-through memory update policy causes a very high bus load, which reduces the bus bandwidth available for productive work. It does not guarantee data consistency because other caches are not updated automatically.

16.14 The advantage is that no special facilities (such as an invalidate line) have to be provided by the bus. The disadvantage is that a special memory system has to be used which contains a tag per line of data (to indicate Public or Private).

Chapter 17

17.1 A conceptual model is a conceptual method according to which a computation can be performed. An architecture is an embodiment of a conceptual model.

17.2 A von Neumann computer consists of a CPU, a memory and a connecting tube.

17.3 See Section 17.1.1.

17.4 Self-defining data and the separation of program and data space.

17.5 The semantic gap and the physical and conceptual bottleneck.

17.6 The control mechanism is the mechanism that determines how the computation will proceed. It may be control driven, data driven, demand driven or pattern driven. The data mechanism is the mechanism that defines the way computational units exchange data. It can be based on shared data or message passing.

17.7 Control mechanisms: data driven and pattern driven. Data mechanism: message passing.

17.8 (a) COSH; (b) DAME; (c) DESH; (d) DEME; (e) PASH; (f) PAME.

17.9 (a) Too much parallelism such that memory may be flooded with partial results.

(b) Identical subexpressions will be evaluated each time the result is needed.

INDEX